The Angevin Empire: Or the Three Reigns of Henry Ii, Richard I, and John (A.D. 1154-1216)

Sir James Henry Ramsay

THE ANGEVIN EMPIRE

SIR JAMES H. RAMSAY

THE ANGEVIN EMPIRE

OR THE THREE REIGNS
OF HENRY II., RICHARD I., AND JOHN

(A.D. 1154—1216)

BY

SIR JAMES H. RAMSAY, OF BAMFF, M.A

AUTHOR OF "THE FOUNDATIONS OF ENGLAND"
"LANCASTER AND YORK," ETC

WITH MAPS AND ILLUSTRATIONS

RJH

London

SWAN SONNENSCHEIN & CO LTD

NEW YORK: THE MACMILLAN CO

1903
H

PRINTED BY
HAZELL, WATSON AND VINEY, LD
LONDON AND AYLESBURY.

PREFACE

NO apology seems to be needed for giving to the public a further instalment of my work. I trust that I may again get credit for a verified and consecutive narrative, acceptable to those who ask for facts rather than impressions, and who wish for facilities for forming independent judgments. I continue to give particular attention to chronology. Without sequence events lose half their meaning; the logic of facts cannot be seen until they are placed in the order in which they happened. The political thread is still necessarily the leading one, and the King the central figure round which events have to be grouped; but I have endeavoured as far as possible to bring to light other sides of the national life.

Ecclesiastical questions are prominent throughout, especially in connection with the reigns of Henry II. and John. With regard to the Becket controversy the times seem to call for a careful review of the facts. When men venture to talk of "the Liberty of the Church" it is well that the world should know what those words imported in the days when they had a living meaning.

The disastrous results to himself of the family policy pursued by Henry II., in contrast with the brilliant success of his reign in all other respects, is a point brought out perhaps more fully than has yet been done.

I still give special attention to military affairs. The story of a martial age cannot be told without reference to its modes of warfare. Richard's campaigns in the Holy Land, and the great battle of Bouvines will be found the most interesting chapters

83141

in this connexion. With respect to the latter, I found a careful survey of the locality most instructive. The studies of the battle hitherto published appear to have taken too little account of the testimony of the field itself.

In the matter of commerce and finance I have done the best that I could with the available materials: but it must be admitted that these are far from being as full as we could desire, and that on many points of interest we are still much in the dark.

If there is a subject on which I might claim to have a special mission, it would be that of calling attention to the extraordinary exaggeration commonly found in the Chroniclers in their estimates of numbers, whether numbers of men, or money, or anything else. I have lost no opportunity of testing these, wherever possible, by comparison with more authentic personal or Record evidence, the last being the only authority really trustworthy. The result is that I find again that multiplication by ten might almost be called a normal rate of amplification. Whether dealing with the strength of an army, or the produce of a tax, the student *prima facie* will do well to take one-tenth of any number given if he would arrive at a prudent estimate. In some cases that proportion would be found too large.

On a much contested point I have called attention to the facts indicating that in the England of the twelfth century there was little that could be called at all English. Not only were all the upper classes of society essentially French, but their ranks were perpetually being recruited by foreigners imported from abroad. These people entered every Chapter and Convent, they filled the Episcopate, the Treasury, and the Bench, and found themselves completely at home there.

Architecture was the art of the period. I have indicated some of the more clearly dated monuments, as landmarks for the guidance of the student and the sightseer.

My work continues to be based on an independent survey of the original authorities; but, of course, I have manifold obligations to previous writers to confess, as to Bishop Stubbs, and the other editors of the Rolls Series ; to Mr. J. H. Round, for his valuable monographs, and to Miss Norgate, whose work covers almost the whole of the period embraced in mine. In matters relating to foreign authorities and foreign topography I have found her guidance especially helpful. Only those who have waded through Dr. Giles' *St. Thomas of Canterbury* can appreciate the value of Canon Robertson's *Becket Materials.*

J. H. RAMSAY.

BAMFF, 1903.

CONTENTS

CHAPTER I

A.D.		PAGE
1154	Henry of Anjou, Duke of Normandy, his position and prospects	1
	Affairs in Normandy, crossing to England . . .	2
	Coronation, a Charter, Ministerial appointments . .	3
	Thomas Becket Chancellor; Stephen's supporters; Resumption of grants	4
	William of Aubigny; William of Aûmale . . .	4
1155	William Peverel; Roger Earl of Hereford; Hugh of Mortimer	5
	The Succession; Designs on Ireland; John of Salisbury at Rome	6
	The Bull "*Laudabiliter*"	7
	The Revenue; Expedition abroad	8
1156	Homage to Louis; Fraternal war; Affairs of Brittany .	9
	Geoffrey of Anjou in Brittany; Scutage; History of the Tax	10
	Knight's Service	11
1157	Return to England; Resumption of castles; The Northern Counties regained; Scottish affairs; Scottish homage	12
	Welsh affairs	13
	Royal campaign, a temporary reverse . . .	14
	Owain submits; Crown-wearing renounced . .	15

CHAPTER II

A.D.		PAGE
1158	Affairs of Brittany; trip to France . . .	16
	Matrimonial alliance with France; Occupation of Nantes	17
	Friendly intercourse; overlordship of Aquitaine . .	18
1159	Toulouse, disputed succession, Henry's claim; alliance with Barcelona	19
	Preparations for war, " the Scutage of Toulouse " . .	20
	Yield of taxes; Knights' fees in England; Campaign of Toulouse	21
	Futile ending; gains in the North; pacification; Boulogne, Mortain, and Surrey; marriage of an Abbess	22
1160	Papal Schism, a new Queen of France; marriage of Henry's son	23
	The Norman Vexin : frontier works . . .	24

A.D.		PAGE
1161–1162	Military operations, death of Archbishop Theobald; measures of Reform	25
1162	Fresh homage to the Younger Henry; Nomination, election, and consecration of Thomas Becket as Archbishop of Canterbury	26, 27
	Alexander III. in Gaul, Royal honours	28
	Henry returns to England	29

CHAPTER III

1163	Thomas Becket, his birth, parentage, and early career	30, 31
	Personal appearance, character, and talents . .	32
	Relations to the King as Chancellor; his duties and emoluments	33
	Thomas the Archbishop	34
	Church claims; treaty with Flanders . . .	35
	Gilbert Foliot Bishop of London; Council of Tours .	36
	Welsh affairs, an armed progress; Homages by Scotland and Wales; breach with Becket, the 'Sheriff's Aid'	37
	Courts Christian, immunity of clerks from Lay Jurisdiction	38–40
	King and laity challenged; Henry's response, guilty clerks to be punished	41–42
	Ancient customs of England	43
	Clergy coming round	44
	Becket promises	45
1164	Constitutions of Clarendon	46–48
	Becket protests, but eventually is induced to accept the Constitutions; suspends himself; applications to the Pope	51
	Becket's position, attempts to leave England . .	52–53
	Case of John Marshal, Becket cited . . .	54
	Council of Northampton	54–62
	Flight of Becket from Northampton . . .	63
	Appendix I to Chapter: "Canon Law". . .	63
	Appendix II: "Becket and the Constitutions of Clarendon"	64

CHAPTER IV

1164	Becket goes abroad	65, 66
	Henry and the Pope	67
	Persecution of Becket's friends; Becket, the King of France, and the Pope	68, 69
	Becket and the Cardinals	69
	Becket at Pontigny	70
1165	King over to Normandy; a German Alliance .	71
	Diet at Würzburg; rash pledges . . .	71
	Welsh war	72

A.D.		PAGE
1165	Methods of barbarism; taxation	73, 74
	Becket at Pontigny	74, 75
	Persecution of Nonconformists	75
1166	Assize of Clarendon, circuits of judges; criminal law reforms	76-78
	Inquest of Service, Knights' fees	79, 80
	Assize of Novel Disseisin; the King abroad; William the Lion, King of the Scots	81
	Palestine tax	82
	Becket and Henry; Becket preparing for action .	82, 83
	Henry's Ministers excommunicated; the Constitutions quashed	84

CHAPTER V

1166	Negotiations at Rome	87
	Becket driven from Pontigny	88
	Affairs of Brittany	89
	Henry in possession	90
1167	Affairs of Toulouse and Auvergne	91
	Fresh war with France	92
	Death of Empress Matilda; mission of Cardinals William and Otho	93
	Offers of compromise or arbitration rejected by Becket	94, 95
1168	A Dynastic scheme suggested	96
	Risings in Poitou	96
	And Brittany	97
	Conferences at La Ferté-Bernard	97, 98

CHAPTER VI

1169	Conferences at Montmirail; Henry's dynastic plans; affairs of Becket; Mission of Simon and Bernard	100-103
	Mission of Gratian and Vivian	104
	Excommunication of Bishop Foliot and others .	105, 106
	Further excommunications; meetings with Gratian and Vivian	107, 108
	Fruitless ending	109
	Further moves	110
	Meeting at Montmartre; kiss of peace refused by Henry	111-114
	The young King to be crowned, and by the Archbishop of York; mission of Rotrou and Bernard .	114, 116
1170	The King back to England; Inquest of Sheriffs .	117, 118
	Coronation of young King	119
	Conferences at Fréteval with Rotrou and Bernard; supposed pacification between Henry and Becket	120-122
	A push for the kiss of peace	124
	Last interview of Henry and Becket . . .	125

CHAPTER VII

A.D.   **PAGE**

1170   Return of Becket to England, suspends three prelates in advance 126–127

Attempts to hold a visitation 128

His last sermon ; fresh anathemas 129

Henry loses self-control ; conspiracy against Becket's life   130

Assassination of Becket 131–134

His policy and conduct as Archbishop 135

Henry's position 136

Later history of Becket's murderers 137

CHAPTER VIII

1074–1166   Relations with Ireland; social state of the Island .   138–140

Henry's designs 141

1166–1168   An opening ; Dermot and Strongbow 142

1169–1171   Landings of Welsh adventurers; their successes and conquests 143–146

1171   Landing of Strongbow; capture of Waterford and Dublin   147

Further struggles 148–149

Settlement of Leinster 150

Henry and the Pope 150, 151

Expedition of the King to Ireland 150–153

1172   Synod of Cashel 154

The Papacy and the conquest; the Bull *Laudabiliter* . 155

Return of Henry to England, conquest of Ireland left incomplete 156, 157

CHAPTER IX

1172   Henry passes through England into Normandy . . 159

Reconciled to the Church, and absolved for implication in Becket's murder 160

Henry's treatment of his sons ; discontent of the young King 161

He is re-crowned with his Queen ; second absolution of the King 162

1173   Louis, the Barons and the young King, his demands . 163

Matrimonial alliance with Savoy; homage from Toulouse 163, 164

The young King in revolt 164

Arrest of Queen Eleanor ; league against Henry . . 165

Appointments to six Bishoprics ; Henry accepts the Prior Richard as Archbishop of Canterbury . . 166, 167

General rising against Henry, the leaders at home and abroad 168, 169

The young King in Normandy 170

Unsuccessful attack of Louis on Verneuil; brilliant capture of Dol by Henry 171

A.D.		PAGE
1173	Liberal offers of the King to his sons	172
	The rising in England; siege of Leicester; Scottish inroad; defeat of rebels at Fornham	172-174
1174	Henry's successes abroad; he returns to England	174-175
	Scottish inroad	176
	Course of the rising	177
	Capture of William the Lion	178
	Henry does penance at Becket's tomb	179
	Advances to London, Huntingdon, and Northampton	180
	Goes abroad, and relieves Rouen besieged by Louis	181
	Submission of the King's sons	182
	Terms for liberation of King of Scots	183, 184

CHAPTER X

1175	The young King again fractious	185
	Return of the two Kings to England; Synods and Councils	186
	Homages of the Scots and of Roderic of Connaught	187
	Papal Mission to England of Cardinal Ugo	188
1176	Assize of Northampton	189
	Assize of Mort d' Ancestor; Legatine Synod	190
	Young King still discontented; goes to Paris	191
	First Campaign of young Richard in Poitou	192
	Marriages of the King's daughters, Matilda, Eleanor, and Johanna	193
	Resumption and demolition of castles, Forest prosecutions	194
	King's son John to marry an heiress; homages from Welsh Princes, John to be Lord of Ireland	195-196
	Conquests in Ulster of John de Courcy	197
1177	Henry arbitrates between Castile and Navarre	197
	Crosses to Normandy; elusive treaty with Louis	198
	The King in Berri and Auvergne	199
1178	Religious movement in Languedoc	199-200
	King returns to England	201
	Institution of Court of King's Bench	201
1179	Judicial circuits made systematic; the Grand Assize	202
	Louis VII. on pilgrimage to Canterbury; Coronation of Philip II. of France	203
	Revolts in Aquitaine and Brittany suppressed by Richard and Geoffrey	204

CHAPTER XI

1179	Accession of Philip II. of France, "Augustus"	205
1180	Henry over to Normandy; Treaty of Ivry confirmed	206
	Downfall of Henry the Lion	207
	The King of Scots and the Pope	208
1181	Henry returns to England; Assize of Arms; Lucius III., Pope; Henry's sons supporting Philip of France	210

A.D.		PAGE
1182	The King over to France; Henry the Lion in Normandy	211
	Disaffection in Aquitaine; Richard and the young King	212-213
1183	Fraternal outburst	214
	Revolt of the young King; his illness and death .	214-216

CHAPTER XII

	Henry's efforts on behalf of John	218
1184	Treaty with France; fraternal war	219
	The King to England	220
	Papal demand for a subsidy resisted; vacancy at Canterbury	221
	Election of Archbishop Baldwin	222
X	Forest Assize	223
1185	The Kingdom of Jerusalem; offer of the Crown to Henry	224
	The Patriarch Heraclius in England . . .	225
	The King over to Normandy	226
	Affairs in Ireland; John to be Lord of the Island .	227
	His expedition there : the Papacy and Ireland .	228
1186	Conference with Philip; Henry back to England .	229

CHAPTER XIII

1186	Ecclesiastical affairs; Scottish affairs . . .	230
	Galloway; marriage of William the Lion; death of Geoffrey of Brittany	231
	Strained relations with France	232
1187	Henry over to Normandy; war with France . .	233
	Truce of Châteauroux; fall of Jerusalem . .	234
	Richard and the two Kings take the Cross . .	235
1188	Henry to England; the Saladin Tithe . . .	236
	War in Aquitaine, and with Philip of France . .	237-238
	Henry's last crossing; war with France . . .	239
	Conference at Bonmoulins; Richard joins Philip .	240
	Henry's last Christmas; fruitless efforts for peace .	241
1189	The war pressed; Capture of Le Mans and Tours by Philip	242, 243
	Henry signs Treaty of Azai or Colombières . .	244
	His death	245

CHAPTER XIV

1154-1189	Henry's looks and manners, character and ability .	246, 247
	Success of foreign and domestic policy; mistake of family policy	248
	Legal reforms; Court of King's Bench; circuits; trial by jury	249-250
	His revenue	251-254

A.D.   PAGE

1154–1189 Wages and prices ; the currency ; public works ; Church
                architecture ; the Transition Style . . . 255-257
            Question of fusion of races 257
            The King's issue 259

CHAPTER XV

RICHARD I

1189   First acts ; installation as Duke of Normandy . 262, 263
        Conference with Philip ; crossing to England . . 264
        Queen Eleanor set free ; Royal Progress . . . 265
        Coronation 266-269
        Attack on Jews ; Ministerial and Episcopal appoint-
            ments 269-270
        The Regency ; raising funds for the Crusade . . 271, 272
        Foreign affairs ; Archbishop Baldwin, and the Hacking-
            ton foundation 273, 274
        Treaty of Falaise-Valognes cancelled . . . 274
        Further arrangements for government at home ; Richard
            crosses to Normandy 275, 276
1190   Bishop Puiset and Chancellor Longchamp, struggle
            between them 277
        Outrages on Jews 278, 279
        Puiset and Longchamp, the latter victorious and
            supreme 280

CHAPTER XVI

1190   Richard enters on his Crusade ; his fleet ; Tryst with
            Philip at Vézelai ; compact between them . 282, 283
        Advance to Marseilles and Messina . . . 284, 285
        Affairs at Messina, King Tancred and Henry VI. ;
            Constance and Jeanne 286
        High-handed action of Richard ; Sack of Messina . 287
        Alliance with Tancred 288
1191   Richard to marry Berengaria of Navarre ; final rejection
            of Alais of France ; fresh treaty with Philip . 289
        Affairs in England ; mission of Walter of Coutances ;
            Geoffrey, Archbishop of York. . . . 290
        Richard sails on to Cyprus ; affairs there . . 291
        Marriage with Berengaria 291-292
        Visit from Guy of Lusignan 293
        Conquest of Cyprus 294
        Voyage from Cyprus to Acre. 295

CHAPTER XVII

1191   Siege of Acre ; losses among the Crusaders ; dissen-
            sions 296-297
        Capitulation of Acre 298

A.D.   PAGE

1191   Guy of Lusignan and Conrad of Montferrat ; Philip
            sails home   299
        Breakdown of the Acre capitulation ; massacres of
            prisoners   300
        Advance of Crusaders from Acre   301
        Battle of Arsûf   302–304
        Crusaders at Joppa ; negotiations and intrigues ; advance
            to Beit Nuba   305–306
1192   Retirement to Ascalon   307

CHAPTER XVIII

1190–1191 Affairs at home ; return of John ; war between him and
                Longchamp 308, 309
1191   Treaties between them   310
        Return of Archbishop Geoffrey ; his arrest by
            Longchamp   311
        Coalition against Longchamp ; meeting on Loddon
            Bridge   312
        A race to London ; action of the citizens ; Longchamp
            to be deposed   313
        Grant of Municipality to London ; banishment of
            Longchamp   314
        Return of King Philip ; intrigues with John .   .   315
1192   Longchamp attempts to return and again is banished ;
            Queen Eleanor as peace-maker   316

CHAPTER XIX

1192   The Crusaders at Ascalon ; dissensions. Assassination of
            Conrad of Montferrat ; Henry of Champagne
            King of Jerusalem   318–319
        Capture of Darum ; fresh advance to Beit Nuba .   .   320
        Capture of Great Caravan   321
        Final retirement from Beit Nuba ; Joppa attacked by
            Saladin, but relieved by Richard .   .   322, 323
        Battle of Joppa   324
        Truce with Saladin, and end of Third Crusade .   .   325
        Richard's voyage home ; taken prisoner by Leopold,
            Duke of Austria   326

CHAPTER XX

1193   Affairs in England ; John demands the crown ; civil
            war   327
        Philip invades Normandy ; terms for Richard's liberation   328
        Hubert Walter to be Archbishop of Canterbury .   .   329
        Mission of Longchamp to England .   .   330, 331
        French intrigues   331
        Offers by Richard to Philip and John .   .   332, 333

A.D.   PAGE

1194   Richard at last set free 333

Return to England 334

John's intrigues defeated ; end of the rebellion . . 335

Affairs at home ; finance ; judicial investigations . . 336

State crown-wearing 337

Resumption of grants ; Richard leaves England . . 338

War in Normandy, reconciliation with John . . 339, 340

Flight of Philip from Fréteval ; reduction of Aquitanian rebels ; truce with France 341

Affairs at home ; Grand Juries ; institution of Coroners 342

Registration of Jews' property 343

1195   Archbishop Walter Legate ; visitation of York ; institution of Conservators of the Peace ; Archbishop Geoffrey and his Chapter ; he is suspended by the Pope 344-345

CHAPTER XXI

1195   John reinstated in his estates ; Berengaria again with the King 347

Renewed war with France 348

1196   Treaty of Gaillon ; struggle for the possession of Les Andelys ; Normandy under Interdict . . . 349

War in Normandy ; affairs of Brittany ; Fortifications at Les Andelys ; alliance with Toulouse . . 350, 351

Popular movement in London of William Longbeard ; his execution 352

1197   The war ; Richard's allies ; feeble action . . 353-354

King's Demand for a force to serve abroad for a year refused 355

Question of liability of clergy to foreign service ; St. Hugh of Lincoln and the King . . . 356

Proposed New Assessment for Hidage ; breaking of the Great Seal 357, 358

The Hackington Chapel pulled down ; Hubert Walter resigns the Chief Juticiarship ; Geoffrey Fitz-Peter Chief Justiciar 359

CHAPTER XXII

1198   Death of Emperor Henry VI. 360

Otto IV. elected King of Germany ; fortifications at Les Andelys. 361

Richard's allies ; rout of Philip at Gisors . . 362

A truce ; Pope Innocent III. 363

Papal mission ; suggested pacification . . . 364

1199   Richard besieges Castle of Châlus ; is wounded . . 365

Dies 366

His appearance, military talent, and character . 367-369

A.D.   PAGE
1199 ~Finances; the King's Ransom; the Norman Revenue;
          prices   369–373
      ~Friendly relations with Scotland   373
      ~Relations with Wales   374–375
      ~Governors of Ireland   375

CHAPTER XXIII

JOHN LACKLAND

1199 Question of succession   377
      Anjou and Maine declare for Arthur of Brittany; John's
          supporters   378
      He is installed as Duke of Normandy   379
      Crosses to England and is crowned   380
      Form of election; coronation honours   381
      Scottish demands; John crosses to Normandy; truce
          with France   382
      Conferences with France   383
      Fresh war; truce   384
1200 Matrimonial settlement; young Louis and Blanche of
          Castile   384
      Queen Eleanor to Spain; John to England; taxation   .   385
      John returns to Normandy; treaty of Le Goulet; Louis
          and Blanche married; Isabel of Gloucester divorced   386
      John marries Isabel of Angoulême; crosses to England
          for her coronation   387
      Receives homage from William the Lion; funeral of
          St. Hugh of Lincoln 387, 388
1201 Progress to the North; quarrel with the Lusignans   .   389
      Demand for service over sea resisted: compromised by
          payment of scutage; John crosses to Normandy;
          visits to Paris and Poitou   390–391

CHAPTER XXIV

1202 Philip and the Lusignans; John cited to Paris   .   .   392
      And condemned; invasion of Normandy by Philip   .   393
      Queen Eleanor besieged by grandson Arthur   .   .   394
      Relieved by John; capture of Arthur   395
1203 Arthur disappears   396
      John again cited   397
      Further French conquests in Normandy   .   .   .   398
      Attempted relief of Château Gaillard   399
      John crosses to England   400
1204 Fall of Château Gaillard; surrender of Rouen   .   401, 402
      Loss of Normandy, Maine, Anjou, and Touraine   .   .   403
      Death of Queen-dowager Eleanor   404
1205 John calls for troops for service abroad; the demand
          rejected   405

CHAPTER XXV

A.D.		PAGE
1205	Death of Archbishop Hubert Walter; his administration	406
	Struggle for appointment of a successor; secret election of Sub-prior Reginald	407
	Nomination and counter-election of John Gray, Bishop of Norwich	408
1206	Expedition of John to Aquitaine; advance to the Loire.	409
	Truce; the King returns to England; Innocent III. quashes the election of Bishop Gray . . .	410
	Also that of Sub-prior Reginald; nominates Stephen Langton to be Archbishop of Canterbury . .	411
1207	John refuses his assent	412
	Consecration of Langton; his estates seized; Expulsion of Canterbury monks; levy of a Thirteenth . .	413
	Innocent threatens to lay England under Interdict. .	414
1208	The Interdict proclaimed	415
	Persecution of the Clergy	416
	De Braose and King John ('the murderer of Arthur')	416, 417
	John evading the Papal demands	418
	He is excommunicated	419

CHAPTER XXVI

1209	Relations with Wales and Scotland . . .	420–421
	Further treaty; John's son Henry to be recognised .	422
1210	Royal expedition to Ireland; expulsion of De Braose and the De Lacys; capture of Carrickfergus; Matilda de Braose and her son done to death . .	423–425
	Introduction of English law into Ireland; mapping out of subject counties	425
	John returns to England; taxation of clergy and Jews .	426

CHAPTER XXVII

1211	John's position	428
	Expeditions to Wales; Llywelyn forced to submit . .	429
	Unsuccessful mission to England of Pandulph and Durand	429–430
1212	John contracting Continental alliances; alleged Embassy to Morocco	431
	Inquest of Service	432
	Fresh rising in Wales; disaffection in England, flight of De Vescy and Fitz-Walter	433
	Peter of Pontefract; his prophecy	434
	Innocent III. and his opponents	435
1213	John reopens negotiations; Innocent's ultimatum .	436, 437
	Call to arms in England; preparations in France for invasion of England	437, 438

A.D.		PAGE
1213	John accepts Innocent's ultimatum, and in addition surrenders England to be held as fief of the Holy See .	439
	Execution of Peter of Pontefract	440
	Destruction of French fleet; Archbishop Langton and exiled Bishops come to England	441
	John absolved; terms of absolution	442
	Barons again refuse to serve abroad; civil war imminent	442, 443
	Councils at St. Albans and London; Charter of Henry I. produced	443, 444
	Mission of Papal Legate Cardinal Nicolas; John does homage to him for the Crown	445
	Discussions as to ecclesiastical damages, and appointments to benefices	446, 447
	Death of the Justiciar Geoffrey Fitz-Peter, Earl of Essex	447

CHAPTER XXVIII

1214	Royal expedition to Poitou; Operations in the Valley of the Loire	448, 449
	Flight from La Roche-au-Moine	450, 451
	Campaign and Battle of Bouvines	451–464
	Truce with France; John returns to England . .	465

CHAPTER XXIX

1214	Dissolution of the Interdict; discontented state of England	466, 467
1215	The Barons combine to demand the Charter of Henry I.	468
	Popular approval in England; condemnation by Innocent III.	469
	The Barons in Arms	470
	Negotiations with King; Articles tendered and rejected	471
	War declared; occupation of Bedford . . .	472
	Barons enter London	473
	John accepts *Magna Carta*	474–477
	Ostensible pacification	478
	Text of *Magna Carta*	479–485

CHAPTER XXX

1215	Disturbers of the peace excommunicated by the Pope .	486
	The Crown offered to Louis of France . . .	487
	Archbishop Langton suspended; *Magna Carta* quashed by Innocent	488
	War again; seizure and siege of Rochester Castle .	489
	Reduction of Rochester, and devastation of England by John	490, 491
1216	The Lothians overrun	492
	Reduction of Colchester; the Pope in the field .	493

A.D.		PAGE
1216	Louis forbidden to cross ; mission of Cardinal Gualo .	494
	Landing of Louis	495
	Title made by him	496
	Confederates in East Anglia ; Louis in the South ; his halting leadership	497
	Scottish homage ; balance of parties . . .	498
	Last raid of John	499
	His illness	500
	And death	501

CHAPTER XXXI

199–1216	John's personal appearance, character and government	502, 503
	His Revenue	504–506
	Prices	506
	The public Records (Patent Rolls, Close Rolls, etc.) .	507
	The Boroughs	507–509
	The Gild Merchant	510
	Oxford and Cambridge	511, 512
	The English of the period	513
	The King's issue	514

NOTE TO READER.

Where the *ipsissima verba* of an author are given without modification, double inverted commas (" ") are used. If the words are translated, transliterated, or in any way modified, single inverted commas (' ') are used ; "*Jura sua*," 'their rights.'

ILLUSTRATIONS AND MAPS

		PAGE
FRANCE, A.D. 1166	*To face*	92
PORTRAIT OF RICHARD I.	„	262
FORMATION OF CRUSADING ARMY ON MARCH TO ARSÛF .	„	302
FORTIFICATIONS AT LES ANDELYS.	„	398
BATTLE OF BOUVINES—THE CAMPAIGN	„	454
„ „ ARRAY OF THE ARMIES . . .	„	458
„ „ SALISBURY'S CHARGE . . .	„	463

ERRATA

Page 19. For Raymond "V.," read "IV."

Page 191. For "Count" of Limoges, read "Viscount."

Page 208. For "Peter," Bishop of Aberdeen, read "Matthew."

Page 210. For "stepson," Philip, read "half-brother."

Page 245. For "on Saturday, 8 July," read "Friday, 7 July" (so Cardinal Langton, cited Ann. Waverley, 293).

Page 277. For "Geoffrey," Lucy, read "Godfrey."

Page 310. For "Herts" read "Hertford."

Page 322. For "Toron" (twice) read "Darum."

Page 386 (note 4). For "sister's husband, Amauri of Montfort," read "sister's son, Amauri the Younger of Montfort."

Page 449. For "Hugh le Brun X.," read "IX." and delete note (5).

Page 450 (line 3). For "Hugh, son of the man who was to have married the mother," read "Hugh, the man who was," etc.

Page 505. For "Amauri of Montfort, the 'husband' of her elder sister," read "son."

Page 514. Add to the notice of Queen Isabel that in 1220 she remarried her old love, the Count of La March, by whom she had issue.

Page 515 (line 4). For "of Berkshire and Staffordshire 1221–1222," read "of Berkshire 1221–1222; of Cumberland 1225 (List of Sheriffs)."

CHAPTER I

A.D. 1154-1158

HENRY II. "CURT MANTEL"[1]

Born 25th March 1133;[2] crowned 19th December 1154; died 6th July 1189

Accession and Coronation—Resumption of Castles—Homage to the King's Sons—. Designs on Ireland—Expedition to Anjou—Affairs of Brittany—Scottish Homage. and Recovery of the Northern Counties—Expedition to Wales

YOUNG, rich, and talented, the first-born son of Geoffrey *Plante Geneste* and Matilda the Empress came to the throne under circumstances beyond measure favourable. The Continental dominions already under his sway of themselves made him the most powerful of Western princes. Normandy he might be supposed to hold in right of his mother, who, however, was still living. As a matter of fact he owed the Duchy to his father,—who had conquered it by sheer force of arms; Geoffrey's cession to his son having been duly confirmed by investiture at the hands of Louis VII.[3] Anjou and Maine were Henry's by right of birth; while the hand of the divorced Eleanor made him lord of a territory that extended almost without a break from the Loire to the Adour.[4] Above all he would come · as one appointed to rescue England from the miseries of anarchy, and to restore the shattered organisation of government, a formidable task, but one to which Henry's energy, determination and business capacity proved fully equal. In blood he was partly Angevin, partly

The Young Duke.

His Position and Prospects.

---

[1] Giraldus Cambrensis, VIII. 304. So called from having introduced the short Angevin cloak, instead of the long cloak worn under Henry I.

[2] R. de Monte, Rolls Series, No. 82, Vol. IV. 123; Orderic, V. 46 and note (ed. Le Prevost).

[3] See *Foundations of England*, II. 441, 445.

[4] Eleanor's father, William IX., was Count Poitiers and Duke of Aquitaine; his nominal dominions included the fiefs of Poitiers, La Marche, Saintonge, Angoulême, Limoges, Auvergne, Perigord, Guienne and Gascony, but his actual possessions only extended to the counties of Poitiers and Bordeaux. His rights over the other fiefs were merely those of an over-lord. Norgate, I. 442. Bourges was the only fief held by Louis south of the Loire. Martin, *Hist. France*, III. 461 (ed. 1855).

B

Norman, to all intents and purposes a Frenchman. But he had paid three if not four visits to England, and a sojourn of four continuous years in boyhood[1] must have given him a fair knowledge of the insular tongue.[2]

We parted from the young Duke about the 4th April (1154), when he went back from England to Normandy. A son and **Affairs in Normandy.** heir, William, had been born to him during his absence: the reversion to England had been assured to him by the convention of Winchester, and he had but to abide in patience the falling-in of the inheritance. He had not long to wait. The short interval however was well employed. His first step was to revoke alienations of the ducal demesne, grants made to Norman magnates by his father in times of difficulty. We next hear of a visit to Aquitaine to suppress baronial outbreaks. By the end of June he had returned to Rouen.[3] In August he came to terms with Louis, who accepted him as Duke of Aquitaine,[4] and even agreed to restore Neuf Marché (Seine Inferieure), and Vernon (Eure), places won by him in 1152 and 1153. The restitution was facilitated by the payment of 2,000 marks for the expenses to which the King had been put in besieging, manning, and victualling the forts.[5] In September Henry was laid up by a severe attack of illness; but by the month of October he was sufficiently recovered to lead an expedition into the Vexin—now wholly belonging to France[6]—at the request of Louis, to bring Joscelin Crespin, a troublesome baron, to order. This was followed by the siege of Torigny (Manche), the old Gloucester possession, held against Henry by his rebellious cousin Richard, younger son of the faithful Earl Robert, whose loyal devotion had not been inherited by all his sons. The place apparently had just fallen when the news was brought that Stephen had passed away, having died on the 25th October. Henry immediately conferred with his mother to secure her approval, and then convened a Grand Council of Norman magnates, summoned, apparently, not so much to give constitutional advice, as to **Crossing to England.** grace the voyage to England. The Duke's brothers Geoffrey and William were among those present. Foul winds, however, detained the Ducal party at Barfleur for a whole month. Finally, setting

---

[1] *Foundations*, II. 416, 430, 437, 447.

[2] Walter Map gives Henry credit for some knowledge of all languages 'from the Atlantic to the Jordan' (a Mari Gallico usque ad Jordanem), but says that he only conversed in Latin and French. De Nugis Cur., p. 227 (ed. Wright).

[3] On the 24th June he assented to the election of Robert of Torigny ("De Monte") as Abbot of Bec ; De Monte, *sup.* 179.

[4] Martin, *France*, III. 463.

[5] R. de Monte, 180.

[6] The Norman Vexin had been ceded by Count Geoffrey to Louis in 1151 as the price of his recognition of young Henry as Duke of Normandy. See *Foundations*, II. 443.

sail seemingly on the 7th December,[1] they landed on the morrow at various points on the South coast.[2]

For six weeks England had been without a king, but not a breach of the peace had occurred.[3] At the death of Henry I. one week sufficed to throw both England and Normandy into chaos. The writers give all the credit for the improved state of things to Archbishop Theobald, who, without doubt, had worked strenuously for Henry; but the real causes of the change lay deeper. England was in a state of exhaustion, and sick of non-government; the people felt that they had at last a man with an indisputable title, who both could and would rule.

The first place made for was Winchester, the old capital, where Henry met with an enthusiastic reception, and the Barons did homage. London received him with equal joy. On the Sunday before Christmas Day (19th December), Henry and Eleanor were duly hallowed **Coronation.** at Westminster. Archbishop Theobald of course officiated, but the ceremony must have been one of exceptional magnificence, as some fourteen English bishops assisted,[4] including the late King's brother, Henry of Winchester. Four prelates also came from Normandy, with Stephen's friend Archbishop Hugh of Rouen at their head. Nor were Continental lay magnates wanting : chief of these was Dietrich of Flanders, the old ally of Henry I.[5] A Coronation charter was issued, of course.

But, like Stephen in his first charter, and almost in Stephen's **A Charter.** words, Henry contented himself with making a general grant " by reference," without condescending to specify the points on which he would consider himself bound. That is to say he simply conceded ' all the liberties and free customs ' that his grandfather Henry had granted, likewise remitting ' all the bad customs ' that he had remitted.[6] The Charter is attested by one witness, Richard of Lucy, a man who had been in Stephen's confidence, but who had gained and lived to justify the confidence of Stephen's successor. Probably he had been **Ministerial** already appointed Chief Justiciar, a new post, which he **Appoint-** held for five-and-twenty years. But for thirteen years of the **ments.** time he held the office only in conjunction with Robert of Beaumont the Earl of Leicester.[7] Here however we must note the

---

[1] R. de Monte, 180–182.

[2] Gervase, I. 159. He gives the place of landing as Hostreham, which looks like Horsham in Sussex. Huntingdon says " Applicuit apud Noveforest."   [3] H. Hunt.

[4] So Gervase. R. de Monte brings in the whole Episcopate, seventeen in all.

[5] Gervase, I. 159; R. de Monte; H. Hunt; W. Newb., I. 101; Chron. E. Henry of Huntingdon and the Peterborough Chronicle (E) end here.

[6] Statutes of Realm, Charters of Liberties, p. 4; Select Charters, 129. Bishop Stubbs points out that the word ' customs ' should be taken much in the modern sense, as referring to pecuniary exactions.

[7] Foss, *Judges*. In the convention with Stephen Lucy had been given the charge of the Tower of London and the ' motes ' of Oxford and Windsor; *Fœdera*, I. 18.

trust in his own position evinced by the young King in committing such powers to territorial magnates.[1] His grandfather would never have risked such a step. He only employed men of moderate rank.

Another appointment of the first days of the reign must have been that of Nigel Bishop of Ely as Chancellor;[2] but within a month or so he was recalled to the Exchequer, where his acquaintance with the procedure of the times of Henry I. would be invaluable. The Great

Thomas Becket Chancellor. Seal was then given to Theobald's confidential agent, Thomas Becket, Archdeacon of Canterbury,[3] the brilliant young diplomatist who had contrived to gain .the credit of having prevented the Papal recognition of Stephen's son Eustace.[4]

On Christmas Day, losing no time, Henry held a Grand Council in Bermondsey Abbey, and passed decrees for the expulsion of Flemish mercenaries, and the demolition of ' adulterine ' castles, that is of castles fortified without royal license.[5] A provision for the destruction of such fortresses had been included in the convention with Stephen, and some steps towards carrying out the agreement had been taken by him.

The Flemings gave no trouble. William of Ypres retired without a

Stephen's Supporters. struggle, but apparently on the soothing condition of retaining, at any rate for a time, his Kentish revenues, amounting to no less a sum than £451 8s. 7d.[6] His countrymen mostly went with him. Some of them however were allowed to settle in Pembrokeshire, to strengthen the existing colony there, a very judicious step.[7] But the resolutions of the Council as to castles might be expected to involve struggles with refractory magnates, especially as Henry's views as to

Resumption of Grants. resumption extended to all grants large or small made by Stephen,[8] and even to offices held by old and trusted adherents of his own under grants either from the Empress or from Henry I. Of the five or six Earls whom we could regard as standing by Stephen to the last,[9] one, William of Aubigny, had already come in, and been

William of Aubigny. confirmed in his 'third penny' as Earl of Arundel or Sussex.[10] He however had taken no part in the war, and was not at all a dangerous man. Chief of those who might be considered dangerous were William of Aûmale, created Earl of York by

---

[1] So again we find Patrick Earl of Salisbury acting as Sheriff of Wilts, and the Earl of Norfolk acting for his own county. Pipe Rolls.

[2] See his attestation of a charter, Eyton, *Itinerary of Henry I.*, p. 2.

[3] Becket signs in January, 1155, Eyton, *sup.*, p. 3.

[4] See *Foundations of England*, II. 442, 447.

[5] Gervase, I. 160 ; R. Monte ; W. Newb., I. 101.

[6] See the Pipe Rolls, *Red Book Excheq.*, II. 648, 658 (H. Hall, Rolls' Series No. 99)

[7] Gervase 161 ; W. Newb, *sup.*

[8] W. Newb., 103.

[9] *Foundations*, II. 441.

[10] Eyton, *sup.*, 2.

Stephen; and William Peverel of Nottingham. The former during the
anarchy had ruled as a petty King;[1] the latter in 1153 had
repelled Henry's attack on Nottingham.   Early in January
(1155) Henry started for East Anglia and the North.   Passing
through Oxford he came to Northampton, where he received the shifty
Hugh Bigod, and recreated him Earl of Norfolk; advancing by way
of Peterborough and Lincoln he reached York in February.   There
the Earl, after much hesitation, bowing to superior force, came in,
and submitted to be confirmed in his earldom in consideration of
a large surrender of royal lands held by him, and above of all on
condition of handing over the great fortifications established by
him on the heights of Scarborough.[2] From York the King turned to
Nottingham.   Peverel, who laboured under the imputation of having
poisoned Ralph "Gernons" the late Earl of Chester, did not
abide his coming.   He fled to a cloister, and took the cowl.[3]
Early in March the King is again found in London, where he
again held another Grand Council, in which fresh edicts of resumption
were promulgated, with the immediate result of driving Roger Earl of
Hereford, and Hugh of Mortimer into open revolt.   Roger
was the son of Milo of Gloucester, both father and son having
been among Matilda's staunchest supporters.   Roger held the
Castle of Hereford in his capacity of Earl, and that of Gloucester as
hereditary constable, under a grant dating at least from the time of Henry I.
Both fortresses were demanded of him.   Hugh was the head of a family
that had risen to the first place on the Welsh March on the
ruins of the House of Montgomery.   Bridgenorth, Cleobury,
and Wigmore were his.   He had taken no active part in the
struggles between Stephen and the Empress, but he must have been
required to surrender these strongholds, as he prepared to defend them.
Earl Roger did not persevere in his revolt.   Gilbert Foliot, the Angevin
Bishop of Hereford, said to be his kinsman, brought him round.   On the
13th March he made his submission, being allowed to retain his earldom
in consideration of yielding Hereford and Gloucester.[4] In the course
of the year, he died, leaving no issue.   His brother Walter was allowed
to take up the paternal estates, but not the earldom, which was left in
abeyance.[5]   The struggle with Mortimer involved actual hostilities,
extending over the months of May and June.   Several contingents were
detached to lay siege to Bridgenorth, Cleobury, and Wigmore.   The first

Side notes:
William of Aumale.
William Peverel.
Roger Earl of Hereford.
Hugh of Mortimer.

[1] "Qui sub Stephano rex verior fuerat," Newb., *sup.*, a man of the district.
[2] See Eyton, *Itin.*, 2-5; W. Newb., *sup*. The Earl retained Driffield, valued at £67.
Red Book, II. 676.
[3] *Id.*, Gervase, I. 161 ; R. Monte.
[4] Gervase, *sup.* ; W. Newb, 105; Eyton, *sup.*, 109.
[5] R. Monte, 184, 185.

surrendered after a brief siege, Cleobury making more resistance was captured and demolished; on the 7th July, Hugh made his peace.[1]

To go back to some earlier events of greater interest, on the 10th April Henry had held a Grand Council at Wallingford, when the Barons were required to swear allegiance to his son William, not two years old,[2] and, failing him, to the second son, Henry, only born on the previous 28th February.[3] The introduction of the alternative heir might be due to the fact that the elder brother was delicate, and, in fact he died in the course of the following year.[4] Here we have the first indication of the family and dynastic policy destined to become so conspicuous throughout the reign. A further illustration of it was afforded about the 29th September, when another Grand Council was held at Winchester, and a notable scheme propounded; a scheme on which, so far as we can see, no ruler of any part of Great Britain had ever cast a thought since the time of Agricola,[5] namely, a plan for the conquest of Ireland. We are told that the King thought that it would make a good appanage for his second brother William. It appears that to obtain a sanction for his undertaking, in accordance with the example set by the Conqueror when preparing for his attack on England, Henry had applied to the Papacy for approval of his purpose. The Pope at the time was Adrian IV. an Englishman, the only Englishman who ever attained to that dignity;[6] and the mission was entrusted to a personal friend of his, John of Salisbury, an accomplished man of letters, of whom we shall hear much. He found no difficulty in representing his master's enterprise as one for reforming the lax moral and ecclesiastical condition of Ireland, and bringing it into due relations with St. Peter's Chair. Already the Papacy had been endeavouring to bring Erin within the scope of its authority; and not four years before had reorganised the Irish Sees, establishing them under the four Archbishoprics of Armagh, Dublin, Cashel, and Tuam.[7] Salisbury tells us that his mission was entirely successful, and that he brought back Papal letters 'granting' Ireland,

The Succession.

Designs on Ireland.

John of Salisbury at Rome.

[1] *Id.*

[2] William was born 17th August, 1153; R. de Monte. [3] *Id.* [4] *Id.*

[5] See *Foundations*, I. 69.

[6] Anastasius IV. died December 3rd, 1154. On the same day or the next Nicholas Breakspear, Bishop of Albano, was elected, and took the style of Adrian IV. He was the son of a poor clerk at Langley, who became a monk at St. Albans. The son went abroad, studied at Paris; and afterwards became a canon in the Priory of St. Ruf, near Avignon. A dispute as to the validity of his election to be Prior took him to Rome, where Eugenius III. made him Cardinal-Bishop of Albano. He was sent as Legate to Denmark and Norway, where he remained for some years. He returned to Rome about 1150, and on the death of Anastasius became Pope. See W. Newburgh, I., 109, comparing M. Paris, *Gesta Abbatum*, 70 (Ed. Wats); Norgate, *Angevin Kings*, I. 475.

[7] For the mission of Cardinal Paparo to Ireland, and the Synod held by him at Kells, March 1152, see *Foundations*, II. 439; also Four Masters, A.D. 1152.

as he puts it, to the King, 'as an estate of inheritance,'[1] the grant being based on the known rights of the Church of Rome over all islands. John further tells us that he received a golden ring, set with an emerald, as a symbol of the investiture of Ireland.[2] He adds that the ring was kept in the Royal Treasury; the Papal mandate being also deposited there.[3] Here in speaking of an actual 'grant' of Ireland John was evidently giving the sum and substance of his letter, as he and all the world understood it; because the actual document, the so-called "Bull"[4] *Laudabiliter*, contains

The Bull "Laudabi-liter." no such words.[5] Adrian, with due Papal caution merely commends Henry's declared intention of 'entering' (*velle intrare*) Ireland for the sake of 'extending the bounds of the Church;[6] reducing the people to order, and extirpating all vicious growths of the soil.'[7] But as justification for his conduct in approving of Henry's scheme he does refer to the undoubted rights of St. Peter over 'all Christian islands,'[8] the very point mentioned by John of Salisbury. The "Bull" has been fiercely assailed, for very obvious reasons, by zealous Romanists, and patriotic Irishmen. We believe it to be genuine. But even if it should prove to be a concoction there would still remain ample evidence that the Papacy was accessory, both before and after the fact, to the invasion of Ireland by Henry. The statements of John of Salisbury as to the action of Adrian cannot be ignored. With respect to his successor Alexander III. we shall find letters of his, the authenticity of which is undisputed, strenuously backing up Henry's later proceedings.[9] If the Bull *Laudabiliter* has not been found in the Papal Archives, approving notices of the conduct of Adrian and Alexander in the matter have been traced to subsequent Pontiffs, with, in one case, an unmistakable reference to the very terms of *Laudabiliter* itself.[10] Salisbury's letter was doubtless

---

[1] "Concessit et dedit Hiberniam iure hæreditario possidendam; *Metalogus*, V. 205 (ed. Giles).

[2] "Quo fieret investitura juris in gerenda Hibernia"; p. 206.

[3] Namely at Winchester, Giraldus Camb. V. 316.

[4] It seems that in strictness it should be described as "Letters Commendatory"; Round, *Commune of London*, 172.

[5] See the document Girald, V. 317; R. Diceto, I. 300; and R. Wendover, II. 241 (ed. Coxe). The last gives the date 1155.

[6] "Ad dilatandos ecclesiæ terminos."

[7] "Ad vitiorum plantaria inde extirpanda."

[8] For the Papal claim to all islands, based on the spurious Donation of Constantine, see *Foundations*, II. 110.

[9] Liber Niger Scacc, I. 42–48 (Hearne, ed. 1774).

[10] See the passage from a dispensation of the 13th century (Theiner *Monumenta*, I. 151), and that from the instructions of Innocent X. to Rinuccini as Nuncio to Ireland (Rinuccini's *Embassy to Ireland*, Hutton, p. xxviii., and Aiazzi's *Nunziatura*, p. xxxvi.), given by Mr. Round, *Commune of London*, pp. 199, 203. His own view is that the Bull was forged by Giraldus. The reader is further referred to Miss Norgate's Article in the English Hist. Rev., VIII. 13-52. "The latest German papers appear to be those of

laid before the Winchester Council.   But the Empress, to whose views Henry paid great regard, objected to the proposed invasion.   Perhaps she was afraid of the perils that her son might run ; and so for the time "the strange Crusade" was dropped.[1]

Another significant fact was the retirement about this time, without royal leave and as it were by stealth, of the Bishop of Winchester, Henry of Blois, the ex-Legate, the brother of King Stephen, and in fact the man who had raised him to the throne   Not feeling himself comfortable in England under Henry II. he withdrew to his old home at Cluny. Henry at once dismantled his castles.[2]   But the Bishop's retirement was not of long duration.   The compilement of a Pipe Roll for the first year of the reign, beginning at the coronation, and ending at Michaelmas 1155, of

The Revenue. which a summary has been preserved, may be taken as evidence that the general scheme of the old administration had already been set a-going.[3]   For the reign of Stephen no trace of any Pipe Roll has been discovered.[4]   Altogether "the history of the year furnishes abundant illustration of the energy and capacity of a King of two-and-twenty."[5]

Henry was now called abroad to resist the pretensions of his brother

Expedition Abroad. Geoffrey, an ambitious youth, who in 1152 had attempted to waylay and carry off Eleanor when leaving the court of her first husband ; and later in the year had joined a general coalition against his elder brother.[6]   Geoffrey maintained that under their father's will Anjou and Maine had been assured to him in the event of Henry's succeeding to their mother's possessions of Normandy and England.   The story ran that Henry, in compliance with his father's injunctions to those with him on his deathbed, had sworn to abide by the provisions of Geoffrey's will before they were made known to him ; that when they were made known to him he rejected them, and appealed to the Pope to release him of his oath, on the ground that he had been tricked ; and that the Pope, admitting his plea, absolved him.[7]

Scheffer-Boichort in ' Mittheilungen des Instituts für Österreich Geschicht's fiorschung," Erganzung's Band, IV. (1892), and Pflug-Harttung in 'Deutsche Zeitschrift fur Geschwissenschaft' X. (1897)."

[1] R. de Monte ; Norgate.   [2] *Id. Red Book*, II. 662.
[3] See *Red Book of Exq.*, II. 648–658. Only 25 counties out of 32 are called to account.   The regular county ferms alone figure, without any Danegeld or extraordinary receipts.   The sums paid in or accounted for, as I read them, amount to £827 17s. 10d. to the Exchequer, and £238 to the Chamber or Privy Purse, in all £1,067 6s. 2d., a hint as to the probable amount of Stephen's revenue.
[4] For the Pipe Rolls see *Foundations*. II. 323.
[5] Stubbs, *Const. Hist.*, I. 491.
[6] See *Foundations*, II. 445.
[7] So W. Newb., I. 112, the only authority for this story.   But Henry had been formally invested with Normandy by his father, and, apparently, was with him on his deathbed.

On the 10th January[1] Henry crossed from Dover to Wissant with a
force equipped in part by a scutage levied in regular course on the
bishops and abbots.[2] The lay tenants, we may suppose, would render
their services in person. The charge of affairs in England during
the King's absence was left with the Justiciars, the Earl of Leicester
and Richard of Lucy, with some assistance from the Queen, who remained
at home, as she was expecting her confinement. Becket the Chancellor
followed the King.[3]

By the 2nd February Henry had reached Rouen. His first care was
to safeguard his position by drawing closer the friendly relations already
existing with France and Flanders. On the 5th February he met
Louis VII. on the border, and again did homage for all
his Continental possessions, thus establishing beyond question
his technical right to the territories claimed by his brother.
Returning to Rouen he gave a friendly reception to Dietrich of Flanders
and his Countess Sibylle, who was Henry's aunt.[4] A meeting with his
brother passed off less happily. Geoffrey, rejecting Henry's
offers, fled to Anjou, to set in order his three castles, his
undisputed appanage, namely Chinon (Indre et Loire),
Loudun, and Mirebeau (both in Vienne). Henry followed him up with
his army. Mirebeau and Chinon were besieged and taken: and then
Geoffrey submitted. Loudun he was allowed to retain, surrendering
all else, but receiving a money pension by way of compensation (July).[5]

Within twelve months' time however Henry was able to establish his
brother in a new and more comfortable position, and one moreover that
seemed to promise opportunities for future intervention in the affairs of a
neighbouring state. The over-lordship of Brittany had long been
claimed by the Dukes of Normandy; and Henry I. had actually
received homage from Count Allan Fergant in 1113. The
homage was accompanied by a marriage contracted between Matilda,
a natural daughter of the English King, and the Count's son Conan.
This man shortly succeeded his father as Conan III.;[6] but his marriage

Homage to Louis.

Fraternal War.

Affairs of Brittany.

---

[1] Annales Cambriæ, but A.D. 1157 (Rolls Series No. 21).

[2] See the Pipe Roll of the year as summarised *Red Book of Excheq.*, II. 659; John of
Salisbury, Epp. I. 178.

[3] See Eyton, *sup.* At Dover the King passed a charter re-creating Aubrey de Vere
Earl of Oxford.

[4] Daughter of Fulk V., and originally married to William of Normandy, Duke Robert's
son, but divorced from him through the intrigues of Henry I. The Count of Flanders
drew a liberal subvention from England. He had £71 a year from Crown lands in
Oxfordshire, and £250 in Lincoln, etc.; *Red Book*, II. 674, 675; Pipe Rolls, etc.

[5] R. Monte; W. Newb., I. 113, 114; Eyton, *sup.* De Monte gives the promised
pension as £1,000 sterling and £2,000 Angevin. Nothing was paid from the English
Exchequer, but it might be paid from the Norman Exchequer.

[6] See *Foundations*, II. 271, 339.

with Matilda did not prove a happy one. He disowned her son **Hoel**, and declared a daughter, Bertha, the heiress of Brittany, Hoel being relegated to the subordinate position of Count of Nantes. Bertha first married a kinsman, Allan the Black, the Earl of Richmond who fought on Stephen's side at Lincoln, and by him had a son Conan. Earl Allan died in 1146, and then Bertha took as her second husband Eude, Viscount of Porhoet. Her father, Conan III., died in 1148, whereupon Eude became Count of Brittany in right of his wife.[1] Conan of Richmond, like his father Allan, had sided with Stephen, but he must have made terms with Henry, as we find him drawing 'the third penny' in Suffolk this very year.[2] It was therefore, doubtless, with Henry's consent and with means supplied by him that in September (1156) he went over to Brittany, expelled his stepfather Eude from his capital at Rennes, and obtained for himself extensive recognition throughout Upper Brittany.[3] But Nantes, the capital of Lower Brittany, generally at issue with the Western district, refused to accept Earl Conan; at

Geoffrey of Anjou in Brittany. the same time being dissatisfied with their own Hoel, they made overtures to Geoffrey of Anjou, who, with his brother's entire approval, was shortly installed as Count of Nantes.[4]

We have referred to the scutage imposed by Henry for the war against his brother. The levy in question has commonly been

The Scutage of 1156. regarded as the first tax of the sort ever raised in England, the notion being due to the mistaken assertion of Alexander Swereford, compiler of the *Red Book of the Exchequer*, an official of the time of Henry III., who, from want of proper records, had failed to find evidence of any earlier scutage.[5] For the date of this kind of impost as going back to the time of Henry I., at any rate, we have a charter of his

Earlier Scutages. remitting £40 out of the £100 that the Abbot of Ely 'used to pay for scutage when levied by me.'[6] We have other evidence to the same effect for his reign, and also for that of Stephen, and in particular a charter of Gilbert Earl of

History of the Tax. Pembroke (Strongbow) in which he refers to scutage at Horsted as being usually paid at the rate of ten shillings the knight's fee.[7] As for the tax in itself it was a composition for personal service in time of war, the latter being a primary

---

[1] See G.E.C. Peerage " Richmond," and the notes of Mr. W. G. Watson.

[2] See *Red Book Exchequer*, II. 666.

[3] R. de Monte.

[4] A.D. 1157, before Lent, W. Newb., I. 114 and note ; Lobineau, *Hist. Bretagne*, I. 152, 153 ; Morice, *Bretagne*, I. 103, 104 ; and *Preuves*, I. 104.

[5] *Red Book Exchq.*, I. 6.

[6] " Quando scutagium currebat per terram meam Anglie," MS. Cott. Nero A., 15, cited Round, *Feudal England*, 268. In 1166 Ely, then a bishopric, only returned 40 knights' fees as its quota ; Round, *sup.* 249.

[7] Lewes Cartulary, MS. Cott. Vesp. F. XV. 73 ; Round, *Antiquity of Scutage*, 4-7.

ity, from the burden of which not even church lands had ever been exempt. In Old English days the attendance in the *fyrd* or national host was one of the three requirements of the *Trinoda Necessitas*, from which no man was exempt. When the military system was reorganised by the Conqueror he appears to have laid on the tenants-in-chief, or persons holding directly of the Crown, ecclesiastical and lay,

Knight's Service. certain assessments of *milites*, or fully equipped men-at-arms, according to the value of the estates granted or confirmed to them by the King. The quotas to a certain extent appear to have been based on existing compositions, as effected before the Conquest, between the previous owners of the estates and the Crown.[1] As to the social standing of the men to be provided, the term *milites* has been rendered 'knights.' But men-at-arms or esquires would be more correct term, as the bulk of the men could not be in the position of dubbed knights, their holdings only extending to a few hides of land. The quotas, in the first instance at any rate, must have been fixed orally, as it is clear that no official register of the numbers had ever been drawn up, and the number of *milites*, for which a particular landowner was liable, was often disputed. This *debitum servitium* of 'knight's service' might be provided for by the parties liable in one of two ways; either by keeping a standing body of household retainers, 'house carles' in Anglo-Saxon phrase, or by allotting small estates to suitable men on condition of their being ready to turn out on demand for the requisite forty days' service. These estates were styled *feoda militum*, knights' fees, and the system became so prevalent that an enquiry as to the number of men-at-arms for which a particular landowner was liable usually took the shape of an enquiry as to the number of *feoda militum* held of him.[2] The commutation of the actual attendance of the *milites* in the ranks for a money payment, was an arrangement that on just terms might well suit all parties. Such was scutage, or money paid in lieu of the service of a man equipped with a shield (*Scutum Fr. Ecu.*). It is important to note again that Church lands were liable for military service like other lands, and that in the writings of the period the liability is not questioned, though disputes as to details, or the necessity or propriety of calling for a scutage at a particular time, do occur. Such was the objection raised by Archbishop Theobald, to the scutage of 1159 on which so much has been built.[3]

Henry remained abroad, moving from place to place through Aquitaine and Normandy till the spring of 1157. In the previous summer he had

[1] See Index to *Foundations*, "Fyrd."
[2] On the whole subject see Round, *Knights' Service*, reprinted in *Feudal England* 25, etc. ; also *Foundations*, II. 139, etc.
[3] See John of Salisbury Epp. No. 128 (Giles).

been joined by the Queen;[1] who about the month of June had given birth to a daughter, Matilda.[2]   On the 8th April 1157 Henry sailed from Barfleur for Southampton, the Queen and her children having preceded him.[3]   The spring and early summer were spent in the Eastern Counties, the period being marked by important resumptions.   William, the younger son of King Stephen, Count of Mortain in Normandy, and in England Earl of Surrey by virtue of his marriage with Isabelle of Warenne, was forced to surrender the castles of Norwich, Pevensey, and Mortain, although these had been assured to him by the convention of Winchester; while the old intriguer Hugh Bigot was likewise deprived of his castles and of 'the third penny' of the county of Norfolk.[4]   But we must notice that Henry with his usual moderation in his dealings with powerful men did not drive them to extremities by depriving them of their titles and such other possessions as they might be allowed to retain consistently with public safety.   Both William and Hugh are still found at Court, with their proper rank.[5]

Return to England.

Resumption of Castles.

A much more important gain was the recovery of the three Northern counties, held by the Scots during the greater part of the late reign.[6]   David I. had died 24th May 1153, his son Henry the Earl of Northumberland having predeceased him by nine months.[7]   The Scottish Crown then descended on Henry's eldest son, Malcolm IV., surnamed the Maiden,[8] a boy twelve years old.   His government, fiercely attacked by Celtic chieftains in the North and West, could not venture to insist on the pledges alleged to have been given by Henry to King David at Carlisle in 1149.[9]   Passing through Yorkshire, Lincolnshire, Notts, and the Peak, with travelling expenses liberally provided by his cousin of England, Malcolm joined Henry's court at Chester, and surrendered the Northern counties, receiving in return a renewed grant of the Earldom of Huntingdon held by his father.   On these terms Malcolm did homage; the exact scope of the recognition therefore would still remain an open ques-

The Northern Counties Regained.

Scottish Affairs.

Scottish Homage.

---

[1] She was at Saumur on the 29th August; Eyton, 18.   She returned to England with her children about February.   *Id.* 24.

[2] Bromton, 1047, (Decem Scriptt.)

[3] R. Monte, Eyton, 24.

[4] R. Monte, and Pipe Roll 3 H. II. 75, 76 (Hunter).

[5] See Eyton, 26, 27.

[6] Cumberland was made over in 1136, Westmorland being treated as an appendage to Cumberland.   The earldom of Northumberland was granted three years later.   See *Foundations*, II. 347, 379.

[7] Symeon *H. R. Cont.* 330; *H. D. E. Cont.* 169; W. Newb., I. 70.

[8] "Qui dicebatur virgo," Fordun, 254.

[9] *Foundations*, II. 438.

on.[1] The Scots might contend that the homage was only rendered for Huntingdon; the English would insist that it was rendered for Scotland.

The tryst at Chester was due to the fact that Henry was preparing for an expedition into Wales. The step apparently had been resolved upon late in June, when we are told that Henry called for levies on a reduced scale, only one man-at-arms being required from three 'knights' fees.'[2] The Prelates were required to contribute a 'scutage,' the rate being twenty shillings the knight's fee.[3] On the 17th July he held a Grand Council at Northampton and from thence marched to the Welsh border.[4] As sadly common in Celtic politics the appeal of a native

Welsh Affairs. had afforded an excuse for foreign intervention, if any excuse were needed. But Henry was bound to act unless he was prepared to abandon the Plantation lords, as we must call them, on whom the English position in Wales, and the very defence of the Welsh March entirely depended. Stephen's accession had been followed by a series of reverses,[5] and ever since that time the Anglo-Norman settlers in the Southern districts had been left to their own resources. Pembroke, apparently, had been retained throughout; but Aberystwith, Cardigan, Kidwelly, Caermarthen, and Llanstephan had changed hands again and again. On the English side the prominent

The Welsh and the English. names in the struggle were those of Gilbert of Clare, Earl of Pembroke, and his son Richard, best known by his father's original *sobriquet* of "Strongbow."[6] With them also we have Hugh of Mortimer, and the stout sons of Gerald of Windsor, the constable of Pembroke, by name William and Maurice.[7] In the South they had to battle with the sons of Gruffudd, son of Rhys ap Teudwr, the last king of South Wales, represented at the period we have reached by the surviving brother Rhys, son of Gruffudd and grandson of the king. In mid-Wales Madog son of Maredudd, of the House of Bleddyn,[8] was pleased to style himself lord of Powys; while in the North a more substantial

---

[1] July–August (after 17th July). See W. Newb., I. 103 (given under 1155) ; R. de Monte; J. Fordun, 254, 255 ; Chron. Holyrood, *Anglia Sacra*, I. 161 ; Chron. Melrose ; Eyton *Itin.* 28. According to the Melrose writer Malcolm did homage "eodem modo quo avus suus fuerat homo veteris regis Henrici, salvis omnibus dignitatibus suis."

[2] R. de Monte.

[3] Red Book Exch., II. 659, where a summary of the Pipe Roll of the year is given.

[4] Gervase, I. 163, 165. The circuitous route taken by Malcolm may be accounted for by supposing that he was making for Northampton, when he found that Henry had moved on to Chester.

[5] For the Welsh successes in 1136 and 1137 see *Foundations*, II. 347, 357.

[6] So Chron. Melrose, 82. Richard, it may be noted, is not described as a strong man.

[7] Their mother was Nest, previously mistress to Henry I. ; a third brother was David Bishop of St. David's. See Giraldus Camb. I., ix. note Brewer.

[8] See *Foundations*, II. 180, 218, 242, etc.

independence was maintained by the Princes of Gwynedd, Owain and Cadwalader, sons of Gruffudd ap Cynan. But the encounters with the settlers were but as bye-play in the continuous series of fratricidal struggles, assassinations, and warfare kept up by the native families amongst themselves. Thus Cadwalader, who ruled in Anglesey, had been expelled about the year 1152 by his brother Owain.[1] An appeal by the dispossessed Prince to the King of England was answered by the present enterprise.[2] Madog ap Maredudd of Powys was another ally, who appeared in person.

The campaign, like many an earlier one, proved but a moderate success; and it opened with a distinct reverse, Henry being inclined to take counsel of his regular military advisers,

Royal Campaign.

rather than of the March lords who understood Welsh tactics and Welsh warfare. Having crossed the Dee the army advanced by the road along the shores of the estuary to attack Owain, who with his sons Hoel, Cynan, and David, was entrenching a position at Basingwerk, one mile to the north of Holywell. On reaching Flint Henry was tempted to try a flanking movement, in order to turn the position at Basingwerk, and for that purpose detached a wing of his force to work their way round through the wooded heights of Coleshill or Consilt that overhung his left. But the woods were held

A Reverse.

by the Welsh, who promptly surrounded and overwhelmed the detachment. Eustace FitzJohn[3] of old memory, and Robert of Courcy fell. The defeated survivors falling back on the main body caused a momentary pause. Henry of Essex the constable disgraced himself by allowing the Royal Standard to fall to the ground. The cry was even raised that the King had fallen. Henry however soon rallied his men, and resumed his advance; and then it was found that Owain had abandoned his lines at Basingwerk, and was falling back on the Conway. Henry followed him to find that he had retired up the valley of the Conway to Pennant[4] near Llanrwst. Meanwhile the auxiliary fleet that had been appointed to co-operate with the army had sailed on to Anglesey, where the men landing began to plunder

The Advance Pressed.

in disorderly fashion, not even sparing churches. 'But God brought vengeance upon them.' The natives gathering in force drove the stragglers back to their ships with considerable loss, the King's natural uncle, Henry, son of Henry I. by the Lady Nest, being one of the slain. But between a fleet in the Menai and an army

---

[1] See Ann. Cambriæ and Brut y T. A.D. 1135-1157.

[2] Miss Norgate points to grants of land in Shropshire made to Cadwalader in the Pipe Rolls of 1156 and 1157, pp. 43, 88 (Hunter).

[3] For this man and his position in the North under Henry I. see *Foundations*, II. 336, and Foss, *Judges*, I. 115.

[4] So one MS. of the Brut.

n the Conway Owain found himself as it were between two fires, and
came to terms.   He agreed to reinstate his brother Cadwalader,
Owain Submits. declared himself Henry's man, and gave hostages.[1]   The most
substantial work of the campaign, perhaps, was the rebuilding
of the old fort at Rhuddlan, and the establishment of a new post at
Basingwerk.   Under Rufus Deganwy on the Conway had been the
frontier fort.   We also hear of a Templar's house founded between
Basingwerk and Rhuddlan.[2]   The Templars were greatly patronised by
Henry from the first,[3] possibly out of regard for his paternal grandfather
Fulk, who became a Templar and King of Jerusalem.

From Wales the King went to Oxford to see the Queen, who on the
8th September had given birth to her fourth child by him, a son
named Richard, the future *Cœur de Lion*.[4]   Christmas was kept at
Lincoln, but Henry, we are told, less strong-minded than his predecessor, refused to brave local superstition by wearing his crown within
the city walls, and so was content to wear it, not in the grand Minster
of Remigius, but in the charming little church of St. Mary-le-Wigford
across the Witham.[5]

Once more, and once more only have we to record a State crown-
Crown-wearing Renounced. wearing by Henry and Eleanor in the olden style.   Easter
1158 (20th April) was kept by them at Worcester.   During
Mass, when the time came for them to offer, they laid their
crowns upon the altar, solemnly vowing never to wear them again.[6]
The meaning of the renunciation is not clear.   It has been suggested
that it may have been simply due to Henry's impatience of ceremony
and court pageants.[7]   The crown-wearing involved delicate questions of
etiquette.   The King was not at liberty to place the crown upon his
own head.   That was the prerogative of the Archbishop of Canterbury
or other the leading ecclesiastic present, and awkward scenes had
occurred in connexion with the assertion of the privilege.[8]   Henry might
wish to avoid such scenes; possibly he shrank from the recognition of
ecclesiastical authority implied in the procedure.

---

[1] See Ann. Camb., A.D. 1158; Brut., A.D. 1156; W. Newb., I. 106–109; Giraldus
Camb., VI. 130.   For supplies of wheat and bacon provided for the army, and other
details, see the Pipe Roll of the year.

[2] R. de Monte, 193, 195.

[3] See the allowances to them from the county revenues entered on the Pipe Rolls from
the second year onwards.

[4] R. de Monte; R. Diceto; Eyton.

[5] W. Newburgh, I. 117; R. Hoveden.   For the Lincoln superstition, the origin of
which is unknown, see *Foundations*, II. 428.   Of the existing church of St. Mary-le-
Wigford, part of the tower must be as old as the time of Henry II., if not Saxon.

[6] R. Hoveden; R. Diceto; Pipe Rolls (Hunter), 175.

[7] Norgate, I. 439.

[8] See *Foundations*, II. 92, 266, 293.

CHAPTER II

HENRY II. (*continued*)

A.D. 1158-1162

The King abroad—Matrimonial Alliance with France—Occupation of Nantes and Lower Brittany—Campaign of Toulouse—Recovery of the Norman Vexin—Death of Archbishop Theobald and Appointment of Thomas Becket

FIRMLY seated on his throne, Lord Paramount of Great Britain, undisputed master of the best part of old Gaul, with a family of sons to succeed him, Henry might well have been content to follow a domestic and conservative policy, and so, to a certain extent, he did. The only war of deliberate conquest on which we shall find him embarking was that against Ireland. Towards France he never entertained any sinister intentions, though frequently at war with Louis on petty questions. But he was not a man to throw away an opportunity for family aggrandisement; while his multifarious feudal relations supplied endless claims that might be advanced with a greater or less appearance of justice.

On the 26th July (1158) Henry's brother Geoffrey died at Nantes.[1] The rights conferred upon him by his election by the people of that place as their Count had been purely personal; there was nothing in them that he could transmit to a successor, and Conan IV., surnamed 'The Little,' (Le Petit), Count of the rest of Brittany, at once entered and took possession.[2] But Henry claimed Nantes, as heir to his

Affairs of Brittany. brother. The first and most important step to be taken towards realising that pretence was to secure the support of the King of France. With this object Henry proposed a marriage between his eldest surviving son Henry, aged three years, and Margaret, Louis' daughter by his second wife, Constance of Castile, a baby six months old.

Trip to France. It would seem that to pave the way Becket the Chancellor was sent to Paris, with a retinue that dazzled the French by its magnificence.[3] Henry however must have followed hard on his tracks

---

[1] R. Monte ; Chron. Bec Cont. cited Howlett.

[2] W. Newb., I. 114.

[3] See the glowing account given by Becket's follower and biographer, William fitz Stephen, *Becket Materials*, III. xiv. 29 (J. C. Robertson, Rolls Series No. 67).

s on the 14th August he crossed the Channel, sailing either from Portsmouth or Southampton.   Again the Queen was left behind, as again she
was expecting a confinement.[1]   On the 22nd August the two kings met on
the border river Epte, near Gisors, when the marriage was settled ;[2] Louis
A agreeing by way of his daughter's portion to restore the Norman
Matrimonial Vexin ceded to him by Count Geoffrey eight years before.
Alliance. This grant however would not take effect till the marriage was
solemnised ; but in the meantime, as a material guarantee, Louis placed
the border fortresses of Gisors, Néaufles (Eure), and Neufchâtel-en-Brai
(Seine Inf.) in the hands of three Templars, as trustees and stakeholders
for both parties.   Furthermore the French King not only gave his sanction
to the occupation of Nantes by Henry, but even gave him authority to act
in his name, by recognising to some extent the old claim of the Counts of
Anjou to hold the honorary office of Seneschals of France.   If conferred
in its integrity, and clothed with all its power, the post would have made
Henry the chief executive officer of the King of France, with control both
of the army and of the finances.[3]   In this matter we hardly know which to
wonder at most, the simplicity of Louis in giving in to such arrangements,
or the dexterity of Henry in bringing him into them.   With most men
their domestic relations alone would have been a bar to any friendly
understanding.   The credit must be assigned to the charm of Henry's
manner, which was said to be irresistible.[4]   To this also we would attribute
his successful management of his barons, demoralised as they were by
years of uncontrolled licence.

The way being clear before him Henry called out the forces of Normandy
to muster at Avranches on the 29th of September for an attack on
Conan.   In the interval he paid a state visit to Paris, where he won golden
opinions by his courteous and unassuming manners, declining all clerical
processions, or marks of personal honour.   On leaving Paris he took the
baby bride away with him, as the custom of the times was, to be brought
up under his charge.

With the forces of France and England united against him Conan offered
no resistance.   On the 29th September he appeared at Av-
Occupation ranches, and surrendered Nantes, being confirmed in the
of Nantes. possession of the rest of Brittany.   Henry marched straightway to Nantes, and was accepted by the people, thus becoming lord of

---

[1] R. Monte ; Bp. Stubbs *Itinerary Henry II.*, in Benedict of Peterboro, II. cxxxi.(Rolls
Series No. 49) ; Pipe Roll.

[2] R. Monte, 196 ; Bouquet, *Historiens de la France*, XIII. 300, note.

[3] See Gervase, I. 166 ; Sismondi, *France*, V. 404 ; Martin, *France*, III. 466.   For
the Seneschalship see Norgate I. 430, and the authorities there cited, from which it
appears that as a matter of fact the office at the time was held by Theobald of Blois, but
that the Angevins disputed his right to it ; R. Monte, A.D. 1164, 1169.

[4] Giraldus Camb., V., 303 ; Peter of Blois, Epp., I. 195 (Giles).

C

all the territory between the Loire and the Vilaine,[1] with the command of the entrance to the Loire, the central artery of Gaul.

A trip to Poitou ensued to subdue and chastise a rebellious viscount of Thouars.[2] Five days' siege made an end of his resistance. Returning northwards through Le Mans the King again met Louis, who was bound on a pilgrimage to Mont St. Michel. As in duty bound Henry took his suzerain under his charge, entertaining him royally on his journey through his dominions. On Sunday 23rd November they reached the rock 'In Peril by the Sea,'[3] and heard Mass there. But for their night's quarters they returned to Avranches.[4] Again we hear of friendly arrangements[5] with neighbours, in which it would seem that Louis' influence was exerted on behalf of his vassal of England. Theobald of Blois, Count of Chartres and Blois (second son of Theobald the Great, eldest brother of King Stephen), was induced to surrender the border towns of Amboise[6] and Fréteval[7]; while Rotrou of Mortagne the younger, Count of Perche, restored Moulins-la-Marche, and Bonmoulins,[8] Norman places that his father the elder Rotrou had seized at the death of Henry I. The king however in return made over to him the castle of Bellême, a fortress that did not appertain to Normandy, though often in Norman hands.[9] Christmas was kept at Cherbourg by Henry and Eleanor, the Queen having joined him shortly before. On the 23rd September she had given birth to her fourth son Geoffrey.[10]

Friendly Kings.

Friendly Restitutions.

Still pushing onwards Henry is now found coming forward with pretensions that excited the alarm even of the unsuspicious Louis. Between the Houses of Poitiers and Toulouse a rivalry had long existed as to the theoretic over-lordship of Aquitaine in the widest sense, or the whole country between the Loire, the Rhône, the Pyrenees, and the Ocean. This supremacy since the middle of the tenth century had been claimed by Eleanor's ancestors by virtue of their ducal title. At an earlier period however the over-lordship had been supposed to rest with the Dukes of the Roman Septimania, whose capital was at Toulouse, their line being now represented by the Counts of

The Over-lordship of Aquitaine.

[1] R. de Monte, 196, 197; Bouquet, and Martin *sup.* Henry on his way to Nantes dined at Mont St. Michel with Abbot Robert and his monks.

[2] Deux Sèvres.

[3] "Montem Sancti Michaelis de Periculo Maris;" R. de Monte, 198.

[4] R. de Monte, 198; Gervase, *sup.*

[5] "Concordati sunt."

[6] Indre et Loire. Amboise was within the limits of Touraine.

[7] Loir et Cher. Fréteval does not seem to have belonged to Henry's dominions as it lay within the county of Dunois.

[8] Both in Orne.

[9] R. de Monte; Sismondi and Norgate, *sup.* Bellême also is in Orne.

[10] R. de Monte, 197.

Toulouse. Among the miscellaneous possessions of his wife Henry had
found an old claim on the county of Toulouse. About the year 1088
William IV., Count of Toulouse, by a mysterious transaction
sold and conveyed the county to his younger and more
energetic brother Raymond IV. of Crusading fame,[1] generally
known as Raymond of St. Gilles (Gard). William IV. at his death left an
only daughter Philippa, eventually married to William VIII. of Aquitaine,
Eleanor's grandfather. It would seem that he and his son
William IX. always claimed Toulouse as the lawful inheritance
of Philippa, insisting that her father had no right to dispossess
her of it, and that the sale to his brother was only valid during his own
life. Louis VII., as the husband of Eleanor, had maintained
the same view; and in the summer of 1141 had actually
drawn the sword against Toulouse.[2] But in spite of the
assertion of one writer to the contrary,[3] it seems clear that since 1088
Toulouse had remained in the hands of the house of St. Gilles, the present
Count being Raymond V. grandson of the Crusader Raymond. After
his divorce from Eleanor Louis changed his attitude towards Toulouse,
and, to establish a friendly counterpoise to Henry's power South of the
Loire, gave Raymond to wife his sister Constance, widow of Stephen's son,
Eustace.[4]

The Counts of Toulouse.

Disputed Succession.

Henry's Claim.

As a prudent politician Henry began by securing an ally. He had
one ready to hand in Raymond Berenger IV., Count of
Barcelona, Regent of Arragon, ruler of Provence in the
name of a nephew, and altogether the most formidable
neighbour and rival to the Count of Toulouse. Already as if in
contemplation of war Berenger had been contracting alliances in
Languedoc, evidently aimed against Toulouse. In the month of
January (1159) Henry met him at Blaye, on the Gironde, and came to
an understanding with him. The Count would co-operate against
Toulouse, while his daughter was contracted to Henry's
son Richard, a baby, not six months old. We are also told
that Aquitaine would be settled on the pair when the marriage
came to be celebrated.[5] About the 22nd March the King called out
all his forces. England, Normandy, Anjou, and Aquitaine alike were

The Count of Barcelona.

A Matrimonial Alliance.

[1] W. Malmesbury, *Gesta Regum*, s. 438 (Rolls Series No. 90).
[2] Orderic, 923 (Duchesne), the last event recorded in the work.
[3] R. de Monte asserts that William VIII. of Poitiers had actually been in possession
of Toulouse, and that he had mortgaged it to Raymond of St. Gilles. This looks like
an Angevin improvement of the story to strengthen Henry's claim.
[4] See R. de Monte, 201, 202 ; Sismondi, V. 407 ; and Norgate, I. 454, citing Vic et
Vaissete, *Hist. Languedoc*, III. 465 (ed. 1872). The account in W. Newb., I. 121 is a
mere jumble.
[5] Sismondi, V. 408-409 ; R. de Monte, 200, and note Howlett ; W. Newb., I. 123-125.

summoned to the field. The preparations, which must have been
Preparations for War. taken in hand some time before,[1] were on the largest scale,
in fact on a scale unparalleled in any previous expedition
by an English King. The Abbot of Mont St. Michel tells
us that the King, considering the distance at which the field of
operations lay from England, refrained from calling for the personal
attendance of any but the greater English barons, contenting himself
with pecuniary contributions from the lesser gentry, and the boroughs;
and that with the funds so raised he hired large bands of mercenaries.[2]
To the list of the taxed should have been added the English prelates,
who were not spared. With this addition the Abbot's account becomes
entirely correct. The Baronage must have been called out in all its
strength, as we have even Malcolm of Scotland, and Owain of Gwynedd
following the King's banner;[3] while on the Pipe Roll of the year
nothing appears as taken from the Magnates. The other classes were
taxed in two ways. The King first exacted from the bishops and
"The Scutage of Toulouse." abbots and lesser county gentry a scutage on their
assessed knights' fees, as he had done in 1156, only at an
enhanced rate; in that year the rate had been 20 shillings
on the knight's fee, a mark and a half. Now it was raised to two
marks, or £1 6s. 8d. on the fee. This payment exhausted the legal
liability of the persons on whose account it was paid. But Henry
went on to lay on the bishops and abbots, whose legal dues had thus
been already paid, a further arbitrary assessment,[4] running from three
times to ten times the amount of the legal liability already discharged,
a most unconstitutional procedure, and a clear infringement of Church
rights. This impost was most politely termed a *Donum*, or Gift, like the
Benevolences of later days. A similar tax was laid on Borough towns,
the sheriffs, and a few Jews and others. As Becket was the King's
chief adviser at the time, we may judge how much the future St. Thomas
of Canterbury cared for Church rights when the position of the Church
was not bound up with his own.[5] With respect to the King's action it
should be pointed out that though the tenants in chief accounted
at the Exchequer for the scutages of their enfeoffed *milites*, the money
came from the pockets of the latter. The tenant in chief paid nothing.
Henry evidently thought it fair that the prelates should contribute

---

[1] The war taxes were partly paid in by Easter, 12th April, and must have been
assessed a considerable time before.

[2] R. de Monte, 202.

[3] *Id.*

[4] "Ut pro arbitrio ejus et satraparum suorum conferrent in censum"; John of
Salisbury, *Becket Materials*, V. 372, where the writer clearly refers to the *Donum* and
not to the legitimate scutage.

[5] See the taunts of Gilbert Foliot, and the lament of John of Salisbury, *Becket M.*, V.
379, 525.

something of their own.   As for the total amount raised for *Donum* and
scutages within the year, it came to £7,788 16s. 8d.
Yield of the Taxes. Probably there were some arrears that might be collected in
the following year, but the Roll for that year is lost.   In
justice to the King it must further be stated that no Danegeld was
levied; nor do the names of Archbishop Theobald of Canterbury, or
of Thomas Becket appear among the contributories to the *Donum*
But the Abbot of the rival institution of St. Augustine's, Canterbury,
pays for *Donum* £146 13s. 4d. over and above the legitimate £20
Number of Knights' Fees. from his fifteen *milites*.   Gervase of Canterbury, ventures
to state the sum total actually paid by England at the
amazing figure of £180,000,[1] a precious instance of the
worth of chronicler's numbers.[2]

On the 24th May Henry was still at Rouen: in the first week of
June he had an interview with Louis in Normandy, at Héricourt-en-
Caux.[3]   By the 24th of the month he had reached Poitiers,
Campaign of Toulouse. and on the 30th June he was at Perigueux.   There at last
he conferred the coveted honour of Knighthood on King
Malcolm IV. of Scotland.   Henry himself had received the same
distinction from the sword of Malcolm's grandfather, King David I.
The final muster was held at Agen, in the first three days of July.
On the 6th Henry, having drawn near to Toulouse, had a conference
with Louis.[4]   True to his alliance with the Count, and in answer to
urgent appeals from the clergy and people of Toulouse,[5] the French
King had thrown himself into the city, with a force, at the first, stated
to have been insignificant.   Henry's address having failed to turn Louis
from his purpose, operations of a sort began.   Becket, we are told,
urged an immediate assault, before the French forces had fully come
up.[6]   But Henry, more scrupulous than his Chancellor, shrank from a
direct attack on his suzerain, just as he had refused to attack him in
1151;[7] the siege therefore, apparently, became a mere ineffectual
blockade.   About the 29th of September Henry abandoned the futile

[1] I., 167.

[2] Bishop Stubbs makes the sound suggestion that Gervase may have arrived at his
total by taking the sixty shillings Angevin, stated by Robert de Monte as the rate for
Henry's Continental possessions, applying this in sterling money to England, and
multiplying that by 60,000, the supposed numbers of Knights fees. Bened. Peterboro', II.
xcvi. Mr. Round, *Feudal England*, 292, calculated their numbers at about 5,000.
Mr. A. H. Inman, by further investigation, raises the total to something over 7,000;
Feudal Statistics, 65. The Angevin money was worth one-fourth of the sterling currency.

[3] Seine Inférieure, on the Durdan, near Ourville.

[4] Stubbs' and Eyton's *Itineraries*; Geoff. of Vigeois, Bouquet, XII. 439; Chron.
Bec. Id., 302; R. de Monte.

[5] For these see Norgate, I. 464.

[6] So W. fitz Stephen, *Becket*, III. 33.

[7] See *Foundations*, II. 442.

work, and turned northwards. As the sole fruit of his vast preparations, that must have stirred Europe from the Garonne to the Tay, and in fact from the Pyrenees to the Grampians, the city of Cahors had been taken, and the lands of Count Raymond and those of his friends overrun and devastated—the whole amounting to an utter *fiasco*. An attempt to create a diversion by instigating Theobald of Blois to attack the French frontier came to little, till Henry himself appeared on the field. With the forces at his command he was able to capture Gerberoi (Oise): and better still to induce Simon of Montfort, Count of Evreux in Normandy, but a man of double allegiance, to make over to him his strongholds in the Isle of France, namely Montfort l'Amauri, Rochefort,[1] and Épernon.[2] This last acquisition placed Louis in a fix, as the possession of Épernon enabled Henry to threaten his communications with Étampes and Orleans.[3] However in the course of December a truce was signed, to last till the octave of Pentecost (22nd May, 1160).[4] When that day came the truce was converted into a formal peace, on the basis of a confirmation of the matrimonial arrangements of 1158. Henry made concessions in respect of his recent gains on the Vexin frontier, receiving in return a confirmation of Cahors and other acquisitions in the South; while he again granted a year's truce to the Count of Toulouse and his allies.[5]

Futile Ending.

Gains in the North.

Pacification.

On the return journey from Toulouse Stephen's son William, Count of Boulogne and Mortain, and Earl of Surrey in England, died;[6] leaving his sister Mary, Abbess of Romsey, his heir at law: with his wife Isabelle of Warenne, in whose right he had held the Earldom of Surrey, also surviving. Mortain was at once re-annexed to the royal demesne; while the hand of Isabelle was kept in reserve to be given four years later to the King's natural brother Hamelin.[7] Boulogne, as a French fief, would fall to be disposed of by Louis.

Boulogne, Mortain and Surrey.

Determined not to allow this important border territory to fall into hostile hands, Henry took the bold step of removing Abbess Mary from her convent, and marrying her by Papal dispensation to his cousin Matthew, second son of Dietrich of Flanders, by Sibylle of Anjou. We are told that Becket very properly

Marriage of an Abbess.

---

[1] Both in Oise.
[2] Eure et Loir.
[3] R. de Monte, 206; W. Newb, I. 125; Gervase, I. 167; FitzStephen, *sup.*, 33, 34.
[4] R. Monte, *sup.*
[5] See the summary of the treaty given by Eyton, *Itinerary*, 49, 50; R. Monte; W. Newb., I. 159.
[6] October, 1159; R. Monte, *sup.*
[7] G.E.C. *Peerage*; Doyle, *Official Baronage*.

protested, and did his utmost to prevent the grant of the dispensation at Rome, but without result.[1]

Friendly relations with France were not destined to be of long duration; but in July we hear of concerted action between the two Kings on the important question of the recognition of a Pope. On

Papal Schism. the 30th August, 1159, Adrian IV. passed away. On the 7th September the Conclave met in Rome; the majority of the Cardinals declared for Roland Bandinelli, who took the style of Alexander III.; a minority voted for Cardinal Octavian, and invested him with the Papal insignia as Victor III. Adrian, after crowning Frederic as Emperor, had fallen into the inevitable position of antagonism, and Cardinal Roland had been Frederic's Chancellor, and active on his side. The Emperor, therefore, after a show of deliberation, declared for Victor; but his rival had the support of the clergy, the Monastic Orders, and the anti-Imperial party generally.[2] Under these circumstances Henry, in July (1160) held a Grand Council of the clergy and barons of Normandy at Neufmarché; while Louis simultaneously held one of his people at Beauvais. We are told that the Emperor had sent embassies bespeaking support for his Pope. Both assemblies, however, pronounced for Alexander.[3]

Again in October we hear of a friendly meeting, when the treaty of peace was confirmed, and the younger Henry, a mere infant, was made to go through the form of doing homage for Normandy. But the aspect of affairs was soon to be changed. Already, namely on the 4th October, Louis' Queen Constance of Castile had died in giving birth to a second

A new Queen of France. daughter, Alix or Alais.[4] Within a fortnight or so the King, again disappointed of a male heir, took for his third wife Alais of Blois, sister of the Counts Henry and Theobald, themselves already betrothed to his two daughters by Eleanor. Theobald had been acting with Henry against Louis only a few months before, but Henry professed alarm at the closeness of the alliance now effected between France and the House of Champagne. At all events he found

Marriage of Henry's Son. in it a sufficient pretext for solemnising the marriage between his son Henry, not five years old, and the little Marguerite, not three years old (2nd November). By this step the King, according to the literal terms of the treaty, became entitled to call for

---

[1] "Inaudito exemplo"; R. Monte; H. Bosham, *Becket*, III. 328; Bouquet, XIII. 517; Norgate I., 469. M. Paris, Hist. Angl., I. 314, discredits the dispensation, "sophisticis literis bullatis." The divided state of the Papacy would facilitate the grant of dispensations.

[2] See Milman *Latin Chr.*, III. 418-427, for the extraordinary scenes that took place.

[3] R. Monte, 207; Gervase, I. 167. A Synod of English bishops held by Archbishop Theobald confirmed the decision of the Norman Council; Foliot, Epp., I. 197, cited Norgate.

[4] R. Monte; Bouquet, XIII. 517; Norgate.

the retrocession of the Norman Vexin, and specially of the forts of
Gisors, Néaufles, and Neufchâtel.   The Templars who had
The Norman Vexin. the charge of them, accepting Henry's view of the case
surrendered the castles, and with them the line of the
Norman Vexin.[1]

We have already referred to the friendly relations existing between
Henry and the Temple, due to his grandfather's connexion with the
Order ; in fact one of the three men now in question was Richard of
Hastings Grand Master of the Temple in London [2]

Henry's conduct was tricky, no doubt, and Louis was greatly incensed,
though the treaty in fact seemed only to stipulate that the pair should
be married with the consent of the Church, which condition had been
fulfilled, the ceremony having been performed by two Cardinals, who
happened to be in Normandy, on a mission from Alexander III.[3]   But
the French King had only himself to blame for agreeing to such a cession,
on such loose conditions.   For Henry the recovery of the Norman Vexin
was of the utmost importance, as on the Andelle the French would be
within some ten miles of Rouen.

War was threatened, all along the frontier, but nothing serious happened.   The Counts Henry and Theobald began to fortify Chaumont on
the Loire [4] as a basis for attacks on Touraine.   The King came down
on them before their works were completed, drove them off, and then
placed the Castle in the hands of a trusty adherent, to whom of right
it belonged.   Christmas was kept by King and Queen in peace at Le
Mans.[5]

Taking a hint as it were from recent events Henry now appears as
falling back on a policy of concentration, devoting himself to
Frontier Works. the defences of his long straggling frontiers.   Meulan (Seine
et Oise) a French fief, was taken out of the hands of its
Count, Waleran of Beaumont, and placed under a royal officer ; Gisors
was strengthened ; castles were either established or repaired throughout
Normandy, Maine, Touraine, and Aquitaine.   We also hear of domestic
buildings, such as a royal residence with a park outside Rouen ; and a
hall and chambers added to the castle at Rouen.

After Easter (16th April), say about May, Louis and his brothers-in-law
called out forces, and made hostile demonstrations first on the borders of
the Vexin, and then on those of the county of Dunois.   But Henry

[1] R. Monte ; W. Newb., I. 159 ; R. Hoveden, I. 217 ; R. Diceto, I. 303, 304.
[2] Gervase, I. 177 ; De Invent. Crucis, 38.   The Temple buildings of the time would
be not the existing Temple, but the old Temple, on the site of Staple Inn, Holborn.
[3] R. Diceto, I. 304.   Herbert of Bosham claimed the credit of the success for Becket,
III. 175.   The dispensation granted by the Legates is given Bouquet, XV. 701.
[4] Loire et Cher ; between Blois and Amboise.
[5] R. Monte, 208, 209.

was ready for them at all points, and so no collision took place.   A

Military Operations. fresh truce signed at Fréteval ended the manœuvres.[1]   For further military events we have an expedition to Aquitaine, and the reduction within a week's time of a Castillon, most likely the place on the Dordogne (10th August)[2]; and for a domestic event the birth of a daughter, Eleanor, who came into the world at Le Mans

Death of Archbishop Theobald. (September–October).   Christmas was kept at Bayeux.[3]   But, for the ulterior consequences to follow, the event of the year was the death of the worthy Archbishop Theobald, in the twenty-third year of his pontificate (18th April).[4]   For him the seven years of peaceful administration under Henry must have been in happy contrast to the struggles and turmoil of the days of Stephen.   But the fateful nomination of his successor was not given out to the world for some months to come.

Again for another twelvemonth, through the year 1162, we have Henry staying abroad, and devoting himself to the repression of feudalism,

Reforming Measures. fiscal reform, and the strengthening of his position in general. Geoffrey of Mayenne, a name identified with *Mansel* independence,[5] is forced to make over Ambrières, Gorron, and another fort on the Calmont.   Pontorson is taken out of the hands of a lay baron, and placed in the safer keeping of Robert the chronicler-abbot of Mont-Saint-Michel.   Dol is taken into hand.   In February we have a Grand-Council at Rouen, in which the King found much to quarrel with in the management of his affairs by the bishops, their officers, and his own men.   Apparently the meeting came to no definite conclusion, as we hear that it was adjourned to Lillebonne.[6]   The next recorded event was a fresh step towards assuring the succession to the Crown, naturally the cardinal point in the King's family policy.   Young Henry had already been recognised as heir, conditionally on his surviving his brother William, the first born, an event that had happened.   The King now wished the homage to be repeated, as it were unconditionally; and for this purpose he ordered the boy to be taken over to England under the charge of the Chancellor.   Here we learn that Henry's belief in Becket was such that the Heir Apparent had been committed to his care to be brought up under healthy influences, with other lads of rank, in his household.[7]   The guardianship cannot have lasted long; but short as it

---

[1] R. de Monte, 209–211; R. Diceto.   The pacification placed by Diceto at Fréteval (Loire et Cher) was evidently that recorded by De Monte in connexion with the abortive hostilities in the Dunois, as Fréteval lies in that county, on the road from Paris and Chartres to Tours.

[2] R. Monte, 210, 211.   The writer gives the place as "supra Urbem Agennum," but I cannot find any likely place above Agen.

[3] *Id.*   [4] *Id., Anglia Sacra*, I. 56.   [5] See Index to *Foundations*.   [6] R. de Monte, 211, 212.

[7] So W. Fitz Stephen and H. Bosham, *Becket*, III. 22, 176.

may have been the impression produced by Thomas upon his pupil's mind was indelible. To the end of his brief career young Henry regarded his former tutor with unbounded affection and regard, a fact that must be put to Becket's credit. About the end of April or the beginning of May they sailed for England.[1] As they were taking leave at Falaise the King, at last, divulged his intentions about the vacant throne of Canterbury. Becket might consider himself Theobald's appointed successor. The announcement could hardly have taken the indispensable Chancellor by surprise, but, of course, he protested. The King however declared his purpose as fixed; the Cardinal Henry of Pisa, who was at Court looking after the interests of Alexander III., ordered Becket to submit, and he submitted.[2] Henry doubtless flattered himself that he would find in Thomas the Primate the same useful supple tool that he had found in Thomas the Chancellor.[3] In fact he was doomed to find in him a man prepared to push ecclesiastical pretensions as far as Anselm himself, but one less prepared than Anselm to listen to any reasoning not his own. The King's mistake cost him all his future peace of mind, and Becket his life.

The New Archbishop.

A Mistaken Appointment.

Gilbert Foliot, Bishop of Hereford, the old partisan of the Angevin cause, tells us that the Empress Matilda opposed the promotion of Becket, and that he himself had ventured to raise a warning voice, till silenced by the King's threats.[4] We take it that the world expected to see Becket made Archbishop, but that strict Churchmen rather regarded him as a wolf in sheep's clothing.[5]

The homage to young Henry was rendered without difficulty or demur, Becket setting the example, and swearing allegiance to the boy saving the rights of his father.[6] For the 'election' to Canterbury the proceedings followed the precedents of 1123, and 1138, when William of Corbeil, and Theobald of Bec were respectively appointed, that is to say the King required the form of choice to be gone through in London by a delegation of the Christ Church monks, acting in concert with the suffragan bishops of the Province. The monks had always shown a disposition to be restive on these occasions; the influence of the prelates, therefore,

Fresh Homage to the Younger Henry.

'Election' to Canterbury.

---

[1] Becket signs at Rouen in April; Eyton, *Itin.*, 56. It is clear that he did not return to Normandy during the year.

[2] H. Bosham, *sup.*, 180–182; Gervase, 169; W. Canterbury, *Becket*, I. 8.

[3] So John of Salisbury, *Becket M.*, II. 305; and, in fact, all the writers.

[4] *Becket Mat.*, V. 410, 524. Becket retorted that he had never heard of any opposition except from a disappointed aspirant; *Id.*, 516, 517.

[5] See H. Bosham, *sup.*, III. 183; Anon, IV. 84; Garnier de Pont-Saint-Maxence, a metrical Life of Becket, p. 18 (ed. Hippeau).

[6] Diceto, I. 306. The writer seems only to record homage by the Bishops. The proceedings included something in the nature of a coronation, as a gold crown was provided for young Henry; Pipe Roll 8, H. II., p. 43. See also Grim, *Becket*, II. 366.

would be useful in keeping them in order. One objection in particular here was, that had been raised against previous candidates for the Primacy, to which Becket was open, namely that he had not taken monastic vows. The monks might raise difficulties on that score.

The King's message summoning the Canterbury electors to London was delivered in the Chapter House by Richard of Lucy, the Justiciar, and the Bishops of Rochester, Chichester, and Exeter, with an intimation as to the man on whom their suffrages would be expected to fall. It is clear that considerable discussion ensued, but that the monks finding from the Justiciar's tone that the King was not to be trifled with, eventually agreed that the Archdeacon of Canterbury would be a most acceptable person.[1] On the 27th of May the final election was held at Westminster in the presence of the King's son and of the Justiciars. The **A Suspicious Protest** objection to Becket on the ground of his secular Orders and secular mode of life was taken by Gilbert Foliot, the Bishop of Hereford, an old Cluniac monk, who spoke out, protesting it would seem, against the promotion of a man who could eat meat and drink wine.[2] But whatever scruples may have been expressed or entertained no counter-nomination was attempted; and in the course of the afternoon Henry of Winchester was able to announce in the Westminster Refectory that Thomas, Archdeacon of Canterbury and King's Chancellor, had been unanimously 'elected.'[3] The Archbishop-elect was next presented in due form to young Henry for confirmation, and was of course most gladly accepted. Then the Bishop of Winchester addressing the Regency council demanded in Becket's name a full release from all questions or claims concerning his past administration of the revenue as chancellor and treasurer.[4] The request was granted,[5] but, as we shall see, the validity of this release soon became a matter of dispute between Becket and the King. The clerical party now adjourned to Canterbury. Becket so far had only advanced to deacon's orders. As a necessary preliminary to his promotion to the Episcopate, on Saturday, 2nd June, Thomas was ordained a priest by Walter, Bishop of Rochester, this see being **The Consecration** specially connected with Canterbury. Next day, being Sunday after Whitsunday, or the Octave of Pentecost, he was duly consecrated. The right of officiating belonged, it would seem, of right to the Bishop of London, as Dean of Canterbury. But the see

[1] See E. Grim; H. Bosham; Foliot's letter below, and the Anonymous writer, *Becket*, IV. 14–16.

[2] See W. Cant., *Becket*, I. 8, 9; E. Grim, *Id.* II. 366; W. fitz S., III. 35; H. Bosham, *Id.*, 182–184; Gervase, I. 169, and esp. Foliot's letter, *Becket*, V. 524.

[3] "Nemine reclamante," R. Diceto; "consensu unanimi," H. Bosham, *sup.*, etc.

[4] "Ne cui in posterum pateat exactioni vel calumniæ . . . liberum et absolutum, etc."

[5] E. Grim, II. 357; W. Cant., I. 9; W. fitz S., III. 35; Anon., IV. 17, 18.

had just fallen vacant.[1] The honour therefore was disputed, the main contention lying between the Bishop of Rochester as Vicar[2], and the Bishop of Winchester as Precentor (*Cantor*). Rochester however giving way, the Archbishop was duly hallowed by the hands of Henry of Blois.[3] The Archbishop's first act was to ordain that the day of his consecration should thereafter be held a new festival in honour of the Holy Trinity.[4] "The observance thus originated spread from Canterbury throughout the whole of Christendom, which thus owes to an English Archbishop the

The Pall.

institution of Trinity Sunday."[5] For his *Pallium*, the seal of his apostleship, Thomas was not required to take the usual journey to the Holy See, which at the time was established at Montpellier. A petition for the grant without personal application was graciously received by Alexander III. On the 10th August the sacred badge was brought to Canterbury by the hands of Becket's friend John of Salisbury.[6]

To return to the King and Continental affairs. Confronted by Barbarossa and his anti-Pope; with the Italians, and the Romans themselves divided in their allegiance, Alexander III. found, as other Popes before him in similar circumstances had found,[7] that a retreat to Gallic territory would be the wisest course. Sailing from Terracina with a Sicilian fleet he landed near Montpellier on the 11th April, 1162.[8] Of

The Pope in Gaul.

course he met with a hearty welcome from the Gallican clergy. The Emperor then, by way of a counter-move, proposed to Louis a meeting on the frontier of Burgundy, to be held on the bridge of the Saône at Saint-Jean-de-Losne (Cote d'Or); each side to produce their Pope, and settle the question then

Royal Deference.

and there. Alexander very properly refused to submit to so derogatory a proceeding; but Louis gave in to it, went to the appointed place, and then, taking offence at something or other, rode off without waiting for Frederic's arrival.[9] Some ten days later Louis and Henry met Alexander at Choussy on the Loire, below Blois, and in conducting him to a marquee prepared for his reception

---

[1] Richard of Belmeis II. died 4th May, 1162; *Reg. Sacrum.*

[2] The Bishop of Rochester is described as being the Vicar of Canterbury for ordinations and the dedication of churches; Diceto, 307.

[3] H. Bosham, III. 188, 189; Gervase, I. 170, 171; R. Diceto, I. 306.

[4] Gervase, I. 171.

[5] Norgate, II. 5.

[6] W. fitz S., III. 36; H. Bosham, 189; Gervase, I. 171. 172.

[7] So Gelasius II. in 1119; Innocent II. in 1130; and Eugenius III. in 1147. See Milman, *Latin, C.* III. 308, 337, 396.

[8] R. de Monte, 213; W. Newb., I. 135; Vic et Vaissete, *Hist. Languedoc,* cited Sismondi.

[9] 6th or 7th September; R. de Monte, 215, and note Howlett; Sismondi, *France.* V. 441. For the incident at length see Lavisse, *France* III. 40-43 (1901).

gave the world the striking spectacle of two crowned, anointed kings, testifying their respect for moral force in the person of an exiled Pontiff by meekly leading his mule, one on the right hand and the other on the left.[1]

After four full years of absence from England Henry now prepared to return thither. About the beginning of December he went to Barfleur, but foul winds detained him nearly two months. Christmas had to be kept at Cherbourg.[2] At last, on the 25th January, 1163, the King and Queen landed at Southampton. Becket was there to receive them. Henry gave him the usual friendly kiss, but his looks showed that already their relations had undergone a change. Becket, to Henry's great annoyance, had resigned the Seal, and in other respects also had evinced a disquieting purpose of leading a new life, and adopting independent lines of action.[3]

---

[1] 18th September ; R. de Monte, *sup.* ; Duchesne, *Hist. Fr.*, 620, cited Howlett.
[2] R. de Monte, 216.
[3] R. Diceto, I. 308 ; E. Grim, *Becket*, II. 367 ; H. Bosham, III. 185.

CHAPTER III

HENRY II. (*continued*)

A.D. 1163-1164

Becket Archbishop—His earlier Life and Relations with the King—Altered Attitude—
Ecclesiastical Pretensions—Criminal Clerks—The *Constitutions* of Clarendon—
Council of Northampton—Flight of Becket

THOMAS BECKET, at the time of his consecration (3rd June,
1162), is stated to have been in his forty-fourth year; and he
was in his fifty-third year at the time of his death (29th
December, 1170).[1]   His birth took place on a 21st December,
St. Thomas's Day, the day of the Saint after whom he was
named.[2]   He must therefore have been born in the year 1118.   By
birthplace he was a Londoner, native of Cheapside; by
blood a pure Norman-Frenchman.   His father Gilbert was
sprung from a family of respectable burghers of Rouen;
and his mother, Mahalt or Matilda, from similar ancestry connected
with Caen.[3]   His parents were persons in good position, on terms of
acquaintance with Archbishop Theobald, and able to entertain in their
house barons of high degree, such as Richer of Laigle.   Two other
children they had, both daughters, by name Mary and Agnes.   The
former became Abbess of Barking in 1173.   Agnes married one Thomas
fitz Theobald, had children by him, and, possibly, was the ancestress of
the subsequent bearers of the name of Becket.[4]   Her husband eventually

*Thomas
Becket.*

*His Birth
and
Parentage.*

---

[1] H. Bosham, III. 185, 522; *Angl. Sacra*, I. 300.

[2] Anon., *Becket*, IV. 2.

[3] "Mahalz," Garnier, 77; "Mahalt," "Matildis," W. fitz Stephen, III. 14; E. Grim,
II. 356.   The last supplies the family name " Beket."   The form " à Becket " is modern
—not found in the writers of the time.   The anonymous writer printed by Canon
Robertson in the fourth vol. of his *Becket Materials* gives Becket's mother the name
of Roese. p. 81.

[4] See Foss, *Judges*, I. 217; *Becket*, V. 242, 258.   Thomas fitz Theobald late in
Henry's reign founded the Hospital of St. Thomas on the north side of Cheapside, on
the site of the house in which Becket was born, now occupied by the Hall and Chapel
of the Mercers' Company.   The hospital came to be distinguished as that of St. Thomas
of Acon or Acre, when Becket gained the alternative designation of St. Thomas of Acre
(Aconensis) from the popular belief that the capture of Acre in 1191 was effected through
a miraculous interposition by him.   See Wheatley and Cunningham's *London*.

rose to be *Vicecomes*, presumably Portreeve of London.[1] With some
discrepancy in the authorities we take it that Gilbert Becket was in
trade, as he is said to have been at one time reduced in circumstances
by the fires to which London was so subject. Thomas as a child was
placed for his education with the Canons of Merton in Surrey. After
that he attended schools of higher grade in the City, and ultimately
went on to Paris. From thence he was recalled about the age of
twenty-two, owing to his father's losses, and his mother's death, she
seemingly having been more interested in their son's education than
her husband was.[2] Having to support himself Thomas found employment as a clerk in the house of a well-to-do kinsman, by name Osbern
Huit-denièrs.[3] After two or three years with him he was introduced to

Employed by Archbishop Theobald. Archbishop Theobald, to whom he first presented himself
at Harrow, in good style, with a servant in attendance.[4]
Becket always had an eye to appearances. Theobald at
once took a fancy to the young man, whose quickness and business
capacity soon brought him to a leading position in the household. Two
other men divided their patron's confidence. Roger of Pont l'Évêque,
afterwards Archbishop of York, and John of Canterbury, afterwards
Bishop of Poitiers and Archbishop of Lyons. Roger however was
jealous of Becket from the first, and behaved very unkindly to him,
exposing his comparative want of reading—for Becket was no scholar—
and nicknaming him "Baille-hache," 'the Axe-bearer.'[5] Becket however
held his ground in the archiepiscopal circle. As early as the year 1143

Taken to Rome. we hear of him as going to Rome with Theobald. In 1148
he shared with Roger of Pont l'Évêque the Archbishop's
'swim' across the Channel, to attend the Council of Rheims;
and in 1151 he was the man sent to oppose Henry Murdac's efforts

Diplomatic Success. to obtain the recognition of Stephen's son Eustace by the
Papacy.[6] As soon as he had taken deacon's Orders prefer-
ment was heaped upon him. His first church was St.
Mary-le-Strand; then came Otford in Kent, and again a prebend at

Preferment. St. Paul's, and one at Lincoln. Of course Becket was
non-resident; the duties would be performed by curates at
paltry stipends of a few pounds a year. By Theobald's permission he

---

[1] W. fitz Stephen, *sup.* Becket, Epp., V. 515. Of his parents he says modestly, "nec
omnino infimi."

[2] W. fitz S., *sup.*; E. Grim, II. 359; Anon., IV. 81; Garnier, 9.

[3] W. fitz S. *sup.*; E. Grim, 358–361; W. Cant., I. 3; Garnier, *sup.*

[4] A.D. 1142–1143 (?). W. Cant., I. 4; J. Salisbury, II. 303; W. fitz St., III. 16;
Garnier, 10.

[5] *Id.* "Horum respectu Thomas minus litteratus erat"; W. Fitz., *sup.*, "multi
litteratiores"; J. Salisb., *sup.*, Anon. IV. 10; E. Grim, II. 362. For the word baille-
hache see Godefroy, where no second intention is given to the word.

[6] See *Foundations*, II. 422, 436, 442, 447.

went abroad for a year to improve his education by studying Canon Law, first at Bologna, where the celebrated Gratian was lecturing, and afterwards at Auxerre.[1] It will be remembered that it was through Theobald's zeal for the Canon Law that Vacarius was brought to lecture at Oxford. In 1154 when Roger of Pont l'Évêque became Archbishop of York Becket was chosen to succeed him as Archdeacon of Canterbury;[2] and within a month of Henry's coronation he became his Chancellor.

Personal Appearance. Tall, handsome, and distinguished looking,[3] with regular features and shapely hands, Thomas in outward appearance must have had every advantage over his Royal master, who is represented to us as a man with a large round head, closely-cropped sandy hair, freckled face, grey eyes, bull-neck, a stout figure, and coarse hands.[4] Nor did Becket fail to do justice to his goodly person in the matter of outward attire;[5] a point again on which the King was sadly remiss. As already intimated Becket was neither a scholar nor a theologian. He was a man of the world, fitted to shine in society, politics, diplomacy, or war. Ostentatious in his habits he **Talents and Disposition.** clearly was, and one of his best friends admits that he was a man of considerable vanity and inordinately fond of popularity. But his private life was free from all stain of impurity.[6] Unlike as the two men were the relations of the King and Becket **Relations with the King.** during the time that the latter held the Great Seal were intimate and cordial. We are told that the King would not only visit him, and dine with him in State; but that at times he would ride into the hall without ceremony, have a word with the Chancellor, perhaps take a glass, and retire; perhaps sit down and dine. To the same authority we owe the well-known story of the incident when Henry and Becket, riding through the streets of London

---

[1] W. fitz S., *supra*, 17; Hook, *Archbishops*. Miss Norgate places this period of study between 1143 and 1148.

[2] *Foundations*, II. 439, 455.

[3] "Procerus ad elegantiam," W. Cant, I. 3. "Statura procerus, decorus forma," J. Salisb., II. 302; "Naso eminentiore et parum inflexo," W. fitz S., *sup.* "Frontem amplam . . . . formam manuum oblongarum," H. Bosham, 327.

[4] "Erat rex . . . . vir subrufus, cæsius, amplo capite et rotundo, oculis glaucis, ad iram torvis, et rubore suffusis, facie ignea, voce quassa, collo et humeris aliquantulum demisso, pectore quadrato, corpore carnoso . . . . ventre præamplo . . . . Statura inter mediocres." Girald. Camb. V. 302. "Subrufum . . . . statura ejus mediocris est . . . . caput sphœricum . . . . Ea vero est capitis quantitas ut collo et toti corpori proportionali moderatione respondeat. Cæsaries ejus damna calvitii non veretur, superveniente tamen artifici capillorum tonsura. Manus ejus quadam grossitie sua hominis incuriam protestantur . . . . vestibus utitur expeditis," etc. Peter of Blois, Epp., I. 193. The description, however. was written later in Henry's life.

[5] H. Bosham, III. 193, 194.

[6] "Supra modum captator auræ popularis . . . . quod etsi superbus esset et vanus . . . . admirandus tamen . . . . in corporis castitate"; J. Salisb., II. 303.

on a wild winter's day, met a poor old man thinly clad. 'Would it not,' quoth the King, 'be a charity to give that man a good warm cloak.' Becket having admitted that it would be so, the King proceeded to lay hands on the Chancellor's furred scarlet cloak, and after something of a struggle stripped it from his shoulders and bestowed it on the pauper.[1] Of the splendour and liberality of Becket's house-keeping we get accounts that can only be paralleled by those of Warwick the Kingmaker. Open table was kept. Every child has read how for the accommodation of those who could not find seats on the benches at meal times fresh litter was strewn on the floor every day. No earl could vie with the Chancellor; even the King at times complained that he was eclipsed. If the Chancellor's duties were endless, so were his emoluments. With respect to the former, as Chancellor he was Chief Secretary of State, with a seat *ex officio* both in the Exchequer and the King's Court; we hear that besides the passing of all writs and charters, and the drawing up of decrees, he had charge of the King's chapel and its clerks, and the custody of vacant sees and abbeys, as well as of the King's 'wardships' and escheats.[2] But the range of Becket's actual employment considerably transcended the limits of his office, and extended to every department of business, military as well as civil. For seven years he was the King's absolute factotum. As for his income, besides the preferment already mentioned, he had the provostship of Beverley, the prebend of Hastings, the three constable-ships of the Tower, of Eye, and of Berkampstead.[3] But a still more fertile source of income must have been the gifts and offerings incessantly pressed upon the Chancellor to secure his good offices at Court or on the Bench.[4] In such dealings he might plead the example set to him by the King, who while "appointing him Chancellor for his merits, made him pay his price" for the appointment.[5] Becket's devotion to the King's interests, we are told, was unbounded. But it is satisfactory to hear that at times he could interfere to protect persons who had brought down the King's wrath upon them, as in the case of the Archdeacon of Rouen, and the Bishop of Le Mans, hastily condemned to forfeiture for having ventured to recognise Alexander III. before Henry himself had done so.[6] With respect to Becket's services

His Household.

Duties.

And Emoluments.

---

[1] W. fitz S., III. 24, 25.

[2] *Id.* 18.   See also Bishop Stubbs, Bened. Peterborough, II. lxxvii. (Rolls Series, No. 49).

[3] W. fitz S., 20; so too Pipe Rolls.   [4] Fitz S., 22.

[5] Bishop Stubbs, *sup.* See Foliot's letter to Becket, V. 523; he gives the fact as undeniable and notorious. For Becket as Chancellor, see further E. Grim, II. 363; Anon., IV. 13, etc.

[6] W. fitz S., III. 26, 27.

in war, without giving entire trust to the strength attributed to his contingent in the campaign of Toulouse, we may believe that it was the smartest, best found, and most efficient force in the field.   In the later operations on the Vexin he seems to have had the chief command, and in that capacity, in the spirit of the age, tilted with and overthrew a French knight, Enguerrand of Trie, carrying off his charger as a lawful prize.[1]

But with a new position came a new life. No sooner was Becket installed on the throne of Canterbury than he proceeded to throw off the old man and put on the new, 'crucifying the flesh,' as his

Thomas the Archbishop. friends termed it.   He became sedulous in his attendance at church services, frequent in preaching, and great in alms-giving, this last of course, being a great point with the mediæval Church. Theobald had doubled the amount previously allowed for charity.   Becket redoubled it.   Then we hear of troops of poor men ostentatiously ushered into the dining hall before all other persons;[2] and again of thirteen paupers whose feet were daily washed.   But this work of supererogation was performed in private.   Further we are told that at Mass, at any rate when celebrating in person, Becket would burst into tears of pious emotion.[3]   To indulge Canterbury traditions he put on the monastic habit,[4] wearing it under his canonical vestments, with a penitential *cilicium*, or shirt of hair cloth, next to his skin.   But this piece of self-discipline was only discovered at his death.   Later in life he is said to have taken the vows of an Augustinian canon, but he did not abstain from meat or wine, taking them however only in strict moderation.[5] Foliot on hearing of these devout practices vented his feelings with the caustic remark that a miracle had been wrought by the King, who had 'made an Archbishop of a layman and a soldier.'[6]   Concurrently with this abrupt change in his mode of life Becket embarked on a crusade

---

[1] W. fitz S. III. 33-35. The 700 *milites* ascribed to Becket's contingent cannot be accepted.   The largest contingent for the Agincourt army, that of the Duke of Gloucester, only mustered 142 *milites*, with 406 archers. H. Nicolas, *Agincourt*, 333, 336.   Then fitz Stephen adds that Becket gave his *milites* 3 shillings a day.   But the regular pay was only 8 pence a day; Pipe Roll, 8 H. II. p. 53, cited Round.

[2] "Pauperibus præinductis," J. Salisbury, II. 306 ; Anon., IV. 89; H. Bosham, III. 202.   According to the latter, twenty-four *pauperes* were introduced at one meal, and one hundred 'poor prebendaries' at another meal, and that daily.

[3] "Inter missarum solemnia totus in lacrymas usque in miraculum diffluebat"; W. Canterbury, I. 11 ; see esp. H. Bosham, III. 210.

[4] It was alleged that only two men, not in monastic Orders, had held the See of Canterbury, namely Ælfsige, who perished on the Alps in 959 (*Foundations*, I. 312), and the schismatic Stigand ; W. Cant.

[5] See W. Cant. and J. Salisb., *sup.*; E. Grim, 368-371 ; and for fullest details of the Archbishop's daily life, H. Bosham, III. 192-240.

[6] "Mirum fecisse Regem qui de homine seculari et de milite quodam fecerat archi-episcopum" ; W. fitz S., III. 36.

against all persons who could be taxed with infringing in any way the
rights of Canterbury, or those of the Church in general.
Church Claims. Beneficial grants of land on lease (*firmæ feodales*) made by
previous Archbishops were quashed, and the lands reannexed
to the archiepiscopal demesne; and that, we hear, in some cases without
any process of law. William of Ros was required to surrender an estate
of seven knights' fees; Roger of Clare, Earl of Hertford,[1] was required to do
homage for Tonbridge Castle, and the appurtenant *banleuga* (Fr. *banlieue*),
a possession that had been held by his family as tenants *in capite*, at
any rate since the time of Domesday.[2] Then the King himself was
called upon to deliver up the custody of Rochester Castle.[3] Another set
of persons attacked were the clerics in the King's service, men in Orders
doing secular work in the Exchequer or the Chancery, but also holding
Church preferments. They were summarily deprived of their livings.[4]
This might be regarded as a legitimate work of Church reform. As for
the actual employment of clerics in government business, that was a
necessity, there being no lay class of sufficient education to replace
them; but the King, no doubt, should have requited their services
with proper salaries from his own pocket, and not at the expense of
the Church. But so far as Becket personally was concerned no act
could be more ungracious than his attack on these men, considering
that they had probably been working under him for years, and that
he himself had been in the matter of plurality the grossest offender
of all. The complaints of these men soon filled the ears of the King.
With respect to the clerks of his chapel he was able to retort on Becket
by requesting him to resign the Archdeaconry of Canterbury, an office
that Becket, amazing to tell, had retained till then, and even then would
not surrender without a struggle.[5] But men who will spend must be
grasping. No breach, however, or any direct collision occurred for a
while. On Palm Sunday (17th March) we hear of the King as being
with Becket at Canterbury, and assisting at a procession on the occasion
of the consecration of one Clarenbald to be Abbot of St. Augustine's.[6]
But Henry had not gone to Canterbury merely to visit the Archbishop.
He was on his way to Dover, where two days later he and his
Treaty with Flanders. son sealed a fresh treaty with Count Dietrich of Flanders;
one of those treaties of retainer, so one-sided in their operation,
that had come into vogue with the Conquest. The Count undertook to

---

[1] Younger brother of Gilbert, created Earl of Hertford by Stephen in 1141.

[2] See Ellis, *Introd. to Domesday*, I. 211, 212, 477. The *leuga* or district round the
castle " is even at the present day called the Lowy of Tonbridge."

[3] H. Bosham, III. 250–252. It does appear that the custody of Rochester Castle had
been granted to the See of Canterbury by Henry I.; Flor. Cont., A.D. 1126.

[4] E. Grim, II. 171, 172; W. fitz S., III. 42.

[5] H. Bosham, *sup.*; R. Diceto, I. 308.

[6] R. Diceto, I. 308; Gervase, I. 173.

place 1000 mounted men (*equites*) in the field, at Henry's call, for operations against any person or persons except the Lord Paramount King Louis. For this contingent service Henry would make a standing payment of 500 marks (£333 6*s.* 8*d.*) a year, of course without curtailing the revenues already enjoyed by Dietrich in England.[1]

From Dover Henry returned to Windsor to preside over a judicial combat between the unfortunate Henry of Essex and Robert **Wager of Battle.** of Montfort. Robert had impeached the ex-Constable for cowardice in the Welsh campaign of 1157. The result went against Henry, who was defeated in the lists, but he was allowed to save **Foliot** his neck by retiring to a convent.[2] On the 28th April Gilbert **Bishop of** Foliot received fitting promotion by being translated from **London.** Hereford to London, the latter see being vacant. For his talents, his learning, and his party services Gilbert might well have aspired to the Primacy. It must be admitted however that his relations to Becket were not untainted by personal jealousy. It is curious to note that although the appointment to a bishopric rested with the King, for the translation of a bishop from one see to another Papal consent was held necessary; and so in this case the sanction of Alexander III. had been duly asked for and obtained.[3] In May Becket, Roger of York, and **Council of** the other English Prelates went off to attend a Council that **Tours.** was opened by the Pope at Tours on the 19th of the month.[4]

By Becket's panegyrist we are assured that he was received with exceptional distinction.[5] From an independent source we simply hear that in the inevitable struggle for precedence that ensued between Canterbury and York, Becket had to keep silence, not being able to deliver a speech in Latin.[6]

The King's spring was devoted to another expedition into Wales. **Welsh** Since 1157 Gwynedd and Powys had kept pretty quiet in **Affairs.** their allegiance. But in South Wales Rhys son of Gruffudd had given much trouble. In 1158 he had applied to the King for the assignment of a big Cantref (Welsh Hundred) in return for his homage. The King was willing to assign land to the extent of the

---

[1] *Fœdera*, I. 23. For previous treaties of a similar kind see *Foundations*, II. 92, 248, 270.

[2] 31st March; R. de Monte, 218; R. Diceto; Stubbs, *Itinerary.*

[3] R. Diceto, I. 309 Richard of Belmeis II., the late Bishop of London, had been for some time incapacitated by illness. Becket as Chancellor proposed to Foliot to administer the diocese on the terms of giving Bishop Belmeis a pittance, and paying the rest of the revenues to the King. Foliot utterly refused; see his letter to the King, *Becket*, V. 15.

[4] R. de Monte. For the decrees passed see W. Newburgh, I. 135-139.

[5] H. Bosham, III. 253.

[6] "Hic siluit Thomas antistes Cantariensis, Ut minus edoctus verba Latina loqui." *Draco Normannicus*, Chronicles Stephen, etc., II. 744 (Howlett; Rolls Series, No. 82).

desired Cantref, only not in one block, but in parcels, prudently inter-mixed with the holdings of the Anglo-Norman Lords.[1] Rhys flew to arms, and for several years the districts represented by the modern shires of Cardigan, Pembroke, and Caermarthen suffered from desultory ravages, the struggle being kept up between the Welsh on the one side, and William Clifford, and the Earls Reginald of Cornwall, Roger of Hertford, and William of Gloucester on the other side.[2] In fact the state of Wales

An Armed Progress. had been one of the matters that recalled Henry to England. The campaign proved bloodless. The King led an army through Gwent, Morgannwg (Glamorgan), and Gower as far as Pencader in Caermarthenshire. There Rhys came in, and made his peace, on terms not particularly stated. To create an impression on the natives the King extended his armed progress by a march through the interior 'by Elennyth and Mailennyth,' that is to say through our Caermarthenshire and Cardiganshire to the foot of Plinlimmon, and so round through the South of Montgomeryshire into Radnor.[3]

On the return from Wales a Council was held at Woodstock, when Rhys, who presumably had been brought from home in the King's train, was made

Homages by Scotland and Wales. to do formal homage to Henry and his son, in company with Malcolm of Scotland, Owain of Gwynedd, and other Welsh chiefs.[4] And now according to Becket's biographers, the King and he came to open variance. That much is probable, because the cases of the Earl of Hertford and William of Ros above mentioned must have already come under discussion, as shortly afterwards they were submitted to legal decision, when the Archbishop's claims were rejected;[5] while other matters of contention, in which the King had taken part, had also come

Breach with Becket. forward, as we shall see. What happened at Woodstock does not seem to be open to much doubt, though the inexactness of the writers has led to misapprehension. We are told of a hot altercation as to the appropriation of a sum of money, an annual payment, alleged to be one of two shillings on the hide of land, made to the sheriffs

The 'Sheriff's Aid.' as part of their emoluments. The King proposed to deprive them of this, and to have it enrolled as an item to be accounted for by them to the Exchequer. Becket protested. 'Saving your pleasure my Lord King, we will not pay this as revenue, but if the

---

[1] Lhoyd and Powel seem to give Dynevor, near Llandilo in Caermarthenshire, as Rhys' seat; *Hist. Wales*, 161.

[2] So I interpret the " comes Bristolliæ " of the *Annales Cambriæ*, q.v. A.D. 1158–1164 (given as 1159–1165); see also the *Brut y T.* for the same years, and the Annals of Margam, A.D. 1158, 1161 (Luard, Rolls Series, No. 36).

[3] Giraldus, VI. 138. For the costs of the campaign a special *assiza* or composition was laid on the *milites* of Staffordshire, Worcestershire, Gloucestershire, and Hereford-shire; Pipe Roll, 9 H. II. p. 9. But a full scutage was also levied in the ensuing financial year; Pipe Roll, 10 H. II.

[4] R. Diceto, I. 311; R. de Monte, 218.   [5] R. Diceto, *sup.*

sheriffs deserve well of us and our men we will not refuse them an aid (*auxilium*).' Henry in a passion swore by his favourite oath "*Par les oelz Deu' tut ierent enrullé,*" (' By God's eyes the whole shall be enrolled '). ' By those same eyes' retorted the undaunted Archbishop ' Not a penny of this shall be paid [to you] from my lands or the possessions of the Church.' The King overpowered by his firmness gave way.[1] Now the only payment of two shillings on the hide of land of which we know anything was Danegeld, and Danegeld has been supposed to have come to an end in consequence of Becket's action on this occasion.[2] But **Danegeld not in Question.** Danegeld did not form part of the *corpus comitatus,* or revenues for which the Sheriffs compounded ;[3] it was always accounted for by them as a separate item. Then no question could be raised as to the legality of so old a Tax as Danegeld. Lastly as a matter of fact it had already been dropped by the King, presumably as not being worth the trouble of collection. For extra revenue he preferred to tax his subjects by way of *Donum,* an arbitrary tallage, unhampered by established assessments, compositions, or remissions, and not even restricted to landowners, but applicable to all classes of the community.[4] What then were we to make of this Woodstock incident ? If we strike out the mistaken rate of two shillings on the hide given by the writers it becomes clear that the discussion simply turned on the payment of the ' Sheriff's Aid ' or *Auxilium vicecomitis,*[5] a contribution taken by the Sheriffs from the Hundreds as their fee for holding the Hundred Courts and County Courts, as we learn from the fuller records of later reigns.[6]

But questions between the King and Becket of far greater moment than any sheriff's percentage were already pending. The severance of the ecclesiastical from the civil courts introduced by the Conqueror **Courts Christian.** had led to startling results when worked by the bishops in the spirit of the Hildebrandine ideas prevalent at the time. In England before the Conquest no real distinction of Church from State was known. The Church was but the ecclesiastical side, as the *fyrd* or host was the military side of the national organisation. Thus spiritual cases, and cases affecting clergymen were tried in the mixed national courts

---

[1] W. Cant, I. 12 ; E. Grim, II. 373 ; Anon, IV. 23 ; Garnier, 20. The last two are in close correspondence, and I believe that Garnier abridged from the former. None of the other writers have the incident.

[2] Norgate, *Angevin Kings,* II. 15. *Cnf.* Stubbs, *Const. Hist.,* I. 500.

[3] See *Foundations,* II. 325-328.

[4] Danegeld was levied for the last time in the 8th year, 1161-1162, having been levied only once before. Donum had been raised most years ; Pipe Rolls.

[5] "Auxilium"; W. Canterbury, *sup.* "L'aide al vescunte"; Garnier, *sup.* See Round, *Feudal England,* 497, where this point was first cleared up.

[6] For the Auxilium Vicecomitis in Essex and Herts see *Red Book of Exchequer,* 774-777. Lands exempt from suit to the County Court were seemingly not liable to this tax ; Pipe Roll, 5 John, p. 8.

of the Hundred and Shire. On the Continent the Church had enjoyed a more independent status ; and so, in accordance with Con- **The Anglo-** tinental views, William I. introduced ecclesiastical courts, **Saxon Church.** Courts Christian as they were called, forbidding the bishops and archdeacons to hold ecclesiastical pleas in the Hundred Courts, and requiring them to decide spiritual causes in courts of their own, according to Canon or 'Episcopal' law, and without any intervention of laymen. How far he intended the jurisdiction of the bishops to extend does not appear, probably only to strictly spiritual questions. He himself kept the clergy under strict control. He refused to do homage to Gregory VII. ; he kept Lanfranc from paying the usual visit to the Pope at Rome ; he did not even shrink from laying hands on his brother Odo, Bishop as he was.[1] But the development of the Canon Law in the following century gave a more definite position to the ecclesiastical courts, and brought into them a mass of business with which previously they had no concern.[2] But that Henry I. held the clergy amenable to the jurisdiction of his courts cannot be doubted, as in the case of the clergymen fined for being married,[3] a clear invasion of the spiritual domain of the bishops against which Anselm protested, but protested in vain. Stephen's Charter it was that by granting full liberty to the Church enabled the clergy to carry their pretensions to any lengths.[4] The hearing of all suits in any way affecting **New Views.** a cleric was claimed by them, including prosecutions of clergy for criminal offences. Thus crimes committed by clerks could only be punished by spiritual censures, such as degradation, or **Clerks not** confinement, the only penalties recognised by the Canons.[5] **Amenable** To make the thing more complete "every individual who had **to lay** **Jurisdiction.** been admitted to the tonsure, whether he afterwards received holy orders or not, was entitled to the clerical privileges."[6]

Two flagrant cases had recently been brought under the King's notice, **Murder.** one of a murder, the other of a sacrilegious robbery, committed by clerks. Both apparently had been convicted in spiritual **Robbery.** courts, one of them having been subjected to the ordeal as applicable to clergy.[7] Henry wanted the culprits to be handed over to the

---

[1] See *Foundations*, II. 113, 124.

[2] See Stubbs' *Const. Hist.*, I. 307 ; also *Foundations*, II. 146, and for Canon Law the Appendix to this chapter.

[3] *Foundations*, II. 140.   [4] *Foundations*, II. 351.

[5] For the Canon Law, and its latest embodiment the *Decretum of* Gratian see Appendix I. to this chapter. It was a digest of alleged ecclesiastical law, largely based on spurious authorities, the exaltation of the clerical order being the constant aim.

[6] Lingard, *Hist. England*, II. 64. See also W. Newb. I. 140, and John of Salisbury Epp. Nos. 122, 305, 310 (Giles).

[7] See H. Bosham, III. 264, where the case appears to have been this, that the accusers not being able to produce direct evidence, but only probable, or circumstantial evidence,

lay courts, to be re-tried, or at any rate properly punished.[1]   But Becket would not consent to either alternative, ordering the men to be degraded, one being sent into monastic confinement, the other, it would seem, being branded 'to pacify the King.'[2]   Probably the Archbishop's contention was the plea subsequently maintained by him, namely that a man ought not to be twice tried for one offence.[3]   That argument would apply to a re-trial, but not to punishment inflicted by a lay court for a conviction obtained in a spiritual court, for which distinct authority could be found.[4]   Becket was determined to push ecclesiastical claims to the very farthest.

Another case was that of Philip of Broi or Brois, a canon of Bedford, who, having been accused of murder in the court of the Bishop of Lincoln, had cleared himself on oath.   But at an Assize for the county of Bedford, held subsequently by one Simon fitz Peter, Sheriff of Northamptonshire and Justice in Eyre, Philip was again summoned to answer for the murder.   He refused to appear, alleging his previous acquittal, and utterly rejecting the jurisdiction of any lay court.   In stating his case, he made use of language held insulting by the Justice, who, in reporting the occurrence to the King, represented the canon's behaviour as amounting to contempt of court.   The King,

Contempt of Court.

accepting Simon's view, swore "*Par les oelz Deu*" that Philip should be tried by his court.   But again Becket interposed with effect, refusing to permit any fresh trial, except before his own own court at Canterbury.   The end of it was that Henry had to depute bishops and others to prefer his charge against the canon in the Archiepiscopal Court; that a re-trial for the murder was refused; but Philip condemned to suspension for two years for the offensive language used to the King's Judge.   He was also required to present himself before the offended Justice 'naked' according to English custom, to offer a humble apology and amends.[5]

A contention of a different character broke out over an appointment to a living.   The cure of Eynsford, a manor held of the See of Canterbury,

the accused was put to his 'purgation,' and condemned by it.   "Canonica indicitur purgatio accusato . . . fama consentiente. . . . Eo in purgatione deficiente, etc."   For compurgation and the ordeal as applicable to clergy see *Foundations*, I. 280.   Mr. F. W. Maitland points out that the Courts Christian could not really boast of the superior rules as to procedure and evidence with which they are sometimes credited; *Engl. Hist. Rev.*, VII. 234.

[1]   "Hunc clericum rex volens judicio curiæ laicæ examinari et judicari"; W. fitz S., III. 45.   As the writer was a lawyer and man of business his words are worthy of attention.   They seem to me to imply that in this case at any rate the King wanted a re-trial.

[2]   W. fitz S., H. Bosham, *sup.*

[3]   *Summa Causæ*, IV. 202.

[4]   See Mr. F. W. Maitland, *sup.* 231-233.

[5]   W. Cant, I. 13; E. Grim, H. 374; and Anon., IV. 24; the last, the best account, is followed by Garnier, 30.

having fallen vacant, Becket instituted a clerk, one Lawrence, on the
ground that the patronage of all livings on estates held of
Presentation to Livings. Canterbury belonged to the Archbishop. The lord of the
manor, William of Eynsford, expelled Lawrence, and was excommunicated by Becket. Henry immediately ordered the ban to be
removed, because William was a tenant-in-chief in respect of other
lands held of the King, and therefore under the Conqueror's rules
could not be excommunicated without royal license. Becket protested
that the King had no right to interfere, and did not give way till
Henry had been exasperated to the last degree.[1]

Yet another matter in which Becket must have set himself to thwart
the King was that of the proposed marriage between Henry's
A Marriage Forbidden. brother William and Isabel of Warenne, the heiress of
Surrey, left a widow in October 1159 by the death of a
prior William, the younger son of King Stephen. The Archbishop
forbade the union, apparently on some grounds of consanguinity. The
young Angevin William, crushed by the disappointment, went over to
Normandy to pour his griefs into the sympathetic ear of his mother,
and then shortly sickened and died at Rouen.[2] The curious thing is
that a few months later Isabel was married to the King's natural brother
Hamelin, without any opposition.[3]

Becket's conduct so far, since his accession to the Primacy, was
neither more nor less than a challenge to the King, and in
King and Laity Challenged. fact to the whole lay portion of the community. The matter
of the criminal clerks was but a small portion of the broad
question whether England was to be governed by the Archbishop of
Canterbury and the Canon Law, or by the King and the national
tribunals. Henry promptly took up the gauntlet. That he
Henry's Response. had already resolved to reduce the action of the ecclesiastical
courts within proper limits, clearly appears from the orders
transmitted to John of Canterbury, one of Becket's friends, recently
appointed Bishop of Poitiers, and appointed to that bishopric, as was
understood in Becket's circle, for the express purpose of getting him
out of England.[4] Richard of Lucy, the Chief Justiciar, was sent out
to warn him that in future he must not hold pleas relating to wills, or
the distribution of intestates' effects, or to real estate claimed by clerks.
John was also informed that he would not be at liberty to excommunicate
a baron without assent.[5] To bring matters to an issue Henry summoned

[1] W. fitz. S., III. 43 ; R. Diceto, I. 311.
[2] 30th Jany. 1164, R. de Monte, 221. See *Draco Normannicus, sup.*, 676.
[3] R. de Monte, *sup.*
[4] So W. fitz S., III. 46. John of Canterbury was consecrated Bishop of Poitiers by
Alexander III. in September 1162 ; Diceto, II. 120.
[5] August (?) 1163. See the Bishop's letter to Becket, V. 38. See also Becket

the bishops to appear at Westminster on the 1st October. He began
Guilty by complaining of corrupt and oppressive practices in the
Clerks to be courts of the Archdeacons ;[1] then taking up the question of
Punished. the immunities he demanded the assent of the prelates to an
ordinance for the trial of clerks charged with criminal offences. The
measure propounded may be taken to have been to the same effect as
the provision on the subject found in the well-known *Constitutions of
Clarendon* a few months later. A clerk charged with any offence to be
summoned in the first instance to appear before the King's Court to
answer the complaint brought against him : if a *prima facie* case should
be made out, the accused to be remitted to his ecclesiastical court for
regular trial, one of the King's Justices being present to see that the
case was fully gone into. If convicted the culprit to be degraded, and
so, stripped of his Orders, to be sent back to the King's Court for
final judgment and punishment.[2] Henry knew that he could not venture
on so bold a measure as to try or punish an actual clerk in a lay
tribunal. But he thought that after trial and conviction in an ecclesiastical
court the degraded culprit, now no longer in Holy Orders, might be
committed to a lay court for punishment.[3] On the King's side it was
asserted that his proposal would simply revive the law of the time of his
grandfather, while Becket's own friends were forced to admit that authority
for Henry's scheme could be found even in the Canon Law itself.[4]

letters to the Pope and Cardinals anticipating an attack by the King on the
immunities of the clergy, *Id.* 48-53 ; also an earlier letter, Epp. J. Salisb., I. 81
(Giles).

[1] See W. fitz S., III. 43.

[2] The clause in the *Constitutions* is as follows : "Clerici rettati et accusati de
quacunque re summoniti a Justicia regis venient in curiam ipsius, responsuri ibidem
de hoc unde videbitur curiæ regis quod ibidem sit respondendum ; et in curia
ecclesiastica, unde videbitur quod ibidem sit respondendum ; ita quod Justicia regis
mittet in curiam sanctæ ecclesiæ ad videndum qua ratione res ibi tractabitur. Et
si clericus convictus vel confessus fuerit, non debet de cetero eum ecclesia tueri."
Select Charters, 132. Diceto, a man of the time, and in good position gives the
following account of the King's proposal in the Westminster assembly · "Rex
Anglorum volens in singulis, ut dicebat, maleficia debita cum severitate punire, et
ordinis dignitatem ad iniquum trahi compendium incongruum esse considerans, clericos
a suis justiciariis in publico flagitio deprehensos episcopo loci reddendos decreverat
ut quos episcopus inveniret obnoxios præsente justiciario regis exauctoraret, et post
curiæ traderet puniendos," I. 313. These two ·passages supplement each other,
Diceto omitting the preliminary examination before the King's Justices but bringing
out even more clearly than the clause in the *Constitutions* that the accused was to
be tried by his own bishop, but ultimately punished by the lay court. See also
Summa Causæ, IV. 202 ; and H. Bosham, III. 266.

[3] See this question cleared up by Mr. F. W. Maitland, *English Historical Review*,
VII. 225.

[4] See E. Grim, II. 376 ; Anon, IV. 96 ; H. Bosham, III. 266. The passage in
the *Decretum* of Gratian to which the last refers (Causa XI. 91 ; s. 18) ordains that

The King, then, having propounded his views, the Bishops retired to consider them, when some difference of opinion became **The Bishops Refuse.** manifest. At last however Becket carried the assembly in favour of resistance. In giving their reasons for dissent, the Archbishop, according to his secretary, who was present, treated the King to a Hildebrandine harangue on the "two Swords," worthy of Gregory VII. himself. The clergy as such could recognise no head but Christ, and no law but His law, as expounded in the Canons : they were the makers and judges of Kings, not subordinate to them.[1] The utmost that he could concede was that a clerk who had once been degraded and reduced to the *status* of a layman should, for any subsequent offence, be amenable to lay jurisdiction.[2] According to another account Thomas took a dry dialectic line. A decision of the Church must be either just or unjust; unjust it could not be,[3] therefore it must be just, and being just, it must be final, one way or the other. To subject a man to further penalty after condemnation and degradation would be trying him twice for the same offence.[4] No sophistry could be more transparent.

After some argument, the King, taking up the position taken up by **The Ancient Customs of England.** Henry I. as against Anselm, asked if they were prepared to observe the ancient customs of the realm.[5] The Bishops answered, as William of St. Carilef had answered in 1188, that they could only observe the customs 'saving the rights of their Order,'[6] a reservation that left everything open. Henry, refusing to accept a mere collective response, proceeded to extort an individual answer from each prelate in succession. Only one man, Hilary of Chichester, would accept the 'customs' without reservation. The angry discussion lasted till almost nightfall; the King finally leaving the apartment abruptly and in a passion.[7] Next day he went out of Town

if a clerk offends against his bishop then "*depositus mox curiæ tradatur, et recipiat quod inique gesserit.*" Of course, passages in a contrary sense could also be quoted. See Mr. Maitland's article, sup. 229-232, where it is pointed out that a 'system substantially the same as that proposed by Henry had been introduced in Gaul by a Merovingian King as far back as the year 614, and had probably ruled the procedure in Normandy ever since. After Henry's time Innocent III. gave his sanction to the punishment of clerks by lay courts for offences of certain sorts.

[1] "*Regibus non subsunt sed præsunt, etc.*"

[2] See H. Bosham, 268-272, who professes to give the substance of the address "*si non eadem verba . . . tamen dictorum virtus et materia.*"

[3] "*Sed non dabis injustum.*"

[4] "*Si ergo damnatur reus, dum exauctoretur non debet alium judicium inchoari ad ejusdem condemnationem peccati,*" *Summa Causæ,* IV. 202.

[5] "*Consuetudines avitas*"; W. Cant.; T. Grim; "*consuetudines suas regales*"; *Summa Causæ*; and H. Bosham.

[6] "*Sauf lur ordre*"; Garnier, 32.

[7] H. Bosham, 273-275.

without taking leave of his Bishops; while Becket was ordered to give up all royal castles and honours still in his keeping.[1] But the two nevertheless were able to meet in Westminster Abbey on the 13th of the month (October), the occasion being the first Translation **First Translation of the Confessor.** of the remains of the Confessor, when they were removed from their original resting-place, to a new and costly shrine.[2]

Another personal interview is recorded as taking place outside Northampton, in the open air, and on horseback, as the way was in those times. Henry taxed Becket with ingratitude, reminding him of the benefits that he had heaped upon him. The Primate, after hinting, rather ungraciously, that his thanks were due to God as much as to the King,[3] answered that he always had been and still was truly faithful to his King in all lawful matters, but that to disregard the will of God would not be for the King's true interests or his own. 'He must obey God rather than man."[4]

Becket had been able to sway the voices of the Bishops at Westminster, **The Clergy Coming Round.** but he could not prevent misgivings as to the possible consequences of continued resistance to the King's will. Archbishop Roger of York and Gilbert Foliot of London joined Hilary of Chichester in recommending submission. Fresh defections followed, till the Archbishop and his secretary found themselves almost alone.[5] Another coadjutor to the King appeared in the person of Bishop Arnulf of Lisieux, a clever diplomatist, who having incurred Henry's ill-will came over to act as 'mediator.'[6] Then the Pope's answer to Becket's appeals, while urging him to stand on his rights, only promised such support as could be given 'with justice and reason.'[7] But the Papal letter, apparently, was accompanied, on the system pursued in the struggle between Anselm and Henry I., by verbal representations[8] committed to the Cistercian Abbot, Philip of L'Aumône,[9] a personage of admitted weight and character. We are told that this man, associating with himself the distinguished

---

[1] *Id.*

[2] H. Bosham, III. 261; Ann. Waverley, & Winton; M. Paris, *Hist. Angl.*, I. 329. For the application to the Pope for leave, see *Becket*, V. 19. The Bermondsey Annals give the day as the 13th October but under the year 1164.

[3] "Beneficiorum . . . quæ non simpliciter tu sed Deus tribuens," etc.

[4] Anon, IV. 27-29. The words attributed to Becket "a quo temporalem tantum præstolabar dignationem" imply a broad distinction in his mind between his duties to God when holding lay office, and those when holding spiritual office; as his career showed.

[5] "Pauci nobiscum . . . soli sic sedimus." H. Bosham, III. 276; Anon., IV. 30; *Id.* 97; E. Grim, II. 377.

[6] For Arnulf's position and career see Norgate, *Angevin Kings*, I. 500.

[7] "Quantum salva justicia et ratione poterimus"; *Becket*, V. 54.

[8] For communications that the Pope would not commit to writing, see the letter of the Bishop of Poitiers to Becket; V. 56.

[9] Otherwise Little Citeaux, between Blois and Chartres.

scholar Robert of Melun,[1] just named for the vacant See of Hereford, and John, Count of Vendôme, had an interview with Becket at Harrow, in order to point to the divided state of the Church, and the danger of alienating the King of England.[2]   Pressed on all sides not to distract the Kingdom for 'a petty verbal dispute,'[3] Becket at last gave way, and, waiting on the King at Oxford, agreed to withdraw the obnoxious saving clause, and promise honest (*bona fide*) observance of the customs.[4]

Becket Promises.   Grim, William of Canterbury, and the Anonymous writer allege that this promise was obtained on the faith of assurances given through the Abbot Philip to the effect that Henry intended nothing derogatory to the 'Order,' and that he merely wanted a nominal submission for appearances' sake.   But Becket's secretary has nothing of this. At any rate if such an assurance was really given Becket had no business to be taken in by it or to listen to it.   But Bosham's plain assertion is that his patron yielded from mere charity, and wish for peace.   The Archbishop, then, having given this promise, the King resolved to bring his submission to a tangible shape by publishing an authoritative definition of the 'customs,' and for that purpose summoned a Grand Council to meet at his hunting lodge at Clarendon on or about the 25th January 1164.[5]   We are assured that the plan of reducing the 'customs' to writing was adopted at the suggestion of the Archbishop's enemies,[6] as if the propriety of taking this very natural step could not have suggested itself to the King's own intelligence.

At the appointed time and place bishops, earls, barons, and dignitaries came together in full numbers.[7]   Unfortunately for us there was neither a William of Malmesbury, nor an Eadmer, to report the proceedings,

---

[1] So named from having taught at Melun in succession to Abelard, but John of Salisbury says that he was an Englishman.

[2] So I venture to read the facts. Grim, II. 378, and the Anonymous writer, IV. 31, represent the Abbot as bringing letters from the Pope and Cardinals urging Becket to submit. The former throws doubts on the authenticity of the Abbot's mission; the latter accepts it. William of Canterbury seems to accept instructions given through the Cardinals, but mentions no letters, only verbal assurances ; I. 15. Reuter rejects the mission ; I. 355, 566. I cannot believe in any letters from Alexander, but he may have directed the Abbot to talk over Becket, and keep him within bounds.

[3] "Unius verbuli contentione."

[4] Bosham, 276, 277 ; Anon., IV. 33 ; W. Cant., I. 15. That the interview took place at Oxford also appears from Foliot's letter, V. 527. The Anonymous writer and Garnier, who copies him, place it at Woodstock.

[5] So R. Diceto, I. 312. Gervase, I. 176, gives the 13th January as the day of meeting, but that would prolong the sittings of the Council to seventeen or eighteen days, as it certainly rose 'four days before the Purification,' *i.e.*, on the 29th or 30th January.

[6] H. Bosham, *sup.* The complaint that the customs had been reduced to writing is a constant one on the part of Becket's supporters, *e.g.*, V. 149.

[7] See the names of 14 bishops, 10 earls, and 27 barons given, *Select Charters*, 131 ; 'besides many others.'

only a Herbert of Bosham, and his account in our opinion must be

Grand Council at Clarendon. corrected by reference to the statements of more trustworthy authorities. The reader should be told in the first place that at these Grand Councils the King did not sit with the lieges, but apart in a private chamber with his confidential advisers; the Prelates and Barons again sitting either together, or separately according to circumstances. Communications therefore between the several Estates had to be kept up by verbal messages, carried to and fro by suitable envoys.[1] A day or two may have elapsed before the assembly was fully constituted.[2] When it was constituted and business entered upon, the course of affairs, according to Becket's biographers, was that the King began with the very superfluous proceeding of requiring Thomas to repeat in public his Oxford promise, still in the dark as it were, and without being enlightened as to what observance of the 'customs' would entail. These accounts go on to say that Becket, who had begun to suspect the King's intentions, drew back, and refused to renew his pledge, whereupon there ensued a prolonged struggle to extort the desired concession, and that it was not until that had been obtained that the customs were produced in writing. This version, no doubt, till now has found general acceptance, but we venture to discard it,[3] on the strength of counter-allegations, by men who took actual part in the discussions, whose word we think better entitled to credit than that of Herbert of Bosham. As we take the facts, therefore, Henry on the first day of actual sitting, after some preliminary discussion, produced his 'customs' in the shape of his

The Constitutions. celebrated *Constitutions* of Clarendon,[4] sixteen ready-drafted articles, intended to be enacted by the assembly as an Organic Statute, or fundamental Law of the Constitution to determine the relations of Church and State. Since the innovations of the Conqueror the law had been in a very indeterminate state, and since Stephen's time in a state of absolute chaos. The clergy took their stand on the Canon Law, but that had never been recognised as part of the Law of England, except in a very general way by the ordinance of William I. He and his sons had followed a hand to

---

[1] See the proceedings at Rockingham, *Foundations*, II. 194, and below those at Northampton.

[2] "Infra paucos dies conveniunt universi"; H. Bosham, 278.

[3] See the Appendix to this chapter, where I trace the seeming development of the popular account; accepting the recorded incidents, I simply transpose them, placing them after instead of before the production of the Constitutions.

[4] This is clearly stated by Bosham, 279, who thus leaves no room for the three days' struggle detailed by the others, which therefore must have come after the production. Bosham, in fact, ignores all the incidents of the struggle, contenting himself with a general statement that the Constitutions were produced "facta obligatione," *i.e.*, after Becket had agreed to them. W. fitz Stephen also gives the production of the Constitutions as the first thing done; II. 46.

mouth policy, content to carry any point they wanted to carry by the exercise of their prerogative. Henry of Anjou wanted a clear and settled state of the law, and Becket's militant attitude had greatly assisted to settle him in that purpose.[1]

Of the Constitutions the principal provisions were as follows :—

All suits relating to advowsons, whether between layman and layman, or between a clerk and a layman, to be heard and determined in the King's Court (s. 1).

All clerks charged or accused of any matter (*de quacumque re*) to be bound upon the summons of the King's Justiciar to appear before the King's Court to answer there, for such things as the Court shall hold to be answerable there, and in the ecclesiastical Court for such things as shall appear to be answerable before that tribunal; the Justiciar to send an officer to watch the proceedings in the ecclesiastical Court; no further protection to be given by the Church to any clerk convicted of or confessing an offence (s. 3).[2]

No archbishop, bishop, or [ecclesiastical] person whatever (*persona regni*) to leave the Kingdom without the King's leave (s. 4).

Laymen not to be accused in the Episcopal Courts except by lawful (*legales*) witnesses, and with due regard to the rights of the archdeacons. In the event of witnesses being afraid to come forward against persons of high position, the Sheriff, on the requisition of the Bishop, to impanel twelve lawful men of the vicinity (*de vicineto*)[3] or township to declare the truth on their consciences (s. 6).

No tenant in chief or any King's officer to be excommunicated, or his land laid under interdict without a previous reference to the King, or, in case of his absence abroad, a reference to his Justiciar, so that right may be done, and matters appertaining to the King's Court be decided in the King's Court, and matters appertaining to the Ecclesiastical Courts be decided in Ecclesiastical Courts (s. 7).

Appeals (in spiritual cases) to be carried in due course from the Archdeacon to the Bishop, and from the Bishop to the Archbishop; with an ultimate reference to the King; the matter to go no further without his leave (s. 8).

Archbishops, bishops, and other ecclesiastical persons holding in chief to be deemed to hold in Barony, and under liability to render all dues, and perform all suits and services incidental to such tenure, including that of sitting on the King's Court, except in cases involving penalties of life or limb (s. 11).

The rents and issues of all vacant sees, abbeys, and priories to go

---

[1] See Foliot's letter already cited, *Becket*, V. 527, where his best point against Becket seems to be that of having unnecessarily forced the King into hostile action.

[2] See the text above, p. 40.

[3] Hence our "venue."

to the King as part of his demesne. Canonical elections to take place under the King's writ, in his chapel, with his assent, and by the advice of persons deputed by him for the purpose; the Elect before conse-cration to do homage and fealty to the King of life and limb and earthly honour, 'saving his Order' (s. 12).

The goods of men under forfeiture to the King not to be protected by Church Sanctuary (s. 14).

Actions for debt, even when involving questions of trust, to be tried in the King's Court (s. 15).

Sons of villeins not to be ordained without the assent of the lord on whose land they were born (s. 16).[1]

These Articles give an insight into the encroachments of the ecclesiastical courts that they were intended to remedy. Of their legitimate spiritual jurisdiction Henry had no wish to deprive the clergy. He allows the prelates on appointment to do homage 'saving the rights of the Order'; his officers are directed in certain cases to back them up; bishops are even authorised to hold pleas relating to land where the land in question has been determined by the verdict of twelve lawful men to be frankalmoin—*i.e.* Church land, and not lay fief.[2] The article giving the King the revenues of vacant sees was clearly indefensible. The practice had been abjured by Henry and his grandfather; but as a matter of fact all vacant sees had been regularly farmed out for the King's benefit since the time of Rufus; and we shall find even such a Pope as Innocent III. prepared to acquiesce in the practice. The prohibition on clerks leaving the Kingdom without leave would place them at a disadvantage as compared with laymen, as Becket complained, but the restriction was necessary to check the endless appeals to Rome, that, like other abuses, had sprung up during the Anarchy.[3] The bearing of the important third clause we have already considered. We found that Henry was prepared to leave the trial of criminal clerks in the hands of the Bishops, only requiring the convicted offender to be handed over for adequate punishment after degradation. We would therefore read the clause as providing for a preliminary investigation before a Royal Justice—say, to ascertain if the accused was really a clerk or not—if found to be such he would be sent to his Bishops for trial; if found guilty he must be stripped of his orders, and then sent back as a layman to the King's Court for judgment. But of course even the preliminary investigation that we suggest would involve the appearance

---

[1] See the *Constitutions* in Bishop Stubbs' *Select Charters*, 131, from the Cotton MS. Claudius B 2, one of the original copies. They are also given by W. Cant., I. 18, and among the Becket Letters, V. 73, where the articles condemned by the Archbishop are noted. Only clauses 2, 6, 11, 13, 14, and 16 had his approval.

[2] See clauses 9 and 10.

[3] See *Foundations*, II. 440.

of clerks before secular tribunals for criminal matters, the concession most strenuously resisted. As a whole, however, the *Constitutions* "must seem moderate and reasonable to any man who does not exalt the Mitre above the Crown."[1] To the Churchmen of the period they seemed intolerable, as involving the subordination of ecclesiastical to lay authority, at a time when they aspired to making the Church supreme.[2]

Against all the leading provisions Becket protested vehemently, and at length. With respect to the article that dealt with criminal clerks he repeated the old sophism that it would involve a double trial for one matter.[3] 'It would be bringing Christ again before Pontius Pilate.' The restriction on clerks going abroad was unfair, and would stop pious pilgrimages; the Archbishops were bound to admit appeals to Rome; a pledge to that effect was required of them when receiving their *Pallia*.[4] In short Thomas refused to sanction the Constitutions as a whole, and his suffragans, as in duty bound, took post behind him.[5] Without their assent it is clear that the statute could not be enacted, and indeed without their concurrence it could not be worked, even if passed. But the constitutional theory of the time evidently required the several assent to a new law of each of the three Estates of the Realm, namely, the King and the Lords Spiritual and Temporal.

Becket Protests.

Indignant as Henry was at Becket's refusal, he so far kept his temper that we next hear of successive attempts to influence the Archbishop by mediators approaching him from different sides, and in fact with a certain regard for dramatic effect. First two Bishops are put forward, Joscelin Bohun of Sarum and Roger of Norwich, men understood to be out of favour at Court, and so likely to be among the first victims of the King's wrath if he were to be thwarted. Their pleadings having failed, two Earls come forward, men of the greatest standing, Robert of Leicester and Reginald of Cornwall; their cue is to deprecate the measures that it might fall on them to execute if the King should be driven to extremities. Becket still proving obdurate the King's cause is taken up by two Templars, men whose position appealed both to lay

Mediators.

---

[1] C. H. Pearson, *Hist. England*, 499.

[2] See Bishop Stubbs, Bened. Peterborough, II. *xxix.*; and Reuter, I. 369. The writers of the time only notice Henry's 'customs' to condemn them. If old, they were old abuses "Non consuetudines sed abusiones." So the letters of John of Salisbury, *passim.* W. Newburgh, while doing justice to Henry's wish to introduce much-needed reforms, thinks that he went too far; I. 140.

[3] "Bis judicabuntur in idipsum."

[4] H. Bosham, 280-283.

[5] W. fitz S., III. 46. See also the speech of the Bishop of Chichester, reported *Id.* 66, and the letter of Foliot, V. 527. As he was addressing Becket he could not venture to tamper with facts equally well known to both. All the three give the contest as occurring after the production of the *Constitutions.*

E

and clerical sentiment, namely, Richard of Hastings, the Grand Master for England, and one "Otes" of Boulogne,[1] otherwise Tosty of Saint Omer.[2] They implored the Archbishop to have mercy on his Church, which might be wrecked by resistance to the King. The third day of

A Climax. the struggle had now been reached. King and Barons had lost all patience; armed men invaded the conclave of the clergy, throwing them into utter confusion and alarm.[3] Then the Archbishop, feeling himself overpowered, according to an assertion that we can hardly reject, retired for a brief consultation with his private advisers. Returning to his Episcopal brethren he said 'If my lord the King will have me to perjure myself (*i.e.* take an oath he could not keep) so be it; I must hope to do penance in the future.'[4] He then proceeded

Becket Accepts the Constitutions. formally to declare his acceptance of the Constitutions 'on his word of truth . . . honestly, legally, and without reserve' ("*in verbo veritatis . . . bona fide, legitime, sine dolo malo*").

At his bidding the other Bishops did the same.[5] It would seem that the King then, by way of further guarantees (*ad cautionem majorem*) for the observance of the articles suggested that they should be sworn to and sealed. With respect to the swearing he was proudly told that a bishop's word was as good as an oath; as for the sealing we hear that Becket managed to evade that formality without irritating the King by a direct refusal. 'It could be done at any time';[6] a very palpable shuffle.[7] For his own satisfaction, however, he consented to take away one of the copies of the Constitutions, the Statute having been engrossed in triplicate. The Archbishop of York took another copy, and the third was consigned to the Royal Archives.[8] On

---

[1] "Otes," Garnier, 22; "Hosteus de Bolonia," Gervase; "Hostes," Anon., VI. 35.

[2] So Reuter, *sup.* I. 362.

[3] W. Cant., I. 16, 17; E. Grim, II. 381, 382; Anon., IV. 34, 35; and esp. Foliot's letter, V. 527. The others of course place all this before the promulgation of the *Constitutions*.

[4] "Est domini mei voluntas ut pejerem; ad præsens subeo, et incurro perjurium, ut potero pænitentiam acturus in posterum." Foliot, *sup.* He could hardly invent these words when writing to the speaker of them, but his suggestion that Becket set his followers the example of flight is most unfair.

[5] W. fitz. S., *sup.*; Foliot, V. 529; and the speech of the Bishop of Chichester, *sup.*, 66.

[6] "Archipræsul . . . dissimulat regem exacerbare tunc nolens. Et caute quidem non de plano negat, sed differendum dicebat," etc.; H. Bosham, 288; and the Bishop of Chicester, *sup.*; also W. Cant., I. 33. Fitz Stephen says that Becket did seal, but that clearly seems wrong.

[7] Becket wrote to the Bishop of Poitiers to inform him that he had not promised to observe the customs absolutely 'as their author boasts' ("non absolute sicut illarum innovator gloriatur"!) and that he had not sealed ('scripti munimento roborasse'), *Becket*, V. 112.

[8] Bosham, *sup.*

the 29th or the 30th of January the assembly broke up, business
apparently having taken up four days or thereabouts.[1]

Deeply humiliated at his own weakness, and inwardly resolved to be

Suspends
Himself for
so doing.
guilty of no such backsliding in the future, Becket suspended
himself from all priestly functions until absolved by the
Pope.[2] That he never intended to keep his promise may
be taken as clear from his subsequent acts and words, and those of his
friends. Their view was that the laws of the Church were the laws of
God, and that whatever was contrary to the laws of God could not
stand or be respected.[3] For this position Becket had Papal sanction;
because, about the time of the meeting of the Clarendon Council he
must have received a letter from Alexander releasing him from his
Oxford pledge, and charging him to consent to nothing that could
interfere with the 'liberty' of the Church, and more especially with the
rights of the See of Rome.[4] Henry had not neglected diplomatic

Application
to the Pope.
efforts to obtain from Alexander concessions that might be
used against Becket. About November [5] he sent over Arnulf
of Lisieux and Richard of Ilchester, Archdeacon of Poitiers,
with a double request: one that the grant of the Legatine commission
formerly held by Theobald, but not conferred on Becket, should be
given to Roger of York; the other for directions to Becket and the
Bishops to pay due regard to the customs of England, and the prerogatives of their King. The envoys were greatly delayed by bad weather,[6]
and apparently only returned to England about January. With respect
to the Legateship they brought encouraging assurances.[7] With respect to
the customs the answer given to them personally is not recorded, but the
outcome of their mission, apparently, was the inhibition to Becket.

Henry, on the other hand, after Clarendon, despatched a fresh embassy
to Sens, where Alexander was, the envoys being Geoffrey Riddel, Archdeacon of Canterbury, and John of Oxford. They were instructed again

---

[1] "Quarta die ante Purificationem"; *Summa Causæ*, IV. 208. Some read this as
equivalent to the 29th, some as equivalent to the 30th January.

[2] See J. Salisb., II. 312; H. Bosham, III. 291-293; and for Alexander's letter
absolving Becket, V. 88. A first suggestion that he might not perhaps have known
what the customs were to be, seems thrown out by the Pope (ignorantia, sicut
dictum est).

[3] See Becket's words below, uttered at Northampton, and reported by his own
follower Fitz Stephen, III. 66. "Quod contra fidem ecclesiæ debitam et contra
leges Dei est non potest in bona fide et legitime observari." John of Salisbury regarded
Becket's concession at Clarendon as merely a form of words. "Verbo tenus annuit,"
II. 311.

[4] *Becket*, V. 84. The letter was clearly written after the meeting at Oxford, and
probably reached Becket bef. Clarendon; Reuter, I. 359.

[5] Reuter, I. 265.

[6] R. Diceto, I. 312.

[7] See the Pope's letter, V. 85.

to pray for the Legatine commission and the recognition of the 'customs,' as accepted by the Bishops.   But it would seem that Henry refrained from sending the actual text of the *Constitutions*, contenting himself with sending some general summary, as we are expressly told that the *Constitutions* as enacted had never been seen by the Pope, or the Cardinals, till produced by Becket at Sens late in the year.[1]   In their prayer for the acceptance of the customs the King's agents were supported by letters from both Roger of York and Becket, the concurrence of the latter being a transparent device to humour the King.   It was probably on the strength of this concession that he wrote to the French King saying that he had made his peace with Henry and had regained his favour.[2]   Rotrou Bishop of Evreux is also named as concurring in this mediation.[3]   On neither point did Henry receive anything very satisfactory.   The Pope, seeing through Becket's application, declined to ratify the Constitutions.[4]   At the same time he urged Thomas, in the

His Action.   strongest terms, considering the needs of the times, to consult the King's wishes as far as he possibly could, 'saving the honour of his Order.'   The Legatine commission in favour of Roger of York Alexander granted, but under conditions that made it impossible for the King to make any use of it, and so it was returned as a mere mockery and delusion.[5]

Henry now resolved to take the offensive against the Archbishop,

Becket's Position.   who was in a very isolated position.   The Pope was prepared to stand by him, but the majority of the Cardinals were too much in awe of Henry to do anything that might offend him.   Louis also feared the King as well as hating him. Becket's friends abroad agreed in urging him if possible to come to terms with Henry.   A retirement to France was suggested, and a plausible excuse for doing so laid before him, in the shape of a personal appeal to the Pope in the matter of Clarembald, the Abbot of St. Augustine's, Canterbury, who refused to make profession of obedience.[6]   We hear of Becket taking ship at Romney, one of his

[1] See below, and H. Bosham, 343.

[2] See his letter to Louis, V. 80.   In an earlier letter he had declined gratefully the offer of a refuge in France, 70.

[3] W. Cant., I. 24 ; Anon., IV. 37.

[4] " Petitionem istam nequaquam admisimus."   Becket, referring to the Pope's action in the matter, could only venture to say that the 'Constitutions had been rather condemned than approved by him' (" potius improbatæ quam approbatæ ").   W. fitz S., III. 67.

[5] See the Pope's letter, V. 86 ; W. Cant., I. 24 ; Cf. Grim, II. 383, 384 ; Anon., IV. 37, 38.   For the Legatine commission see the letters, V. 85, 87, 91, 94, 113.   There again Becket was impracticable.

[6] See the various letters, V. 70, 80, 97-103, 113, 114.   The contumacy of Clarembald weighed heavily on Becket, *Id.* 113.   The question of the Archbishop of York's cross was another sore subject ; *Id.* 67-69, 82, 83.

manors, to leave the country, secretly, and without leave, a clear infringement of one of the Clarendon regulations, and that a
Attempt at Flight. regulation, without doubt, not introduced by Henry, but
as old as the time of the Conqueror. Foul winds frus-
trated the Archbishop's attempt. Conscious of his mistake he went to
Woodstock to see the King, and explain his conduct. He was
admitted to a bare formal audience, but nothing more, the King contenting himself with asking him sarcastically if England was not big
enough to hold them both.[1] Meanwhile the ostensible root of the
trouble remained where it was, Henry endeavouring to bring guilty
clerks to justice, and Becket systematically resisting him.[2]

At last, however, the King found an opportunity for bringing Becket's
attitude towards the *Constitutions* to a final test. Among other legal
reforms he had introduced a rule, obviously intended to control the
action of the private courts of *Sac* and *Soc*, under which a suitor who
had failed in the court of his lord might carry the proceedings up to
the King's Court, on taking an oath, supported by two compurgators
to the effect that justice had not been done to him in the manorial
court.[3] John Marshal, a leading magnate,[4] brought an action in the
archiepiscopal court to recover certain lands to which he
Case of John Marshal. laid claim, and having failed, took advantage of this
opening to appeal to the King. Henry at once cited
Becket to appear on the 14th September to answer for the failure of
justice to Marshal. The Archbishop did not attend in person, being,
as some said, unwell;[5] but he sent four *milites* with letters from
himself and the Sheriff of Kent to put in an appearance for him. They
Becket Pleads by Attorney. were instructed to plead in bar of the appeal; first that no
wrong had been done to Marshal; and secondly that the oath
on which the appeal was based was null and void. The
objection taken was that John had been sworn not on the Gospels, or
on any relics of Saints; but only on a 'troper,' a sort of hymn-book,

---

[1] H. Bosham, III. 273; Foliot, *Becket*, V. 529. This letter refutes the account of
Grim, II. 389. Fitz Stephen combining the version has two attempts, III. 49; he also
alleges that Becket was refused an audience at Woodstock.

[2] W. Cant., I. 25-29; E. Grim, II. 385-389; Garnier, 39; J. Salisb., II. 312.

[3] Glanville, *De Legg. Angl.*, XII. 7; extracted by Bishop Stubbs, Hoveden, I. 225;
also in substance Anon., IV. 41. Henry's regulation, as suggested by Reuter, I. 399,
probably only reduced existing custom to more definite shape. We cannot suppose the
private courts to have been exempt from all liability to revision.

[4] "Quidam ex proceribus," Anon., IV. 41; 'Quidam regni nobilium,' Foliot, V. 530.
He was probably Matilda's old supporter and the father of William Marshal, afterwards
the great Earl of Pembroke.

[5] So E. Grim, II. 390, and Anon., IV. 41. But neither William fitz Stephen nor
Bosham, Becket's personal attendants, allege any illness, and so the fact must be
considered doubtful. Foliot taxed Becket with having simply refused to appear;
V. 530.

a collection of 'tropes' or versicles to be sung during Mass at certain festivals.[1]   Henry, who, apparently, was sitting in person to hear the case, was most indignant at Becket's non-appearance, treating it as contempt of court, and, presumably as a direct breach of the 12th

Fresh Citation. article of the *Constitutions.*   A fresh citation was immediately issued calling on Thomas to appear before a Grand Council to be held at Northampton on the 6th October, then and there to answer for his conduct in connection with Marshal's case.   Grand Councils, like the Witenagemots of earlier times, could always sit as High Courts of Justice in State trials.   The Archbishop would thus be forced to accept the *Constitutions* or else be condemned in default.   As one of the greater Barons he was entitled to receive a special writ of summons, addressed to himself in person.   But on this occasion he only received a general summons through the Sheriff, as if he had been a minor Baron, the King refusing to address him personally with the greeting incidental to a special writ.[2]

Council of Northampton. On the appointed day Becket came to Northampton.   Herbert of Bosham and William fitz Stephen were in attendance, the latter probably as his legal adviser.   Next morning (Tuesday 7th October) after Mass the Archbishop waited on the King in the Castle, but was not admitted to the kiss of peace.[3]   Becket then asked leave to go abroad to see the Pope on the question of the Archbishop of York's cross.   This was refused.[4]   Thomas then referred to the case of the Marshal; Henry told him that that would be taken on the morrow.[5]

On Thursday, 8th October, before a full sitting of English prelates, earls, and barons, with some from Normandy, Becket was formally charged with treasonable contempt of the King's 'majesty,' and breach of his homage bond, and oath of allegiance, as Archbishop and tenant-in-chief, in that he had neither appeared in person on the 14th September, nor sent any sufficient excuse, whether of bodily infirmity or pressing ecclesiastical duty, to account for his absence.[6]   His pleas that the case had been properly tried in his court and full justice done, were

---

[1] "Super librum troporum"; W. fitz S., III. 50; "Troparium"; Anon., IV., 41. See Canon J. C. Robertson, *Life of Becket*, 111.

[2] W. fitz S., III., 49-51; E. Grim, II. 390, 391; Anon., *sup.*

[3] W. fitz S., *sup.*

[4] E. Grim and Anon., *sup.*; Garnier, 52.   Roger wanted to be allowed to have his cross, the emblem of an archbishop, borne before him outside his own Province.   That was quite inadmissible.   See below, p. 59.

[5] W. fitz S., *sup.*   He was present.   Herbert of Bosham, who also was there, clearly states that business did not begin till Thursday, 8th October (p. 296).

[6] "Neque corporis infirmitatem, vel necessariam quæ differi non poterat ecclesiastici officii administrationem," etc.

rejected as inadmissible; and the King pressing for judgment, he was declared guilty, the consequent penalty to be forfeiture of all
A Doubtful Judgment. his goods and chattels 'at the mercy of the King' (*ad misericordiam Regis*), that is to say, unless the latter should be pleased to accept of a composition.[1]   So far everything had gone smoothly, all were at one.   But when it came to the point of uttering the sentence, a slight hitch occurred to betray the difficulties of the King's position.   Barons and prelates alike shrank from the invidious task of condemning a man invested with the halo of the *Pallium*.
Who shall Declare it? Each order sought to throw the burden on the other.   The Barons thought that an ecclesiastic should be sentenced by ecclesiastics.   The Prelates protested that they only sat there as barons.
Henry of Blois. The irony of fate threw the duty on the senior Prelate, Henry of Blois, the Bishop of Winchester,[2] a thorough-going Churchman, who, by making his brother Stephen King of England, had done most to bring about the present deadlock.   According-ing to some of his friends Becket protested, utterly rejecting the right of any court to try an Archbishop of Canterbury.[3]   But, whether with or without protest, he was persuaded to bow to the decision
Becket Compounds. of the assembly, and tender a special composition.   His offer was accepted, the bishops, all but Foliot, joining in security for the amount.[4]

Marshal's own case was then taken up.   But there Becket gained the day, the King being content to accept his declaration that John's claim had been rejected on its merits, and that he had not taken a proper oath.[5]   Probably Henry saw that it would be wiser not to press a case where the feelings of the Magnates would not be with him. Interference with their private jurisdictions was a matter of which they were very jealous.[6]   The King so far had vindicated his *Constitutions*; at any rate he had forced the Primate of all Britain to submit to the

---

[1] Becket subsequently asserted that there were standing compositions for *misericordia* in different localities, and that by the custom of Kent he ought to have been let off with forty shillings.   That might be so in some cases, but the Pipe Rolls show amerciaments running up to £200 and more; *e.g.*, 7 Henry II., p. 29.

[2] W. fitz S., 52, 53.

[3] See H. Bosham, III. 297, and Anon., IV. 42.   Foliot in the letter already cited, suggests. perhaps sarcastically, that Becket yielded to the consideration that the King by virtue of his consecration was clothed with something of an ecclesiastical character; V. 531, 532.   Fitz Stephen says "sustinuit consilio episcoporum . . . quasi concessione judicii," p. 53.   Reuter rejects any protest.

[4] Fitz S., H. Bosh., and Anon , *sup,*; Grim, II. 391.   Fitz Stephen and Bosham are silent as to any composition.   Grim and the Anonymous writer notice it, and give it as £500; so does Diceto, I. 313.   W. Canterbury, I. 30, gives it as £50, and Garnier, 32, as £300.   Diceto says the amerciament was 'taxed' at £500 (habita taxione).

[5] Grim, *sup.*; W. Canty., I. 31; Anon., 43.

[6] Anon., 40, 41.

sentence of his court. Probably for his own credit he would have done well to rest there for the time, ready to renew the struggle, if needful, when a fresh case should present itself. But Henry was a self-confident man, spoiled by success, and utterly intolerant of opposition. He had not had the early lessons of adversity that had taught his grandfather self-restraint and patience. He proceeded to follow up his **Mean Proceedings.** first victory by a series of mean pettifogging attacks on Becket, in the shape of pecuniary demands, going back to the time of his tenure of office as Chancellor. The first call on him was for £300 received from the constableships of Eye and Berkhampstead. Becket protested, very rightly, that he was not bound to answer a claim of which he had received no notice, but, under protest, he declared that he had spent the whole and more on public works in London and elsewhere.[1] But Henry refused to accept these payments as sufficient vouchers, and demanded judgment. Then Thomas declaring gracefully that no mere money question should come between the King and himself submitted, and eventually produced sureties, the King's cousin William Earl of Gloucester being one of them. So ended the first day.[2]

But the King had not done yet. On Friday 9th October Becket **Fresh Demands.** received demands for 500 marks lent to him by Henry for the Toulouse campaign; and another 500 marks for which the King had stood surety for him to a certain Jew; and finally for an account of all his receipts from vacant sees during the time that he held the Seal, the total being supposed to amount to the prodigious sum of 30,000 marks (£20,000).[3] Again Becket declared that he could not be justly called to account without notice, but that at the proper time and place his accounts would be forthcoming.

Security Wanted. Henry sent word that the Archbishop could not be allowed to leave the Castle without giving security. Becket replied that for security he must consult his clergy. At last however he was allowed to retire. But we are told that from that time no more barons called at the Archbishop's quarters at St. Andrew's monastery.[4] The breach with the King seemed complete.

On the morning of the third day (Saturday, 10th October) all the higher clergy came to Becket's lodgings. Separate consultations were

---

[1] The receipts from Berkhampstead were fully accounted for on the Pipe Roll, 9 Henry II., p. 24. For Eye there is one payment of £150 3s. 7d. without further detail, p. 34.

[2] W. fitz S., III. 53.

[3] So H. Bosham. But in such matters chroniclers' estimates are of little worth.

[4] Fitz S., 53, 54. I follow him, as a lawyer and the clearer-headed man of the two, in preference to Herbert of Bosham, who, with other differences, places the demand for the accounts on the Saturday; III. 290. Reuter follows him.

held by him with the bishops and the abbots.[1]   Foliot, the Bishop of
London, thought that, considering Becket's previous relations
with the King, and the interests of the Church, entire submission, even to the point of resigning the Primacy, would
be the wisest course.[2]   Hilary of Chichester took the same view; and
so did Robert of Lincoln, and Bartholomew of Exeter, the last holding
that it was better that one man should suffer rather than the whole
Church be exposed to ruin.   Roger of Worcester, the King's cousin,[3]
declined to give any advice.   But Henry of Winchester protested against
such an utter surrender on the part of the Church.[4]   Others not named,
probably men of minor position, urged Becket to honour the King
without sacrificing his dignity, by standing his trial for the accounts,
from which they assured him he had nothing to fear; while others
again said that if he were to give up every penny of income, he ought
never to divest himself of his sacred office.[5]   Eventually it would seem
that they went to the Castle, by the advice of the Bishop of Winchester,
to offer on Becket's behalf a composition of two thousand marks.   The
offer was rejected;[6] and then again at the suggestion of the same Prelate
they retired, pleading the release given to Becket when appointed
archbishop.[7]

Clergy in Council

Sunday was spent in further deliberations at St. Andrew's, the Archbishop never leaving the premises, and at night he fell ill,[8] breaking
down under the prolonged strain.   In consequence he failed
to appear on the Monday.   Henry swore that he must be
shamming, and eventually sent the Earls of Leicester and Cornwall to
ascertain the facts.   Becket told them that if he had to be carried in
a litter (*lectica*) he would come on the morrow.[9]

Becket ill.

Tuesday, 13th October, witnessed the crisis of the painful drama.   The
principles that Becket identified with the name of Christ would have
paralysed all government, and relegated England to the theocratic
imbecility of Anglo-Saxon days.   The *Constitutions* were the enactment
of a duly qualified assembly.   Becket evidently did not intend to be
bound by them.   He had already committed a distinct breach of them

[1] Fitz S.   Reuter, *sup.*, holds these consultations to have been carried on at the
Castle, but I think that very unlikely.

[2] Cf. Foliot's letter, V. 535.

[3] Son of Earl Robert of Gloucester.

[4] Allan of Tewkesbury, *Becket*, II. 326–328; Fitz S., III. 54, 55.

[5] Fitz S., *sup.*

[6] *Id.*

[7] H. Bosham, 300.   So I harmonise the accounts of the two eye-witnesses which
are not altogether at one.

[8] The attack was apparently one of lumbago.   "Renes frigore et dolore contre-
muerunt"; "cervicalia" (poultices?) had to be heated and applied; Fitz S., *sup.*

[9] Fitz S., 56; Bosham, 300, 301; Grim, II. 393.

by attempting to go abroad without leave. On this point the feeling of the country was against him. We fail to trace any indication **Lay Feeling against him.** of that lay sympathy that Anselm in his struggle with Rufus had enlisted at Rockingham.[1] The Barons were solid for Henry II, though his unjust attacks on false issues gave every moral advantage to his antagonist.

The day opened with a final effort on the part of the Bishops to frighten Becket into submission, and resignation of his office. It was credibly reported, they said, that if he went again to court, without having come to terms with the King, he was to be impeached for breach of his allegiance through infringement of the Clarendon articles, and imprisoned—if not worse.[2] The hopelessness of contending with the King was also insisted on. The Bishops' attempt failed signally. Revoking the concessions that he had previously been induced to make, Becket at once assumed an attitude of uncompromising defiance. Going back **Becket throws away the Scabbard.** to the matter for which he had originally been brought to Northampton, the case of John Marshal, he took his brethren to task for having sat in judgment upon him, and condemned him to a penalty greatly exceeding the established composition, which, he averred, ought to have been simply forty shillings for him as a Kentish man; or at most a hundred shillings, according to the rule in London. He inhibited them from again sitting on him for any matter anterior to his promotion to the Primacy,[3] appealing in the meantime to the Papal Chair; lastly, if any attempt should be made to give effect to the judgment of any lay tribunal upon him, as popular rumour anticipated, he charged the prelates on their canonical obedience to visit the offenders with immediate excommunication. Against this last injunction Gilbert Foliot at once entered a counter-appeal to the Pope. The Bishops then retired, all but Henry of Winchester and Joscelin of Salisbury, who stayed to speak in private some words of comfort to the Archbishop.[4]

The Bishops having dispersed, Becket, as if to nerve himself for the final struggle,[5] went to a chapel in the monastery dedicated to the protomartyr St. Stephen, and celebrated the Mass of that Saint with " its significant introit " " *Etenim sederunt principes.*" (The rulers take counsel together against the Lord and against his anointed.)[6] Still further to

---

[1] See *Foundations*, II. 195.

[2] " Imminere captionem aut quod deterius," H. Bosham, 301.

[3] So W. fitz S. the lawyer and man of accuracy; Bosham extends the inhibition to any matter touching Becket personally. See also Becket's letter " Appellavimus et appellati sumus."

[4] W. fitz S., 62 : H. Bosham, 302, 303 ; Foliot, V. 535, 536.

[5] " Parat se ad palæstram."

[6] Psalms II. 2. Cnf. Becket's offensive protest that at Northampton Christ was again brought to trial in his, Becket's, person, V. 494.

emphasise his proceeding he donned his archiepiscopal Pall, a sacred
badge usually reserved for high festivals. Of course the
injudicious act was immediately reported at court, where it
excited intense indignation, being naturally regarded as at
once a challenge and an insult; a suggestion that the tyrannical King
might be prepared to send his Archbishop to a martyr's doom; but that
the Archbishop was still prepared to face him.[1] Becket's intention had
been to go to court in full pontificals, barefooted, and carrying his own
cross. Friendly remonstrances, however, induced him to abandon that
purpose, and to content himself with riding to the Castle in his usual
garb and style. But under the influence of the alarmist rumours that
surrounded him he thought it prudent to prepare for the worst by carrying
the Eucharistic-wafer secreted on his person.[2] Dismounting at the Castle
gate he took the cross from his Welsh bearer, Alexander Llywelyn,
and entered the hall, carrying it in his own hands, to the
consternation of all present.[3] Hugh of Nonant, the Archdeacon of Lisieux, who had come with Becket, being one
of his household, addressing himself to Gilbert Foliot, asked him if he
could allow the Primate to carry his own cross. 'Good Sir,' was the
answer, 'he always was a fool, and always will be one.'[4] Nevertheless
Foliot joined Robert of Melun, Bishop of Hereford, the distinguished
dialectician and teacher, in begging the Archbishop to lay down his
cross. 'If the King now were to draw the sword, forsooth,' said they,
'King and Archbishop would be fairly matched.'[5] 'Let the King draw
the sword if he will,' was the answer, 'I will cling to the emblem of
peace.'[6] Cross in hand Becket marched through the hall to the inner
chamber where the prelates sat,[7] the others taking their seats beside
him in due order. Last of all appeared Roger of York, with his cross
borne before him, in equal defiance both of recognised usage, and of
recent Papal prohibition.[8] The prelates, all but Thomas, were shortly

Side notes: Mass of St. Stephen. Entry to the Castle.

---

[1] W. fitz S., III. 56; H. Bosham, 304; W. Cant., I. 32; E. Grim., II. 393;
Anon., IV. 45.

[2] W. fitz S., and Bosh., *sup.* For Becket's fear of personal violence, see his
letter, V. 495.

[3] "Qui aderant obstupuere omnes"; Fitz S.; "Videntes stupent universi, anguntur
pontifices, indignantur proceres"; Bosham.

[4] Fitz S., 57.

[5] "En bene ornatum regem, bene ornatum archiepiscopum."

[6] Fitz S., *sup.*; Bosham, 305.

[7] Grim, II. 393, 394; Anon., IV. 46.

[8] Fitz S., 57, 58. The Archbishop of York was never allowed to carry his cross
within the Province of Canterbury. For attempting to do so Thurstan had seen his
cross-bearer turned out of the chapel at Windsor; *Foundations*, II. 307. Application
had been made to the Pope on Roger's behalf in this matter, and he vouchsafed a
truly Papal concession, granting nothing: that is to say he authorised Roger to carry
his cross—as he might do in his own Province; and to crown kings—as he might

summoned to the Royal presence in an upper chamber; the Primate, cross in hand, remaining in his seat, with his two attendants, Herbert of Bosham and William fitz Stephen, sitting at his feet in silence.   In fact Becket was somewhat in the position of a man in custody, with a Royal marshal, wand in hand, keeping guard over him.   Fitz Stephen having risen up to speak to his master was peremptorily ordered to sit down again and hold his tongue.[1]

Prolonged and animated discussions took place in the upper chamber ("*in cænaculo*").   Henry had been sufficiently irritated by Becket's entry with his cross, and the imputations it suggested; but more serious matter followed when the Bishops reported the morning's proceedings at St. Andrew's, and the inhibition, and the appeal to Rome.   Eventually a deputation of lay magnates was sent down to enquire if Thomas admitted

The King's Require-ments. having broken the Clarendon regulations as alleged;[2] the breach of these being claimed as involving a breach of his personal allegiance to the King.   Henry also wanted to know if the Archbishop was prepared to give the required security for rendering his accounts, and for standing by the decision of the Court.

The Primate's Answer. In a calm well delivered speech Becket repeated his old pleas. His homage and fealty to the King had only been given saving 'his obedience to God, his ecclesiastical dignity, and archiepiscopal honour';[3] he had not been cited to answer any suit but that of the Marshal; all that he had received as Chancellor, with more of his own, he had spent on the King's service; before consecration he had been released from all secular demands, as they all well knew; security for accounts he could not be called upon to give before trial, and all his friends were already overwhelmed with liabilities on his account; as for the inhibition and the appeal he frankly admitted both, renewing them, and finally committing himself personally, and the Church of Canterbury, to the protection of God and the Pope.[4]

The breach of the *Constitutions* having been thus admitted Henry began to press the Bishops to concur with the Barons in passing an immediate sentence on their Archbishop.   But to do so in the teeth of the inhibition

do in the absence of the Archbishop of Canterbury. *Becket*, V. 21. The grant, however, had been interpolated, or interpreted to extend to carrying the cross in all England, whereupon Alexander on Becket's remonstrance wrote to correct the misapprehension; *Id.* 67, 68, 69 ; 82.

[1] W. fitz S., 57-59; H. Bosh., 306.

[2] The inhibition was charged as a contravention of the article that required bishops to sit on the King's Court.

[3] The homage and fealty of a bishop to a King were in fact only given "salvo ordine suo" (*Constitutions Clarend.*, 12).   But a general saving clause could not overrule specific provisions to which a definite assent had been given.

[4] W. fitz S., 63, 64. With respect to the release Henry denied that his son had authority to grant it ; Diceto, I. 314.

would involve on their part a defiance of spiritual authority, a sacrifice
of all Church principles, and a risk of censures that no
Pressure on
the Bishops. ecclesiastics could be expected to face. They protested
vehemently, and the King after considerable discussion was
obliged to recognise the force of their objections. But if they could not
go as far as the King wished, they were able to propose a middle course;
A Middle they would enter an appeal to Rome, praying for the deposi-
Course tion of Becket on the ground of 'perjury,' *i.e.* the breach of
Suggested. his Clarendon promise, pledging themselves to prosecute the
appeal to the utmost of their power. The offer having been accepted, they
returned to the chamber where the Archbishop had been left sitting.
Hilary of Chichester in declaring the appeal addressed the Primate in
bitter words. 'Truly My Lord,' he said, 'By your inhibition you have
placed us between the hammer and the anvil.' He then recapitulated the
proceedings at Clarendon, laying stress on the fact that when the King had
asked that his *Constitutions* should be sworn to, and the records attested
by the bishop's seals, he was told that a bishop's 'word of truth' was as
good as an oath, and that they would observe his customs 'honestly,
legally, and without reserve' (*bona fide, sine dolo malo, et legitime*). By
inhibiting them from sitting on him in judgment the Archbishop had
broken that word, because the duty of sitting on the King's Court was
expressly laid on the Bishops by the *Constitutions*. To his inhibitions they
would bow for the time, but on the rights of the case they appealed to the
Pope.[1] Becket's answer, reported, as well as Hilary's speech, by his own
follower, is painful reading. 'Whatever he had promised at Clarendon
was promised saving the rights of the Church (*salvo honore ecclesiastico*):
the very words "*bona fide, sine dolo malo, et legitime*" implied as much;
Pledges not no pledge that was contrary to the rights of the Church (*fidem*
Binding. *debitam ecclesiæ*) and the laws of God could be honestly
observed. The Pope had condemned the *Constitutions* rather
than approved of them : if through the weakness of the flesh they had
lapsed at Clarendon, they were bound to take breath (*spiritum resumere*)
and renew the struggle.[2] Now, here with regard to the tacit reservation
claimed by Becket, we must bear in mind the fact that the whole point
of his submission at Clarendon was his surrender of the saving clause
"*salvo ordine suo*," on which till then he had insisted.[3] He now contends
that the abandonment of the clause made no difference, a monstrous
pretence. Again we may point out that if the immunities of the Church
were then to Becket's conscience as the laws of God, that view of them
had only come upon him as Archbishop.

---

[1] W. fitz S., 65, 66 ; H. Bosham, 308, 309.
[2] W. fitz S., 66, 67. Miss Norgate, Becket's apologist, omits all notice of this speech.
[3] So expressly H. Bosham, III. 379 ; " Nulla omnino conditione adjecta," J. Salisby.,
II. 311.

The Prelates having announced their appeal to the Pope retired to leave the declaration of the finding of the Court in the hands of the Barons. To make up for the retirement of the Bishops the King had reinforced the Court by calling in Sheriffs and other minor personages not usually summoned to Grand Councils.   In the general reluctance to face the painful duty of passing sentence on an Archbishop the task **Becket to be Condemned.** had to be undertaken by the Earl of Leicester, joint Chief Justiciar with Richard of Lucy, the Peer of greatest weight and standing.   It is clear that Becket was to be found guilty of 'perjury,' and presumably of treason also ;[1] and it was understood that the sentence would be imprisonment.[2] But the fact cannot be stated positively, because the judgment was never delivered.   When the Earl, after going over the facts to the same effect as the Bishop of Chichester, came to the point ; Thomas, springing to his feet, stopped his mouth. 'Do ye pretend to judge me ? Ye are but laymen ; I am your spiritual father, and I refuse to listen to you.'   Abashed by his resolute attitude, and **Sentence Eluded.** probably in some fear of having an immediate excommunication fulminated at them,[3] the Barons retired.   After a short pause Becket rose again, and took his departure, cross in hand.   He had eluded actual condemnation ; further stay might expose him to fresh assaults.   As he passed through the crowded hall he stumbled over a faggot of sticks, but without actually falling.   Insulting cries of 'Traitor,' 'Perjured traitor' followed him.   Becket turned fiercely on his assailants. 'If it were not for this gown I would show you if I was perjured or a traitor.' The door had been closed during the day, but it was now opened for him.   Outside he found his horse, but Herbert of Bosham could not find his animal in the crowd, and so Becket took him up behind him, and the two rode back to St. Andrew's on the one steed. In the course of the evening the Archbishop's military tenants renounced their homage, some of his clergy following their example.[4]

Determined to get away from Northampton Becket sent for the Bishops of Worcester, Hereford, and Rochester, men under special ties with him,[5] and instructed them to apply for leave to depart on the morrow, with a safe-conduct to take him abroad.[6] They found the King in excellent

---

[1] See Herbert of Bosham. "Cum . . . de reatu perjurii tangeret, volens jam, ut adverti poterat, pronunciare perjurum, et forte (ut conjectabatur) ut proditorem" ; p. 310; "perjurum et proditorem archipræsulem, ut postea nobis intimatum, judicarunt"; 309.

[2] "Captio, aut quod durius" ; *Ib.* "Ut redactus in vincula in carcerem retrudatur" ; E. Grim, II. 397.

[3] Herbert of Bosham had urged Becket to be ready with an excommunication, W. fitz S., 58.

[4] W. fitz S., 67-69 ; H. Bosham, 309-312, two accounts in excellent accord.

[5] Rochester was his vicar and chaplain, and the other two had been consecrated by him.

[6] W. fitz S., H. Bosham, "postulans securum de terra sua egressum."

;pirits.   He replied that he would send an answer next day.   But Becket did not care to wait for the morning's light.   Concealing his purpose by declaring an intention of 'invigilating' in the chapel, about **Flight from Northamp-ton.** cock-crow he rode off in torrents of rain, with four horses procured in the town, and three attendants, one of them a Gilbertine Brother from Sempringham.   Passing through the North gate he escaped, making his way that night to Grantham, and next day, after a rest, to Lincoln.[1]

It may be taken as clear that Becket left Northampton greatly fallen ih the eyes of his countrymen ; both the natural sense of loyalty, and the natural love of plain dealing would be shocked by his repudiation of his pledge to the King.   Then his hasty flight would be held a confession of guilt.[2]

APPENDIX I. TO CHAPTER III.

CANON LAW

FROM early times the   Christian Churches had endeavoured to dissuade their members from going to law before pagan tribunals.   As St. Paul wrote to the Corinthians, "Dare any of you having a matter against his neighbour go to law before the unrighteous, and not before the saints?" (1 Cor. vi. 1).   This disposition seems to have been encouraged by the Christian Emperors, who gave the Bishops a definite jurisdiction over their flocks.   But when Christianity was introduced into England this authority had to fit itself into the pre-existing system of national judica-ture, the mixed courts with which the reader is familiar being the result.   As for the principles on which the episcopal jurisdiction should be conducted, the canons established by the great Councils held in the East during the fourth and fifth centuries became "the nucleus" of a new body of law, primarily theological and dogmatic, but secondarily juridical.   Towards the end of the fifth century a collection of canons and Papal letters was made by a Roman monk, Dionysius Exiguus.   In the middle of the ninth century there appeared in Gaul the celebrated False Decretals, published under the name of Isidore Mercator, a compilation of passages from the Bible and the Fathers, canons and decretals, some genuine, some spurious, with maxims from the Roman Law, the whole arranged to establish the sanctity and authority of the priest-hood, the supremacy of the Pope, but above all the rights and privileges of the Episcopate in general.   Other collections followed, best known of which were those of Burchard of Worms, who wrote early in the eleventh century, and of Ivo of Chartres who died early in the twelfth century.   But the work that established itself as the "authoritative text-book" on the subject was the *Decretum* of Gratian of Bologna, published between the years 1139 and 1142.   The authorities quoted included the Isidorian forgeries, with a like mixture of canons, decretals, Biblical texts, and legal maxims.   By the clergy it was at once proclaimed 'God's Law,' and the value set on it for controversial purposes may be seen by a glance at the Becket correspondence, where references to the *Decretum* occur on every page.   But it never

---

[1] E. Grim, 399 ; W. fitz S., 69 ; H. Bosham, 312, 323, 324 ; Anon., IV. 53–55.   At Lincoln they lodged with a fuller, by name Jacob, an Israelite?

[2] See the elaborate apologies for the flight in Bosham, 318–322 ; "unde et commen-dabilis hæc Thomæ fuga."

received any sanction as authoritative Church law. That recognition was reserved for the Code in five books published by Gregory IX. in 1234. A sixth book or 'Sext' was added by Boniface VIII. in 1298; and the 'Clementines' by Clement V. (1313). We may add that the forgeries of the original Isidore were never questioned till the fifteenth century, and not exploded till the sixteenth century. But the practical instincts of the laity enabled them to resist pretensions that they could not critically refute. In England, of course, the Canon Law was the law of the Courts Christian. See Pollock and Maitland, *History of English Law*, I. 111; Mr. Maitland's essay, *Canon Law in England*, *English Hist.*, *Rev.* vol. XII.; Bishop Stubbs, *Lectures on Modern History*, 292; and the article on Canon Law in the *Encyclopædia Britannica*.

APPENDIX II. TO CHAPTER

BECKET AND THE *CONSTITUTIONS* OF CLARENDON

THE commonly accepted version of the events at Clarendon, according to which Becket and the other bishops were induced to accept the *Constitutions* before seeing them, goes back, no doubt, to the account of Herbert of Bosham, who in a very brief, confused notice asserts that the 'customs' were only produced in writing "incontinenti facta obligatione," *i.e.* after Becket had pledged himself to them (III. 279). But I have already pointed out that he tells us that the *Constitutions* were produced on 'the first day of the Council,' so that the three days' discussion, of which we hear from other sources, must have come after the publication of the 'customs.' The short reference to the matter in John of Salisbury is simply this: that the King required his customs to be publicly rehearsed and confirmed by the unqualified assent of the bishops ("Ut consuetudines . . . publice recenserentur . . . et absoluto omnium episcoporum assensu firmarentur" (II. 311), where the rehearsal is evidently placed before the assent. Grim, II. 379, with no personal knowledge of what happened, goes distinctly beyond Bosham, because he introduces a preliminary demand by Henry for a fresh pledge to observe the 'customs,' of which Herbert says nothing, and on this point the whole struggle, and the overtures of the successive envoys are made to turn (p. 381). The 'customs' are not recited till Becket and his bishops have given in to them. When it comes to the King's demand for the sealing the Archbishop, with his eyes at last opened, utterly protests, 'Not while I live.' Bosham has told us that he tactfully avoided a direct negative. Grim goes on that the King's agents had assured Becket that the 'customs' should never be reduced to writing, never recorded (p. 383). The Anonymous writer No. 1 (IV. 33–37) has just the same story as Grim. The King begins by demanding a renewal of the Woodstock (Oxford) promise. The Archbishop, who has begun to have misgivings as to the Abbot of Aumône's assurances, draws back, and then the contest begins. But the writer outdoes Grim in averring that the 'customs' were not even reduced to writing till after the pledge to observe them *bonâ fide* had been extorted. Like Grim, he makes Becket reject the sealing with an oath. Lastly William of Canterbury (I. 18) boldly asserts that, which to a certain extent has been hinted at by the Anonymous writer, namely that the 'customs' were not merely not reduced to writing, but not even hunted up and ascertained till after the promise to observe them. The gradual development of the current version seems therefore clearly traceable. It is sufficiently refuted by the authorities cited in my text. I should repeat that in the subsequent references to Becket's acceptance of the *Constitutions*, we never have any suggestion that he was entrapped; he himself says that he was coerced "observantia per vim et metum extorta" (VI. 521). With his followers, as already mentioned, the great complaint seemed to be that he had been compelled to assent to customs reduced to writing (III. 341; V. 149).

CHAPTER IV

HENRY II. (*continued*)

A.D. 1164-1166

Controversy with Becket—Henry, Louis, and the Pope —Alliance with Germany—Welsh War—Nonconformist Visitors—*Assize* of Clarendon—*Inquest of Service*—Excommunication of the King's Ministers

On the 14th October (1164) the eventful council of Northampton held its last sitting. Becket having absconded, the King, in some trouble, asked what was to be done. He was induced to respect the appeals to the Pope, and to allow them to run their course; pending their decision the Archbishop to be left in the enjoyment of his revenues, and his men under the protection of the King's peace. Proclamations in that sense were immediately issued. For the prosecution of the Bishop's appeal Roger of York, Gilbert of London, Hilary of Chichester, and Bartholomew of Exeter were selected.[1] It would seem, however, that at the same time orders were issued to watch the coasts to prevent Becket leaving the Kingdom,[2] a matter of great importance for the King. Within the four seas he would have his adversary pretty much under his thumb; abroad Becket could defy him with impunity. Foliot, William Earl of Arundel, and Richard of Ilchester were entrusted with a mission to King Louis;[3] while a warning was sent to the ruling Count of Flanders, Philip son of Dietrich, the latter having gone off to Holy Land.[4]

Proclamations and Missions.

At Lincoln Becket assumed a disguise and a feigned name, 'Brother Christian Dearman.'[5] From Lincoln he passed down the river Witham to a hermitage belonging to Sempringham, and after three days' rest there went on to Boston, and from thence again to the Gilbertine Priory of Haverholme in the Parts of

Becket's Movements.

---

[1] H. Bosham, III. 322, 323; W. fitz S., 70.

[2] Anon., IV. 55.

[3] Anon., 58.

[4] R. Monte, A.D. 1168, when Dietrich died.

[5] "Derman," E. Grim, II. 399; "Christianus," H. Bosham, III. 326. I put the two names together.

Kesteven.[1] His next recorded stage was to Chicksand Priory, near Ampthill in Beds; finally he made his way to his own manor of Eastry near Sandwich; where he lay for a week, while a vessel was being found for him. On the 2nd November he made out his crossing, landing on the open beach, between Oye and Gravelines. By a curious coincidence the King's envoys passed over on the same day to Boulogne (*Portus Magnus*).[2] Exhausted by his tossing on the waves, the Archbishop soon found himself unable to walk, and had to sit on the ground till his attendants procured a draught horse, on which he rode bare-backed to Gravelines. At the inn there at supper he was recognised, but not betrayed; and so was enabled to continue his journey up the river Aa to the Cistercian Abbey of Clairmarais, near St. Omer. There he was joined by Herbert of Bosham, who had been waiting for him at St. Omer, with 100 marks of silver (£66 13s. 4d.) and some plate that he had secured at Canterbury. On hearing that the King's ambassadors were at St. Omer, Becket retired to a cell or hermitage called Eldminster, and lay there for three days to allow the envoys to get ahead of him. When the coast was clear he moved on to St. Omer, where of course he took up his quarters at the great Abbey of St. Bertin.[3] Concealment now became impossible, and in fact Thomas found himself confronted by no less a personage than Richard of Lucy, who had been sent on an embassy to the Count, to forestall Becket's movements, and deprecate support to him.[4] The Justiciar did his best to induce Thomas to return, promising his good offices with the King. Finding Thomas not to be shaken, he renounced all ties with him.[5] But the fugitive Archbishop was not yet on safe territory. Count Philip was closely leagued with Henry; and besides that had a personal quarrel with Becket, who had opposed the marriage of his brother Matthew to King Stephen's daughter, Abbess Mary, the heiress of Boulogne.[6] Thomas therefore failed to obtain from the Count the desired safe-conduct, and so had to make out another stage in secret, starting by night with the help of Milo Bishop of Thérouanne. In due course, however, he reached Soissons, within the dominions of the King of France.[7]

He Crosses the Channel.

And Reaches France.

Henry's envoys found Louis at Compiègne. They presented a letter from their master, indited on the spur of the moment at Northampton,

[1] Four miles N.E. from Sleaford. H. Bosham, III. 324.
[2] *Id.*; W. fitz S., III. 70.
[3] H. Bosham, 325-332; W. fitz S., 70, 71; Anon., IV. 57.
[4] H. Bosham, 332.
[5] W. Cant., I. 43; E. Grim, II., 400; W. fitz S., 71; Anon., IV. 57.
[6] H. Bosham, 328; above p. 22.
[7] W. Cant., *sup.*; E. Grim, 400, 401; H. Bosham, 338, 339.

requesting his 'lord and friend' to withhold all protection from a convicted traitor 'Thomas formerly Archbishop of Canterbury.'[1]

Henry's Agents Abroad. King Louis, with some surprise, asked who had deposed the
Archbishop. 'He in his kingdom could not depose the
humblest clerk.'[2] Discussing the question with Foliot and the Earl of
Arundel, Louis declined to admit that his ties with Henry were incompatible with showing hospitality to so distinguished an exile as the
Archbishop; and he utterly refused to use his influence with the Pope
against Becket.[3]

From Compiègne the ambassadors went on to Sens, where they were
received by Alexander in full Consistory. In their several speeches they
complained of Becket's hot-headed, self-willed action, undertaken apart
from his suffragans, whereby he had precipitated an unnecessary crisis,
disturbed the peace of the Church, and put the devotion of the King to
the severest test. Foliot having ventured to quote the Psalm 'The wicked
fleeth when no man pursueth,' with reference to Thomas' escape,
brought down a prompt rebuke from Alexander. 'Spare brother,
spare.'[4] 'I will spare him my Lord,' answered the Bishop. 'Nay
brother but I meant spare thyself.' It would seem that the difficulties of the English Bishops over their Latin excited some amuse-
ment. The Earl of Arundel prudently confined himself to his own
tongue, presumably French.[5] The sum of their petition was that the
Pope would be pleased to send Becket back to England, with a Legate
or Legates commissioned to hear and determine all questions between
the King and the Archbishop.[6] For Henry it must be said that to
entrust the decision to ecclesiastical arbitration implied considerable
confidence in his own position. The Biographers suggest that Henry
hoped to solve the question with a golden key.

Alexander was in a position of extraordinary difficulty. "To Henry
he almost owed his pontificate." Louis had shown a disposition to
treat his claims as an open question.[7] Henry had been staunch
throughout. Then Becket's uncompromising attitude was

Henry and the Pope. quite out of keeping with his own cautious, patient policy;
while, more than half of the *Curia* were on the King's
side. But it was impossible for the Pope to desert the champion of

---

[1] See the letter, *Becket*, V. 134, from Bouquet, XVI. 107.

[2] H. Bosham, 332.

[3] Anon., IV., 58; W. Cant., I. 44.

[4] "Parce frater."

[5] "Comes eleganter sed in lingua sua." William of Aubigny, of course, was a
Frenchman.

[6] Allan of T., II. 337-340, a much better report than that of Herbert of Bosham,
III. 335, 336, though he was present; compare E. Grim, II. 402; W. fitz S., III.
73; Anon., IV. 61.

[7] See above for Louis' proposed interview with Frederic, p. 28.

Church rights. To gain time, therefore, and avoid giving a direct negative, he requested the ambassadors to wait for Becket's coming, as he could give no answer till he had seen the Primate. The ambassadors replied that their instructions would not warrant their staying on, and so, having failed to elicit any further response, they left Sens, their errand unsped.[1]

Returning to England, they reported the failure of their mission to the King at Marlborough, where he was keeping his Christmas Feast.[2] Orders were immediately issued for confiscating the archiepiscopal revenues, and the preferment of all clergy who had had any intercourse with Becket since his flight.[3] The impounding of the Primate's estates might be expected; but there could be no justification for meddling with the effects of the other clergy. But Henry went to still greater lengths by directing all Becket's innocent relations to be be sent into banishment, to hamper and distress him.[4] The cruel orders were strictly enforced. All such of Becket's connection as could be found in London were brought to Lambeth, and sworn to leave England with the first fair wind, and join their friend wherever they could find him. In consequence we hear that in a short time a dismal crowd of fugitives, old and young, had gathered round Becket in his retirement, his sister Agnes and her children among them.[5] It also appears that the sheriffs were directed to arrest any persons, clerical or lay, who should attemp to carry any 'appeal' to Rome; while the payment of Peter's Pence was suspended.[6]

Persecution of Becket's Friends.

At Soissons Becket had the honour of a visit from the King of France, who condoled with him in his troubles, and furnished him with means to continue his journey to the Papal court at Sens. By Alexander, again,[7] Thomas was received with equal cordiality, the Pope sympathising with him in the hardships and perils of his wanderings. With great consideration he refrained from calling on Becket for any account of his proceedings, leaving it to him to offer an explanation at his own convenience. Accordingly, at the end of a few days, Thomas, at his own request,[8] was

The King of France.

Becket and the Pope.

---

[1] H. Bosham, 337, 338.

[2] W. fitz S., III. 75.

[3] "Qui circa ipsum fuerant post fugam suam." See the writ, *Becket*, V. 151. The Canterbury estates were farmed by Ralph of Broc for £1,562 15s. 5d., besides sundries accounted for separately; Pipe Roll, 11 H. II.

[4] W. Cant., I. 46, 47; J. Salisb, II. 313, 314; H. Bosham, III. 359.

[5] W. fitz S., *sup*, and the letter, V. 242.

[6] See the supposed writ, V. 152.

[7] Fitz Stephen's assertion that a 'large part' of the Cardinals went out to meet Becket is one of the statements of that writer that lacks confirmation. None of the others have it.

[8] So H. Bosham, who was present, p. 340.

received in private conclave, and gave his account of his quarrel with the King, ending by producing the actual text of the *Constitutions*, which, till then, had never been laid before the *Curia*.[1] Needless to say, that by such a tribunal the bulk of the articles would be condemned as monstrous (*abominabilia*). We need only to refer to the provision intended to check appeals to the Papacy. What could a Pope say to a measure framed with such a purpose? Alexander, it would seem, took Becket sharply to task for ever having given his assent to such 'tyrannical usurpations,' 'enslaving the Church of God.'[2] Some of the Clarendon regulations, however, the Pope, as if to leave room for future negotiation, admitted to be tolerable, but only just tolerable. Finally, changing his tone towards the Archbishop, he said that if he had sinned much he had suffered much, and deserved especially well of the Church; and so again granting him absolution from his Clarendon promise, dismissed him with the Apostolic blessing, charging him, however, at the same time, never again to agree to anything doubtful, except ' saving the rights of the Order.'[3]

However strongly the *Constitutions*, as a whole, may have been reprobated by the *Curia* we take it that no official condemnation was passed on them, for this reason, among others, that while the Pope admitted that some of them might be tolerated, it seems clear from the report of Herbert of Bosham that the tolerable articles were not specified, or distinguished, from those that were not tolerable. By refraining from an authoritative declaration Alexander would avoid a direct collision with the King of England; on the other hand, the informal reprobation would enable Becket and his friends to treat all the *Constitutions* as utterly condemned and void.[4]

The Constitutions not Condemned Officially.

Once more we must point out that in the discussion on the *Constitutions* nothing was said to suggest that Becket had assented to them without seeing them.

But Thomas had to face another and a more trying discussion with the Cardinals, who criticised his course of action as ill-timed and impolitic. William of Pavia is mentioned as taking the lead against him.[5] A variety of speeches are given to us as delivered by the Archbishop, all different. Herbert of Bosham has one

Becket and the Cardinals.

---

[1] " Scriptura . . . quam ante nunc nec papa nec cardinales, etsi de ipsa, non tamen ipsam audierant ; " *Id.*

[2] " Qui Dei ecclesiam ancillaverint ; " *Id.*

[3] H. Bosham, III. 340—343; Anon., IV. 62; also Becket's own reference to the events, V. 321.

[4] See Becket's own letter, VI. 205. "Consuetudinibus quas dominus Papa Senonis de unanimi fratrum consilio . . . condemnavit."

[5] See the cautious admission of Bosham, " a quibusdam cardinalium . . . amicabili est asperitate objurgatus," 343 ; " Cardinales tamen . . . multam vexationem beato viro in sua causa præstiterunt ; præcipue Guillelmus Papiensis." Anon., IV. 63. " Tepide receptus a cardinalibus," Allan, II. 341 ; Grim, 403.

impossible oration, of twelve pages in length, contemptuous to the Sacred College, and breathing fire and sword against all 'schismatics,' and infringers of the 'liberty' of the Church.[1] We also have 'Becket's Cause' in the shape of an address to the Pope, rightly described as an "effusion;"[2] but which does enunciate the position, to which we shall find Becket persistently adhering, namely, that on the question as to what things are Cæsar's and what things are not, the last word must rest with the Spiritual, not with the Temporal authority; in ultimate resort the State must bow to the Church, not the Church to the State.[3] To this ocasion we may perhaps attribute the offer of resignation of which we hear from several of the biographers. Allan of Tewkesbury represents the offer as based by Becket on a recognition of the painful fact, that he, Thomas, was not a true Shepherd, not having entered the Fold by the right door, inasmuch as his appointment was in fact due to the King's nomination, and not to a *bona fide* canonical election,[4] a most pharisaical piece of affectation, if Becket was guilty of it, as not a prelate on the whole English Bench could be found whose position would not be open to the same objection. But, if made, the offer of resignation was certainly not accepted, the Archbishop being fully confirmed in all his rights.[5]

After a stay of three weeks at the Papal court Thomas removed to the Cistercian Abbey of Pontigny,[6] "the second daughter of Citeaux," within the borders of Burgundy, about forty miles from Sens, a convenient retreat outside the dominions of King Louis,[7] so as not to bring him into trouble. Becket's peace there, however, was soon disturbed by the report of the banishment of his friends, followed shortly by the actual appearance of many of them, as applicants for food and shelter. Eventually, however, through Becket's influence they were taken up and provided for in various ways by charitably disposed persons, and especially by religious Houses.[8]

In the course of Lent (17th February—28th March ?)[9] 1165, the King went over to Normandy, apparently for the sake of having an interview with

Becket at Pontigny.

---

[1] Pages 344—356.

[2] So Bishops Stubbs, R. Diceto, I. 316, where the speech is copied.

[3] *Becket*, V. 138; also copied by Diceto and Hoveden.

[4] II. 343. For the offer to resign see also W. fitz S., III. 76, "Ut dicitur;" "ut mihi pro certo dictum est;" E. Grim, II. 403; "ut pro certo cognitum est," *Summa Cause*, IV. 210. Bosham is silent as to any resignation, but on such a point his silence is not conclusive.

[5] *Id.*; W. Cant., I. 46. Herbert of Bosham, who was present, is the only writer who seems to distinguish rightly the proceedings of the two days.

[6] Yonne, on the Serain, a little below Ligny-le-Châtel.

[7] H. Bosham, III. 357. The chief Cistercian Houses had taken Alexander's part as against the Emperor, and they likewise declared for Becket as against Henry; Reuter, *Alex. III.*, Vol. I. 468.

[8] H. Bosham, 358—375; also J. Salisb. V. 252.

[9] 17th February, Ash-Wednesday; 28th March, Palm Sunday.

Louis. The meeting was held on the 11th April, near Gisors.[1] Nothing is
told us of the matters discussed, but the conference must have
The King in Normandy. had reference to the contest with Becket. We hear of efforts
to arrange for the Archbishop's presence. Always regardful of
appearances, Thomas required provision to be made for a fitting suite;
larger provision in fact than the French King felt called upon to provide.
But the proposal came to nothing, because Henry refused to meet his
adversary.[2] Returning to Rouen Henry received an embassy from the
Emperor, Frederic Barbarossa, the chief envoy being Reginald, Archbishop
of Cologne. He was charged to propose a double matrimonial
A German Alliance. alliance, asking for the hands of the King's two daughters;
Matilda, the eldest, to be married to Henry the Lion, Duke of
Saxony and Bavaria,[3] and Eleanor, the younger, to the Emperor's son,
Henry, born only that same year.[4] Negotiations on the subject had
already been opened in England, the Archbishop having gone over
apparently to approach the Queen and bespeak her consent.[5] The
proposed alliance with the Emperor's son fell through, but two years
later Matilda, being then in her twelfth year, was sent to Germany, and
married to Duke Henry.[6] Of course the ultimate object of the Emperor's
proposals was to detach Henry from Alexander III.; and the King's
action in consenting to receive such an embassy would, in itself, be held
significant. We are told that the Empress Matilda refused to see the
Germans.[7] Strict churchmen, like Earl Robert of Leicester, would consider
themselves contaminated by intercourse with schismatics.[8]
Diet at Würzburg. But Henry went farther. He sent John of Oxford and Richard
of Ilchester back with Reginald to Würzburg, to assist at a
grand Diet held there by Barbarossa at Whitsuntide,[9] for the express purpose

---

[1] R. de Monte.

[2] *Becket*, V. 160, 162, 169, note.

[3] R. de Monte, 224.

[4] Boehmer, III. 438, cited Reuter, *Alex*. III. v. II. 194.

[5] R. Diceto, I. 318; Pipe Roll 11 H. II., 77, 108. Diceto represents the Archbishop as
entertained by the King at Westminster. If so Reginald must have come in the winter;
but most likely he came during Lent, and was received by the Queen, who remained in
England till towards May. See Eyton, *Itin*. 78.

[6] Pipe Roll, 13 H. II., 2, 18, 37, 194; R. de Monte records the marriage under the
year 1168; but the entries on the Pipe Roll show that she must have left England before
Michaelmas, 1167. The expense of her outfit was met by an aid *pur fille marier*,
properly 13*s.* 4*d.* on the knight's fee, and exigible only from tenants in chief; but Henry
extended the tax so as to include all classes of the community from the highest to the
lowest. See Pipe Roll, 14 H. II. *passim* and below.

[7] See the letter of Rotrou, late Bishop of Evreux, and now Archbishop of Rouen,
V. 194.

[8] According to Diceto, *sup*. he refused to give the kiss of peace to the Archbishop
when in England; the altars at which Reginald had celebrated were thrown down.

[9] In 1165 Whitsunday fell on the 23rd May.

of renewing and perpetuating the Schism, and pledging his subjects to support Pascal III., and to reject, not only Alexander III., but also any future Pontiff to be elected by his partisans. The Germans for the most part swallowed the pledges prescribed by their Emperor.   The

Bad Pledges. English envoys also took an oath on behalf of their master, but the exact form of words used by them seems doubtful. According to Frederic they swore to discard Alexander and stand by Pascal.[1] According to reports sent to the Pope they swore to follow the Emperor's lead in the matter of the Schism.[2] According to an account preserved by John of Salisbury, they swore to support the Emperor 'as against all men,'[3] the real aim of the alliance being of course well understood.   But even in this shape, if it was so taken, the pledge of the envoys was a bold one, and more than English feeling could support. Accordingly Rotrou of Beaumont, late Bishop of Evreux and now Archbishop of Rouen, was directed to issue a contradiction declaring that the King had neither himself personally, nor through his agents, given any promise to support the 'Schismatic one,' or abandon the Church.[4] By Becket and his friends, however, the guilt of John of Oxford and Richard of Ilchester was considered indisputable.[5]

From his conferences with the German ambassadors at Rouen Henry went back to England for operations against the Welsh. In the course

Welsh War. of the previous year, the indomitable Rhys ap Gruffudd had again gone to war with Roger of Clare, the Earl of Hertford, and won back the whole of Ceredigion, finally managing to unite the nations of North, South, and Middle Wales in a common rising against the English yoke.[6] Reprisals had been resolved upon in the council of Northampton, and writs for assessments for foot soldiers had been issued,[7] but no further action had as yet been taken. The King's steps were directed in the first instance towards the modern county of Flint, where David, son of Owain Gwynedd, had been committing wholesale depredations, carrying off all the people with their cattle. Henry advanced as far as Rhuddlan, where he rested three days. Then, finding that the enemy had withdrawn to the Vale of Clwyd, he fell back, and after refortifying Basingwerk and other places went home to raise a more sufficient army. The muster for this second campaign was apparently held at Shrewsbury, from whence the King

---

[1] See his letter and his proclamation, *Becket*, V. 183, 193.

[2] *Id.* 187, 189, 190.

[3] "Cum . . . operam . . . et consilii promitteret contra omnes homines," *Id.* 433.

[4] *Id.* V. 194 and . . . Henry's explanations addressed to the Pope through Foliot.

[5] See Becket's . . . munication of them *Id.*, 394. On the whole episode cf. Reuter, II. 19 . . .

[6] Ann. Camb. . . . 1163.

[7] 14th October, . . .

advanced to Oswestry.[1] Crossing the border he entered Powys. The
Ineffectual Campaigning. natives under Owain Gwynedd from the North, and Rhys from South Wales, with the representatives of the old House of Bleddyn from Powys, were all encamped at Corwen. The forces apparently, advancing concurrently towards each other, reached the banks of the river Ceiriog, and confronted each other there. Some skirmishing took place, but Henry eventually forced the passage, cutting his way through woods, and so led his army on to the foot of the Berwyn, a mountain range running along the south border of our Merionethshire. There he halted. Bad weather came on, his provisions ran out, and he had to retire. We must suppose that he made his way to Llangollen, as he returned to England *viâ* Chester. There he consoled himself by
Methods of Barbarism. barbarously mutilating the children of Gruffudd and Owain, and other unfortunate hostages who had been placed in his hands.[2]

But before the year was out Rhys was again up and doing, and captured the fort of Aberteify, *i.e.* Cardigan.[3]

The expenses of the two campaigns were met by the proceeds of the assessments voted, as already noticed, at the council of Northampton.
War Taxation. These were in form voluntary undertakings, 'promises,' to find contingents of foot-soldiers (*servientes*), the finding of a soldier meaning simply a payment of 15s. 3d., being apparently a man's wages at a penny a day for six months.[4] Of course the two expeditions together did not last half that time; but that did not matter. The contributions are not styled scutages, as in fact they grossly exceeded any legal scutages in amount. The Bishop of Lincoln, whose scutage at £1 the Knight's fee would have been £60, paid £152 10s.; the Abbot of Abingdon, who at the same rate would have paid £29, paid £79; the Bishop of Exeter owing for 17½ fees gave £75. The Bishop of London had 'promised' £114 5s. But Gilbert Foliot was a man to whom the King was much beholden, and so he was excused his 'promise,' and let off with the minimum scutage of one mark the fee, £13 6s. 8d.[5] It has been suggested that the gross sums accounted for by the tenants in chief under the head of 'promises' included legal scutages.[6] If the scutages were in fact paid by the enfeoffed *milites*, the men liable for the actual service in the field, as seems to have been the case,[7]

---

[1] *Brut. sup.*; Girald., VI. 138 (*It. Camb.*); Pipe Roll, 11 Henry II., cited Eyton.

[2] July-August; *Brut.* and Ann. Camb., *sup.*; Eyton, *Itinerary*, 82; and for the mutilation of the hostages, Ann. Waverley. An entry on the Pipe Roll, 12 H. II., p. 109, distinctly refers to two campaigns in Wales.

[3] *Brut.* and Ann. Camb. *sup.*

[4] See this worked out by Mr. Round, *Feudal England*, 283.

[5] Pipe, 11 H. II., 19, 37, 74, 81.

[6] Round, *sup.*

[7] So I gather from the fact that when in any given case part of a scutage accounted for by a tenant in chief is remitted, the remission is given as made, not in favour of the

then the difference between such scutage and the amount of the 'promise'
Tenants in Chief made to Pay. would represent the contribution actually paid by the tenant in chief out of his own pocket, and as it were out of his desmesne lands, which properly were not liable to direct taxation. From that point of view the assessments, though illegal, might not seem altogether so iniquitous.

With respect to the expenditure of the money we find the King importing mercenaries, *cotterels*, from abroad. A body of nine hundred of these received uniforms in London at his expense.[1] But the 'promises' for the Welsh war were not the only noticeable exactions of the year. Hugh Bigod, Earl of Norfolk, found it convenient to compound with the King at Nottingham for a fine of £1,000, one third paid down, and that independently of £227 10s. for the war.[2] Then we have long lists of *misericordiæ*, amerciaments, again irrespective of contribution to the war,[3] running from 40s. to 100 marks, 200 marks, and 300 marks, and culminating in one huge fine of 2,000 marks (£1333 6s. 8d.) imposed on Abraham son of Rabi of London (nothing paid).[4] In no case do we get any hint as to the misdemeanour for which the penalty is inflicted.

In the refreshing seclusion of Pontigny, with his hours divided between
Becket at Pontigny. study, meditation, and prayer,[5] Becket nevertheless kept a watchful eye on the outer world, determined to lose no opportunity of prosecuting his contest with the King, a contest that he was resolved should end in one way, and one way only, namely, in his own unconditional reinstatement, and the absolute surrender of the King.
His Purpose. "For this one object he laboured, pleaded, argued, censured during the next six years without ceasing ; his own suffragans, the monastic orders, Pope, cardinals, the Empress Matilda, the King of France, none of them had a moment's peace from his passionate endeavours to press them into a service which he seemed to expect them all to regard as a matter of life and death, not merely for England but for all Christendom."[6] The Pope while instructing Foliot to remonstrate with the King on his attitude to the Church,[7] and annulling the sentence passed on Becket at Northampton in the Marshal's case[8]—a

---

accounting tenant in chief, but of some subordinate whose name is specified, doubtless the *miles* liable for service, who had made out some case for indulgence. Pipe Rolls, *passim.*

[1] Pipe Roll, 11 H. II., 31.
[2] *Id.* p. 7.
[3] *E.g.* the Bishop of Lincoln besides his £152 10s. for the war, is amerced 400 marks, and pays in £133 6s. 8d. on account ; p. 37.
[4] *Id.*, p. 33.
[5] So at least H. Bosham, III. 358, 376 ; and Anon., IV. 65.
[6] Norgate, *Angevin Kings*, II. 52. See the Becket correspondence, *passim.*
[7] *Becket*, V. 173, 200–211. Henry allowed Peter's Pence to be again collected.
[8] *Id.*, 178.

wonderful piece of interference—had nevertheless forbidden Thomas to take any measures against Henry till Easter, 1166.[1] But so keen was the Archbishop for action that we find him opening up a fresh ground of quarrel. The See of Bangor had been vacant since the year 1161

See of Bangor. when Maurice the last bishop died.[2] Alexander's attention having been called to the fact, he issued a mandate to the clergy of the diocese ordering them within two months to elect a bishop to be presented to Becket for confirmation; failing that election the Primate to present. Owain Gwynedd, fearing doubtless to be embroiled afresh with Henry, wrote humbly to Becket praying that during his exile any bishop appointed to Bangor might be consecrated by some other prelate. Thomas sent a curt refusal, and then went on to attack Owain for his marriage to a kinswoman (*cognatam*).[3] The end of it was that Becket excommunicated the Prince, and under that ban Owain died (1168).[4]

The year 1166 opened with two noteworthy Councils. The first, apparently a Synod of Bishops,[5] held under the King's order, met at Oxford, and was concerned with the heretical teaching of a humble band of Nonconformists, men and women, some sixteen in number,[6] who had

Nonconformist Visitors. appeared in England. They were said to come from Germany, perhaps more likely from Flanders, their leader being one Gerard, described as a man of some education.[7] The exaggerated pretensions and dogmatic teaching of the Hildebrandine Church had provoked a widespread spirit of revolt, of which the South of France was the chief centre. Throughout the twelfth century Western Europe was traversed by teachers, "Biblical Anti-sacerdotalists," mediæval Protestants, who appealed to the Scriptures against the existing ecclesiastical system.

Attacks on Church Teaching. The spiritual claims of the priesthood, their Sacramental doctrines, their wealth and social position were points specially attacked. On the Continent the holders of these new views were known by various names Paterini, Idonii, Publicolæ, Publicani, Cathari. About the time that we have reached Peter Waldo of Lyons was founding in the valleys of the Alps the well-known sect that still commemorates his name. On English soil the doctrines were now being broached for the first time, and they had made but little progress, only one woman having been converted. The persons brought before

---

[1] *Id.*, 179.

[2] *Registrum Sacrum* (Bishop Stubbs).

[3] *Becket*, V. 225-239. December 1165-March 1168. Bangor remained vacant till 1177.

[4] Giraldus, VI. 133; *Brut.*, A.D. 1169.

[5] "Episcopale concilium," W. Newb.

[6] So Walter Map. Wm. of Newburgh raises the number to thirty.

[7] "Nationis et linguæ Teutonicæ"; W. Newb.

the bishops are spoken of as Weavers,[1] a designation that seems to connect them with the "Tisserands" of France. Probably they were descended from the followers of Tanchelin of Antwerp, who, for a time, had ruled his sect "with the power and state of a King."[2] The doctrines of the 'Weavers,' when examined by the Bishops, were found, like those of Tanchelin, to be anti-sacramental. Having refused to recant

'Heretics' Punished. they were handed over to the King as declared heretics. Henry was not a persecutor, but under existing circumstances he could not afford to be thought lax; the offenders were all branded on their foreheads, scourged, and then turned out of doors half-naked in mid-winter.[3]

In this Synod Henry was understood to have bound down the bishops to have no communication either with Becket or the Pope, except through him.[4] The second assembly of the winter was another Grand Council, held at Clarendon apparently in February;[5] and its work was the sanctioning of a measure published as the King's act, and known as

Assize of Clarendon. the *Assize of Clarendon*. This important Ordinance was aimed at the suppression of crime, and the establishment of a more efficient and uniform administration of the law, to be effected through the judicial circuits of itinerant justices. These

Circuits of the Judges. iters, initiated by Henry I., and disused during the anarchy, had already been revived to a certain extent by Henry II.[6] But from the entries on the earlier Pipe Rolls of the reign we may gather that the judicial business in the counties had remained mostly in the hands of the sheriffs, local magnates, with private interests to serve. From the year 1166 onwards we are told that the visitations of the King's justices become "annual and general"; and such no doubt

[1] "Hæresis texentium"; Ann. Tewkesbury.

[2] See Milman, *Latin Christ.*, IV. 174-180.

[3] See W. Newburgh, I. 131, where the incident is placed under the year 1160; W. Map, *De Nugis C.* 62; R. Diceto, I. 318; Ann. Tewkesbury; Ralph of Coggeshall, 122 (Rolls Series); Newburgh asserts that the band perished miserably; *contra* all the others. Bishop Stubbs suggests that they may have been connected with the movement "which in France was crushed for the time by the council of Lombers"; and he points out that their punishment was mild as compared with those under the Forest laws, or even under the ordinary criminal law; R. Hoveden, II. liv. But it was effectual, "the next case of heresy is late in the reign of John."

[4] Anon., IV., 65, where however the pledge is given as exacted at Clarendon.

[5] For the date see Bishop Stubbs, B. Peterboro', II. lix., where it is shown that the Council must have been held in 1166, after the Synod at Oxford, and before March, when the King went abroad.

[6] For evidences of judicial circuits prior to 1166 see Foss, *Judges*, I. 174; the case before Simon fitz Peter above, and W. fitz S., I. 45; the iters identified by Bishop Stubbs, Ben. Peterborough, II. lxiv.; and the reference in the *Polycraticus* of John of Salisbury, V. 15, written between 1159 and 1162 to "Justicias errantes"; *Id.*, lviii.; W. Newburgh also speaks of these as reinstated early in the reign, I. 102.

vas the case.   But we must remark that if the earlier circuits had been
partial or intermittent, the fault rested with the King, with whom it lay
o appoint and instruct the judges.   But for some of the provisions of
iis new regulations the assent of the Lords Spiritual and Temporal
would be requisite, as their privileges would, to a certain extent, be
infringed.

We would regard as the essential innovations now introduced the absolute
Subordina- subordination of the sheriffs to the Royal justices ; and the
tion of breaking down of the barriers offered by the private franchises
Sheriffs. of *soc* and *sac*, both of these reforms being entirely in
keeping with Henry's anti-feudal, centralising policy.   That there were
large arrears of unpunished crime to be dealt with, and that the ordinance proved very drastic will be seen.   The measure begins by requiring
inquests to be held, either before the King's Justices or the Sheriffs, in
every county by its Hundreds, by juries of twelve of the better (*legaliores*)
Presentment men of the Hundred, and four good (*legales*) men from each
of Criminals. Township, the jurors being sworn to present all persons accused
or reported guilty (*si aliquis rectatus vel publicatus*) of theft,
robbery, or murder ; those so presented to be put to the ordeal by
water ;[1] inquests to extend to offences committed at any time since the
beginning of the reign (ss. 1 and 2).   Bail to be granted if demanded
by the lord of the accused, or his steward, within three days of the
man's arrest (s. 3).   The Sheriffs to be bound to report each presentment to the nearest Justice, and to produce the culprit, as and when
The Ordeal. required to do so, with two men from the Hundred and
Township to record the presentment ; the ordeal to be
undergone in the presence of the Justice (s. 4).   No lord of a franchise
Lords not to to claim any jurisdiction over any man presented ; the King
Interfere. to have the culprit's chattels (s. 5).[2]   All criminals arrested
under any circumstances to be brought by the Sheriffs before
the Justices (s. 6).   Jails to be built in counties where there were none
(s. 7).   All persons to be bound to attend the county court and to serve
on these juries[3] ; no one to be exempt by reason of holding
Frank- any 'liberty' or soke (s. 8).   The Sheriffs to enter all castles
pledge. and franchises to 'view the frank-pledges' ; *i.e.* to ascertain
that every man was under the standing bail for his good conduct required

[1] For ordeals see Index to *Foundations*.

[2] So too *Dialogus de Scaccario, Select Charters*, 220; the chattels to go to the King,
the land to the lord, where the *Assize of Clarendon* is evidently referred to as the
King's 'assiza arctior' against criminals.   Bishop Stubbs also points to the fifteenth article
of the *Constitutions* of Clarendon as showing that Henry had already introduced some
regulation to the same effect, "an innovation on the older law ;" Benedict af Peterborough, II. cliii.

[3] For methods of evading this burden see F. W. Maitland, *Eng. Hist. Rev.*, III.
417; and Pollock and Maitland's *English Law*, I. 537, etc.

by the old Anglo-Saxon law (*frithborh*) [1] (s. 9). No lord of a soke or other person to have in his house or on his land any person not under frank-pledge, or for whom he himself will not be personally responsible (s. 10). No lord of any franchise or castle to hinder the Sheriff from arresting persons charged or presented (s. 11). Persons presented, but cleared by the ordeal, if of very bad character to be required

Abjuring the Realm. to leave the country (s. 14). Strangers not to be entertained except in boroughs, and then for one night only, except in cases of sickness (ss. 15, 16).[2] Fugitives from justice to be followed from county to county; when found in counties other than

Hue and Cry. their own, liable to be arrested (s. 17). Lists of fugitives to be made out by the Sheriffs, and returned to the Justices, so that their goods may be seized for the King's use (s. 18). The Sheriff on the summons of the Justices to convene a full county court to meet them (s. 19). The 'renegades' branded at Oxford not to be harboured (s. 21).[3] With respect to the culprits who 'perished' under the ordeal it does not appear that they were necessarily hung. From the *Assize of Northampton*, a republication of the present Ordinance, we learn that the loss of a foot was the ordinary penalty.

The interest and importance of the *Assize of Clarendon* cannot be over-estimated. It illustrates the continuous character of our institutions, and the slow course of their development. It exhibits the old

County Courts. gemots of the Hundred and Shire, meeting, no doubt, not under the Bishop and the Earl as of old, but under the Sheriff; while from this time onwards the Sheriff, as a judicial officer, has to bow to the King's Justices, and take his orders from them. Then again we still

Soc and Sac. have the old franchises of *soc* and *sac*; but they can no longer claim jurisdiction in cases of serious crime. On the other hand the fetters of the old law of *frithborh* are preserved intact. Every man of moderate position must still be under standing bail for his good conduct, whether it be the personal bail of a responsible lord, or the collective guarantee of a 'frank-pledge,' tithing, or guild. The ordeal is still the ultimate test of a man's guilt or innocence, compurgation

Continuity of Institutions. falling into the background. But now, if we turn our eyes forward to the law of our own times, we shall find that the Commissions of Assize under which our Judges hold their circuits go back to Henry's Ordinance,[4] while the liability to serve on juries

---

[1] For Frithborh see Index to *Foundations of England*.

[2] Bishop Stubbs, *sup.*, points out that this was an increase of stringency on the old law, which admitted of three nights' entertainment. *Leges Henrici Primi*, VIII. 5; Schmid, etc.

[3] *Select Charters*, 137; also printed by Bishop Stubbs in his B. Peterboro', II. cxlix., etc.

[4] Blackstone, III. 394 (ed. Stephens 1848) traces these Commissions to the *Assize of Northampton* of 1176. But that was merely a republication of the *Assize of Clarendon*.

comes from the same source.[1] The presentment of guilty persons by the twelve men of the Hundred and the four men of the Township carries us back still farther, standing as it does as a link between the accusation by the twelve sworn thegns in the old English gemot and the presentments of our own Grand Juries.[2] If we might venture on one remark more we would point out how much the old localism interfered with the administration of justice. Even apart from the private franchises—hotbeds of crime—we gather from the *Assize of Clarendon* that it was not altogether an easy matter to follow a criminal from one county to another: the old provisions of Hue and Cry had to be repeated. A county still retained something of the character of a Heptarchic Kingdom.

A first circuit under the provisions of this Assize was shortly held by William Mandeville II., Earl of Essex, and Richard of Lucy. The vigour of their proceedings is shown by the entries on the Pipe Roll of the year (12 Henry II.) swelled by long lists of the names of men and women whose goods had been forfeited to the King, either because they had shirked attendance at the courts, or fled from justice, or been apprehended and convicted. It is clear that there had been large arrears of petty crime to be dealt with; but the fiscal results were not great. From the fugitives in general nothing was obtained; the total realised, we are told, would barely make up £400.[3]

To this same period, the winter of 1166, we must ascribe another important Inquest directed by Henry, namely one as to the amount of military service due by the tenants-in-chief.[4]

Inquest of Service.

This service, of course, was the cardinal point of the new feudalism introduced by the Conqueror. In granting or regranting an estate to a tenant, old or new, it would seem that he declared verbally the number of *milites*, fully-armed cavalry soldiers, that the grantee would have to provide, if called upon, for service in each year, the recognised term of service being forty days. Now it has been shown that the tenant might provide for the performance of this duty

---

[1] Bishop Stubbs, Ben. Peterborough, II. cli., note.

[2] See Laws of Æthelred, III. 3 (Schmidt); Pollock & Maitland, *English Law*, I. 90, 140 bowing it would seem to German authorities, seem to question the connexion of Henry's procedure with that of the Anglo-Saxon gemot. But apart from the fact that the former met under a Royal writ I do not believe in much practical difference between the "accusation" of the one and the "presentment" of the other. The summoning of a jury by Royal writ of course was a practice that came in with the Conquest. A Frankish origin has been suggested.

[3] See Bishop Stubbs' Preface to the Roll; Pipe Roll Society, 1888.

[4] For the year see the *Red Book Exchequer*, I. 186, and the entry on the Pipe Roll (12 H. II.) of the purchase of a chest (huchia) for keeping "curtas Baronum de militibus"; p. 72. For the time of the year see p. 412, where it appears that the returns were to be sent in by the First Sunday in Lent (12th March).

(*servitium debitum*) in one or other or both of two ways. He might keep in his household or on the lands in his own hands (*super dominicum suum*) a body of retainers for the purpose, the house-carles of Anglo-Saxon times. But such men were expensive and troublesome to main-

Knights' Fees. tain. The more favourite plan was to grant out little estates to suitable men, to be held of the tenant-in-chief, in return for the obligation of turning out when required. The form of conveyance was termed enfeoffment or subinfeudation, and the estates themselves were known as *feoda militum*, rendered 'knights' fees,' a misleading term, as implying that the *milites* would be dubbed knights, whereas the fees in question were mostly quite inadequate to support men of such position, as they varied from two hides to fourteen hides each.[1] Of course the reader is aware that by the· time that we have now reached, through the introduction of scutages, the number of *feoda militum* for which a man was liable was more a fiscal than a military question. The Crown must have known pretty well how many *milites* were due from each tenant-in-chief; but there does not appear to have been any strict register of them kept, and disputes sometimes occurred. Henry might well wish to come to a final understanding on the point. But the tenor of his writs, as reflected in the returns to them, suggest that he may have had something farther in view. The tenants-in chief are required to state (i.) how many *milites* they had enfeoffed before the day of the death of the late Henry ; (ii.) how many they had enfeoffed since that day ; (iii.) how many they had on their demesne lands ; and (iv.) whether any of these men had not as yet done personal homage to the King, in which case they must render it by the first Sunday in Lent

Old and New Feoffments. (12th March).[2] The rather singular line drawn by the King between the fees created before, and those created after his grandfather's death, suggests that the Exchequer officials or the King himself had discovered that during the troubles of the Anarchy some of the magnates, for their own purpose, had enfeoffed *milites* over and above the number that they owed to the Crown, and that having made that discovery Henry proposed for the future to treat these as part of their *servitium debitum*, and assess them for scutage accordingly. Anyhow the returns of the Barons (*cartæ*) to the King's writs became the basis of a new assessment, "in no case to the advantage of the tenant, but in many to the advantage of the Crown."[3] In the subsequent scutages of the reign the tenants are charged both on their old and their new feoffments, the *milites* on the demesne

---

[1] Round, *Feudal England*, 52. On the whole subject see *Foundations* II. 140.
[2] See the return of the Archbishop of York, *Red Book*, I. 412 ; Round, *sup.*, 238.
[3] Round, sup., 242.

being included amongst the old.[1] The Barons' returns at last supply us with authentic data for ascertaining the number of 'Knights' fees' in England, estimated by Orderic at 60,000. The most laborious **Total Number.** investigations of modern scholarship only bring the total up to 7173 fees.[2] But to this eventful winter, again, it would seem that we must ascribe the issue of another Ordinance, perhaps published in **Assize of Novel Disseisin.** the shape of instructions to the Justices, the *Assize of Novel Disseisin.* The text of the measure has not come down to us, but it was destined "in the long run to prove itself one of the most important laws ever passed in England." It provides that if a man be disseised, that is to say dispossessed of his freehold, unjustly and without due process of law, he shall have his remedy by application for a royal writ, under which a jury will be summoned, and the case tried before a royal Justice. The *Assize* stands parallel to that of Clarendon. As by the latter the cognisance of crime was taken from the county courts and private franchises, to be placed under the King's Justices, so now likewise a certain class of suits relating to land is taken from the same courts to be placed under the protection of the King's authority.[3]

Early in Lent, probably in the course of the second week (13th-18th March) Henry went over from Southampton to Normandy.[4] He **Henry Abroad.** was shortly followed by the young King of Scotland, William the Lion. His elder brother Malcolm the Maiden had passed away on the 9th December, unmarried. On Christmas Eve William **William the Lion King of Scots.** was hallowed by Richard Bishop of St. Andrews, and installed at Scone.[5] We are told that William went over on the business of his lord the King of England; and he certainly went at his expense.[6] Doubtless he had been called upon to render homage; while he himself would be anxious to obtain a confirmation of the earldom of Hun-tingdon and other estates previously held by his brother. The earldom was not confirmed; but some other estates were granted.[7] William's visit may

---

[1] For the *cartæ* themselves see Liber Niger Scacc. (Hearne), 49-340; and *Red Book Exch.*, I. 186-445. On the whole subject see Mr. Round's masterly article *Feudal England*, 225-314; *Foundations*, II. 139.

[2] See the Tables compiled by Mr. A. H. Inman, *Domesday and Feudal Statistics*, 65. Mr. Round, *sup.*, 272, was inclined to put the total at 5000.

[3] See Pollock and Maitland, *Histy. Eng. Law*, I. 137. 146. The *assize* is ascribed to this year on the ground that in the next year's Pipe Roll, 12 Henry II., p. 65, we first have a fine for "dissaisina super assisam"; so again 13 H. II., p. 134.

[4] R. de Monte; R. Diceto, I. 318; Eyton, *Itinerary*, 92.

[5] Chron., Melrose; J. Fordun, 258, 259; Eyton, *sup.*

[6] Chron., Melrose; Pipe Roll, cited Eyton.

[7] Malcolm however must have been deprived of the earldom before Michaelmas, 1164, as the revenues of the county, and those of Cambridgeshire, not previously accounted for, appear on the Pipe Roll of that and the following years. William was allowed to succeed to considerable estates in Northants, apparently including Althorp and Earl's Barton ("Berton") evidently relics of Waltheof's inheritance; Pipe Roll 13, H. II. 117-123.

also have had some reference to the affairs of Brittany where his sister was the reigning countess.

At Easter Henry was at Angers,[1] and had an interview with Louis VII., who urged him to follow his example by levying contributions from his subjects for the relief of the kingdom of Jerusalem, a matter in which the French King as an old Crusader felt deeply interested.   Henry accordingly held Grand Councils of his Continental subjects at Le Mans, on the 10th and 17th days of May, and induced them to vote a tax on all rents and movable property of twopence on the £1 for one year, and a penny on £1 for four years, the money to be paid on the simple oath of the contributor, into boxes in the churches; all classes of the community, from the highest to the lowest, to contribute.[2]

Palestine Tax.

But the term of the armistice imposed by Alexander on Becket (Easter Day, 24th April, 1166) had already expired.   In anticipation of the time the Pope had given Thomas special authority to excommunicate all persons guilty of invading Canterbury property; leaving his position with reference to the King more open.[3]   A Legatine commission over all England except the Province of York had at last also been granted to Becket on Easter Day.[4]   But as Alexander had now left France, and gone back to Rome [5] that could not reach the Archbishop for some time.   Reading the Papal authority in his own way Thomas opened hostilities without the loss of a single day.   Before the rising of the Councils at Chinon Henry had received from Pontigny three successive calls to surrender at discretion.[6]

Becket and Henry Again.

According to Herbert of Bosham his master began with 'sweet and peaceable words,'[7] gradually rising in tone as the King continued obdurate.   As a matter of fact the missives, though not without some expressions of more gentle feeling, are so uniformly imperious and threatening that critics have had some trouble in making up

---

[1] J. Salisb., Epp., I. 219; *Becket*, V. 350.

[2] See the order, Gervase, I. 198; R. Monte.   Contributions were also levied in England, Pipe Roll, 13 H. II., 194.

[3] " De persona regis speciale tibi mandatum non damus, nec tamen in aliquo jus tibi pontificale quod in ordinatione et in consecratione tua suscepisti adimimus, sed et ipsum volumus, auctore Deo, illæssum et integrum tibi conservare."   Two beautifully worded utterances, the one exactly balancing the other !   V. 316, 317.

[4] V. 328, 329.   The first letter is misdated at Anagni in October, but the mistake is corrected in the second letter, which refers to it, and is dated 24th April.   Notice of the appointment was received at St. Paul's on 30th June ; p. 417.

[5] Alexander having received an invitation from Rome left Sens in April, 1165, and travelling by slow stages reached Montpellier on the 10th July.   Becket accompanied him as far as Bourges.   About the end of October the Pope sailed from Maguelonne, and after landing in Sicily, was sent on to the mouth of the Tiber, and entered Rome 23rd November.   Reuter II. 184-188, from Jaffé, *Regesta*.

[6] The letter " Desiderio desideravi " generally regarded as the last ultimatum, is stated by Grim, II. 419, to have been delivered at Chinon in Council.   See also the letter, V. 381.

[7] " Suavia et pacifica " ; III. 384.

their minds as to their sequence.[1] The position taken up throughout is this, that as things spiritual are above things temporal, the spiritual authority must control the temporal authority. Kings derive their powers from the Church, but not the Church from kings.[2] 'Christ bought the liberty of the Church (not the salvation of mankind) with His blood';[3] Henry must listen to words of wholesome correction, mend his ways, and 'liberate the daughter of Sion,' lest the kingdom be taken from him and given to another. The last word is that the Archbishop must be fully reinstated. 'Otherwise know that ye shall feel the vengeance of the Almighty.'[4] The first two missives were entrusted to an agent of suitable rank, one Urban, Abbot of a Cistercian House dependent on Pontigny. In his verbal instructions he was directed to press for a meeting between Becket and the King. The last letter was committed, as if in deliberate insult, to one Gerard, a tattered, shoeless, enthusiast of a monk.[5]

A Call to Surrender.

Henry, in natural trepidation as to the excommunication so plainly threatened, consulted his prelates who had not yet left Chinon. The only suggestion was the old one of a counter-appeal to Rome,[6] to tie Becket's hands for another year. The Archbishop of Rouen and the Bishops of Lisieux and Séez were sent to Pontigny to give notice of this proceeding; but to their great disappointment Thomas was not there; warned of their coming he had taken himself off; and so they had to return to Court to report their failure.[7] Becket had betaken himself on pilgrimage to Soissons, more than 100 miles off, to worship at three noted shrines, namely those of the Virgin, of St. Augustine of Canterbury, and of St. Drausius. The last, a seventh century bishop, was considered the patron Saint of battle wagers, and his altar in consequence was much sought to by men about to engage in such encounters. Here, we are told, had Robert of Montfort found strength for his combat against Henry of Essex; and here Becket sought to nerve himself for the renewed attack on Henry and the *Constitutions of Clarendon*.[8] Having invigilated for three nights at Soissons, on the

Preparing for Action.

---

[1] See Reuter, II. 577. He is quite at sea as to the date of these events, which he places in 1165.   [2] V. 281.   [3] P. 280.

[4] See the three letters, "Loqui de Deo"; "Exspectans exspectavi"; and "Desiderio desideravi"; V. 266, 269, 278, given in the order generally accepted.

[5] H. Bosham, III. 383-385.

[6] John of Salisbury very fairly smiles at Henry for endeavouring to forbid appeals to Rome, and then himself appealing; V. 381. But what was the King to do?

[7] J. Salisb., *sup.* H. Bosham, 393, places the fruitless visit of the prelates to Pontigny after the Vézelay excommunications. According to this writer the bishops declared an appeal by word of mouth, to which the technical objection was taken that the appeal ought to have been in writing and affixed to the church door. But Salisbury in two places reports that they lodged no appeal, 382, 385.

[8] J. Salisbury, 382; J. C. Robertson, *Life of Becket*, 184.

morrow of Ascension Day (3rd June) Thomas left the city, making for Vézelay,[1] a place of some ecclesiastical note, situate about thirty-five miles South of Pontigny, and endowed with an abbey and a fine church, dedicated to St. Mary Magdalene. On Whitsunday (12th June), after celebrating Mass, Thomas ascended the pulpit, and after ex-

Becket at Vézelay. pounding his causes of difference with the King proceeded to excommunicate by name, and in most solemn form,[2] John of Oxford, Richard of Ilchester, Richard of Lucy, Joscelin of Bailleul, Ralph of Brock, Hugh of St. Clair, and Thomas fitz Bernard. John of Oxford and Richard of Ilchester were condemned for their

War Declared. intercourse with the Imperialists at Würzburg and elsewhere; the former having already been excommunicated for having dared to accept the Deanery of Sarum notwithstanding an inhibition by Becket.[3] Lucy and Bailleul were denounced for having drafted the *Constitutions of Clarendon*; and the other three for invasions of Canterbury property. But Thomas was not to be content with attacking Henry through his agents, or by any mere side wind. The King was solemnly warned to repent under penalty of anathema; while his ecclesiastical legislation was quashed and abrogated. Becket utterly condemned the

The Con- stitutions Quashed. 'document' (*scriptum*) embodying the so-called 'customs,' denouncing them all, as well as all persons who should either pay any regard to them themselves, or exact any regard to them from others.[4] He also released the bishops from their oaths to observe them, including himself, we must suppose. Six or seven articles of the *Constitutions* were held up to special opprobrium, including those bringing criminal clerks, and questions of tithes and advowsons before secular tribunals; also those forbidding the excommunication of the tenants in chief, and appeals to Rome without the King's leave.[5]

Immense was the sensation created by these extraordinary proceedings; but Becket's cause was not greatly furthered by them. He

Public Feeling. was generally felt to have overshot the mark; and in fact his anathemas fell a dead letter.[6] The Empress Matilda almost laughed. 'Of what use was it,' said she, 'to excommunicate such men? They were mostly excommunicate already!'[7] Within twelve days from Whitsunday a Synod was held in London, under orders sent by the King to Richard of Lucy, who as Justiciar was acting as Regent in his absence.

---

[1] Dept. Yonne.

[2] "Accensis Candelis"; R. Diceto, I. 318.

[3] Bishop Joscelin of Salisbury was suspended by Becket for having instituted John of Oxford on the King's nomination. See V. 346, 364, 397, 399.

[4] "Tam observatores quam exactores earum."

[5] See John of Salisbury's letter, V. 383; and Becket's Notifications, 386, 389, 392.

[6] So John of Salisbury, writing to his friend Radulfus Niger, VI. 3.

[7] V. 421. Matilda doubtless referred to John of Oxford and Richard of Ilchester who had already been excommunicated; V. 392.

The names of those present are not fully recorded, but Foliot, Robert of Melun, the Bishop of Hereford, and Joscelin of Salisbury were among them. The Bishops of Winchester, Rochester, and Exeter, and the Canterbury monks sent excuses for not appearing.[1] The assembly however, taking upon them to speak in the name of the whole Province, entered a fresh appeal for Ascension Day, 1167.[2] Lengthy, bitter recriminations between the two parties ensued; the old positions being reasserted over and over again, with untiring iteration. The most valuable contribution to the correspondence was the letter of Foliot, to which we have already referred, giving in very sarcastic language, but apparently with considerable accuracy, the history of the quarrel down to the time of Becket's flight.[3]

A Counter-Appeal.

Perhaps the most significant fact with respect to the Vézelay excommunications, and the effect that they produced on the public mind, is the unmistakable disposition of the Biographers to ignore them. The Anonymous writer No. II. (the Lambeth MS. of Dr. Giles) is actually the only one who makes a specific reference to these anathemas.[4] John of Salisbury, who in private had written such a full report to his friend Bishop Bartholomew of Exeter, skips in his published Life from the time of Becket's establishment at Pontigny to that of his removal from it in November (1166). Allan of Tewkesbury jumps from the same point to the events of 1169. William of Canterbury and Grim are equally silent about the occurrences of Whitsunday, though both insert documents referring to them. William fitz Stephen has a vague reference to excommunications, but apparently not those fulminated on the 12th June. But the most glaring *suppressio veri* is that to be found in the pages of the Archbishop's own secretary, who, having taken his master with all solemnity up to the pulpit at Vézelay, brings him down again after a simple utterance of warning to the King, without one word of any sentence uttered. And yet the wretched sycophant goes on to assure us that he and his friends were horrified at what they heard.[5] This bold attempt to mislead the world must be placed on a par with his more successful performance in giving out that Becket had not seen the *Constitutions* when he promised to obey them.

Again, on the point of popular feeling Becket's friends claimed that the lower clergy were with him. The lay magnates were declared to be utterly hostile.[6] But considering that Thomas fought simply and solely for

[1] Gervase, I. 200; W. Cant., I. 56, 57, and John of Salisb., V. 15.
[2] 24th June, V. 403, 408.
[3] See V. 459–518; and for Foliot's letter, 520.
[4] Vol. IV. 111.
[5] H. Bosham, III. 391. "Nos . . . ex inopinato audientes sic, mox obstupuimus." He gives the day as the 22nd July, wrongly, no doubt.
[6] So Arnulf of Lisieux, V. 309.

the exaltation of his Order, the wonder is that any clerics should have gone against him.   The humblest curate might be proud to think that Peter's cause was to some extent his own.   Among the higher clergy alone could men be found with sufficient breadth of view to realise how impracticable and mischievous Becket's aims were.

CHAPTER V

HENRY II. (*continued*)

A.D. 1166–1168

Controversy with Becket (*continued*)—Negotiations at Rome—Marriage of the King's son Geoffrey to Constance of Brittany—Henry takes Possession of the County—Hostilities with France—Abortive Mission of the Cardinals Otho and William—Fruitless Conferences at Gisors and La Ferté Bernard

THE appeal to the Pope presented in the name of the Canterbury clergy, was not allowed to lie dormant. To back it up Henry sent off an embassy consisting of John Cumin, Ralph of Tamworth, and, strange to say, the thrice condemned John of Oxford.[1] Not

Negotiations at Rome. only had he been at Würzburg, pledging his master to the schismatic Frederic; not only had he escorted schismatic envoys to England[2]; not only had he been excommunicated at Vézelay; but before that, as already mentioned, he had incurred Becket's censures for having accepted the Deanery of Sarum conferred upon him by Bishop Joscelin, in defiance of the Archbishop's inhibition. The appointment had been quashed, John excommunicated, Joscelin suspended, his diocese laid under Interdict, and the Pope, before the report of the Vézelay sentences had reached him, supported Becket's action.[3] Now we find all

The Pope Coming Round. this reversed. John meets with quite a friendly reception at Rome; is allowed to clear himself of the charges connected with the Diet at Würzburg by his own simple oath; and then receives at the hand of Alexander a triumphant investiture in his Deanery of Sarum.[4] For the King the results of the mission were not less satisfactory. Writing to him in terms of marked friendliness the Pope announces the appointment of a Legatine Commission to settle all questions

---

[1] V. 68, 114.

[2] Pipe Roll, 11 H. II., p. 77.

[3] See all the letters, V. 346, 364, 375, 392. 397–399; VI. 31, 32. Alexander's confirmation of the sentences against Richard of Ilchester and John of Oxford (p. 392) must I think, have reference to matters prior to Vézelay.

[4] VI. 141, 147, 170, 198, 200, 203.

—the very concession refused at Sens the previous year—he forbids Thomas to utter any fresh sentences ; and gives conditional authority for absolving those already excommunicated by him.[1]   The explanation of the change in the Pope's attitude is clear.   Becket had attempted to force his hand,[2] but Alexander refused to have his hand forced.

A petty move of a less justifiable character in which Henry was equally successful, was that of Becket's expulsion from Pontigny.   He had begun to intrigue for this before the Vézelay excommunications were uttered.[3]   A formal demand for the removal of Becket was laid before the annual general Chapter of the Order, held according to custom, at Citeaux in September. The King in effect declared that he would hold the Cistercian communities in his dominions responsible for the conduct of their Pontigny brethren.   Of course the special solidarity of the Cistercian Houses would make this threat a very telling menace.   The Chapter over, Gilbert Abbot of Citeaux, and William Bishop of Pavia, an old Cistercian, hastened to Pontigny to lay the **Becket** state of the case before Becket, leaving it to him to act as he **Driven from** should think proper.   It was obvious that his continued stay **Pontigny.** at Pontigny would involve the whole Cistercian Order in considerable risks.   Nevertheless two months must have elapsed before Thomas had the grace to retire.[4]   Louis having already pressed offers of hospitality upon him,[5] and repeating them now, Thomas moved to Sens, where he was established in the Benedictine Abbey of Sainte Colombe, the King of France providing liberally for his maintenance.[6]

About the end of May Henry had moved northwards from Chinon to engage in operations of secular warfare.   Uniform success attended his path.   His forces were directed in the first instance towards the borders of Normandy and Maine, to reduce to order the representatives of the great House of Talevas-Montgomery.   The present head of the family, William **The House** Talevas, styled Count of Sées by the Abbot of St. Michael's **of Talevas.** Mount, was of course the son of the notorious Robert of Bellême by Agnes daughter and heiress of Guy of Ponthieu, the man who laid hands on Harold.   Robert, again was the eldest son of

---

[1] VI. 82, 84, 86, 123, 125, 126.   1–20 December.

[2] See the tone of Becket's demand for ratification of his sentences, " Necesse est . . quod a nobis gestum est ratum omnimodis habeatis " ; V. 388.

[3] See his letter threatening the Cistercians, dated at Chinon, and so presumably in May, V. 365, also 389.

[4] H. Bosham, III. 397-404.   He says that they left Pontigny after two years' residence there, " Biennio Pontiniaci expleto."   They were there on the 30th Nov., 1864.   Gervase dates the retirement about the 11th Nov. ; I., 201.

[5] V., 44.

[6] H. Bosham, III. 402-407.   His narrative, and the terms of Louis' letter seem quite to negative the personal visit of the King to Pontigny, and the escort of 300 men alleged by Garnier, Diceto, and Gervase.   At every step in the narrative we have to encounter the grossest exaggeration and misrepresentation from the friends of St. Thomas of Canterbury.

the great Roger of Montgomeri, Earl of Shrewsbury by Mabille Talevas of Bellême. William Talevas had surrendered Ponthieu to his eldest son Guy, but with the aid of a younger son, and of a grandson, both of the name of John, he had been oppressing the people round the ancestral holds of Alençon and La Roche Mabille, old centres of brigandage. Henry forced them to surrender both.[1]

From Maine the King turned into Brittany to reap the fruits of a well-planned scheme. We have seen that in the year 1156 Henry had established Conan Earl of Richmond as Count of Upper Brittany, with his capital at Rennes; that shortly afterwards Henry's brother Geoffrey became Count of Nantes and Lower Brittany; and that at his death in 1158 Henry succeeded in making good his claim to Nantes as his brother's heir. In 1160 Conan married Margaret, sister of King Malcolm of Scotland,[2] a match probably arranged by Henry to keep the Count within the circle of his influence. The issue of the marriage was a daughter, Constance, born in 1162, and therefore one who in course of time might make a nice match for Henry's third son Geoffrey, born in 1158. Friendly help, therefore, from Normandy was always at Conan's call in time of need. Ralph of Fougères, a leading Breton, who also had the custody of Dol and Combourg,[3] as guardian of an heiress, having risen against Conan on behalf of the rival Count, Eude of Porhoet, Henry sent his Constable Richard of Humez[4] with an army, and deprived Ralph of both Combourg and Dol.[5] Ralph then put himself into communication with the discontented barons of Maine and Poitou with a view to establishing a 'defensive' league against the King.[6] Henry very properly gave his first attention to the domestic foes. These having been subdued, and all other matters disposed of, in the month of June he led out his forces to punish the fomenter of the recent troubles, Ralph of Fougères. On the 28th of the month the King was drawing near to the place.[7] Ralph had made every preparation for a stubborn resistance; and Becket's friends were eagerly looking forward to Henry's discomfiture;[8]

Affairs of Brittany.

Ralph of Fougères.

---

[1] June. R. de Monte, 227. Mr. Eyton in his Itinerary places the campaign before Easter, but a letter written after July 28th refers to the settlement with 'the barons of the Cennomannian Diocese' as among the latest news, *Becket*, V. 421. Sées, Alençon, and La Roche Mabille are all the dept of Orne.   [2] Chron. Melrose.

[3] Ille and Vilaine; between Dinan and Fougères.

[4] Now Le Hommet, Manche.

[5] Lobineau, *Bretagne*, I. 154; Morice, *Bretagne*, I. 105.

[6] Lobineau, 155; R. de Monte, p. 288. Before March, 1166.   [7] *Becket*, V. 421.

[8] See the letter of John of Salisbury to Becket, quoting a prophecy of Merlin to the effect that a bit was being forged for the boar, *i.e.*, Henry, in Armorica; V. 436. We may conjecture that his attention had been called to the prophecy by Alexander Llewelyn, Becket's cross bearer.

but about the 14th July the place fell.[1] An advance into the interior
of Brittany followed, and then the unfortunate Conan had to consent
The Heiress of Brittany. to the immediate celebration of a marriage between the two
infants, Geoffrey and Constance.[2] At the same time he
was induced to commit the government of his unruly subjects to the more capable hands of the King of England, reserving for
himself only the county of Guingamp (*Côtes du Nord*).[3] We next hear
of Henry as being at "Toas," "Toarz,"[4] or "Thoarcium," a place
Henry in Possession. that we are inclined to identify with Thouaré on the Loire,
as Breton nobles did homage to him there.[5] But wherever
the place may have been he went from thence to Rennes,
to establish his authority. From Rennes he returned to Normandy
by way of Combourg, Dol, and Mont-Saint-Michel, where he paused
to 'offer,' passing on, however, for the night to Genest.[6]

At Genest, curious to hear, we are told that Henry received a second
visit from the King of Scots, who brought with him the Bishop of Man,
as envoy from the Western potentate Godfrey or Guthfrith, King of the
Isles.[7] William accompanied the King to Caen, some matter of importance being under discussion, probably that of the Earldom of Huntingdon.[8] According to reports sent to Becket, Richard of Humez having
ventured to say a word on behalf of the Scottish King, Henry gave
way to one of his fits of ungovernable fury, throwing off his robes and
biting and tearing bits of straw from the floor with his teeth.

From the same source we hear of conferences held during the
autumn, in Normandy and Touraine, with the Count of Flanders,
with Theobald Count of Blois, with the Poitevins, and with Matthew
of Boulogne.[9] Three of these parties, at any rate, had grievances to

---

[1] So the Cartulary of Mont-Saint-Michel cited by Mr. Howlett, R. Monte, *sup.*

[2] The Papal dispensation for the marriage was obtained late in the year by John
of Oxford; it is spoken of as confirming the marriage (*Becket*, VI. 170); if so the
marriage must have been celebrated earlier, W. Newb., I. 146.

[3] So R. de Monte and Lobineau, *sup.* That Henry assumed control over Brittany
appears from a Charter of this year in which he confirms possessions held by the Abbey
of Redon under Conan III.; *Morice, Bretagne, Preuves,* I. 657. "Apud Thoarcium."

[4] R. Monte.

[5] Loire Inf. The charter (Morice, *sup.*) refers to the holdings of the Abbey "in
Garrandia vel in tota Media tempore Conani Grossi." Garrandia looks like Guerande,
also in Loire Inf.

[6] Manche, near Avranches. See R. de Monte; R. Diceto, I. 329; W. Newb. I. 146.
and the Itineraries, *sup.* Martin, *France,* III. 480.

[7] R. Monte, *sup.*; Guthfrith was son of Olaf, by Afreca, daughter of Fergus of
Galloway, by "Elisabeth," reputed natural daughter of Henry I.; E. W. Robertson.
Scotland under Early Kings, I. 357. De Monte notices the connexion with the
English Royal House.

[8] The Earldom was not granted to William till about 1173.

[9] *Becket*, VI. 71-76, and the Itineraries, *sup.*

complain of. The Poitevins will be found a year later in open revolt.

Henry and his Neighbours. Philip of Flanders was not in receipt of the English revenues enjoyed by his father Dietrich. Matthew had not been allowed to take up the county of Mortain, claimed in right of his wife, as Stephen's heiress;[1] while lands in England previously held by Matthew himself are also now found in the King's hand.[2] The Count was pacified with the promise of a pension of £1000 a year, but his attitude had been so hostile that a descent on the English coasts was feared. The neutrality of Theobald of Blois was gained by the grant of another pension of £500 a year.[3]

Thus the year 1167 opened under gloomy auspices, and in fact for the greater part of the twelvemonth the soil of Gaul was a prey to turmoil and war. In Lent (22nd February, Ash Wednesday—2nd April, Palm Sunday) we hear of a conference between Henry and **Henry and Toulouse.** the Count of Toulouse at Grammont.[4] Raymond V. had forfeited the support of King Louis by repudiating his sister, and so Henry may have thought it a good opportunity for reasserting old pretensions. No war was declared by Henry, but in the autumn the Count was again attacked by a coalition of Southern powers, who may have been instigated by the King. These hostilities, however, were cut short by the death of the Count, assassinated at Béziers, in church, by some of his own subjects.[5] After Easter (9th April) came an expedition to Auvergne, where Henry as over-lord had been called in **Henry in Auvergne.** to decide a disputed succession as between an uncle and a nephew, both of the name of William. The elder William being in alliance with King Louis, the King overran his lands on behalf of the nephew. It would seem however that Henry was able to effect a partition, from whence sprang the two noble Houses of the Counts of Clermont and the Dauphins of Auvergne.[6] On the 4th June we have a meeting between Louis and Henry in the open air near **Conference at Gisors.** Gisors.[7] Of questions between the two monarchs there was no lack. The loss of the Vexin border fortresses must still have rankled in Louis' mind; the course of affairs in Brittany was most alarming; while a petty squabble had broken out as to the hands by which the money collected for Holy Land should be transmitted.

[1] Pipe Roll, 11 H. II., p. 26.

[2] Pipe Roll, *sup.*

[3] *Becket*, VI. *sup.*; Gervase, I. 203; cnf. de Monte, *sup.*

[4] "Apud Magnum Montem"; R. Monte. I would identify the place with Grammont, near Lavit, in Tarn et Garonne. There is a Gramond in Aveyron, but that seems a different name. I can find no other "Grammont" near the borders of Toulouse.

[5] 14th October. Sismondi, *France*, V. 548; Martin, *France*, III., 470, note.

[6] R. de Monte; Martin, III. 480; Sismondi, V. 458.

[7] "Sub climate nudo." *Draco Norm.*, p. 679.

The silver was lying at Tours, within Henry's dominions ; so he contended that it ought to be taken out by agents of his.   Louis claimed the sending of the money on the ground that the Archbishop of Tours was his man.[1] In the conference Louis apparently put forward territorial requirements that Henry could not comply with.[2]   Breton affairs probably also came in question.   Anyhow the Kings parted in anger.   Louis drawing

War with France. the sword in his aimless way began ravaging the lands between Mantes and Pacy.   Henry retorted by a vigorous attack on Chaumont, in the French Vexin (Oise), a place where stores and supplies for the war had been collected under the charge of Louis' brother Robert, Count of Dreux.   The French sallied out boldly to encounter the English outside the gates ; but meanwhile a party of Welshmen, detached by Henry for the purpose, entering the town through the channel of the river Tröesne, fired the place in the rear of the French.   Thus taken on two sides they dispersed in confusion.   The whole town outside the citadel was destroyed.   Louis then made a fresh inroad into Normandy, through Gasny on the Epte, advancing as far as Les Andelys.   This town, we are told, he was allowed to destroy, the inhabitants having been previously removed by Henry.   This was done in pursuance of an arrangement suggested by the Count of Flanders, and approved of by the Empress.   Louis would waive

A Truce. further hostilities if his honour were satisfied by inflicting on his enemy some set-off to the destruction of Chaumont.   On this singular condition in August a truce was signed, to last till Easter 1168.[3] After a pause of a month or so in September, Henry again entered

Henry in Brittany. Brittany, where the people, by no means reconciled to their fate, showed a disposition to rally round the ex-Count Eude of Porhoet.   They had looked to Louis for support, and his inroad into Normandy may have been undertaken partly on their account ; but, as we have seen, it led to nothing.   The Bretons themselves were not organised for resistance.   Henry therefore marched through the County meeting with little opposition, except in the extreme West.   Eude was forced to give up his daughter as a hostage.   A few but only a few castles had to be reduced by force.[4]

---

[1] R. Monte, 230.

[2] " Francigeni juris terras, quas detinet ille, Is (sc. Rex. Gallus) petit " ; *Draco N.*, 677.   The writer was living in Normandy at the time.   A bitter enemy to Becket, he represents him as present at the conference, and makes him responsible for the rupture, p. 676 ; but if Becket was there we surely should have had some notice of the fact in his voluminous correspondence.

[3] July-August, R. Monte ; and the long detailed account in the *Draco N.*, 681-695 ; R. Hoveden, A.D 1169.

[4] See R. de Monte, who only specifies Saint Pol-de-Leon (Finisterre, on the N. coast) held by the brother of Eude's second wife, and " alia nonnulla " as stormed ; see also *Draco Norm.* 695.   Mr. Howell would refer the final abdication of Conan and the homages of the Bretons to this year.

While engaged in this campaign Henry received the news of the death
Death of the of his mother, the Empress Matilda. Born early in 1102;
Empress baptised as Adelaide; married first in 1114 to Henry V. of
Matilda. Germany, for whom she changed her name to Matilda; united
in second wedlock to Geoffrey of Anjou in 1129;[1] she died on the 10th
September (1167), at the monastery of Notre Dame Des Prés, otherwise
De Bonne Nouvelle, by Rouen, where she had lived for years. By her
own request she was buried at Bec.[2]   In Germany she created a favourable
impression; in her struggle with Stephen for the crown of England she
did not appear to advantage, she was not equal to the situation; her head
was turned by it. With her son as King her relations were most kindly
and loyal. Subjected to constant pressure by Becket and his partisans she
refused to take any step that might prejudice her firstborn. As a friend
said to the Archbishop, ' After all she was the daughter of tyrants.'[3]

The campaign in Brittany over, the King returned to Normandy,
Mission of probably late in October, to hold the long delayed meeting
the Cardinals with the Cardinals William and Otho. The emissaries of St.
William and Peter had left Rome in the middle of March;[4] but the
Otho. presence of the Imperial forces obliged them to take a circuitous
route through Venice; and from thence across Lombardy to the Mont
Cenis: finally they rested at Montpellier about the middle of April.[5]
Their further progress was delayed partly by the disturbed state of Gaul;
partly by the hostility of Louis to their mission, as having been granted
at the request of King Henry;[6] partly, we might add, by well-founded
misgivings as to Becket's acceptance of their mediation.[7] Otho was his
friend; but William of Pavia was a man devoted to the King's interest,
and therefore an enemy, one, who, in Thomas' delicate phrase, ' thirsted
for his blood.' In his private correspondence Becket openly
Becket's disclaimed any intention of submitting to William's decision;[8]
Tone. while in letters addressed to the Cardinal himself, he made use
of language, ' not fit,' as John of Salisbury felt obliged to point out, ' not fit
to be addressed to the Pope's running footman.'[9] The disturbances in

---

[1] For these facts see *Foundations* and the Index.

[2] R. Monte; *Draco*, 712, 713.

[3] *Becket*, V. 149.

[4] VI. 262.

[5] See Otho to Becket, VI. 199; Reuter, II. 338.

[6] VI. 249.

[7] For the limitation of their authority to friendly intervention see Alexander's letters to them, VI. 201, 232.

[8] *Id.*, 154, 226; ' Presumptio et insolentia domini Willelmi Papiensis;' 229. See also 203.

[9] " Profecto ego nec domini papae cursorem sic alloquendum fuisse arbitror," p. 218. For letters indited by Thomas, but withheld at the remonstrances of John of Salisbury; see 209, 210.

Gaul having died down, and other obstacles been smoothed over, the Legates resumed their journey.   Passing through Sens, they had an interview with Becket, and notified their mission to him.   From Sens they went on to pay their respects to the King of France, finally joining Henry's Court at Caen, about the 1st November.[1]   An immediate invitation for a conference on the 11th of the month was forwarded to the Archbishop. But at his request, in order to give him time to muster his friends, and arrange for a fitting retinue, the meeting was adjourned to the 18th November; and on that day the parties met at the well-known

Conferences at Gisora. trysting place, between Trie and Gisors.[2]   The Archbishops of Rouen, and York, and the Bishops of London, Salisbury, Chichester, and Worcester were present;[3] while Thomas was supported by John of Salisbury, Herbert of Bosham, and some ten or more chaplains and others.[4]   Louis, who had defrayed Becket's expenses, if not actually present, was certainly at hand, at Trie.   The Cardinals opened the proceedings with an address in which they ran over the salient points of the situation, such as the needs of the times, the great influence of the King of England, his past favours to Becket, and his present grounds of complaint against him.   One of Henry's charges, by the way, that of having fomented the war with France, was refuted next day by the Royal word of King Louis himself.   The Legates then proceeded to sound Thomas[5] as to a series of suggestions, one or other of which, it was thought, might serve as a basis for a settlement.   As might have been anticipated he refused to give in to anything that would involve the smallest semblance of concession on his part.   Asked if he could not bring himself to pay a loyal deference to the will of his lord, King Henry, the answer was, 'Certainly, saving the liberty of the Church, his, Becket's own dignity, and the possessions of the Churches.' Asked if he would stand by the law as recognised in the times of his

Compromise Offered. predecessors, he said that he could give in to nothing that would curtail the 'liberty' of the Church.[6]   This answer, of course, amounted to an indirect admission that some of his claims at any rate were novel.   The Cardinals then propounded the one plan that, apparently, had been looked forward to as offering a way out of the difficulty,[7] namely that, if the King was willing, Thomas should return

---

[1] H. Bosham, III. 409; VI. 246, 262.   For their interview with Thomas see 281.

[2] VI. 247.

[3] *Id.*, 193, 270.

[4] *Id.* 262.   Henry, of course, was not there.

[5] The Cardinals were very careful to insist that they had come not to advise Becket, but to receive advice from him; " Se non venisse ut ei sed ut eum consulerent;" 249, 257.   Neither party would undertake the responsibility of surrendering Church claims.

[6] It is important to point out that the Pope seemed prepared to accept the "antiqua jura," and the measure of 'liberty' enjoyed under Henry I., VI. 201.

[7] So H. Bosham, III. 410.   He treats this as the only serious proposal, and in fact it was on this footing that Becket returned to England in 1170.

to England sinking all question as to the *Constitutions*, the tacit understanding being that they would not be enforced. They urged that under
this arrangement the Archbishop would have gained the day, but that the
King would be spared the humiliation of avowed surrender. The answer
was that in such a case silence would be tantamount to assent.
And Rejected. Then, producing the text of the *Constitutions*, Becket boldly
asked if such abominable Articles could be allowed to pass
uncondemned.   Thomas was then asked if he would submit to the
decision of the Legates on the points in dispute between the King and
himself.   Evading a direct answer, as he himself boasted to the Pope,[1] he
said that litigation meant money ; that he and his were in a
Arbitration Likewise. destitute condition ; but that when they had been restored to
their possessions he would always be ready, at due time and
place, and as and when required, to submit to the judgment of any person
authorised by the Supreme Pontiff. The same response served as an
answer to the final query whether he would submit to their decision in the
matter of the appeal of the Bishops.[2] The unfortunate Legates having
failed, as they were bound to fail, received no thanks from either side.
By Becket they were overwhelmed with abuse.[3]   Returning to Normandy
they met the King at Argentan (26th November).   Henry, who, at their
arrival, went out two leagues to meet them, next day after a private
audience was so enraged to find that they neither would nor could depose
Becket, that he almost turned them out of the house, muttering audibly
that he trusted his eyes might never see the face of another Cardinal.
Further colloquies between the King, the Cardinals, the English Bishops,
and the courtiers, resulted in nothing but the entering of fresh appeals to
Rome, for the 11th November, 1168. This would restrain
Failure of Mission. Becket for another period, the appeals of the previous year
having expired.   On the 5th December the Cardinals left
Argentan, having effected nothing.[4]

Another year of considerable war and confusion (1168) ensued ; the
diplomatic struggle with Becket never flagging. The spring season however opened with negotiations for peace. With that object the Counts
Philip of Flanders [5] and Henry of Champagne sought King Louis at
Soissons, to suggest a pacification on the footing of his accepting a plan
of which we now hear for the first time, a plan fondly conceived by

---

[1] VI. 251.

[2] See Becket's own report to the Pope, and two other accounts, apparently penned by
John of Salisbury, all in perfect accord ; VI. 245—266 ; also H. Bosham, *sup.*

[3] VI. 293, 296, 368, 370.

[4] See the letters, VI. 269—274 ; 276 ; 283—291. The Cardinals remained in Gaul
till August or September, 1168 ; William apparently was with Henry at La Ferté
Bernard on the 1st July ; *Id.* 455, 481.

[5] Full Count now through the death of his father Dietrich, which happened about this
time. De Monte.

Henry for the future administration of his dominions through his sons,
mere boys, whose fitness to be entrusted with such respon-
A Dynastic sibilities must have been utterly uncertain.　Anjou and
Scheme. Maine would be ceded to young Henry, who would do
homage to the King of France as against all men ; Poitiers would be
made over on the same terms to Richard as his mother's heir, while
Louis would bestow upon him the hand of a daughter.　Another
daughter, of course, was already married to the younger Henry.　Just
as the Count of Champagne was on his way to the King's Court, to
announce Louis' approval of the scheme, a revolt in Aquitaine was
reported ; and Henry, in his haste to suppress the movement, left the
prosecution of the negotiations to his Ministers, namely Rotrou of
Beaumont, the Archbishop of Rouen, Richard of Humez or Le Hommet
the Constable, and Richard of Lucy the Justiciar.　Louis, thinking that
Henry was shuffling, followed him to Berry, to make common cause with
the insurgents ; accepted their homages, and took hostages.[1]　We have
already seen that the Poitevin Barons were in a state of discontent ;
Risings in curtailment of feudal ' liberties ' was of course their grievance.[2]
Poitou. To them, no less than to Becket, State control seemed
objectionable ; and they probably had an understanding with the
Bretons.　Among the leaders were Adalbert IV. Count of La Marche,
William Taillefer IV. Count of Angoulême, Geoffrey of Lusignan,[3] and the
Viscount of Thouars.[4]　Henry having reduced the Castle of Lusignan, where
the rebels had prepared for resistance, and so broken the neck of the
movement, went back to reopen the negotiations for peace with Louis ;
Aquitaine being left under the charge of the Queen and Earl Patrick of
Salisbury.　On the 7th April Henry had an interview with French magnates
between Pacy and Mantes.　Louis had refused to appear.　The Soissons
proposals however were accepted on both sides, except that Louis would
no longer give his daughter to young Richard.　But the negotiations were
much complicated by recent events in the South, the French insisting
on compensation for injuries done to the barons who had become their
King's men.[5]　Louis however was induced to agree to a meeting on the
12th May for the ratification of the treaty.　How he could hesitate to
close with proposals so obviously promising for the future of his kingdom
it is not easy to understand.　Probably he was suspicious of anything
emanating from his wily vassal.　On the other hand Henry's well-meant
scheme must damage our opinion of his wisdom and forethought as a
politician.

---

[1] February–March.　See John of Salisbury's letter, *Becket*, VI. 407, 408.
[2] Gervase, I. 205.
[3] Vienne, on the Yonne.
[4] Deux Sèvres.
[5] " Omnibus qui regi adhæserunt."

But meanwhile the hostilities in Poitou were going on, and Earl Patrick
had fallen by the hand of Geoffrey of Lusignan.[1] This again was
disturbing.   But before Henry could do anything to avenge his loss a
fresh rising in Brittany had to be dealt with.   The ex-Count

And Brittany. Eude, following the example of the Poitevins, had renounced
his allegiance to Henry, and given hostages to King Louis.
Henry came down upon him at once ; burned Josselin, his chief seat ;
took the town and county of Vannes into hand, and captured and
garrisoned Auray.[2]   Turning northwards the King then attacked Eude's
allies Geoffrey of Montfort, and Roland of Dinan.   Hédé, Tinteniac,
and Becherel[3] were successively attacked and taken, and the whole
country round Dinan on both sides of the river Rance devastated.   The
district of St. Malo fared no better.[4]

With these troubles going on the meeting originally fixed for the
12th May had been postponed to the 1st July ;[5] and for that day both
Kings drew near to the appointed place, La Ferté Bernard.[6]   There again

Conferences at La Ferté-Bernard. the conferences came to nothing, as the kings failed to meet
face to face.   Louis was assailed beforehand by the Bretons
and Poitevins with charges against Henry.   Eude had a
domestic insult to complain of, in that Henry had taken as his mistress
Eude's daughter, Henry's own cousin, placed in his hands as a hostage.[7]
Then the Poitevins were loud in demanding compensation for damages
inflicted after a truce had been taken.   Henry was prepared to admit
the claims of the Barons, but not those of a certain Abbot of Charroux,[8]
who claimed to hold immediately of France, and not at all of Henry.   ' At
any rate,' said the King, ' if I do give in it will not be out of regard for
the rights of the King of France, but out of regard for Cardinal William
and the Count of Flanders.'   Deeply offended at the report of these
ungracious words, and mortified to find that the Legate was still in
Henry's company, Louis went down to the river bank, stayed there till

[1] J. Salisbury, *sup.* Benedict of Peterborough, I. 343 (Rolls Series, No. 49) ;
R. Diceto, I. 331, enf. R. Monte, 236.   For the refutation of the story in Hoveden,
I. 273, that the Earl was killed when on pilgrimage by Guy of Lusignan afterwards
King of Jerusalem, see Norgate, *Angevin Kings*, II. 59.   "There is nothing to show
that Patrick was not killed in fair fight" ; Bishop Stubbs.

[2] All three places are in Morbihan.

[3] Ille et Vilaine, all three.

[4] R. Monte ; Lobineau, 155, 156.   Roland of Dinan had considerable estates in
England ; Pipe Rolls.

[5] R. Monte.

[6] Sarthe, on the river Huisne, on the borders of Maine and Perche.

[7] " Quod filiam ejus virginem, quam illi pacis obsidem dederat impraegnavit."   There
seems nothing in these words to support this charge of forcible outrage repeated by
modern writers.   The young lady's mother Bertha, was daughter of a natural daughter
of Henry I. ; while Henry II. was the son of the legitimate Matilda.

[8] Vienne.

H

evening, and then, after washing his hands in the water, went off, denouncing Henry for having failed to keep his word. Then Henry in turn, when it was almost dark, hastened down to the river with a band of armed men, thus giving the French an opening for taxing him with treasonable intentions.

Envoys from Scotland, Wales, and Gascony were said to be in Louis' train ; also Becket, brought by the Count of Flanders, it was said by Henry's directions.[1] But the Archbishop's presence might account for the King's reluctance to come to a personal interview with Louis. Not many days later the Cardinals took final leave. Otho made a last effort

No Conclusion. to bring Henry to terms. But the King stood firmly on the rights of his ancestors : the question of restitution, however, he was prepared to listen to. But this was not thought enough ; and so the Cardinal on taking leave felt bound to utter a solemn word of warning.[2]

No truce had been taken ; but as neither King wanted war,[3] peace need not have been broken but for an unmannerly act on the part of the Count of Ponthieu, John grandson of William Talevas.[4] Henry having at last effected a compromise with Matthew of Boulogne as to his claims on Mortain,[5] the Count, wanting to come to Normandy on Henry's

Petty Hostilities. summons, to settle the affair, was refused a passage through Ponthieu, and had to go by sea. Henry avenged the slight by ravaging Vimeu.[6] Louis retaliated by a feeble inroad into Normandy, burning one small place ;[7] and then Henry repaid him, with interest, by extensive destruction in the Chartrain and Perche. Advent brought a truce, and an agreement for another conference on the 6th January, 1169.[8]

In the course of the autumn the Anti-pope Pascal III. had died at Rome in ostensible possession of the Holy See (20th September)[9]. Within

A New Antipope. the month the vacancy was filled by the election of John of Struma, Cardinal Bishop of Albano, who took the style of Calixtus III. No time was lost in proclaiming his accession, and Barbarossa had the ingenuity to convey the notification

---

[1] J. Salisb., *Becket*, VI. 455--458, 479 ; R. Monte, 237, 238.

[2] *Becket*, VI. 482 ; *Circa* September ; Reuter, II. 391, 631.   [3] *Becket*, VI. 482.

[4] John's father Guy, spoken of as Count in 1166, must have died since ; R. Monte, pp. 227, 238, 251.

[5] On the Pipe Roll, 14 H. II., p. 60 (1167-1168), we have a grant of £200 a year to Matthew in Lincolnshire by a writ from the King himself from abroad.

[6] *I.e.* the part of Ponthieu between the Somme and the Bresle. Ponthieu as a whole extends from the Canche to the Bresle, with its capital in the grand hill-fortress of Montreuil.

[7] " Chesnebrut "; (Le Chesne ? Eure, near Breteuil).

[8] R. Monte ; Gervase, I. 207.

[9] Pascal had been established at Rome by Barbarossa 20th July, 1167.

in the shape of proposals for putting an end to the Schism. The ambassadors accredited to England and France were Philip the new Archbishop of Cologne,[1] Christian Archbishop of Mayence, and Duke Henry of Saxony, Henry's son-in-law. They reached Normandy towards the close of the year. Becket's friends and the French were much perturbed at the prospect of an alliance between England and Germany.[2]

But Henry had no need to damage his position by committing himself to the schismatic party. He was on good terms with the **No Support from Henry.** Pope and Cardinals ; he had Becket still at arm's length ; he was in the quiet enjoyment of the revenues of four Sees in England,[3] and five Sees abroad.[4] As against his feeble overlord King Louis, whose rights as such he always respected, he had no need whatever of any allies. The embassy led to no perceptible results.[5]

The death of the Earl of Leicester, Robert of Beaumont II., ought perhaps to be noticed. A faithful and trusted servant to the King he had held the office of Chief Justiciar jointly with Richard of Lucy since the beginning of the reign. He passed away on the 5th April (1168).[6]

---

[1] Successor to Reginald, who succumbed to the pestilence at Rome in August, 1167.

[2] See the letter of Mary, the Countess of Boulogne, to Louis, putting him on his guard ; Bouquet. XVI. 144 ; *Becket*, VI. 487.

[3] Namely, those of Canterbury, Lincoln, Hereford, and Bath ; Pipe Roll, 13 II. II.

[4] So Becket to the Pope, VI. 253. He speaks of seven vacant Sees in England and Normandy, besides Canterbury and Tours.

[5] On the embassy see Reuter, III. 7-11 ; R. Monte. The *Draco Norm.*, 718-724, has a long account of the interview with Henry, and represents the Emperor as offering to invest young Henry with the crown of France, a proposal that would certainly shock Henry's one "feudal superstition." (Bp. Stubbs.)

[6] R. Monte, and for the day of the month G. E. C. Peerage ; Doyle ; Foss., *Judges*.

CHAPTER VI

HENRY II (*Continued*)

A.D. 1169–1170

Controversy with Becket continued—The King's Dynastic Schemes—Conferences at Montmirail—Fruitless Mission of Brothers Simon and Bernard—Further Excommunication of King's Ministers—Fruitless Mission of Masters Gratian and Vivian—Conferences at Montmartre—Inquest of Sheriffs—Coronation of the Young King Henry—Mission of the Archbishop of Rouen and Bishop of Nevers—Conferences at Fréteval—Agreement for Becket's Return to England

ON the 6th January, 1169, the Kings duly met at Montmirail.[1] A double programme lay before them. The first part, or that personal to Henry and Louis, presented no difficulty. The scheme propounded at Soissons was accepted and ratified, with the modifications introduced by the French in April. Henry renewed the homage to Louis that he had rendered both before, and since his accession to the throne ; while Louis released to Henry the rights over Brittany and Poitou that he had acquired through the recent homages, Henry being bound down to make due restitution and compensation, as previously stipulated. Next day young Henry did homage to Louis for Anjou and Maine ; Normandy he had already done homage for. At the same time Richard was allowed to do homage for Poitou.[2] According to the Abbot of Mont-Saint-Michel young Henry also did homage for Brittany, Louis thus recognising the superiority of Normandy over Brittany ; but the under-lordship was shortly afterwards granted by this young Henry to his brother Geoffrey. Louis also granted to the younger Henry the Seneschalship of France, an honorary post claimed of old, as already mentioned, by the Counts of Anjou.[3] By the French, naturally, this 'distribution of honours' was viewed with great satisfaction. If we have thought Henry's conduct rash, we must recognise the fatherly wish to make provision for all his

Marginal notes: Conferences at Montmirail. / The Dynastic Scheme. / Young Henry. / Richard. / Geoffrey.

---

[1] Sarthe, on the borders of Maine and the Chartrain.
[2] So the letter of John of Salisbury, VI. 506, 507.
[3] R. Monte, 240. Sismondi and Martin accept his statements.

children.[1]   A sense of the insecurity of testamentary dispositions made
him anxious to see the arrangements made sure in his life-
time.   Perhaps he may have called to mind the questions
that had arisen between his own brother Geoffrey and himself
at their father's death.

Henry's Motives.

The second part of the Royal programme referred of course to Becket
and his affairs.   A fresh mission had been sent by the Pope to succeed
that of the Legates Otho and William.   Monks were selected this time,
as if in the hope that monastic fervour might succeed where the worldly
wisdom of the high-born Cardinals had failed.   The men chosen were
Simon, Prior of Mont-Dieu,[2] and Bernard of La Coudre,
Prior of the Order of Grammont or Grand Mont.[3]   To these
a third man, Engilbert, Prior of Val-Saint-Pierre, was subsequently added, probably because the peculiar strictness of the Grammont
rules forbade the writing of letters by its members, even of letters addressed
to a Pope.[4]   The instructions to these agents show an intention of putting
greater pressure, certainly on Henry, and apparently on Becket also,
than had as yet been attempted.   Alexander evidently felt that the
existing state of things could not be allowed to continue ; that, in one way
or other, the quarrel must be brought to an end.   The envoys therefore
received two several credentials to the King, one a letter
of friendly warning (*litteras commonitorias*), the other of
a distinctly threatening character (*comminatorias*) ; the latter
to be delivered only if the first should fail, and in presenting it the
bearers were to give verbal notice that the suspension of Becket's
authority would end with Lent (5th March 1169).[5]   Having reached
Henry's court   few days before the appointed time of meeting the
envoys presented their gentler mandate.   Its tone, though friendly, is
distinctly colder than that of the communications of the previous year ;
and the King is expressly warned that the Pope will not on any account
'keep the Archbishop's mouth shut much longer.'[6]   All parties having
gathered at Montmirail, including Thomas, brought by ' the
Most Christian King,' stress was laid upon the Archbishop
by all the mediators, including Louis and the Papal envoys,
to induce him ' to humble himself before the King and appease him by

Mission of Simon and Bernard.

Their Instructions.

Conferences at Montmirail.

---

[1] See his words to Cardinal Otho, " Dixit se et liberos suos," etc., *Becket*, VI. 433.

[2] Ardennes.

[3] The Pope styles him ' Brother Bernard,' but he seems to have been Prior ; see
Reuter, II. 623, 624.   Grammont is a hill in the dept. of Corrèze, six leagues from
Limoges ; the Order at first was established at Muret.   It was specially favoured by
Henry.

[4] See VI. 490, 519 ; Reuter, *sup*.

[5] VI. 438.

[6] " Nec præfato archiepiscopo os de cœtero aliqua ratione claudemus, quin officii su
debitum libere prosequatur." *Ib.*

deferential submission.'[1]   In their report to Alexander the envoys state that they had felt bound to 'warn and advise' Thomas (*monuimus et consuluimus*) to follow this course.[2]   It will be remembered that at the meeting between Trie and Gisors in November 1167 the Cardinals had pointedly disclaimed offering any advice to Becket.   The question remains, What did the King demand as the price of reconciliation? What amount of submission was Becket required to offer?   The report of the envoys does not indicate this.   John of Salisbury in his account **Henry's** of the proceedings represents Henry as affecting to ask only **Require-** for a public expression of submission, without any real con- **ments.** cession on the crucial question.[3]   This most improbable version, utterly incompatible with the position consistently maintained by Henry both before and afterwards, may be safely discarded on the strength of the more detailed narrative supplied by Herbert of Bosham, who was also present.   From him we learn that the essential point of the King's requirements had been clearly stated, and the formula of submission to be used by Thomas keenly discussed.   Becket had been informed by intermediaries, expressly stated to be friendly to him, that Henry would not be satisfied with anything short of an absolute sub-mission, without saving words,[4] that is to say he required in effect a repetition of the Clarendon promise.   Herbert further tells us that Becket had suggested a new saving clause that might be accepted by the King, namely, 'Saving the honour of God' (*salvo honore Dei*), but that the proposed words had been condemned by the intermediaries, as sure to give offence.   The Secretary goes on to say that the *eruditi*[5] of Becket's circle, afraid to give advice one way or the other, held their tongues.   We need not discard this very probable account because the offensive writer goes on to say that at the last moment, one man, and one man only, 'the disciple who wrote these things,' whispered in his master's ear to stand firm, and not repeat the lapse of which he had once been guilty.[6]

Breathless must have been the suspense when the Archbishop was led into the Royal presence by William of· Blois, the newly consecrated Archbishop of Sens.[7]   After more than four years of bitter estrangement

---

[1] "Ut se coram rege humiliaret, et rigorem ejus humilitate precum et sedulitate obsequii studeret emollire."   So the envoys to the Pope, *Becket*, VI. 488.

[2] *Ib.*

[3] "Si modo dominus Cantuariensis ei coram hominibus speciem humilitatis prætenderet," etc.; VI. 507.

[4] "Ut poneret se de tota quæ inter ipsos vertebatur querela in misericordia regis, et absolute sic, absque omni additamento"; III. 419.

[5] This phrase must be taken to refer to John of Salisbury at any rate.

[6] III. 418–422.

[7] *Ib.* and VI. 486.   William was son of the late Theobald of Champagne, King Stephen's brother, and himself brother to the Counts Henry, Theobald, and Stephen; Reuter, II. 404.

Henry and Thomas again looked at each other face to face. Becket fell on his knees before his lord, who at once took him by the hand, and made him rise. The Archbishop then, in a speech in which after bewailing his own unworthiness, he made an appeal for mercy to the **Becket's** suffering Church of England, ended with words to this effect: **Submission.** 'My lord, I place myself in God's hands and yours for God's honour and your own.'[1] It will be noticed that however willing to make a general profession of submission and loyalty, Becket was still, as ever, determined to make no surrender except with saving words **Saving** that would enable him to nullify any confession that he might **Words.** be supposed to have made.[2]

As the intermediaries had anticipated the 'honour of God' was rejected with scorn; the formula simply meant the 'Liberty of the Church' over again, but with an offensive insinuation that the Archbishop had a regard for God's honour, while the King had none. A long argument ensued. Henry again declared that he only required Becket to observe the customs of former reigns that he had already promised to observe, and that he was prepared to grant the full measure of liberty enjoyed by Becket's predecessors, some of them Saints and workers of miracles. At this Louis, as if in a spirit of prophecy, exclaimed 'My lord of Canterbury, do you want to be more than a Saint?'[3] To this Thomas could only reply first, that his original homage vow saved the rights of his Order, and that no more binding pledge could ever be demanded of him; and secondly that none of his predecessors had been called upon to make such a declaration as was now required of him.[4] Neither argument, of course, was at all to the point; the latter allegation was simply untrue, as Anselm under similar circumstances had been required to conform to **Fruitless** custom; a fact to which Becket's attention was subsequently **Ending.** called.[5] But, in spite of all remonstrances, Thomas, standing alone, with magnificent assurance, remained obdurate, and again the meeting broke up without result.

With respect to the pressure put upon Becket it is right to point out

---

[1] "Posuit se in Deo et rege, ad honorem Dei et regis." So the envoys report, VI. 488. "Parati fuimus . . . ponere nos omnino ad honorem Dei et suum in misericordia Dei et sua"; Becket's own account, VI. 490. Again "Ad honorem Dei et vestrum paratus eram me ponere omnino in misericordia Dei et vestra," 514. John of Salisbury again agrees with the envoys, giving the words in the *Oratio recta* as "Miseremini mei, domine, quia pono me in Deo et vobis ad honorem Dei et vestrum"; 508.

[2] See the subsequent letter of Becket to his friend the Bishop of Poitiers, severely rebuking him for having suggested that he might possibly withdraw the saving words, VI. 491, 493.

[3] H. Bosham, III. 424, 425; and the letter, VI. 488, 515. Allan, II. 347, gives a good summary.

[4] VI. 489, 509.

[5] VI. 509-510.

that another Crusade was being loudly called for; and that it was felt that without a reconciliation with Becket no support could be expected from the King. In fact he had told the envoys as much.[1] But on whatever grounds it is clear that even Becket's own friends, including King Louis, were annoyed by his obstinacy.[2]

Under the circumstances the Papal envoys could not take it on them to present the minatory letter at once.[3] It was reserved for another interview held between the Kings on the 7th February, at some place not clearly specified. Henry took the Pope's threats very calmly, repeating that he would receive Becket on the terms already stated, but not otherwise.[4]

But with the coming Ash Wednesday (5th March) the restriction on Becket's powers would expire. To anticipate probable action on his part Henry despatched Reginald Archdeacon of Sarum,[5] and Ralph Archdeacon of Llandaff to Benevento, where the Pope then was, to try if by any means Alexander might yet be induced to depose or translate

A Third Mission. Becket. That was found to be impossible. But the Pope announced the appointment of a third mission to work for a reconciliation. As a fresh experiment two men of the Law were selected, namely Gratian, Subdeacon and Notary, and Vivian Archdeacon of Orvieto, a practising advocate in the Papal

Gratian and Vivian. Court.[6] These men would be quite fitted to deal with any questions as to the wording of a compact between the contending parties. But for some reason or other their departure must have been delayed for months, as we shall find the Pope again announcing their mission on the 10th May.[7]

But the time was not wasted by the King's ambassadors, their efforts

Keeping the Pope in Hand. being directed, very sagaciously, towards keeping the Pope in hand by winning support for him—possibly with English gold—among Roman nobles, and Lombard citizens. The Sicilian alliance was also mooted at this time, through the offer of the hand of the King's daughter Johanna to King William II. According to Becket the ultimate aim of these intrigues was to get him assassinated in Italy, if the Pope could be induced to summon him to his presence.[8]

---

[1] *Becket*, III. 419; VI. 499.

[2] See W. fitz S., III. 96; H. Bosham, 430, 437.

[3] VI. 499.

[4] VI. 511-512, 516.

[5] Son of Bishop Joscelin, and afterwards Bishop of Bath; Angl. Sacra, I. 561, note; Reuter.

[6] VI. 538; VII. 31. Gratian was nephew to Eugenius III.

[7] See the letters, VI. 521, 537, and VII. 25. The original notification of the mission is dated 28th February.

[8] VII. 25-27. Thomas assures his correspondent, the Archbishop of Ostia, that under no circumstances will he submit to a citation to Italy.

A man who felt himself specially bound to guard against attack from
Becket was his old antagonist Gilbert Foliot of London. On
Becket and the 18th March he held an Episcopal Synod at St. Paul's, and
Foliot with the concurrence of the Abbot of Westminster and others
entered a fresh appeal to the Holy See for the 9th February, 1170.[1]

In Becket's eyes all opposition was criminal. But opposition within
his own Province, organised by a suffragan, was simply flagitious. At
Clairvaux, on Palm Sunday (13th April), he discharged another broadside
of anathemas, excommunicating by name Foliot, Joscelin of
Fresh Salisbury, Hugh Bigod Earl of Norfolk,[2] Ralph of Brock, and
Anathemas six others of minor note. In his notification to the London
clergy he intimates the probable excommunication on Ascension Day
(29th May) of a further batch of six, the list to include Geoffrey Riddel
Archdeacon of Canterbury, Richard of Ilchester now Archdeacon of
Poitiers, and the Chief Justiciar, Richard of Lucy.[3] In his personal
communication to Foliot Thomas almost outdoes himself in vehemence
of language. 'The gentleness of his patience could no longer endure
such intolerable provocations,' etc., etc.[4] Foliot, of course, had all along
been leader of the clerical opposition to Becket; but the tone of Thomas's
letter would incline the reader to suppose that the Bishop had been recently
guilty of something very offensive. As a matter of fact during the last two
years, that is to say since the conferences with the Cardinals in November
1167, he had, so far as we can see, taken little part in the struggle. In the
voluminous correspondence of the period his name hardly appears. The
truth seems to be that the crowning iniquity was simply that of having
ventured to appeal from Thomas of Canterbury to Alexander of Rome.[5]
It will be noticed that Becket wholly ignored that appeal. On his behalf
it has been urged that the Pope in October, when apologising for the
further suspension of Becket's powers, had ‘undertaken when that term
expired to leave him a free hand 'without appeal.'[6] But in the
contemporary discussions on the case this point is not taken; the

---

[1] See the notification to the Pope and to Becket, etc., *Becket*, VI. 534, 535, 539,
540, 619. R. Diceto, I. 333. Joscelin of Sarum joined in the appeal. The letter
to Becket however, Reuter would refer to the year 1166.

[2] The case of the Earl of Norfolk was not connected with Becket's quarrel with the
King. He was anathematised for a dispute with the Augustinian canons of Pentney as
to the right to some lands, a clear case for the ordinary courts of law, and one that had
been brought before the King in person in 1166. See VI. 543-557; and Bishop
Stubbs, Hoveden, I. 232.

[3] VI. 558.

[4] " Excessus vestros dum licuit supportavimus . . . mansuetudo patientiæ nostræ,"
etc., 541. The letter is also given by Diceto, who must have seen the original.

[5] So the Abbot of Reading, VI. 629; and in fact so Becket himself to the Pope, 581.

[6] So Reuter, II. 427. " In die tibi concessa potestatem tuam libere sine appellationis
remedio exercere tibi plenam concedimus potestatem "; VI. 485.

excommunication is admitted to be irregular, but is upheld as in fact necessary.[1]

The sentences, however, though uttered on the 13th April, were not notified in London till the 29th May (Ascension Day), and even then they **Publication of the Sentences.** were published, as it were, by a *coup de main*, to elude the vigilance of the King's officers. Foliot had received private warning of the coming blow, and had discussed the matter with the Barons of the Exchequer, so that the authorities must have been quite on the alert.[2] The opportunity chosen for the delivery of the letters was the celebration of High Mass at St. Paul's. The Gospel had been read, and the Offertory sentences begun, at which point of the service, we are told, the congregation would begin to disperse, having already attended ordinary Mass in their parish churches.[3] Becket's emissary, a young **A Coup de Main.** French layman of the name of Berenger, stepped up to the altar, and kneeling held out a packet to the celebrant as if it were an oblation. The priest having taken hold of it as such, Berenger clutched his hand with the packet in it, and then, apprising him of the contents, charged him in the name of the Pope and the Archbishop to deliver the letters to the Bishop and the Dean, neither of whom was present. Then turning to the people he cried aloud ' Know all men that Bishop Gilbert has been excommunicated by Thomas Archbishop of Canterbury and Apostolic Legate.' A confederate who was standing by to witness and attest his proceedings threw a cloak over him, and so, before any one could lay hands on him, he plunged into the crowd and vanished, to reappear some days later at York, where again he proclaimed the sentences.[4] Two days later (Saturday, 31st May) Foliot held a meeting of his clergy at Stepney. The letters were read and considered ; the sentence on their Bishop was condemned as unjust and irregular, and a fresh appeal to Rome entered. But in this the Canons of St. Bartholomew's, St. Martin's, and Holy Trinity declined to concur.[5]

Foliot Submits. Gilbert however did not attempt to ignore the excommunication. Bowing to the censure he abstained from all sacerdotal functions, and even from attendance at church.[6] But the feeling in his favour is shown by a series of protests addressed by influential churchmen to the Pope.[7] Henry wrote in most sympathetic terms giving

---

[1] *Causa Inter Cantuariensem et Londiniensem, Becket* IV. 226-227. So too John of Salisbury, VII. 3.

[2] See the report to Becket, VI. 606, and W. fitz S., III. 89.

[3] So W. fitz S., 90.

[4] VI. 603, 604 ; W. fitz S., *sup.*

[5] VI. 606.

[6] R. Diceto, I. 334 ; W. fitz S., II. 91.

[7] See VI. 607-615, and 618-635. Among those who wrote were the Archbishop of Rouen, Arnulf of Lisieux, the Abbots of Westminster, Chertsey, Ramsey, etc.

the Bishop leave to come abroad, and offering to defray his expenses for a journey to Rome.[1]

Meanwhile Becket had been as good as his word, and had condemned to eternal perdition seven-and-twenty other men, with a general clause sweeping in all who had meddled either with land or preferment belonging to Canterbury.[2] Such hasty, independent action could not fail to annoy the Pope, especially when a mission had been announced. But he could not go the length of annulling the Archbishop's sentences. At the same time, in language as strong as he could use short of absolute command, he pressed Thomas to recall his anathemas.[3]

Yet more Sentences.

The envoys Gratian and Vivian, first commissioned in February, and finally in May,[4] did not cross the Alps till July. By the 22nd of that month they had reached Vézelay, and were interviewed by John of Salisbury, eager to learn what might be expected of their mission.[5] But Henry was far away, in Gascony, where he had been, coping with rebellion, since Lent; so the envoys, after a visit to King Louis at Souvigny,[6] remained for some time at Sens, Becket apparently not being there.[7] At last, on the 15th August, their credentials were forwarded to Henry at Argentan, and on the 23rd of the month they were welcomed by him at Domfront, on his return from a day of hunting, young Henry being there also.[8]

The Third Mission.

Becket's resolute action had undoubtedly altered the situation, and thrown the burden of the initiative upon the King. Hitherto it was the Archbishop, as the man out in the cold, who had to bestir himself to obtain restitution. Henry could afford to let things drift. Now he had to press for the absolution of his Bishops and Ministers. In consequence the discussions that ensued were of a more acrimonious and protracted character than any that had yet taken place; and were marked by repeated outbursts of temper on Henry's part. On the 24th August, when business was taken up in the envoys' chamber, the King enquired at once about the absolutions, and was told that the excommunicates would be required to swear beforehand to abide by such terms as the envoys might impose.[9] Henry

Altered Situation.

Meeting at Domfront.

---

[1] *Becket*, VI. 595-599.

[2] VI. 601, 602.

[3] "Monemus, consulimus, volumus, et hortamur"; VII. 1. See also the letter VI. 564 written before Alexander had heard of the sentences.

[4] VI. 537, 563-567.

[5] VII. 2.

[6] "Silviniacum"; Loir et Cher, or Indre et Loire?

[7] See H. Bosham, III. 441, and Becket's letter, VII. 8.

[8] The young Duke and his companions are described as coming in blowing the death-note of a stag in true old French style. See VII. 71.

[9] See the reports, VII., 71, 79, 83.

became very indignant, complained of the Pope, and swore 'by God's eyes' that he would 'do something soon' (*faciam aliud*). Gratian told
Stormy Discussion. him not to attempt to threaten them, as their *curia* was wont to give its orders to Emperors as well as Kings. After a long stormy day the conference was adjourned for a week.[1]

On the 31st August Gratian and Vivian again made a formal opening of negotiations with the King at Bayeux, to be told to meet him next day at Bures,[2] to which place he had summoned all the leading clergy of his allegiance, including the Archbishops of Rouen and Bordeaux.[3] The
Meeting at Bures. meeting was held in the open air; in a park, that is to say a paddock or close. None but invited persons were admitted to the enclosure. The King again began by asking if the excommunicates were to be absolved unconditionally (*sine juramento*). Being again told that that could not be, he mounted his horse, threatening
Threatened Rupture. to break off all further parley then and there. The Norman prelates, however, gathering round Gratian and Vivian, implored them to save a rupture by making the desired concession, and to this, with much hesitation, they gave in.[4] Henry then dismounted and returned to the circle. Once more he declared
c that he had never banished Thomas, and that he was quite willing to have him back at the request of the Pope. This of course, in a sense, was strictly true. Henry had always been willing to have Thomas back on certain terms. But Thomas insisted on being taken back on terms that were wholly different. For the moment however all minds felt relieved; but clouds began to gather again when the conditions of Becket's return came to be more precisely defined. Henry first required that three of the excommunicates, who were present, should be absolved at once, and that the two envoys should go over to England to absolve the others. Gratian flatly refused, and again the King called for his horse.[5]
Fresh Efforts. Another effort on the part of the prelates brought the parties together once more, and eventually it was agreed that the Three should be absolved at once, and that Vivian should go to England leaving Gratian to report to Becket.[6] But whatever the stipu-

---

[1] *Becket*, VII. 71.

[2] Calvados, near Troarn, to the East of Caen ; there is another place of the name further South in the same Dept., near Campeaux.

[3] See the list in Henry's letter to the Pope, VII. 83.

[4] "Cum summa difficultate concesserunt," p. 72, the private report to Becket. I agree with Reuter in thinking that the writer, though at Bures at the time, was probably not within the enclosure. Vivian, in his rather summary report to the Pope, slurs over this incident, but he certainly implies that at the close of the day the King's require-ments had been conceded, p. 79.

[5] So the report to Becket, VI. 73.

[6] So Vivian, *Id.* 79; Henry, 84; Archbishop Rotrou, 86; and the Bishop of Nevers, 88.

lations on either side may or may not have been, the end of the weary day
clearly was that Henry promised to reinstate Becket and his friends,[1] 'to
the honour of God and the Church, and that of himself and his sons,'[2]
the compact to be reduced to writing on the morrow.[3] By the use of the
words 'the honour of God' Henry seemed to accept Becket's formula of
the month of January (Montmirail) and so to agree to take him back on
his own terms. But next day (2nd September)[4] he began to draw back.
First he asked to substitute 'his heirs' for 'his sons.' That having been
granted, and the question of a kiss of peace to Thomas having been
waived, the three excommunicates, namely Geoffrey Riddell, Nigel of
Sackville, and Thomas FitzBernard were absolved,[5] but not unconditionally, a declaration on their 'word of truth' being exacted from them that
they would abide by the final decision of the Papal envoys.[6] The absolution, however, having been obtained, Henry came forward with a final
addendum to the record, 'saving the rights of his realm

All in "Statu Quo." (*Salva dignitate regni sui*), words which clearly meant the
'customs' and the *Constitutions* of Clarendon. Of course the
clause was rejected, and then the conference broke up, after nightfall.[7]
The parties were clearly still just where they had been all along.

From Bures Henry went off to Rouen for a meeting with the Count of
Flanders, leaving Gratian and Vivian to be taken to Caen under the
charge of the Archbishop of Rouen. On being again pressed to accept
the clause 'saving the rights of the realm' the envoys suggested that they
might do so if they were allowed to tack on a counterbalancing clause
'saving the liberty of the Church.' The Bishops declared that the King
would never grant that; but it would seem that a proposal that Becket
should be allowed to return sinking all questions (*nulla conditione apposita*)
met with approval on both sides. From Caen the Papal agents were taken
on again to Rouen, to receive a message from the King to the effect that
he adhered to the stipulation 'saving the rights of his realm'; and there
in effect the third mission ended, with as little fruit as either of those that
had preceded it. The absolved men were warned that if peace should not

---

[1] " Omni integritate, sicut habuit ante quam exiret "; *Becket*, VI. 79.

[2] *Id.* (Vivian), cnf. 84, 86, 88, where the 'honour of God' is coupled with words
introduced, as I think, on the morrow.

[3] " Et in scriptis totum quod promittebat redigere debebat," 79. This seems more
trustworthy than the allegation of Becket's informant that Henry said that he would add
on the morrow anything more that was needed. "Si quid modo minus feci cras
consilio vestro supplebo," 74.

[4] The date is given by Becket's correspondent (the only one who gives dates) as the
1st September; but this must be corrected.

[5] " Absolutione autem illorum trium postmodo facta "; 79.

[6] 74-80, and especially Gratian's warning to the three, 115. For an attempt to throw
the decision of the question of the oath on the Archbishop of Sens see 94-96.

[7] 74, 75, 79, 80.

be made before the envoys left the sentences would revive.   As a last
effort to forestall any charge of having broken off negotiations
Third Failure. unnecessarily one Master Peter, Archdeacon of Pavia, was
sent to the King with one more appeal in the name of the
Pope to make peace.   He was somewhat curtly dismissed.   On his way
back he fell into the hands of thieves, who robbed him of some of his
effects.   Gratian then made ready to go; Vivian, who was accused of
sympathy with Henry, remaining in Normandy.[1]

With the departure of the envoys, and the end of the mission the tacit
armistice or *Interim* as it has been called,[2] would come to an end.
Gratian started for Rome on the 29th September.[3]   Becket, treating the
Moves and Counter-moves. mission as ended, though Vivian remained,[4] at once began to
prepare for a renewal of hostilities.   A double attack on Henry
was planned, as if to cut the ground from under both of his
feet.   Thomas, as Papal Legate, would lay England under Interdict unless
Henry should come to terms by the 2nd February, 1170; while the Archbishop of Sens, one of Becket's strongest supporters, would go to Rome
with Gratian to press for authority to lay Henry's Continental dominions
under the like ban.[5]   The reader need not be informed that the Interdict
was the last and most dreaded of Papal sentences.   Under an Interdict all
public services, all religious ministrations to laymen, except the baptism of
infants, and the confessions of the dying, would cease.   No church bells
would ring; but the clergy might celebrate low Mass for themselves, in
private, with closed doors.[6]

Henry met the double attack by a double move, and that independently
of the efforts of his diplomatic agents at Rome.   On the one hand,
ordinances of a most stringent character were framed and sent over to
England, to guard against the introduction of letters of Interdict; the
bearer of any such mandate after the 9th October be held guilty of high
treason; any bishop, clerk, or layman paying any regard to an Interdict to
be subjected to forfeiture and banishment; all clergy deriving any income
from England to return home by the 13th January, under penalty of

---

[1] *Becket*, VII. 80, 81, 117, 201; H. Bosham, III. 444.   Vivian's report seems very
brief, but he tells us that Gratian wished it still briefer, as if he thought the less they
said of their mission the better.

[2] So Reuter, *passim*; see also Becket's letter to the Pope, VII. 240: " Non attenditis,
pater, hoc interim quam sit dispendiosum ecclesiæ," etc.

[3] Bouquet, XVI. 394; Reuter, II. 456.

[4] In fact the 11th November had been fixed as the term of the conditional absolution
of the Three; VII. 75; the armistice would properly last till then.

[5] See VII. 170, 171, 175, 177, 190.   For Becket's letters to all the ecclesiastical centres
in England proclaiming a conditional Interdict for the 2nd February, see 97—115.   It
may be doubted if the missives were ever delivered or even sent.   It is certain that they
never were acted on.

[6] See the directions, VII. 100, 103, 377, etc.

forfeiture; no appeal to Pope or Archbishop to be allowed; nor any regard paid to any order of theirs: all laymen coming from over sea to be searched; no clerk, canon, or monk to be allowed to pass in or out of the kingdom without letters from the King, nor any Welshman; and all Welsh students to be expelled from the schools in England; the sheriffs to exact oaths of conformity to these ordinances from all freeholders over fifteen years of age in county courts, cities, and boroughs.[1] Efforts were made to obtain the concurrence of the English bishops in these measures, but with little success. The Bishop of Winchester, old Henry of Blois, who was still living, took the lead in refusing; Exeter and Norwich followed his example; while he of Chester retired into Wales.[2] But with or without the co-operation of the Bishops the King's measures proved effectual. Not a shaft from Becket's quiver reached its mark in England.

Henry's other step was to reopen negotiations through Vivian. He expressed a purpose of making a pilgrimage to the shrine of St. Denis at Mortmartre, and a wish to be introduced to his future Suzerain, Louis' little son Philip, born so late in time.[3] He also suggested that the occasion might be utilised for a meeting with the Archbishop in the presence of the King of France. With undisguised reluctance Thomas gave in to the proposal, and Sunday, 18th November, was fixed for the interview.[4] In anticipation of the meeting Henry thought it well to sound Becket on the important questions of restitution and arrears. The Archbishop of Rouen and the Bishop of Séez were sent to ask for an enumeration of the lands to which Thomas expected to be admitted on his return, with the amount that he would claim for mesne profits.[5] Becket showed more clearly than ever that he was determined to beat the King at every point, and make him drain the cup of humiliation to the very bottom. With respect to the estates that he would claim, he declined to commit himself to any

A Suggestion.

Becket's Requirements.

---

[1] Gervase, I. 214; cnf. *Becket*, VII. 147, which seems a less authentic version in several particulars, and specially because it omits the oaths to be exacted in the counties. In a subsequent letter from the Pope the ordinance is evidently referred to as the oath recently exacted from the men of England, VII. 216, a reference that does not tally with the text given, VII. 147. From this last document, however, we learn that the ordinance was brought to England by Walter of Grimsby, described as Sheriff of Lincolnshire. He became such at Easter, 1170; Pipe Roll, 16 H. II., 140.

[2] So Becket to his agents at Rome; VII. 175, 176. What the other bishops said or did we do not hear.

[3] H. Bosham, III. 445. Philip was born in 1165; five years after Louis' marriage to his third wife Alais or Adelaide of Champagne, and eight-and-twenty years after his marriage to his first wife "Aliénor" of Aquitaine; R. de Monte, *in annis*.

[4] *Becket*, VII. 152, 153, 154, 162; H. Bosham, III. 445.

[5] "Immobilium nomina possessionum quas nobis cum ecclesia Cantuariensi restitui petebamus;" VII. 173. Reuter, II. 461, treats this enquiry as only made on the 18th November, at Montmartre. It seems to me more likely to have been put beforehand.

list, demanding everything that had been held either by Theobald, or by himself, down to the time of his quarrel with the King.   Not content with that, he further required the delivery of certain disputed estates of which he had never been in possession, such as the Ros estate of which we heard before, Saltwood forfeited by Henry of Essex in 1163, and lands claimed in virtue of Henry's convention with Stephen in 1154.   On the subject of the arrears Thomas was equally uncompromising.

The Utmost Measure. He refused to make a definite remission of one single penny. One half of the total he demanded down, the other half to be reserved for further consideration.   What the total was estimated at does not appear in the letters and documents that may be considered official. But if we can trust Herbert of Bosham the sum named was 30,000 marks (£20,000).[1]   Now the rent or composition at which the archiepiscopal estates had been farmed to Ralph of Brock was in round numbers £1463 a year,[2] so that down to Michaelmas, 1169, the total accounted for to the King would be under £7,365.   In a letter subsequently addressed to his agents at Rome, Thomas pointed out that without restitution there could be no remission of sin ; and that the suspended moiety of arrears might be usefully kept *in terrorem* over the King's head.[3]

The mediating Prelates had offered Becket 1,000 marks (£666 13s. 4d.) for an outfit.   To promise all that he might demand under the head of arrears was clearly impossible.   On the other hand, if there was a point on which a man with any sense of moderation would feel bound to make concession for the sake of peace, it would be that of arrears.   But Thomas had no compunctions on the subject.   To prevent any misconception he writes to the King to repeat what he had said in conversation to the mediators ; he would require the fullest measure of restitution, including that of all benefices appertaining to Canterbury that had fallen vacant during his exile.   As the King had presented clergymen to these livings Becket's demands involved the expulsion of those in possession.[4]

Thus Henry would go to Montmartre with little hopes of any result. The two Kings first met in private.   With Louis Henry had

Meetings at Montmartre no difficulty ; he could always manage him.   The King expressed himself charmed with little Philip, asked to be allowed to give his own son Richard the benefit of an education at the Court of Paris ; and suggested that the Count of Toulouse should be summoned to Tours to do homage to the young Count of Poitiers.[5]   The two then advanced to the chapel at Montmartre, where Becket was waiting to

---

[1] *Becket*, III. 448.

[2] Pipe Roll, 11 H. II., 108, etc.

[3] VII. 173—176.

[4] 154—156.   It would seem that the question of the benefices had been raised at Bures, 74.

[5] So Becket to the Archbishop of Sens, VII. 162 ; II. Bosham, III, 445, 446.

receive them. The Kings took up a position in a field outside, the discussion being carried on through intermediaries, as on other
And the Chapel occasions of which the reader has heard.[1] Thomas opened the
proceedings by presenting a humble petition for reinstatement
on the terms already intimated by him, offering in return ' to render to the
King whatever an archbishop was bound to render to a prince.[2] Henry
demurred to the arrears, and the eviction of the clerks whom he had
instituted, and offered a reference to the Court of the King of France, or
to the University of Paris.[3] Becket evaded this by saying that he hated
litigation, and would prefer an 'amicable' (!) settlement with his King. As
we have already seen, Thomas never would face the risk of an arbitration,
obviously because it might possibly go against him on some point or other.

At last, after the interchange of many messages, the Archbishop sent in
his final demand, in writing, as an irreducible minimum, requiring reinstatement in all the possessions held by him as Archbishop, with the
disposal of the livings that had fallen vacant : in return he would render
all due service to the King, 'saving the honour of God and his Order.'[4]
Henry made an answer off-hand[5] to the effect that the Archbishop might
have 'all that his predecessors had had, and on the same terms' (*sicut
habuerunt*); words that were supposed to cover a reservation
No Agreement. of the *Constitutions*.[6] To this no response was made, and
so the King, as we hold, very justly, refused to give the kiss of
No Kiss of Peace. peace on a bargain that was not concluded. 'His son might
give it,' he said, 'but he would not ;' adding that he had
vowed never to give it.[7] This was unfortunate because otherwise the
King's position was a sound one. The formula 'saving the honour of
God' had acquired a technical force, equivalent to 'the liberty of the
Church.' Henry could not possibly accept it. Then we must point out
that Becket's silence as to the arrears involved no real surrender on his
part. His saving words were a trump card up his sleeve, with which he
could substantiate any claim not formally abandoned. That he had not
abandoned the arrears appears clearly from his subsequent letter to his
agents already quoted.[8] For not accepting Becket's terms *simpliciter*

[1] Bosham, III. 446.

[2] " Offerentes nos paratos esse exhibere illi quicquid archiepiscopus principi debet."

[3] See Becket's letter, VII. 163, 164, and Diceto, I. 336, 337.

[4] See the paper, VII. 158, 168 ; R. Diceto, *sup.*

[5] The King's answer is stated to have been made 'in his mother tongue' (*materna lingua*), p. 164, doubtless as contrasted with Latin. That Henry's language would be French may be gathered from the fact that on another occasion Henry when addressed by a petitioner in English gave his answer in French, though evidently understanding what was said to him. Giraldus Camb. V., 290.

[6] So Both Becket and Vivian, VII. 164, 168. See next note but one.

[7] H. Bosham, III. 450, and esp. the Pope's letter, VII. 198—201.

[8] Id. 175. See also the reports of the Bishop of Paris and of Vivian, where the fact transpires, though it is obviously slurred over ; also the Pope's letters, 198, and below.

I

Henry is taxed with sophistry and evasion,[1] but, if our view be correct, the equivocation was on the side of the Archbishop.   But the dignitaries who were present, weary of the struggle, and anxious to be relieved of it, were naturally much disappointed at the fresh breakdown.   Great efforts were made to induce Henry to give the kiss of peace.   Louis was urged to use his influence in that behalf, but with well-bred courtesy he refused to put pressure on a man who was in the position of his guest.   But he told **Fresh Breakdown.** Becket that he would not have him go to England without the kiss of peace for all the gold that he (Louis) was worth ; and Count Theobald of Blois was of the same opinion.[2]

As, for the time, there was nothing more to be said or done, Henry went back to Normandy, Louis accompanying him to Mantes, and in fact as far as the frontier near Pacy.   At parting he enquired about the education and custody of young Richard.   To his evident disappointment he was told that that would be discussed when they met at Tours.[3]   Vivian also took his departure, mortified and irritated with the King.   His last act was to write to Henry, rejecting with proper scorn an offer of money. He urges Henry to accept Becket's last demands, and to be liberal in the matters of arrears ; an interdict and excommunications are declared to be impending ; 'The time is short.'[4]

The family arrangements announced by Henry in the spring were being **The Dynastic Scheme.** carried out step by step.   Geoffrey had done homage for Brittany to his brother Henry—to keep up the link with Normandy—and had received the homage of the Bretons at Rennes (May).   The chief of these, again, had been required to attend the King's Court in Normandy on his return from the South (August) ; and he himself with his son kept Christmas at Nantes.   A progress through Brittany ensued, in the course of which the unfortunate ex-Count Eude of Porhoet was subjected to further degradation and confiscation.[5]   The coronation of young Henry was the one part of the programme yet to be **Young Henry to be Crowned,** carried out.   For the hallowing of a son in his father's life-time no precedent could be found in English history.   Stephen for very obvious reasons had been anxious to get his son Eustace crowned, but his relations with the Church made that impossible.[6] Henry's anxiety on the subject is not so intelligible, as his title was indisputable, he being in fact the first of the Norman Kings whose title

---

[1] "Sophisticus est et captiosus" ; Vivian, 169. "Ut simplicioribus videretur universa concedere, cautioribus autem perversas et non ferendas immiscere conditiones," *Becket*, VII. 164. Reuter, II. 462, 463 holds that Becket had not surrendered anything.

[2] *Becket*, VII. 164, 169.

[3] 165.

[4] VII. 170.

[5] R. Monte, 241-244. Benedict of Peterborough I. 3.

[6] See *Foundations*, II. 441, 446.

was indisputable.　But precedents for the step contemplated were not
wanting in France, and Henry as a Frenchman might naturally look to that
country for guidance.　The purpose had long been cherished by him,
probably ever since the first recognition of his son in 1162.　For the
performance of the rite he was looking to Archbishop Roger of York,
a purpose that promised a fresh rupture with Becket, if all existing

And by the Archbishop of York. difficulties had been removed.　But the King recked nought
of that.　The envoys sent to Benevento to give his account
of the meeting at Montmartre were apparently instructed to
apply for authority for the coronation by Archbishop Roger.[1]　They were
to point to the liberality of the last offers made by the King to Becket, and
to renew the same.　Their representations apparently met with a favourable
reception.　Alexander, to clench the matter, at once nominated a fourth

A Fourth Papal Mission. commission, drawn not from the circle of the *Curia*, but from
that of the Gallican Church.　The men chosen were Rotrou
Archbishop of Rouen, and Bernard Bishop of Nevers, the one
a subject of King Henry's, the other a subject of the King of France.
They were directed to negotiate an accord on the footing of the Montmartre terms, if better terms could not be obtained.　They were to urge
the King to give the kiss of peace, unless Thomas would be satisfied with
the kiss from the son.　If necessary they were to waive all question of the
arrears, and even of the 1000 marks, though in the first instance they would
press for this last grant.　On the other hand they were to urge Becket to
accept the kiss from the son.　No question as to the 'customs' was to
be raised in the first instance ; but if peace were secured they might
approach the King with a view to procuring a modification of the more
objectionable provisions.　In the last resort however, failing compliance
on the part of the King ' within forty days from receipt of our warning '[2],
they would lay all his Continental dominions under Interdict, 'unless it

Alexander and the King. should appear to them that the King would come to terms
very shortly after the expiration of the forty days, or that the
Archbishop would accept the son's kiss,'[3] a saving clause that
would give the negotiators all the latitude that they could possibly wish.
Writing to the King to announce the new mission Alexander begins by
referring to petitions presented to him to which he could not lend an ear—

---

[1] See Becket's letter to his agents at Rome, warning them ; VII. 181.

[2] " Infra quadraginta dies post commonitionem nostram " : VII. 200.　How the date
of the warning would be reckoned does not appear, probably it was not intended to be
too clearly defined.

[3] " Nisi forte vobis omnino constaret quod sæpefatus rex Henricus in brevi post
quadraginta dies elapsos [promissa] adimpleret, aut archiepiscopus osculum filii pro suo
velit suscipere." *Ib.* 19th January, 1170.　See also the several instructions to the two
Prelates, 202, 203.　On the other hand letters were addressed to the clergy of all Henry's
dominions, laying stress on the threatened Interdict, 212-214, 218.　But it seems that they
were never delivered, or not till after the coronation, 318.

presumably the matter of the coronation—but he thanks Henry for the offer to receive Becket back with all his former possessions ; urges him to give the kiss of peace ; and to enable him to do so, absolves him from the oath not to give it. Not a word is said of any impending censures.[1] On the contrary Alexander intimates that he will receive appeals down to 18th October, and that the envoys are authorised to give absolution to certain excommunicates appointed to be absolved.[2]

This further concession had reference to the case of Foliot, to whom a month later a grant of conditional absolution at the hands of the Arch-bishop of Rouen was vouchsafed.[3] Gilbert had come over from England in October, and had been present at the meeting at Mont-

Absolution of Foliot. martre.[4] Continuing his journey to Italy by a circuitous course through Querci, Toulouse, and Montpellier, he received the Papal letter at Milan. Returning at once to Normandy he was finally absolved by Rotrou on Easter Day (April 5th).[5] Becket's indignation knew no bounds.[6] By the Pope's orders the matter had been kept secret from him till it was actually concluded.

Henry, on the whole, was fairly well pleased with the Pope's letter to him, but still more so with the verbal reports brought by his envoys, who boasted that they had obtained leave for the coronation by Roger. In face of the reiterated inhibitions that followed it is not easy to give any credence to this assertion, but it would seem that there was a Papal Bull extant, not as yet revoked, that gave the Archbishop of York express authority to crown young Henry.[7] The King's agents may have founded on this ; but more likely they had put their own interpretation on general assurances of goodwill. Anyhow Becket and his friends were alarmed, while Henry at once announced an intention of going over to England to arrange for the coronation ; making that an excuse for throwing over an appointment previously made for a meeting with Becket at Pontoise.[8]

On the 2nd March, presumably, Henry embarked, as he landed at

---

[1] See also *William of Canterbury*, I. 76, who gives the mission of Rotrou and Bernard without any threat of Interdict.

[2] January ; VII. 204–208. " Excommunicatis qui fuerint absolvendi."

[3] 18th February, p. 208.

[4] P. 194.

[5] R. Diceto, I. 337, 338 ; *Becket*, VII. 273–277, 295.

[6] See his letters to Rotrou, and the Pope, 278–282, 294, ' Again had Barabbas been released and Christ put to death.'

[7] VI. 203. The date and authority of this document have been much disputed. The day of the month that it bears, 17th June, proves that it could not belong to the year 1170 as Henry was crowned before that day, but it may be referred to June 1166, when the siege of Rome was being pressed by the Emperor. See Canon Robertson's note *ad loc*, and Reuter, II. 682–684. Yet in April 1166 Alexander had written to York forbidding him to crown a King without the consent of Becket, V. 323,324. For earlier vacillations of the Pope on the subject see above, p. 59, note 8.

[8] February. See the various letters of complaint and remonstrance, VII. 225–236.

Portsmouth on the 3rd of the month, after having encountered a
The King back to England sudden gale, in which the Royal squadron suffered severely, one ship at least being totally lost.[1] Easter was kept at Windsor, King William of Scotland and his brother David being in attendance.[2] The festivities over, the King moved to London
A Grand Council and held a Grand Council, at which the arrangements for his son's coronation were settled, and Sunday, 14th June fixed as the day. But the Magnates took the opportunity of calling the King's attention to complaints that were running through the land of extortions practised by the sheriffs during the years of his absence. To satisfy them Henry gave orders for a general fiscal enquiry,
Inquest of Sheriffs since known as the Inquest of Sheriffs, an investigation to be carried on throughout the counties by commissions of barons, clerical and lay. The sheriffs would be bound to appear, and also all freemen, summoned to give evidence upon oath. The sheriffs would be required to render account of all their receipts since the King's departure in 1166, whether from Hundreds, townships, or individuals, distinguishing sums exacted under judicial decision from money levied without such warrant (s. 1). So too the lords of franchises, ecclesiastical and lay, were to state what they had exacted from their men, whether with or without legal process (s. 2): so of the officials or farmers in charge of vacant Sees, or other lands in hand (ss. 3, 4); so of the Foresters having view of the Royal Forests; and to these men a special enquiry would be addressed as to possible remissions of penalties through corrupt or personal motives (s. 7). Another head of enquiry would be as to the chattels of 'fugitives' from justice under the Assize of Clarendon, a source of revenue that had proved disappointing.[3] In connexion with this head of enquiry we have a further very proper demand for information as to innocent parties unjustly charged, or guilty parties improperly let off, or amerciaments to the King unduly remitted; so again as to corrupt bargains or compositions made since the King's home-coming was announced, the King requiring a full return of all bribes or hush-money taken or given (ss. 5, 9, 10). Lastly the Commissioners were directed to enquire as to any persons who had not yet rendered homage to the King or his son (s. 11); and as to the stocking and general state of the King's demesnes (s. 12).[4]

Thus it will be seen that the enquiry ostensibly granted on behalf of

---

[1] Benedict of Peterborough, I. 3; Gervase, I. 216.

[2] Benedict, *sup.* 4; Chron. Melrose; J. Fordun, 261. According to the Melrose writer David was knighted by the King on 22nd May.

[3] See the Pipe Rolls, *passim*, where the common return in such case is " Non est inventus. Nihil inde quod nihil habuit." Petty crime is always penniless.

[4] See the Inquest printed from the MS. Bodl., Rawlinson C., 641, *Select Charters*, 141; also Benedict P., I. 4, 5. Gervase, I. 216. The last also gives the names of the commissioners for seven of the Southern counties.

the tax-payer as against the tax-collector, becomes very much an enquiry
Practical Bearing of the Enquiry. on behalf of the King as against both tax-collector and tax-payer. From the King's point of view, at least so far as the sheriffs were concerned, it would be an attempt to get behind the ordinary investigations of the Exchequer audits. At these they could only be called upon to account for known liabilities; now they would be asked to state whatever else they might have received, with the parties concerned to confront them. With respect to the community in general the Inquest might be regarded as an attempt to find out how
Direct Taxation. far direct taxation could be carried. A few fragmentary returns from private lords are extant, and they give all the extraordinary payments that had been made to the lord by his under-tenants, whether on the King's account, or under his writ (as for the Aid *Pur fille marier*), or on the lord's account, and without royal writ (as to pay the lord's debts, or to knight his son).[1]

With respect to the causes of popular discontent the Pipe Rolls give us sufficient information. No scutage nor any *Donum* so called had been levied within the period. An Aid *pur fille marier*, of course, had been levied. This as taken from the tenants-in-chief at the rate of one mark (13*s*. 4*d*.) per rated knight's fee was a perfectly legal impost. But Henry had levied it from all classes of the
Henry's Imposts. community, whether resident in town or country, without regard to tenure. Then the circuits of the judges had been used as opportunities for wholesale exactions from Hundreds, townships and individuals, for real or supposed offences, and sometimes with no offence at all alleged. Lastly we hear of a *Communis assiza*, a levy on the counties as collective units, said to have been first directed by Henry before sailing for Normandy in 1166.[2] As this is sometimes described as a *misericordia* imposed for some default or other it may be that this and the preceding head to a certain extent run into one another.[3] Of what malversations the sheriffs may have been guilty we cannot say,
Sheriffs Dismissed. but the King, as it were making scape-goats of them, and without waiting for the results of the Inquest, turned fifteen of them out of office, as from Easter, leaving nine to remain in possession of their offices.[4]

A few days before the appointed 14th June the King's son young Henry was brought over from Normandy by the Bishops of Séez and

---

[1] See these, *Red Book of Exchequer*, II. clxvi.

[2] So Red Book, *sup.* cclxxviii.

[3] For Communis Assiza see *e.g.* Pipe Roll 15 H. II., 7, 29. This levy is noticed in the Dialogus de Scacc. *Select Charters*, 224, 226. We have an *assiza comitatus* in Norfolk on the Roll 2 H. II.

[4] Pipe Rolls 15 & 16 Henry II. Ow'ng to the linking of counties the number of Sheriffs was much less than that of counties.

Bayeux. His young wife Margaret of France was not allowed to accompany him; she was left at Caen with Queen Eleanor. Henry would not allow her to be crowned along with her husband, an intentional slight, as it was considered, to her father King Louis.[1] But we may here state that a little later she was permitted to come to England, and that the King, as if to make amends, ordered her a very handsome outfit.[2]

Young Henry, 'The King, the King's son,' as he is oddly styled on
Coronation the Pipe Rolls,[3] was now in his sixteenth year. By rights
of the Young he should have been knighted before being crowned; as till
King. admitted to knighthood he would not be held of full age, or entitled to have a seal of his own. The honour must have been purposely withheld in order to keep him in a state of tutelage. Three years later the sword of William Marshal, afterwards Earl of Pembroke, conferred the lacking distinction, to enable 'the young King' to act, not for his father, but against him.[4] Thus then, on the 14th June, Henry, without being knighted, was duly hallowed and crowned in Westminster Abbey. The service was performed by Archbishop Roger. Hugh of Puiset Bishop of Durham, Gilbert Foliot Bishop of London, Joscelin Bishop of Sarum, and Walter Bishop of Rochester assisted; while the Bishops of Chester, Exeter, St. Asaph, and Llandaff, and the Norman Bishops of Evreux, Bayeux, and Séez were present, without taking part in the rites.[5] The coronation
oath followed the regular formula, without adopting the novel
The Corona- clause that the Pope wanted to introduce pledging the King
tion Oath. to observe the rights and 'liberty' of the Church, and those of Canterbury in particular.[6] Neither on the other hand did it contain any declaration in favour of the *Constitutions*, as alleged by Becket's friends.[7]

But all this time the Pope had not been idle. Since the King left Normandy, a series of inhibitions against the coronation by York had

---

[1] So the letters t) Becket, VII. 309–311.

[2] *Id.* 317. See the Pipe Roll 16 Henry II., *passim*, where, not having been crowned, Margaret is only styled 'the daughter of the King of France.'

[3] "Rex, filius Regis."

[4] See the Earl's Biography, *Willaume le Mareschal*, I. 77, II. 187 (P. Meyer).

[5] Bend. Pet., I. 5; Gervase, I. 219; the report to Becket, VII. 316, and for the exact list of offending prelates the Pope's letters, 356, 358, 360: for the Bishop of Evreux see his own admission, 422.

[6] On this point see the letters, VII. 216, 346, 366, 427. The correct formula was 'to hold church and people in good peace,' without reference to any special immunities claimed by the clergy. Of course the Coronation Oath was much older than either the Canon Law or the 'liberty' of the Church. See *Foundations*, I. 318, 338, II. 44.

[7] *Becket*, VII. 356, 358, 362; and esp. the declaration of the Bishop of Evreux who was present, 422; that of Archbishop Rotrou, 426; and that of Roger of York, 502.

been issued.[1]   But with some discrepancy among the authorities, we
take it that none of them had been delivered, certainly not
**Suppressed
Inhibitions.** formally published.[2]   More strange it is to hear that the
attempt to have them transmitted had been delayed by
Thomas out of regard for some silly prophecy,[3] probably brought under
his notice by his Welsh cross-bearer Alexander Llewelyn, who was with
him to the last.

With respect to the mission of the Prelates Rotrou and Bernard,
Alexander, on hearing that the King had crossed the Channel, being
afraid of possible delays, sent renewed instructions ordering them to
follow Henry to England.   But the King managed to put them off,
assuring them that he was coming back to Normandy directly,[4] and so
he did, after the coronation.   The notifications to the Gallican clergy
that Henry's Continental dominions would be laid under Interdict, if he
did not make peace with Becket within forty days, likewise had not been
delivered, having also lain dormant in Becket's hands.[5]

On the day after the coronation, 15th June, the earls, barons, and
Homages to freeholders of the realm, with William of Scotland and his
the Young brother David at their head, were made to do homage to
King.   the young King, and to swear fealty to him saving their
allegiance to the elder King.   Some nine days later, about the 24th of
the month, Henry recrossed the Channel, the young King being left
behind as Regent, with a Regency seal specially struck for him.[6]

The King having come back to Normandy Rotrou and Bernard could
Mission of no longer withhold the Papal letters threatening Interdict.
Rotrou and Henry at once repeated the offer made at Montmartre,
Bernard.   namely the grant to Becket of peace and goodwill (*gratia*),
with reinstatement in all possessions, but without the kiss of peace.
These proposals were duly reported to the Archbishop of Sens about
the 16th July.   As it happened Louis and Henry had arranged to meet

---

[1] *Becket*, VII. 216, 217, 256–263.

[2] William fitz Stephen asserts that the inhibitions were delivered to Roger and Foliot
the day before the Coronation, III. 103 ; Bosham more vaguely says that some of the
bishops received their letters, III. 459 ; and so said Becket to the King at Fréteval
(below), VII. 330.   Against this we have the report to Becket which states that the
Pope's letters had crossed the Channel, but having been committed to untrustworthy hands
had never been delivered or published. but destroyed, VII. 3c9.   Then we have a pressing letter, apparently written at the last moment, by Becket to one Idonea, doubtless a
nun, urging her to deliver the Papal letter to the Archbishop of York, 307.   Foliot's
agent at the Papal court formally denied that the inhibitions had been received, VII. 480,
and so did Roger of York, 502.

[3] "Subtilitatem vestram vaticinia quæ non erant a spiritu deluserunt."   See the letter
of John of Salisbury rebuking Thomas for superstition and impiety, VII. 319.

[4] VII. 210, 300, 338 ; Gervase, I. 219 ; William of Canterbury, I. 76–81.

[5] For the letters, see VII. 210–218 ; for their non-delivery, 319.

[6] So Ben. P., I. 6.

on the 20th July, near Fréteval,[1] on the borders of the Chartrain and

Touraine, and Becket was persuaded by his friends to present

Conferences at Fréteval himself at Fréteval, unbidden and on his own responsibility, in the hope of effecting a settlement.   The Kings met as appointed.   On the afternoon of the second day, their business having been transacted, a request for an audience was presented on behalf of Becket, and Henry agreed to receive him on the morrow (22nd July).[2] They met on horseback in the open air, in the presence of a large concourse of magnates.   Henry pressed forward to meet the Archbishop with elaborate courtesy, behaving in fact as if there had never been a word of difference between them, doffing his cap (*capite detecto*) and anticipating Thomas' salute.   The attendants having retired, a private conversation ensued, according to Becket, of most friendly character.[3]   Thomas, how-

The slight to Canterbury. ever, at once broached the question of the recent coronation. Henry, protesting that he had intended no offence, asked who had crowned the Conqueror and subsequent kings.   'Was it not the Prelate of the King's choosing?'   Becket answered that the Archbishop of York had been allowed to crown William I. because Canterbury was then in bondage to Stigand, a condemned schismatic.   In the case of Henry I., Anselm being in exile, the coronation had been performed, not by the Archbishop of York, but by a suffragan of Canterbury.   Here we may point out that Becket ignored the fact that Archbishop Thomas I. of York was not brought to London on that occasion simply because he was too old and infirm to travel.[4]   The other Norman kings, William Rufus, Stephen, and Henry II. himself, Becket continued, had been crowned by Archbishops of Canterbury, without protest from any Archbishop of York. Thomas ended by demanding reparation for the wrong done to him.[5] Henry answered that he was protected by Papal authority, and even produced a Bull empowering him to have his son crowned by whatsoever prelate he might choose.   Becket replied that the mandate relied on had been revoked by subsequent missives ; and that the letter produced had been issued at a time when Canterbury was vacant.[6]   Again he insisted on 'condign satisfaction' being rendered to the Almighty, and to the Saints resting at Canterbury.   For this he pleaded if only for the

---

[1] Loir et Cher.   The place had been ceded to Henry, above, p. 18.

[2] See the letter, VII. 338–340.

[3] "Soli duo"; see the letters, *Becket*, VII. 327, 341.

[4] See *Foundations*, II. 229.

[5] "Ut hujus lœsionis nostræ jacturam repararet."

[6] The Bull here referred to cannot be identified.   There is no Papal letter extant on the subject of the coronation that was either written during the vacancy of Canterbury, or that gives the King power to choose his own consecrator.   There are the two letters already noticed that authorise the Archbishop of York to crown kings, but these are dated the one 13th July, 1162, after Becket's consecration, and the other probably in June, 1167; V. 21, and VI. 206.

sake of the King's own son and his crown. The King answered with a laugh. 'My son? Why he loves you so well that he cannot look at one

The Young King and Becket. of your enemies. He will avenge you only too well as soon as he has the opportunity. He would have done so already but for his regard for me.'[1] These words, so full of interest in themselves, acquire a double significance when viewed in connexion with events that Becket did not live to witness. Henry ended by declaring that he would discuss the question of the amends due to Canterbury with the Archbishop. 'As for the men who have betrayed you and me with God's help I will give them their deserts.'[2] Thomas, interpreting these very ambiguous utterances in his own way, sprang from his horse to do obeisance. But the King promptly dismounted also; and then, laying hold of the Archbishop's stirrup made him remount. Then returning to the general circle Henry ordered the Archbishop to present his petition in due form. This was done by word of mouth, through Becket's especial friend, William of Blois, the Archbishop of Sens. Following the words of the Montmartre offers, as recently renewed by Henry, he asked for peace and favour to him and his; and reinstatement in his and their possessions, a written list of these being tendered. But he also prayed that the King would 'mercifully amend'[3] the injury recently done to him and his Church in the coronation of young Henry. The King nodded assent, and the great pacification was supposed to have been at last effected. In truth

A Hollow Accord. it was the hollowest possible sham. If no word had been said of the *Constitutions*, as Becket boasted,[4] that was because Henry intended to enforce them, and Thomas intended to defy them. If the question of the arrears was passed over, Becket was still careful to inform the Pope that he neither could nor would remit one fraction of what was due. Still, by consenting, as he did, to return to England sinking all questions, he undoubtedly surrendered the position he had previously maintained. Lastly we must point out that the King's words as reported by Becket himself gave him no free hand with regard to the men concerned in the recent coronation.

The day ended with a proposal addressed to Becket through Arnulf of Lisieux, that as the King had extended his favour to

Reciprocity Refused. Becket's friends, Thomas might do the same by the King's friends. The Archbishop cleverly evaded the concession by pointing to the distinctions between the various cases: some men had been sentenced on one ground, some on another; some by this or that Prelate, some by the Pope himself. No one judgment could be passed

---

[1] *Becket*, VII. 332.

[2] " Illis autem qui me et vos hactenus prodiderunt, Deo propitio, sic respondebo ut exigunt merita proditorum "; 332.

[3] " Ut misericorder emendaret."

[4] Page 326.

on all. If any of them should eventually fail to obtain peace it would not be through his, the Archbishop's fault.[1]

Whatever the pacification might ultimately prove to be worth in itself, for the King it served the immediate purpose of staving off the Interdict; while he might anticipate that Becket in England would be a man more under control than Becket abroad. In fact it was to escape control that Becket had originally taken flight.

Declining an invitation to accompany the King to Normandy,[2] Thomas returned to Sens. Four more months were destined to elapse before he could make up his mind to leave the sheltering soil of France. The persistent refusal of the kiss of peace might well excite misgivings as to the honesty of the King's intentions; while Becket was determined to punish the prelates who had taken part in the recent coronation. To exact due 'amends' from them Papal authority had to be obtained.

The slight to Canterbury. Alexander at first seemed to take a moderate view of the slight to Canterbury. Other things appeared to him to be more important. Writing to Henry on receipt of the news of the pacification he presses for the satisfaction of the arrears, and complains that the young King had not taken any oath to respect the 'liberty' of Canterbury. But he makes no other complaint with regard to the coronation.[3] Writing to the Archbishop he promises him that the recent infringement of his rights shall not be allowed to become a precedent;[4] as if Thomas ought to be content with that assurance. But Thomas was not at all content with it; and so at his instance,[5] Alexander

Becket to be Avenged. took the fatal step of entrusting him with letters suspending all the nine English and Welsh Prelates who had assisted at the coronation; while as a further penalty on the Bishops of London and Salisbury their excommunications would be revived. But as if sensible that the coronation by itself would hardly justify such severity, Alexander in his prefatory indictment goes back to the original acceptance of the *Constitutions* at Clarendon, and the general misconduct of the offending Prelates since that time[6].

Meanwhile, beyond a general notification of the peace, nothing had been done by Henry towards the reinstatement of the Archbishop. John of Salisbury and Herbert of Bosham had been sent into Normandy to press

---

[1] See Becket's report to the Pope, VII. 326–336: comparing the hearsay letter, 338–342, where of course the scope of Henry's concessions is considerably extended. So with all the chroniclers. See also the King's notifications from which we learn that the question of the livings was also conceded by him, 343. Miss Norgate ventures to call the arrangement "A complete mutual amnesty," *Angevin Kings*, II. 73.

[2] VII. 334, 342. [3] VII. 315. [4] *Id.* 354.

[5] See the letter, *Id.* 370; and Becket's own complaint that he had not been allowed freer action, 385; also the letters of the Cardinals urging moderation, 372, 374.

[6] 10–16th September, VII. 355–368.

Henry on the point, with special demands as to the disputed Ros estate, as to Saltwood, and as to Rochester Castle. They found the King at Ger,[1] in the Côtentin, seriously ill of a tertian fever,[2] and had to wait till he was well enough to see them. When they were admitted to an audience, the question of the Ros estate was apparently evaded, the demand for Rochester Castle, as might be expected, being flatly refused.[3]

Orders for Reinstatement. But some days later Henry at last sent orders to the young King in England, proclaiming peace to Becket and his friends; directing them to be admitted to all that they held 'three months before Thomas left England,' with an inquest as to the right to the Honour of Saltwood.[4] This writ was apparently issued while the King was on a thanksgiving pilgrimage to Rocamadour[5], a retired valley in Querci, the resting place of a popular Saint.[6] Armed with the King's mandate, Becket's agents went over to England, and, after a visit to Canterbury, proceeded to London, where they had an audience of the young King and his council, with his grand-uncle Reginald Earl of Cornwall assisting as chief adviser (5th October). They were told to come again on the 15th, evidently in order to defer the restitutions till after the conclusion of the Michaelmas Audit.[7]

From his pilgrimage into Querci the King returned to Tours for a meeting with Theobald of Blois, to be held on the 13th October. Becket, apprised of Henry's plans, presented himself on the 12th to press for reinstatement, and for money in hand; also to make a push **A Push for the Kiss of Peace.** for the kiss of peace, if even by a *ruse*. With that object, as was supposed, he appeared next morning (13th October) at the King's early Mass, when the service would give him an opportunity of offering Henry a kiss in a way that could not be evaded. The King, however, warned by Nigel of Sackville, described as Keeper of the Seal,[8] ordered the celebration of a Mass for the Dead, at which the *pax* would not be given.[9] A day or two later another, and the last, interview between

---

[1] Manche. between Mortain and Domfron*.

[2] August-September, Ben. P., I. 6; R. Monte, 247; H. Bosham.

[3] H. Bosham, III. 467.

[4] VII. 346.

[5] Lot, near Gramat.

[6] Bend. P., I. 7; R. Monte, 248. The writ is dated at Chinon, and therefore I judge that it was issued on the King's way South, but the want of dates makes it very difficult to settle the sequence of events. The pilgrimage was undertaken late in September. Herbert of Bosham speaks of earlier writs to England, but I think that that must be a mistake, III. 467.

[7] VII. 389, W. fitz S. III. 113. Again we hear that the young King was all for Becket, but that in the presence of his advisers he had to restrain himself; VII. 390.

[8] "Sigillifer." W. fitz S.

[9] Robertson, *Becket*, 248; Bosham, III. 468, 469; W. fitz S., *Id.* 115; the latter places the incident at Amboise, meaning Chaumont, where the next meeting was held, mixing up the two. See also Anon., IV. 67, and for the date Ben. P., I. 8.

the two antagonists was held at Chaumont, between Blois and Amboise.

Last Interview of Becket and Henry. Henry said playfully (*familiarius et jocundius*) 'Why wilt thou not do my will? Then would I give all things into thy hands' —words that, according to the Secretary, Becket afterwards said reminded him of the Temptation in the Wilderness.[1]

Finally Henry told Becket to go to Rouen, whither he would follow him to provide him with money, and send him, perhaps accompany him, to England. 'Depart in peace.' 'My lord,' Thomas was reported to have said, 'My soul tells me that we shall meet no more in this life.' 'What! rejoined the King, 'Takest thou me for a traitor knave?' 'Far be it from thee, my lord.'[2] To Rouen Becket proceeded, as ordered, but only to receive there an apology from the King for his non-appearance, Henry excusing himself on the ground that he had been called to Auvergne, to resist attacks by the French. But he directed Becket to proceed to England forthwith. Thomas was also much mortified to find that the man appointed to conduct him to England was his old adversary, John of Oxford, Dean of Sarum. Nor was any money forthcoming from the Royal treasury for the settlement of Becket's debts. But the Archbishop of Rouen kindly presented him with £300 from his own pocket.[3]

Henry was bound to resist the Archbishop's pretensions. He was fighting the battle not only of the Crown, but of all lay rights as against intolerable aggression. But it must be admitted that he conducted the struggle in a mean and petty spirit. Of course he had only carnal weapons to fight with, while Becket had all the resources of the spiritual armoury at command.

[1] H. Bosham, III. 470.

[2] So W. fitz S., *sup.*; Bosham, however, does not record this colloquy. That the meeting at Chaumont was the last appears clearly from the letter of John of Salisbury, VII. 395.

[3] See the King's letter, VII. 400; W. fitz S., III. 116; and the letters of John of Salisbury, VII. 409, 410.

CHAPTER VII

HENRY II. (*continued*)

1170

Return of Becket to England—Suspension of Prelates—Further Anathemas on Christmas Day—Assassination of the Archbishop

FROM Rouen Thomas returned once more to Sens (October); but only to pack up and take leave of his French hosts. 'Always great' (*semper et ubique magnus*) as his Secretary informs us, he had got together some 100 horses for his journey.[1] On the 1st November he left the walls of Sainte Colombe, six years within a day from the time when **Becket preparing to return.** he had sailed from Sandwich.[2] At Witsand he must have tarried some time ; perhaps in hesitation, as many of his friends thought the return to England perilous. Actual threats, apparently, had reached Thomas himself.[3] But we incline to believe that he waited in hope of receiving from the Pope amended letters for which he had applied. Alexander, as we have seen, had in part based the proposed suspension of the Prelates who had officiated at the recent coronation on their original acceptance of the *Constitutions*. Becket wished the sentences to be based solely on the matter of the coronation, without any reference to the *Constitutions* ; as without doubt any condemnation of those articles would be an infringement of the tacit agreement of Fréteval ; as Becket delicately puts it, it might give offence to the King, and cause a breach of the recent pacification which he was most anxious to avoid.[4] He further petitioned for alternative letters of varying degrees of severity, to be used at his discretion, the case of the Archbishop of York, as the chief offender,

---

[1] H. Bosham, III. 471.

[2] H. Bosham, *sup.* ; Anon. IV. 68 ; and VII. 395. Becket had sailed on the 2nd November, 1164.

[3] See John of Salisbury, II. 315 ; W. fitz S. III. 113 ; and the violent threats ascribed to Ralph of Brock by Becket, VII. 394.

[4] " Quia timemus ne teneras viri prepotentis aures verbum mordax exulceret, et nuper initam pacem impediat." And again, " Quia veremur ne pax recens ex variis causis impediri valeat aut turbari " ; VII. 336.

being always reserved for the decision of the Holy Father himself.[1] Becket's wishes were complied with, and the desired documents made out and forwarded ; but not in time to reach his hands alive.[2] Thomas therefore, who with all his love of peace[3] was resolved to herald his home coming by a fresh declaration of war, had to content himself with the original letters. To ensure their delivery they were sent on in advance in charge of a lad or acolyte (*puer*) by name Osbern, whose apparent insignificance may have enabled him to escape search at Dover, a point

Fresh Suspension of Prelates. that we cannot otherwise explain. By a curious coincidence the three men primarily aimed at, Roger of York, Foliot, and Joscelin of Sarum were actually at Dover apparently superintending the measures to prevent the introduction of Papal letters. They were immediately served with their sentences in the church of St. Peter's Dover, the lad Osbern, like Berenger at St. Paul's in 1166, making good his escape.[4] This unpardonable action on the part of Becket must have dashed the hopes of those, if any such there were, who still believed in the possibility of a real pacification.[5] But once more we must point out that in Becket's view 'peace' meant his own absolute victory on all points. Having hurled this preliminary bombshell into the enemy's camp, Thomas on the evening of the next day, after hearing that the sentences had been duly delivered,[6] loosed from Witsand. Steering clear of Dover, on the

Landing of Becket. morning, apparently, of Tuesday, 1st December,[7] he landed at Sandwich among his own people. He was promptly confronted by the Sheriff of Kent, Gervase of Cornhill, accompanied by Reginald of Warenne,[8] and Ralph of Brock, late farmer of the Canterbury estates. They came to challenge the Archbishop's proceedings and demand his authority for landing. John of Oxford satisfied them on this point. But the Sheriff could not refrain from telling Becket that,

---

[1] *Ib.*

[2] See these dated Tusculum, 24 Nov., VII. 397, 399.

[3] " [Nos] omnibus modis caventes rescindere pacis initæ conventionem " ; *Id.* 375.

[4] W. Cant., I. 87. 89, 95 ; H. Bosham, III. 471, 472 ; Anon. IV. 68 ; and the letter of John of Salisbury, VII. 410. W. fitz S., III. 117 places the delivery at Canterbury. Becket's own account is ambiguous ; VII. 403.

[5] See the despondent tone of the report of Becket's agents already cited, VII. 390 ; also the clear condemnation of Becket's conduct by W. Newburgh I. 161 ; the Anonymous writer, *Becket*, IV. 123 ; and Rotrou of Rouen, VII. 426. " Rediens, durum et triste dedit sui adventus principium."

[6] H. Bosham, III. 472. If we may trust this man Becket was filled with righteous joy. " Gaudio magno gavisus est, lætante juste eo quod vindictam desideratam jam vidisset."

[7] See Becket's letter to the Pope, VII. 403 ; W. fitz S., III. 118 ; H. Bosham, *sup.*, and 476. Fitz Stephen, William of Canterbury, I. 99, and Diceto, I. 339, all give 1st Dec. as the day of landing. Gervase, I. 221, has the 30th Nov. Bosham says that they sailed either on the 30th Nov., or 1st Dec., landing next day.

[8] Brother to Earl William who died on Crusade in 1148.

coming as he did, he was bringing fire and sword with him.[1] Next day the party reached Canterbury. We are told that clergy and people received them with joy. As a matter of fact the monks had shown themselves rather indifferent to Becket's cause, but we cannot doubt that the tenants would welcome the return of their proper landlord.[2]

On the following day again (3rd December) officers from the Regency appeared to demand the immediate recall of the sentences against the Prelates. After some discussion Becket offered to hold friendly inter-course with Foliot and Joscelin if they would swear to abide by the Pope's decision. By Roger's advice this offer was declined, and then the three went over to Normandy to consult the King.[3]

Thomas now found time to write to the Pope to report his proceedings. He condescended to offer excuses for having delivered the sentences.

Becket explains his Conduct. These were that the Fréteval compact was not being honestly observed by the King, either as to the lands, or the Livings: some of the latter were still being kept back ; the farms were in a wretched state, and all the rents had been anticipated ; then he had been informed that the three Prelates had been urging the King not to allow him, Thomas, to return, except under condition of accepting the *Constitutions* ; lastly he understood that there was a scheme on foot for filling up the vacant bishoprics by summoning to Normandy delegacies of six men from each diocese whose voices would be held to represent canonical election. ' And so,' as John of Salisbury puts his case for him, ' he had frustrated their designs as best he could.'[4] The reader must be left to judge if Thomas' previous acts did not indicate a settled purpose, independently of these considerations. As to canonical election we repeat that it had never obtained in England at any time ; and that the suggested plan carried with it as much concession to the clergy as was at all usual.

After eight days' stay at Canterbury we hear of Becket as announcing **Attempts to hold a Visitation.** an intention of paying a visit to the young King at Winchester ;[5] this visit to be followed by a general visitation of the Province to assert his position. We have already seen how well-disposed the young King was to his former tutor.[6] But the Regency Council

---

[1] " Dixit ei vicecomes quod in igne et gladio terram intraverat," W. fitz S. 118. So too said Arnulf of Lisieux to the Pope, VII. 424.

[2] See W. Cant., I. 99-102 ; W. fitz S., and H. Bosham, *sup.*, and the reports to the Pope, VII. 402, 410.

[3] See the letters, VII., 405, 411, etc.

[4] " Conatus eorum via qua potuit elisit," VII., 410, and Becket's own letter, 402, 403. But from the way that he puts it I gather that the last point did not emerge till after that he had landed. So too clearly W. Cant. I. 106.

[5] So W. Cant., I. 106 ; W. fitz S, III. 121 ; and the Anonymous writer, IV. 126, of whom the two former were at Canterbury at the time. Diceto, I. 342, thought that the young Henry was at Woodstock, doubtless wrongly.

[6] See above, 122 ; also John of Salisbury, VII. 408 ; H. Bosham, III. 482.

had also to be consulted, and for this purpose Richard Prior of St.
Martin's Dover, Becket's future successor, was sent in advance. His
reception was chilling ; but Thomas was not to be deterred, and without
further ado, he left Canterbury with a modest escort of five mounted men-
at-arms for protection from outrage. The way to Winchester in those
days—as in fact now also—lay through the Metropolis. At Rochester the
Archbishop was received in procession by the Bishop and clergy, and so
again apparently on the third day, on reaching Southwark, where he was
met by the Canons of St. Mary's Overey amidst a great concourse of citizens.
For the night, being that of the 18th December, he was entertained at the
quarters of the Bishop of Winchester. Next morning he received a formal
Ordered to order from the Regency to discontinue his visitation tour,
remain at return to Canterbury, and remain there till further orders.
Canterbury. Under protest he obeyed.[1]

John of Salisbury writing at this very time from Canterbury admits that
their prospects were most gloomy, and that they had no hope but in the
prayers of their friends.[2] The Brock family who had been fattening on the
archiepiscopal estates were still established at Saltwood, which had not
been adjudicated to Becket, and was still held for the King. From this
base of operations, distant fifteen miles from Canterbury, they waged
a discreditable war on the Archbishop : they hunted his game ; plundered
a ship laden with wine for him ; and finally in wanton insult, cut off the
tail of a sumpter-horse laden with supplies for his household.[3] On
Christmas Day Thomas once more mounted the pulpit and gave out as his
A last text the words, as they appear in the Vulgate, ' Peace on earth
Sermon. to men of good will.'[4] His tone at first was subdued, even
mournful. He reminded the people of the fate of St. Ælfheah ;
and warned them that ere long Canterbury might witness the martyrdom
of a second Archbishop.[5] Then rising with his theme[6] he excommuni-
cated by name Nigel of Sackville and his curate for retaining
Fresh possession of the church at Harrow ; a priest appointed to
Anathemas. another Canterbury living ; and Ralph and Robert of Brock.[7]
According to one witness as a final climax he ended by denouncing the
Prelates concerned in the coronation of the young King, as excommunicate.
' Accursed of Jesus Christ be all they who shall sow discord between me

---

[1] See W. Cant. I. 105-113; W. fitz S., III. 121-123 ; H. Bosham, 481-433; and
Salisbury's letter, VII. 412.

[2] *Ib.*

[3] See W. Cant., I., 116, 117; W. fitz S., III. 126 ; Bosham, 483; and the letter,
VII. 394.

[4] W. fitz. S. III. 130 ; Luke, ii. 14.

[5] W. fitz S , *sup.*; H. Bosham. III. 484.

[6] " Post priores lacrymas tam ferus, tam indignabundus," H. Bosham, *sup.*

[7] W. Cant., W. fitz S., and H. Bosham, *sup.* Diceto I., 342. Robert of Brock was
the man who mutilated the animal.

K

and my lord the King; blotted out be their memory from the company of the saints.'[1] If these awful words were uttered with reference to the offending Prelates it is plain that what they had done they had done by the King's orders, and of his own determined purpose. It is equally clear that their misdeeds after all only amounted to a breach of ecclesiastical

Crisis. etiquette. The acts of the Brocks, however disgraceful, were matters for the cognisance of an ordinary criminal court. But Becket was determined to keep the law in his own hands, and he paid the penalty. This fresh attack caused the cup of the King's patience to boil over.

Henry, after leading an expedition into Berri in November, in hopes of securing the appointment to the Archbishopric of Bourges, just fallen vacant, had returned to his hunting seat at Bures, near Bayeux, for Christmas. Though sufficiently infuriated by the news of the original delivery of the sentences at Dover, he had nevertheless contented himself with writing to the Pope to protest against Becket's action, and to beg for a suspension of the sentences.[2] At the report of the renewed anathemas

Henry loses self-control. of Christmas Day, as we take it, he lost all self-control, and broke into curses on the worthless servants by whom he was surrounded, who, while eating his bread, could allow their lord to be so bearded by an upstart priest.[3] The hasty words fell on ears only too ready to act on such a hint. Four knights connected with the Royal Household, Reginald fitz Urse, Hugh of Morville, William of Tracy, and

Conspiracy against Becket. one Richard, a Breton, bound themselves by an oath to force Becket to submission in one way or another. Leaving court hastily and in secret, after a smooth and successful crossing, they landed on December 28th, at a creek or inlet that has not been identified. The place is described as situate near Dover, and its name is rendered in Latin as *Portus Canum* (Dogshaven). Probably it should be sought for at or near Hythe or Limpne, the natural landing points for Saltwood, to which place they were bound, and where they spent the night

---

[1] "A Jesu Christo maledicti sint quicunque inter me et dominum meum regem odium et discordias seminabunt;" E. Grim, II. 428; followed by Garnier, p. 173. Grim had gone on a visit to Becket a few days before his death—doubt'ess a Christmas visit—and so presumably heard the sermon. Herbert of Bosham and William of Canterbury must also have heard it; but they omit the denunciation of the Prelates. Of course it was not a formal sentence.

[2] VII. 418. See also the letters of Giles of Evreux, Arnulf of Lisieux, and Rotrou of Rouen to the same effect, 420-426.

[3] See E. Grim, II. 429; H. Bosham, III. 487; and Anon., IV. 69. I take it that the King's final outburst must have been occasioned by the report of some fresh incident, and that could only be the sentences of Christmas Day. The Biographers represent him as goaded to fury by the Prelates. Becket's sermon was preached early in the day; the news might reach Bures on the 26th. The murderers reached England on the 28th. For Henry's utterances as the final occasion of the murder see his own admission at Avranches in 1172, as reported by Herbert of Bosham, VII. 514.

at the Castle.[1]　The King, on hearing of the knights' departure, suspecting mischief, had sent after them in all haste, to arrest their progress, but without success.[2]　Next day, Friday, December 29th, the conspirators gathered a party of supporters, and then rode to Canterbury.　It must have been about a quarter to 3 o'clock p.m. when they reached the gates of the convent buildings.　Dinner was partly over; Becket had retired to his chamber, the domestics being still at table in the hall.[3]　Leaving the bulk of their followers outside, in a house facing the convent gate, to keep a watch on the townspeople,[4] the Four with a few attendants entered the precincts.　Declining refreshment they asked to see the Archbishop. Having been admitted to his presence they seated themselves in front of **Becket and** him, on the floor, among the clergy and monks, Thomas being **the Con-** seated on his bed.　After an awkward pause Becket greeted **spirators.** them in God's name. 'God help thee rather,' was the sarcastic answer, wherewith the Archbishop, with a sudden intuition of what lay before him, coloured up to the roots of his hair.[5]　Fitz Urse, who seemed to take the lead, then said, 'we have somewhat to say unto thee from the King, shall we say it in public or in private? After a moment's consideration Thomas answered ' In public '; and therewith recalled the clergy who previously had been told to leave the apartment.[6]　Reginald then told the Archbishop bluntly that they were come to summon him to appear before his lord the King to answer for his conduct[7] in violating the recent peace by suspending the Prelates who had crowned the young King ; as also by excommunicating the King's ministers and advisers ; the sentences on the Prelates being tantamount, he said, to an attempt to

---

[1] E. Grim, II. 429 ; Gervase, I. 224 ; H. Bosham, III. 487, 488. The last and other writers allege that the conspirators crossed by different ways, but all agree that they met at night at Saltwood.

[2] Grim, *sup.*

[3] E. Grim, II. 430 ; W. fitz S., III. 132. "Circa diei vesperam ;" H. Bosh., *sup.* (he gives the day, wrongly, as the 28th Dec.) " Hora diei erat quasi decima ;" W. fitz S., *sup.* To explain these *data* it has been pointed out that owing to the incorrect state of the Calendar the 29th Dec., 1170 would correspond to the 5th January, New Style, when the sun would rise at 8 7 a.m, and set at 4 5 p.m. Then we are told that vespers were always sung one hour before sunset, that would be a little after 3 p.m. Lastly, with reference to " hora decima " we are told that the mediæval Church divided the periods of light and darkness into 12 hours each of varying length, according to the time of the year. Thus ten-twelfths of the light of a day beginning at 8.7 a.m. and ending at 4.5 p.m. would bring us to 2.40 p m. Thus all the *data* fit in well. See a letter to the *Athenæum*, 21st January. 1899.

[4] W. fitz S., 132.

[5] Grim and fitz S., *sup.* For the sitting on the floor see the Passio of Benedict Becket, II. 1.

[6] E. Grim, 430, 431 ; W. Cant. I. 129 ; W. fitz S., *sup.*

[7] "Adversus dominum tuum . . . operatus es." The homage tie bound a man to consult his lord's interests at all hazards.

discrown the young King.[1] Becket stoutly defended his conduct: he
entertained the best feelings towards the King's son, and would invest him
with three crowns instead of one, and the amplest dominions, if he could:
the Prelates had been sentenced not by him, but by the Pope, and he
alone could absolve them: they might go to the Pope if they pleased; for
himself he was glad to have such a protector (*patronus*) to avenge his
wrongs; as for the officials excommunicated he was bound to punish
injuries done to him; and he appealed to his interlocutors to say if the
King had not, in their presence, given him free leave to do so (*permisit
depravata corrigere*). The knights, however, refused to admit that any
such permission had been given, and in that, no doubt, they were quite
right. Henry had only promised to concert measures of redress with
Becket, not to allow Becket to do as he pleased. Being again pressed to
submit his grievances, if any, to the King, Thomas, repelling a last word
of advice by John of Salisbury,[2] answered that he could not have
recourse to court for every trifle, and, in fact, he had been forbidden to
leave Canterbury; there he intended to remain, and if any injury were
done to Christ's Church the sacerdotal sword would not remain idle.
'Threats,' exclaimed his antagonists, 'you threaten us!'[3] Then with a
final warning they added, 'Mind, thy life is in danger.'[4]

Mutual Defiance. 'Oh,' said he defiantly, 'are ye come to kill me? Try to
frighten somebody else.[5] If all the swords in England were
hanging over my head ye would still find me fighting the Lord's battle
against you hand to hand, foot to foot.'[6]

The conspirators then retired to arm themselves, and make all safe for
the prosecution of their work. As they went out they charged the little
crowd of clergy and others who had gathered at the sound of the voices
raised in altercation not to allow Becket to escape.[7]

To harmonise accounts that do not seem to be altogether in accord, we
must suppose the conspirators to have gone out to their men stationed
outside, calling them to arms. The convent gate was then seized and
secured, to prevent interruption from without;[8] while the knights threw
off their robes, and girt on their weapons of offence; this they did in the

---

[1] E. Grim, 431. The charge of excommunicating ministers and advisers of the King
clearly pointed to the case of Nigel of Sackville and Brock, sentenced on Christmas Day.
For the peremptory summons of Becket to court see also W. Cant., 129.

[2] Fitz S., 134.

[3] "Ad hauc vocem . . . exclamant Minæ! Minæ!" W. Cant.

[4] "In capitis tui periculum locutus es;" E. Grim.

[5] "Quærite qui vos fugiat."

[6] "Pede ad pedem;" E. Grim and fitz S.; both have the words.

[7] See W. Cant., I. 129, 130; E. Grim, II. 431-433; W. fitz S., III. 132-135. All
three were present. Herbert of Bosham was absent, having been sent to France on a
mission on the 26th December.

[8] W. fitz S., 136.

court-yard, under the branches of a spreading mulberry tree.[1]   Returning
to the hall they found the door closed against them.   But Robert of
Brock, being well acquainted with the premises, led them into the ad-
joining garden or orchard, where they found an external staircase leading

Convent Buildings broken into. up to a side door.   The steps were broken down, and under
repair; but the workmen's ladder, and workmen's tools, found
there, enabled them to climb up, and break through the door.[2]
Other accounts speak of clambering in through a window.[3]   In short they
reached the hall,[4] and from it the chamber where Becket had been left.

In spite of all remonstrances the Archbishop had remained undauntedly
in his place, refusing to stir.   But when the crash of splintered wood-
work, and the patter of flying footsteps reached their ears, the terrified
attendants, overcoming all resistance, insisted on his taking refuge in
the Cathedral.   Vespers had begun,[5] and he was bound to attend.   To
reach the sanctuary in safety as things now stood, with the enemy
attacking the hall behind them, they had to descend to the cloisters,
their access lying by a door that of late[6] had been kept locked.   The
question was, would they be able to open it?   Providentially the lock
gave way at a touch, and the party, pressing through the cloisters, entered
the North arm of the Western transept of the church.[7]

Becket refused to allow the transept door to be closed behind him:

Becket in the Cathedral. the house of prayer was not to be turned into a fortress.
Moving slowly and reluctantly, he had ascended but a few
of the side-steps that at that time led up from the transept
to the choir, when the knights rushed in, flourishing drawn swords
in their right hands, and battle-axes in their left hands.   The transept
at that time had a central pillar supporting the vaulting of the roof.[8]
This, standing between the doorway and the choir-steps, would, for a
moment, hide the Archbishop from their view.   Passing some to the
right and some to the left of the pillar, they shouted out, 'Where is
that traitor Thomas Becket?   Where is the Archbishop?'   Proudly

---

[1] "In ipso pro-aulo;" W. fitz S.; " Sub moro ramosa;" W. Cant.; "Prope hortum;"
H. Bosh.

[2] W. Cant., 130; E. Grim, 433; W. fitz S., 137.   Grim's "ligneum obstaculum"
I take to be the side-door; and so also the broken *paries* of fitz Stephen.

[3] "Per fenestras," H. Bosham.   "Rupta fenestra," Anon., No. 2, IV. 130.   A garden
entrance might be spoken of as a window.

[4] So W. fitz S., 137, clearly, and W. Cant., ' perscrutato palatio."

[5] Circa 3.15 p.m.   See above p. 131 note.

[6] As fitz Stephen speaks of descending from the hall to the church (per gradus
descendere), 137, there must have been a descent from the chamber also.

[7] Grim, 434, 435; W. Cant., 131; W. fitz S., *sup.*; "l'ele del Nort," Garnier, p.
192; "Ad partem ecclesiae aquilonarem," Anon., IV. 76.

[8] "Ad medium postem cui testudinis onus innititur," W. Cant., 132.   See also R.
Willis, *Canterbury*, and Dean Stanley's *Memorials of Canterbury*, p. 86 plan.

repelling the taunt, as he had repelled it at Northampton, Thomas turned to bay, descending the steps. 'Here am I, no traitor, but a priest of the Lord.'[1]   He confronted his adversaries between the central pillar and the altar of St. Benedict, an apsidal chapel forming the East side

The Conspirators' Ultimatum of the transept.[2]   Once more the Knights thundered out their ultimatum, literally at the point of the sword. 'Recall the sentences; absolve the excommunicates, and restore the Bishops to their offices'!   The answer as ever was, 'They have made

Rejected. me no amends, I will not absolve them.' 'Then take thy deserts and die, or come with us.' Thomas calmly answered that he was ready to die for his Lord and the liberty of the Church; but he charged them in the name of the Almighty to touch none of his men.[3] A desperate struggle to drag the Archbishop from the church ensued, the knights wishing perhaps to avoid the crime of sacrilege; perhaps only wanting to carry off Thomas and put him in bonds,[4] or force him to appear before the King.   But he laid hold of the pillar, roughly repelling fitz Urse with insulting language. 'Touch me not Reginald, vile pander,[5] thou who owest me homage and subjection.' It appears that fitz Urse at one time had been in Becket's service, and by him had been introduced to the King.[6]   'I owe thee nothing as against my

Murder of the Archbishop. lord the King,' cried the infuriated ruffian, brandishing his sword over his victim's head. Feeling that the end was come, Thomas folded his hands in prayer, and, bending his head, commended his spirit to God, the Blessed Virgin, and St. Denis—a French Saint.   A stroke from Reginald's sword slashed off part of his scalp, and severely wounded Edward Grim, his biographer, in the arm. This young monk, an Englishman and a native of Cambridge,[7] who had joined the Archbishop but a few days before, was bravely holding him in his arms, shielding him, and helping him to resist.   Thomas withstood a second cut on the head; at a third, dealt apparently by William of Tracy, he collapsed, while the Breton Richard gave him the *coup de grâce*, cleaving his skull as he lay on the floor with such violence that the sword was broken on the pavement.[8]

[1] *Id.* "Occurrit iis ex gradu quem pro parte ascenderat"; J. Salisby., II. 319, "Occurrit e gradu quo delatus fuerat a monachis"; Grim, 435; W. fitz S. 138-140.

[2] Grim, 436. See Willis and Stanley, *sup.*

[3] So Grim, 436; see also W. fitz S., 131, and W. Cant., 133.

[4] So the Anon., IV. 128.

[5] "Lenonem eum appellans"; Grim. William of Canterbury paraphrases the offensive word by "vir abominabilis."

[6] W. Cant.

[7] "Anglicus natu"; W. Cant., 134; H. Bosham, 498.   As the latter speaks of Cambridge as a 'castellum' we may infer that the town was still comprised within the walls of the old Roman camp.

[8] See E. Grim, 437; W. Cant., *sup.*; W. fitz S., 142; Anon., IV. 139.   Generally

The tragic day ended with the plunder of the archiepiscopal palace. Everything of value was carried off, including books, charters, even old Papal privileges. The horses found in the stables were seized, and the whole household turned out of doors. Papal Bulls were sent to the King as his share of the spoils.[1]

In the Cathedral, when the first panic had subsided, a crowd soon gathered round the remains of the fallen Archbishop. The **His Burial.** corpse was placed on a bier, and laid out before the high altar in contemplation of burial with all due ceremony. But in the morning, at a warning from the Brocks, Thomas was buried quietly in the crypt without Mass, the church having been desecrated by the spilling of blood. It was then discovered that he wore not only a penitential shirt of hair (*cilicium*), but also tightly fitting drawers of the same, both foul with vermin. It was also found that he had on him a monk's gown, over the *cilicium*, and under his regular canon's vestments.[2] "St. Thomas of Canterbury" thoroughly deserved the supreme post of honour to which he has been raised by Rome, and those who **His Policy and Conduct as Primate.** take their inspiration from Rome. An undoubted martyr, but no true saint, he fought and fell in the cause of sacerdotalism pure and simple. The ascendency of the clergy in matters temporal was the ultimate end for which he strove. He would have subjected England to a virtual hierarchy, of all known forms of government perhaps the very worst. No sense of patriotism, no regard for the cause of the poor, for the advancement of education, or even of religion, except as a resultant from clerical domination, can be traced in his words or acts. Fighting what might be supposed to be a spiritual cause, and with spiritual weapons, he conducted the struggle in a thoroughly secular spirit. With all his Biblical jargon he fought as a politician, and the leader of a political party, and such but for his end would have been the unanimous verdict of History. No man was ever less disposed to do justice to the position of an adversary than Thomas Becket; while on his part personal motives, and personal considerations generally are much too perceptible. We cannot but admire his courage, constancy,

the reader may compare the accounts of Herbert of Bosham (written fifteen years later), III. 491-508; of Garnier, 178-190; and of the Anonymous writer, IV. 69-77, all compounded from the earlier narratives. Grim clearly attributes the first blow to fitz Urse; so does Wm. of Canterbury in his narrative; but on the next page he suggests that as Tracy subsequently boasted of having cut off John of Salisbury's arm, he perhaps was the man who wounded Grim; l. 133, 134; see also H. Bosh., 493, 498. The broken point of the sword was preserved as a relic. J. Morris, *Relics of St. Thomas.*

[1] J. Salisb., II. 320; E. Grim, 439, 440; W. fitz S., III. 144; H. Bosh., 513; and the letter, VII. 466, 467.

[2] J. Salisb., II. 321; E. Grim, 441, 442; W. fitz S., III. 146-149; H. Bosham. 519-521.

independence, and integrity. His determination of purpose eventually bent all wills to his own. As for his inner convictions we must bear in mind that his views as to the supremacy and indefensibility of Church rights were considerably exalted after his accession to the Primacy. Modern opinion must be shocked at the recklessness with which he could consign human souls (as he believed) to everlasting perdition, on grounds that to us seem trivial. Such, however, was mediæval Christianity; and in Becket's mind nothing was trivial in which he was personally concerned.

Miracles wrought through invocation of the martyr St. Thomas soon **Miracles.** began to be noised abroad; beginning in fact three days after his death, when the wife of a Sussex Knight recovered her eye-sight on pronouncing him 'a precious martyr to Christ.'[1] Within a very few years if not months two bulky records of reported wonders had been compiled at Canterbury.[2] On 21st February 1173 his name **Canonization.** was inscribed by Alexander III. on the authentic Calendar of Saints.[3] But popular opinion had canonized him from the day of his death.

For the King the consequences of the crime seemed likely to be disastrous, and it certainly wrecked his ecclesiastical policy. It put him out of court with the public opinion of Europe, gave every handle to **Outcry against Henry.** his enemies, and placed the game as it were in their hands. Indignant calls for vengeance were sounded on every side.[4] To show his horror of the deed and his sense of the possible consequences he shut himself up for three days, refusing to see anybody.[5] William of Sens, perhaps Becket's most thorough-going supporter, applying the Pope's mandates of the previous year to present circumstances, took it on him to lay Henry's Continental dominions under Interdict (25th January, 1171). But the Norman clergy refused to recognise the sentence. Archbishop Rotrou entered an immediate appeal, and, accompanied by the Bishops of Worcester, and Evreux, and by Richard Barre and others, started for Italy.[6] The end of it was, as we shall see, that after the usual Papal threats, and the usual amount of diplomatic fencing, Henry was reconciled to the Church on terms costing him little beyond personal humiliation and apology.

One word as to the subsequent careers of the murderers. And here

---

[1] See *Becket*, II. 37, 440.

[2] See these collections, one by Benedict, Prior of Canterbury, and afterwards Abbot of Peterborough, *Becket*, II. 1–281; the other by the Biographer William of Canterbury, I. 136–546. On the whole subject see Dr. Abbot, *St. Thomas His Life and Miracles*, 1898.

[3] *Becket*, VII. 544.

[4] See the letters to the Pope of King Louis, Theobald of Blois, etc., VII. 428–436, and 446–460.

[5] See the letters of Arnulf of Lisieux to the Pope, VII. 438; Henry's own letter, 440, and Bened. P., I. 14.

[6] See the letters, VII. 440–446.

we get an illustration of the practical working of the 'liberty' for which Becket contended. Cases affecting the clergy were to be decided in clerical courts, and in none other. The assassination of an Archbishop **Impunity of the Murderers.** was a case affecting the clergy, and so on Thomas' own principle the perpetrators could only be arraigned before an ecclesiastical tribunal, with excommunication as the maximum penalty that could be imposed.[1] Thus clerical immunity when pushed to its logical conclusion would involve clerical outlawry. But whatever the cause may have been no attempt was made to interfere with the culprits. Without orders from the King no Justice could move in such a matter[2]; and Henry could not in conscience take any proceedings. The men however finding that their action was disavowed at court retired to Knaresborough Castle, a place in Morville's keeping, and there remained for some time in seclusion.[3] According to monastic report Henry sent them to the Pope, who ordered them to expiate their crime by a pilgrimage to Holy Land, where they died, Tracy succumbing to illness in Italy on the way out.[4] Of this story the only bit that has **Their subsequent Lives.** been substantiated is that Tracy did go as a penitent to the Papal court[5]; and that he went on to Calabria, where, presumably in illness, he made a grant of lands to Canterbury for the good of his soul and that of St. Thomas. But he lived to return to England, and became Justiciar of Normandy, 1174—1176.[6] As for Hugh of Morville, whose chief seat was at Burgh on Sands, he had been an Itinerant Justice in Cumberland in 1169–70, but was not subsequently reappointed.[7] Apparently he lived till 1202–1203, when the wardship of his daughter and co-heiress Johanna was sold to William Brewer for 500 marks.[8] Fitz Urse made over his estates in Somerset and Thanet partly to his brother Robert fitz Urse, and partly to the Knights of St. John; and then disappeared. The family however lived on in Somersetshire, their patronymic eventually assuming the modern shape of Fisher (Filsours, Fyshour, Fisher).[9]

[1] See the circular of Archbishop Richard, Becket's successor, to his suffragans, deploring the fact that the perpetrators of the recent murder of a priest could not be adequately punished, and urging a reduction of ecclesiastical pretensions; Peter of Blois, *Epp.*, I. 217.

[2] See the complaint, *Becket*, IV. 150 (Lansdowne MS. f. 398).

[3] Ben. P. I. 13; Pipe Roll, 17 Henry II., 63

[4] W. Newb. I. 163; H. Bosham, III. 335-338.

[5] So Bosham's letter, VII. 511.

[6] Stanley, *sup.* 108-112, and the charters there referred to.

[7] Pipe Roll, 16 H. II., p. 33.

[8] Pipe Roll 4 John, f. 18; Foss, Judges, I. 279.

[9] Stanley, *sup.*, and Collinson, *Somersets*, III. 487.

CHAPTER VIII

HENRY II. (*continued*)

A.D. 1170-1172

Early Relations of England with Ireland—Social state of the Island—Interference invited by Dermot King of Leinster—Landings of Welsh Adventurers and of Richard Earl of Pembroke ("Strongbow")—Reductions of part of the East coast of Ireland—Expedition of Henry to Ireland

OF intercourse between Great Britain and the Sister Isle, the reader as yet has heard but little, and that little at scattered intervals. Most interesting was the successful co-operation of Irish missionaries in the work of converting the Anglo-Saxons to Christianity. Mission work was that for which the poetic and enthusiastic temperament of the sons of Erin, and their wonderful gifts of speech, specially fitted them.[1] Later in time we had Ireland becoming a base for Wicking attacks on England;[2] and later still an occasional refuge for magnates in trouble;[3] while of commercial intercourse the chief point noticed was a nefarious trade in slaves, exported from Bristol and Chester.[4] A step towards the establishment of ecclesiastical relations was taken in 1074, when Godred the Norse King of Dublin sent one Patrick, a priest, to be consecrated as his Bishop by the hands of Lanfranc. Patrick made profession of obedience to Lanfranc, "and for the next seventy-eight years the bishops of Dublin were suffragans not of Armagh but of Canterbury."[5] In 1096 the men of Waterford, another Wicking settlement, followed the example of King Godred by taking for their Bishop one Malchus consecrated by Anselm.[6] But in 1152 the whole Irish Church was reorganised under the four Archbishoprics of Armagh, Dublin, Tuam, and Cashel, by Cardinal John Paparo, in the Synod of Kells, as already mentioned.[7]

[1] See *Foundations* I. 186-196.
[2] *Id.* 276, 284, 295, etc.
[3] *Id.* 455; II. 64.
[4] *Id.* II. 146, 202, 247.
[5] Norgate, *Angevin Kings*, II. 88; *Foundations*, II. 166.
[6] Norgate, II. 89.
[7] *Foundations*, II. 439.

Of Old Ireland and its institutions the reader has had a sketch mainly
based on the evidence of the *Senchus Mor*, that precious record of
early Aryan society.   But the work in question, a curious mixture of
ancient texts and modern glosses and commentaries, was probably not
compiled before the period of which we are now treating;[1] and therefore
the latest social phases there described should be applicable to the
12th century.   Thus we take it that by that time Primitive

Social State of Ireland Feudalism had probably run its course, that is to say that
society had reached the stage implied in the maxim that
to every tenant his landlord (*flath*) is as a king.[2]   But we must recognise
the fact that, apart from the mensal lands or public endowments of the
kings, chiefs, clergy, Brehons, and the like, the ownership of land was
vested rather in the family than in the individual.[3]   Generally speaking
but little advance on the most primitive conditions had been achieved.
Personal ties, and landed relations were still the only bonds of society.

Of social organisation, as we understand it, as little as ever
No Organisation can be discovered.   There are no regular political or
legislative assemblies, only turbulent fairs, or casual conferences—there are no laws, no courts of judicature, no judges with
No Law. any coercive authority.   The so-called Brehon Laws were
but customs sanctioned by old usage, to which right-minded
persons were expected to conform ; but if a headstrong individual
refused to be bound by precedent there was no appeal but to the sword,
or to speak more accurately the battle-axe.[4]   A reference to a Brehon
judge was simply a reference to arbitration.   Social ostracism was the
only penalty that could be called down on the head of the man who
rejected the Brehon's decision.   Of any sort of police the
No Police or Currency. country was wholly innocent ; and coinage, except in the
towns occupied by the Norse, or Ostmen as they were called
in Ireland, was equally unknown.   Cattle, and, for large sums, ounces of
gold, were the only currency.   But we notice with satisfaction that the
female slave was no longer a standard unit of value.   On the other hand
the incestuous connexions that scandalised the Roman clergy proved
that Christianity had failed entirely to eradicate primitive polyandry.[5]   Of

[1] The oldest MS. only dates about 1350.

[2] *Foundations*, I. 16, 17.

[3] *Id.* and p. 19.   The laymen enjoying ecclesiastical privileges of whom we hear
should be Brehons ; Giraldus Cambrensis, *Topographia Hibernica*, V. 171. (Dymock,
Rolls, Series No. 21.)

[4] For the battle-axe as the favourite weapon see Girald ; *sup.* ; and 165.

[5] See *Foundations* I. 9 ; and for the later state of things Giraldus, V. 164 ; the
letter of Anselm to the Irish King, *Epp.* No. 142 ; Migne, vol. 159, C. 173 ; the
life of St. Malachi by St. Bernard, Migne, vol. 182, C. 1100 ; and the letter of
Alexander III. to Henry, *Liber Niger Scacc*, I. 45, and *Fœdera*, I. 45.

Kings there was still no lack, but the title was not quite so freely granted as in earlier days. We no longer have village kings, but kings of the four Provinces of Ulster, Leinster, Munster, and Connaught, with, as of old, a High-King (*Ardri*), the theoretic over-lord of the whole Island rising over them. But the position of this dignitary gave him little more than an honorary precedence. The mischievous custom of Tanistry still prevailed, that is to say the election during the life of each king or chief of an appointed successor, to stand as it were on the steps of the throne, watching an opportunity of getting rid of him. The political relations of these princes were of the most unsettled and in fact hostile character. The apologist of Hibernian institutions frankly tells us that the Kings "fiercely battled like bulls for the mastery of the herd"; and again that "a normal Irish King had to clear his way through the provinces, battle-axe in hand, gathering hostages by the strength of his arm."[1] No wonder that the Irish annals present a continuous record of strife and bloodshed. "The anarchy of the Irish State was reflected in that of the Church. . . . It had in fact scarcely advanced beyond the primitive missionary stage; . . . the bishops were for the most part merely heads of ever-shifting missionary stations."[2] Their dependence on the abbots of the monasteries, a system peculiar to Ireland, had deprived them of the status and authority elsewhere enjoyed by the Episcopate. The payment of tithes was unknown; the endowments of the Church had been largely invaded by lay impropriators; and so the clergy, high and low, were left almost wholly dependent on the fees and offerings of their flocks. The general character of the priesthood, however, is praised by Giraldus, who finds little else to eulogise in Ireland. Unfortunately he adds that excessive fasting by day led to rather hard drinking at nights.[3]

Kingly Rule.

The Church.

Averse to exertion, except under the spur of excitement, and intolerant of discipline or restraint the Irishman has always loved a free, casual, hand to mouth, out of doors sort of existence. Their dwellings in the 12th century were still built of wicker-work and mud, stone being reserved for ecclesiastical edifices; their agriculture was most primitive, the climate in fact being better suited for pasturage than for the raising of grain crops; they had few fruit trees, no mines, no manufactures; the chief article of importation that we hear of was wine, brought from Poitou in return for hides and wool. Defensive armour was unknown; the battle-axe, ready for use at the slightest provocation, was constantly carried in the hand. The entire equipment of a horseman was a rope bit and a switch. For clothing we hear of the *phalanga* or *falach*, a plaid or

Domestic Arts.

[1] Standish O'Grady, *English Hist. Review* IV. 286, 292.
[2] Norgate, *Angevin Kings*, II. 91.
[3] V. 172.

blanket, trimmed with fringes and hanging down to the heels. Under this, presumably, they wore a tunic or kilt, and below that the breech-hose or hose breeches (*braccæ caligatæ, seu caligæ braccatæ*) described by the Romans in Gaul ; while the head and shoulders were protected by a hood that came down to the elbows, as seen on sepulchral monuments.[1]

Music and Poetry. But if an orderly life and domestic comfort had no charms for the Irish, we must in justice to them remember their musical, literary, and artistic gifts. The beauty and delicacy of their MSS. are well known. Their monumental crosses in size and richness of ornamentation greatly surpass those of England, Wales, or Scotland. The "magic" of their legends and tales has captivated the world,[2] while Giraldus, who has so few good words for them, declares their music incomparable, both for the sweetness and brightness of the tunes, and for the technical skill of the performers.[3]

Henry's Designs on Ireland. The reader is aware that early in his reign, namely in the year 1155, Henry had entertained the idea of invading and conquering Ireland in order to provide an appanage for his brother William ; that the English Pope Adrian IV. had graciously sanctioned the scheme ; but that it had been dropped owing to the objections of the Empress Matilda.[4] Eleven years later Henry was pressed to intervene in the affairs of the island, the invitation of course coming from an Irishman. During the century the position of High-King (*Ardri*) or Over-lord of all Ireland had been battled for between the O'Neals of Ulster, descendants of the hero-King Nial of the Nine Hostages, and the O'Briens of Munster, representatives of the famous Brian Boromha, killed at Clontarf in 1014. But in 1166, at the death of Murtogh O'Lochlainn of Ulster, the Lordship of Ireland fell to the King of Connaught, Roderic O'Connor (Ruaidhri Ua'Conchobhair). The Ostmen of Dublin acknowledged him ; and so did all the princes of Southern Ireland, including Dermot MacMurrough (Diarmid MacMurchadha), King of Leinster,[5] or

[1] Girald., V. 150-153.

[2] As a specimen of the Irish style of the period see the poetic diction of the letter to Earl Strongbow, below p. 146. 'The storks and swallows, the summer birds, have come ; they have come and gone again at the blasts from the North. But neither east wind nor west wind hath brought thy long-wished for presence,' etc.

[3] "In musicis . . . præ omni natione quam vidimus incomparabiliter instructa est," etc., V. 153-160. Their instruments were the harp (cithara, clairseach), and the tabor (tympanum).

[4] See above, p. 7.

[5] Ireland of old had been divided into five Provinces, originally Ulster (Uladh), Meath (Midhe), Leinster (Laighin), Munster (Mumha), and Connaught (Connacht). Meath however had been taken out of the list, and appropriated to the *Ardri*, as his mensal territory, and so after that the fifth Province was made out by splitting Munster into two, namely Desmond (Deas Mumha) or South Munster, and Thomond (Tuadh Mumha) or North Munster ; literally Right-hand Munster and Left-hand Munster, the Celts reckoning the points of the compass with their faces to the East. (Giraldus V. 31 *Song*

more properly of the Hy Kinselagh, his territory lying mostly in the modern county of Wexford to the East of the river Barrow, and on the whole corresponding to the modern diocese of Ferns.   This man however had a bitter enemy in Tiernan O'Rourke (Tighearnan UaRuairic) Under King of Breifny (Leitrim and Cavan) whose wife Devorgil (Dearbhforgail) Dermot had carried off fourteen years before.   In other ways too Dermot had misgoverned and made himself unpopular, and the injured Tiernan, after years of watching, at last found an avenger in the new High-King Roderic who joining forces with him fairly drove Dermot out of Ireland.

An Opening. Sailing from Cork he landed at Bristol, and after some stay there eventually made his way to Henry's court in Normandy (1166).[1] The King took his homage, but, engrossed as he was with his quarrel with Becket, and other affairs, all that he could do for Dermot was to give him a letter authorising him to enlist followers among his, Henry's, subjects, English, Norman, Welsh, or Scotch.[2]

Dermot returned to Bristol, where he fell in with the famous "Strongbow,"[3] Richard of Clare, second Earl of Pembroke, but commonly styled Earl of Striguil, now Chepstow,[4] that doubtless being his chief seat.   The two soon came to terms, Dermot promising Richard the hand of his **Dermot and Strongbow.** eldest daughter with the succession to the crown.[5]   From Bristol the exiled king went over to South Wales, where he met with a friendly reception from the Prince Rhys ap Gruffudd, and his cousin the Bishop of St. David's, David son of the Lady Nest by Gerald of Windsor, the former Constable of Pembroke.[6]   In fact Dermot's appearance helped to solve a difficulty by which the Bishop and his family were much disturbed.   David's uterine brother Robert, son of Nest by her second husband Stephen, Constable of Aberteivy or Cardigan, a post in which Robert had succeeded his father, was at the time a prisoner in the hands of Rhys, who demanded as the price of his liberation the renunciation of his allegiance to Henry II., and the adoption of the cause of Wales as against that of England, a hazardous step, that Robert naturally hesitated to take. Through the mediation of the Bishop and of another brother, Maurice,

---

of Dermot, etc., notes, 256, 289).   The modern names Ulster, Leinster, and Munster appear to have been formed by appending the Scandinavian suffix "ster" to the native appellations.

[1] Giraldus, V. 225, 226.   For the earlier events see the Four Masters (O'Donovan) and the other authorities cited by Miss Norgate, II. 85-91 and 97 ; also *Song of Dermot and the Earl*, 3-21 ; (G. H. Orpen, 1892).   [2] See the letter, Girald., 227.

[3] "Strangbo," annals Loch Cé, I. 142 (W. M. Hennessy, Rolls Series No. 54) ; Chron. Melrose A.D. 1170 "Stranboue," where however the name seems applied to his father Gilbert the first Earl.

[4] It appears that strictly Striguil was the name of the castle, and Chepstow that of the village that grew up beside it, but that in course of time the latter name prevailed; Archæol. XXIX. 25 (Cokayne).   [5] Giraldus, V. 228, *Song*, pp. 26-29.

[6] See *Foundations* II. 275, 339 ; and the Table at the end of this chapter.

Rhys was induced to grant Robert his liberty on condition of his leaving Wales for Ireland. What else Rhys was to get does not appear; but Dermot concluded a treaty with Maurice and Robert, promising them the

Welsh Allies. town of Wexford, and two cantreds of land in return for their support. Dermot then returned to Ireland with a small band of men-at-arms and archers raised in Pembrokeshire, and led by one Richard fitz Godibert.[1]

Roderick of Connaught and Tiernan of Breifny soon appeared to show fight. Two petty battles were fought at Killiestown, in the modern county Carlow, with doubtful results. A pacification ensued. Dermot was allowed to retain part of his territory on condition of giving hostages for allegiance to his over-lord Roderic; he was also required to make compensation to the injured King of Breifny by paying him a proper fine (*eineach*) for the abduction of his wife. The sum demanded is given as the large amount of one hundred ounces of gold, equivalent to £600.[2] Peace was maintained all through the year 1168, and on till May, 1169,[3] when at last Robert the

Landing in Ireland. son of Stephen, otherwise fitz Stephen, landed at Bannow, a little to the North of Waterford, with three ships, conveying some 90 men-at-arms, and 300 archers. Next day a further force, said to have been raised in the Flemish district of Ros, reached the shore under the lead of one Maurice of Prendergast. He brought ten men-at-arms and a considerable body of archers, but all conveyed in two ships. Among the men of position who joined the expedition we have Hervé of Montmorency, a man of broken fortunes sent to represent Strongbow's interests, and described as his uncle;[4] also of a notable band of kinsmen, namely, Meiler fitz Henry, Milo, son of Bishop David, and Robert of Barry,[5] brother to the historian Gerald, all of them descendants of the Lady Nest.[6] Thus the enterprise had quite a family character that would account for the concurrence of Prince Rhys.

As men born in an atmosphere of border warfare, holding their possessions at the point of the sword, the adventurers were eminently fitted for the work in hand.

---

[1] August 1157; Giraldus V. 229. *Song*, 30-32.

[2] Four Masters A.D. 1167; for the system of fines see *Foundations* I. 13.

[3] I agree with Miss Norgate in thinking that the language of Giraldus, p. 230, suggests that Robert came over in 1168; but that there is no distinct evidence for this date, nothing to set against the precise 1169 of the Four Masters.

[4] " Patruus "; Giraldus, *sup.* " Avunculus "; Gervase I. 234. Hervé was apparently the Earl's half-uncle, being the son of his grandmother Adeliz of Claremont by her second husband, a Montmorency. See Round, *Feudal England*, 523; and the Nat. Dict. Biog.

[5] Giraldus, with his usual classical affectation, always gives the family name as " Barrensis." Two charters cited to me by Mr. Round show that they signed " De Barry." I would connect the name with Barry on the coast of Glamorgan, where the ruins of an old castle may be seen; Lewis, *Topog. Dict.*

[6] See Table at the end of this chapter.

The Irish King having joined his friends an attack on the rebellious town of Wexford was at once taken in hand. The place resisted all assaults the first day, but on the morrow it submitted. In accordance with the compact Wexford was made over to Robert fitz Stephen and Maurice fitz Gerald, Hervé receiving two cantreds of land.[1]

Capture of Wexford.

After a pause of three weeks at Ferns, to rest and recruit, Dermot led his forces, swelled by native levies estimated as 3,000 strong, to invade Ossory (Osraigh), or the parts of Leinster lying to the West of the river Barrow, and corresponding in the main with the county Kilkenny and Queen's county of the present day. This district was ruled by one Donnell Mac Donough (Domhnall Mac Donnchad), a bitter enemy to Dermot, whose son had been blinded by him some years before.[2]

The rebel chief took up a position in a pass on the line of Dermot's advance, with his front protected by triple earthworks and a stockade. But the Anglo-Normans by dint of resolute fighting carried the entrenchments and scattered the Irish. Ossory was then overrun and plundered. The only other engagement recorded was an attack on Dermot's rear, as he was leaving Ossory, and approaching the Barrow. His army had to traverse a wooded valley before reaching an open plain where cavalry could act. But the enemy, apparently, delayed their attack until the men-at-arms were practically clear of the wood, and able to charge with effect; this they did, driving the men of Ossory back upon a party of archers who had been left behind in ambuscade. Two hundred heads were laid at Dermot's feet in the evening.[3] But Donnell had not given in his submission; nor had the Prince or Under-King of Offelan (Ui Faelain)[4] done so, nor yet the men of Dublin; nor O'Toole (Ua Tuathail) of Glendalough (co. Wicklow). Successive raids at intervals therefore had to be undertaken from Ferns against Offelan and Glendalough;[5] as well as a second inroad into Ossory. Again we hear that Donnell took up a defensive position in a pass, by a river, with trenches and stockades both in front and rear. For two days he held his own against the assaults of Dermot's Irishmen: on the third day the English were brought up, and then Donnell broke and fled to the South. The name of the locality is given as Achadhur, now Freshford in Kilkenny, and the actual site of the struggle has been placed on an affluent of the Nore, between Freshford and Kilkenny.[6]

War against Ossory.

---

[1] Giraldus, 230-233; *Song*, 34-39.

[2] Giraldus, V. 233. See *Song*, notes, 267.

[3] *Song*, 40-59; Giraldus, 233, 234. Dermot probably entered Ossory by the Pass of Gowran and the Valley of the Nore. He returned to the Barrow at Leighlin, having probably crossed the wilderness of the Dinin. See *Song*, note Orpen, 267.

[4] "The north-eastern part of the present co. Kildare, including Naas"; Orpen, *sup.*, 269.

[5] *Song*, 64-69.   [6] *Song*, 72-79 and notes, 270.

The current of Dermot's success now received a certain check through the desertion of Maurice of Prendergast and his party. They asked to be allowed to return to Wales, thinking perhaps that their stipulated term of service had expired. Dermot sent orders to Wexford to withhold all shipping from them, and detain them. The result was that they made terms with Ossory, joined his camp, and began raiding Kinselagh.[1] Then Roderic of Connaught, and Tiernan of Breifny, and the men of Dublin gathering in strength, made a combined advance against Dermot. Efforts were made to seduce his allies, and when those overtures were rejected by fitz Stephen, they endeavoured to persuade Dermot to dismiss him. The end of it was that another treaty was concluded, Dermot recognising the suzerainty of Roderic, and giving up his son and heir Conor (Conchobhar) as hostage.[2]

An Irish Coalition.

The loss suffered by the defection of Prendergast was now counterbalanced by the arrival of a fresh force under Maurice fitz Gerald, son of Nest, half brother to Robert fitz Stephen, and progenitor of all the Irish Fitz Geralds. He brought ten men-at-arms, thirty horse-archers, and about a hundred archers on foot, all conveyed in two ships.[3] With this reinforcement Dermot resumed active operations. First we hear of an incursion into Leix (Laeighis)[4] to succour the King of Kings, O'More (Ua Mordha), who had been attacked by Donnell of Ossory and Prendergast. At Dermot's approach they retired; while O'More gave hostages for his submission to Leinster.[5] Then we have an attack on the city of Dublin, in the course of which much territory was wasted, until the citizens made terms and did homage.[6] An indirect gain was the retirement of the hostile Prendergast, who, finding that the men of Ossory were plotting against his life took "French leave" of his employers, and slipping away from Kilkenny by night, made his way to Waterford, and so got back to Wales.[7] Lastly, either in the course of the winter or of the ensuing spring (1170) fitz Stephen was sent to Limerick to assist Dermot's son-in-law Donnell O'Brien (Domhnall Ua Briain) King of Thomond or North Munster in throwing off the yoke of Roderick of Connaught.[8]

Landing of Maurice fitz Gerald.

Dermot had now regained all that he had lost. But with success his views had expanded. He now aspired to the supremacy of Ireland. But

---

[1] *Song*, 80-87; Giraldus, 237. Kinselagh, as already stated, was the part of Leinster immediately subject to Dermot.

[2] Giraldus, 238-244; *Four Masters*.

[3] Giraldus, 244; *Song*, 86. The date of the landing seems uncertain.

[4] Leix is the district round Maryborough in the present Queen's County.

[5] *Song*, 88-95. Nothing of this is given by Giraldus.

[6] Giraldus, 245.

[7] *Song*, 94-103.

[8] Giraldus, 245; *Four Masters*, A.D. 1170; *Song*, notes, 273.

L

for that enterprise further reinforcements would be needed. A letter couched in beautiful language was addressed to Strongbow, to remind him of the compact which he seemed to have forgotten. 'We have watched the storks and the swallows. The summer birds have come; they have come, and gone again; but neither east wind nor west wind hath brought thy wished for presence.'[1] With respect to the Earl it is clear that in spite of his high connexions he was in difficulties. One writer tells us that he was deep in debt.[2] It is clear from the account of Giraldus that he was not in the enjoyment at any rate of some of the estates to which he was entitled by descent;[3] while from other sources we expressly hear of his being under forfeiture;[4] and Giraldus again tells us that he pressed the King either to reinstate him, or give him leave to retrieve his fortunes elsewhere; and that Henry 'ironically' bade him go.[5] With reference to the surname "Strongbow," by which he has been commonly distinguished, it appears that he did not earn the designation himself, but inherited it from his father Gilbert,[6] and that he had no other right to the appellation than that of descent. He is described as tall, slight, fair, and delicate in appearance; tactful and conciliatory, ready to take advice, and in all matters of importance led by others.[7] The requisite permission having been obtained Richard began his preparations in earnest. In anticipation of his own coming he sent over another descendant of the Welsh Princess, namely Raymond surnamed the Stout (*Le Gros*),[8] the son of William eldest son of Nest by Gerald of Windsor. About May 1st, 1170, Raymond landed, a little to the east of Waterford, a city still the seat of a Norse or "Ostman" settlement. His force mustered ten men-at-arms and seventy archers. Their first care was to fortify a camp on a cliff, and well it was that they did so, because their indiscriminate plundering raised the whole country against them. A grand assault on the camp was signally defeated, but the victors disgraced themselves by butchering seventy prisoners in cold blood.[9]

A Poetical Appeal

Raymond fitz William

---

[1] "Cigonias et hirundines observavimus; venerunt aves æstivæ; venerunt et circio jam flante reverræ sunt"; Giraldus, V. 246. Mr. Round would condemn the letter because it opens with a quotation from Ovid. But if we consider the extensive acquaintance of the writers of the time with the Latin poets (see the Becket correspondence, *passim*) I do not see why Dermot's secretary, or "Latinier" as he was called, should not have known something of Ovid.

[2] W. Newburgh, I. 167.   [3] V. 247.

[4] W. Newburgh, *sup.*; Dugdale, *Baronage*, I. 208; Gervase, I. 234. The last places the forfeiture in 1168; Norgate, II. 103.

[5] V. 247, 248.

[6] "Stranboue": Chron. Melrose, A.D. 1170; Brut y T., A.D. 1171.

[7] Giraldus, 272.

[8] So the *Song*, *passim*, "Carnosa superfluitate ventre turgescens"; Girald.

[9] Giraldus, 247-253; *Song*, 104-111; and for the locality, notes, 275.

Four months later, on the eve of St. Bartholomew, Earl Strongbow finally landed at Waterford, with an army of two hundred **Landing of Strongbow.** men-at-arms, and 1,000 others. Next day they rested, presumably keeping the Feast, but on the morrow (Tuesday, 25th August) the city was attacked in form. Two assaults were resisted; but at the third the stout man Raymond, who had joined his lord, effected a breach by pulling down a wooden house that projected **Capture of Waterford.** over the wall, being partly supported on posts outside. Waterford was stormed, including the keep or citadel known as Reginald's Tower. Two of the Ostman rulers, both of the name of Sibtric, were put to the sword. Reginald, a third, was saved alive, along with a native potentate, Melaglin or Malachy O'Phelan, chief of the Deisi (Decies).[1]

Dermot hastened to join his new ally, bringing with him his daughter Aoife or Eva, to cement their alliance. Her marriage with the Earl was forthwith celebrated, and then the whole force started for the city of Dublin, another old Norse conquest. To avoid an army under Roderic, reported as posted at Clondalkin, five miles to the South-West of Dublin, the allies took an arduous route by Glendalough, right through the Mountains of Wicklow, perhaps debouching at Rathfarnham.[2] Thus on the 21st September they found themselves under the walls of Dublin.[3] Negotiations for terms of peace and the delivery of hostages were opened under the mediation of Laurence O'Toole (Lorcan Ua Tuathail), the Archbishop of Dublin.[4] But while the terms were being discussed Raymond fitz William and one Milo of **Sack of Dublin.** Cogan, treacherously burst into the city and cruelly sacked it. The Ostman chief however Asculf or Asgall son of Thorkil, fought his way to his boats, and so got away in safety to the Orkneys.[5] After a few days' rest the allies retired from Dublin, Cogan being left in charge.[6] Strongbow went back to Waterford; while the indefatigable Dermot, now in his sixtieth year, turned aside to attack Meath. East Meath, that some time had been under Dermot, but was then held by Tiernan O'Rourke, submitted. West Meath was subject to Roderic of Connaught; and there, according to the native annals, Dermot was repulsed, and had to pay the penalty of losing his son and

---

[1] Giraldus, V. 254, 255; *Song*, 112; Four Masters. Reignald's tower, now known as the Ring Tower, still stands on the quay at Waterford. *Id.* notes.

[2] Giraldus, 256; *Song*, 112-121, and notes, 279.

[3] As the old parts of Dublin are on the right bank of the Liffey, there would be no river to cross.

[4] This man was canonised by Honorius II. as St. Lawrence on the 11th Dec., 1225; *Song*, notes, 286.

[5] Giraldus, 256, 257; *Song*, 120-127. *Cnf.* Four Masters who tax the Ostmen with desertion.

[6] 1st October. *Song*.

heir, a hostage in Roderic's hands for his peaceable behaviour.[1] From the battle-fields of Meath King Dermot returned to Ferns, to pass away about the ensuing 1st of May (1171). During his long reign of forty-six years,[2] his hand had been against every man, and every man's hand against his.[3]

Death of Dermot.

Dermot's death was the signal for a general uprising of the Irish, who gladly joined hands to get rid of the foreigners Almost the only man who remained true to the Saxons was Donnell Kavanagh, natural son of Dermot, a very gallant warrior who had led his father's forces in battle.[4] Then Henry, who was not particularly well disposed towards the Earl, becoming jealous of his reported successes, forbade any further reinforcements or supplies to be sent to him; and in fact recalled him. To procure a reversal of this edict Raymond fitz William was immediately sent off with a humble letter from the Earl, placing himself and his conquests at the King's absolute disposal.[5]

Strongbow in disgrace.

But before the Irish could muster their forces for combined action the Ostmen lately expelled from Dublin made a bold attempt to recover their footing there. We hear of sixty vessels landing on the Steine, a flat space to the East of the city, now in part occupied by Trinity College, and in front of the " Hogges," or Thingmote, a mound fort of Danish type.[6] But the force must really have been a very moderate one, as Milo Cogan ventured to march out to engage them. He was driven back; but his brother Richard having sallied from a postern on the South side of the city, and taken the enemy in the rear, they were utterly routed and scattered. Asgall the leader was taken prisoner, but his demeanour was so defiant that Milo ordered his head to be cut off.[7]

The Ostmen again.

Much more serious was the attack on Dublin shortly undertaken by the natives. Their annals speak of conflicts and skirmishes for a fortnight [8]; but they attempted no direct assault on the city, keeping at a safe distance from the walls, and contenting themselves with establishing a blockade, in which they were assisted by

Native Siege of Dublin.

---

[1] Giraldus, *sup.* ; Four Masters, and for the partition of Meath *Id.* A.D. 1169 and *Song*, notes, 256. The hostages of East Meath likewise were put to death by Tiernan.

[2] 1171. So the Book of Leinster, p. 20. cited *Song*, notes, 284. Other writers make Dermot reign longer.

[3] Giraldus, 238, 263 ; *Song*, 127 ; Four Masters.

[4] *Song*, 128.

[5] Giraldus, 259.

[6] *Song*, 170. This mound formerly stood at the angle of Church Lane and Suffolk Street ; *Id.* notes, 291.

[7] *Circa* 16th May, 1171 ; Giraldus, 263-265 ; Four Masters, II. p. 1185 ; Annals of Loch Cé ; and the long story in the *Song* 164-183, where the attack is placed after Strongbow's passage to England.

[8] Four Masters.

a naval squadron under Guthred King of Man.[1] Thus we hear that the

Blockading Forces. King of Connaught was established at Castleknock, on the North side of the Liffey, to the West of Dublin, with the men of Uladh (Ulster, counties Down and Antrim) lower down the river at Clontarf. O'Brien of Munster was posted at Kilmainham, to the South of the river, and West of the city ; and the revolted Leinster men, eight miles off, at Dalkey on the coast.[2] These last men were led by Murtough MacMurrough, brother to the late Dermot, who had been appointed King by Roderic in 1167, when Dermot was expelled.[3] On the other hand Cogan had been reinforced by Strongbow from Waterford ; with as many more men as could be spared by fitz Stephen from Wexford. Two months, we are told, the blockade lasted ; victuals were beginning to run short in the city when a hasty messenger came in to say that Robert fitz Stephen was being pressed by the men of Wexford

Wexford in danger. in his fort at Carrick on the Slaney outside Wexford. Failing succour within three days or so all would be lost with him. In this extremity a council of war was held, and the resolution come to was to put a bold face on the situation and calmly to offer peace to Roderic on condition of their recognising him as over-lord, while he would accept the Earl as King of Leinster. This tempting offer was rejected with scorn ; Dublin, Wexford, and Waterford they might retain, Roderic said, but nothing more.[4] About midday the Anglo-Normans in three bodies, probably not six hundred strong in all,[5] crossed the Liffey and

Rout of the Irish. fell on Roderic's force at Castleknock,[6] where they were found keeping no watch, probably preparing for their dinners, and many of them bathing in the river. Among these was Roderic himself. The whole force was scattered with great slaughter, the king himself escaping with difficulty. His discomfiture involved the retirement of the other Irish divisions, and the blockade was at an end. In the course of the afternoon the Earl and his men returned to Dublin, laden with booty and provisions. To the estimates given of the Irish numbers we pay no attention, but the names of the chieftains recorded as present show that apart from the men of Connaught, and those from Leinster and the South, tribesmen from the modern counties of Louth, Meath, Dublin, and Kildare, must have joined in the operations.[7] On

[1] Giraldus, 265.

[2] See *Song*, 128–130, and notes, 284.

[3] See *Song*, notes, 383.

[4] Giraldus, 266 ; *Song*, 130–138.

[5] Giraldus gives the men-at-arms in the three divisions as 20, 30, and 40 respectively, or 90 in all ; the numbers of the others he does not give, V. 268. The *Song* gives 120 men-at-arms, with a total of 600 men.

[6] The *Song* after placing Roderic at Castleknock, says that the English took the road to Finglas, but at the first that would coincide with the road to Castleknock.

[7] See Giraldus, 268, 269 ; *Song*, 128–144 ; Four Masters ; and annals of Loch Cé.

the English side the only casualty admitted was that of one foot soldier slightly wounded.[1]

Without the loss of a single day, Strongbow posted off on the morrow, in hopes of rescuing fitz Stephen. He took the 'upper road,' through Idrone (county Carlow). Dispelling an attempt to obstruct his passage through the Leinster Mountains, on the road to Newtownbarry, he reached Wexford, to find the little fort at Carrick fallen, and fitz Stephen a

Wexford lost. prisoner. At Richard's approach the Irish fired Wexford, retiring with their prize to the island of Begerin within the harbour.[2] Satisfied that he could do nothing to help his follower the Earl moved on to Waterford to make all safe in that quarter.[3]

Strongbow now appears as endeavouring to strengthen his position by peaceable means, and in particular by organising a government for

A Government for Leinster. Leinster on something of an English plan, with native chiefs to work under him. Thus we hear that he agreed to recognise Murtough the brother of Dermot as under-King of Hy Kinsellagh, apparently with the authority of an English Earl; while Donnell Kavanagh was appointed to hold pleas, or as we should say to act as Justiciar for Leinster.[4] Again we may point out that the institution of an authoritative court of justice would be an absolute novelty in Irish history.

While engaged in this useful work the Earl received a summons to join his lord King Henry, who had returned to England, and in fact was preparing to come over to Ireland. Richard obeyed, and, crossing the channel found the King at Newnham in Gloucestershire.[5]

We left Henry in Normandy in great anxiety as to the possible consequences of the ghastly crime supposed to have been committed at his

Henry and the Pope. instigation. Archbishop Rotrou of Rouen did not prosecute his journey to Italy, leaving the mission in the hands of the Archdeacons of Salisbury and Lisieux, and Richard Barre. They met with a very cold reception at Tusculum, where the Papal court was. Hardly a Cardinal would speak to them. Alexander III. had been overwhelmed with agony at the report of Becket's death, for which he might feel himself somewhat to blame. His conduct throughout the struggle has been much criticised.[6] Between two such antagonists as Henry and Becket he had to temporise—to use no stronger term. But on the whole in our opinion he had only given in too much to the Archbishop. He had to keep Henry in hand; but, while doing what he could

---

[1] *Song, sup.*
[2] Giraldus, 270-272; *Song,* 144-148.
[3] *Song,* 148; Giraldus, V. 273.
[4] *Song,* 160.
[5] September, Giraldus, V. 273; *Song, sup.*
[6] See *e.g.* Norgate, *Angevin Kings,* II., 50.

to keep on terms with him, he had never committed himself to the surrender of any essential point in dispute. With respect to affairs at Tusculum Henry's agents became very uneasy at the approach of Maunday Thursday (25th March), a day specially appointed for the utterance of Papal sentences. To avert a condemnation of their master they had to swear in his name that he would submit absolutely to the Pope's decision with respect to himself. The agents of the suspended Prelates had to take the like oath on behalf of their principals. But we are told that the promise of 500 marks (£333 6s. 8d.) had been extracted from them before they could even be admitted to an audience. Thus when the day came the Pope contented himself with excommunicating the murderers, and all those who should harbour or assist them. At the same time **Maunday Thursday.** he announced the intended mission of two Cardinals to deal with the case of the King. Somewhat later, after Easter (28th March), Alexander confirmed the Interdict laid by the Archbishop of Sens on Henry's Continental dominions. But as a set-off to that blow again he authorised the conditional absolution of the Bishops of London and Salisbury.[1]

Pending the declaration of the Pope's intentions, Henry remained quietly in Normandy, on the borders of Brittany. There all question of **Succession in Brittany.** the succession had been finally set at rest by the death of Conan IV. (20th February 1171).[2] The rights of his daughter Constance and her husband Geoffrey could no longer be disputed; while the revenues of the Honour of Richmond would become available for the Royal Exchequer.[3] The King also bethought him of directing an inquest as to the Royal demesnes in Normandy, probably on the lines of the Inquest of Sheriffs already held in England. The new enquiry, we are told, was attended by results not less satisfactory to the Treasury than the former one.[4]

Henry's anxiety as to Papal censures having been relieved by the reports from Tusculum he was able to turn his attention to events happening in Ireland. He could not be blind to the dangers of allowing an indepen- **Henry and the Irish Adventurers.** dent state to be built up by subjects of his own across the Irish Channel. The close ties of relationship by which so many of the adventurers were linked together made the situation more disquieting. It seemed as if Ireland was to become the appanage of the sons of Nest.[5] To calm the King's fears Strongbow's uncle Hervé of Montmorency had been sent to Normandy with renewed

[1] See the reports of the different envoys, *Becket*, VII. 471–480.
[2] Bouquet, XII. 563, cited Norgate; R. Monte, 249.
[3] R. Monte; Pipe Roll 17, Henry II., 117.
[4] R. Monte 251. For the Inquest of Sheriffs see above, 117.
[5] See the Table at the end of this chapter; also Miss Norgate's note, *Angevin Kings*, II. 107.

protestations of allegiance. But Henry resolved to see for himself what
was going on. A Grand Council of Barons was held at Argentan in July,
and a general approval of the measures in contemplation secured. In the
first days of September[1] the King landed at Portsmouth. Advancing to

Death of the Bishop of Winchester. Winchester, he paid a death-bed visit to old Henry of Blois,
then in the forty-second year of his eventful episcopate.[2] A
thorough-going churchman he never hesitated to sacrifice the
interests of his country to those of his Order. Having been promoted by
Henry I. he discarded his uncle's heir for his own brother, in order to gain
the 'liberty' of the Church. Stephen having disappointed his expectations
the Bishop turned from him to Matilda ; and when Matilda proved even
less manageable than Stephen he went back to him. Finally he had to
give up the fraternal dynasty and reconcile himself to the triumphant
accession of young Henry of Anjou. For the novel appeals to Rome,
that had thrown the Church of England into such confusion, Bishop
Henry was largely responsible.

Troops for an invasion of Ireland were now called out, while the young
King was sent over to Normandy, to take charge of affairs there during his
father's absence. The muster was probably held at Newnham in Gloucestershire, where Strongbow joined the King.[3] About the 8th September

Henry in Wales. Henry crossed the Usk.[4] For a wonder, coming as an English
King, at the head of an army, he nevertheless came peaceably.
Relations with the Welsh for the moment were friendly. The
"gentle poet-statesman" Owen Gwynedd of North Wales had died in
peace in November 1169.[5] Next year his eldest son Howel was
assassinated by a younger brother David, and the new Prince was prepared
to keep quiet. The bellicose Rhys actually hastened to meet the King

Peaceable Princes. across the border, with an offer of tribute in the shape of 300
horses, and 4,000 head of cattle. The seizure of Cardigan
Castle, and the imprisonment of Robert fitz Stephen were
acts for which the Prince might have been called to account ; but on the
contrary we are told that Rhys was confirmed in the possession of
Ceredigion, and allowed to refortify "Aberteivy" (Cardigan) ; the tribute
also being ultimately remitted. In fact Rhys' command of the road to
Ireland now gave him quite a novel importance.

By the third week of September[6] the King had reached Pembroke,
where he was detained a considerable time by foul winds. He took

----

[1] 3rd September, Ben. P.; 6th September, Diceto.

[2] Henry of Blois was consecrated 17th November, 1129 ; he died 8th August, 1171.
Reg Sacr. R. Diceto, I. 347.

[3] Giraldus, V. 273.

[4] So Brut y T ; a very detailed narrative.

[5] *Id.*; R. de Monte, A.D. 1170.

[6] 14th Sept. Ben. P., 27th Sept. *Brut.*

advantage of the delay to make out a pilgrimage to St. David's, where he was entertained by Bishop David fitz Gerald (26th-29th Sept.). Finally on Sunday, 17th October, Henry sailed from Milford Haven, landing next day at Crook, in Waterford Harbour.[1] His force was estimated at from 400 to 500 men-at-arms, with a grand total of 4,000 of all sorts.[2]

Henry in Ireland.

But whatever the actual numbers may have been no resistance could be offered by the natives, who had been unable to hold their own against the paltry forces of the first adventurers. The men of Wexford therefore promptly brought FitzStephen to Waterford as a peace-offering.[3] Within a few days Dermot MacCarthy (Diarmid MacCarthaig), King of Desmond or South Munster, with his capital at Cork, had come in. A Royal advance to Lismore and Cashel was followed by the submission of O'Brien, King of Thomond or North Munster: the princes of Ossory and Decies followed suit. After a return to Waterford the King started for Dublin, journeying by way of Ossory. No itinerary of his route has been preserved, but it was attended by important results. In the first place all the princes of Leinster, Meath, Breifny, Uriel (South Ulster), and Uladh (East Ulster), accepted Henry's supremacy. Only the men of Aileach (West Ulster) kept altogether at a distance. As to the behaviour of Roderic of Connaught accounts differ. It would seem that he condescended to meet Henry's envoys, namely Hugh de Lacy and William fitz Aldelin, on the Shannon.[4] On the other hand again we are told that he refused to bow to the supremacy of the King of England, but that owing to the wetness of the season no expedition to reduce him could be undertaken.[5] More real and important in our opinion than the homages of the lay chiefs was the adhesion given in by the Irish clergy. According to our best authority the four Archbishops, with their suffragans, swore allegiance.[6]

General Submission.

The Irish clergy.

---

[1] See the *Brut*. which here clearly represents a contemporary account; the writer gives the day of Henry's sailing as the 17th October, and Giraldus states that he landed on the 18th October. Benedict, who records the landing at "Croch," gives the 16th October as the day of sailing, and the 17th as that of arrival.

[2] Giraldus, V. 275; *Song*, 189. Among those with the King, at any rate at Pembroke, were the Earls of Cornwall and Hertford (Charter cited Round, *Commune*, 152). For supplies sent by the sheriffs for the army, wheat, bacon, and cheese, with hand-mills to grind the corn, see Pipe Roll, 17 Henry II., 2, 11, 19, &c. The army must have consisted mainly of feudal levies, as we only hear of 163 "coterels" or hired mercenaries; Pipe Roll, 18 H. II., 144; some of the tenants in chief sent men, some sent money to the King direct—a fact to be noted. From those who had sent neither men nor money a legal scutage of £1 the Knight's fee was taken in the next year; Pipe Roll, *sup.*, 9, 15, etc.   [3] Giraldus, 276; *Song*, 192.

[4] Giraldus, V. 278, 279; Annals Loch Ce, I. 145.

[5] Ben. P., I. 25, 26; R. Diceto, I. 348.

[6] See Bend. P., *sup.*, where a full list of the Irish Episcopate seems to be given. Gervase, I. 235, copies him.

In the case of these men we can believe in a wish for a change of system.
We have already heard that the position of the Irish clergy was not at all
equal to that of their brethren in other countries.   Their envy might well
be excited by reports of the *status* to which the priesthood had attained
elsewhere; and a certain ecclesiastical connexion with England had
already been established.   Nor would it be too much to give them credit
for desiring some reform in the manners of their countrymen.   It was
probably to meet their wishes that Henry on the 6th November issued
orders for the holding of a grand Synod of the Hibernian Church.[1]

Five days later Henry reached Dublin, taking up his quarters in a
wicker-work palace, after the native fashion,[2] specially built for him outside
the walls, near St. Andrew's Church.   His Christmas entertainments there
made a great impression on the native chieftains, who had never before
seen such choice of viands, or such sumptuous attendance.[3]

Early in 1172[4] the King's Synod was held at Cashel under the
presidency of Christian or Gilchrist O'Conarchy, Bishop of Lismore, who

Synod of
Cashel.

took the lead by reason of having been appointed Apostolic
Legate for Ireland.   The Archbishop of Armagh[5] excused
himself on the plea of age; but the other three Primates
appeared with their Suffragans.   Seven canons were passed, the provisions
giving interesting evidence as to the social condition of Ireland.   Intercourse with female relations and connexions (*cognatarum et affinium
contubernium*) is condemned, the people being ordered to confine
themselves to legitimate marriages (c. 1): children to be baptised in
church, and catechised at the door of the church (c. 2): tithes of animals,
fruits, and all other products (*cæterarum proventionum*) to be paid to the
parish church (c. 3): Church property to be free from all secular
exactions; Kings and great men (*potentes viri*) and their families not to
quarter themselves on the clergy, nor to exact from them 'food-rents'[6]
(*cibus ille detestabilis* c. 4): clerks not to contribute to fines (*eric* = A.S.
wer) due for murders committed by relatives (c. 5).   The 6th Canon
seems to authorise, or at any rate to encourage and regulate the making of

[1] Ben. P., I. 28.
[2] *Scotice,* a "creel-house."
[3] Giraldus and Ben P., *sup.*
[4] So expressly Giraldus, 281, Henry being still in Ireland.
[5] Gilla MacLiag, a man much reverenced by the people.   He subsequently came to
Dublin to pay his respects to the King, bringing with him his white cow, on whose milk
he chiefly lived; Giraldus, 283 and note.
[6] The right of being entertained at free quarters, known as coinium or coiguy, with
that of receiving 'food-rents' or contributions of victuals in kind, were among the
chief emoluments of the Celtic Kings.   See *Foundations*, I. 16; for the like rights in
Scotland see Skene, *Celtic Scotland*, III. 227; in Wales, Seebohm, *Tribal System in
Wales*, 25, 155, etc.   From the Cashel Canon we learn that the *cibus* was levied
quarterly, a regular rent.

wills of personalty. In the case of a man leaving a widow and children
it provides that the clear residue, after payment of wages and debts, shall
be divided into three parts : one for the widow, one for the children, the
third to be at the man's disposal (c. 6). The 7th and last Canon provides
for the due performance of funeral rites.[1]

Reports of the submission of the Irish Kings, and of the proceedings at

The Papacy and the Conquest. Cashel were now forwarded by Henry and the Irish bishops to the Pope, with requests for his approval.[2] Their petitions were not ignored. On 20th September (1172)—Henry in the
meantime having been reconciled to the Church, as we shall see—Alexander
issued three letters from Tusculum ; one addressed to Henry ; another to
the Irish prelates ; and the third to the Irish Kings and Princes. In these
communications the Pope expresses his entire approval of Henry's conduct
in entering Ireland ; condemns the native practices condemned at Cashel ;
and orders the Irish chiefs to remain faithful to the obligations entered
into with the King of England under pain of ecclesiastical censures.[3] It
would seem that the letters when received were sent over to Ireland by

The "Bull" *Laudabiliter.* Henry under the charge of William fitz Aldelin, together with the original 'Bull' of Adrian, and a further alleged 'Privilege' of Alexander, expressly confirming the 'concession' of Ireland
made by Adrian. Both these lost documents have been questioned : the
'Privilege' may safely be rejected as spurious.[4] But the whole batch,
apparently, were published in a Synod immediately held at Waterford for
the purpose.[5]

Henry stayed in Dublin till the month of February, when he moved

---

[1] Giraldus, V. 282, 283 ; Ben. P., I. 28. Diceto refers to the Synod as held at
Lismore, I. 351.

[2] Ben. P., *sup.* He places the sending of the reports before the meeting of the Synod
of Cashel. But as he tells us that they were carried to Italy by Ralph, Archdeacon of
Llandaff, who assisted at the Synod (Gir. 282) ; and as the Pope, in his answers specially
notices the verbal communications of Archdeacon Ralph, it is clear that the reports were
not sent out till after the Synod.

[3] See the letters, *Liber Niger Scacc.* (Hearne) I. 42-47. The day of the month is
given, but not the year, which is supplied from other data.

[4] See the document, Gir. 318, the only authority for it. But he need not be regarded
as the author of it, as in another place (*De Instr. Pr.* VIII. 197) he tells us that it was
much questioned—a man would hardly record such evidence against a fabrication of
his own.

[5] Mich. 1172-Mich. 1173. See Giraldus, V. 315-319, where no date is given, the
marginal 1174-1175 being an addition by the editor. But Mr. Round, *Commune,* 182,
cites an entry from the Pipe Roll, 19 H. II., p. 145, showing that fitz Aldelin was sent
to Ireland during the above period. Again, it must be stated that the three undisputed
Papal letters preserved in the *Liber Niger,* are not noticed by Giraldus ; but it does not
seem unreasonable to supplement his narrative by supposing these letters to have been
sent over with the documents that he does mention. See the whole matter discussed by
Mr. Round, *Commune,* 180-194, though my conclusions are not quite the same as his.

towards Wexford, where he took up his quarters about the 1st March. The season continued to be wet and stormy, in fact inclement enough to supply the King with an excuse for not invading Connaught. Communications with England were almost cut off,[1] and he became very anxious for news. At last he heard that the mission announced by the Pope had been despatched, and that the Legates, the Cardinals Albert and Theodine were actually in Normandy.[2] Disagreeable rumours also reached his ears of intrigues to set up his sons in opposition to him; some of Queen Eleanor's relations being mentioned in this connexion.[3] About the

Henry returns to England. middle of March Henry sent the bulk of his force on to Waterford, as a more convenient place for shipment than Wexford; he himself remaining at Wexford. At last on Easter Day (16 April), the army sailed from Crook, near Waterford, to Milford Haven; the King himself crossing next day from Wexford to the coast near St. David's.[4]

Towards strengthening the English hold on Ireland, Henry, apart from **The Irish Measures shortsighted.** the relations established with the Irish clergy, had done nothing. His arrangements for the government of the territory conquered, being mainly dictated by jealousy of Earl Strongbow,[5] were calculated, perhaps intended to foster discord in the chosen land of discord. Hugh de Lacy, a man who had taken no part in the conquest, was appointed Justiciar of Ireland, with a grant of Meath in fee; Dublin also was placed under him, with Maurice fitz Gerald and Robert fitz Stephen as his subordinates.[6] But an independent element would be introduced into that city by the grant of municipal and trading rights to the men of Bristol.[7] Wexford was placed under the charge of William fitz Aldelin, and Waterford under that of Humphrey of Bohun and Robert fitz Bernard,[8] all three officials brought over by Henry. With respect to Strongbow his position is not very clearly defined. He had surrendered

---

[1] " Vix una navis transnavigasset ; " Giraldus. The words must not be pressed too closely.

[2] They must have arrived by December (1171), as they granted the authority under which the Cathedral at Canterbury was ' reconciled ' on 21st December, 1171. Gervase, I. 236 ; Chron. Melrose (A.D. 1172).

[3] So Diceto, I. 350, who names Hugh of St. Maur, and Ralph of Faye, uncle to Queen Eleanor. The traitor had large estates in Surrey, Pipe Roll, 19 H. II., 95.

[4] Ben. P., I. 29, 30 ; Giraldus, V. 284-286 ; *Song*, 196-201 ; R. Diceto, I. 351.

[5] " Ut . . . comitis partem redderet exiliorem ; " Giraldus.

[6] Giraldus and Ben. P., *sup.* ; Hoveden, II. 34 ; *Song*, 198 and notes 297. De Lacy's fief would include Meath, West Meath, with parts of Longford and King's County ; the whole estimated at some 800,000 acres ; Gilbert, *Viceroys*, 35.

[7] Historic Documents of Ireland, p. 1 (J. T. Gilbert, 1870). Bristol of course was the old head quarters of the Angevin party. A later charter granted by Henry gives the men of Dublin exemption throughout his dominions from all tolls, pontages, market and harbour dues, etc. *Id.* p. 2. For such exemptions see below under the reign of John.

[8] Giraldus, *sup.*

to Henry all regalian rights that he might claim through his wife[1]. Apparently he was established in an outpost at Kildare,[2] with the style of seneschal or constable of Ireland.[3] But that title would imply the chief military command. In Henry's arrangements we trace no effort to bring the natives into peaceable co-operation, as attempted by Strongbow, only imperfect military measures. Thus the conquest, such as it was, remained incomplete, as was pointed out from the very first ;[4] and the English occupation became a mere buccaneering settlement, demoralising to all within the sphere of its influence. The natives refused to learn from the foreigners ; and the foreigners soon sank to the level of the natives, if not lower. For the native gentry the conquest involved wholesale eviction, such as the Britons had suffered at the hands of the Anglo-Saxons, and they in turn at the hands of Danes and Normans.[5]

[1] Giraldus, 382.
[2] *Song*, 196.
[3] R. de Monte, p. 252.
[4] See the lament of Giraldus, 383.
[5] See the list of estates in Meath and Leinster granted out to their subordinates within the next few years by Earl Richard and Hugh of Lacy ; a sort of Domesday Book, *Song of Dermot*, etc., pp. 223-231, with Mr. Orpen's identifications of the places, Notes 303-316 ; also Giraldus, V. 314.

ISSUE OF NEST,

CONNECTED WITH THE INVASION OF IRELAND.

(*See Song of Dermot, xliii., ed. G. H. Orpen and Giraldus V. c, and notes Dymock.*)

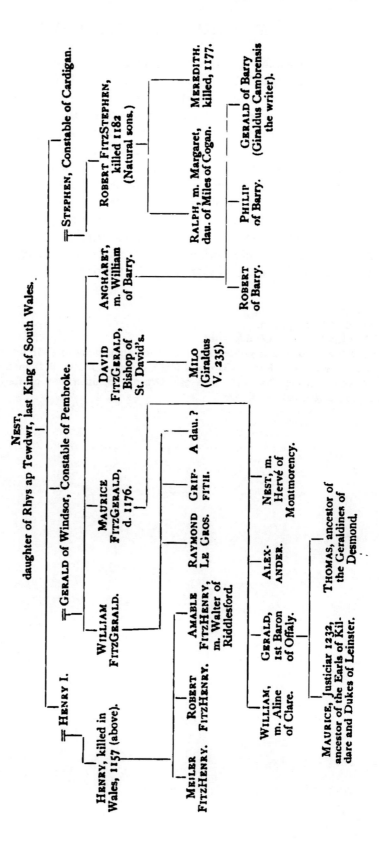

CHAPTER IX

HENRY II. (*continued*)

1172-1174

Reconciliation of the King to the Church—Treaties with Savoy and Toulouse—Revolt of the King's sons, abetted by Queen Eleanor, Louis VII. and the greater Barons— Civil War in Normandy, Brittany, England, and Poitou—Capture of William the Lion at Alnwick—Henry does Penance at Becket's Tomb—Collapse of the Rebellion

FROM the haven on the coast of Pembrokeshire where he had landed on the 17th April, Henry moved by easy stages[1] to Porchester, and so across the Channel to Barfleur in the first half of May.[2] **Crossing to Normandy.** The Legates duly apprised of his coming advanced to meet him in the Côtentin. On the 16th May they exchanged friendly kisses of peace at a place given as "Gorham" or "Gorram." Next day moving on to Savigny[3] the Papal envoys propounded their terms, which as formulated at first Henry could not accept. 'If such was to be the price of reconciliation he would go back to Ireland.'[4] The Legates then took Arnulf of Lisieux and the Archdeacons of Poitiers and Sarum into their counsels, and with their help two days later presented at Avranches a more palatable set of conditions (19 May). Henry accepted them at once; but he asked that the formal proceedings should be deferred for two days more to allow of the presence of his son the young king.[5] The reconciliation accordingly took place on Sunday 21st May at **Henry reconciled to the Church.** Avranches. Henry began by taking a voluntary oath[6] in the cathedral that he had neither ordered nor sought for (*neque mandavit neque voluit*) the death of the Archbishop; and that he had been

---

[1] He only reached Newport (Monmouth) on the 22nd April; Giraldus, V. 289.

[2] *Id.*; R. Dicero, I. 351; Ben. P., I. 31.

[3] Manche, near Coutances.

[4] See the letter of Herbert of Bosham, VII. 514; also Henry's own account, p. 519. "Quamquam eos in principio duros invenissem," etc.

[5] Benedict of Peterborough asserts that the King brought his son over with him from England. But the younger Henry was at Bures at Christmas as told by Robert de Monte, who notices no voyage of his to England till that in August.

[6] "Propria voluntate"; *Becket*, VII. 514, 521.

utterly distressed when he heard of it. He added however that he felt that the murder had been committed on his account; and in consequence of words uttered by him.[1] The Legates then declared their **The Conditions.** conditions of forgiveness. Henry to find money for the support of 200 men-at-arms (*milites*) for one year for the defence of Jerusalem; and himself to take the cross at Christmas for a three years' crusade, unless excused by the Pope. Appeals to Rome in ecclesiastical matters to be freely allowed (*libere fiant*), the King however being at liberty to exact guarantees from appellants against possible intrigues against himself or his realm. Customs introduced during his reign to the detriment of the churches of his dominions to be wholly disclaimed.[2] Full restitution to be made to Canterbury of all possessions enjoyed by her one year before the Archbishop's exile, with amnesty and restitution to all persons who had suffered on his account. Lastly the King would pledge himself to stand by Alexander III. and his Catholic successors in the Papal chair.

Henry took the oaths, the son concurring in the articles not personal to his father. The King was then led out of the church to receive **Absolution.** plenary absolution at the door, meekly kneeling on a block of stone that still stands there to commemorate the event.[3]

As a whole the conditions involved a distinct abandonment of Becket's extreme demands. Of the points for which he had contended, the only one insisted on in its entirety was the freedom of appeals, a vital matter for the Papacy, as Thomas had always maintained. The omission of all specific reference to the *Constitutions* of Clarendon was also remarkable. Henry was thus left free to maintain as he always had maintained, and with substantial truth, that he had introduced no new customs. If we might venture on a conjecture as to the modification of their conditions accepted by the Legates on the 19th May, we would suggest with some confidence that it was just the omission of any reference to the *Constitutions*, because in the version of the conditions given by Herbert of Bosham, the condemnation of the *Constitutions* does appear, a point on which he is clearly refuted both by the King and the Cardinals. Apparently he was following the original, and not the amended draft of the terms.

The absolution is stated to have been given in the presence of a large concourse, but probably it was only a concourse of people from the neighbourhood. Apparently no representatives of France were present, and on that account it was agreed that the ceremony should be repeated, and

---

[1] *Ib.*

[2] "Consuetudines quæ inductæ sunt contra excelsias terræ vestræ tempore vestro penitus dimittetis," p. 517.

[3] See the several reports of King, Legates, and H. Bosham; *Becket*, VII. 513-523; also Diceto, I. 351, and Bened. P., I. 32, but the latter gives the terms as propounded on the 27th September.

at an early date ;[1] Caen was named as the place. But as things turned out the renewed absolution was not given till the month of September, and then again at Avranches.

Another laudable task undertaken by the Legates as peacemakers was

Discontent of the young King. that of endeavouring to establish more cordial relations between Henry on the one hand, and his eldest son and the King of France on the other hand. We have seen that in the great Becket controversy the young king's sympathies were not with his father, but with his old tutor the Archbishop. Then the King though kind and well-meaning was the most trying of fathers. He had carved out magnificent positions for his sons, positions that would naturally excite

The King and his Sons. aspirations after independence and freedom of action. The young king had been invested with the crown of England ; while just at this time Richard, with his mother's approval, was being installed as Count of Poitiers, and Duke of Aquitaine.[2] But their father gave them no scope. Young Henry was treated as a mere puppet, obliged to take orders on every point ;[3] his allowance was shabby ;[4] and he had been subjected to the gratuitous humiliation of seeing regal honours withheld from his wife ; uncrowned, and therefore no Queen. King Louis also felt deeply aggrieved in this matter, Henry's action being generally supposed to have been chiefly prompted by the wish to mortify his over-lord. Such pettiness must lower our estimate of Henry's ability as a statesman. Now however, in his humbled frame of mind, he was prepared to give Margaret her due. A conference was held with Louis, when as we may suppose details were settled.[5] With respect to the prelate to be appointed to officiate Canterbury was still vacant ; Roger of York had been absolved and reinstated ;[6] but under all the circumstances of the time his ministrations could hardly be accepted. The man selected was Rotrou, the Archbishop of Rouen, with the Bishops Giles of Evreux, and Roger of Worcester to assist. It was also, apparently, suggested that in view of the doubts that might be thrown on the young king's coronation in 1170, as having been performed in the teeth of Papal prohibitions, it might be well to take the opportunity of having him re-crowned. Accordingly the party were sent to England, landing at Southampton on the 24th August. On the following Sunday, being the 27th of the month young Henry and

---

[1] *Becket*, VII. 516, 518.

[2] Richard was installed at Poitiers on the 11th June ; Geoffrey Vigeois, Labbe, *Nova Bibliot.*, II. 318.

[3] See the expression of Gervase with regard to Henry's advisers ; "Magistros magis quam ministros" ; I. 240.

[4] So W. Newburgh I. 170; and the Pipe Rolls, *passim*, where the young king's 'corrodies' seem distinctly moderate.

[5] R. Monte, 254 ; Gervase, I. 237.

[6] 6th Dec., 1171 ; Diceto, I. 348 ; *Becket*, VII. 498-506.

Margaret were duly hallowed and crowned by the appointed Prelates, in **Recoronation of the Young King.** Winchester Cathedral.[1]   The choice of that church for the ceremony, instead of the traditional St. Peter's Westminster, suggests a certain grudgingness on the King's part; nor were the expenses allowed very liberal.   The chief items on the Pipe Roll are **Coronation of his Queen.** £95 18s. 4d. for robes for the Royal pair; with £55 4s. 4d. for their coronation banquet.[2]   But the chief outlay apparently was that required to make the palace in the castle at Winchester habitable.   A quantity of roofing had to be brought from France.[3] Margaret however at last appears as 'the Queen the daughter of the King of France,' in exact correlation to her husband 'the King the King's son.'[4]

The officiating Prelates shortly returned to Normandy, the young King remaining in England by his father's orders to preside over futile efforts to come to an agreement with the Canterbury monks as to the choice of a new Archbishop.[5]   Thus he was unable to assist at the renewed **Second Absolution of the King.** absolution of the King, which took place at Avranches, as already mentioned, on Wednesday 27th September.[6]   Henry had been on a tour through Brittany and the ceremony took place immediately on his return to Normandy.   About the beginning of November the young King received a summons from the King that brought him over to Normandy, much against his will.[7]   His discontent had not been allayed by the coronation of his wife, and now, to show his ill-humour, instead of joining his father and mother at Chinon, he went to Gisors, to hold an interview with King Louis, who received him and Margaret with open arms,[8] and pressed them with insidious counsels— counsels that had already been tendered from other quarters.   We have mentioned the intrigues of which the King had heard in Ireland.   Ralph

[1] Bened. P., I. 31 ; Gervase I, 237.   Diceto, I. 352, adds that the Archbishop of York and the Bishops of London and Sarum were forbidden to appear; but he gives the 21st August, a Thursday, as the day.

[2] Pipe Roll, 18 Henry II., 87, 144, 145.

[3] See *Id.*, p. 87, £200 paid in one account; and again p. 98, etc.

[4] "Regina filia Regis Franciæ . . . Rex filius Regis."   Pipe Rolls, *passim*.

[5] Windsor 1st September, Diceto, I. 353 ; see Gervase, I. 239, 240.

[6] See Ben., P. I. 31-33, copied by Hoveden, II. 35-37; also Gervase, I. 238. Neither of these writers notices the first absolution; but in fact the account given by Benedict as that of the second ceremony is really that of the first, because the presence of the young King is noticed.   Now he was certainly present on the first occasion, but not on the second.   *Cnf.* R. de Monte.   The stone on which the King knelt, being as I am informed, almost the only relic of the once magnificent Cathedral, bears an inscription record ng the second absolution, but not the first one.   Apparently no one authority notices both.

[7] "Multum invitus."

[8] See R. Monte, 255.   Benedict, I. 34, represents the young couple as sent by Henry to visit Louis, but this seems hardly consistent with his own admission that Henry was most suspicious of Louis.

of Taye, uncle of Queen Eleanor, and her chief confidant,[1] and Hugh of
Saint-Maur,[2] an Angevin Baron, had been urging young Henry to demand
an establishment on a footing of independence, either in England or
Normandy.[3] Louis now backed up their suggestions with the weight
of his authority.[4] In so doing he was probably thinking more of France
than of the true interests of his son-in-law. As for the Barons,

Louis the Barons and the Young King. they only spoke the voice of Feudalism, long repressed, and
panting for an opportunity of breaking out. Such an opening
might now seem to have presented itself. Henry's position
had undoubtedly been weakened by the Becket catastrophe, and the
posthumous glory acquired by St. Thomas of Canterbury. Then the King's
hand had been heavy on all classes of his subjects; and the arbitrary
taxation disclosed by the Pipe Rolls was enough to create wide-spread
discontent. Lastly Queen Eleanor had her domestic grievances, and was
prepared to avenge them by supporting her sons as against her husband.

From the French court the young King and Queen went off to Bonne-
ville, to spend a quiet Christmas apart, instead of joining the family circle
at Chinon,[5] where Henry and Eleanor were holding the last Yule Feast that
they were destined to spend together for many a day. Summoned to

The Young King's Demands. Anjou early in 1173 young Henry confronted his father with
a demand for an independent establishment, as advised by
King Louis; that is to say he asked to have the reins
of government either in England or Normandy placed in his hands. Of
course the request was refused.[6] Henry had been providing for the future
welfare of his children, but he did not propose to divest himself of his
clothing before going to bed. The son was taken on to Auvergne
to witness a series of diplomatic triumphs gained by his father as the
consummation of his foreign policy. Henry had been careful

Diplomatic Triumphs. to cultivate friendly relations with all powers on his Southern
borders, probably with especial reference to his cherished
designs on Toulouse. A prince in a position of great importance, as
holding the key to the passes from Southern Gaul to Italy, was Humbert
III. Count of Maurienne, whose dominions North of the Alps included the
Tarentaise, and Savoy properly so called; while to the South of the Alps
the lordships of Aosta, Châtillon, Susa, and Turin gave him the proud title
of Marquis of Italy. In short he commanded all the passes from the Lake
of Bourget to the Mont Genèvre, if not to the Col di Tenda.[7] The Count

---

[1] See *Becket*, V. 197 (Norgate).
[2] Indre et Loire, near Chinon?
[3] Diceto, I. 350.   [4] Benedict, *sup.*
[5] R. Monte, *sup.*
[6] Bened. P., I. 35, 42 ; R. Hoved., I. 46 ; Gervase, I. 242.
[7] See Freeman, *Historical Geography*, I. 286 ; Norgate, *Angevin Kings*, II. 131 ; and
the treaty, Ben. P., I. 36.

had no son, but a little daughter Alix or Alais, a good match for Henry's youngest son John, "Lackland,"[1] now five or six years old,[2] for whom no provision had as yet been found. Humbert accepting the offer a meeting was arranged to be held at Montferrand[3] in February, when two other potentates, Alphonso II. of Arragon, and Raymond V. of Toulouse, were invited to appear, in order to take the opportunity of disposing of certain matters in which all were interested. Raymond, the old enemy, now hemmed in between Maurienne and Arragon, had to resign himself to a compromise, by accepting Henry as his over-lord; while Alphonso, the old ally, was content to accept of Henry's mediation in making friends with Toulouse. The marriage contract between John and Alix was formally sealed at Montferrand, the Count settling all his possessions on the young couple, provided that he should leave no male issue at his death.[4] The distinguished party then adjourned to Limoges, probably for more commodious quarters. There the questions between Alphonso and Raymond were settled, and Raymond did homage to the two Henries, undertaking to do the like at Whitsuntide to young Richard as Duke of Aquitaine.[5]

The Reversion of Savoy.

Over-lordship of Toulouse.

So far everything had gone smoothly and happily. But the conferences did not end there. Count Humbert having enquired very naturally what land the King would give to his son John, Henry said that he would give Chinon, Loudun, and Mirebeau (Vienne), three important castles, in fact the former appanage of his brother Geoffrey. At this the smouldering discontent of the young King burst into flames. He protested that he would never agree, his consent being necessary as he had been invested with Anjou.[6] It would also seem that he had been irritated by the removal from his household of some young men of whom the King was suspicious.[7] Thus father and son left Limoges no longer on speaking terms. They travelled together as far as Chinon, where the King halted for the night. But the younger Henry, slipping away without leave, pushed on with such expedition that next night he rested at Alençon, distant from Chinon 100 miles as the crow flies. The King, traversing the same stage with equal rapidity, reached Alençon just as his son was entering the gates of

A Rupture.

Flight and Pursuit.

[1] "Cognomento Sine Terra," Diceto; "Quartum, natu minimum, Johannem Sine Terra agnominans (sc. Henricus)"; W. Newb., I. 146.

[2] John was born late in the year, either in 1166 (Diceto), or in 1167 (R. Monte).

[3] Puy de Dôme.

[4] See Ben. P., I. 35–41, where the treaties are given in full; R. Monte, 255; Diceto, I. 353. The last gives the 12th February as the day of the meeting at Montferrand.

[5] Ben. P., I. 36; R. Diceto, I. 353. Geoffrey of Vigeois gives the 25th February as the day of Raymond's homage; the conferences lasting seven days; p. 319.

[6] Ben. P., I. 41.

[7] R. Monte, 255, 256.

Argentan.   Leaving Argentan at cockcrow the young King made his way to Paris by a circuitous route, through Mortagne, the fief of Robert of Dreux, King Louis' brother (Thursday, 8th March ?).[1]   Finding

War imminent.

that he could not catch his son, Henry, seeing that he must prepare for the worst, at once sent warning to the constables of all his castles, himself going the round of those in. Normandy to set everything in order.[2]

Henry in truth had need to be on the alert.   The situation was most alarming, and everything seemed to be going against him.   Queen Eleanor

Queen Eleanor arrested.

sent her sons Richard and Geoffrey to join their brother in Paris, while she herself went off to Poitou to canvass support for Richard.   She was found disguised in male attire, arrested,

and placed in close confinement by the King's orders.[3]   Louis seized the opportunity that seemed at last to have presented itself for raising up an effectual adversary to his great rival.   He convened a Grand Council of magnates in Paris.   His summonses were attended not only by old enemies of the House of Anjou, such as Theobald of Blois, but also by old allies, such as Philip of Flanders, and his brother Matthew of

League against Henry.

Boulogne, both of whom Henry had alienated by shabby treatment.[4]   Oaths were interchanged.   Louis swore to support young Henry and his brothers against their father,

and they pledged themselves to make no peace without Louis' concurrence.   Young Henry then declared a series of lavish grants to purchase support.   The King of Scots was offered Carlisle, with all Westmoreland[5]; and his brother David a restoration of the Earldom of Huntingdon with Cambridgeshire.   The Count of Flanders would have all Kent, with Dover and Rochester Castles; his brother would have the county of Mortain, and Theobald the Castle of Amboise, and so forth.

---

[1] The chronology of these events is very uncertain.   Diceto, I. 355, gives the 23rd March, a Friday, as the day of the young King's ride from Argentan.   Benedict, I. 42, more specifically gives as the date of his arrival in Paris Thursday, 8th March.   " Octava idus Martii, feria quinta ante mediam Quadragesimam."   The eighth of the Ides fell on a Thursday, before Midlent Sunday, but it was not the Thursday next before Midlent Sunday, which fell on the 18th March.   The words therefore " ant. med. Quad.," seem true but not exact.   On the previous page the writer refers to events as happening before Midlent in the same vague way.   For the restoration of the word " mediam," omitted in the printed text, see Diceto, II. xxxvi. note.   The earlier date also fits best with the date of the meetings at Limoges, and leaves more time for the proceedings in Paris, which are given as happening before Easter.

[2] Ben. P., *sup.*

[3] Ben. P., *sup.* ; Gervase, 242 ; Peter of Blois, *Epp.*, II. 93.

[4] The money engagements with them had never been kept ;   the English Honour of Boulogne was in hand.   Pipe Roll, 18 H. II., 45.

[5] So Jordan Fantosme, who at the time was apparently living in the North of England.   Benedict, p. 45, represents the grant as one of Northumberland to the Tyne. William's subsequent operations support Jordan's version.

To enable him to pass the requisite charters a new seal was provided for the young King, his own Seal having been carried off by Richard Barre the Keeper, who loyally delivered it to the old King.[1] Among the first to join the rebellion were Hugh II., Earl of Chester, just returned from a pilgrimage to Compostella; and Robert of Beaumont, Count of Meulan.[2] All this happened apparently before Easter (8th April).

The elder Henry acted with great coolness and judgment. His first

The King's measures.

care was to strengthen the friendly relations recently established with the Church, so as to secure the support of the clergy, and in this matter the presence of the Legates stood him in good stead. One obvious scandal there was that loudly called for remedy, namely the amount of Church preferment kept vacant for the King's benefit. He had at the time in England alone no less than seven bishoprics and six abbeys in hand, the whole being farmed out for rents

Vacant Sees to be filled.

amounting in the aggregate to £5,000 and upwards.[3] Already in the previous year steps had been taken towards filling up the Primacy. The difficulty was that the Canterbury monks wanted a freer hand in the matter than the King was disposed to grant

Canterbury.

them. After an abortive meeting at Windsor, under the presidency of the young King, held on the 1st September (1172)[4] as already mentioned, the Prior Odo went over to Normandy to see the King, but could not be prevailed upon to accept the King's

The King and the Monks.

nominee, Henry of Beaumont, Bishop of Bayeux. Another meeting held in London on Odo's return, late in the year, led to nothing. Early in 1173, however, the monks, afraid of being thought to throw too great difficulties in the way of an appointment, agreed among themseves upon a list of three, to be laid before the Bishops and the Chief Justiciar. This was done at a third meeting held in London in February, when, apparently, Roger Abbot of Bec was accepted by all parties.[5] But it would seem that owing to wrangling over points of precedence and etiquette his election was only proclaimed at Lambeth on the 3rd March.[6] Odo again crossed the Channel to report the election

Abortive Election.

to the King; but, unfortunately, Abbot Roger, from whatever motives, absolutely declined the proffered honour; and the Legates, eventually had to 'absolve' him from the burden.[7] The Cardinals then urged Henry to fill up the other Sees, leaving Canterbury to stand over for the time. In accordance with this advice

---

[1] Ben. P., I. 43-45.
[2] R. Monte, 256.
[3] See the entries in the Pipe Roll, 18 H. II., under the several heads.
[4] Diceto, I. 353.
[5] Gervase, I. 240, 241.
[6] So Diceto, I. 354.
[7] Sainte Barbe (Eure), 5th April; Gervase, 242; R. Monte, 256; Diceto, *sup.*

orders were at once sent over to England, in pursuance of which before
many days were over Richard of Ilchester was named Bishop
Six Sees filled. of Winchester; Geoffrey Riddel Bishop of Ely; Robert Foliot
Bishop of Hereford; Reginald of Bohun Bishop of Bath; John
the Dean of Chichester becoming at the same time Bishop of Chichester,
while lastly the rich See of Lincoln, let for £1,004 a year, was conferred
upon Geoffrey the King's natural son,[1] a mere boy, perhaps fourteen or
fifteen years old.[2] A more thoroughly courtly set of nominations could
not have been made;[3] yet Henry writing to the Pope at this time ventures
to claim credit for having granted free canonical election to the Church
in England.[4] The result however of this conciliatory attitude on the
King's part was that both in England and Normandy the whole bulk of
the clergy remained loyal to him. During the ensuing crisis only Hugh
of Puiset the Bishop of Durham, and Arnulf the Bishop of Lisieux
were accused of playing a double game.[5] It was in hopes of con-
ciliating the refractory Prior Odo that Henry at this time gave the
Abbey of Berking to Becket's sister Mary.[6] But the struggle over
the appointment to Canterbury still went on, being kept up in
appearance between the Bishops on the one hand and the monks
on the other hand, the latter standing out for their
Struggle at Canterbury. Prior, or at any rate one of their own number, a demand for
which no warrant could be found in the history of Canterbury.
As for the intervention of the suffragans in the choice of an Archbishop,
that, so far as we can see, only dated from the election of William of
Corbeil in 1123, the bishops having then been put forward by Henry I.
to counteract the monastic fervour of the Chapter, who then as now
demanded the appointment of a monk.[7] Odo again crossed the Channel
in company with one of his brethren, namely Richard Prior of St. Martin's,
Election of Richard of Dover. Dover. But still the King would not stoop to overt submission.
He preferred to write privately to his uncle of Cornwall and
Richard of Lucy; and under the instructions sent to these
Odo so far gained his point that at last on the 3rd June Prior Richard
was elected at Westminster.[8] Great was the jubilation when on the same

---

[1] Gervase, 243; Diceto, 367, 368; Bp. Stubbs; *Reg. Sacr.*

[2] See Foss, *Judges*, I. 293.

[3] "Ad libitum Regis et curialium electi"; Gerv. *sup.*

[4] *Becket*, VII. 553.

[5] Bishop Stubbs, Ben. P., II. xlviii. Bishop Hugh openly joined the rebels, as we
shall see. Of Arnulf we only hear generally that he gave them support; but the King
never forgave him, and eventually forced him to surrender the Bishopric of Lisieux.
Ben. P., I. 278; R. Monte; A.D. 1181.

[6] Gervase, I. 242. [7] *Foundations*, II. 279.

[8] Gervase, I. 243, 244; R. Diceto, I. 368, 369. I disregard the date given by the
latter. But again Dr. Liebermann's *Geschiches-Quellen*, 6, gave the 15th June as the
date of Richard's election (Howlett).

day the Papal Bull, for the canonisation of St. Thomas of Canterbury, was produced.[1]   On the following Saturday being the 9th June[2] the Archbishop-Elect was received at Canterbury, to be hallowed as was understood, on the morrow.   But when the parties met to arrange the

A Veto.   procession they were confronted by a letter from the young King forbidding the consecration of a Pontiff elected without his assent, and appealing to Rome.   Richard had to submit.   He sent a statement of his case to the Pope, and, following it up by a personal application,[3] was eventually consecrated by Alexander himself at Anagni on the 7th April, 1174.[4]   Reginald of Bohun, who had gone out with Richard as representative of the newly appointed bishops, was unable to procure confirmation at the actual hands of Alexander, who wished to force the King to come to terms with his son.   But under a tacit permission, doubtless given by the Pope, he was consecrated by Archbishop Richard on the way home at Saint Jean de Maurienne, on the 23rd June, 1174.[5]

To return to secular affairs.   After the 'close of Easter' (April 15th),

General Rebellion.   we are told, the storm of rebellion burst over the whole of Henry's dominions.   Everywhere the royal demesnes were overrun and pillaged.   Of the foreign barons in revolt we have lists of names given to us that supply representatives for Normandy, Brittany, Maine, Anjou, and Aquitaine.   We have John Talevas Count of Ponthieu, Gilbert of Aumâle, Simon of Montfort Count of

Leaders abroad.   Evreux, Robert of Montfort-sur-Rille, William of Tancarville, the Chamberlain of Normandy, Ralph of Fougères, Guionon of Ancenis, Guibert of La Guerche, John Count of Sonnois (*i.e.* Alençon), Bernard of La Ferté Bernard, Hugh of Sillé, Robert of Sablé, Geoffrey son of the Count of Vendôme, Geoffrey of Lusignan, Hugh of Sainte-Maur, Ralph of Faye, the Count of Angoulême, Saher de Quincy, William Marshal.[6]   But the focus of the disturbance clearly lay in Normandy and Brittany,[7] as the largest proportion of names comes from those districts.   Dislike to Angevin rule would count for something both

[1] Diceto, *sup.*   For the documents see *Becket*, VII. 544-550.
[2] So Gervase, *sup.*   The 8th June of Diceto, 372, a Friday, is clearly wrong, as he agrees that the consecration was to take place on the morrow, while the rite would certainly be performed on a Sunday.
[3] Gervase, I. 244, 245 ; Diceto, I. 372 ; R. Monte, 257.
[4] Gervase, 247, *Reg. Sacrum.*   For details of Richard's journey, and of the difficulties he had to contend with at the Papal Court, see R. Diceto, I. 387-391, and especially the Bishop of Bath's letter to the King, Ben. P., I. 69 (3rd May, 1174).   Richard duly received his Pall, and also the Legateship over the Province of Canterbury.
[5] Ben. P., 74 ; the Bishop's letter, *Id.*, 69, and *Reg. Sacrum.*
[6] See Ben. P., I. 45-47 ; R. Monte, 257 ; R. Diceto, I. 371 ; and for identification of the places, Norgate, II. 136-139.   It was at this time that the young King was knighted by William Marshal.   [7] So Miss Norgate points out ; *sup.*

with Bretons and Normans.   In England among those who rose against
the King we have Robert III. of Beaumont, Earl of Leicester,
Leaders at Home. son of the late Chief Justiciar; Robert III. of Ferrers Earl
of Derby; Hugh Bigod Earl of Norfolk; Hugh II. Earl
of Chester; Roger Mowbray of Axholme; Geoffrey of Coutances; and
Richard of Morville, with their allies the King of Scots and his brother
David, styled Earl of Huntingdon.[1]   Under their control they had,
apart from Berwick and other places North of the Border, the castles of
Mountsorrel, Groby, Leicester, Tutbury, Framlingham, Duffield, Bungay,
and Huntingdon,[2] a formidable show.   On the other hand, through the
zeal of Richard of Lucy and the Sheriffs, the royal castles throughout
the kingdom had been promptly repaired, manned, and supplied with
provisions.[3]

Scottish co-operation in any English disturbance might be looked for
almost as a matter of course, but Henry had been mean in his dealings
with William and David, as with other feudatories.   The loss of the
Earldom of Huntingdon was a great blow to David.   As for the other
men in revolt, all of them much more French than English in their ways
Grievances of the Insurgents. and sympathies, "the necessity of submitting to the law"[4]
would be a primary source of discontent.   Some of them,
like Hugh Bigod, could remember the good old days of the
Anarchy, when they did as they pleased.   Others, like Hugh of Chester,
must have heard of the parts then played by their fathers.   The garrisoning
of baronial castles with royal troops,[5] a right freely exercised by Henry,
and the resumption of Crown demesnes, of which we have heard from
the very beginning of the reign, would be special grievances.[6]   A more
justifiable complaint might be based on the arbitrary taxation of which,
in England at least, we have had such abundant evidence.

On Henry's side were his natural relatives, his uncle Reginald Earl of
Cornwall, his brother Hamelin Earl of Warenne or Surrey, his
Loyal Barons. cousin William Earl of Gloucester; he had the two de Clares
Roger of Hertford and Richard (Strongbow) of Pembroke;
also William of Mandeville Earl of Essex, William Earl of Salisbury,
William of Beaumont Earl of Warwick, and Simon III. of St. Liz Earl of
Northampton.[7]   More trustworthy and important was the adhesion of the
officials—such as the Lucys, Glanvilles, and Stutevilles—of the clergy, and

---

[1] Ben. P., 47, 48; Diceto, *sup.*   [2] Ben. P., 48.

[3] See the Pipe Roll, 19 H. II., *passim.*

[4] Palgrave, *Normandy and England*, IV. 25; Stubbs.

[5] Bishop Stubbs describes this as "a chief prerogative of the dukes of Normandy";
Ben. P., II. xlvii.

[6] So Diceto, I. 371.

[7] See the full list, Ben. P., 51 (MS. B.).   Salisbury was the son of Earl Patrick who
fell in Poitou in 1168.

of the English population generally, which now, as under Henry I., stood by their King as against their Norman lords. Still with Louis of France and William of Scotland, with Eleanor of Aquitaine and her sons all on the side of rebellion, the odds must have seemed "dead against Henry." But with all their strength and numbers his adversaries had no programme, no leader, no watchword. What they seemed to contemplate was a scramble, in which each man might get what he could. "The whole rebellion was crushed in a few months."[1]

Weakness of the Rebels.

No serious operations were undertaken till after Midsummer, both sides being busy concentrating their forces for the main trial of strength, that would be fought out in Normandy. Thus we find Henry enlisting Brabançon mercenaries, and bringing over Strongbow and Hugh de Lacy from Ireland; while the Earl of Leicester and William of Tancarville, under pretence of joining the King, left England and went to Paris.[2]

Mustering of Forces.

About the first week in July[3] the confederates at last set their forces in motion. The young King supported by Philip of Flanders and his brother Matthew of Boulogne laid siege to Aumâle. After a show of resistance the place yielded; William of Aumâle, the ex-Earl of Yorkshire, and Simon of Northampton falling into the hands of the Flemings; Eu was surrendered by Count Henry without being subjected even to the form of a siege.[4] The invaders then advanced to Neufchâtel.[5] Feeling unable to hold out the garrison applied for and obtained the King's permission to surrender. The next place attacked was Arques.[6] But during some skirmishing that took place there on July 25th the Count of Boulogne fell mortally wounded. He was taken home to die, and there the young King's campaign ended.[7]

The Young King's Campaign.

On the 6th of the month[8] Louis had laid siege to Verneuil with a well-equipped army. We are told that the town consisted of three detached quarters or wards (*tres burgi*, Fr. *bourgs*), each with its own wall and ditch,

[1] Bishop Stubbs, Ben. P., II. xlix.

[2] W. Newb., I. 172; Diceto, 371, 375; Ben. P., I. 49, 51.

[3] So Ben. P., I. 49; R. de Monte, 257; R. Diceto, I. 372. William of Newburgh gives June as the month.

[4] Diceto, 373.

[5] "Castellum Novum," W. Newb., I. 173; "Novum Castrum quod diciter Dringcurt"; R. Monte, 258, mixing up two distinct places.

[6] Diceto, *sup*. The writer, however, interpolates an expedition to Driencourt (Somme, near Peronne) between the attacks on Neufchâtel and Arques, which seems impossible.

[7] Diceto, *sup*.; W. Newb., *sup*. This writer, however, gives Matthew as wounded at Neufchâtel; while R. Monte, 258, and Benedict I., 49, represent him as struck at Driencourt. The Count's brother Peter, Bishop Elect of Cambrai, was chosen to succeed him.

[8] So Ben. P., *sup*. Diceto gives July 1st as the date of the mustering of Louis' army, and July 15th as that of the actual operations against Verneuil; 372, 374.

besides the citadel (*castellum*).[1]   The constables Hugh de Lacy and Hugh
of Beauchamp, safely established in the Keep, could laugh at
Louis' efforts; but at the end of a month the principal ward,

Louis'
Campaign

known as Bourg la Reine, crowded with non-combatants, was
reduced to extremities.   On 6th August apparently a truce was signed,
under which the men of this *bourg* promised to surrender on the third
day if not previously relieved, Louis guaranteeing them all their property.
Henry, hastening to the rescue from Rouen, halted on the night of the
7th August at Conches; next 'day, having passed through Breteuil, he
was drawing out his forces in battle array, near Verneuil, when a proposal
came in from Louis for a truce of twenty-four hours, and a conference on
the morrow.   Henry accepted the offer, and then very carelessly retired to
a distance, without providing for the safety of the compromised people
of Verneuil.   On the 9th he came to the appointed place of meeting,
and waited there, and waited, till clouds of smoke from the direction of
Verneuil told him how grossly he had been duped.   Pushing on he found
that King Louis had demanded the surrender of the *bourg*,

A base
Trick.

for want of relief; and then conscious that he could not hold
part of the town without the rest of it, had plundered and
fired the surrendered quarter.   Finally, not daring to face Henry in the
field, he posted off in ignominious flight.[2]   A more deplorable exhibition
of mingled bad faith and poltroonery was never witnessed.

Returning to Rouen Henry sent his mercenaries to the frontier of
Brittany, where the Earl of Chester (hereditary Viscount of

Campaign in
Brittany.

Avranches and Bayeux) with Ralph of Fougères, the ex-Count
Eude of Porhoet—no friend either—and a host of discontented
Breton gentry, were running riot.   They had burned St. James de Beuvron,
and Le Teilleuil; and obtained the surrender of Combourg and Dol.   On
Monday, 20th August, an action ensued outside Dol in which the Bretons
were defeated by Henry's troops.   Eude made off; but the Earl with
Ralph of Fougères and many others had to take refuge in the castle.   A

Forced
March.

report of the state of things at Dol reached Rouen the next
evening, Tuesday, 21st July.   By the morning Henry was on
the march, and reached Dol on the 23rd of the month.   Three
days later the castle yielded.   What with the men taken in the action, and

A Haul.

what with those found in the fortress, some hundred gentlemen
of name and position fell into the King's hands; a perfect
haul, that cleared Brittany of unruly elements.[3]

The transmission of a message from Dol to Rouen in one day; and the
march of a body of troops over the same distance in two days are facts

---

[1] Ben. P., 49, 50; Diceto, 374.

[2] See Ben. P., 49-55, the best account. *Cnf.* Diceto, 374, 375; R. Monte, 257, 259.

[3] Ben. P., I. 56-58. R. Monte, 259, 260. R. Diceto, 378. The former names 97
men. All three agree that Henry did the journey in two days.

worth noting. If the message was really carried in twenty-four hours or so, that would imply an organised system of posting with relays of horses. But the statements as to the time taken for the message may not be strictly accurate; on the other hand it seems perfectly clear that Henry left Rouen on the Wednesday, rested that night at Tinchebrai, and reached Dol on the Thursday. The distance as the crow flies would be 140 miles. We may conjecture that Henry rode by way of Bernay, Merleherault, Argentan, Tinchebrai, Mortain, and Pontorson, 170 miles at the least.

Affairs in Normandy now seemed so far settled down that Henry went off to Le Mans, where he spent most of September, returning, however, to hold a conference with Louis at Gisors on the 25th of the month; the **Henry and his sons.** meeting being held in the hope of effecting an arrangement between the King and his sons. He made them liberal offers, offers that might remind the reader of those made by Henry I. to his brother Robert on the eve of the battle of Tinchebrai. The young King might have half the revenues of England with four castles, if he liked to live there; or half the revenues of Normandy, with the whole of those of Anjou, and three castles, if he should prefer an establishment abroad. Richard might have half the issues of Aquitaine with three castles; Geoffrey would have the inheritance of his bride as soon as the marriage with **His offers rejected.** Constance could be celebrated. But these proposals did not meet the views of the French, who wanted to see the Royal youths placed in positions of absolute independence, an impossible concession for Henry to make. A second meeting held on the morrow between Trie and Gisors proved equally fruitless.[1] We are told that on the latter occasion the Earl of Leicester utterly lost his temper, abusing the King, and finally laying his hand on his sword as if to strike him.[2]

At the outbreak of the rising the Earl had left England for Normandy, **The Rising in England.** as offering the most promising field of action. Finding the game in Normandy now played out he hastened back to England, where he landed at Walton in Suffolk about the 18th October.[3] At home the initiative had been taken by the King's men, and just about the very time when operations began on the Continent. On **Leicester besieged.** the 3rd July the Earl of Cornwall and Richard of Lucy laid siege to Leicester; an arduous and expensive undertaking as matters turned out. Towards the end of the month, however, great part of the city was burned down by an accidental fire; and then the

---

[1] Ben. P., I. 59; Hoveden, II. 53.
[2] Hoveden, 54.
[3] Ben. P., 60. Diceto, I. 377, gives the date as the 29th September. But the extreme improbability of the Earl's being able to collect troops and land in Suffolk four days after attending a council at Gisors leads me to follow the dates of Benedict for Leicester's campaign rather than those of Diceto, which differ entirely

eople came to terms, paying the Royalists £200 to be allowed to march
ut with all their goods and chattels. With the garrison in the castle a
ruce to Michaelmas was taken, and so, on the 28th July, the siege was raised.[1]

Scottish Inroad. In fact Lucy was called off to resist a Scottish inroad. King
William had drawn the sword to give effect to the generous
'grant' of Northumberland made by the young King. After
n effectual attack on the stubborn little fortress at Wark, he pushed on
nto Northumberland, where the men of Galloway and the Highlanders [2]
ommitted the usual ravages, sparing however the possessions of the
riendly Bishop Hugh of Durham. Returning homewards by the favourite
restern route they laid siege to Carlisle, but again without result, the
Lucy and Bohun to the Rescue. approach of a relieving army inducing them to retire on Roxburgh. Lucy and Humphrey of Bohun, the constable, followed
them up, burning Berwick, and committing retaliatory ravages
n Lothian, till the news of the landing of the Earl of Leicester in the
South induced them to sign a truce to the 13th January, 1174.[3]

Having disembarked at Walton near Felixstow about the 18th October
Campaign in East Anglia. Earl Robert had wasted four days in fruitless assaults on
Walton Castle, a fortress that had been duly manned and
victualled.[4]   He then joined the Earl of Norfolk at Framlingham, and the two together proceeded to attack the castle of Haughley,
near Stowmarket, held for the King by Ralph of Brock. After four
days' siege the place yielded (1 to 6 Nov.)[5] Content with this achievement the two Earls apparently returned to Framlingham, as we are told
that Leicester would willingly have prolonged his stay there, but that
finding that his presence, or that of his foreign retainers was becoming
burdensome to his hosts, he resolved to make for his own home at Leicester.
But Lucy and Bohun, hurrying back from Berwick, had reached Bury St.
Edmunds, and were preparing to intercept him with 300 mercenaries,
besides reinforcements brought by the Earls of Cornwall, Gloucester, and
Arundel. Robert endeavoured to give them the slip by passing a little
to the North of Bury; but on crossing the river Lark at Fornham St.
Battle of Fornham. Geneveve, he found himself face to face with the Royal army.
One charge of the mercenaries' settled the affair. The Earl's
rather motley force was dispersed at a blow, some killed,
some drowned, some taken prisoners, the Earl himself and his spirited
wife Peronelle or Petronilla of Grand Mesnil among the number ; also

---

[1] *Id.* 376.

[2] Per montanos Scottos . . . et Galwalenses ;" J. Fordun, p. 262. J. Fantosme specially
mentions a contingent from Moray and Ross ; p. 242 (Howlett, Rolls Series, No. 82).

[3] See Chron. Melrose followed, and apparently copied, by J. Fordun, 262 ; also R.
Diceto, 376 ; Ben. P., 61 ; R. Hoveden, 54, and J. Fantosme, 242—274.

[4] Pipe Roll, 19 H. II., p. 131.

[5] Ben. P., I. 60. Diceto, I. 397, gives the date as 13th October. See note last page.

the Earl's cousin Hugh of Château-Neuf-en-Thymerais, besides another Frenchman of rank who was with them (15th or 16th November).[1] The Earl and Countess were sent to Normandy by Henry's orders, to keep the Earl of Chester company at Falaise.[2]

A considerable force had now rallied round the King's officers in defence of the cause of order. But somewhat to the surprise of the nation they did not press their advantage by reducing Bigod to submission. On the contrary they signed a truce with him to the 19th May 1174, on the simple condition of his dismissing some Flemish mercenaries in his service. The men were taken to Dover under safe-conduct and from thence shipped home at the King's expense.[3] We

A Fire of Straw. may take it that this lenient policy had its warrant in the King's instructions. He evidently regarded the whole rising as a mere fire of straw that might be left to burn itself out.

On the continent the tide of affairs showed the same quiet drift in favour of the elder King. He himself had paid a hasty visit to England, making his way as far as Northampton, where he rested four days.[4] The date of his journey is not indicated, but we incline to believe that he went over after Michaelmas, as if following on the track of the Earl of Leicester. Anyhow he went and returned "so quickly that neither friends nor foes seem ever to have discovered his absence."[5] In the course of November he led an army across the Loire, and received the

The War abroad. submission of the rebel castles of Champigny (near Richelieu), La Haye, and Preuilly[6]; returning Northwards he reinstated Count John I. of Vendôme, who had been ousted by his eldest son Bouchard.[7]

---

[1] 16th November, the Cotton MS. of Diceto, I. 378, reading "XVI. Kal. Dec." for the "XVI. Kal. Nov." (17th October) of the printed text. Benedict, whose dates so far seem the best, after telling us that Haughley was taken in the first week of November, gives for the battle the absurd date of 16th October; "XVII. Kal Nov.," where of course again we should read "XVII. Kal Dec." = 15th November. Diceto who places the taking of Haughley on the 13th October, and the battle on the 17th October, discredits himself by telling us that a considerable period of inaction had intervened between the two events. As for the numbers engaged the 300 mercenaries on the King's side (Benedict) a very probable estimate, may be used to correct the talk of 3,000 Flemings (Diceto) or 12,000 Flemings (Benedict) on Leicester's side. See also W. Newb., I. 178, 179; and R. Monte, 261 and note.

[2] Benedict, 62. [3] Diceto, *sup.*

[4] Pipe Roll, 19 H. II., pp. 33, 35.

[5] Norgate, II. 343. She would place the visit in June; but we have warrants passed by the King himself, as if he was in England at the time, sanctioning payments extending to Michaelmas, with one for wages running 8th September–18th October (Pipe Roll, p. 134). Of the King's movements in October we have no record.

[6] Indre et Loire, all three.

[7] Bened., 62, 63; Norgate, II. 151; Hoved., II. 56, note Stubbs; a younger son, Geoffrey of Lavardin was also in revolt.

So again went affairs in 1174. The year opened with a truce with France taken to last from the 13th January to the octaves of Easter, 31st March. The young King apparently did not consider himself included, as he made an attack on Sées in concert with the Counts of Blois, Perche, and Alençon. The attempt failed, the stout burghers repelling the assaults without the help of King or captain.[1] On the 30th April Henry started on a triumphant progress through Maine, Anjou, and Poitou. On the 12th May he was at Poitiers. Hearing that

Royal Successes. Saintes[2] was being held for his son Richard, he hastened thither to find the rebels ensconced in three strongholds, namely, two castles and the cathedral, the latter having been fortified for the occasion. Henry stormed all three in successive assaults, beginning with the fort that stood at the entrance of the town; advancing to the original castle in the interior; and finally ending with the church. Some sixty men-at-arms and four hundred archers fell into his hands.[1] Returning Northwards by easy stages, Henry on the 11th June recovered possession of Ancenis, on the Loire, where he ordered the fortifications to be greatly strengthened, as if to keep both Brittany and Anjou in check.[4] On reaching Normandy Henry would probably hear of an apprehended invasion of England by the Count of Flanders; of the actual descent of

Confusion and alarm in England. a body of Flemings on the coast of Norfolk; and of a general state of war and confusion harassing the country. In view of an immediate crossing, he summoned a Grand Council to meet at Bonneville-sur-Touques[5] on the 24th June. There he found his trusty confidant Richard of Ilchester, late Archdeacon of Poitiers, and now Elect of Winchester, charged to deliver a last urgent appeal for help, the centre of disturbance having now crossed the Channel, and lying over Great Britain. Henry lost no time. In the early hours of the 8th July

The King returns. he took ship at Barfleur with some hired troops, and his whole household, but no Norman levies.[6] His retinue included the two Queens, Eleanor and Margaret, both in custody; the affianced brides of his younger sons;[7] his son

A Family Party. John, his daughter Johanna, the Earl and Countess of Leicester, the Earl of Chester and other captives. The wind was fitful and squally, and the sailors seemed doubtful of the weather. But when the King heard that the direction of the wind was favourable,

---

[1] " Sine principe, etiam sine duce;" R. Diceto, I. 379.

[2] Charente Inf. [3] Diceto, 379, 380; Ben. P., 71.

[4] Ben. P. and Diceto, *sup.* The latter speaks as if he supposed the fortifications to be of wood, as he gives the *faber lignarius* as the chief artificer.

[5] Calvados. See Round, *Calendar*, 46.

[6] R. Diceto, 380–383; Ben. P., 72. R. Monte, 263, 264.

[7] "Uxores filiorum suorum," namely, Alais of France, Constance of Brittany, and Alais of Maurienne ; Norgate, II. 158.

he said solemnly ' If I seek the peace of Church and people ; if the God of Heaven has decreed peace at my coming, then let Him in His mercy grant me a haven of safety. If He intends to visit my kingdom with a rod then let me never reach the shore.' Before night set in the fleet had reached Southampton water.[1]

At that very time the young King and the Count of Flanders were going down to the coast preparing to cross. But Louis, on hearing that Henry had gone over, recalled them.[2]

The King came none too soon, as since Easter the Kingdom had been a prey to every disorder. Nevertheless when he landed the worst of the storm was already passed. Just as in Normandy the year had opened with a truce to cover the Easter season ; so in England the armistice with the Scots that would have expired on the 13th January was extended by Hugh of Puiset to the 31st March. For this respite £200 were paid by the Northumbrian barons. Unfortunately the use made of the truce by the Bishop was to fortify his castle at Northallerton in the rebel interest ; while Roger of Mowbray, having set Thirsk and Kirkby-Malzeard (near Ripon) in order, proceeded to restore a decayed fort at Keadby in Axholme.[3] With respect to Bishop Puiset we must remember that he owed his promotion to King Stephen, being closely connected with the House of Blois.[4] He was all for the rebels ; and was making arrangements with his nephew and namesake Hugh of Puiset, Count of Bar, for bringing over troops to England.[5]

The War in England.

The only connected operations were those of the Scots. At the expiry of the truce (April) William, advancing from Berwick, made a demonstration against Bamborough, sacking Belford and over-running a certain amount of country. But Bamborough, apparently held by William of Vesci,[6] was impregnable, so the King fell back on Berwick with his booty.[7]

A fresh start was made in May, when William, at the solicitation of Mowbray and Adam of Port (Calvados) a man under forfeiture, sent his brother David to reinforce the garrison at Leicester ;[8] while he himself advanced to lay fresh siege to Wark. But there again Roger of Stuteville, the Sheriff of Northumberland, was found quite prepared, so the King of Scots, with a heavy heart, moved on to attack William of Vaux at Carlisle.[9] At Leicester David was received

The Scots again.

---

[1] R. Diceto, I. 380–382. Ben. P., *sup.*

[2] Diceto, 381 ; Ben., I. 71, 73.

[3] Ben. P., 64 ; R. Hoveden, II. 57. The name of the place is given " Kinardeferia."

[4] See *Foundations*, II. 434.

[5] Ben. P., I. 67. Hugh the nephew held the county of Bar-sur-Seine in right of his wife Peronelle daughter of Count Milo II. ; Hoveden, II. 63, note Bp. Stubbs.

[6] Pipe Roll, 20 Henry II., 106.

[7] J. Fantosme, 300, 302 ; Ben. P., 64.

[8] Fantosme, 296, 314 ; W. Newb., I. 180.

[9] Fantosme, 314 ; Ben. P., *sup.*

with open arms by Robert Ferrers Earl of Derby, who was established there; and the two at once swooped down upon the unfortunate town of Nottingham, inflicting on it all the miseries of another sack—

Sack of Nottingham the third within the half-century.[1] About the same time, as we suppose, that is to say late in May, Ansketill Mallory, the Constable of Leicester, emulating their example, made a successful attack on Northampton, defeating the citizens in a pitched encounter

And North-ampton. outside the walls.[2] But meanwhile the Royalists had not been idle. On the 5th May Geoffrey the young Elect of Lincoln had taken and destroyed Mowbray's fort in Axholme; then rallying the Yorkshiremen he captured Kirkby Malzeard, finally reducing Roger to impotence by setting up Topcliffe as a counterwork to Thirsk, his one remaining castle.[3] Simultaneously Rhys of South Wales, who kept loyal, was attacking Ferrers' Castle at Tutbury.[4] Again going back a little, we hear that on the 8th May Richard of Lucy laid siege to Huntingdon. Earl David was clearly not there; we must suppose that the place was being held by the tenants of the estates still retained by the King of Scots in the neighbourhood.[5] The old castle resisted all the Justiciar's efforts, so he had to content himself with building a counterwork at its gate, which he entrusted to Simon of St. Liz, the Earl of Northampton. Simon claimed Huntingdon and its earldom as his by rights, and the King had said that he might have it if he could win it.[6]

So far the successes were on the whole on the side of the Royalists, who were fairly confronting the rebels in their strong central position in the Midlands. On the other hand a reverse had been suffered in East Anglia,

The War in East Anglia. where Bigod had perhaps been dealt with too gently in the previous year. The Count of Flanders, who had pledged himself to invade England in person after Midsummer, had sent over an advanced column of 418 picked men. They landed in the Orwell on the 15th May, and at once placed themselves under the orders of Earl Hugh. An attack on Dunwich was repelled, but Norwich fell into their hands, having been betrayed to them, it was said, by a Lorrainer (18th June).[7]

But the decisive triumph of the war fell to the share of the loyal Yorkshire Barons. The King of Scots, whom we left at the siege of Carlisle, after a short stay there in person, went on a ravaging tour through

---

[1] See index to *Foundations*. Ben. P., I. 69; J. Fantosme, 298.

[2] Ben. P., 68.

[3] Id., 68, 69; W. Newb., I. 182; Diceto, 384; Giraldus, IV. 364-367 (Norgate).

[4] Diceto *sup.*

[5] See above, 81. In fact Diceto speaks of the Castle as belonging to William; I. 104.

[6] Diceto *sup.*; Ben. P., 70, 71.

[7] R. Diceto, 1. 381; Ben. P., I. 68; J. Fantosme, 272-280. W. Newb., I. 184, follows Jordan in mixing up these events with Leicester's landing of the previous year.

Northumberland, capturing the Border forts of Liddel and Harbottle; the
The War in the North. one held by a Stuteville, the other by an Umphraville.[1]
Having returned to Carlisle he led another expedition into
Westmoreland, capturing Appleby and Brough-under-Stane-
more.[2] Vaux now finding his communications with Richmond and the
West Riding cut off and provisions running short, was induced
Raids of the Scots. to enter into one of the usual conventions by which he
agreed to surrender on Michaelmas Day, if not previously
relieved.[3] Having secured this advantage the King of Scots struck,
along the line of the old Roman wall, from Carlisle to Prudhoe, half-way
between Hexham and Newcastle. On Tuesday, 9th July, apparently,
he laid siege to Prudhoe Castle. On the Thursday, the Scots, hearing
that the Yorkshiremen were gathering at Newcastle, resolved to drop
the siege; and in fact next day they rode off, William himself making
Retirement on Alnwick. his way as far as Alnwick.[4] But the greater part of the army
under Gillebride Earl of Angus, Duncan II. Earl of Fife, and
Richard of Morville were sent in detachments to plunder far
and wide. By one of these parties Warkworth was burnt, St. Lawrence's
Church and all.[5] In the course of the ensuing night,[6] at any rate before
sunrise next morning, the Royalists started from Newcastle under the lead
of Ranulf of Glanville, William of Vesci, Bernard of Balliol, Odinel of
Umphraville, and Robert of Stuteville, and his son William. Archbishop
Roger of York had sent his Constable with sixty men.[7] The thirty-three
miles between Newcastle and Alnwick were traversed without a check.
As they drew near to Alnwick they found themselves in a mist that
overhung the valley of the Alne. When the mist cleared away the King
of Scots was discovered in a meadow outside the town, quite off his guard,
with only his ordinary Household in attendance, some sixty men all told.[8]
William the Lion did not disgrace his name. Quickly donning his armour
and mounting his steed he led his men to engage the enemy. 'The first
whom he met he struck to the ground.'[9] Next moment a common soldier

[1] Ben. P., I. 64, 65. I correct his list by reference to the topography and subsequent
events.

[2] J. Fantosme, 324–330; W. Newb., I. 181, 182 ; Ben., P. *sup. Cnf.* J. Fordun, 263,
an utter jumble. Fantosme and Newburgh have nothing of the first tour, and Benedict
mixes up the two tours, adding the capture of Warkworth, that came still later.

[3] J. Fantosme, 340 ; Ben. P., and W. Newb. *sup.*

[4] J. Fantosme, 344 ; Ben. P., 65, 66.

[5] Fantosme, 346 ; Ben. P , *sup.* With respect to the atrocities ascribed to the Scots
in this war by the latter writer, and after him by Hoveden, Bishop Stubbs has pointed
out that their descriptions are copied from Henry of Huntingdon's account of what the
Scots did in 1138; Hoved., II. 57, note.

[6] "La nuit;" Fantosme.

[7] Ben. P., 65, 66.

[8] W. Newb., I. 184.

[9] Fantosme.

(*serjant*) speared his horse bringing down the animal and his rider.   There
the King lay prostrate and helpless, with his legs under the horse's belly
Capture of till Glanville secured him.   The Household, like good and
William the true vassals,[1] bound to share their master's doom, fought
Lion. it out till they were either killed, or unhorsed and taken
prisoners.   Mowbray and Adam of Port being bound by no such ties
made good their escape.   The Royal prisoner was taken by Glanville first
to Newcastle, and from thence to Richmond, Ranulf's official residence,
to await orders.[2]   Of the prisoners mentioned it is worth noting that all
were bearers of Anglo-Norman names, except one, and he was a Fleming.[3]
The presence of Flemings in the service of the Kings of Scots, is a fact
worth noting; so is the circumstance that Jordan Fantosme, the writer of
the time, always speaks of Scotland as ' Albany,' the old Pictish name.

We left Henry at Southampton, just landed, on the 8th July, the
Monday of this eventful week.   His first care was to place his captives
in safe keeping;[4] his next to seal his reconciliation with the clerical world,
and to testify to the sincerity of his remorse for the death of St. Thomas
by submitting to an act of personal humiliation more signal than any that
he had yet undergone.   Leaving Southampton on the 9th[5] he reached
Henry does Canterbury on the 12th July.   At the church of St. Dunstan,
Penance at at the West gate of the city, he dismounted, put on a plain
Becket's woollen gown, bared his Royal feet, and so walked through
Tomb. rough and muddy streets to the Cathedral.   A large concourse
of prelates, monks, and others had gathered there to receive the King, but
by his orders all customary ceremonial was dispensed with.   At the threshold he knelt down and said a prayer; on being led to the spot where
Becket fell he kissed it and bathed it with tears;[6] having then confessed
to the bishops he descended with reverential trembling[7] to the tomb in the
crypt; there he lay for some time at full length, prostrated in prayer.
The Bishop of London then addressed the people on the King's behalf,
protesting once more his innocence of the fatal deed, but begging for their

[1] " Cil d' Aubanie (Albany, Scotland) furent mult bons vassaus ; . . . En mi la
bataille serrunt pris communaus." Fantosme, 356.

[2] Saturday 13th July.   I follow Fantosme, who was with the English force, presumably
as their chaplain, 348–362.   His presence there was doubtless the *raison d'être* of his
poem.   *Cnf.* W. Newb., I. 183, an account evidently taken from Fantosme.   A stone
marks the spot where William was unhorsed.

[3] Ben. P., 67 ; Hoved., 63.   So at the Battle of the Standard we heard that the Scots
King's bodyguard were either English or Norman ; *Foundations*, II. 370.   For names of
English barons taken on William's side see Fantosme, 356–360.

[4] Ben. P., I. 72.   Eleanor was sent to Salisbury, the young Queen to Devizes ;
Norgate, II. 159 ; G. Vigeois, 319.

[5] Ben. P., 72.

[6] " Rigavit lacrymis et osculatus est."

[7] " Tremore multo et reverentia."

intercession in prayer for forgiveness for the hasty words of which such unfair advantage had been taken ; he added that the King confirmed the church of Canterbury in all her fullest rights, granting her a further endowment of £30 a year from the Royal revenues. Henry with his own mouth ratified Foliot's pledges ; then divesting himself of his outer garment he knelt down with his head and shoulders inside one of the apertures in the outer sarcophagus of the tomb,[1] and in that position received five formal stripes from each prelate, and three from each monk present, the number of the latter being given as about eighty. The flagellation concluded Henry was at last once more solemnly absolved. But there he remained, fasting as he had come, crouching humbly on the bare floor of the crypt through the night,[2] just like a Greek suppliant of old. When the time of Lauds came (3 a.m.) he rose and went the round of the altars and shrines in the upper church ; at daybreak he attended Mass, and so finally in the course of the morning was dismissed in peace from Canterbury. At parting he was given a drink of holy water in which some of the Martyr's relics had been dipped, with a further portion of the same to carry away in a phial. Leaving Canterbury on Saturday 13th July Henry next day entered London.[3]

Great as the moral effort involved in Henry's elaborate act of penitential humiliation may have been, his reward in the eyes of the world was certainly prompt and signal. The day following his vigil at Canterbury

Report of William's Capture. witnessed the capture of his most dangerous enemy, as the reader knows. The news, brought by a mounted messenger sent by Glanville, reached Westminster on the Wednesday evening, after the King had retired for the night (17th July).[4] A fuller report from the Archbishop of York having been received next day, the King at once started for Huntingdon.[5] But the capture of King William

Collapse of the Rebellion. had knocked the bottom out of the rising. On the 21st July Huntingdon surrendered ;[6] an advance on the 24th July to Sileham, close to Framlingham, brought Bigod to terms. Next day he came in, and yielded Framlingham and Bungay, obtaining leave, but not without difficulty, to send off his Flemish and French auxiliaries in peace.[7] During the discussion, conducted apparently on

---

[1] "Scapulis et capite inclinato in unam fenestrarum tumuli." These apertures were made to allow pilgrims to have a view of the actual coffin in which the body was enshrined.

[2] See the account of E. Grim, *Becket*, II. 445–447, who was doubtless present.

[3] Gervase, I. 248, 249 ; Ben. P., I. 72.

[4] J. Fantosme, 364–372. The distance from Alnwick to London by the old posting road is 308 miles.

[5] *Id.* Ben. P., 72.

[6] Huntingdon having surrendered Henry apparently kept his word to Simon of St. Liz III., who became Earl of Huntingdon.

[7] Ben. P., 72, 73 ; Diceto, 384, 385.

horseback, the King received a severe blow on the leg from the kick of a horse.   On the 26th July, notwithstanding, the Royal army moved to Northampton, a loyal town.   There William the Lion was brought in with his legs ignominiously tied under his horse's belly ;[1] and there on the 31st July all the outstanding rebel chiefs made their submission.   Hugh of Puiset yielded Durham and Northallerton, on condition of dismissing his nephew the Count of Bar, who had landed at Hartlepool on the day of William's capture.   Leicester's men yielded Leicester, Mountsorrel, and Groby ; Ferrers gave up Duffield ; and loyal assurances were received from William, Earl of Gloucester, and Richard, Earl of Hertford, who had somewhat suspiciously kept aloof.[2]

Thus in three weeks time Henry had restored peace to England.   But for himself personally no time of rest as yet had come.   Louis,

The War Abroad. thinking that an opportunity had offered itself when Henry went over to England, had recalled the young King and the Count of Flanders from their intended invasion of England, and had taken them to make a bold attack on Rouen.[3]   But the Norman

Rouen besieged. Barons were not to be tempted from their allegiance to Henry. Louis' own forces were barely sufficient to invest the East side of the city, leaving communication with the West across the bridge of the Seine entirely open.   Thus provisions flowed into Rouen, while supplies for the French camp had to be brought from a distance, through hostile country.   The chief incident of the siege was a treacherous attempt at escalade made by Louis on St. Lawrence's Day (10th August), after that he had voluntarily proclaimed a truce in honour of the Saint.   His movements, however, having been detected from the top of a church tower, a prompt alarm rung out from the great bell " La Rebol " brought the citizens to arms.[4]

Henry, having settled affairs in England, had sailed from Portsmouth on the 6th August, landing next day at Barfleur.[5]   He brought

Henry goes over. with him his Brabançon mercenaries, and by way of a novelty, a Welsh contingent under Rhys.[6]   The unfortunate Earls of Chester and Leicester, who had gone over with the King a month before

---

[1] Hoveden, II. 64.

[2] Ben. P., I. 73 ; Diceto, I. 385.   The Earl of Gloucester, son of the loyal Robert, was married to Leicester's sister Hawise ; Richard of Clare, 3rd Earl of Hertford, succeeded his father Roger in 1173 ; he was married to Amicia, daughter of the Earl of Gloucester.   R. Monte, p. 258 ; G.E.C. Peerage.

[3] 22nd July, Diceto, 386.   [4] W. Newb, I. 192.

[5] Ben. P., 74.   Diceto, 385, gives the 7th August as the day of sailing.

[6] Benedict gives their number as 1000.   They received from the Sheriff of Hereford-shire £4 18s. 11d. for corredy or journey money, presumably from Wales to Southampton, with £2 14s. 8d. from the Sheriff of Gloucestershire for drink (*Pro potu Wallensium*), Pipe Roll, 20 H. II., 21, 121.   The corredy money would be 1187 pennies.   But how many pennies would each Welshman require to support him on the way from the Wye

had now to recross the Channel, with William the Lion as a companion in adversity, all three bound for Falaise.   At Barfleur by an odd coincidence the King found the newly consecrated Prelates, Richard of Canterbury and Reginald of Bath, on their way to England from Italy.[1]   On the 11th August Henry entered Rouen.   On the very next day he sent out his Welshmen to cross the river, recross it higher up, and scour the woods in the French rear.   A convoy of forty waggons laden with victuals fell into their hands.   On the 13th August Henry threw open the gate leading to the French camp, filled up the foss, and assumed the offensive.   That was enough for Louis.   He begged for a truce to allow him to retire to Malaunay, some ten miles on the road to Dieppe, promising an interview there on the morrow.   Under cover of this pretence he burned his engines, and made off to France (14th August).   But through the mediation of the Archbishop of Sens and his brother Count Theobald a conference was agreed upon, to be held at Gisors on 8th September.[2]

The Siege raised.

The French and Flemings, sick of their losses, and satisfied of their inability to contend with Henry, had now made up their minds to abandon the cause of his sons.   But when the parties met at Gisors no final arrangement could be effected ; because Richard was still at large and defiant.   An agreement, therefore, was entered into for a fresh conference to be held at Michaelmas between Tours and Amboise, with an interim truce from which Richard was expressly excluded in order to enable his father to bring him to terms.   Henry at once entered Poitou chasing his son from place to place, till the lad (he was only seventeen years old) finding himself helpless, threw himself at his father's feet, begging for forgiveness.   On 23rd September the two rode into Poitiers together as friends.[3]   A week later the three sons, Henry, Richard, and Geoffrey made their formal submission to their father at Montlouis,[4] near Tours.   "Henry's victory was so complete that he could afford to be generous ; "[5] all that he required was submission, with reasonable guarantees against fresh outbreaks in the future.   Pledges of reciprocal amnesty and restitution were exchanged ; no estates were confiscated ; but all the castles fortified since the beginning of hostilities would be dismantled.   Further, the King granted to his sons

Conferences.

Richard hunted down.

Submission of Henry's Sons.

Generous Terms.

to Southampton ? By so many, roughly speaking, must the estimate of 1000 be reduced. A penny a day was the regular wage of a foot-soldier.   Perhaps the Welshmen would only receive a halfpenny a day.

[1] Ben. P., *sup.*, see above, 168.

[2] See Ben. P., I. 74-76 ; Hoveden, II. 65, 66 ; Diceto, I. 386, 387 ; W. Newb., 195 ; R. Monte, 265.

[3] Ben. P., 76 ; Diceto, 393, 394 ; Gervase, I. 250 ; J. Hoveden, 66.

[4] "Mons Laudatus ;" Ben. P., I. 77, and note ; Gervase, I. 250 ; Hoveden, II. 67.

[5] Stubbs, *Const. Hist.*, I. 519.

endowments somewhat on the footing of the terms so liberally offered in the previous year. The young King would have two castles in Normandy (of his father's choosing), with £15,000 *Angevin* (£3,750 sterling) *per annum*; Richard, as a more dangerous man, would have two non-fortified residences[1] in Poitou, with half the money revenues of the county; Geoffrey would have half the inheritance of his affianced bride Constance; while the young King was taken bound to respect Henry's prospective benefactions in favour of John; these would include the castle and earldom of Nottingham, and the castle of Marlborough in England; with sundry scattered castles and revenues in Normandy, Maine, Anjou, and Touraine, an arrangement fraught with endless possibilities of trouble in the future. It will be remembered that John's appanage was the question that provoked the final rupture between young Henry and his father. Three notable prisoners were excluded from the amnesty, namely the King of Scots, and the Earls of Leicester, and Chester, with all hostages already actually in the King's hands. Finally Richard and Geoffrey did homage to their father for the grants conferred upon them; but young Henry was excused the ceremony, out of regard for his Royal dignity.[2]

The settlement with William the Lion ran on similar lines. Neither ransom nor cession of territory was required of him; only an **The King of Scots.** absolute recognition of the suzerainty of England. Since the Conquest, at any rate, the homages of the Scottish Kings had been couched in general terms, so as to leave it an open question whether the recognition was rendered in respect of the Scottish Crown or only in respect of lands held in England.[3] By the present treaty William was **Liege Homage for Crown of Scotland.** required to declare himself the liege man and sworn feudatory of the King of England for Scotland and all other his possessions; his undertenants, the Scottish Baronage, ecclesiastical and lay, being also bound to render direct homage to Henry, as under the rule laid down by the Conqueror at Salisbury. To complete the subordination of the Northern Kingdom it was stipulated that the Church of Scotland should render to the Church of England ' such submission as it ought to render, and had rendered under Henry's predecessors,' a pretension of course for which there was no historic authority whatever.[4] As security William was required to give up as

---

[1] " Duo receptacula idonea unde Regi damnum nou possit provenire."

[2] See the terms as finally drawn up apparently on the 11th October (Diceto, 394) at Falaise, *Fœdera*, I. 30 ; Ben. P., I. 77. Diceto, *sup.*, gives the notification sent over to England by the King. He also gives the number of prisoners of gentle rank (milites) set free by the King without ransom as amounting to 969; while the young King liberated rather more than 100 men, but not without ransom.

[3] See *Foundations*, II. 174.

[4] The claim of the Archbishops of Canterbury to be held Primates of all Great Britain had never been recognised in Scotland ; see *Foundations*, II. 294, and the notice of Eadmer in the list of authorities at the end of Vol. I.

hostages his brother David (not styled Earl), four Earls,[1] and a string of Scottish magnates, with the castles of Berwick, Roxburgh, Jedburgh, Edinburgh, and Stirling as material guarantees. The treaty, drawn up at Falaise, probably at the same time as that with the King's sons, was ratified at Valognes on the 8th December.[2] Three days later William was

William set free. taken over to England to be set at liberty as soon as the castles had been duly surrendered.[3] About the beginning of February (1175) he reached his home.[4] The prompt acceptance of the treaty by the Scots, who might have left William in bonds, and made David king, suggests that the ruling class, the Anglo-Norman Baronage, were not by any means averse to union with England. In fact many of them had interests on both sides of the Border.[5]

The rising of 1173-1174 "was the last struggle in English history in which the barons were arrayed against the united interests of the Crown and people." The rebel Earls rose in the cause of feudal insubordination, and seignorial rule, just as former Barons had risen under the Conqueror, and under Rufus, and under Henry I. But the Baronage had now learned their lesson, and accepted their proper position. In the next struggle we shall find them siding with the people in resistance to the tyranny of an arbitrary despot. Henry's clemency to them was one of the most politic and laudable acts of his reign. With respect to the other parties concerned in the rebellion the arrangement of Montlouis was less successful. It gave the King no real guarantees for the future ; it satisfied no aspirations, neither those of the French ; nor those of the continental Feudatories ; nor those of the King's own sons.

[1] The Scottish Earls were Duncan II., Earl of Fife ; Waltheof, Earl of Dunbar ; Gilbert, Earl of Mar ; and Gilbride, Earl of Angus.

[2] See the treaty tested at Falaise without date, *Fœdera*, I. 30 ; and Ben. P., I. 96 ; tested at Valognes 8th December, Diceto, I. 396 ; and (without date), *Liber Niger*, Hearne, I. 36.

[3] Diceto, 198 ; Norgate, II. 167.

[4] Chron. Melrose ; J. Fordun, 265.

[5] John of Fordun, the fourteenth century writer, makes a vague allegation of a general rising and massacre of French and English settlers, both in Scotland and in Galloway ; p. 264. Mr. Skene accepts his statement as evidence of a general rising of the Gaelic population against the Norman and English barons (Celtic Scotland, I. 475). The evidence to me appears very insufficient. In Galloway no doubt a fratricidal struggle for the lordship broke out between Uhtred and Gilbert, sons of Fergus. But the question with them was not one of resistance to English supremacy but to Scottish supremacy. They wanted to be annexed to England. John of Hoveden the chronicler was sent to settle their affairs, but found the matter too delicate for him to meddle with. Fordun regarding the matter in a fourteenth-century light totally misrepresents it.

CHAPTER X

HENRY II. (*continued*)

1175-1179

Measures for Restoration of Order—Dismantling of Castles—Judicial Circuits system-
atised—*Assize of Northampton*—Rivalry of Canterbury and York—Campaign of
Young Richard in the Limousin—John Lord of Ireland—Arbitration between
Castile and Navarre—Treaty of Ivry with France—Establishment of Court of
King's Bench—Further Campaigns of Richard in Aquitaine

RESUMPTION and demolition of castles, general measures of dis-
armament, and the filling up of blanks in the English Church were
the work of the year 1175; as of a time of clearing after a
storm. But indications that the clearing would be short-lived
were not long of appearing. In January the King was called
from Normandy into Anjou. By the 2nd February he had returned as far
North as Le Mans.[1] There we hear that Richard and Geoffrey did homage
to their father, as if in fact they had not done so before, or their previous
homage had in some way been incomplete or irregular. Richard was then
sent off to Poitou, and Geoffrey to Brittany, the latter under the guardianship
of Rowland of Dinan, who had made his peace.[2] Henry then went on
to Normandy for an interview with King Louis (Gisors, 25th February).
Another visit to Anjou followed; Henry going back to Normandy towards
the end of March. He then announced an intention of going over to
England, his eldest son to accompany him. But the misguided
youth refused to join his father. He was still lending an ear
to insidious counsels from Paris, and was or affected to be
suspicious of the King's purpose in declining to take his
homage along with that of his brothers at Montlouis. The homage tie as
the reader knows implied mutual obligations. At length, under much
gentle pressure,[3] he came to his father's court at Bures on the 1st April,

Marginal notes: Henry's Movements. — The young King again giving trouble.

---

[1] Ben. P., I. 81.
[2] Diceto I. 398; R. Monte, 267; Ben. P., I. 81, 83. Geoffrey and his tutor were
successful in ousting Eude of Porhoet from Vannes, Ploermel, and Auray; R. Monte, *sup.*
See Ben. P. 101, for his doings and for those of Richard in Aquitaine.
[3] Ben. P., 81, 82.

begged to be forgiven ; was allowed to do homage ; swore oaths of allegiance, and gave pledges for his good conduct in future.[1] The young King was then allowed to pay a visit to his father-in-law, returning to spend Easter (13th April) with the King. On the 22nd April the two received Philip of Flanders at Caen. The Count had taken the Cross on Good Friday (11th April), and naturally wished to make his borders safe before leaving home. At last, in May, the two Henrys sailed from Barfleur, landing at Portsmouth on the 9th of the month.[2]

Return to England.

Their English subjects found them apparently living on terms of the closest intimacy, dining together, and occupying the same chamber at night.[3] In fact it would seem that the King never allowed his son to pass out of sight. They reached London in time to assist at a Synod held by Archbishop Richard on the 18th May. Some nineteen Canons were promulgated ; but, as the Primate admitted, there was not much that was novel in them. The chief novelty was a provision based on a Decretal of the existing Pope Alexander III.[4] under which married clerks in minor orders (Doorkeepers, Acolytes, Exorcists, and Readers) were allowed to retain their wives on condition of sacrificing all Church emoluments.[5]

Synod at Westminster.

A thanksgiving pilgrimage to the shrine of St. Thomas followed (28th May) ; and then the Court moved on to Reading for Whitsunday (1st June). From Reading the King turned Westward to compel the Earl of Gloucester to surrender Bristol Castle, a matter about which he had made some demur. William having been brought to his duty, the two Henrys moved on to Gloucester, where they held a Grand Council to settle measures for the maintenance of peace on the Welsh March (29th June). Rhys ap Gruffudd and other Welsh Princes were in attendance.[6] In connexion with this progress we begin to hear of a series of disgraceful prosecutions instituted by the King. During the rising, to conciliate the gentry and clergy, he had proclaimed free hunting in the Royal forests. Now all who had taken advantage of this license, high and low, 'learned and lay,' were brought to justice and amerced, though Richard of Lucy, the Chief Justiciar, boldly produced the King's warrant for the liberties taken.[7]

Grand Council.

---

[1] See the notification published by the King in England on the 20th May, Diceto, 400.

[2] Ben. P., I. 83 ; Diceto, I. 399.

[3] Diceto, *sup.*

[4] *Epp.* Foliot No. 368, cited Bishop Stubbs.

[5] For the Synod see Ben. P., 84 ; Hoveden, II. 72 ; Gervase, I. 251. Of course the standing questions with York came up. Roger would not appear, because he could not carry his cross within the Province of Canterbury. Then he claimed Lincoln, Chester, Worcester, and Hereford as Suffragan Sees, etc.

[6] Ben. P., 91, 92. The carrying of arms was forbidden, Diceto, 401. See also *Brut.*, 224.

[7] See Ben. P., 92, 94 ; Diceto, 402 ; R. Monte, 267.

In July the Court is found at Woodstock, and there on the 8th of the
month Henry held another Grand Council, largely attended
Grand Council. by ecclesiastics, as the chief business was to provide abbots
for no less than eleven vacant monasteries.   This was done :
while John of Oxford at last had his reward by appointment to the See
of Norwich that was also vacant.   Next day the election of the King's
natural son Geoffrey to the See of Lincoln was confirmed by Archbishop
Richard, under Papal Dispensation.   The young man was not in England
at the time.   He came over a few days later, and was allowed to make a
processional entry into Lincoln on the 1st August.   But the King did not
ask to have him actually consecrated as yet, and sent him to Tours for
a further course of study.[1] From Woodstock the Kings proceeded through
Lichfield and Nottingham to York, which they reached on the 10th
August.   The business at York was to receive the stipulated
Homage of the Scots. homages of the under-tenants of the Scottish Crown.   William
and his brother David duly appeared with a long train of
bishops, earls, barons, knights, and freeholders.   The ceremony took place
on the 15th August,[2] and within the walls of St. Peter's Minster, where
liege homage, as against all men, with oaths of fealty, was rendered to
Henry and his son.   The Scottish Bishops also took the oath that they
would render to the Church of England such obedience as
Canny Bishops. their predecessors had rendered, and they ought to render;
a very safe pledge to take.   It is interesting to hear that
William did homage specifically for Galloway, as distinguished from
Scotland.   From this we learn that Galloway, presumably representing the
old Kingdom of Reged, and at any rate being the unabsorbed kernel of
the Kingdom of Strathclyde, still retained something of an independent
character.[3]

Again at York we hear of Forest prosecutions, to which the sporting
tastes of the cathedral clergy laid them open.[4] The two
Homage for Ireland. Kings then turned Southwards to London, and from thence
again to Windsor, there to score another triumph in receiving
the vicarious submission of Roderic of Connaught.   What had brought

[1] Diceto, I. 401 ; Ben. P., I. 92, 93.   For the names of the abbots chosen see Bishop
Stubbs' note to Hoveden, II. 79.

[2] J. Fordun, 265.

[3] Ben. P., I. 94-99 ; R. Hoveden, II. 79-82 ; W. Newb., I. 198 ; J. Fordun, *sup.*
Henry very properly authorised William to reduce the rebellious Lord of Galloway,
Gilbert son of Fergus, who wanted to throw off all allegiance to Scotland, and hold
directly of England.   Henry would not listen to the proposal.   See Benedict I. 79, 80.
99 ; J. Fordun, 266.   William reduced Gilbert to subjection, and then brought him to
Feckenham where he did homage to Henry on the 9th October, 1176 ; Ben. P., 126.
Henry's action in this matter gives another illustration of his regard for the rights of an
over-lord.

[4] Ben. P., *sup.*

the Irish King to this point does not appear, as in fact the English settlement had been in a struggling condition since Henry's departure in 1172.[1] Cadhla or Catholicus Archbishop of Tuam was the principal envoy, and through him a treaty was arranged and published in a Grand Council held on the 6th October. The compact took the peculiarly insulting and in fact preposterous shape of a 'grant' by Henry to his liege man Roderic of the liberty to rule under him, so long as he should serve him faithfully, pay tribute, and keep both the districts directly, and those indirectly subject to him,[2] in peace and good order, and tributary to the King of England. The districts not in any way subject to Roderic, but under the direct control of the King of England, or of his Barons, for which Roderic would not be held responsible, were defined

The English Pale. as comprising Dublin and its pertinents ; Meath and its pertinents, including West Meath ; Wexford with all Leinster ; and Waterford and its county up to Dungarvan. The tribute expected from the Irish was stated as one merchantable hide from every ten head of cattle. The Council closed with the appointment by Henry of one Augustine to be Bishop of Waterford.[3]

The year ended with the appearance of a Papal Legate, Cardinal Hugh,

Papal Mission. Ugo, or Ugoccione, of the family of the great Semite Peter Leonis.[4] He came at Henry's invitation, the first Legate seen within the four seas since the King's accession. On the Continent Legatine visits had been frequent. Ugo's mission might seem an invasion of the rights of Archbishop Richard, who held a commission as Papal Legate for the Province of Canterbury ; but as the Cardinal came ostensibly to settle differences between Canterbury and York no objection could be taken to his coming. He was received at Winchester

Canterbury and York. on the 31st October by the two Kings.[5] In the discussions that followed the question of the jurisdiction over St. Peter's Gloucester, dating at latest from the time of St. Oswald,[6] was settled in favour of York by the disclaimer of Archbishop Richard. The more vital question of the cross-bearing had to stand over.[7] At Canterbury, it was whispered that the Legate had been really brought over in hopes of effecting a divorce of the King from Eleanor.[8] But Hugh gained the

---

[1] See Giraldus, V. 308-313 ; *Song of Dermot*, notes, 301.

[2] " Terram suam . . . et totam aliam terram."

[3] Ben. P., I. 101-104 ; Hoveden, II. 83, etc.

[4] " Hugo Petrileonis " ; Diceto, 402 ; " Hugozun " ; " Hugezun " ; Ben. P., 104, 112.

[5] Diceto, I. 403.

[6] Say from A.D. 971, when Oswald, being Bishop of Worcester, was appointed to be lso Archbishop of York ; *Foundations*, I. 318.

[7] Ben. P., I. 104.

[8] Gervase, I. 256.

execrations of the entire clergy by sanctioning the King's proceedings against them for Forest offences.[1]

The judicial iters of the King's justices had been regularly kept up since 1166, but not apparently on any settled plan. Some years one set of counties was visited, some years another set, just as the King might direct. He now resolved to extend and systematise the provincial administration of justice. At a Grand Council held at Northampton on the 25th January 1176 he divided England into six circuits, appointing three standing Itinerant Justices for each, almost all of them men of experience in the discharge of judicial functions.[2]

Judicial Circuits.

At the same time by way of fresh instructions to his Justices he published the well-known *Assize of Northampton*, described as a re-issue of the *Assize of Clarendon* of 1166, but being in fact a new Ordinance, with some of the old provisions retained. The presentment of suspected culprits by the twelve freemen of the Hundred and the four good men of the Township, with the ultimate reference to the Ordeal by Water, is still the basis of the system of criminal justice. But the condemned culprit will now lose a hand as well as a foot ; while persons charged with murder or grosser felony, even if absolved by the Ordeal, are required to abjure the realm within forty days (s. 1). Again, as before, strangers are not to be harboured in any borough or township for more than one night, except for reasonable cause (s. 2). On the other hand, the clauses of the Clarendon Assize intended to meet possible opposition to the Justices by the sheriffs and the lords of franchises are now rather oddly omitted, as if those personages had sufficiently acquiesced in the new state of things. Measures suggested by recent events were the direction to the Justices to exact oaths of allegiance to the King from all and sundry, from the earl down to the villein (*rusticis*) (s. 6); and the direction to see to the effectual demolition of castles ordered to be destroyed (s. 8).[3] The Justices are given cognisance of all suits concerning the King, and all pleas of the Crown, down to the value of half a Knight's fee, 'or less'; unless the matter should seem so doubtful or of such importance as to demand a reference to the King himself 'or his representatives'[4] (s. 7). Of course the Justices are charged to attend to all the King's interests, and to make careful enquiry after escheats and vacant benefices, and heiresses and widows at the King's disposal (ss. 9, 10, 11).[5]

Assize of Northampton.

But perhaps the most important section of the measure is the fourth,

---

[1] Ben. P., 105 ; Gervase and Diceto, *sup.* ; and especially Henry's letter, Diceto, I. 410.

[2] Ben. P., 107 ; Hoveden, 87. For notes on the men see Foss. ; Judges, I. 176.

[3] "Quod prorsus diruantur."

[4] "Ad illos qui in loco ejus erunt."

[5] Ben. P., 108–111 ; Hoveden, 81–91 ; *Select Charters*, 143.

by which the celebrated Assize of Mort d'Ancestor seems to be instituted.
Assize of Mort d' Ancestor. By this clause it is provided that where a man has died seised, that is possessed, of a freehold of inheritance his heir is to obtain possession as a matter of course; if the lord should attempt to interfere with the succession of the heir the latter will have his remedy by applying for a royal writ, to be followed by an inquest by a jury of the neighbours. Here we have an extension of the principle of the Assize of Novel Disseisin, in the withdrawal of a further class of cases relating to the ownership of land from the cognizance of the local and private courts, and the placing of them under the protection of the royal courts.[1]

The Council of Northampton was attended by William the Lion, with his bishops and abbots, summoned by Henry to make definite profession of their subjection to the Church of England, as supposed to have been stipulated at Falaise. But when it came to the point the Scottish **The Church of Scotland.** ecclesiastics, with one voice, protested that no such subjection had ever been recognised by their predecessors, and that none could be recognised by themselves. Roger of Pont l'Evêque then rose producing documents to show that the Sees of Whithern, or Galloway, and Glasgow, at any rate, had at times admitted the supremacy of York.[2] But that did not suit Archbishop Richard, who interposed at once to point out that if there was to be any submission it must be to Canterbury. So the King had to allow the Scottish prelates to depart in peace, without making any profession to either Province.[3]

Some two months later the rivalry of the two Archbishops led to a most disgraceful scene. The Legate having made a visitation tour of **Legatine Synod.** cathedrals and abbeys summoned a general Synod to meet at Westminster on Mid-Lent Sunday (14th March). The question then arose who was to sit at the Cardinal's right hand? Roger claimed precedence on the ground of seniority, as no doubt originally directed by Gregory the Great.[4] Richard on the other hand maintained that the precedence of Canterbury under all circumstances had long been fully established. The dispute must have arrested all business in the Synod for several days, as we are told that it was not till the Thursday, the 18th March, that the Legate finally took his seat

---

[1] See s. 4 of the *Assize of Northampton*; Pollock and Maitland, *Histy. Engl. Law*, I. 147.

[2] For early Anglian bishops at Whithern, see Stubbs and Haddan, *Councils*, II. 7, and later, 25; and for bishops of Glasgow subject to York, pp. 14, 21, 26. Jocelin, the Bishop of Glasgow, however, was able to cite the recent Privilege of Alexander III., declaring the See of Glasgow under the immediate protection of Rome; *id.* 40, 41.

[3] Ben. P., 111, 112; Hoved., 91, 92.

[4] See *Foundations*, I. 177; Bæda, *Hist. Ecc.*, I. cc. 27-32. Alexander III. approved of Gregory's arrangement. See his letter condemning the notion of any subjection of York to Canterbury; Diceto, I. 406.

in St. Katherine's Chapel, Westminster, being a chapel attached to the
monks' Infirmary.[1] Archbishop Richard having taken his
place at the Cardinal's right hand and close to him, Roger
coming in afterwards, and finding the place of honour occupied,
squatted down on Richard's knees endeavouring to squeeze himself in
between him and the Legate. The Canterbury suffragans of course flew
to the rescue; Roger was thrown down, kicked, cuffed, beaten, and finally
turned out of the chapel with his mantle (*cappa*) torn.[2] So at least the
Canterbury writers. William of Newburgh the North-country man gives
the more probable account that Roger having entered the chapel first,
and taken his seat at the Cardinal's right hand, was assaulted and dragged
from his place by the Canterbury clergy.[3] The unseemly scuffle ended
with a shower of citations to Rome, hurled at each others' heads by
the chief actors in the scene. But neither appeals nor Synod went any
farther.[4]

A Struggle for Precedence.

The young King, as might be expected, soon began to chafe at the
tutelage in which he was kept, never allowed to leave his
father's side, in fact a state prisoner. He pressed to be
allowed to go on pilgrimage to St. James of Compostella.
The King refused his consent; but eventually gave his son leave to go
over to Normandy. Acting on this permission young Henry and his
Queen went down to Porchester, and were there waiting for a favourable
wind to sail, when on Good Friday (2nd April) Richard and Geoffrey
landed at Southampton. Richard came to ask for help against a formidable rising in the Limousin, Angoumois, and Saintonge. The Counts
of Limoges, and Angoulême, and the Viscounts of Chabanais,[5] Ventadour,
and Turenne[6] were up and in arms,[7] while Wulgrin son of the Count of
Angoulême, had actually invaded Poitou.[8] What Geoffrey wanted does
not appear; but the three brothers, very properly, went together to
spend Easter with their father. About April 20th Henry and
Richard recrossed the Channel; the young King going to
visit King Louis, while Richard went back to Poitou. There
the young Count began his military career with a brilliant campaign, in
which the mercenaries hired with his father's gold carried all before them.

Discontent of the Young King.

He leaves England.

[1] Diceto, I. 405; Ben. P., I. 112.
[2] Gervase, I. 258; Birchington, *Angl. Sacr.*, I. 9.
[3] I. 204. The accounts of Benedict, *sup.*, and Hoveden, II. 92, are compatible with
either story. The Canterbury story really goes too far. But, in fact, the account given
by Gervase in his *Actus Pont.* (II. 399) is also compatible with the York version.
[4] The Legate left England 3rd July; Diceto, I. 410, *q.v.* for a supposed letter from
the King to the Pope abjuring all that he contended for in the Constitutions of Clarendon.
[5] Charente.
[6] Both in Corrèze.
[7] Ben. P , 115.
[8] For his doings see Diceto, 407.

First we hear of a victorious engagement fought in Saintonge, between
Saint Maigrin [1] and Bouteville; [2] then of a march into the
Limousin; and of the capture of Aixe-sur-Vienne,[3] where some
forty men-at-arms were taken prisoners. Limoges was then
attacked, and reduced after a few days' siege. Richard then fell back to
Poitiers to meet his brother Henry, who had been charged to co-operate
with him (after 24th June). Advancing Southwards again the two brothers
laid siege to Châteauneuf near Angoulême, and took the place within a
fortnight. Satisfied with this achievement, Henry, who was not at all in
earnest in his opposition to the rebellion, went back to Poitiers, leaving
Richard to prosecute the war alone. Nothing daunted the Count went
on with his work, and, having isolated Angoulême by the reduction of
Moulin-Neuf,[4] finally attacked his adversaries in their chief stronghold.
Within a week Angoulême had capitulated, and Count William Taillefer IV.,
and his son Wulgrin, Aimery Viscount of Limoges, Eschivard Viscount of
Chabanais, and Ebles Viscount of Ventadour, had to place themselves
and their remaining castles in Richard's hands.[5] Viscount Wulgrin and
certain others held especially responsible were sent to England to make
their peace with the King. On the 21st September they were admitted
to terms at Winchester.[6] Bertran de Born the great troubadour, who had
done his best to stir up Henry's sons against their father, was now equally
zealous in urging patriotic resistance to Count Richard.[7] But the young
King's attitude was again fractious and disquieting. He was gathering
round him at Poitiers the men who had already sided with him against
his father. His acting chancellor, one Adam of "Chirchedune,"[8] being
found sending a confidential report to the old King was cruelly flogged
and imprisoned by the young one. In fact he would have put him to
death, had not the Bishop of Poitiers claimed him as a clerk.[9]

Richard's First Campaign.

At home the King had been busy arranging for the marriage of another
daughter; endeavouring to settle the quarrel between the two
Archbishops; and drawing the teeth of Feudalism by depriving
it of its castles.

Marriage of the King's Daughters.

With respect to the marriage Henry had been as careful to provide for

[1] Charente Inf.
[2] Charente, near Cognac.
[3] Haute Vienne, near Limoges.
[4] Charente, near Aubeterre.
[5] August? See Ben. P., I. 114, 115, 120, 121; Hoveden, II. 93, and Bishop Stubbs' notes.
[6] Ben. P., *sup.*; Diceto, 414.
[7] Martin, *France*, III. 496; Sismondi, V. 519. Dante saw Bertran in hell, carrying his own head in his hands, as a punishment for the bad advice he had given to 'the young King,' "il re Giovane"; *Inferno*, XXVIII. 118-142, cited Sismondi .
[8] Churchdown, Gloucestershire?
[9] Ben. P., 122, 123; Hoved., 94.

his daughters as for his sons. Matilda, his eldest, born in 1156, had **Matilda.** been married in 1168 to Henry the Lion, Duke of Saxony and **Eleanor.** Bavaria.[1] Eleanor the second, born in 1161, had been married in 1170, during the heat of the Becket struggle, to Alphonso III. of Castile, a youth in his fifteenth year.[2] A twelvemonth earlier, namely in 1169, the hand of Johanna, the third daughter, had been **Johanna.** offered to William II., 'The Good,' King of Sicily and Duke of Apulia.[3] The relations of the two Courts, of common origin and parallel history, were naturally friendly.[4] But Henry's proposal was not taken up at once. In 1176 however the negotiations were reopened. In the spring of the year Elias Bishop-elect of Troja, Arnulf Bishop of Carpaccio, and Count Florio di Camerota, Justiciar of Sicily, appeared under the escort of Archbishop Rotrou of Rouen—a connection of the Sicilian King—to ask for the definite settlement of the marriage.[5] Henry gave his assent in a Grand Council held in London on 20th May. His pledge was given in the form of an oath taken by three men of rank, at his bidding, and on his soul. A mixed deputation was then sent to Palermo to notify Henry's agreement and obtain William's ratification. That formality was given on 23rd August.[6] On receipt of the concluded compact, as we may suppose, Johanna was sent across the Channel under the charge of the Archbishop of Canterbury. Her brothers Henry and Richard were directed to escort her through Gaul.[7] On the 9th November she was handed over to the representatives of King William at St. Gilles, near the mouth of the Rhone.[8] After a tedious voyage she reached Sicily about the end of January, and was finally married and crowned on Sunday, 13th February, 1177,[9] having then reached the nubile age—as it was then considered—of twelve years.[10]

As for the matter of the Archbishops' quarrel a Grand Council was held

---

[1] Minden, 1 Feby. ; charter cited Green, *Princesses*, I. 223.

[2] R. Monte, 211, 247 ; Mariana, *De Rebus Hisp.*, p. 526 (ed. 1592).

[3] *Becket*, VII. 26.

[4] Peter of Blois was tutor for a time to William II. ; Master Thomas Brun, a man who was found very useful in the business of the Exchequer came to Henry from Sicily ; *Dialogus De Scacc. Select Charters*, 170, 181. In 1172 we find William and his mother interceding with the Pope for the ex-communicate Bishop Joscelin of Salisbury, *Becket*, VII. 509 ; while in 1173 the King of Sicily, alone of European princes, had written in sympathetic terms to Henry on the conduct of his sons ; Ben. P., I. 55 ; Hoved., II. 48.

[5] Ben. P., I. 115 ; Hoved., II. 94, and Bishop Stubbs' notes.

[6] Ben. P., 117, and esp. William's letter to Henry, Diceto, 413.

[7] Ben. P., 119, 120. The writers differ as to the date of Johanna's sailing, but she certainly sailed before Michaelmas, as the charge for her squadron of seven vessels appears in the Pipe Roll of the year.

[8] Dept. Gard ; Diceto, 415.

[9] See Ben. P., I. 157, and the marriage settlement, p. 169 ; Hoved., II. 95.

[10] She was born in October, 1165 ; R. Monte.

at Winchester on the 15th August in the hopes of settling it.   Roger of
The Primates' Quarrel.   Pont-l'Evêque taxed the Bishop of Ely with having laid violent hands on him in the Legatine Synod at Westminster. Geoffrey Riddel repelled the charge ; and Roger accepted his assurances.   But no final settlement could be effected between the two **A Truce.**   Primates.   All that the King's efforts could obtain was a truce for five years, during which time each Archbishop pledged himself to abstain from aggressive action against the other.[1]

As for the resumption of castles, that was being carried on in a very **Resumption and Demolition of Castles.**   thorough-going fashion.   Even the long and faithful service of Richard of Lucy could not secure him in the possession of his castle at Chipping Ongar.   In Normandy the Justiciar William de Courcy having died the Bishop of Winchester was sent over to succeed him, with orders to take into hand all castles there.[2]   So again in Ireland.   Strongbow on his return to Ireland had been appointed Justiciar, vice Hugh de Lacy ; he died 5th April (1176) ;[3] whereupon William fitz Aldelin was appointed in his place ; and his first act was to take possession of all castles previously held in the name of the Earl.[4]   As for demolitions we hear that the fortifications at Leicester, Groby, Framlingham, Bungay, Thirsk, and Kirkby Malzeard were pulled down ; Huntingdon had been dismantled in the previous year.[5]

In another department the newly appointed Justices in Eyre were carrying out the instructions of the *Assize of Northampton* very fully, especially in **Forest Prosecutions.**   the matter of the Forest prosecutions.   In 1175 the Pipe Roll of the year (21 Henry II.) showed only one fine, a heavy fine of £100, but that was suspended.   But in the following year we have one hundred and fifty persons in Yorkshire fined sums varying from £100 downwards ; while in the year after that again (1176–1177), the Roll shows four hundred and twenty-five persons in eleven counties fined in sums running from ten marks (£6 13s. 4d.) to £100.[6] If the five hundred and seventy-five persons fined in the two years had only paid ten marks each, the lowest figure given, the total would come to some **Their Yield.**   £4000.   These amerciaments (*misericordiæ*) were very difficult to exact, but with every allowance in that respect we could not estimate the total got in at less than £8000–£12,000 ; a very substantial

---

[1] Ben. P., I. 118 ; Hoved., II. 99.

[2] Ben. P., 124, 125 ; R. Monte, 271.

[3] Diceto, I. 407.

[4] Ben. P., 124, 125 ; Hoveden, 100 ; Gilbert, *Viceroys*, 33, 35, 37.

[5] Ben. P., 126, 127 ; Hoveden, 101 ; Diceto, I. 404.   The works at Thirsk, Kirkby Malzeard, and Huntingdon apparently were never rebuilt.

[6] See these figures given Madox, *Hist. Excheq.*, I. 541.   The Pipe Rolls after the 21st year of the reign have unfortunately not been printed.

addition to a revenue that even before the troubles of 1173-1174 did not amount to £21,000.[1]

The arrangements of the year included one of a very singular character for the fresh endowment of the King's son John. This had become **A new** necessary because the affianced bride of Maurienne had died **heiress for** within a year of her betrothal. The inheritance for which **John.** the King now manœuvred was that of the great Earldom of Gloucester, with its English, Welsh, and Norman estates. Earl William, son of the loyal Robert, had no son living. According to one authority he had a grandson, Philip son of a deceased son Richard.[2] At all events he had three daughters; Mabille or Mabel married to Amauri of Montfort, Count of Evreux; Amice or·Amicia married to Richard of Clare, Earl of Hertford; and Isabel still unmarried. Henry required the Earl to pass over his grandson—if he really had one—and at any rate to disinherit his two elder daughters and concur in settling the Earldom and estates on Isabel and John; if the Pope would grant the necessary dispensation, the two being third cousins. The elder sisters would receive from the King annuities of £100 each by way of compensation.[3]

The year 1177 was marked by a series of Grand Councils, the King being evidently anxious to put the home government on a thoroughly satisfactory footing before going back to his Continental dominions, where events might detain him for an indefinite length of time. The **Grand** first meeting was held at Northampton, about the middle of **Councils.** January, when the Earls of Leicester and Chester were pardoned and reinstated; the castles, however, of Mountsorrel and Pacy (Normandy) being withheld from the one, and that of Chester from the other. William of Aubigny II. was also admitted to the Earldom of Arundel or Sussex, his father having died in the previous year.[4] In March a Grand Council of a special character was held in London, to which we shall revert; and a third at Geddington (Northants) on the 2nd May. The business in hand proving heavy, the meeting was adjourned in the course of the week to Windsor. There the custody of the chief castles in the North, and specially of the Scottish strongholds in the **Northern** King's hands, was rearranged. Roxburgh was given to William **Strongholds.** of Stuteville, *vice* Archbishop Roger of York; Edinburgh to Roger of Stuteville; Norham to William Neville, vice Roger of Conyers; while the Archbishop was put in charge of Scarborough, and Conyers in

---

[1] So the total for the 15th year, 1168-1169, as added by myself.

[2] So R. Monte, 269, under this year. " Ricardus filius comitis Gloecestriæ obiit et successit ei Philippus filius ejus ex sorore Roberti de Monte Forti." No other notice of this Philip seems to be known.

[3] 28th September, Diceto, I. 415; Ben. P., I. 124; R. Monte, 308; and for the names of the ladies, *Complete Peerage.*

[4] Ben. P., I. 125, 132-135. All three sign as Earls on the 16th March; *Id.* 154.

charge of Durham. Bishop Puiset's other castle at Northallerton was ordered to be pulled down, and he himself fined 2000 marks for his recent rebellious conduct.[1] A further adjournment about the middle of May was then made to Oxford; and there we hear in the first place of a conference held with a host of Welsh magnates, headed by Rhys son of Gruffudd, of South Wales, and David son of Owen Gwynedd, of North Wales; all appearing in answer to the King's writs. To secure them in their allegiance Rhys, 'the King's most beloved friend,'[2] received a grant of Melenith or South-East Radnorshire; while David, who in 1174 had been honoured with the hand of the King's natural sister Emma,[3] was now given an endowment from the lands of Ellesmere in Shropshire.[4]

Welsh Princes.

A more important affair was the Irish programme arranged. The King's son John would be Lord Paramount of Ireland,[5] with the Earl of Chester to act as his guardian or chief adviser, presumably in the event of his going over to take possession. For the actual government of the Dominion Hugh de Lacy was reappointed Justiciar, vice William fitz Aldelin, who had proved unequal to the situation, de Lacy also receiving a confirmation of his great Meath fief; while fitz Aldelin was relegated to his old position at Wexford. Waterford was placed in the hands of one Robert le Poer; while Limerick, a possession yet to be won,[6] was assigned to Herbert fitz Herbert and two other men, all three being relatives of the late Earl of Cornwall.[7] The concession, apparently, was offered to them by way of compensation for the property of their deceased kinsman which had been seized by the King. The kind offer however was not accepted, and so the grant was cancelled in favour of Philip of Braose, a man prepared to undertake the conquest. As for the original adventurers their claims would be sufficiently recognised by the grant of Cork to Robert fitz Stephen and Miles Cogan. Those men, we are told, had rendered the King good service during the late troubles.[8] Henry's

Irish Programme.

John Lord of Ireland.

---

[1] Ben. P., I. 160, 161.

[2] *Brut. y. T.*, 227.

[3] Diceto, I. 397; Pipe Roll, 20 H. II., 16, 20, *Brut.*, 225.

[4] Ben. P., 162; Hoved., II. 133. £10 a year was the amount of the allowance; Pipe Rolls.

[5] Benedict, I. 162; and Hoveden, II. 133, have it that Henry created John King of Ireland. But as John never on any occasion styled himself King of Ireland, only "Dominus," their statement must so far be corrected.

[6] Raymond fitz Gerald, "Le Gros," had captured Limerick in October, 1175; but found it prudent to evacuate the place after Strongbow's death; Giraldus, V. 320–333; *Song of Dermot*, 247, 317. Henry recalled Raymond and sent Robert le Poer to replace him at Wexford and Waterford; Giraldus, 326–328.

[7] Reginald died 1st July, 1175; Diceto, I. 401; Pipe Roll, 21 Henry II., 37.

[8] See Benedict P., I. 161–164, 172, 221; Hoveden, II. 134; comparing Giraldus, V. 347–349.

dispositions again suggest a general distrust of all men holding rule in Ireland, and especially of the first invaders. *Divide et impera* was his motto for the Dominion.

The King made no reference to Downpatrick and the conquests in Uladh (modern Down and Antrim), achieved since the beginning of the year by the enterprise and determination of a subordinate, in defiance of the prohibitions of the King's representative. John de Courcy, a man

John de Courcy. sent out under fitz Aldelin in the previous year, stands pictured to us as an ideal leader of Wicking or buccaneering enterprise.

Tall, fair, and large of limb, of indomitable strength and courage, he had a perfect passion for fighting and adventure, always to the front in time of danger. In time of peace, we are assured, he was gentle and orderly, as men of such stamp commonly are.[1] He found the garrison at Dublin discontented through inaction, and mutinous from want of pay. Despising the injunctions of fitz Aldelin he gathered round him a little army of twenty-two men-at-arms and some 300 others to exploit new fields in the North. Four days of rapid marching brought them a hundred miles to the gates of Downpatrick which, taken by surprise, was carried by a *coup de main* (*circa* 1st February, 1177).[2] But the Ulster men did not belie their ancient reputation. Within ten days'

His Conquests in Ulster. time Roderick MacDunleve, the local King, appeared to challenge a trial of strength. De Courcy went out to meet him, and defeated him after a severe struggle. But four more battles with alternate results had to be fought out before de Courcy was established in his little principality.[3]

But the telling incident of the year, a great personal compliment to Henry, chronicled at due length, was the reference to his arbitration of

International arbitration. territorial disputes of long standing between the courts of Castile and Navarre. The King's son-in-law Alphonso III. and Sancho VI. of Navarre, weary of fruitless warfare, had agreed to submit their differences to the decision of the King of England, as the Prince of greatest personal reputation and territorial influence in Europe.[4] The litigant monarchs were doubly related, being cousins by paternal descent from Sancho the Great, King of Navarre (1000–1035); while Sancho VI. is further described as uncle, presumably maternal uncle, to the King of Castile. In connexion with this affair three deputations, each headed by a Bishop, appeared in England early in March ;

---

[1] So Giraldus, V. 334, 344. De Courcy's parentage has not been discovered, but he came of a family settled in Oxfordshire and Somerset ; Natl. Dicty. of Biog. (J. H. Round).

[2] Giraldus, 338 ; Ben. P. I. 137.

[3] Ben. P., *sup.* ; Giraldus, 343. The sites of these battles are given as Downpatrick (24th June, 1177), Firlee, Uriel, and Newry Bridge (all in 1178) ; *Id.*, Four Masters.

[4] See the agreement for the reference, dated 25th August, 1176 ; Ben. P., I. 140 ; Hoveden II., 122.

one for each party ; while a third or umpire-embassy, appointed by common consent, came to hear and report the King's decision. Two doughty champions also were there, men of approved ' worth ' and courage,[1] prepared to defend their master's causes in the lists if Henry should wish to enlighten his judgment by an appeal to a battle-wager. On the 9th March the deputations were received at Windsor. On the 13th a Grand Council, that to which we have already referred, was held in London to hear the several cases. An adjournment to the 16th of the month followed. On that day the Council, through the mouth of the Archbishop of Canterbury, pronounced the King's award, a careful
The Award. compromise adjudicating to either side a part of their demands. But Alphonso was also ordered to pay 3000 maravedis *per annum* to Sancho for the term of ten years.[2]

On the 1st July Henry held another Grand Council, at Winchester, to make the last arrangements before leaving England for Normandy. The King of Scots attended the meeting. On the 9th the court was at Stokes Bay, ready to sail ; but the King being troubled with the injury to his leg received at Sileham in 1174, did not put to sea till the 17th August, landing next day at Caplevic. On the 11th September he
Henry in Normandy. entered Rouen. The young King and Richard were there to receive him.[3] Geoffrey had accompanied him from England. But the King at Rouen was also confronted by a Papal Legate, Peter of Pavia, Cardinal of St. Chrysogonus, charged by the Pope—of course at Louis' instigation—to insist on the celebration
Demand for the marriage of Richard to Alais. of the long contracted marriage between Richard and Alais the French King's daughter, who, as usual under the circumstances, was in Henry's keeping.[4] The Cardinal had been authorised to threaten a general Interdict. Henry parried the blow by proposing an interview with Louis. The meeting was held on the 21st September at the ford of Saint Rémy-sur-Arve, near Nonancourt.[5] Henry declared that the marriage would take place as soon as
Elusive Treaty. the French King was prepared to make over Bourges, and also the French Vexin[6] now alleged to have been included in the dowry promised to the young Queen Margaret.[7] The end of it was that Louis allowed himself to be put off with a solemn treaty arranging for a joint Crusade, with a complete defensive alliance between

---

[1] " Miræ probitatis et audaciæ." Fighting ' worth ' of course is meant.

[2] Ben. P., I. 139-154 ; Hoveden, II. 120-131.

[3] R. Monte, 273.

[4] Sismondi, *France* V. 525, thought the Papal action brought about by scandalous rumours concerning *Henry's* relations with Alais, the ground on which Richard eventually refused to marry her.

[5] R. Monte, 273 ; Eure et Loir.

[6] This district extended from the Epte to the lower Oise.

[7] Hoveden, 143.

the two Kings and their subjects. In the event of the death of either King on the pilgrimage, the other to succeed to the undivided command.[1]

Complete as the accord was to be, Henry had the dexterity to keep out two or three matters in which he was interested. One was the right to the custody of the heiress of Déols and Chateauroux in Berri, who had been spirited away by her relatives to keep her from the hands of
Henry in Berri and Auvergne. the King of England. Henry entered Berri in force, and compelled the surrender of the girl.[2] Another matter was the question of the respective rights of the King of France and those of the Duke of Aquitaine over Auvergne. The Auvergnat Barons were prepared to concede everything to the Duke except the appointment to the Bishopric of Clermont. But this matter had to be referred to arbitration. Yet another piece of business transacted by Henry while in the South was the treaty for the purchase of the county
The County of La Marche. of La Marche, another fief held of Aquitaine. Count Aude-bert V. being childless, and intent on joining the Crusade, sold his inheritance to the King for a sum of money. We are told that Henry paid the price.[3] But if he did for once he was outwitted, as the purchase was never completed, the Lusignans succeeding in keeping him out of it.[4]

The proposed joint Crusade of course came to nothing; but we do hear of joint action by the two Kings for the suppression of the heretical views
Religious Movement in Languedoc. that, in spite of the decrees of the Council of Lombers,[5] still kept spreading in Languedoc. In fact the sectaries were so bold and strong that the Bishop of Alby at this time was a prisoner in their hands. They are spoken of as calling themselves the *Bons Hommes*,[6] an appellation that would seem to connect them with Poor Men of Lyons. But with respect to their tenets we labour under this difficulty that, as we shall see, under the pressure brought to bear on them they tendered an orthodox creed on all points save one. To judge by the

---

[1] Ben. P., I. 178-194 ; Gervase, I. 272 ; Hoveden, *sup.* The treaty was concluded at Ivry.

[2] See Ben. P., I. 132, 194, 195 ; R. Monte, 274.

[3] Ben. P., 196, 197 ; G. Vigeois, 324. The former gives the price as 15,000 *livres* (*Angevin*), the latter as 5,000 marks (English), not quite so much.

[4] "The Lusignans had possessed themselves of half the county. Matilda of Angou-lème, the next of kin to Count Audebert, was admitted to the remainder by Richard as over-lord, who, according to Geoffrey of Vigeois, intended to marry her. She ultimately married Hugh Le Brun IX. of Lusignan, and thus united the two portions of La Marche ;" Ben. P., *sup.*, note Bp. Stubbs.

[5] For the Acts of the Council of Lombers (near Alby) the reader is referred to Labbe, *Conc.* X. 1470, and Mansi, XXII. 159. A careful abridgment is given by Hoveden under the year 1176, but 1165 seems the accepted date ; see Hoved, II. 106, note Bp. Stubbs.

[6] Qui se Bonos Homines appellari fecerant, Ben. 198.

articles on which they were pressed by their opponents, they seem, besides holding independent views as to infant baptism and the Eucharist, to have entertained tenets of Manichæan character, such as that of the Two Principles of Good and Evil; extreme asceticism in conjugal relations; denial of the merit of alms-giving, and the like.[1] To meet the growing

Measures to check it. evil the two Kings at first proposed a personal expedition to Toulouse to clear the land of such sinners. On second thoughts they contented themselves with appointing an ecclesiastical commission to reason with them, and convert them (1178). The Cardinal Peter took the lead, with the Archbishops of Bourges, and Narbonne, and the English Bishop Reginald of Bath, and others to support him; while Count Raymond V. of Toulouse, and the Viscounts of Turenne, and Châteauneuf would provide the support of the secular arm. The Bishop of Alby having been rescued from captivity, the Cardinal on reaching Toulouse was able to lay hands on one Pierre de Mauran, a

A Recantation. man of wealth, and a chief supporter of the sectarians. He allowed himself to be frightened into submission, and by way of penance to be publicly flogged through the streets by the Bishop of Toulouse. His punishment induced many others to come in and conform. But two 'false brethren,' by name Raymond and Bernard, men who had been active in preaching, asked for and obtained leave to come under safeconduct to explain their views. The Legate received them in the church of St. Stephen, when they gave in a written profession that he was obliged to admit seemed orthodox. When however he came to ask for further explanations on certain points, he found that the men were

The Vulgar Tongue. unable to converse in Latin; and so, as he tells us, he had to stoop to the absurdity of discussing doctrinal questions in the vulgar tongue.[2] The party then adjourned to the church of St. James, where in the presence of an excited crowd Raymond and Bernard repeated their confession. On the question however being put whether they had always held the same views, the Count of Toulouse and others sprang up to declare that they had often heard them preach doctrines wholly different. The Legate then asked if they would swear to the honesty of their present profession; but there the men drew back, averring that they held oaths to be unlawful. 'Swear not at all,' was their principle.[3] As on this point they remained contumacious they were formally excommunicated and 'handed over to Satan.'[4]

---

[1] On these points compare the proceedings at Lombers *ubi sup.* most singularly on a par with those at Toulouse, as below; see also G. Vigeois, 326.

[2] " Necesse fuit nos illis condescendere, et de ecclesiasticis sacramentis . . . quamvis satis erat absurdum, vulgarem sermonem habere."

[3] Matt. V. 34.

[4] "Satanæ traditos." See Ben. P., and the report issued by the Cardinal, I. 199-206; also a report by Henry Abbot of Clairvaux, 213; Hoved. II., 151-166; also generally Vic et Vaissete IV. 273-279.

Henry, who apparently had remained abroad to hear the result of the proceedings at Toulouse, returned to England in July, landing on the 15th of the month at a place given as ' Dighesmuta.' His first care we are told was, as usual, to visit the shrine of St. Thomas of Canterbury. On the 6th of August, being at Woodstock, he knighted his son Geoffrey, who straightway went off to emulate his brothers by practising feats of arms on the borders of France and Normandy.[1] Tournaments of which we hear little or nothing in England, were of frequent occurrence abroad;[2] so much so that a year later they were expressly forbidden by the Third Lateran Council.[3]

In the course of the autumn and of the following spring further important changes were made in the judicial system of England. Henry's legal reforms, his Assizes of Clarendon and Northampton, and other measures had greatly increased the amount of business brought before his courts. The feigned actions for the ratification of contracts or the conveyance of land known as " Fines " (*finalis concordia*) begin to appear about this time.[4] To meet this increase the King evidently tried various experiments.[5] The Pipe Roll for the year 1175 (21 Henry II.) shows a group of three judges in attendance on the King in his progresses ; so that his peregrinations became an extra judicial circuit. The matter brought before these judges is entered as " *In curia Regis* " ; the business transacted by the Justices in Eyre not being so entered.[6] We now hear that the King

Origin of the Court of King's Bench. having heard complaints of the multiplicity of the circuit judges—eighteen in number at the time—' chose five men, two clerks and three laymen, who were not to depart from the King's Court, but were to remain there to hear complaints from all men ; matters that they could not decide to be brought before the King and his Wise Men.'[7] *Prima facie* a bench of judges attached to the King's Court would be an itinerant body. But the tribunal that does emerge from the legal records of the next few years is a permanent central court, sitting mostly at Westminster, a *Curia Regis* in a restricted and special sense, the original of our Court of King's Bench. This tribunal would be distinct from the Court of Exchequer, although the same men might often sit on both ; it would also have to be distinguished from the King's ordinary Council or *Curia Regis* in the larger and older sense.[8] The reservation of special

---

[1] Ben. P., 198, 206, 207 ; Diceto, I. 426.

[2] See *Guill. Le Mareschal*, II. pp. 90–182. The young King figured in several of these engagements.

[3] Ben. P., I. 226.

[4] The first " Fine " so far traced belongs to the year 1175 ; Round, *Feudal England*, 509.

[5] See Diceto, I. 434, 435.   [6] Round, *sup.* 510, 511.

[7] Ben. P., I. 107. It is worthy of notice that this passage is omitted by Hoveden, a man acquainted with the business of the Courts.

[8] See Bishop Stubbs, Ben. P., II. lxxi.; and Pollock and Maitland, *Hist. Eng. Law*, I. 153, 154.

cases for the hearing of this body (the King and his Wise Men) takes us back on the one hand to the old Witenagemot; and on the other hand brings us down to the Judicial Committee of our Privy Council.

That the chronicler was mistaken in thinking that the King in establishing his new Central Court was influenced by complaints as to the number of his justices in eyre appears plainly enough from the fact that in the following spring their number was increased. In 1176 the country had been mapped out in six circuits with three judges for each. In a Grand Council held after Easter (1st April) 1179 the circuits were rearranged, and reduced from six to four; but the number of judges on each was raised to five and in one case to six. The judges appointed in 1176 had apparently all been laymen; now the names of the trusty Bishops of Winchester, Norwich, and Ely head the lists on three of the circuits, with

Judicial Circuits Systematic. that of Ranulf Glanville on a fourth.[1] The orbits of the circuits, and the judges to serve on them might vary at the King's pleasure. But with all modifications the institution has become permanent. Hardly a year passes by without a visitation of some part of England.[2] To this same Council of Windsor has been

The Grand Assize. ascribed the institution of the Grand Assize, a fitting complement to the Assizes of Novel Disseisin and Mort d'Ancestor. This measure in effect brings all suits for the possession of land under the protection of the King's justice. It declares that no man need answer for his freehold without royal writ, and further that any suit for the possession of land brought in a feudal court may at the instance of the 'tenant' be removed into the King's Court to be tried by the verdict of a jury of his neighbours.[3]

In connexion with these affairs we must notice the retirement and

Death of Richard of Lucy. death of Richard of Lucy, the Chief Justiciar, who for five-and-twenty years had been faithful to his master without being unjust to the people. He resigned his office about the month of April, taking the habit of an Augustinian Canon in the Priory of Lesnes or Lessness (Kent), just founded by himself, and there

Glanville Chief Justiciar. he passed away in July.[4] The great post left vacant was given just a year later to Ranulf Glanville,[5] who for nine years filled it with not less ability but with greater posthumous fame than his predecessor.

In August England was honoured by a visit from the King of France. Louis' son Philip, the Heaven-sent *Dieudonné*, the future 'Augustus,'

---

[1] See the names all given, Ben. P., I. 238; Hoveden, II. 190.

[2] Pollock and Maitland, I. 156, 157.

[3] See Pollock and Maitland, I. 147. The dating of the Assize is due to Mr. J. H. Round, *Athenæum*, 28th January, 1899.

[4] Ben. P. and Hoved., *sup*; Gervase, I. 292, 293.

[5] April, 1180; Hoveden, II. 215.

being on the point of completing his fourteenth year,[1] his father, undeterred by Henry's experiences, resolved to have him crowned
by anticipation, as, no doubt, he himself had been.   The
15th August was fixed for the ceremony.   But the lad fell ill from fatigue
and exposure, and the shock of being run away with by his horse when
hunting in the forest of Compiègne, and so benighted, and lost, until
found and brought home by a grimy charcoal burner.[2]   The King then,
in obedience to a monition conveyed to him in his sleep by
apparitions of St. Thomas, thrice repeated, resolved on a
pilgrimage to the shrine of the Martyr.   A safe-conduct having
been duly obtained he landed on the 22nd August at Dover, where Henry
was in waiting to receive him.   The two went on next day to Canterbury.
Louis' offerings at the tomb were commensurate with the occasion.   They
included a gold cup; a grant of 100 *modii* of wine in perpetuity to be
received at Poissy[3]; with an exemption from Customs' duties for all
articles to be exported from France for the use of the monks.   After a
stay of two days, Louis, still escorted by Henry, returned to Dover.   On
the 26th he recrossed to Wissant.   Philip having recovered
his health, fresh orders were issued for his coronation, to take
place on the 1st November.   The ceremony this time duly
took place, the hallowing being performed by Becket's friend William of
Blois, late Archbishop of Sens, and now of Rheims, and brother to Queen
Alais.   Among the dignitaries present was the young King Henry, who
carried the crown, while the Count of Flanders carried the sword of state,
"Joyeuse," the reputed sword of Charlemagne.   Poor King Louis was
unable to appear.   On his return from England he took a chill, and was
prostrated by a stroke of paralysis, affecting his whole right side.[4]

If all the world stood in awe of Henry, as we are told,[5] his authority in
Aquitaine and Brittany, at any rate, was not undisputed.   In those
districts disaffection was chronic.   Not a year passed but the young
Count of Poitiers had to take the field against rebels.   In less than six
months after the successful Limousin campaign of 1176 Dax
and Bayonne were in revolt, and had to be reduced.   Richard
took the opportunity of endeavouring to establish order on the
Navarrese frontier for the protection of pilgrims to Compostella (December

Side notes: Louis VII. — On Pilgrimage to Canterbury. — Coronation of his Son Philip. — Revolts in Aquitaine

---

[1] He was born 22nd August, 1165; R. Monte; Rigord, *De Gestis Philippi*, Bouquet,
XVII. 5.

[2] Rigord, Bouquet, XVII. 4, 5; Sismondi, *France*, V. 558; Lavisse, *France*, III. 74.

[3] Poissy being on the Seine below its junction with the Yonne, the wine would
presumably be the produce of the vineyards of Burgundy and Champagne.

[4] Ben. P., I. 240-243; Hoveden, II. 192-194; Gervase, I. 293; *Grandes Chron.*,
IV. 10.

[5] So Walter Map, *De Nugis Cur.*, 60.   " Rex noster Henricus, cujus potestatem totus
fere orbis timet."

1176–January 1177).[1]   Late in 1177 his brother Geoffrey was sent with
and Brittany. a force to bring Guiomar of Léon to subjection[2]; while the
King himself, as we have seen, had to invade Berri to assert his
rights over the hand of an heiress.[3]   In 1178 the insubordinate Count of
Bigorre fell into the hands of Richard, and had to purchase his liberty by
the surrender of Clermont and Mont Brun.[4]   An ineffectual siege of Pons,
the seat of Geoffrey of Rancogne ended the year.[5]   The warlike young
Count, however, returned to the charge in 1179, with more complete
Successes of success.   Towards Easter (9th April) the investiture of Pons
Richard and was resumed.   In Easter week a force led by Richard in
Geoffrey. person captured Richemont; and in the following week he
won Gensac, Marcillac-Lanville, and Anville.   In each case the fortifications
were immediately razed.[6]   At the beginning of May siege was laid to
Taillebourg, a place fenced in with triple works, and generally considered
impregnable.   The Count began his attack in the remorseless style of the
old Conqueror, namely by devastating the country far and wide to cut off
supplies.   A sally undertaken as if for very shame's sake on the 8th May
ended disastrously, Richard not only repelling the attack, but forcing his
way into the town pell-mell with the fugitives; two days later the castle
surrendered.[7]   Geoffrey of Rancogne, brought to the end of his resources,
then yielded Pons.   By the end of the month Wulgrin Taillefer III., the
rebel of 1176, who had just succeeded his father, had to inaugurate his
accession to the title by giving up the walls of Angoulême to be
dismantled.   Crowned with laurels Richard went over to England to
be congratulated by his father.[8]   In Brittany Geoffrey had found it
necessary to deprive Guiomar of almost all his possessions.[9]

[1] Ben. P., I. 131, 132.
[2] R. Monte, 274, 275.
[3] Ben. P., 175, 176.
[4] Gers or Haute Garonne?   Both names are found in each department.
[5] Both in Charente; Ben. P., 213; *cnf.* G. Vigeois, 327.
[6] *Id.* All these places are in Charente.
[7] Diceto, I. 431, 432.   Benedict, *sup.*, gives the siege of Taillebourg as only lasting
3rd-5th May.
[8] Ben. P., *sup.*; R. Monte, 281, 282.
[9] Ben., 239; Monte, *sup.*

CHAPTER XI

HENRY II. (*continued*)

A.D. 1179–1182

Accession of Philip II. of France, "Augustus"—Treaty of Ivry renewed—Henry
    mediating between Philip and his Relations—Henry's Sons supporting Philip in
    the Field—Troubles in Aquitaine—Dissensions in the Royal Family—Richard
    renouncing Allegiance to the Young King—The Young King and Geoffrey
    supporting Aquitanian Insurgents against the Elder King and Richard—Death of
    the Young King Henry

WITH the coronation of his son the reign of Louis VII. came practically
to an end. During the remaining months of his life (1st Novem-
Accession of Philip II. of France. ber, 1179–18th September, 1180) no account was taken of the
paralytic King. Young Philip II. began to reign ; and he soon let
the world see what the working of boy-government might prove
to be. His first recorded act was an unprovoked attack upon
Boy-government. the Jews. We are told that he had heard from his playmates
of the wicked people who used to crucify a Christian child on
Good Fridays by way of mockery—a slanderous and preposterous legend
only too widely current.[1] Having made enquiry, and found, as he
supposed, that the charge was well-founded, Philip ordered all
Persecution of the Jews. the Jews in his kingdom to be arrested in their synagogues on
a given Saturday ; while all their valuables were to be seized.[2]
Philip's next step was to break with his father's advisers, namely his own
mother Alais, and her four brothers Theobald of Blois, Henry
Breach with his Mother. of Champagne, Stephen of Sancerre and Archbishop William,
late of Sens and now of Rheims. Discarding these he took
for his Mentor his God-father Philip of Flanders. At his suggestion he

---

[1] A case, that of St. Richard of Paris, had been alleged in 1179, W. Le Breton and
Rigord, Bouquet, XVII. 66, 6. For the celebrated case of " St. William of Norwich,"
A.D. 1144, see *Monastic Annals*, IV. 25, and R. Monte, 251 ; for cases at Blois, A.D.
1172, and Gloucester, *Id*. and 250 ; at Bury St. Edmunds, 1181, Chron. Melrose ; at
Winchester, 1192 ; R. Devizes, 56 (Eng. Hist. Socy.) ; also Gervase, I., 296, for the
Bury case.
[2] Rigord, *sup.* ; Diceto, II. 4.

proceeded to marry the Count's niece Isabel, daughter of Baldwin V.
of Hainault by Margaret of Flanders (April 1180). The match
was by no means a bad one as it gave the French Crown the
first accession of territory that it had yet enjoyed, namely the
County of Artois with St. Omer and Arras, given over by the Count as
his niece's portion[1]; while he further proposed to make the lady his
heir, and failing issue of his own to settle on her Flanders South of
the Lys, with the Vermandois, the latter a French fief that he held in
right of his wife Isabel.[2] From another point of view the marriage was
considered to shed lustre on the house of Capet by linking it with
that of Charlemagne. But the French Magnates thought fit to rail
against the alliance as disparaging. Isabel however having been married
at Bapaume in Artois, was brought to Paris to be crowned. The
ceremony was performed at St. Denis on the 29th May, by Guy Archbishop of Sens, a direct slight to the Archbishop of Rheims.[3] Lastly
we hear that the old King was deprived of his Seal, lest he should in
any way interfere.[4]

His Marriage.

To report on the situation created by the practical advent of a new reign
the younger Henry had gone over to England at the end of March.[5]
About the middle of April he and his father came over to
Normandy together; on the 28th June they had a conference
at the familiar place between Trie and Gisors with Philip and
the French Magnates; when Henry came forward to play the graceful part
of mediator as between the young King of France and his relatives of the
House of Blois, Henry's old enemies. Philip was induced to make friends
with his uncles; to make an immediate provision for his mother; and to
agree to respect her appointed dower in the future. With Henry he
concluded a treaty confirming that of Ivry as a league of amity
and defensive alliance; but without any agreement as to taking
the Cross. In view of the influential position at the French
Court held by the Count of Flanders Henry thought it expedient to revive
the old treaty of retainer, granting Philip 1000 marks (£666 13s. 4d.) a
year, in consideration of his being ready with 500 men-at-arms for forty
days' service in each year, if called upon.[6] Louis VII., the weak petty
King, having passed away, as already mentioned, on the 13th September,

Henry in Normandy.

Treaty of Ivry confirmed.

---

[1] Lavisse, *France*, III. 85.

[2] Sister of Raoul or Ralph II., whom she succeeded in 1163; Giraldus, VIII. 229
note Warner.

[3] Ben. P., I. 244-246; R. Monte, 289, 290; Diceto, II. 5; Giraldus, VIII. 228;
Rigord, 7 and note.

[4] Diceto, II. 6.

[5] 30th March, Ben. P. *sup.* 1st April, Diceto, II. 5.

[6] Ben. P., I. 246-249; Diceto, II. 6. See also the letter of Henry to Glanville,
Giraldus, VIII. 188. Glanville, as chief Justiciar, acted as Regent in the King's
absence.

a fresh confirmation of the treaty of Ivry was immediately sealed by Philip and Henry.[1]

A blow much felt by Henry as a domestic calamity, though his own **Downfall of Henry the Lion.** position was not affected by it, was the fall of his distinguished son-in-law Henry the Lion, Duke of Saxony and Bavaria; "one of the most interesting characters in mediæval history." He had incurred the ill-will of the Emperor by withdrawing his support in Italy in 1175, during the war with the Lombard cities. He had many enemies among his own feudatories, and the German nobility, and an especial one in Philip of Heinsberg Archbishop of Cologne. At the return of Frederic to Germany in 1178 Henry was attacked on all sides. Having attempted to remonstrate he was treated as the guilty party, and called upon to answer. He failed to appear. At a final citation issued for a Diet to be held at Würtzburg on the 13th January 1180 he refused to come except under safe conduct; whereupon he was declared guilty of treason, and sentenced to utter forfeiture. On the 13th April his great inheritance was broken up, and distributed among his adversaries. The King was much distressed, and all the more so because he felt that he was powerless to intervene.[2]

Henry having spent the winter abroad was preparing for a visit to England in the spring (1181); but was detained for three months by successive incidents. In contemplation of his crossing he had an interview on the 27th April with Philip at the ford of Saint-Rémy-sur-Arve, near **Appeals to Henry.** Nonancourt. There they were presented with copies of a Papal Encyclical loudly calling for help to Jerusalem, now **Help for Jerusalem.** openly threatened by Saladin, but under the helpless rule of a leper, Baldwin IV.[3] The Kings were deeply moved by Alexander's representations; but could not promise any immediate assistance.[4] Next day, Henry having moved towards the coast he was met by Bishop Puiset's nephew Hugh Count of Bar. This man in 1174 had brought over troops to support the rebels in England, but he now had the assurance to ask the King for a subvention to enable him to **Crusade in Spain.** carry out a crusade against the Moors and *Publicani* of Spain enjoined on him by the Pope. Henry answered that if the Count would go to Palestine instead of Spain he might give him something. The progress towards Barfleur was resumed, to be again arrested by the appearance of William the Lion and his brother David.[5] Henry had summoned them in the hope of settling an ecclesiastical trouble that

---

[1] Ben. P., I. 250; Hoveden, II. 197, 198; Diceto, II. 7.

[2] See Boehmer, *Regests*, 140, cited Bishop Stubbs; Hoved. II. 200; Ben. P., I. 240; Green, *Princesses*, I. 242, etc.

[3] So the Pope, " Non est rex Baldewinus qui terram regere possit."

[4] Ben. P., I. 272-275; Hoveden, II. 255-259, and the Papal letters there.

[5] Chron. Melrose.

involved a trial of strength between King William and the Pope. The See

A Scottish
Episcopal
Appoint-
ment. of St. Andrews having fallen vacant in 1178 or 1179,[1] the Chapter without consulting the King elected one John Scott.[2] But William refused to recognise this appointment; and instead nominated one Hugh, his chaplain, and had him consecrated and installed. John went off to Rome, and at his instance Alexander III. sent the sub-deacon Alexius, afterwards a Cardinal, to investigate the facts. Passing through England under Henry's safe conduct he gained admission to Scotland, much against William's will.[3] Of course he decided in favour of John, and, after a fierce struggle, in the course of which the whole diocese of St. Andrews was laid under Interdict, got him consecrated in Edinburgh, in the month June 1180, by the hands of his uncle Peter Bishop of Aberdeen. But both John and Peter found it prudent to retire promptly to Normandy.[4] Henry, after discussing the matter with the parties, suggested as a compromise that Bishop Peter should be allowed to return to Aberdeen, and that John should resign St. Andrews as soon as another See could be found for him. The plan was approved of and forthwith sent to the Pope for his consideration.[5] This matter having been so far settled, Henry, who had reached the coast, was actually preparing to sail, when his plans were again interrupted by an appeal from the young King of France. Intolerant of control or advice Philip had already broken with the Count of Flanders, who, having left Paris in a huff, was actually threatening hostilities. Henry hastened back to the French

Mediation
between
France and
Flanders. frontier; had an interview at Gisors with the two Philips, and for the moment succeeded in patching up a seeming reconciliation. Then, at last free, taking ship at Cherbourg, he

Return to
England. landed at Portsmouth on the 25th or 26th of July. The King of Scots came back with him.[6]

Hitherto we have found Henry's legislation chiefly directed to matters connected with the revenue or the administration of justice. Now we

Assizes of
Arms. have him taking up the subject of national defence. In the previous autumn he had published an Assize of Arms for his Continental dominions.[7] On his return to England he issued a similar set of regulations for his insular possessions. Every holder of a knight's fee of land to be provided with a helmet (*cassis*),

[1] Bishop Richard died in 1178 (Chron. Melrose), or 1179 (Chron. Holyrood).

[2] " Magister Johannes cognomine Scottus "; Melr.

[3] " Rege Willelmo vix permittente "; Melr.

[4] See Chron. Melrose, A.D. 1178-1180; Benedict, I. 250, 263-266; Hoveden, II. 208-212, and the Papal letters there.

[5] Ben., 276, 277; Hoveden, II. 259.

[6] 25th July, Diceto, II. 7; 26th July, Ben. P., *sup.*, Hoveden, II. 260.

[7] Ben. P., 269.

coat of mail, shield, and lance; a similar equipment to be kept for every knight's fee on the demesnes; men worth 16 marks (£10 13s. 4d.) in personalty (*in catallo*) or rents to be similarly provided; men with 10 marks (£6 13s. 4d.) to have an iron skull cap (*capellet ferri*), a hauberk (*aubergel*), and a lance; burgesses and freemen of the common sort[1] to have a wambais, or quilted jacket, with iron skull-cap, and lance; the prescribed weapons not to be sold or parted with under any circumstances, but to be allowed to descend from father to son. Jews not to be allowed to retain arms at all. To ensure the execution of the Ordinance the Justices in Eyre would hold inquests upon oath in the Hundreds and Boroughs, and return lists of the men liable under the different categories; defaulters would be punishable with mutilation,[2] not with mere fines. A "Foreign Enlistment" provision, the **Foreign Enlistment.** first on record, forbids men to serve out of England without the King's orders; while a parallel clause prohibits the exportation of ships, or even of ship-timber. With his frequent crossings Henry might well be anxious about the keeping of the Channel seas.[3] The Assize was a re-organisation of the *fyrd*, the ancient national militia, that had not been superseded by the special liability to service in connection with feudal tenure. Comparing the Assize for Henry's Continental dominions, we notice that abroad the highest class were required to serve on horseback, not so in England. Cavalry was still the main arm of foreign armies, not of English levies.

Two conspicuous figures in the ecclesiastical world passed away in the course of the autumn. On the 30th August Alexander III. closed his "long and eventful pontificate."[4] He had beaten and out-**Deaths of Alexander III.** lived four successive anti-Popes; had reduced Barbarossa to sue for peace; and brought together the whole hierarchy of Western Europe to sit under his presidency in Œcumenical Council, the Lateran Council, third of the name.[5] Roger of Pont-l'Evêque died on the 26th November;[6] a man of letters and a courtier, **And Arch-bishop Roger of York.** but not perhaps a zealous churchman; at any rate a hater of all monks. The archiepiscopal estates throve under his careful management, and were left in most flourishing condition. He rebuilt the choir of York Minster and the palace there;[7] but of his work nothing seems to remain. He also left considerable treasure, of which great part was bequeathed to various charities at home and abroad.

---

[1] " Tota communa liberorum hominum."
[2] " Dominus rex capiet se ad eorum membra."
[3] Ben. P., I. 278; Hoveden, II. 261.
[4] N. Nicolas; Chr. Melrose.
[5] A.D. 1179, 5th–19th March; Ben. P., I. 210-238; Gervase, I. 278, etc.
[6] *Reg. Sacrum*; Stubbs, *Decem Script.*, 1723.
[7] Stubbs, *sup.*

Henry however laid his hands on the whole, exacting a strict account of every penny that belonged to the Archbishop.[1] Roger's last act had been to excommunicate William the Lion, and lay all his dominions under Interdict in pursuance of Papal instructions, Alexander having refused to sanction the compromise suggested by Henry, and William still refusing to accept John Scott as Bishop of St. Andrews.[2] But a

Lucius III. Pope. new Pope, Lucius III., had ascended St. Peter's chair. William lost no time in applying to him; and was rewarded not only by a reversal of the sentences passed by Archbishop Roger, but also by an actual gift of the Golden Rose.[3]

The reconciliation patched up by Henry between the two Philips proved hollow and short-lived. The Count joined hands with the discontented magnates of the House of Blois. Henry the Count of Champagne had died; but his place was filled by his son Henry II., under the tutelage of his mother Mary, daughter of Louis VII. by Queen

Coalition against Philip of France. Eleanor. She hated her stepson Philip. The coalition was also joined by Hugh III. Duke of Burgundy, and the Counts of Hainault and Namur. "France" was to be attacked from North and South. But the actual rupture was provoked by the action of the Count of Sancerre, who occupied Saint-Brisson-sur-Loire;[4] and then to protect himself did homage for it to the Count of Flanders. Philip, refusing to recognise this transaction, expelled Sancerre, and recovered Saint-Brisson; whereupon the Flemish troops advancing in force sacked Noyon, overran the district of Clermont, invested Senlis, occupied Pierrefonds,[5] and carried their ravages to within fifteen miles of Paris. Matters might have gone hard with King Philip

Intervention of Henry's Sons. had not Henry's sons hastened in the most chivalrous manner to the rescue of their boy-suzerain. Their *Brabançons* soon turned the scale. The county of Sancerre was harried; the Countess of Champagne and the Duke of Burgundy forced to retire; Philip of Flanders put to flight.[6]

But for winter storms the report of these events would have brought Henry with all speed back to Normandy. As it was he could only loose

---

[1] See W. Newb., I. 225; R. Monte, 299; Ben. P., I. 282, 283, 289; Hoveden, II. 264, 265. Diceto, II. 12, gives an inventory of Rogers' valuables, the cash being alleged to amount to £11,000 of 'old money,' and 300 "aurei." New money was issued in November, 1180; Gervase, I. 295.

[2] Ben. P., I. 281, 282; Hoveden, II. 263.

[3] Ben. 283, 286; Hoveden, 264, 267, 268; Chr. Melrose, A.D. 1182. Ubaldo Bishop of Ostia was elected Pope on the 1st September, and took the style of Lucius III. H. Nicholas; Milman.

[4] Summer of 1181; Loiret, near Gien.

[5] Oise, all four.

[6] 1881; November; Ben. P., I. 283, 284; Hoveden, II. 265: Diceto, II. 8-10; Gervase, I. 297. *Cnf.* Lavisse, *France*, III. 87, a very loose account.

from Portsmouth on the 3rd March, 1182, landing next day at Barfleur.[1]

Henry in Normandy. He lost no time in seeing young Philip, and was able to arrange for a conference with the Count of Flanders and his allies. The parties met on the 4th April, between Gournay and Gerberoy. Henry's tact again succeeded in establishing peace, and the terms were apparently settled on that day.

Pacification. But owing to the absence of the Duke of Burgundy, and the Countess-mother of Champagne, it was found necessary to arrange for another meeting, to be held between Senlis and Crépy-en-Valois, on the 11th April. According to the reports sent to England by Henry the Count of Flanders surrendered Pierrefonds to the King of France with all claim to the over-lordship of Amiens, Clermont, or Coucy; and quashed certain engagements entered into with the young King during the rebellion. All the French feudatories would return to their allegiance, and all captures and damages be made good by mutual restitution. With respect to the Vermandois a new situation had been created by the death of the Countess Isabel who had passed away on the 26th March.[2] Her rights should have passed to her sister Eleanor, married to Matthew of Beaumont. But she was ignored,[3] the French claiming the Vermandois as an escheated fief; while the Count insisted that he had expended large sums on the improvement of the property, and that till these were repaid he could not be required to surrender it.[4]

Henry appears to have taken advantage of the happy moment of concord subsisting between himself, France, and Flanders to induce the two Philips to concur in an intercession to Frederic Barbarossa on behalf of the unfortunate Duke of Saxony, who, driven from one possession after another, had been obliged finally to throw himself on the Emperor's mercy (Erfurt, 1181). Frederic had condemned him to seven years' exile. Now we are told that he was induced to remit four years of the banish-

Henry the Lion in Normandy. ment, and in other ways to mitigate the sentence. Bowing to necessity Henry retired to Normandy with his wife and family. They were received with open arms, and, through the King's kindness, established on a comfortable footing at Argentan.[5]

But the dissensions at the French Court were not the only matters that had called the King from England. He had to succour Richard in Poitou,

---

[1] Diceto, II. 10; Ben. P., 285.

[2] Ben. P., I. 309, note Bishop Stubbs.

[3] De Serres, cited Engl. Hist. Rev. XIV. 546.

[4] See Henry's report of the first meeting, Giraldus, VIII. 189; and that of the second meeting, Diceto, II. 11; also Giraldus, 229. According to Benedict, I. 286, the Count renewed his promise to leave Flanders South of the Lys to Philip at his death failing issue.

[5] Ben. P., I. 287, 288; Hoveden, II. 269; Diceto, II. 12. Green, *Princesses*, I 248, 250.

where matters were going badly.   Successful in war the Count failed altogether
as an administrator.   His governing had united all classes
Disaffection in Aquitaine. against him.   The Barons protested that his rule was intolerable.   If after a fashion he was a lover of 'justice' and order,
it is admitted that his temper was arbitrary, and his methods sanguinary.
He solved all difficulties in his own way, and with the sword.[1]   Then the
Barons further complained that no lady's honour was safe from his assaults.[2]
In the previous summer "the voice of Bertran de Born had once more
given the signal for a general revolt."[3]   Richard had been obliged to rase
the walls of Limoges, as he had rased those of Angoulême in 1179.   In
the course of the month of May Henry, having pacified Philip's enemies,
moved Southwards.   On reaching the borders of La Marche he found that
his purchase had been nullified by the Lusignans, who had made themselves masters of the county, and were too strongly established to be
Henry and his Sons in the Field. attacked.   Efforts at negotiation with the leading Poitevin
rebels having come to nothing, the King took the field,
marching hither and thither, assisting Richard in his sieges.
Then Geoffrey came forward to lend a helping hand; while finally the
young King joined his father and his brothers under the walls of Périgueux,
the city at the time being assailed by Richard (1st July).   Within the week
the place surrendered; and peace to a certain extent was restored.[4]   But
the miseries of the land were not ended.   The suspension of hostilities let
loose hordes of disbanded *Brabançons*, as they were called, the scum of
all Western Europe, who, retiring to Auvergne and Berri, pillaged the
country till at last, the peasantry driven to desperation organised themselves
for resistance in the brotherhood of the *Caputii*.[5]

It is not without pain that we confess to a misgiving that the alacrity of
Henry's sons in coming to the rescue of young Philip may
The Royal Family. have been prompted by the hope of securing an ally against
their father.[6]   The young King and Richard were still as
ungrateful and disloyal to him as ever; while we now find that, naturally
enough, they were equally destitute of all proper regard for each other.

We hear that Richard was detected secretly fortifying Clairvaux,[7] a
place described as situate between Loudun, Chinon, and Ile-Bouchard,[8]

[1] See the portrait of him given Giraldus, VIII. 246, 247.
[2] Ben. P., I. 292.
[3] Norgate, II. 220.
[4] G. Vigeois, Labbe, *Nova Bibl.*, II. 330, 331; Norgate, II. 220, 223; Eyton,
Itinerary.
[5] So called from the linen hoods that they wore as badges. See Gervase, I. 301;
Grandes Chroniques, IV. 20, from Rigord, 10.
[6] See Hoveden, II. 266.
[7] "Castellum Claræ Vallis;" R. Monte, 302; Ben. P., I. 294; Diceto, II. 18.
[8] So Bertran de Born, p. 44 (ed. Clédat). cited Norgate. I cannot find the place in the
Gazetteer of France.

just within the borders of Poitou, but belonging to Anjou.   There could
be but one interpretation as to the meaning of such an act.   It
Brotherly Love. showed an aggressive purpose, not only as against the old
King, but also as against the young King, to whose heritage it
belonged ; and Bertran de Born, always on the look-out to make mischief,
was prompt in calling attention to the fact.[1]   But the younger Henry in
turn was quite prepared to accept any opportunity that might offer itself
for stripping Richard of his possessions.   He was in communication with
the Aquitanian Barons, who, in their despair now turned to him.[2]   Moreover he was still pressing his impossible demands for the
A fractious Son. absolute cession of Normandy, or some other district.   With
respect to this matter it is clear that though Henry might
allow Richard to take possession of his mother's lands, and Geoffrey to
enter on his wife's rights : yet that he himself could not without loss of
dignity and position surrender any part of his own inheritance.   To have
done so in favour of such a youth as the young King had shown himself to
be would have been mere culpable folly.   Besides, Henry had already
gone as far as he safely could, as we hear that when he last went over to
England he had given his son a free hand as Regent of Normandy during
his absence ; and that all the appointments during that time had been
made with young Henry's concurrence.[3]   His demands now meeting with
the inevitable refusal he went off to Paris, threatening to take the Cross.
Repeated embassies, and much pressure were needed to induce him to
return.   He only came on condition of receiving the liberal allowance of
100 *Livres Angevin* (£25 sterling) for himself *per diem*, and 10 *Livres* for
his Queen.   On these terms he took a solemn oath of future obedience to
his father's will.[4]

Christmas 1182 was kept by Henry at Caen, in the midst of his family.
The young King and Queen, Richard, Geoffrey, the Duke and Duchess of
Saxony were there.   The only absentees were John who was in England,
and Queen Eleanor, who was also in England, still a state prisoner.
The gathering was the prelude to an outburst of domestic passions
worthy of the annals of ancient Greece.   The Court having moved to
Le Mans Henry, to bind his sons once more to the acceptance of his
dispositions, suggested that the young King should again receive the
homage of his brothers for their respective possessions.[5]   On the part of
Geoffrey no difficulty was raised ; and the ceremony was performed at
Angers, the Court having advanced to that place.   But with respect to

---

[1] *Ubi sup.*
[2] Ben. P., 292 ; Diceto, *sup.*
[3] Diceto, II. 8.
[4] Ben P., 290 ; Hoveden, *sup.*   The Angevin Livre was one-fourth of the pound
sterling.
[5] Ben. P., I. 291 ; Hoveden, II. 273.

Richard young Henry demurred to recognising his position in Aquitaine,[1] he complained of the fortification of Clairvaux, and informed his father of his own relations with the insurgent Barons. At last, however, yielding to the personal influence that Henry could always exercise, he promised to accept the homage, if only Richard would also take a fresh oath of

Fraternal outburst. fealty to himself.[2] At this the Count burst into a fury, declaring that he owed no subjection to his elder brother; and that if the first-born son succeeded to the father's land, the second-born had an equal right to his mother's heritage. With that he took himself off in open revolt.[3]

But meanwhile the Poitevin Barons who had come to terms in the previous summer were again in arms against Richard.[4] The King, who, however much irritated with his son, could not abandon him, sent first Geoffrey, and then the young King to reason with the insurgents who had gathered at Limoges. Instead of doing so they joined their ranks. Kept out of Limoges Richard revenged himself by barbarous cruelty to any rebels who fell into his hands. At the end of a month Henry himself

Father and Sons. marched to Limoges, to be received with flights of arrows by his graceless sons (1st March). His surcoat was said to have been pierced.[5] It would seem however that he gained admission to the city; the young King being established in the citadel. He kept going backwards and forwards, to and from his father's quarters, in the most unblushing manner, pretending to negotiate on behalf of the rebels; but in fact merely manœuvring to give Geoffrey time to raise more troops.[6] At one time he told the King that he had taken the Cross to atone for his sins against him. Henry, having exhausted himself in efforts to induce his son to renounce what seemed a rash vow,[7] ended by saying that if his son had really taken the Cross from conscientious motives he would provide an outfit. Then we hear of the son bringing men from the castle to sue for peace on their knees, promising hostages. But when the King sent for the hostages his men were shot at.[8] In like manner Geoffrey, 'the son of iniquity,' in turn came to his father to ask for a twenty-four hours' truce to enable him to enter the citadel, to reason

---

[1] On this point see also W. Newb., I. 233; who clearly makes that the cause of the rupture.

[2] "Dummodo Ricardus, homagio sibi præstito, ligantia facta, fidelitatem sibi . . . repromitteret." From this we gather that Richard had already sworn fealty as well as done homage.

[3] See the clear account given by Diceto, II. 18, 19; comparing the two muddled versions of Benedict, 292, 294; also the brief word in Geof. Vigeois, 332.

[4] See the list G. Vigeois, *sup.*

[5] G. Vigeois, 332, 334; Ben. P., I. 293, 295, 296; Hoveden, II. 274.

[6] G. Vigeois, 332, "Habitis . . . percunctis inter se colloquiis"; Diceto, II. 19. *Cnf.* Ben. P., 296, 297.

[7] "Incauto voto."   [8] Ben. P., I. 297, 298.

with his brother Henry. Under cover of that protection he came and plundered the shrine of St. Martial, the local patron-saint, carrying off a mass of gold and silver.[1] Having kept Easter (17th April) at Limoges the King retired, as if sick of the siege; while the younger Henry about the same time went off to Angoulême, to stir up the spirit of resistance there.[2] Bertran de Born hoping for Henry's downfall began to call for a general rising in Flanders, France, and Normandy,[3] and the King in evident alarm sent orders to England for the imprisonment of the men who had been most implicated in the rising of 1173.[4] But as at that

The Young King rejected. time, so again now, the fire soon burnt itself out. When the young King after a while returned to Limoges he found the gates of the citadel closed against him. The people, who by that time had had their eyes opened as to the real characters of Henry's rebel sons, would have nothing to say to him. Falling back in disgust on the 23rd May he captured Aixe, a town loyal to Richard.[5] From Aixe he went to Grammont, a House of Religion especially reverenced by the elder King,[6] who wished to be buried there. But the Grammont monks were not spared: all their valuables were carried off, including a golden pyx in the form of a dove, the King's gift. The monastery of La Couronne near Angoulême and other churches suffered likewise. On the 26th May Henry was at Userche, where Hugh of Burgundy and Raymond of Toulouse joined him with reinforcements. Their action however would be directed, not against the elder Henry, but against Richard. But in the utter confusion of the moment it was not easy to distinguish friends from foes. On the 27th the army moved on to Donzenac,[7] without any other apparent aim than plunder, as next day they advanced through Martel to Rocamadour.[8] This again was "the most famous of the holy places of Aquitaine," the seat of a shrine to which the King himself had turned for comfort and support in time of trial.[9] But his son cared no more for St. Amadour than he did for St. Martial. The place was

His Illness stripped. Retracing their steps they were arrested at Martel by the illness of the young King, who, having been unwell since the 25th or 26th of the month, was laid up with fever in a blacksmith's cottage. Dysentery followed.[10] A message was sent to the King begging him to come.[11] The father who had trusted, and trusted, till he

---

[1] *Id.*, 299; G. Vigeois, 335, 336. The writer was at Limoges at the time, but he thought that the sacrilegious Geoffrey was the Elect of Lincoln, not the Count of Brittany.

[2] G. Vigeois, 336.

[3] Clédat, *Bertran*, 52.

[4] Ben. P., 294.

[5] G. Vigeois, 332, 336.

[6] *Id.*, 330.

[7] Both this place and Uzerche are in Corrèze.

[8] Both in Lot.

[9] Above, p. 124.

[10] G. Vigeois, 336; Ben. P., I. 300; Hoveden, II. 278; Norgate, II. 226.

[11] The King was apparently at the junction of the Briance with the Venne, *i.e.* at Aixe; G. Vig., 338.

could trust no more, fearing some filial snare, refused to come; but he sent Bertran Bishop of Agen, who found the young man in a dying condition.[1] On Whitsunday (5th June) he had received no Sacrament. But on the Tuesday he was visited by the Bishop of Cahors and other Aquitanian Prelates who received his confession, and administered the Holy Communion.[2] Bishop Bertran having arrived the young King committed to him a last prayer for forgiveness, to be carried to his father, with a petition that his followers might be paid what was due to them. On Saturday 11th June he confessed again, and received the *viaticum* and extreme unction from the Bishop. He asked to have the cloak with the crusader's badge that he had assumed at Limoges laid upon his shoulders; and then gave it to his faithful friend and servant William

And Death. Marshal to be carried to Holy Land. He asked to be buried at Rouen, and so passed away in the 29th year of his age. On receipt of the news, the King, who loved his son with all his faults, was overwhelmed with grief.[3] On Ascension Day (26th May) he had directed the clergy at Caen to excommunicate all those who were making mischief between him and his son. But the chief offender, the young King himself, was to be specially excepted.[4]

In compliance with his directions young Henry's remains were embalmed for transmission to Rouen. But at Le Mans, where they **His Burial.** were deposited for the night in the Cathedral Church, a hitch occurred. The Bishop and people of Le Mans refused to part with the corpse, and insisted on burying it there. But the men of Rouen declined to waive their claim, and so the King, at their petition, ordered the body to be exhumed and taken to Rouen. There it was finally laid to rest on the 22nd July in St. Mary's Cathedral.[5]

Weak and unstable, treacherous and ungrateful; without one good deed to be placed to his credit, the young King was undoubtedly **Estimate of his popularity.** popular, and regretted to an extent at first sight surprising.[6] The mystery, however, does not seem insoluble. In the first place the young man certainly had gifts which, whether accompanied by more sterling qualities or not, go far towards winning popular favour. He had good looks, his father's pleasant manners and address, and spent freely; his liberality being extended to deserving and undeserving alike. He also

---

[1] Ben. P., *sup.*; and the Bishop's report to the Pope, printed by Bishop Stubbs, Hoveden, I. lxvii.   [2] G. Vigeois, 337.

[3] See Geoffrey Vigeois, 337, 338; Ben. P., I. 300, 301; Hoveden, II. 278, 279; Diceto, II. 19; and the Bishop of Agen's report, *sup.*

[4] Ben. P., 300.

[5] Ben. P., 301, 303, 304; Hoveden, II. 280; Diceto, II. 20. For the date Bishop Stubbs cites the *Chronicle* of Rouen.

[6] See the extravagant encomiums of Giraldus, VIII. 173, 174. "Omnibus amor;" and "plus homine dilectus;" where however, the writer balances and explains his assertion by adding "Pater vero cunctis infestus et odiosus."

shone in the tilt-yard. On these points all the writers are agreed.[1] Then
the mere fact that he had been on Becket's side would with a large class
cover a multitude of sins. If we scrutinise the list of those who try to
make a case for the young King, we shall find that apart from one or two
courtiers and sycophants, like Peter of Blois,[2] and the Abbot of Mont-
Saint-Michel, who sought to reach the King's heart by eulogising his
Absalom, they were men who from one point of view or another hated the
elder Henry; namely, either for his antifeudal policy, like Radulfus Niger;[3]
or for his ecclesiastical policy, like Gervase, and Thomas Agnellus the
Archdeacon of Wells;[4] or from personal pique, like Giraldus, and Walter
Map. So again Bertran de Born might well write elegies on the young
man who had been weak enough to lend an ear to his fiendish suggestions.[5]
On the other hand, the worthy Dean of St. Paul's (Diceto) thought that
young Henry had lived quite long enough.[6] Hoveden says that nobody
mourned him but his father;[7] while William of Newburgh utterly condemns
him, and laughs at the attempts to make a martyr of him.[8]

Henry's dying charge to William Marshal was not disregarded. True
to his master's wishes he undertook the vicarious pilgrimage,
A Vicarious Pilgrimage. on which he spent two years. As we are told that on his
return he took leave of King Guy of Jerusalem his journey
must have fallen in 1184-1186.[9]

With the death of the young King his following fell to pieces, the
scattered relics being fiercely hunted down by Richard. On the 24th
June Limoges surrendered; the King ordered all the fortifications to be
utterly demolished. Some of the baronial castles were likewise dismantled;
while all those previously held by Richard were taken into hand. The
King of Arragon who had brought succour—probably out of opposition to
Toulouse—was handsomely rewarded, and sent home.[10] Geoffrey, whose
previous conduct seems inexplicable, except from a Satanic passion for
mischief and intrigue, came to Angers, and made his peace with his father
(3rd July); and also with Richard; but like Richard he was deprived of
all his strongholds.[11]

---

[1] " Decorus facie, blando sermone, dulcis et amabilis;" Ben. P., I. 302; " Militiæ
splendor . . . in armis . . . atrox . . . viribus Achilles . . . ore Paris;" Giraldus, 174.
" Non tam largus quam prodigus;" Geoff. Vig. 335 ; " Dapsilis muneribus;" R. Monte,
305. See also Gervase, I. 303 ; W. Map, *De Nugis*, 139.

[2] See his letter to the King, *Epp.*, I. 4.

[3] Bp. Stubbs, Hoveden, II. lviii.

[4] See his sermon printed by Bp. Stubbs, *sup.*, lvii., where the young King is held up as
a martyr in the cause of civil and religious liberty.

[5] See two of these Elegies, Clédat, *sup.*, 53, 54; Norgate.

[6] II. 19.   [7] II. 279.   [8] I. 233, 234.

[9] *G. Mareschal*, I. 261, 350.

[10] Ben. P., I. 303; Hoveden, II. 280.

[11] Ben. P., 304 ; and for the date, Bp. Stubbs' *Itinerary, Id.* II. cxlv.

CHAPTER XII

HENRY II. (*continued*)

A.D. 1183-1186

Attempts to obtain from Richard the cession of Aquitaine for John—Appointment to Canterbury—*Forest Assize*—Offer of the Crown of Jerusalem to Henry—Expedition of John to Ireland

THE death of the young King undoubtedly cleared the situation. But it might also open up fresh questions. We hear with amazement that Henry, as if incapable of profiting by the lessons of experience, was actually prepared to suggest that Richard should surrender Aquitaine to John, as if to provoke between Richard and John the jealousies that as **Richard and John.** between the young King and Richard had given so much trouble. The King's first step after the burial of his son was to order Glanville the chief Justiciar to bring John over to Normandy, to do homage to Richard on that footing. When the proposal was laid before Richard he asked to be given time to consider his answer. As soon as he was at a safe distance he sent to say that under no circumstances would he part with Aquitaine.[1]

Then King Philip kept demanding the retrocession of Gisors and the Norman Vexin ceded by Louis VII. as the portion of the young Queen Margaret. This restitution might be claimed on the ground that she had left no child. Philip was also pressing for the assignment of her dower. With respect to the Norman Vexin, or the territory between the Epte and the Andelle, this had been given up by Count Geoffrey *Plantegeneste* to Louis VII. in 1151 as the price of his recognition of Henry as Duke of Normandy;[2] and Louis had been induced to restore it as his daughter's portion, as already stated.[3] The demand for the surrender of the Vexin was one with which Henry could not possibly comply. The loss of it would have brought the French frontier almost within sight of Rouen; and so Henry insisted that the Norman Vexin was part and parcel of Normandy,

---

[1] September; Ben. P., I. 304, 305, 307, 308 ; Hoveden, II. 282.
[2] See *Foundations*, II. 443.
[3] Above, 17, 23, 24.

and that the retrocession by Louis was final and absolute. The dower ought to have been granted at once; but Henry evaded it under a shallow pretence. He said that he had made the lands in question part of Queen Eleanor's dower, at the same time ordering her to be admitted to all her dower. Repeated conferences were held on the subject. At last an agreement was effected at a meeting held on the 6th December between

Treaty with France. Trie and Gisors, under the accustomed elm tree.[1] Henry submitted to do fresh homage in person to Philip for all his Continental dominions; he also settled 2,700 Livres Angevin on Margaret during her life; Philip resigned all claim on the Vexin, on condition that Henry should celebrate the long-deferred marriage of Alais, giving him the option of uniting her either to Richard or John.[2]

Henry kept his Christmas Feast (1183) at Le Mans, John being with him. Again we hear of efforts made to induce Richard to cede at any rate some part of Aquitaine to his brother. Again the Count answered defiantly that he would not part with a foot of land. To punish him Henry placed his troops at John's disposition for an invasion of Poitou. Geoffrey

Fraternal War again. joined in with alacrity, and so the King's sons were again at war with each other; Richard retaliating by attacks on Brittany. It would seem that these princes did not necessarily go to war with any definite end in view. They did not seek the fruits of victory; they loved war for its own sake, they revelled in the excitement of danger, the licence of pillage.[3] Apart from sieges we hear of no direct encounters; only of the sacking of homesteads, and robbing of monasteries. Having no compunctions, they could sheath their swords, and make friends again at a moment's notice. So later in the year we shall find Henry, alarmed at the conflagration that he himself had kindled, ordering the three to come over to England; when they went, without demur, and, apparently, in perfect amity.[4]

About the end of May or beginning of June we have the King again called upon to mediate between the two Philips on the question of

Vermandois. Vermandois. When the Count in 1180 promised to leave the territory to his niece Isabel, the Queen of France, his own wife Isabel, in whose right he held the Vermandois, was still living. But she died on the 26th March, 1182,[5] as already mentioned. As she left no child her inheritance ought to have devolved on her younger sister Eleanor of Beaumont. But this lady's rights were passed over, the King of France claiming the county as an escheated fief, and the Count of

---

[1] Sismondi, *France*, VI. 29. The tree stood on the border line, with its branches extending on either side.

[2] Ben. P., I. 304-306; Hoveden, II. 280, 281. The latter omits the stipulation as to the marriage.

[3] Sismondi, *France*, VI. 26.

[4] Ben. P., I. 311, 319.   [5] Ben. P., I. 309, note Bp. Stubbs.

Flanders struggling to retain possession under one pretext or another. Henry, to assist him, now very kindly set himself to find him a new wife, as if to raise up an heir who might intercept the promised legacy to France. He discovered a willing bride in Theresa or Matilda daughter of Alphonso I. of Portugal. Henry's hand in the matter is shown by the fact that his private yacht was sent to Lisbon for the Princess, and landed her at La Rochelle; while from La Rochelle she was passed on through the King's dominions, till she was delivered to the Count, on the borders of Ponthieu in the last days of December, 1183. The marriage was then celebrated at Poix, being the nearest town of Philip's allegiance.[1] King Philip was prompt to declare that no child born of that union should be allowed to interfere with the existing arrangements as to Vermandois. The Count demurring war ensued. Henry then, naturally, came forward to allay a trouble of his own creating: a conference was held at Choisi—presumably Choisi-au-Bac [2]—in the last days of May or beginning of June. The King failed to bring the parties to an agreement as to the Vermandois, but negotiated a truce to last for a year from Midsummer.[3]

From Choisi Henry passed through Flemish territory to Witsand, from whence he sailed to Dover, landing on the 10th June. Two days later the Duchess of Saxony followed him. She went by the usual route, that is to say *via* Canterbury and London, from Dover to Winchester, where shortly afterwards she gave birth to her youngest son, William of Winchester, ancestor of the Ducal House of Brunswick, and of the Royal families of Hanover and England.[4] At Matilda's request her mother Queen Eleanor was released from stricter custody, and allowed to join her daughter at Winchester.[5] According to the Waverley Annals the King had been 'reconciled' to her in 1179. In seeming accord with that statement we notice that in 1180 £133 15*s*. 8*d*. was allowed for her maintenance,[6] and again in the following year £110 6*s*. 8*d*. through the hands of Ralph fitz Stephen, Sheriff of Gloucestershire.[7] In 1183 we heard that Henry had ordered Eleanor to be admitted to her dower lands.[8] These might mark successive steps towards liberation. But as a matter of fact except for special occasions she was kept at Winchester during the rest of the King's life.

The King to England.

The Duchess of Saxony

And Queen Eleanor.

[1] *Id.* 310; Hoveden, II. 283; R. Monte, 310; Pipe Roll, 30 H. II., cited Eyton.
[2] Oise. There are two places of the name in the Department.
[3] Ben. P., I. 311, 312; Gervase, I. 309.
[4] Ben. P., 312, 313, the Duke came over in July, 316. See also Gervase, I. 309, 310; Diceto, II. 21.
[5] Ben. P., *sup.*
[6] Eyton, *Itin.* 231.
[7] *Id.*, 241.
   Ben. P., 308.

In the spring, while the King was still abroad, a fresh move in the
way of Papal aggression had been met and defeated in
A Papal Move defeated. England. Lucius III. had applied to Henry for leave to
tax the English clergy to provide him with means for his
struggle with the Romans, who had driven him from the city.[1] On a
previous occasion application had been made to Louis VII. and Henry
for pecuniary help. But that was for the relief of Palestine, not for
the mere support of the Papal Government. Henry, who since the Becket
catastrophe seemed to have lost all spirit of resistance, left the bishops
to defend themselves. Being left to themselves they proved equal to
the occasion. By the King's orders they met in Council, under the
presidency of Glanville, and agreed in reporting that in their humble
opinion a dangerous precedent would be set if the Pope's agents were
allowed to come to England to levy contributions.[2] But they added
that if the King of his own good pleasure should think fit to send a
subvention to the Pope, assistance from their purses would not be
wanting.[3] The attempt was thus resisted, but the mere fact that it had
been made was ominous for the future. That the meeting of the bishops
was held under the presidency of the Justiciar was probably due to
the fact that both Primacies were vacant. Roger of Pont l'Evêque had
died in 1181, and no successor had as yet been appointed. On the
night of the 16th-17th February (1184) Richard the gentle, unassuming
Archbishop of Canterbury, who took so sound a view of the
Vacancy of Canterbury. ultimate consequences of exaggerated clerical pretensions,
had also passed away.[4] The appointment of a successor
involved the usual struggle between the King and the Canterbury monks,
but the contest, though well sustained, was not so prolonged
Struggle for the Appointment. as on the last occasion. The drama opened with a letter
from the Pope, who, evidently fearing that Henry might
allow the See to remain vacant, wrote to the suffragan Bishops and the
monks ordering them to proceed at once to an election 'without fear
or favour.'[5] The King then, in due course, having directed the monks
to prepare for an election, they agreed among themselves that they would
put forward their late Prior, Odo, then Abbot of Battle, the man who
had fought the King on the last occasion, and in fact had made Richard
Archbishop. A supplemental list of four other names however was also
prepared, in case Henry should object to Odo. But when privately
sounded as to these men he rejected them all.[6] A state discussion on

---

[1] See Milman, *Latin Chr.*, III. 539.

[2] "Quod in consuetudinem verti posset ad detrimentum regni si permitteret nuncios domini papæ in Angliam venire ad collectam faciendam."

[3] Ben. P., I. 311.

[4] Gervase, I. 308 ; Diceto, II. 21 ; Ben. P., I. 311.

[5] "Omni gratia et timore postposito ;" Diceto, II. 22. [6] Gervase, I. 309, 310.

the subject then took place in a special Grand Council held at Reading on the 4th or 5th August.[1]   The Canterbury delegation was headed by the Prior Alan, Becket's biographer, afterwards Abbot of Tewkesbury. The contest between the King and the monks as to the choice of the Archbishop was carried on ostensibly as a struggle between the bishops and the monks, namely, on the question whether the suffragans could be allowed a voice in the election or not.   Neither party being disposed to bate their pretensions nothing was done.[2]   Another conference, held at Windsor on the 21st or 23rd October, gave no better results, the bishops pointing to the recent letter of the Pope as proof of their right to concur.[3]   Finally at a third sitting held at Westminster on the 2nd December the bishops taking one name out of a list of three produced by Prior Alan declared that the only man they could accept was Baldwin, late Abbot of Ford in Dorset, and then Bishop of Worcester. To clench the matter Gilbert Foliot then and there pronounced him

Election of Archbishop Baldwin. duly elected.   The *Te Deum* was sung, and the Archbishop-Elect at once presented to and accepted by the King and his three sons, who were all at Westminster at the time.[4]

But the matter was not quite ended yet.   The monks protested against these proceedings so resolutely that, after further negotiations through the King's sons Geoffrey and John, Henry himself had to go down to Canterbury to bring back the Prior and his monks to London, to satisfy them by allowing them to go through the form of re-electing Bishop Baldwin.[5]   The new Archbishop was a man of humble origin, born at

His antecedents and Character. Exeter, and therefore might be claimed as an Englishman; a scholar, and a man of high character.   He became Archdeacon of Exeter, but he resigned that office to take vows at the Cistercian abbey of Ford, where he soon was elected abbot.[6] He became Bishop of Worcester in 1180.   In the month of July in the current year he had shown his independence and sense of justice by rescuing from death Gilbert of Plumpton, a young man of rank, whom Glanville wanted to hang because he had run away with an heiress, whose hand the Justiciar intended for a friend of his own.[7]

In the course of the year Thomas fitz Bernard, Master Forester and

[1] 4th August, Diceto ; 5th August, Benedict.

[2] Diceto, II. 22 ; Ben. P., I. 317, 318 ; Gervase, I. 311, 312 ; the latter gives the real secret history.

[3] Diceto, *sup*. Gervase, 313-318.

[4] Gervase, 318-321 ; Ben. P., 319 ; Diceto, 23, and the bishops' report to the Pope there given.

[5] 15th December ; Gervase, 322-325 ; Diceto, 23, 24 ; Ben. P., 320.   Baldwin was not required to go to Italy for his Pall.   He received it at Canterbury, and was enthroned on the 19th May, 1185 ; Gervase, 325, 326.

[6] Gervase, II. 400.

[7] Ben. P., 314-316.

Chief Forest Justiciar for all England, had died. Henry abolished the
office, and sub-divided England into divisions with four

**Forest
Assize.**

Forest Justiciars, two clerks and two laymen, for each.[1] He
also took the opportunity of issuing a Forest Assize, or new
code of Forest Law. Of all the King's rights the Forest prerogatives were
those that pressed most harshly on his subjects. Stephen had been forced
to resign all Forests created by Henry I., retaining only those of the time
of Rufus. Henry II. probably had re-established matters as under his
grandfather. We have seen how heavily his hand came down on those
who had been rash enough to act on his permission to kill game in the
time of the rebellion. But then he had only exacted pecuniary fines.
Now he re-establishes the law on the footing of its pristine severity. The
first clause of the Assize informs the lieges that in future pecuniary
compositions will no longer be accepted; there will no longer

**Retrograde
Provisions.**

be place for *misericordia* in such matters. The Forest offender
will have to suffer 'full justice,'[2] as in the time of Henry I.,
i.e. barbarous mutilation. So too the Royal Forester who allows the
King's wood to be destroyed will answer for it with his body.[3] Within the
limits of the Forests no man may keep bow and arrows, or dogs, or
greyhounds (*leporarios*) (s. 2). Big dogs (*mastivi*), kept near a Forest,
to have the ball of one foot cut out (*expeditatio* s. 14). In every county
in which the King has any Forest twelve *milites* to be appointed to have
charge of his vert and venison, or in proper English his greenhow and
game (s. 7). All persons, no matter of what rank, to be bound to attend
pleas of the Forest, when summoned by the Master Forester (s. 11). We
are told that the King's Forest rights might extend not only over land of
the Royal demesne, but also over lands admittedly private property; while
again outside the limits of the Forest proper, there were the purlieus (Fr.
pourallée), a further area within which the King's game might not be
meddled with.[4] Persons owning land within these limits are forbidden
to sell or give away timber; or to cut any, except for necessary estate
repairs (*estoveria*, *Anglice* botes).[5] The Assize as a whole grievously detracts
from the character for merciful dealing for which otherwise we are
inclined to give Henry credit.[6]

Christmas was kept at Windsor, with an unwonted family assemblage,
Queen Eleanor, Richard, John, and the Duke and Duchess of Saxony with

---

[1] Ben. P., I. 323; Hoveden, II. 289.

[2] "Plenariam . . . justiciam " s. 1 ; so of Clerks too, s. 8.

[3] "Nihil aliud capiatur . . . nisi proprium corpus " ; s. 8.

[4] "Boscos extra metas reguardi . . . in quibus venatio domini regis pacem habet ";
s. 4. See Blackstone (Stephens), I. 634.

[5] S. 4.

[6] Woodstock ; 16th August? See *Select Charters*, 150; Hoveden, II. 245, Benedict
I. 323, gives a summary.

their children all being present. Richard, who had been summoned to England about the beginning of November, obtained leave to return to his beloved Poitou before the year was out.[1]

Early in 1185 Henry received a last despairing appeal for help to the unfortunate Kingdom of Jerusalem, now tottering to its fall **Kingdom of Jerusalem.** before the assaults of Saladin. Its history since the loss of Edessa in 1143 had been a mere record of continuous decay, due mainly to internal causes. Neither the constitutions nor **A Record of Decay.** the habits of the settlers were suited to the climate; while the feudal organisation given to the state proved a source of weakness. The holders of the great fiefs, such as the Counts of Antioch, Edessa, or Tripoli, aiming at independence, pursued private lines of policy, regardless of central interests. "Jerusalem was to them only a secondary consideration; the zeal that set Europe from time to time in a blaze found no answer in the land for which so much was being sacrificed." Then the men passed away so quickly that the chief offices were perpetually in the hands of minors or women. In the course of the twelfth century Jerusalem had witnessed eleven Kings, while during the same period France and England had only seen four each. The only "sound element" in the country were the military orders of the Hospital and the Temple, who could introduce fresh and healthy blood from Europe.[2] **Baldwin IV.** The reigning King at the period that we have reached was Baldwin IV., a leper, and childless. Two sisters he had, Sibyl and **Montferrat and Lusignan.** Isabel. The former and elder was given in marriage to William Longaspata, Marquis of Montferrat, by whom she had a son, afterwards Baldwin V. The Marquis having died a fresh regent was found by marrying Sibyl to Guy of Lusignan,[3] a gallant soldier, and an able captain; an honest man who with fair play might have kept things going. But the opposition of rival magnates of higher connexions proved too strong, and Baldwin was obliged to remove him, in order to place the conduct of affairs in the hands of Raymond of Tripoli. There was also talk of a scheme to divorce Sibyl from Guy in order to marry her to Raymond, himself a married man.[4] It was apparently at **Offer of the Crown to Henry.** this juncture that Baldwin, in failing health, and anticipating a disruption at his death, resolved to make an offer of the Kingdom to the head of the House of Anjou, his second cousin, Henry II. (1184).[5] The embassy accredited was the strongest

---

[1] Ben. P., I. 319, 333, 334.

[2] See Bishop Stubbs, Memorials Richard I., Vol. I. lxxxv.-cvii., a brilliant sketch.

[3] Brother of Hugh le Brun who established himself as Count of La Marche in defiance of Henry II.

[4] Ben. P., I. 343, 358, 359. Cnf. W. Newb., I. 255.

[5] Memorials, *sup.*, cii., ciii. Henry was grandson of Fulk V. by Eremberge of La Flèche; Baldwin IV. was his grandson by Melisende, daughter of Baldwin II.; p. ci.

that he could find, comprising Heraclius the Patriarch of Jerusalem, a dignitary who claimed homage even from the King,[1] and the Grand Masters of the Hospital and Temple, namely Roger de Moulins, and Arnold de Toroge, the latter however died on the journey.[2] They were instructed to invite the King to accept the succession to Baldwin, and to tender by way of investiture the Banner of the Holy Cross, and the keys of the Sepulchre, with those of the strong places of Jerusalem. They visited the Pope at Verona on their way, and obtained from Lucius a letter to Henry, urging the necessity of the case; pointing to the family connexion with Palestine; and gently reminding him of his former pledges.[3] With respect to these, apart from various vague expressions of purpose, and gifts of money, Henry had been charged as the price of his absolution for his share in Becket's death to take the Cross within three years from May 1172; and had only been granted an extension of time on condition of founding three monasteries. He had apparently in fact founded a small Carthusian House at Witham; but the other two foundations were provided in very simple fashion. For the one he turned out the Secular Canons at Waltham, to make room for Regulars; while for the other the Sisters at Amesbury were replaced by nuns from Fontevrault.[4] In the treaty of Ivry with Louis VII. Henry had renewed his crusading pledge. Anyhow he was the one prince of Christendom who could save the situation.[5]

His Crusading obligations.

The envoys probably landed at Dover about the 28th January, as next day they visited the shrine at Canterbury.[6] Henry who was in the North at the time hastened Southwards on hearing of their arrival, and received them in audience at Reading some time in February. The Patriarch in tendering his credentials drew a picture of the state of Palestine that moved his audience to tears; but, however sympathetic, Henry could decide nothing without his Barons.[7] A Grand Council, accordingly, was held at Clerkenwell on the 18th March,[8] the King of Scots and his brother David being present. Henry begged for honest advice as to the course he ought to adopt, but he enquired if a personal expedition to Holy Land would be

---

[1] "The Kingdom of Jerusalem was looked upon as a fief of the Holy Sepulchre." Stubbs, *sup.*, cxiv.

[2] Ben. P., I. 331 and notes; Diceto, II. 32.

[3] Ben., 332; W. Newb., I. 245; Giraldus, VIII. 204.

[4] The change at Amesbury was only effected in November 1186, Ben. P., I. 354. For the distinctions between *nunnan*, lay sisters or canonesses, not bound by perpetual vows; and *mynecena*, female monks, see *Foundations of England*, I. 316, 361, 442.

[5] Bishop Stubbs, *sup.* cxiii.; Giraldus, VIII. xxvi. (G. F. Warner).

[6] Gervase, I. 325.

[7] Ben. P., I. 332; Diceto, II. 32; Giraldus, VIII. 202. The last places the reception at Winchester.

[8] So Diceto, who was doubtless present. Benedict, 336, and Hoveden, II. 301, place the meeting on the 10th March.

Q

quite consistent with the obligations of his Coronation oath, considering that those pledges bound him to keep Church and people in good peace, and put down all wrong-doing. To such a question there could be but one answer. With two such sons as Richard and Geoffrey to **The Crown declined.** keep in order, even a temporary visit to Palestine would have been the height of folly. Henry declined the proffered crown, but said that he would give money, and would allow such of his subjects as were prepared to take the Cross to do so. To the question whether he would allow one of his sons to accept the proposed succession he gave an evasive answer.[1]

From London the Court removed to Windsor; and there on the 31st March John, being in his nineteenth year, was knighted by his father **John Knighted.** in all due form. In honour of the occasion Henry invested the King of Scots with the coveted earldom of Huntingdon, vacant by the death of Simon of St. Lis III.[2] The King might remember that six-and-thirty years before he himself had been dubbed by the sword of William's grandfather and his own great uncle, David I.[3]

Henry now prepared to cross the Channel, Continental affairs again calling for his presence. Philip of France and Philip of Flanders were still quarrelling over the Vermandois, and actually at war, with their armies confronting each other in the valley of the Somme. Then Richard was reported to be making himself strong in Poitou, and waging war on Geoffrey, in defiance of his father's orders.[4] Lastly Henry had told the Patriarch that he would discuss the question of the Crusade with the King of France. On the 16th April the Court sailed from Dover to **Crossing to Normandy.** Witsand, the Royal circle including the Patriarch and the Bishop of Durham.[5] Philip of France promptly came to visit the King, being probably anxious to avert any interference with his Flemish campaign, that was progressing favourably. For three days they held friendly colloquy at Vaudreuil.[6] On the question of the Crusade the French King agreed with Henry in thinking that for the time a money

[1] See Diceto, II. 33 ; Gervase, I. 325 ; Giraldus, VIII. 208 ; W. Newb., I. 247 ; Ben. P., and Hoveden, *sup*. With respect to the offer of the Kingdom of Jerusalem to Henry, or one of his sons see Peter of Blois, Epp. I. 350, where writing to the King's natural son, Geoffrey, he says that he was present when it was made. Giraldus asserts that John was anxious to go, but he is always on the look out to contrast somebody to Henry's disadvantage, and he alone of the writers condemns Henry's course. Diceto, Gervase, and William of Newburgh emphatically approve of it.

[2] Ben. P., 336, 337 ; Diceto, II. 34 ; Chron. Melrose. The latter implies that William had been deprived of the earldom in 1173 or 1174. "Sicut habuit ante guerram." I cannot make out that he ever had it. It would seem that William now passed on the earldom to his brother David, who appeared as such at Christmas, 1186 ; Ben. P., II. 4.

[3] See *Foundations of England*, II. 438.

[4] Richard had only left England after Christmas ; Ben. P., I. 333.

[5] Ben. P., 334, 337.

[6] Diceto, II. 34.

subvention was the only assistance that could be given; and so the Patriarch went home deeply disappointed with the results of his mission.[1]

Eleanor reinstated in Aquitaine. As for Richard, Henry, unable to tolerate him any longer, suspended him. He sent for Queen Eleanor; and then, under threats of invasion, ordered his son to surrender Aquitaine to its rightful mistress. Unable to contend with his father in open war the Count submitted, and came to Court.[2] To make the submission effectual the King undertook a progress through the South; and remained there, lost to the ken of our chroniclers, till November.[3]

The knighting of John had a special meaning at the time. The King still clung to his family policy, and his purpose of promoting his youngest son. **The Family Policy again.** Unable to procure Aquitaine for him, he now fell back on the Irish scheme mooted in 1177, namely that of establishing him as under-King or Lord of all Ireland. For England no scheme more fraught with mischief could well be devised than that of building up a nationality in the sister isle; and Henry had shown his own appreciation of the danger by the jealous eye that he had kept on his lieutenants there, limited as their powers were. **Affairs in Ireland.** As for the course of events since 1177, in Munster Robert fitz Stephen had barely been able to hold his own against the natives, without gaining any ground.[4] In Meath and Leinster Hugh de Lacy by steady castle-building, and firm but conciliatory attitude towards the Irish had been successful to the point of exciting Royal jealousy. Twice he had been recalled, and twice allowed to return as indispensable.[5] In Ulster de Courcy had added Armagh to his conquests, and signalised his position by contracting a marriage with the daughter of Guthred King of Man.[6]

On the evening of the 24th April John embarked at Milford Haven, **Expedition of John.** Glanville the Justiciar having been deputed to convoy him safely through Wales. Next morning he landed at Waterford; he is said to have had the imposing force of 300 men-at-arms, with a suitable complement of archers, some mounted, and some on foot.[7] Among the clergy in attendance on him was *Giraldus* the historian, otherwise Gerald of Barry, a grandson of the Lady Nest, and so one of the innermost circle of the original adventurers.[8] John lost no time in showing how lamentably unfit he was to be trusted with authority. When

---

[1] Ben. P., I. 338 ; Hoveden, II. 304.

[2] Ben. P., 337, 338 ; Hoveden, *sup*.

[3] For his proceedings in Aquitaine, occupying strongholds, etc., see Diceto, II. 40.

[4] Giraldus, V. 317-350.

[5] *Id.* 352-356, 359 ; *cnf.* W. Newb., I. 239, 240. De Lacy attests a charter passed by John confirming his father's charter granting trading rights at Dublin to the men of Bristol; and attests it as constable ; *Historic Documents Ireland*, 49 (Gilbert).

[6] Giraldus, 345.

[7] The native Annals of Loch Ce give John's force as 60 ships ; I. 171.

[8] Giraldus, V. 380, 381. Giraldus had already been in Ireland in 1183 pp. 351, 352.

friendly Irish chieftains hastened to Waterford to tender their allegiance,
the new Lord of Ireland and his young friends allowed
Lamentable
Failure. themselves to make merry at their expense, and even to take
liberties with their beards.   In utter affront they went home to
organise revolt.   An expedition sent by John against North Munster ended
disastrously.[1]   Then he proceeded to make enemies of all classes of any
influence in the country.   Native allies were robbed of their land ; old
settlers turned out of their posts to make room for inexperienced favourites,
or greedy sycophants ; the frontiers were neglected, and left open to raiding
parties.   Then the money that should have been applied to the pay of the
soldiers was squandered by John on his amusements, till the men became
disorderly and mutinous, or joined the ranks of the enemy.[2]   After nine
His Recall. months of inglorious rule he was recalled by the King.   On the
17th December he returned to England,[3] the military command
being left in the hands of de Courcy, who as a man of war seemed better
fitted to retrieve matters than de Lacy, who was essentially a man of peace.[4]
But Henry had not yet been cured of his infatuation.   Shutting his eyes to
all the facts of the case he made prompt application to the new
The Papacy
and Ireland. Pope, Urban III., for authority to crown his son King of
Ireland.[5]   It would seem that Lucius had been approached on
the subject, but had refused his consent.   Urban however was quite willing
to see John made king ; and with his Bull of approval sent him a crown of
peacocks' feathers intertwined with gold.[6]

After six months' disappearance in the South, Henry is again heard of
as in Normandy.   On the 7th November he held a conference at Aumâle
with the two Philips, and, apparently did his best to reconcile the Count
to his loss of territory, viz., the Amienois and part of the Vermandois, finally
extorted from him as the result of the hostilities of the spring.[7]   Friendly
relations continuing, we hear two days later of a visit by the King of France
to Henry, who was ill and laid up at Beavoir-en-Lyons.[8]

Again on the 10th March, 1186, we hear of another conference near
Gisors, at which the two Kings, the young Queen Margaret, and the Count
of Flanders were present.   Henry was not ashamed to pledge himself once

---

[1] Four Masters, III. 67.

[2] Giraldus, V. 388-392 ; Ben. P., I. 339 ; Hoveden, II. 304, 305.

[3] Diceto, II. 39.

[4] Giraldus, V. 392.   For description of de Courcy and de Lacy see *Id.*, 344, 354.

[5] Lucius III. died at Verona 25 November, 1185 ; Jaffé cited Bp. Stubbs ; Hoveden,
II. 305.   On the same day Uberto Crivelli, Archbishop of Milan, was elected Pope as
Urban III.

[6] Ben. P., I. 339 ; Hoveden, II. 306.

[7] Diceto, II. 38.   For the campaign see Sismondi, *France*, VI. 42, and Lavisse,
France, III. 89.   The latter gives the final treaty as settled at Boves, near Amiens,
in July.

[8] *Id.* Seine Inférieure.

more to pay Margaret's jointure of £2,750 *Angevin*, and to celebrate without further delay the nuptials of Richard and Alais, the latter promise, at any rate, now given for the fifth time or so, being one that he certainly never meant to keep. Philip, on the other hand, once more renounced all claim on Gisors.[1]

Having thus settled affairs on the Continent Henry went back to England. On the 27th April he landed at Southampton, from Barfleur, Queen Eleanor coming with him, and in the same ship. But we are surprised to hear that the King, with his usual self-confidence, left Richard behind him, and moreover with considerable forces at his disposal. But these were given him for war against Toulouse,[2] in concert with and on behalf of Alphonso II. of Arragon.[3]

---

[1] Diceto, II. 40 ; Ben. P., I. 343 ; Hoveden, 308. See Margaret's charter of the 11th March, accepting the arrangement ; Round, *Calendar*, 382. The exact ratio of sterling to Angevin money is there given as 13*s.* 4*d.* sterling = 54 Angevin, slightly more than four to one. In August, Margaret went off to Hungary, to be married to King Bela, III. ; Ben., 346 ; Diceto, 41.

[2] Diceto, *sup.* ; Ben., 345, 347 ; Gervase, I. 334.

[3] Martin, *France*, III. 510.

CHAPTER XIII

HENRY II. (*continued*)

A.D. 1186–1189

Domestic Affairs—Altered Relations with France—Richard acting with Philip—Fall of Jerusalem—Crusading Movement—War with France—Henry refusing to recognise Richard as his Heir—Attacked by Philip and Richard—Submits to Treaty of Colombières—His death.

ECCLESIASTICAL affairs occupied the King's first attention on his return to England. The bishops were summoned to arrange for the filling up of vacant sees. No less than eight bishoprics were again vacant, namely Carlisle, York, Chester, Salisbury, Worcester, Exeter, and Lincoln. Carlisle had been vacant since 1137; York since 1181; the others had fallen in within the last three years. The Synod was held at
Episcopal Appointments. Eynsham on the 25th May,[1] when arrangements were made under which William de Vere became Bishop of Hereford, and William of Northall Bishop of Worcester; while the Lincoln Chapter, under pressure from the King, accepted as their shepherd their future patron Saint, then Prior of Henry's Carthusian foundation at Witham in Somerset, Hugh of Avalon.[2] An election was also made to Exeter, but the nominee declined the proffered honour.[3]

A turn of Scottish business followed. Two years before, William the
Scottish Affairs. Lion, who was unmarried, had applied for the hand of the King's granddaughter Matilda, daughter of the Duchess of Saxony. The parties being related in blood the matter was referred to the Pope who refused his consent.[4] Henry was now prepared
A Bride for the King. to offer the hand of a lady more remotely connected with himself, namely Ermengarde of Beaumont, daughter of Richard Viscount of Beaumont-le-Vicomte; he being son of Viscount of Roscelin, by Constance, natural daughter of Henry I. The King of Scots and his Barons having been summoned to court to consider the proposal it was duly accepted, William however being required first to reduce to order Ronald mac Uhtred of Galloway, who in the previous year

---

[1] Diceto, II. 41.

[2] *Id.* 41–43; Gervase, I. 335; Ben. P., I. 345, 346. Lincoln became vacant in 1186, through the translation of Walter of Coutances to Rouen. Walter had been appointed to Lincoln in 1183, Geoffrey having resigned in 1182.

[3] Ben., 346, 349 Hoveden, II. 309.   [4] Ben., 313, 322.

at the death of his uncle Gilbert mac Fergus had seized the district. Henry felt called upon to interfere because Gilbert's son Duncan was at the time a hostage in his hands.[1]

The submission of Ronald was not obtained without difficulty, involving the march of a Royal army to Carlisle, and repeated embassies to Galloway. At last however he came to Carlisle, did homage, and was allowed to retain the lands formerly held by his father Uhtred mac Fergus, on condition of submitting to an enquiry in the King's Court as to the land properly belonging to his cousin Duncan.[2] The settlement was a thoroughly equitable one, as Ronald's father Uhtred had been dispossessed by his younger brother Gilbert. We might also point out that the requirement of Ronald's appearance before an English court was the only case of which we hear in which Henry attempted any intervention in Scottish domestic affairs. The King's stay at Carlisle was utilised by an attempt to fill up the See, but the man elected by the Canons, though approved of by the King, rejected the appointment.[3]

Affairs of Galloway.

The Royal marriage however went on. The lady was brought over by her parents, and on the 5th September William and Ermengarde were married at Woodstock. Archbishop Baldwin performed the service. Henry gave away the bride, and endowed her with Edinburgh Castle as her portion. He also gave up his palace at Woodstock to the Scots for four days' bridal festivities, retiring to other quarters for the time. The four days over the Queen of Scots was sent to her new home under the charge of Joscelin Bishop of Glasgow, her Royal spouse following the King of England to Marlborough for another ecclesiastical council.[4] The meeting was held on the 14th September. Nominations were made for the Sees of York and Salisbury, but came to nothing through differences between the King and the Chapters. But John the Precentor became Bishop of Exeter.[5]

Marriage of William the Lion.

On the 19th August Henry's son Geoffrey Count of Brittany had passed away in Paris, apparently of fever.[6] For the third son of Henry and Eleanor no writer has a word of praise to offer. Clear-sighted and astute, with a fatal gift of persuasive speech, he is described as irretrievably crooked in all his ways.[7] His father and

Death of Geoffrey of Brittany.

---

[1] Ben. P., I. 336, 339 ; Chron. Melrose ; *cnf.* Fordun, 269, whose account seems to reflect the views of a later period.

[2] August, Ben. P., 347, 349 ; Hoveden, II. 309 ; Chron. Melrose ; Fordun, *sup.*

[3] Ben., 349 ; Hoveden, *sup.*

[4] Ben. P., I. 350, 351 ; Chron. Melrose.   [5] Ben. P., 352.

[6] So Rigord and G. Le Breton, Bouquet, XVII. 20, 21, 67 ; Diceto, II. 41 ; Giraldus, VIII. 176. But Benedict, I. 350, and Hoveden, II. 309, say that Geoffrey died of injuries received in a tournament.

[7] " Eloquens et astutus, et quia de facili falli non potuit, fallere si nollet, prudentissimus . . . mirabili industria rerum omnium simulator varius et dissimulator ;" Giraldus, VIII. 178, also 176. " Filius proditionis Gaufredus." Ben. P., I. 297.

King Philip are said to have been the only persons who mourned his
loss.   Yet to his father he had been persistently ungrateful,
His character. and at the time he was intriguing against him and Richard.
He was proposing to hold Brittany directly of Philip, rejecting
all homage to his father, and had been appointed Seneschal of France,[1] an
honour conferred on Henry in 1158.   He left a daughter Eleanor,[2] while
seven months after his death Countess Constance gave birth to a son, who,
The Wardship of Brittany. to please the Bretons, was christened Arthur.[3]   Philip meanwhile as over-lord claimed the wardship of the heiress, and
of Brittany ; he also insisted on the cessation of Richard's
hostilities against Toulouse.[4]   Events came rapidly to a head.   On the
Strained Relations with France. 9th October Walter of Coutances the Archbishop of Rouen [5]
had to make counter-complaint to Philip of attacks on
Normandy ; unable to obtain any satisfactory assurance he
hastened back to England to report to Henry.   The King hoping to effect
a diplomatic settlement at once sent over Glanville, who, after an interview
with Philip at Noyon, returned to England bringing envoys who were
instructed to say that the attacks on Normandy would cease when Richard
ceased warring on Toulouse.[6]   Henry however succeeded in obtaining a
truce to the 13th January, 1167, with, apparently, an eventual prolongation
to Easter (29th March)[7].   But the relations of the two countries—so
friendly since Philip's accession—had been further strained by a rash
attempt on the part of Henry de Vere, Constable of Gisors, to interfere
with the building of a new French border fortress near Gisors, in the
course of which Ralph, son of Richard of Vaux the lord of the place,
was killed.[8]

Henry himself did not cross the Channel until February, 1187, when
Henry over to Normandy. he landed at Witsand on the 17th of the month.   He brought
in his train a Papal Legate, the Cardinal Octavian, who had
just been sent to England to crown John King of Ireland.[9]
Archbishop Baldwin, feeling incommoded by his presence, had persuaded

---

[1] Giraldus, 176 ; Ben., 350.

[2] Diceto, II. 41, gives him two daughters, but this seems wrong.

[3] 29th March, 1167 ; Ben., 361.

[4] Gervase, I. 336 ; Diceto, 43, 44 : cnf. Ben. P., 347.   See for the hostilities against
Toulouse Vic et Vaissete, *Hist. Languedoc*, V. 3.   The Count of Toulouse had sided
with the young King against Richard in 1183 ; *Id.* IV. 290, 296 (ed. 1842).

[5] Walter, previously Bishop of Lincoln, was translated to Rouen in 1185, in succession
to Rotrou of Beaumont, who died 25th November, 1183 ; Ben. P., I. 308, 335, and notes

[6] Diceto. II. 43, 44.

[7] Ben. P., 353, 354.   The accounts of these negotiations are rather confused.

[8] Ben. P. I. 354 ; Hoveden, II. 315.   Diceto, II. 44, gives a different account of the
incident with the date 28th November.

[9] Ben. P., II. 4 ; Diceto, II. 47.   Octavian had landed at Sandwich on Christmas
Eve, under the escort of Hugh of Nonant, Bishop-Elect of Chester.   On the next day
they went to Canterbury ; where they gave great offence by wearing mitres and having

he King to take him abroad.[1] John had preceded his father by a few
days.   Richard too was there, waiting to receive him ; so that
A Papal   the hostilities against Toulouse must have ceased.   An ap-
Mission.   pointment was shortly made with King Philip for a conference,
o be held at the Gué-Saint-Rémy, near Nonancourt.   The parties met
on the 5th April.   But Henry's plausibilities could no longer carry him
hrough.   To the question of the wardship of Brittany had now been
dded the revived question of Gisors ; as it was clear that Henry after all
is promises would neither allow Richard to marry Alais, nor pay Margaret
er promised jointure.   With respect to the latter default his excuse now
would be that Margaret had taken a second husband, having just been
narried to Bela III. of Hungary,[2] and so forfeited her jointure.   Of
course no agreement was come to, and Philip went off to prepare for
war.[3]

Henry, on his side, content to assume a defensive position, placed four
armies in the field ; one under Richard, one under John, one
War with   under his natural son Geoffrey, no longer ex-Elect of Lincoln,
France.   but filling the office of Chancellor ; and one under William of
Mandeville II., Earl of Essex and Albemarle,[4] a man much employed by the
King.   Philip, in the latter half of May mustered an army at Bourges, his
southernmost stronghold ; captured Graçay (Cher), and Issoudun ; and
then laid siege to Châteauroux.[5]   Richard and John had concentrated
there ; but the siege was pressed so closely that Henry himself had to
come to the rescue.   Philip drew out his forces to meet him.   For nearly
a fortnight the two Kings faced each other as if for battle, on opposite
sides of the Indre.[6]   But the state of affairs in Palestine was now so
critical that the idea of war between France and England was shocking.
The Legate Octavian, under orders from the Pope, among others, took up
the work of mediation.   But though nobody wanted war there was the

crosses carried before them, Hugh of Nonant giving himself the airs of a Legate.
Archbishop Baldwin was not at Canterbury, his terrible quarrel with the monks having
begun.   On the 1st January, 1187, the Cardinal and Hugh were received by the King
at Westminster ; Gervase, I. 345, 346.

[1] Ben. P. and Diceto, *sup.*

[2] Margaret left Paris on the 24th August, 1185, to be married to Bela ; Diceto, II.
41 ; Ben. P., I. 346 ; G. le Breton, *sup.* 67.

[3] Ben. P., II. 5 ; Gervase, I. 336, 346 ; Rigord, 23 ; Le Breton, 68.   According to
Giraldus, VIII. 230, the Count of Flanders, indignant at Henry for having gone against
him on the question of the Vermandois, egged on Philip to war.

[4] Mandeville, second son of the old intriguer of Stephen's time, became Earl of
Albemarle or Aumâle by his marriage with Havise, daughter of Count William, 14th
January, 1180 ; (Diceto, II. 3).   William of Aumâle was son of Stephen set up against
Rufus in 1195 ; *Foundations*, II. 201.

[5] May. Ben. P., II. 6 ; Grandes Chron., *sup.*   Both Issoudun and Châteauroux are in
Indre.

[6] So Norgate, II. 245, citing *Bertran de Born*, Clédat, 71 ; Gervase, I. 369-371.

usual difficulty in adjusting the terms of peace. Suspicion and intrigue were rife. Richard displayed a spirit of opposition to his father; and well he might, if, as asserted by Giraldus, Henry had privately offered to accept the alternative suggested in 1183, namely that of marrying Alais to John, with all the Continental dominions, except Normandy. Of course Philip had earned Richard's gratitude by informing him of the plot.[1] Then we hear that Philip found that his best troops had been bought over by Henry.[2] Finally a truce for a couple of years was sealed on the 23rd June. Philip allowed the credit of negotiating it to fall to Richard; but as the price of it he was allowed to retain Issoudun, and the border town of Fréteval (Loir et Cher).[3]

Truce of Châteauroux

The truce settled, Richard, to Henry's great alarm, went off with his new friend King Philip, and in spite of all remonstrances lived with him on terms of the closest intimacy for weeks, just as Geoffrey had done. Then under pretence of going to his father's court he went to Chinon, and carried off the treasure deposited there. At last, however, on condition of being reinstated in Aquitaine he returned to his duty, and did public homage to his father at Angers.[4]

Richard off

And back Again.

But the final crash in Palestine had come at last, and Europe was in consternation at the news. Heraclius had gone back to Jerusalem to find young Baldwin V., nephew of Baldwin IV., established as King. But he shortly passed away, and then the crown having been held to devolve on his mother Sybille, she, in spite of all opposition, gave it to her husband, Guy of Lusignan.[5] An existing truce with Saladin was renewed at his request for three years; and the aspect of affairs was so peaceful that pilgrims who had gone out with Heraclius began to return home.[6] But the end was near. To the disgrace of Christianity the truce was treacherously broken by Reginald of Châtillon, Lord of Hebron and Kerak, who pillaged a caravan of Moslem pilgrims going down to Egypt.[7] Saladin, provoked beyond measure, called out all his Emirs for a final assault on

Fall of Kingdom of Jerusalem.

[1] Giraldus, VIII. 231-233. Here we further hear for the first time that the opposition to the match with Alais came from Richard, who maintained that she had succeeded the Fair Rosamund in his father's affections. For Henry's purpose of promoting John, see also Gervase, I. 435. Hoveden assigns the proposal to marry Alais to John to the conference at La Ferté Bernard in June, 1189; II. 363.

[2] So *Bertran de Born*, 71, 72, cited Norgate, II. 246.

[3] Giraldus, *sup.*; Diceto, II. 49; Ben. P., II. 6, 7; Gervase, I. 369-373; Rigord, 23, 24.

[4] September—October? Ben. P., II. 9; Hoveden, II. 318.

[5] August—September, 1186; Diceto, II. 47; Ben P., I. 358, 359 and notes.

[6] *Id.*

[7] 1186. See *Memorials of Richard I., Itinerary*, I. c. and 12; Lane-Poole, *Saladin*, 198.

the Kingdom of Jerusalem.   After two days' fighting near Tiberias the
Christians were totally defeated; King Guy and the True Cross fell into
the hands of the enemy; Guy's life was spared, but Reginald of Kerak
and all the Templars and Hospitallers were beheaded on the spot.[1]   In
the course of the month (July) Acre, Haifa (Mount Carmel), Cæsarea, Sidon,
were taken in quick succession; Beirout was reduced in August, Ascalon
and Gaza in September: while finally on the 3rd of October, after an
eight days' siege, the Holy City fell.[2]   The report of the loss of the True
Cross killed Urban III.[3]   His successor Gregory VIII. spent his short

Richard takes the Cross. pontificate in appeals for help to Holy Land.[4]   The first to
respond was young Richard, who, without consulting his father,
took the Cross from the hands of the Archbishop of Tours
in November.[5]

After keeping Christmas at Caen, Henry was on his way to Barfleur,
for a visit to England, when again he was called back to face the demands
of the King of France.   They met at the old spot between Trie and
Gisors, the Count of Flanders being also present.[6]   King Philip, in view
of Richard's expected departure for Holy Land, wanted to make one
more push to get his sister Alais married.   But the ear of the assembly
was gained by the Archbishop of Tyre,[7] who having come to Europe to

The Kings likewise. call for help, preached the word of the Lord with such effect,
that all three Princes took the Cross, then and there; a host
of minor personages following their example.   For the sake
of distinction it was arranged that the French should wear red crosses,
the English white crosses, and the Flemings green crosses.[8]   A wooden
cross, to be followed by a church, was set up to mark the 'Holy Field'
(*Saint-Champ*), where the Princes finally pledged themselves.[9]   As a

---

[1] Hittin, 4th July, 1187; *Itinerary, sup.* 12-17; and the letters printed, Ben. P., II. 11, 13.

[2] *Itin.*, 17-20; Ben. P., II. 20-24, and Hoveden. II. 321, and notes, Bp. Stubbs.   For
the earlier career of Saladin see below under the year 1190.

[3] Urban III. died 20th October.   Next day Cardinal Albert, who had been Legate in
Normandy in 1172, was elected as Gregory VIII.   He died, 17th December.

[4] Ben. P., II. 15-19.

[5] Giraldus, VIII 239; Diceto, II 50.   For Henry's attitude see W. Newb., II. 271;
cnf. Gervase, I. 389.

[6] 21st January, Ben. P.; *circa* 22nd January, Gervase, I. 406.

[7] Perhaps William the famous historian of the Crusades; perhaps a successor of the
name of Joseph.

[8] Ben. P., II. 29, 30, and notes; Diceto, II. 51-54, *q. v.* for Henry's letters to
Frederic, the King of Hungary, and Isaac Angelus for leave to pass through their
dominions; for his notification to the Pope see *Epp. Cantuar*, 160 (*Memorials Richard
I.*, Vol. II., Bishop Stubbs; Roll Series No. 38).   Gregory VIII. having died 17th
December, 1187, on the 19th of the month Paolo Scolaro was elected as Clement III.;
H. Nicolas.

[9] Grandes Chroniques, IV. 58, from Rigord, 25; *q. v.* for the fullest list of the names
of the magnates who took the Cross.

necessary preliminary to an expedition the Kings agreed to call on their
subjects for a subsidy, to be levied in the shape of a tenth
of all their rents and movable or personal property for one
year, being the well known Saladin tithe, celebrated as a new
departure in the matter of taxation.[1]   For Henry's Continental dominions
the tax was settled in a Grand Council of magnates, ecclesiastical and lay,
held in the course of the next few days at Le Mans, doubtless as being a
central place.[2]

The Saladin Tithe.

On the 29th January Henry sailed from Dieppe, landing next day at
Winchelsea.[3]   A Grand Council was immediately summoned
to arrange for the levy of the Saladin tithe in England.   The
assembly met at Geddington in Northamptonshire on the 11th
February, when the tax was agreed to on the same footing as for the
Continental dominions.   All persons not prepared to take
the Cross would be put under contribution.   The whole of
their rents and personal property would be assessed, except
the horses, arms, and clothing of the military or gentry classes (*milites*);
the horses, books, clothing, or vestments of the clergy, with all church
furniture; and all precious stones, whether belonging to clerks or laymen.
But even persons prepared to take the Cross would be assessed on the
produce of their demesne lands; the money to be collected by parishes
(parochiis), in the presence of the priest, the archdeacon, a Templar and
a Hospitaller, with agents severally appointed by the King, the lord of
the manor, and the bishop, respectively.   In case of dispute, the amount
to be paid by any individual to be referred to the decision of a little jury
that might comprise from four to six men of the parish.   Along with
this ordinance the chroniclers give an ordinance of 'the Pope'—which
Pope they do not say—demanding a tenth on terms so similar to those
on which the tithe was actually granted that we may suppose the idea of
the tax to have emanated from the financial genius of Italy.[4]   The
student of History has been invited to compare the regulations for the
levy of the title framed by Henry with those framed by Philip with " purely
feudal" machinery.[5]   The contrast is indeed striking.   In England the
money is collected by royal commissioners; and paid to the
King; but under provisions for securing justice to all parties
interested.   In France the money is simply collected by the
lord, the lord of the manor as we should say in England; and if he

The King to England.

Assessment of the Tithe in England.

The French Assessment.

---

[1] An earlier levy for Palestine had been granted in 1166.   But the amount then was
only two pence on the £1 for one year and a penny on the £1 for four years afterwards,
while the proceeds were simply to be paid into collecting boxes in the churches. See
the Ordinance, Gervase, I. 198, and above p. 82.

[2] Ben. P., II. 30-33; Hoveden, II. 335-338.   [3] *Id*; Gervase, I. 406.

[4] Ben. P. and Hoveden, *sup.*; also Gervase, I. 409, and W. Newb., I. 273.

[5] Bishop Stubbs, *Select Charters*, 152.

has the higher rights of judicature (*haute justice*) he keeps the money, under condition of taking the Cross.[1] If not prepared to take the Cross we may conjecture that he would hand the money over to the next higher over-lord who might be prepared to accept the condition.

Having arranged for the levy of the tax in his own proper dominions **Efforts to** Henry then made efforts to bring in the dependencies. **obtain** Bishop Hugh of Durham was sent to the Border, and had a **contributions** meeting with the Scots, on the Tweed, between Wark and **Scotland** Birgham, near Coldstream. According to one account William, who was anxious to get back his castles, was disposed to agree, but his Barons refused their consent.[2] According to another version William offered a sum of 5,000 marks down for tithe and the restitution of his castles; but the English could not accept that,[3] and so the mission came **And Wales.** to nothing. An attempt was also made to get something out of Wales. Archbishop Baldwin went off to preach the Crusade there. He was assisted in his work by the historian "Giraldus," a man as zealous in the cause as himself; and to this tour we owe the writer's interesting *Itinerarium Cambriæ.*[4] For five months the King remained in England, chiefly occupied with the raising of the Saladin tithe, and efforts to settle the great quarrel between the Archbishop and **The** the Canterbury monks, arising out of Baldwin's attempts to **Canterbury** found at their expense a great Church and College of Secular **Quarrel.** Canons, men who would be less attached to Rome, and more amenable to episcopal influence than themselves. In this scheme the King of course sided altogether with the Archbishop.[5]

But already Aquitaine was all ablaze, the inflammable material there having again taken fire. First we hear that Aimar of Engoulême,[6] **Revolt in** Geoffrey of Rancogne, and Geoffrey of Lusignan (elder brother **Aquitaine.** of King Guy), all three old enemies, had risen against Richard. But Richard soon stamped out that fire, and drove the Lusignan to find a refuge with his brother in Palestine.[7] A more serious quarrel with

---

[1] See the Ordinance, given by Rigord, Bouquet, XVII. 26.   [2] So Ben. P., II. 44.

[3] So Hoveden, II. 338.   [4] Giraldus, I. 23, 24; VI. 13, 14; Gervase, I. 421.

[5] For this dispute begun in 1186, and not finally settled until 1201, see the correspondence *Epp. Cantuar*, and Bishop Stubbs' Introduction; also Gervase, I. 332-587.

[6] Brother to Wulgrin Taillefer III. whom he succeeded in a portion of the county in 1181 in opposition to the will of Richard, who supported the rights of Wulgrin's daughter Matilda; Ben. P., II. 34, note Bp. Stubbs.

[7] Ben. P., *sup.* Hoveden, II. 339; Diceto, II. 54. *Itinerary*, 26, Norgate. I disregard the allegation of Diceto that Henry supported the Poitevin rebels as pure calumny, invented to excuse Richard's later conduct. The story is quite worthy of Giraldus, VIII. 245, who treats Raymond also as having been suborned by Henry to attack his son. The Crusade question is here the disturbing element. Richard was all for the Crusade, and so became the hero of the Church. Henry laboured under the imputation of being lukewarm in the matter.

Raymond V. of Toulouse followed. He was accused of having arrested and
Richard at War with Toulouse. maltreated some merchants of Richard's allegiance. Richard made a raid on his territory,[1] and carried off one Peter Seilun, a confidential minister of Count Raymond. He again retaliated by laying hands on two English knights, Robert le Poer and Ralph Fraser, men on their way home from Compostella. The plunder of such pilgrims, we are told, formed no inconsiderable part of the revenue of a Count of Toulouse. Raymond then proposed an exchange of prisoners. Richard affecting to treat the arrest of pilgrims as sacrilege, would hear of no compromise. Then King Philip came forward to mediate; but finding the parties impracticable went off in disgust, leaving them to their own devices. Richard, taking Philip's retirement as tacit leave to draw the sword,[2] again invaded Toulouse in greater force, capturing Moissac[3] and sundry other towns in Quercy (June).[4] Philip then raised protests against the attack on his vassal; and taking advantage of the opportunity of
Philip invades Berri. Richard's absence, he marched an army into Berri, surprised Châteauroux,[5] and captured Argentan, Busançai,[6] and other places. But at Richard's approach he retired northwards, without risking any battle. Montrichard however fell into his hands, while still farther North Vendôme was surrendered to him by Count Bouchard IV., a man who had sided with the young King in 1173; Troô on the Loir was also burnt. Richard following hard on Philip's tracks ravaged the lands of all who had submitted to him.[7] These hostilities undertaken without due preliminaries, and between men actually under crusading vows would be held indefensible by all church people.

Meanwhile reports, remonstrances, and explanations were flying backwards and forwards across the Channel. Philip complained of Richard; the King demanded explanations of his son, and he ventured to assert that he had done nothing without Philip's leave.[8] After sending over first
Henry's last Crossing. the Archbishop of Canterbury, and then his son John, to discuss matters with Philip, Henry resolved to go over himself, and so, having called out an army, left England for the last time, to sink under the heartless intrigues of ungrateful young men, banded

---

[1] April? See G. Le Breton, Bouquet, XVII. 68, comparing Rigord, *Id.*, 25.

[2] So I interpret Richard's bold assertion to his father that he had attacked Toulouse with Philip's consent; Ben. P., II. 40; Hoveden, II. 340.

[3] Tarn et Garonne.

[4] Ben. P., II. 34-36; Hoveden, II. 339, 340; Rigord, 27; Diceto, II. 55.

[5] 16 June Diceto.

[6] Indre, all three.

[7] Ben. P., II. 39, 40; Diceto, *sup.*; Gervase, I. 432; Rigord, 27; Montrichard, Vendôme, and Troô, are all in Loir et Cher.

[8] Giraldus, VIII. 246. "Nihil nisi per licentiam regis Francorum"; Ben. P. *sup.*

together against him.   On the 10th July he sailed from Portsea, and next day landed at Barfleur.[1]

Henry, who did not want war, and was always scrupulous of direct attacks on his suzerain, took up a defensive position within his own borders;[2] the French however meanwhile indulging in petty raids.   Thus the martial Bishop of Beauvais burned Blangy and Aumâle.   Henry however asked for a conference to discuss matters, and, accordingly, one was held at the old trysting place between Trie and Gisors.   The discussion lasted some three days; but it seems doubtful whether the two kings actually met.   Anyhow no agreement was effected; and Philip, in a fit of silly temper, cut down the historic elm, vowing that no more conferences should be held there.[3]

Fruitless Conference.

Henry then issued a formal declaration of war, renouncing his allegiance to France.   To follow up this blow he moved from Gisors through Vernon to Pacy; and from thence on the 30th August led his forces for a one day's raid on the soil of France. Sweeping round the walls of Mantes, and laying waste all before him, he returned at nightfall to his own territory at Ivry.   Philip was at Mantes at the time, but he was not tempted to accept the challenge, and the only engagement that took place was a skirmish between champions, in which *Cœur de Lion* distinguished himself by unhorsing and taking prisoner William des Barres, a noted French lance.   The latter, however, to Richard's great annoyance, managed to escape on a sumpter horse.[4]   But the Count seemed to be getting past keeping up any appearance of cordiality with his father. On the very next day he obtained leave to go off to Berri, by way of retrieving matters there, but of course under promise of true and faithful service.[5]

War with France.

But the state of war between the crusading Kings of England and France was still distressing to all those who were interested in the recovery of Holy Land; and few throughout the length and breadth of Europe were not interested in that recovery. Theobald of Blois and Philip of Flanders gave King Philip to understand

Movement for Peace.

---

[1] Ben. P., *sup.*; Hoveden, II. 343; Diceto, *sup.*; Gervase, I. 433.   Henry is said to have had a large force of Welshmen (multi Wallenses); but from the Pipe Roll as cited by Mr. Eyton we learn that this contingent only numbered 300 men.

[2] Diceto, II. 55.

[3] 16th August; Diceto, *sup.* Benedict, II. 45-47, makes two of this one conference, placing the one before, and the other after Henry's march on Mantes; the elm being cut down after the last meeting.   The metrical Life of William Marshal (*W. Mareschal*, I. 280-282) supports Diceto on both points; showing that the conference and the cutting down of the elm happened before the advance to Mantes.   Benedict however notices the presence of William Marshal.   *Cnf.* Le Breton 68, 69 and 148 a very questionable account.

[4] Diceto and *Mareschal, sup.*   Ben. P., II. 46; Hoveden, II. 344.   The account given by Gervase, I. 433, 434, of this little campaign is absolute bombast.   He raises the number of the Welshmen to thousands (millia Gualensium).

[5] Ben. P. and Hoveden, *sup.*

that he need look for no further support from them. Under this pressure he asked for another conference. The parties met on the 7th October at Châtillon on the river Indre, when peace was suggested on the footing of restitution by Philip and Richard of the conquests recently made by them respectively in Berri and Quercy ; but we are told that Philip wrecked the scheme by demanding the surrender of Pacy as a pledge of Henry's good faith.[1] But in view of the general disinclination for war both parties began to disband ; and another conference was held on the 18th November at Bonmoulins,[2] on the borders of Normandy and Perche.

This meeting we are told was arranged at the instance of Richard,[3] *Conference at Bonmoulins.* acting plainly in concert with Philip, with whom he had renewed relations. The two rode to Bonmoulins together.[4] Richard wanted to come to a definite understanding with his father as to the succession. Philip wanted to bring the father and son to loggerheads. He began by proposing a restitution of all conquests made on either side since they had taken the Cross. But the objecting party this time proved to be Richard, who protested that it would be unfair to ask him to part with his acquisitions in Quercy—demesne lands worth 1,000 marks a year—in exchange for the barren over-lordship of a few castles in Berri.[5] *A joint Move.* The two then developed their grand move to checkmate Henry ; Philip, acting as spokesman, once more demanded the solemnisation of Richard's marriage with Alais, with his recognition as heir to all Henry's dominions.[6] For the King, now growing elderly, and enfeebled by over-exertion and illness, to have recognised Richard in the disposition that he had been showing would have been a suicidal act ; and at any rate it would have interfered with the proposed settlement even of Ireland on John. The King therefore was able to make the dignified answer that to give in to such demands under such circumstances would be derogatory. Then Richard in the sight of the *Richard does Homage to Philip.* whole assembly threw off his sword, and, crossing over to Philip's side, fell at his feet and did homage to him for all the Continental possessions, saving however his allegiance to his father. That broke up the conference, but the Kings had been able to agree on a truce to the 13th January, 1189. In return for Richard's adhesion Philip gave him Issoudun, with the promise of all Berri.[7]

[1] Ben. P., II. 48, 49 ; Hoveden, II. 345.
[2] Orne, near Moulins-la-Marche.
[3] Diceto, II. 57.
[4] *Mareschal.* [5] Diceto, 58.
[6] Ben. P., II. 50 ; Hoveden, II. 354. Diceto, *sup.* however, and Gervase I. 435 represent the demand for the marriage as preferred by Richard himself. So do Rigord and Le Breton. But, considering the rooted aversion to the match that he afterwards evinced, this on his part would be really too barefaced. Gervase moreover makes the conference last three days, but without giving any date.
[7] *Ibid.* ; also W. Newb., I. 276, 277, and Giraldus, VIII. 254.

Henry held his last Christmas at Saumur, as if to keep an eye on his
son's doings.   But his court was visibly thinned by the retire-
Henry's last ment of men who had gone to worship the rising star of the
Christmas.   young Count Richard.[1] The truce that expired on the 13th
January 1189 was renewed, at Henry's instance, first to the 2nd February
and finally to the 18th April, but little regard was paid to it on either side.[2]
Henry was suffering from a fistula, and depressed in body and mind.   So
ill did he seem that the prelates in attendance induced him to make a
confession—a perfunctory and inadequate confession Giraldus thought it.
During the whole spring the King remained inactive at Le Mans;[3] his
                    efforts being directed towards effecting a reconciliation with
Efforts to   Richard.   Conferences were proposed, and one actually held
conciliate
Richard.   at Bonmoulins on the 18th April.   But the son, who, not
without cause, was suspicious of his father's intentions with reference to
John, turned a deaf ear to all his overtures.[4]   Richard then went off to
the South to prepare for more active war.   Henry, by a great effort, rode
after him as far as Le Dorat (Haute Vienne); returning to Chinon and
Le Mans.[5]

At this juncture a final effort was made by the Pope.   Clement III. had
                    been greatly distressed by the breakdown at Bonmoulins.   He
Papal   sent off Cardinal Henry Bishop of Albano to mediate; but the
Efforts.   Legate turned aside to preach the Crusade in Germany; and
so never got beyond Flanders, where he died in the course of the year.[6]
A fresh emissary was accredited in the person of John de' Conti, Cardinal
of St. Mark.   Leaving Rome in March he went to Paris, and from thence
to Le Mans, where he was with Henry on the 19th May.[7] Through his
exertions yet another conference was held at La Ferté Bernard about the
4th June, Henry having then somewhat recovered his health.[8]   Again
Another   Philip demanded the celebration of the marriage between
Fruitless   Alais and Richard; with a guarantee to the latter of the
Conference.   succession at his father's death; but he now added the further
requirement that John should join the Crusade, while Richard protested
that he would not go unless his brother went also.[9]   Cardinal John was
indignant with Philip for being so stiff and unaccommodating, and

---

[1] Ben. P., II. 61; Hoveden, II. 362.

[2] Gervase, I. 338, 339; Girald., VIII. 260; *Mareschal*, I. 290, 291.

[3] Giraldus, *sup.*, and Gervase, I. 443.   Giraldus was in attendance at court at the time.

[4] *Mareschal*, I. 291-295; Giraldus, *sup.*; Diceto, II. 62.

[5] 5th May.   See the *Mareschal*, 296-299.   The writer's details, though not free from
confusion, seem in the main trustworthy.

[6] Ben. P., 51, 55, 56; Hoveden, II. 355, 356; Norgate, II. 256.

[7] Ben. P., 61, *Epp. Cantuar.* 286-290.

[8] Hoveden, II. 362; Giraldus, VIII. 260.

[9] Ben. P., II. 66; *cnf.* Gervase, I. 446; and Diceto, II. 66. Hoveden, II. 363, as
already mentioned, introduces the offer to marry Alais to John here.

R

threatened to lay his dominions under Interdict. Philip answered defiantly that he would pay no regard to any such sentence: the Church had no right to interfere between the King of France and a contumacious vassal.[1] The conference left the parties more bitterly hostile than ever.

Philip and Richard resumed operations without the loss of a single day, attacking and reducing in quick succession La Ferté-Bernard, *The War Pressed.* Maletable, Beaumont-sur-Sarthe, Ballon, Montfort.[2] Geoffrey of Mayenne, Guy of Laval, and Ralph of Fougères joined them.[3] On the 12th June, a Sunday, they appeared before Le Mans, to which place Henry had retreated in a state of helpless fury.[4] To throw him off his guard Philip pitched his tents in a wood across the Huisne, making as though he would move on towards Tours on the morrow. But when the morrow came[5] he drew out his men, and prepared for an assault on the city. To clear his front the English governor, Stephen of Turnham, Seneschal of Anjou, set fire to a suburb. The flames spreading laid hold of the main part of the city; while the French boldly attacked and carried the bridge over the Huisne, to the South of Le Mans[6] thence entering Le Mans pell-mell with the flying garrison, across the other bridge over the *Henry driven from Le Mans.* Sarthe. Henry, panic-stricken, evacuated the city, with all his following, riding twenty miles under a scorching sun to Fresnay-le-Vicomte, on the road to Alençon.[7] With him went two sons, John, 'whom he loved and in whom he greatly put his trust,' and Geoffrey the Chancellor.[8] Richard pressed his father in hot pursuit till his horse was killed under him. It was said that the animal was killed by the lance of William Marshal, who prudently sparing the Royal Count brought his steed to the ground by a dexterous stroke.[9] Next day the King, changing his mind, and against the advice of his followers, who saw that his strength lay in Normandy, resolved to return to Anjou, with a slender escort, while sending off the bulk of his force into Normandy. He bound the commanders, namely, the Earl of Essex and William fitz Ralph by an oath that *Sends John into Normandy.* if anything should happen to him they would deliver the castles to John and to John alone.[10] Thus it is clear that he was bent upon disinheriting Richard. Geoffrey the Chancellor, was allowed to accompany the main force as far as Alençon, being charged

---

[1] Ben. P., and Hoveden, *sup.*

[2] Maletable is in Orne; the other places are all in Sarthe.

[3] Ben. P., II. 61, 67; Diceto, II. 63; Hoveden, II. 362; *Mareschal*, 301, 302.

[4] "Molt iriez qu'il perdeit sa terre . . . De l' ire et del corruz le rei," *Mareschal,* *sup.*

[5] "Lendemain," *Mareschal*, 307.   [6] *Mareschal*, 303, and note.

[7] "Freesnei," *Mareschal*, 317, 320, 321; "Frenellas," Giraldus, IV. 369.

[8] Le conte Johan, qu'il amout, E en cui il molt se fiout," *Mareschal*, 308. John had been made Count of Mortain.

[9] *Id.* 317-320; Ben. P., and Diceto, *sup.*, Giraldus, *sup.* and VIII. 282, 283, 286.

[10] Giraldus, IV. 369.

after that to rejoin his father, who clung to his society. The journey from Fresnay to the Loire must have been one of considerable peril, as the roads were beset with Philip's troops. But Henry kept well to the West of
Himself Le Mans, as we hear that he rested at Sainte Suzanne ;[1] and so
retreats to got through in safety. Geoffrey rejoined him at 'Savingni'[2]
Chinon. either Savigné in South Maine, or Savigny on the Loire ; from the place, whichever it was, they went on to Chinon.

Meanwhile Philip was pursuing his victorious career, reducing Mont-doubleau, Troô, La Roche L' Evêque, Montoire, La Chartre, Château du Loir, Chaumont, Amboise, Rochecorbon.[3] Having thus cleared the country all round Tours on Friday 30th June he appeared before that city, fording the Loire—half dried up with heat—and establishing himself on the South bank of the river.[4] It would seem that negotiations had already been opened with Henry, as a meeting had been arranged for that very day, to be held between Tours and Azai, but Henry being attacked with fever was too ill to attend. Philip and Richard, however, brutally scoffed at his sickness as a mere pretence.[5] On the Sunday, 2nd July, the King was visited by Philip of Flanders, the Duke of Burgundy, and the Archbishop of Rheims, zealous Crusaders, anxious for peace ; but the French King had told them that he would grant no truce till he had taken
Tours Tours. Next day he recrossed the river with scaling ladders,
stormed by and stormed the city from the river front, the garrison being
Philip. evidently insufficient.[6] On the 4th July Henry, conscious that
Henry he must now surrender at discretion, dragged himself to
Surrenders Colombières,[7] between Azai and Tours, to which place he had
at Discretion. been summoned for a final interview. Awaiting the arrival of the French he rested at Ballan, a small commandery of the Templars close to Colombières.[8] Geoffrey the Chancellor was not with him. He had begged to be excused the sight of his father's humiliation.[9] For the meeting Henry had to be supported on his horse by his attendants. A sudden

[1] Mayenne, *Mareschal*, I. 321.

[2] Giraldus, IV. 369 ; VIII. 286. We have Savigné-sous-le-Lude in Sarthe, and another Savigny farther south in Indre et Loire ; either would suit.

[3] Ben. P., II. 68, 69. All these places lie within a moderate compass in the depart-ments of Loir et Cher, Sarthe, and Indre et Loire.

[4] Ben. P., *sup.*

[5] Giraldus, VIII. 286. See also *Id.* IV. 370, and *Mareschal*, I. 323—325, from whence it clearly appears that there was an abortive interview on whatever day it may have been held. But neither Benedict, Hoveden, Diceto, nor Gervase have anything of this.

[6] Ben. P., *sup. Mareschal*, I. 322.

[7] The date and name of the place come from Le Breton, Bouquet, XVII. 28, 158. The date is confirmed by the statement of Matthew Paris that Henry who died on the 6th July, passed away within three days of the treaty ; "infra triduum."

[8] *G. Mareschal*, 323, and note Meyer.

[9] Giraldus, IV. 370.

clap of thunder so shook his nerves that he nearly fell off. An absolute
submission to any terms that he might dictate—a simple *ad*
misericordiam—was Philip's first requirement. Henry next
had to do homage, to purge his recent opposition to his over-
lord; and then Philip propounded his demands, which in fact were
moderate enough, no territorial cession, apart from restitution, being
required, except the surrender of all rights over Auvergne. Henry would
simply bind himself to deliver up Alais, to be married to Richard on his
return from Holy Land; would recognise Richard as heir to all his
dominions; and pay Philip an indemnity of 20,000 marks. Lastly he was
required to remit, at least till he should join the Crusade, all claim to
allegiance from such of his subjects as had taken part with Richard. On
these conditions the treaty was sealed.[1] Henry then gave Richard the
necessary kiss of peace, but gave it with a muttered curse that the son
overheard, "and was not ashamed to repeat."[2]

Treaty of Colombières.

Broken down in mind and body, with his fever rising to a height, Henry
left Colombières. But ill as he was the remorseless Canterbury monks
were in waiting for him at Azai, to pester him with their interminable
quarrel with Archbishop Baldwin. He dictated a letter to the Convent—
probably his last—urging them to think over matters pending his return to
England.[3] But the unkindest cut of all yet awaited him. The list of
those whose allegiance he was to forego had to be tendered. When the
schedule was produced the first name on it was that of the Count of
Mortain—'What? John his best beloved, John for whom he had risked so
much?—it was impossible.' The name having been repeated
Henry turned on his couch with a groan. 'Now,' said he, 'Let
all things go as they will, I care no more for myself, nor for
anything in the world.'[4] "His heart was broken and his death blow
struck."[5]

A Death Blow.

From Azai the King was carried in a litter to Chinon, there to linger on
for two more days, tenderly nursed by the faithful Geoffrey. But in the
bitterness of his heart he could not refrain from cursing his sons, and cursing
the very day on which he was born.[6] 'Shame on a beaten King,' he kept
repeating.[7] With his dying breath, however, he was able to express a hope
that Geoffrey might get either Winchester or York. He gave him his
favourite gold ring, engraved with a 'panther' or leopard, and his blessing;

---

[1] Ben. P., II. 70; Hoveden, II. 365; Giraldus, VIII. 294; Diceto, II. 63.

[2] Giraldus, *sup.* 296; Bishop Stubbs.

[3] Gervase, I. 448, 449. He clearly states that the monks saw Henry after the conclusion of the treaty, and at Azai, but he makes Gisors (!) the place of the treaty. For
the letter dated at Azai, see *Id.* 450, and Epp. Cant. *Memorials Richard*, II., 295-297.

[4] Giraldus, VIII. 294, 295; Hoveden, II. 366; *Mareschal*, I. 327.

[5] Bishop Stubbs, Hoveden, II. lxx.   [6] Hoveden, 366.

[7] "Proh! pudor regi victo," Giraldus, VIII. 297.

also a sapphire ring to be given to his son-in-law, the King of Castile.[1] Finally he had his bed removed into the chapel : said some words of confession ; partook of the Sacrament in both kinds,[2] and so **End of Henry II.** passed away on Thursday, 6th July, being the seventh day of his fever, in the 35th year of his reign, and the 56th year of his age.[3]

A scene ensued, unfortunately not without parallel under similar circumstances in those times. The attendants plundered the Royal apartments and even the Royal corpse, which was left half naked till a young man threw a woollen cloak over it. On the morrow the **His obsequies.** remains were taken by Geoffrey to the nunnery of Fontevrault, not ten miles distant, being the House of Religion most revered by his father next to that of Grammont, which was out of reach.[4] The corpse was laid out in the chapel, with such regalia as could be extemporised. Richard hastened to appear. At his coming the cloth was removed from his father's face to give him a last look at it. As he looked he shuddered with compunction ; then falling on his knees said a brief Paternoster. Of course tradition had it that the body bled as he entered the chapel. On Saturday 8th July, apparently, Henry II. was finally laid in his grave, the Archbishops of Tours and Treves officiating.[5]

[1] *Id.*, IV. 371.

[2] " Communionem Corporis et Sanguinis Domini devote suscepit ; " Hoveden, 367.

[3] Ben. P., II. 71 ; Hoveden, *sup.* ; Diceto, II. 64.

[4] See the legacies in Henry's will below.

[5] See Giraldus, IV. 371, 372 ; and VIII. 305, 306 ; *Mareschal,* I. 332-337 ; Ben. P., II. 71 ; Hoveden, II. 267 ; Diceto, II. 64, 65.

CHAPTER XIV

HENRY II. (*continued*)

A.D. 1154–1189

Personal appearance and character of the King—His Foreign and Domestic Policies —
Legal Reform—The Revenue—Prices—Architecture—Literature—The King's
Issue.

IN bodily make, as already intimated, Henry II. was a stout, thick-
necked, bandy-legged man, of middle height, inclined to corpulence,
only kept down by abstemious diet, and constant exercise. He
had a high complexion, freckled skin, quick, grey, choleric
eyes, a good nose, square jaws and a full round head,
thickly covered with sandy hair, kept closely cropped for fear of baldness ;
in his latter days it became tinged with grey. His chest was full, and his
arms long and sinewy. His hands were coarse and ill-kept. Gloves he
never wore, except when hawking ; his whole attire was light
and simple, if not untidy. When not under the influence of
temper, his speech was most pleasant, and his manner affable
and urbane. But when thwarted, he was liable to fits of passion almost
demoniacal.[1] A keen sportsman, and a man of restless activity, he hardly
ever sat, except on horseback, or at meal times. His followers complained that there was neither peace nor rest for any one in his household.
Confession he shunned.[2] At Mass he was a regular attendant ; but
without even affecting to pay any attention to the service, being engaged
either in conversation with the courtiers, or staring about him.[3] But to
all matters of business in which the Church or clergy were concerned he
gave careful attention—as at Azai in his last illness. Scholarly in his
tastes, and fond of the society of clever men, he was endowed with a
wonderful memory, and never forgot a name or a face.[4] Walter Map gives
him credit for some acquaintance with every language from the Channel to

*His
Looks and
Build*

*His
Manners
and Attire.*

---

[1] *E.g.*, see above, p. 90.
[2] Giraldus, VIII. 259, 260.
[3] Giraldus, V. 305. Radulfus Niger, 169 (Metcalfe, Caxton Society).
[4] " Erat . . . subrufus, cœsius, amplo capite et rotundo ; oculis glaucis, ad iram torvis,
et rubore suffusis, facie ignea, collo ab humeris aliquantulum demisso, pectore quadrato,
brachiis validis, corpore carnoso ; . . . cibo potuque modestus ac sobrius, et parsimoniæ

the Jordan, but admits that he only spoke Latin and French.[1]   We should

His Knowledge of English. have thought that with the years that he spent in England in his boyhood Henry must have learned English.   He certainly understood it, if he did not condescend to speak it, as we find him answering in his own tongue a verbal petition presented to him in English, in a way that showed that he understood what was said to

Private Life. him.[2]   His private life was not domestic ; but his irregularities were as nothing compared to those of Henry I.[3]   He was surrounded by enemies, eager to make the most of any scandal, while again his character has probably suffered from the publicity of his connexion with Rosamond Clifford, and the romantic interest that has always attached to their loves.   Walter Map in one passage implies that Henry was really ascetic in disposition.   Licentious habits would not be easily compatible with the active life he led.[4]   The offences that the clerical party never forgave were first his marriage with a divorced woman ; secondly his quarrel with Becket ; and thirdly his shirking personal co-operation in the Crusade.   With " Giraldus " the last was the worst sin.

Henry was a clever, plausible, self-confident, assiduous man of

Character and Ability. business ; industrious and prompt in action, subtle, tricky, and unscrupulous ; a master of the diplomatic arts of procrastination and evasion ;[5] one who never spared himself, but who, to all appearance, took little counsel of any one but himself. His strong point was the charm of his manner, which, when he chose to make himself agreeable, was irresistible.   To this we must attribute his success in all his personal interventions in the field of diplomacy, which was remarkable.   Being little troubled with sense of honour he could stoop to be utterly mean and paltry.   In reviewing his career as a whole, and forming our estimate of his ability as a ruler and a man, we are confronted by a startling contrast.   We have on the one hand a reign that was undoubtedly successful at home and abroad, and, for England, fruitful of the best results ; on the other hand we have the final collapse

quoad principi licuit per omnia datus. . . . Vel ante cænam vel post rarissime sedentem conspexeris, etc. . . ."   Giraldus, V. 302-306.   "Oculi . . . in ira . . . quasi scintillantes ignem ; . . . leonina facies . . . eminentia naris, . . . equestres tibiæ, thorax extensior, lacerti pugiles ; . . . manus ejus quadam grossitia sua hominis incuriam protestantur, earum enim cultum prorsus negligit ; nec unquam nisi aves deferat utitur chirothecis. . . . Nisi equitet vel comedat nunquam sedet."   Peter of Blois, Epp., I. 193, 194 (Giles).   See also W. Map, *De Nugis Cur.*, 227, 228.

[1] *De Nugis*, 227.

[2] See the incident recorded, Giraldus, V. 290.

[3] So W. Newburgh admitted, I. 280.

[4] I cannot conceive where Sismondi and Martin get the evidence on which they base their charges of Henry's utter license.   The worst charges against him were those in connexion with the Breton hostage (above 92-97), and Alais of France.   These affairs, of course, were disgraceful.

[5] *De Nugis*, 227.

and a tragic ending.   Henry's management of foreign affairs was
undeniably successful.   He held France in the hollow of his
Empire built hand.   He built up and kept together in a marvellous manner
up by him. a Continental dominion in which the antipathies of Norman
and Gascon, of Breton and Poitevin, as well as all the instincts of
Feudalism had to be mastered and held down.   These possessions were
protected by friendly alliances with Germany, Maurienne, Arragon,
and Castile.   He established a footing in Ireland, and effectually
asserted the supremacy of England over Wales and Scotland.[1]   With
respect to the latter country we must especially praise the tact with which
Henry kept his hold on William the Lion without irritating the Scots by
interference in their domestic affairs.   All this was due to the moderation
of his aims, and his persistence in following them up.   That he had no
great Imperial policy is plain from the fact that he spent his life in making
Mistake of arrangements for the break-up of his dominions at his death.
his Family His personal subsidence at the last was of course due to his
Policy. family policy, a misguided course of action that after all proved
him short-sighted, and obstinate ; ignorant of human nature, and of
the world in which he lived.   In pursuit of this scheme, well-meant as it
may have been, he committed a series of mistakes.   The first was that of
crowning young Henry, when the succession could not possibly be in
doubt.   Having made his eldest son King he made him his enemy by
treating him as a child, and by declaring Richard heir to Aquitaine.   The
young King could not possibly share his brother's view that a second son
was the mother's legal heir.   When Henry was relieved of the young King,
and of all the trouble that he had given, he started a fresh source of
bitterness by his efforts to deprive Richard of Aquitaine in favour of
John ; while his proposal to set up John in Ireland was utterly inexcusable.
The universal prejudice—if such it must be called—in favour of
primogeniture could not but be shocked at such proceedings, and to that
prejudice Henry succumbed.[2]

As a legislator and administrator Henry left more enduring results
Enduring behind him.   His *Constitutions of Clarendon* pointed out the
Results of lines on which the relations of Church and State were to be
Domestic regulated.   In the history of our Law and Judicature his reign
Policy. marks a distinct era.   He made an end of feudalism as a
system of Government, leaving it as a system of land tenure.   By

---

[1] With respect to Henry's achievements it may be well to quote the latest French
view on the subject.   " Quand on voit Henri II. livrer à la fois toutes ces batailles et
résister à tant d'ennemis différents, on admire l'audace de l'entreprise et le prodigieux
labeur de l'ouvrier.   Mais cet empire Anglo-Français . . . ne pouvait survivre longtemps
a la forte intelligence qui l'avait créé et le maintenait comme par miracle."   Lavisse,
France, III. 49.

[2] For a very fair estimate of Henry's character and rule see W. Newb., I. 230-238.

establishing the judicial circuits as a permanent institution he secured the
uniformity of the law, rescuing it from the chaos of local custom, and the
conflicting usages of West Saxon, Danish, and Northumbrian codes.
That these were not yet dead appears from the fact that according to
Uniform Law. Hoveden, Glanville, after his appointment as Chief Justiciar,
that is to say, in or after the year 1180, republished the so-
called Laws of William the Conqueror, being, in fact, the Laws
of the Confessor, in which these local customs are recognised [1]; while in
his own treatise on the laws of England, Glanville distinctly refers to the
different customs obtaining in different counties. [2] Along with the
systematising of the judicial circuits, we have the appearance of the Court
of King's Bench, not as an itinerant court, in attendance on
A Central Court. the King in his progresses, but as a standing central court,
established at Westminster. [3] The Exchequer was still but a
Board of Audit, meeting twice a year to collect revenues; but armed
with judicial powers for dealing with defaulters. The very style of those
sitting on the Board, 'Barons of the Exchequer,' points to the fact that
they were not strictly justices: while the title of the office, 'Receipt of
the Exchequer Board' (*Recepta Scaccarii*) indicates their essential duties. [4]
With all these institutions, a class of professional lawyers begins to spring
up. Still more important were the measures withdrawing the cognisance
of cases of serious crime, and of suits for the possession of land, from the
jurisdiction of the local and feudal courts, and putting them under the jurisdiction of Royal justices. By the *Assize of Clarendon* in 1166, the
Extended Jurisdiction of Royal Justices. judicial courts were regulated, and the authority of the King's
justices over presented criminals, declared paramount to all
rights of private courts. [5] To the same year is ascribed the
introduction of the *Assize of Novel Disseisin*, under which a man unjustly
deprived of his freehold is given a remedy by application for a royal writ,
to be followed by a trial by a jury of his neighbours. [6] By the *Assize of
Mort d'Ancestor*, promulgated in 1176, the succession of an heir to the
estate of which his ancestor died seized is in like manner protected by
royal writ, and a legal trial. [7] A still further step in advance was gained,
apparently in 1179, by the *Grand Assize*, under which all suits for the
possession of land are brought under the protection of the King's justice.
From that time no man could any longer be forced to defend his rights by
the barbaric use of a battle wager. [8] Provisions of a similar character were

---

[1] See Hoveden, II. xxii., 215.
[2] *De Legibus Angliæ*, XII. c., 23.
[3] Pollock and Maitland, *Histy. Eng. Law*, I. 153.
[4] See Round, *Commune of London*, 79, 80; Pollock and Maitland, *sup.* 109, 191.
[5] See above, 76.   [6] See above, 81.
[7] See above, 190, and Pollock and Maitland, *sup.*, I. 147.
[8] See above 202; Pollock and Maitland, *sup.*, 149; Glanville, II. c. 7; XII. cc. 2, 25.

introduced by Henry in the delicate sphere of questions relating to advowsons, and disputed Church lands. The Church, in the twelfth century, arrogated to herself not only the decision of all questions relating to lands, given to God and the Church in 'pure and perpetual alms' (or lands in Frankalmoin), but also the decision of the question that might easily arise, as to whether a given parcel of land was Frankalmoin or lay fee. She also claimed jurisdiction over litigation concerning advowsons. In the *Constitutions of Clarendon*, Henry had claimed that the latter sets of cases should be decided under the presidency of a royal justiciar.[1] Effect was subsequently given to these provisions by the *Assisa Utrum*, and the *Assize of Darrein (Dernière) Presentment*. By the first of these, a recognition by twelve lawful men is to decide whether the land in dispute is Frankalmoin or not[2]; under the latter, a right is given of applying for an inquest as to who presented last; the person who presented last time to present again, but saving all questions of right.[3]

An ulterior result of these measures was the introduction of proper trial by jury. Sworn inquests under Royal writs had been known in England at any rate since Domesday, which was compiled from the verdicts of juries. Under Henry II. the sworn inquest "begins to make its way into our ordinary civil procedure." Partly under the four above named Assizes, partly by voluntary agreement among litigants, trial by jury "creeps in." Through the ordinances of Henry II., it becomes "part of the usual machinery of civil justice. Already before the end of the reign it fills a large space in Glanville's text-book. The old modes of proof are not abolished; proof by battle we shall have with us until 1819, proof by oath-helpers (compurgation) until 1833; but from this moment onwards they are being pushed into the background."[4]

Trial by Jury.

The credit of these reforms must undoubtedly be ascribed to Henry himself. His enemies taunted him with them, as being simply dictated by the wish to fill his pocket.[5] His ends may have been selfish, but as has been remarked of his grandfather, his selfish ends coincided with the wants of the nation.

For the student of constitutional institutions the reign does not present many points of interest. Henry's government was essentially personal; but he showed the instinct of any wise ruler whose throne does not rest on bayonets in taking his subjects along with him as much as possible in all measures of importance. His Grand Councils are a distinct feature of his rule. All his ordinances were passed

Grand Councils.

---

ss. 3, 9. If the land was found to be Frankolmoin the jurisdiction of the al courts could not be questioned.
: and Maitland, *sup.*, 145, 240-251 [3] Pollock and Maitland, *sup.*, 148, 149.
), 150; Stat. 59 Geo. III., c. 49; Stat. 3 and 4 Will. IV., c. 42, s. 13.
   quæstu satiatus abolitis antiquis legibus, singulis annis novas leges, quas it edidit," R. Niger, 168. Stubbs.

n these assemblies, consisting of the *Sapientes*, the Witan of earlier days,
or the bishops, abbots, earls, barons and others whom the King chose to
summon. What amount of deference he paid to their counsels we cannot
say, but the formality of one reign might easily become a reality in another
reign.[1] By reducing the Baronage to subjection Henry undoubtedly
cleared the way for orderly, and through that, to constitutional government.

Of Henry's English revenue, as shown by the Pipe Rolls, we cannot give
a very glowing account. Of his foreign revenues we know
nothing at all. Of the way in which the net surplus paid into
the treasury at Winchester was expended, the Pipe Rolls tell us nothing,
but we believe that they give us a fair account of the receipts. It may be,
of course, that at times money was paid to the King direct; in the first
year of the reign, we have some £280 paid into the Chamber, or King's
Privy Purse; after that, we do not seem to hear of any payments into
Chamber, possibly they might have been paid direct without passing
through the Exchequer audit. Certainly in the case of the war in Ireland,
we have references to those who ' had neither gone in person, nor sent men
or money,'[2] suggesting that money for the war, not entered on the Roll,
had been sent to the King in Ireland. Fines for special favours perhaps
might occasionally be handed to the King in person ; but as the total of
fines is not really great, we believe that the Pipe Rolls fairly represent the
revenue. Henry though fond of money, and keeping a sharp eye on his
servants, was not a financier ; he never succeeded in devising a fertile tax.
His financial dealings betray arbitrary and capricious action, and in short
his revenue was small, considerably below that which we ascribe to his
grandfather.

I. The mainstay of the revenue, the branch that on the whole was paid
with least irregularity, was that comprising the county farm
rents, the rents of the counties and boroughs, with the returns
from the special Crown estates, such as Windsor, Bray, New
Forest, etc., entered separately, the Sheriffs being accountable for all these.
The total, if paid in full, would come in round numbers to £12,000.[3]
But from this amount would have to be deducted the value of the *terræ
datæ* or Crown lands alienated by the King since the time when the
Sheriffs' farm-rents were fixed. The returns from these, though passed
through the accounts, went to the alienee and not to the King. Other
fixed charges also there were, such as *decimæ constitutæ* and *eleemosynæ
constitutæ*, which we would deduct in estimating the King's effectual

Revenue.

*County
Farm-rents.*

___

[1] On the whole subject see Bp. Stubbs, Ben. P., II. lxxvi., etc., and his *Constitutional
Hist.*, I. ch. 12.

[2] " De scutagio militum qui nec abierunt in Hiberniam nec milites nec denario
miserunt," Pipe Roll, 19 Henry II., p. 27, etc.

[3] See *Sheriffs' Farm*, G. J. Turner, Eng. Hist. Soc. with some supplement
added by myself. So too Bishop Stubbs, Ben. P., II. lxxxviii.

revenue. Arrears also of course there always were. With these deductions the farm rents might be reduced to about £8,000, the sum actually named by Giraldus.[1]

II. The next item of revenue that Henry at his succession would find
Danegeld. to his hand was the Danegeld, which at the close of the reign of Henry I., yielded him an annual sum say of £2500, and if exacted in full, might have yielded £4500.[2] Strange to say, Henry II. allowed this tax, the legality of which could not be disputed, to drop He levied it in the second year of his reign, 1155–1156; driblets of arrears kept coming in till the eighth year (1161–1162), when it was again exacted; but after that we hear of it no more.

III. Then Henry had the legitimate feudal Aids that he might call for,
Feudal Aids. namely, the Aid to knight his eldest son, and the Aid to marry his eldest daughter.[3] Of the Aid to knight the son we hear nothing; doubtless for the simple reason that the young king was never knighted by his father. But the Aid for Matilda's outfit was duly raised in the 14th year (1167–1168). The legal impost apparently was 13s. 4d. the knight's fee from military tenants. But Henry did not stop there; all classes were called on to contribute, town and country, rich and poor, according to assessments doubtless fixed by the King's justices.

IV. Another feudal incident would be Scutage, or commutation for
Scutage. personal service, as introduced by Henry I., at the King's option, he calling for men or money according as it suited him.[4] Seven times in the reign Henry II. called on his subjects for Scutage; namely, in the second year, for the war against his brother Geoffrey; in the 5th year for the war of Toulouse; in the 7th and 8th years for war with France; in the 11th year for the war in Wales;[5] in the 18th year for the war in Ireland; and lastly, in the 21st year, for the expedition to Galloway. Thus Henry did not call for Scutage except when he had a fair right to do so, but he varied the rate according to his requirements. Sometimes he took 1 mark (13s. 4d.), sometimes a mark and a half (£1), sometimes two marks (£1 6s. 8d.); while in some cases we find him taxing some of his subjects at one rate, and some at another rate;[6] while from some he took money, from others service in the field. Thus the scutage proper of the 5th year (1159) at the rate of £1 6s. 8d. the knight's fee as actually levied

---

[1] VIII., 316. 12,000 marks is the figure he gives.

[2] See *Foundations*, II. 328, where the total of Danegeld actually paid should be read £2,500, with an addition of ⅓ for the counties whose accounts are missing. Mr. Maitland gives the assessed total without any remissions as £5,135, *Domesday and Beyond*, 474. I make it £4,453.

[3] Glanville IX. c. 8.

[4] See above in connection with the Scutage of the 5th year, 1159, p. 20.

[5] This Impost is not described on the Pipe Rolls as a Scutage, but as 'Assessment for soldiers in Wales.' I treat it as in effect a Scutage.

[6] So in the 7th year; Round, *Feudal England*, 281.

is estimated by Mr. Round at £2440.[1]   The Scutage for Ireland as paid within the year, we make £2114.   But in both these cases we know that a large proportion of the tenants were called out in person.   The latest estimate of the number of knights' fees in England raises the total to 7000 and upwards.[2]   At the medium rate of £1 the fee, the tax if taken from all would have yielded £7000.   But even with regard to those from whom money was demanded there were always remissions and arrears not settled for years afterwards.

V.   Among the regular yearly receipts were the incidents of the administration of justice, penalties, fines, and forfeitures *(placita, oblata, conventiones, misericordiæ).*   The fines taken by the King have long been held up to opprobrium.   "Justice was avowedly bought and sold.[3]   The bribes given for the expedition, delay, suspension, and, doubtless, for the perversion of justice, were entered in the public registers of the royal revenue, and remain as monuments of the perpetual iniquity and tyranny of the times."[4]   Henry's justice, no doubt, was venal.   But it must be said that on the whole these fines do not come to much.   We have occasionally crushing fines *(misericordiæ)* imposed on great men ; but these are generally modified or remitted ; while we frequently hear of money agreed to be paid to the King being withheld, because the party had not received the favour for which he had bargained.

(side note: Judicial Penalties, Fines, and Forfeitures)

VI.   Of the miscellanea, the most considerable were the receipts from vacant sees farmed out.   These from the time of Becket's flight in 1164 became considerable, rising to over £5000 in 1172.   Considerable sums were also received from estates in hand, reliefs, and the sale of heiresses.

(side note: Vacant Sees and Estates in Hand.)

VII.   But throughout his reign, Henry largely relied on arbitrary assessments, styled *Donum* from the counties, and *Auxilium* from the boroughs.   The difference of term is significant. The boroughs were considered part of the King's demesne, and so could lawfully be called upon for an Aid to meet his requirements. The counties not being so liable, were asked to contribute by way of a gift, like the Benevolences of later days.   The *Donum* however at times appears to be styled with less ceremony *Assiza Comitatus,*[5] while late in the reign we find *Donum, Assiza, Tallagium,* treated as identical.[6]   The *Donum* from the counties alone in the 2nd and 4th years of the reign is given by

(side note: Arbitrary Assessments.)

---

[1] *Ib.*   [2] Inman, *Feudal Statistics*, 65.

[3] So Giraldus of Henry ; "Justitiæ venditor et dilator."

[4] Hume, *England*, II. 131 (ed. 1792).   His facts are taken through Madox from the Pipe Rolls.

[5] I take the two to be much the same, but the subject is very obscure.   The assiza comitatus however is often spoken of as a penalty.

[6] Pipe Roll, 20 Henry II., p. 23.

Mr. Maitland as £2077 and £2070 respectively.[1] With respect to the
5th year, our summation of the items paid in for *Donum* and Scutage
together comes to £7788 ; deducting from this Mr. Round's £2440 for
the Scutage, would leave £5348 for *Donum*. This *Donum* however was
only exacted from the higher clergy, the boroughs, the sheriffs, and a few
Jews, and others.[2] The year was altogether financially an exceptional one.
On the other hand, we have many years, as notably those when the receipts
from the vacant sees were at the highest, when no *Donum* at all was levied.
After the rebellion of 1174, we have tallages on the lands of those who had
acted against the King; and in some of the last years of the reign he
contented himself with tallages on the demesne lands. We have heard
that Henry was a thrifty man.[3] He only took what he needed, but it mattered
little to him whether he took it by regular or irregular methods. On the
whole however he must be cleared of the charge of oppressive
taxation. £20,000 is the highest estimate that we could form
of his average revenue. Of four years that we have added up
only one reaches that amount.[4]

Total Revenue.

REVENUES OF HENRY II.

From the Pipe Rolls.

	£
2nd year (1155-1156) Including Danegeld, *Auxilium, Donum*, and Scutage from clergy	12,548
5th year (1158-1159) Great Scutage (*Donum* and Scutage together equal £7,788)	19,960
15th year (1168-1169) No extras except vacant sees and arrears of daughter's Aid	20,658
35 Henry II. and 1 Rich. I. (1188-1189)[5] No *Communis Assiza* or *Donum*	15,347

It would have been interesting to know what the proceeds of the Saladin
Tithe came to; but no accounts of the yield seem to be forthcoming. In

[1] *Domesday and Beyond*, 474.
[2] See above, 20.
[3] Giraldus, *sup.*
[4] I must here with all deference express my amazement at the totals given by Bishop
Stubbs for the revenues for the 2nd and 35th years, namely, £22,000 and £48,000. I
can only suggest, as I suggested with reference to his adding up of the Pipe Roll, 31
Henry I., that the person to whom the task was entrusted took in all the *terræ datæ*
remissions and arrears; that might make up the sums. See Ben. P., II. xciv., xcix. I
fully recognise that within a few hundreds of pounds opinions might differ as to what ought
and what ought not to be reckoned part of the King's available income, but within those
limits I think that I may guarantee the accuracy of my figures. It is only a work of
humble patient drudgery.
[5] Mr. Hunter gives the year as 1189-1190, a clear error.

fact the tax was still under collection when Henry died.[1] Prices do not seem to have varied much since the beginning of the century;
Wages and Prices. 1*d.* a day is still the wage of a common soldier, or an able-bodied labourer; 1*d.* a day or £1 10*s.* 5*d.* a year is a sufficient allowance for a respectable pensioner. An ox or a cow may be bought for 3*s.*, a bull for 4*s.*, a farm horse (*affer*) may cost from 3*s.* to 5*s.*, a sheep 4*d.* But in Herefordshire we have five sheep going for 12*d.*[2] Among the supplies sent for the army in Ireland we find the sheriffs paying 1*s.* 10*d.* for the *summa* (quarter?) of wheat, and 1*s.* for the same measure of beans. A weigh (*pensum*) of cheese cost them 5*s.*, a flitch of bacon 1*s.* 4*d.*[3]

Throughout the reign the silver penny was still the only current coin.
The Currency. Twice in the reign, namely in 1158 and 1180, the currency was called in, as having been clipped and defaced, and a new coinage issued; but no change either in the weight or standard of purity was introduced. In 1180 a foreigner from Touraine, one Philip Aymery, was brought over to superintend the proceedings. Unfortunately he was found guilty of malversation and was dismissed. On both occasions we have murmurings at the change. The holders of the old coin would suffer; and all King's taxes would have to be paid in the new medium. We also hear of severe proceedings against moneyers and coiners.[4]

On military and domestic buildings, and works of public utility, Henry was always willing to spend money. He spent largely on the
Public Works and Buildings. fortifications at Scarborough; the massive Keeps of Dover and Newcastle belong to the reign. He built palaces at Rouen, Caen, Tours, and Chinon; parts of the last three still remain. Hospitals and Lazar Houses found in him a liberal patron. We hear of his draining a marsh at Oxford. But his greatest work in this line was the levee or embankment that for thirty miles from Bourgueil to the mouth of the Mayenne still retains the flooded waters of the Loire.[5] It was in this reign too, that the building of London Bridge in stone was first taken in hand by Peter of Colechurch (1176).[6] It "stood about 200 ft. East of the present structure, in the line of Fish Street Hill, and consisted of twenty arches, a drawbridge for larger vessels, and a chapel and crypt in the centre, dedicated to S. Thomas of Canterbury."[7] But for building Churches and Abbeys Henry had little turn. The nascent glories of the

---

[1] Diceto, II. 73.

[2] Pipe Roll, 13 Henry II., 16, 36, 102, 115.

[3] Pipe Roll, 17 Henry II. 11, 12, 19, 91, etc. In the 15th year we have the summa of wheat going for 1*s.*, more or less; Pipe Roll, 137.

[4] See Diceto, I. 302, and II. 7; Ann. Waverley, A.D. 1158; Ben. P., I. 263; W Newb. I. 225.

[5] R. Monte, A.D. 1169; Norgate, II. 196-200.

[6] Ann. Waverley; Ann. Cambriæ.

[7] Wheatley and Cunningham, *London*, II 418.

Pointed Style made no impression on his eye. In England, apart from the forcible conversions at Waltham and Amesbury,[1] the only **Church Architecture.** foundations with which he is credited are an Augustinian Priory at Newstead in Sherwood, and the small Cistercian House at Witham in Somerset. To start the Abbey on a proper footing Hugh of Avalon, the future St. Hugh of Lincoln, was brought to England from the mountains of Dauphiné. From lack of Royal patronage, therefore, and other causes, the ecclesiastical monuments of the reign are not great, though the period was one of marked development of style, the Norman-Romanesque reaching its maturity, and passing into the Transition Style, with the pointed arch appearing. The bulk of our richer Norman doorways with their varied ornamentation is assignable to the period 1130–1175.[2] Of the greater works probably the best known is the rebuilding and enlargement of Conrad's choir at Canterbury by William of Sens (1175–1178?), the work being carried on by English William (1179–1184). "The pillars of the choir, pier-arches, and clerestory above, are wholly the work of the former.". To the latter we owe the Trinity Chapel and Corona of Becket.[3] More familiar to the general reader will be the round Temple Churches of London and Cambridge. St. Sepulchre's Cambridge is purely Norman in style, and understood to date from about the year 1140. In London the Templars removed from their original establishment at the **The Transition Style.** Old Temple, Holborn, on the site of the present Staple Inn, to the New Temple, Fleet Street in 1184. This church, which is distinctly Transitional, was dedicated by the Patriarch Heraclius during his visit to England in the spring of 1185.[4] Some ten years earlier in date was the Transition Galilee added to the West end of Durham Cathedral by Bishop Hugh of Puiset (*circa* 1175).[5] At Oxford we have a most interesting Transition building in the Cathedral, or Church of St. Frithswyth, or Frideswide as the name is generally given in its Latinised form. The shrine of the patroness was translated in 1180.[6] That may be taken as marking the completion of the choir at any rate as far West as the crossing; but there is nothing in the main fabric of the nave inconsistent with that date. The attempts made to connect the existing building with Anglo-Saxon or early Norman periods seem quite mistaken. The arrangement of the triforium-clerestory belongs to the most developed Norman Romanesque; so does the door of the Chapter House, which is admittedly older than the church. The steeple of course is later; while the vaulted roof of the choir is Tudor work.

[1] See above, 225.
[2] See the Paper read by Mr. C. E. Keyser before the Society of Antiquaries, *Athenæum*, 10th March, 1900.
[3] See Willis's *Canterbury*; and Britton's *Cathedral Antiquities*.
[4] Wheatley and Cunningham, *London*; and above, 225.
[5] See Canon Greenwell's *Durham Cathedral*, 49, 50. [6] Ann. Waverley.

With this Church should be compared St. Peter's Northampton, a beautiful specimen, and very similar in the ornamentation of the capitals. The two Western bays of Worcester Cathedral, again, show the architecture of the time. St. Joseph's Chapel Glastonbury, and the West front of Croyland Abbey Church also belong to this reign. But for two singularly perfect specimens of Transition style, blending Romanesque with Early Pointed, we would refer to Dublin's two Cathedrals, Christ Church, and St. Patrick's. Christ Church, originally a Danish Priory for Secular Canons, was refounded by Archbishop Lawrence O'Toole, about the year 1163, and there Earl Strongbow's bones rest unto this day. St. Patrick's is the work of Lawrence's successor, John Cumin, appointed by Henry in 1181.[1] The English settlement in Ireland therefore, after all, meant something more than mere havoc and destruction.

On the obscure question of the fusion of the two races we cannot throw much light. We must however point out that the well-known passage in the *Dialogus De Scaccario*, to the effect that Norman and English could no longer be distinguished, only applies to the offspring of mixed marriages, and at any rate to children born in England;[2] while the concluding words of the sentence imply that all persons of any position passed as Normans, as he adds 'except the villeins who cannot change their condition without the leave of their lord.'[3] As for the language in which the upper classes conversed we have on the one hand the wife of Hugh of Morville, father of Becket's murderer, warning her husband against a supposed danger in English "Huge de Morevile, ware, ware, ware, Ligulf has his swerd drawen."[4] Here however we note that the husband's name "Huge de Morevile" is clearly French. On the other hand the one utterance in the final altercation between Becket and his murderers that has been preserved in the original vernacular is French. Reginald fitz Urse in answer to Thomas' statement of his wrongs exclaims "Avoy." 'Oh, indeed.'[5] We might also point out that the only historical writings that have come down to us not composed in Latin are composed in French.

The English language we find undergoing considerable transformation ; the vowel sounds are modified ; final syllables are weakened or dropped,

Margin note: Question of Fusion of Races.

---

[1] Ben. P., I. 180, Lewis *Topog. Dicty.* "Ireland." See also a Paper read by Sir Robert Drew ; Archl. Inst., Dublin ; August, 1900.

[2] "Jam cohabitantibus Anglicis et Normannis et alterutrum uxores ducentibus vel nubentibus sic permixtæ sunt nationes ut vix discerni possit hodie de liberis loquor quis Anglicus, quis Normannus sit genere." Select Charters, 193.

[3] "Exceptis duntaxat ascriptitiis qui villani dicuntur quibus non est liberum obstantibus dominis suis a sui status conditione discedere," *Ib.*

[4] W. Canty., *Becket*, I. 128. Out of many variants I give what I understand to be the Northern reading.

[5] *Becket*, II. 5. For the word see Godefroy, *Dictionnaire de l'Ancienne Langue Française.*

S

inflections lost, while the spelling becomes chaotic. The infusion of

English of the Period. Romance is limited to a few "significant" words such as *castel, justise, prisun*. The religious needs of the people saved the native tongue from literary extinction. We have a modernised translation of the Gospels (Hatton Gospels), with new glosses to the Psalter, and a considerable mass of Homilies based on, if not simply adapted from, the works of Aelfric Grammaticus. Popular songs, too, of course there were, but of these little remains. Latin literature however

Latin Literature. flourished throughout the reign; the wide acquaintance with the Latin poets showed by all the writers is very remarkable. During this reign John of Salisbury, Peter of Blois, Walter Map, Gerald of Barry, composed their various works. Joseph of Exeter sang of the Trojan war, and Alexander Neckam gave to the world Natural History and Grammar in metrical form. Of the historical writers whose names we associate with the reign William of Newburgh, and Roger of Hoveden wrote somewhat later. An especial outcome of the period was the development of the romances connected with the Holy Grail. Much as these productions may have been appreciated at the court of Henry, it does not appear that any English writer contributed to the cycle.[1]

To turn to a very different subject, with the work of Ranulf Glanville

Ranulf Glanville. *De Legibus Angliæ*, English jurisprudence makes a fresh start. The treatise, however, is only a handbook of procedure in the *Curia Regis*, or court of King's Bench, mainly organised by himself, as well as of proceedings in all Crown cases civil or criminal; procedure in lower courts not originating in any Crown writ does not come within the scope of the work.

If Normans settled in England were becoming English, we must bear in mind that the ruling class in England was being constantly recruited from abroad. A large proportion of the bishops were still foreigners. Such were Archbishops Theobald, Roger of Pont l'Evêque, and Richard; such likewise were Adam of Paris (St. Asaph, 1175); Peter de Leia (St. David's, 1176); Waleran (Rochester, 1182); Walter of Coutances (Lincoln, 1182); Gerard La Pucelle (Lichfield, 1183); St. Hugh (Lincoln, 1186); Hugh of Nonant (Lichfield, 1188).[2]

Henry left a Will, published at Bishop's Waltham in 1182, apparently a day or two before sailing for Normandy (3rd March).[3] The Will simply

---

[1] The connexion of the name of Walter Map with the Grail cycle based on marginal notes to certain MSS. does not seem to bear investigation. The names of the period clearly connected with the Grail seem to be those of Robert of Boron (1160–1170), Wolfram of Eschenbach (1180), and Crestian of Troyes (1180–1200), their productions being based on earlier legends of Joseph of Arimathea, apparently going very far back. See generally Ten Brink, *Eng. Lit.*, Vol. I. 146, 147, 168, 171–174.

[2] See *Registrum Sacrum*.　　[3] Diceto, II. 10; Gervase, I. 298.

deals with charitable legacies, amounting in all to 40,500 marks or
£27,000, more than a year's total of the English revenue that
Henry's Will. we ascribe to the King. The objects of his liberality fall under
five heads (1) the Templars, Hospitallers and Kingdom of Jerusalem ;
(2) Religious foundations in England ; (3) the same in Normandy ; (4) the
same in Anjou and Maine ; (5) special Orders and Houses of Religion
irrespective of country. The first class get nearly half the money, the
Templars and Hospitallers receiving 5,000 marks apiece, 5,000 more
jointly ; 5,000 marks for the defence of Jerusalem ; and yet another
5,000 for the poor and religious of the Holy City. These 20,000 marks
were to be given in addition to money already placed in their hands.
The Monasteries of England get 5,000 marks ; those of Normandy 3,000
marks ; and those of Anjou and Maine 1,000 marks ; all to be distributed
by the bishops of the respective countries. But the monks of Grammont
got 3,000 marks for themselves ; the nuns of Fontevrault 2,000 marks ;
the Carthusians and Cistercians 2,000 marks each ; and the Cluniacs
1,000 marks.[1]

By Eleanor (Aliénor) of Aquitaine, divorced wife of Louis VII.
His Issue. (divorced in March, and remarried in May 1152) Henry had,
(1) William b. abroad, 17th August 1153, d. 1156.[2]

(2) Henry b. 28th February 1155 ; m. Margaret of France November
1160[3] ; crowned King by anticipation 14th June 1180[4] ; d. 11th June
1183.[5] No issue. Margaret remarried 1186-1187 Bela III. King of
Hungary.[6]

(3) Matilda b. 1156[7] ; m. in 1168 to Henry the Lion[8] ; d. 1189,[9]
leaving issue.

(4) RICHARD b. at Oxford, September 1157.[10]

(5) Geoffrey b. 23rd September 1158 ; m. in 1181 Constance heiress of
Conan IV. Count of Brittany[11] ; by her had Arthur and Eleanor ; d.
19th August, 1186.[12] Arthur died in April 1203 murdered by John ;
Eleanor 'the Damsel of Brittany' lived and died a state prisoner in
England. Her mother in 1189 remarried Ralph or Ranulf III. Earl of
Chester ; divorced from him in 1199 she took as her third husband Guy
of Thouars, by whom she had another daughter Constance or Alais who
was recognised as the heiress of Brittany, and married to Peter Manclerc a
scion of the House of Dreux. Her mother died in 1201. (See below 394).

[1] *Id.* and *Fœdera*, I. 147.
[2] R. de Monte ; Sandford, *Geneal. Hist. of Kings of England.*
[3] R. de Monte ; Diceto, I. 304.
[4] Gervase, I. 219 ; W. Canterbury, I. 81.
[5] Ben. P., I. 301.   [6] Ben. P., I. 346.   [7] Brompton, c. 1047.   [8] R. de Monte.
[9] Diceto, II. 65 ; Stederburg, I. 861 (Leibnitz).
[10] Diceto, I. 302.
[11] Morice, *Bretagne, Preuves*, I. 687.   [12] Diceto, II. 41.

(6) Eleanor b. at Domfront, 1161 [1]; m. in 1169 to Alphonso III. King of Castile,[2] and had issue; d. 1214.[3]

(7) Johanna or Jeanne, b. at Angers October 1165 [4]; m. to William II. of Sicily February 1177 [5]; no issue; remarried in 1196 to Raymond VI. of Toulouse; d. 1199 leaving a son.[6]

(8) JOHN b. at Oxford 1166.[7]

Henry also had the following natural sons:

(1) Geoffrey b. about 1152 [8]; elected Bishop of Lincoln in April 1173; renounced the election in 1181 [9]; and then made Chancellor; became Archbishop of York in 1192.   From the date of his birth it would seem that he could not be the son of Rosamond Clifford, as the King's connexion with her did not begin, or at any rate become notorious till 1174.[10]   Walter Map, who had a quarrel with Geoffrey, says that his mother was an abandoned woman of the name of Ykenai or Hikenai; there is reason for believing that in fact she was daughter of a knight, Roger of Akany (Hackney?)[11]   Geoffrey died 12th December 1212.

(2) William, surnamed Longespée, the date of whose birth is quite uncertain, received a grant of Appleby in Lincolnshire in 1188; married in 1198 Ela or Isabella daughter and heiress of William Earl of Salisbury, and in her right was created Earl of Salisbury.[12]

(3) We also hear of one Morgan, born of the wife of a knight, Ralph Bloet by name.   Morgan must have been in Holy Orders, as in 1212 he was elected Bishop of Durham by the monks, but rejected by the Pope on account of his illegitimacy.[13]   He was presumably the son of some Welsh lady.

To revert to the fair Rosamond and her history.   She was the daughter of a Herefordshire Baron, Walter Clifford.[14]   There is no real evidence that she had any son by Henry; she died apparently a considerable time before him.[15]   The story that she was kept in a maze at Woodstock,[16]

[1] R. de Monte.

[2] Diceto, I. 334; Green, *Princesses*, I. 264.

[3] Green, *sup.* 303.   She lies beside her husband in a charming Church of Early Pointed Style and Angevin character, her work, at Las Huelgas near Burgos.

[4] R. de Monte.   [5] Ben. P., I. 157, 169.

[6] Green, *sup.* 361-367.

[7] Diceto, I. 325.

[8] He had barely completed his fourth *lustrum* (his twentieth year) when he was elected Bishop of Lincoln in April 1173; Giraldus, IV. 363; the same writer again says that he was about forty years old in 1192, p. 384.

[9] Ben. P. I., 271, etc.

[10] Giraldus, VIII. 165, 166.

[11] *De Nugis*, 228, 235; Giraldus, VII. xxxvii., note Dymock.

[12] G. E. C. Peerage.

[13] R. Graystanes, *Hist. Dun. Scriptt. Tres.* 35.

[14] Hundred Rolls, II, 93, 94; *Monasticon*, IV. 366.

[15] Brompton, c. 1151; H. Knighton, II. 149 (Rolls Series, No. 91).   [16] *Id.*

to hide her from Queen Eleanor, but that Eleanor found her, and poisoned her, is disposed of by the fact that Eleanor was apparently not released from custody till long after Rosamond's death. She was certainly buried at Godstow nunnery, a house that Henry enriched for her sake.[1] In 1191 St. Hugh of Lincoln, in the course of a visitation of his diocese, came to Godstow, and finding that her body had been laid in a place of honour in front of the altar, ordered it to be exhumed, and buried in the church-yard outside.[2]

The age could not fail to be shocked by the unfilial conduct and general wickedness of Henry's sons. The feeling found expression in suggestions of a diabolical origin[3] for which the lives of the earlier Counts of Anjou gave no warrant. According to Giraldus the Patriarch Heraclius, when at Dover, about to leave England, disappointed at the failure of his mission vented his wrath on Henry by telling him that his sons might well be a trouble to him as they came from the Devil, and would go to the Devil.[4] Such an utterance could only be credited if reported by one who heard it. But Giraldus at the time was not with the king, but with John in the West. Brompton the 14th century writer puts the words in the mouth of St. Bernard as a malediction pronounced on Henry himself in his infancy.[5]

---

[1] *Monasticon, sup.*; Ben. P., II. 231, 232.

[2] Ben. P., *sup.* See the article in the Dicty. of National Biography.

[3] See the wild legend of a nameless Countess of Anjou who vanished into space on being compelled to stay out the whole of Mass. Giraldus, VIII. 301. According to him the Satanic origin was a common matter of jest with Richard I. But Richard was not profane or irreverent in his attitude to religion. Other writers connect the legend with the families of Valence and Lusignan; G. F. Warner.

[4] " De diabolo venerunt et ad diabolum ibunt," VIII. 211.

[5] Scriptores Decem., c. 1040.

CHAPTER XV

RICHARD I. *"CŒUR DE LION"*[1]

*" Ricard li Peitevins
Murra en Limousins."*[2]

Born at Oxford, 8th September, 1157;[3] Count of Poitiers and Duke of Aquitaine, 1171;[4] Duke of Normandy, 20th July, 1189; crowned King of England, 3rd September, 1189; died 6th April, 1199.

A.D. 1189–1190

Accession and coronation—Arrangements for the Government of England during Richard's absence—Sale of Offices—The Hackington Foundation—Treaty of Falaise-Valognes cancelled—The King abroad again—Dissensions at Home—Longchamps and Puiset—Outrages on the Jews.

FROM his father's grave at Fontevrault the young Count of Poitiers and Duke of Aquitaine hastened off to establish himself in his new

First Acts.

dominions, and first and foremost in the rich Duchy of Normandy. His natural brother Geoffrey the Chancellor had already delivered to him the late King's Seal, which had been sealed up with the seals of the barons in attendance at the funeral.[5] Richard met with no opposition; he was not a statesman, or a politician; but he was not vindictive; and he showed good sense by promptly coming to an understanding with the barons who had sided with his father and against himself in the late war. These were at once admitted to make their

---

[1] This epithet seems first to occur in Trivet, a writer of the time of Edward I.; "cor leonis appellatus"; *Annales*, p. 161 (Engl. Hist. Socy.). But the simple 'Lion' is common among the writers of the time; *e.g.*, Hoveden, IV. 84; *Itinerary of Richard*, *passim*. For Lions as the cognisance on his shield see the contemporary Le Breton. "Ecce comes Pictavus . . . rictus agnosco leonum Illius in clypeo." Bouquet, XVII. 154.

[2] M. Paris, *Hist. Angl.*, II. 191; marginal addition. Compare the fellow distich as to John's death (*Ib.*) both evidently being records of past events given as prophecies.

[3] Chronicle of Angers, Labbe, *Bibl. MSS.*, I. 276; Diceto, I. 302; R. Monte, 195. Richard was nursed by an Englishwoman, who appears in the public records under the (Latinised?) name of "Hodierna"; a name that still lives in the parish of Knoyle Hodierne, Wilts, where land was given to her; Bp. Stubbs, Hoveden, III. xviii.

[4] Above 96, 100.

[5] Giraldus, IV. 372. Nevertheless Geoffrey was taxed with having sealed some clerical appointments after his father's death; Hoveden, III. 274.

RICHARD THE FIRST   [To face page 262.

peace, all but the Seneschal of Anjou, Stephen, styled of Turnham in England, and of Marçai in Anjou; who was put into bonds, it has been suggested, for not promptly delivering treasures that he had not got to deliver.[1] But after a short incarceration we shall find him restored to favour, and thereafter showing himself a most useful and faithful servant. With regard to the men who, like Ralph of Fougères, and Geoffrey of Mayenne, had deserted his father for him, Richard, with less good grace, assuming a high moral tone, confiscated their estates for disloyalty to their lord. This principle however was not applied to John, who had disappeared since the day that Henry fled from Le Mans. He was received with all brotherly cordiality.[2] Of course he made no claim to retain the castles lately entrusted to him in Normandy. The Archbishops of Canterbury and Rouen were prompt to greet their new master, coming to meet him at Séez, on his way to Rouen; and at their hands Richard received absolution from sentences incurred by him through his war against his father. But it is curious to note that the *gravamen* of his offence seemingly was not so much waging war against his father, as taking up arms against a brother Crusader,[3] the Church precept overriding the primary moral law. The installation as Duke of Normandy took place on

Installation as Duke of Normandy. the 20th July, in the cathedral at Rouen, when Richard was girt with the ducal sword, and presented with the banner of the Duchy. Homage by the Barons followed.[4] In honour of the occasion a series of royal grants were announced, as if the Duke were already full King of England. But Richard was not a man to stand

Royal Grants. upon constitutional niceties. John was confirmed in the County of Mortain, and the large estates he held in England through his father's grants.[5] Richard also confirmed certain matrimonial schemes, involving the disposition of further fiefs. John would marry Hawise or Isabella[6] of Gloucester; William Marshal would marry Isabella of Striguil and Pembroke, while Gilbert fitz Renfrid received the hand of the heiress of Lancaster. Geoffrey the Chancellor was named

[1] Ben. P. II., 71, 72; *Mareschal*, I. 336-340; for the empty state of the treasury, *Id.* 331; Norgate.

[2] Ben. P., 72.

[3] Diceto, II. 67.

[4] Ben. P., 73; Diceto, *sup.*; *Mareschal*, 344.

[5] Ben. P., *sup.*; W. Newb., I. 301; R. Devizes (Rolls Series, No. 82, Vol. II.) p. 285. Bishop Stubbs questions whether the County of Mortain had been really given by Henry to John. "It was in the King's hands in 1180, and was perhaps promised rather than given by Henry to John." In fact John does not appear to sign as Count of Mortain before Richard's accession. See Mr. Round's *Calendar of Documents.* For the estates and emoluments in England enjoyed by John see Pipe Roll, 1 Ric. I., *passim*, and Hoveden III., xxvi., where I would take the lower of the two sets of figures given by the Bishop.

[6] She makes a convention with the King of France as "Ysabellis" *Trésor des Chartes.*, Cited G.E.C. Peerage "Pembroke." Above 195, 213.

for the Archbishopric of York ; while lastly the hand of Richard's niece Matilda of Saxony was bestowed on Geoffrey, son of the Border potentate Rotrou III. of Perche.[1] This alliance would give protection to the frontiers of Normandy and Maine in case of trouble.

Within two days of his installation as Duke Richard had a conference

Conference with Philip II. with Philip II., between Trie and Chaumont. The historic elm tree of Gisors, of course, was no longer standing. Richard did homage ; but Philip again preferred the old demand for Gisors and the Norman Vexin ; and was again put off with a promise, now formally given by Richard himself, that he would marry Alais. But the Duke had also to undertake that he would pay the 20,000 marks stipulated by the treaty of Azai, with a further subsidy of 4,000 marks for Philip's 'expenses.' Both pledged themselves to start for Holy Land in Lent. With regard to the places won by Philip from Henry II. in Berri, he would retain them for a time, as material guarantees.[2]

About the 12th August, as we may suppose, Richard and John sailed

Crossing to England. from Barfleur, but in separate ships, as Richard landed at Portsmouth on the 13th August, while his brother sailed on to Dover.[3] We are told that Richard was received with much joy.[4] A new reign naturally excites hopes and expectations for the future. But Richard's merits must have been taken very much on trust. An Angevin on his father's side, and a Poitevin on his mother's side, a Poitevin in education and feeling, he was altogether a Frenchman, and to his future Insular subjects must have been an absolute stranger. Since the time of his infancy he had paid just two short visits to England, namely, one at Easter 1176, and one at Christmas 1184.[5] For all popular rights he must have had an absolute contempt. His life, as we have seen, had been spent in ruthless warfare, either against Aquitanian barons, or his own brothers, or his father ; and this warfare, as waged, apart from sieges, meant the raiding of defenceless villages and homesteads. But for the time he was endeavouring, not without success, to win popularity.[6] Before leaving Normandy he had reinstated the Earl of Leicester and others who had suffered for complicity in the rebellion.[7] Orders had also

---

[1] Ben. P., *sup.* and notes ; W. Newb., I. 300. For the disposition of the hand of the Gloucester heiress, third daughter of Earl William, see above 195. For the original promises of Strongbow's daughter to William Marshal, see *W. Mareschal*, I. 299, 300. The Lancaster heiress was Halewise, daughter of William of Lancaster, Lord of Kendal ; Hoveden, *sup.*, note.

[2] 22nd July, Ben. P., II. 73, 74 ; Hoveden, III. 1, 2 ; modified by Gervase, I. 450.

[3] Ben. P., 75 ; Hoved., 5.

[4] Ben, P., *sup.* ; W. Newb., I., 293.

[5] See above, under the years in question.

[6] "Omnibus benigne loquebatur, · qui ad eum veniebant. Unde amabilis valde inprimis effectus est" ; Gervase, I. 451.

[7] Ben. P., II., 75.

been sent in advance for the final liberation of Eleanor,[1] who, except when

Queen Eleanor set free. wanted for great occasions or State appearances had still been kept in detention at Winchester. The relations of Richard to his mother give the most pleasing side of the two lives. Assuming at once the Regency on behalf of her son the Queen started on a progress in Royal style, proclaiming release of prisoners—more especially of those charged with Forest offences—and exacting oaths of allegiance from all freemen to ' Richard lord of England ' (*domino Angliæ*).[2]

Richard's first steps after landing were directed to Winchester, to

Royal Progress. secure the treasure there, and receive homage from a concourse of magnates assembled for the purpose.[3] From Winchester he went on to Salisbury, where he met his mother, continuing his tour through the country while preparations were being made for the coronation under Eleanor's directions.[4] In connexion with this progress we hear of further grants. The hand of Denise of Deols, the heiress of Châteauroux,[5] was given to Andrew of Chauvigny, a follower who had been with Richard in the recent war against his father.[6] It will be remembered that to get the keeping of the heiress of Châteauroux Henry had waged war in Berri in 1177. On the 29th August John's

Marriage of John. wedding to the Gloucester heiress was celebrated at Marlborough, in spite of protests entered by Archbishop Baldwin, on the ground that the parties were related in the third degree.[7] It was at this time most likely that John received confirmation

Further Benefactions. of the whole Honour of Gloucester (£500 a year) with the third penny of the county (£20 a year); the control of the county itself with the castle remaining in the King's hands. Further grants made to John down to the time of the coronation, or any

---

[1] *Id.*, 74; Diceto, II. 67, who here repeats the assertion of other writers that Eleanor had been sixteen years in confinement, 1173-1189. According to the *Mareschal*, I. 343, the order of her release was brought by William Marshal.

[2] Ben. P., II. 74; Hoveden, III. 4; *q.v.* for the terms on which the different classes of malefactors would be set free, as to bail, and the like; Diceto II., 67; W. Newb., I. 293.

[3] 14th August, Gervase, I. 457; 15th August, Diceto, *sup.* Of the amount of the treasure Benedict, p. 77, gives the absurd estimate of £900,000, where perhaps we should, as Bishop Stubbs suggests, read *nonaginta* (90,000) for *nongenta*. Hoveden, III. 8, talks of 100,000 marks, £66,000; but Henry's Will only affected to dispose of 40,500 marks.

[4] Ben. P., *sup.*; Diceto, II. 68

[5] " Dionysia"; Labbe, *Bibl. MSS.*, II. 740; Stubbs.

[6] Ben. P., 76; *Mareschal*, I. 311, 312. There seems to be some confusion about the lady given in marriage to Andrew of Chauvigny: Benedict says that she had been the wife of Baldwin of Redvers Earl of Devon; the writer of the *Mareschal* says that she was unmarried and young (*pucele, meschine*), 398. Baldwin, who died without issue in 1180, no doubt was married to an heiress of Châteauroux (G. G. C. *Peerage*, Doyle). Perhaps she too was dead, and Denise may have been her younger sister.

[7] Ben. P., 78; Gervase, I. 458.

rate down to the time of the Michaelmas audit were ; the farm-rent of Lancaster (£200) ; the Honour of Tickhill (£85) ; " Hecham " Northants (Higham-Ferrers ?) £120 ; Orford (£40) ; Hanley (£20) ; and the Forest of Sherwood (£20) in all £997.[1]   It will be noticed that in no case was any castle committed to John's keeping.   But Richard's wish to court public favour did not restrain him from laying hands on the treasure and effects of Geoffrey Riddel, Bishop of Ely, who died on the 21st August.[2]

For the Coronation the day fixed was Sunday, 3rd September, an odd choice, the day being held one of the *Dies Œgyptiaci*, days pronounced by **The Coronation.** Egyptian astrologers of old to be unlucky ; days on which no business of any importance should be taken in hand.[3] Richard loved pomp, as much as his father hated it, and the etiquette at the new King's coronation was supposed to have set precedents for subsequent occasions.   But the real interest of the proceedings lies in their close conformity to the original rites of which we first heard in the time of Eadgar.   In fact the one set of records may be used to supplement the others.[4]   Among the dignitaries present on the occasion were Queen Eleanor, and the unfortunate Alais[5] ; the Duke of Saxony, with his son William and a daughter ;[6] four Arch-bishops (Canterbury, Rouen, Dublin, and Trèves) with a host of Lords Spiritual and Temporal from England, Wales, and Ireland.[7]

Of the state ride from the Tower to Westminster, found on later occasions as taking place on the day before the hallowing, the institution of which we were inclined to ascribe to the time of the Conqueror, we hear nothing : nor can we say whether the formal election in West-minster Hall, before the move to the Abbey, took place or not, though it is certain that some form of election was gone through, as we shall see ; but in fact the recorded proceedings begin at the King's chamber,[8] from whence he was led to the Abbey in procession, in the following order :—

---

[1] See the entries in the Pipe Roll, 1 Rich. I., which differ materially from the grants alleged in Benedict, 78.

[2] Diceto, II. 68.   The money was sent from Cambridge to London, but not passed through the Exchequer ; Pipe Roll, 1 Rich. I., p. 188.

[3] " Dies mala " ; Ben P. ; " Dies Œgyptiacus " ; W. Newb., I. 294.   For the superstition see Brand, *Popular Antiqq.*, II. 27, and Ducange, " Dies."

[4] See *Foundations of England*, I. 319, 328 ; and the formularies printed, Maskell *Monum. Rit.*, II. 4, 32.

[5] So I understand " Soror regis Franciæ," Pipe Roll, 223.

[6] To avoid accompanying the Emperor on his Crusade Henry had again gone into exile ; Ben. P., II. 62.   See also Pipe Roll, 1 Rich. I., 196, 223, 240, etc.   The Duchess had died in June or July.

[7] See Ben. P., II. 80, and Hoveden, III. 8.

[8] " Ad ostium thalami regis interioris."   Benedict, II. 80 ; Hoveden, III. 9.

The Procession.			
	The lesser Clergy with Holy Water, Cross, Tapers, and Thurible		
	The Abbots		
	The Bishops		
Geoffrey of Lucy (The Cap)		John Marshal [1] (The Spurs)	
William Longsword Earl of Salisbury (The Rod *Virga*) Robert of Beaumont III. Earl of Leicester (Sword of State)	John Earl of Mortain and Gloucester (Sword of State " *Curtana* ") [3]	William Marshal Earl of Pembroke [2] (The Sceptre) David Earl of Huntingdon (Sword of State)	

Baron		Baron
Baron	Chequer Board (*Scaccarium*) with Regalia and Robes	Baron
Baron		Baron

William of Mandeville
Earl of Essex and *jure uxoris*
Earl of Aumâle
(The Crown)

Reginald fitz Jocelin Bishop of Bath	RICHARD DUKE OF NORMANDY under a canopy of silk supported on lances by four Barons of the Cinque Ports. [4]	Hugh of Puiset Bishop of Durham

On reaching the Abbey 'Duke Richard' would take his seat, not on the throne, but on a chair, probably in front of the throne, on a raised platform, with steps leading up to it, in the middle of the crossing. The appeal to the people would then follow. [5] This essential part of the proceedings is not expressly noticed by the writers of the time; but we are bound to assume that either that, or a form of election in Westminster Hall, or both, took place, because Ralph of Diceto, who as Dean of St. Paul's was present and taking

[1] Elder brother of William the newly created Earl of Pembroke. He was probably lord or constable of Marlborough, where he died shortly.

[2] William was not fully invested with the Earldom till the accession of John. Before that time he does sign but only occasionally as Earl; after that he signs regularly as such. Hoveden, IV. 90 ; Diceto, II. 156 ; Round, *Calendar of Docts.*, 495.

[3] This name, however, first occurs in connexion with the coronation of Henry III.'s Queen Eleanor. *Red Book Exche*, II. 756.

[4] Hoveden, III. 9, 10. For the Barons of the Cinque Ports see *Epp. Cantuar.*, 308 ; their privilege is stated to be of ancient date. The canopy (pallium) went to Canterbury.

[5] I venture to take this from the later *Liber Regalis* kept at Westminster, *Coronation Records* (L. G. Wickham Legg). For the appeal to the people see p. 81 ; the sedes in pulpito on which the King first sits is clearly distinguished from the thronus or solium to which he is taken at last, 81, 84, 99.

a part in the ceremony [1] tells us that the coronation oath was only administered 'after formal and due election by clergy and people.' [2] The 'election' having been carried by acclamation the antiphon *Firmetur Manus Tua* would be sung, and the King brought down to the altar to present his offering, namely a vestment (*pallium*) and one pound weight of gold. The Litany followed, the King kneeling; and after that a short sermon, and then the coronation oath. [3] The strict formula was

The Oath. adhered to, Richard swearing to maintain Church and people in good peace to the best of his ability; to put down all wrong doing; and to temper justice with mercy. [4] The fine series of prayers of consecration *Omnipotens Sempiterne Deus—Benedic Domine—Deus Ineffabilis*, would then be uttered, to lead up to the hallowing, the central point of the whole service. [5] For the actual unction the King elect was

The Hallowing. undressed to his shirt and drawers, the disrobing taking place under the cover of a canopy held reverentially over the Royal person. [6] He was then anointed with holy oil in three places, namely, on the chest and the two shoulders. [7] For the anointing of the shoulders slits had to be prepared in the shirt; [8] in front the garment, of course, would naturally be open. The head received a special anointing with chrism, holy oil mingled with balsam, an unguent appointed to be used only at baptism, confirmation, and ordination. Its use, therefore, at the hallowing of a King shows that that rite was reckoned an ordination. The chrism having been administered the head was bound up with a chrism-cloth, not to be removed till the eighth day. The process of redressing the King then began. First he was clothed with tunic and dalmatic, while the Cap

Insignia. of Dignity or Maintenance, was placed on his head over the chrism cloth, and his feet shod with sandals or buskins laced with gold—the boots in which he had walked from the Abbey having apparently been removed for the hallowing. [9] Investiture with spurs, sword,

---

[1] He was filling the place of the Bishop of London, the See being vacant; II. 69.

[2] "Post tam cleri quam populi sollempnem et debitam electionem"; p. 68.

[3] *Coronation Records*, 30, 85–87.

[4] See Diceto, *sup.*, where the oath is correctly given; not so by Benedict and the later writers, who represent Richard as only swearing to keep the church and her ministers in good peace—a clear attempt at clerical aggression.

[5] See *Coronation Records*, 31, 89.

[6] Benedict, II. 82; Hoveden, III. 10; *Liber Regalis*, 91, 92.

[7] "Unxit eum in regem, in tribus locis, videlicet in capite, in pectore, in brachiis"; Hoved., *sup.* Here the writer must have reckoned the anointing of the two shoulders as one act, as with the head the King was touched in four places. Mr. Legg points out that Becket writing to Henry speaks of Kings being anointed "in capite, in pectore, in brachiis"; and that he assigns the same emblematic meanings to the several anointings, namely, gloria, fortitudo, scientia. *Becket* V. 280.

[8] "Camisia dissuta in scapulis"; Ben. P. and Hoveden, *sup.*, *Liber Regalis*, 91.

[9] For the caligæ tantummodo" with which the King was to be dressed in the morning, see *Liber Regalis*, 83.

' armil' or stole, and mantle came next.[1] The King, having thus been symbolically invested with the primary requisites for the discharge of his duties, was led up to the altar to receive the highest emblems of authority. With his own hand taking the crown from off the altar he handed it to **Coronation.** Archbishop Baldwin, by whom it was placed on his head. But we are told that before he was allowed to take the crown from off the altar Baldwin adjured him in the name of the Almighty not to assume it unless he was prepared to keep his oaths; and that Richard answered, that, with God's help, he would. Having been crowned he received the ring, sceptre, and rod, all with the appropriate Benedictions.[2] The chanting of the *Te Deum* followed, while the crowned anointed King was being led up to and established on the throne on the central platform. The *Te Deum* ended, the Archbishop **Enthrone-** pronounced the grand concluding *Sta et Retine*. Mass ended **ment.** the rites, the King communicating.[3]

From the Abbey the King, still wearing his crown, and carrying sceptre and rod, was taken back in procession to his apartments. The usual coronation banquet followed, none but the prelates sitting at **The** the King's table, the earls and barons sitting at tables apart.[4] **Banquet.** Among the supplies laid in for the occasion we have 1900 chickens, at a cost of rather more than a penny apiece, with 1000 platters (*scutellæ*), wooden of course, and 200 tankards (*scyphi*), costing one with another not quite a farthing apiece.[5]

But as if to exemplify the rashness of disregarding times and seasons, and days of good or bad luck, the festivities ended in a ghastly turmoil, a signal for the outbreak of wide-spread disturbances. The Jews, who had flourished under Henry II.,[6] anxious to propitiate the new King—whose crusading ardour might excite misgivings—had gathered in **Attack on** London to present a handsome offering. But Richard on **the Jews.** the day before the coronation had issued an order that no member of their persuasion should show his face either in Abbey or Hall. Notwithstanding this prohibition it would seem that some Jews, having ventured to enter the Hall during the banquet, were roughly handled, and

---

[1] See Benedict and Hoveden, *sup.*, the latter correcting the former in some points, comparing *Liber Regalis*, 94, 95. Benedict and Hoveden, however, have the ' sandals' put on before the anointing, which must be wrong. For the Cap, originally a ducal emblem (so worn by the Doges of Venice), see Mr. St. John Hope's monograph contributed to *Coronation Records*, lxxxii.

[2] Benedict, 82; Hoveden, 11; *Coronation Records*, 35, 96. The sceptre was distinguished by a cross at the top, the rod by a dove.

[3] Benedict and Hoveden, *sup.*; *Coronation Records*, 36, 99.

[4] Benedict and Hoveden, *sup.*

[5] Pipe Roll, 1 Ric. I., 233.

[6] So W. Newb., I. 280; and so too the Pipe Rolls of Henry's reign, which clearly show the Jewish community as numerous and well-to-do.

expelled by the door-keepers.　A cry against Jews was quickly raised out-side; a report that the King had given them up to plunder spread like wild-fire; and London was soon a scene of fighting and pillage, Jews' houses being set on fire, and synagogues desecrated.　Richard contented himself with ordering Glanville to quell the disturbance.　But the mob was beyond control, and the city remained in their hands till the morning, when either the fury of the rioters had spent itself, or the forces of order had rallied.　The King was indignant at the breach of his peace; but he had no sense of the gravity of the affair, or of the justice and protection due to the Jews.　We are told that the few offenders who were punished, suffered only for damage incidentally done to Christian property.[1]　The consequence of this criminal laxity was that outbreaks of similar character broke out shortly in most parts of the country.

With his whole soul bent on Crusading adventure, Richard lost no time in making arrangements for the government of England during his absence. There were several Sees to be filled up, and other appointments to be made, as he did not propose to retain all his father's Ministers in office.

Grand Council.　On the 15th September a Grand Council met at Pipewell Abbey, near Geddington, in Northamptonshire.　Two clerical nominations were the outcome of the first day's sitting. Richard fitz Nigel, the Treasurer, the author of the *Dialogus de Scaccario,* **Episcopal Appoint-ments.** was made Bishop of London, a See convenient to be held by one whose services at the Exchequer Board could not be dispensed with; while Godfrey of Lucy, son of the faithful Richard, became Bishop of Winchester.[2]　On the second day, 16th Sep-tember, a mass of business was transacted.　Richard's follower William of Longchamp, who had already been appointed Chancellor,[3] was named **William Longchamp Chancellor.** Bishop of Ely; Hubert Walter, Dean of York, a man of great ability,[4] who had been much employed by the late King, was made Bishop of Salisbury; and Geoffrey the ex-chancellor was confirmed as Archbishop Elect of York.　These last two appointments **Geoffrey Archbishop of York.** should be considered together.　Hubert, with the support of Eleanor and of Glanville, had been resisting the promotion of Geoffrey to the Northern Province, for which he himself had been proposed in 1186, and again after Henry's death.　His nomination to Sarum therefore might be taken as a compromise to get rid of his opposi-tion to the King's brother.　But in fact he was not reconciled to Geoffrey,

[1] See W. Newb., I. 294–299, the best account; Ben. P., II. 83, 84; Hoveden, III. 12; Diceto, II. 69.

[2] Ben. P., II. 85; Hoveden, III. 15; R. Devizes, Chron. Stephen, etc., III. 387.

[3] Longchamp had been Richard's Chancellor before his father's death, and he was continued in the office afterwards.　R. Devizes, 384; Foss. *Judges,* I. 326.

[4] He was nephew to Glanville's wife, and had been trained by the Justiciar; Hook, *Archbishop,* from Dugdale's *Baronage.*

whose position was attacked persistently throughout the reign, he being, no doubt, hot-headed and quarrelsome, while Richard exhibited much vacillation in the matter.[1]   Sundry minor appointments were also made on the same day, Henry Marshal, brother to William, becoming Dean of York; and Bouchard of Puiset, nephew to the Bishop, Treasurer of York.[2]   On

The Regency. the 17th September the all-important question of the Regency was at last taken up.   Glanville, who, as Justiciar, would have been *ex officio* Regent, was got rid of, being allowed to resign on the alleged ground of age, and a desire to fulfil his Crusading vows.   For this kind permission he was fined the bulk of his available fortune.[3]   For the future the Chief Justiciarship would be divided between the Bishop of Durham and the Earl of Essex, with a consultative committee of five, namely the Earl of Pembroke, Geoffrey Fitz Peter, William Brewer, Robert of Whitfield, and Roger fitz Renfrid.[4]   The composition however of this body was subsequently altered by the substitution of Hugh Bardolf for Whitfield and fitz Renfrid.[5]   The arrangement suggests a division of authority between old men and new.   Richard fitz Nigel, and the Earl of Essex were tried servants of Henry II.; Longchamp the Chancellor was new to office in England; the Bishop of Durham was an old rebel, but a man of high connexions in France.   Of the committee as finally settled all were new men.[6]

But Richard had also his military chest to fill.   The Pipewell council saw the beginning of a disgraceful system of the sale of offices, crown rights, crown property, and royal favours.[7]   Under this last

Filling the King's Purse. head we hear that Richard had obtained from Clement III. leave to excuse from the Crusade men required for the government of the country in his absence, that is to say as Richard worked

---

[1] Geoffrey had been elected by part of the Chapter at York, 16th August ˙(1189), Hubert's friends protesting; while Hubert himself entered an appeal to the Pope: see Ben. P., I. 312, II. 77, 78, 85, 91; Giraldus, IV. 373; Hoveden, III. 17; IV. xlvi.; W. Newb., I. 301.   Of course Archbishop Baldwin endeavoured at Pipewell to raise the old question of supremacy, insisting that Geoffrey should be consecrated by him.   Richard after nominating Geoffrey forbade him to apply for his Pallium; Ben. P., II. 92.

[2] Ben. P., II. 85; Hoveden, III. 15-17.

[3] See R. Devizes, *sup.* 385, 386, who regards Glanville as simply turned out of office, and estimates his fine at 15,000 marks.   He adds that if he had been willing to make over to the King the rest of his means he would have been excused the Crusade, where in fact he died at the siege of Acre in the following autumn; *Epp. Cant.*, 329.   William of Newburgh, I. 302, and Benedict, II. 87, accepted the resignation as voluntary.

[4] Ben. P., *sup.*; Hoveden, III. 16; and Bishop Stubbs' note.   They were all leading Justices and so natural advisers to the Great Justiciar.

[5] Ben. P., 101; Hoved., 28; *W. Mareschal*, I. 349; and especially Richard's letter, Diceto, II. 90.

[6] See Foss, *Judges.*

[7] "Omnia ei erant venalia"; Ben. P., 90.   As Hoveden puts it: "Emerunt a rege sua et aliena jura"; 18; also R. Devizes, 386.

it, leave to sell dispensations from Crusading vows.[1] The Bishop of Durham led the way by buying the Wapentake of Sadberge, with all rights, for 600 marks (£400);[2] also the earldom and county of Northumberland for 2000 marks.[3] Richard boasted that he had made a new earl out of an old bishop.[4] But Hugh was also said to have paid, or promised, another 1000 marks for his share of the Justiciarship.[5] So again Longchamp, though the king's own man, was understood to have given £3000 for the Chancery.[6] Godfrey of Lucy the newly appointed Bishop of Winchester, was allowed to secure the sheriffdom of Hampshire, with the castles of Porchester and Winchester; he also bought the royal manors of Meon and Wargrave, worth exactly £200 a year, for £3000, just fifteen years' purchase.[7] Hugh of Nonant, Bishop of Coventry, a personal friend of the king, managed to get the Priory of Coventry for 300 marks: a scandalous job—and the three sheriffdoms of Warwickshire, Leicestershire, and Staffordshire for the further sum of 200 marks.[8] Another "sworn" follower, Gerard of Camville bought Lincolnshire and Lincoln Castle for 700 marks.[9] It is easy to see how much the Government would be crippled in the future, and what a door for malversation would be opened by parting with such jurisdictions upon such terms. From one point of view it would be a return to that feudal administration that Henry had been so anxious to get rid of. In only seven or eight counties were the old sheriffs allowed to remain. Where they were displaced the king would make a double gain; the outgoing men being fined for supposed misconduct; the incoming men fining for admission. The king at last declared that he would sell London if he could find a purchaser.[10]

Sale of Offices.

Relations with the dependencies had also to be settled. John was commissioned to deal with the Welsh, and Geoffrey with the Scots. Rhys ap Gruffudd, the leading Welsh prince of the time, had taken advantage of Henry's death to seize the important stronghold of Llanstephan in the bay of Caermarthen, with other

Foreign Affairs.

---

[1] Hoveden, III. 17.

[2] See the charter dated Gatington, 18th September; Hoveden 13, and again 38.

[3] Pipe Roll, 2 Ric. I. "Ut . . . esset . . . episcopus simul et comes," W. Newb. I., 304; like Odo under the Conqueror.

[4] W. Newb. I., 305; R. Devizes, 386.　　　[5] Ben. P., and Hoveden, *sup.*

[6] R. Devizes, 387.　　　[7] Pipe Rolls, Henry II., *passim*, and 2 Ric. I.

[8] Pipe R., 2 Ric. I., m. 4, a, Madox I., 458. Having bought the Coventry Priory the Bishop proceeded to expel the monks; Gervase, I. 461. He advised the king to do the same by all the monks in England. 'Monks to the devil!' was his *dictum.* "Monachi ad diabolos," *Epp. Cant.*, 318; Gervase, I., 470.

[9] Pipe R., 2 Ric. I.; Bp. Stubbs, Hoved., III. xxix.

[10] W. Newb. I., 305; R. Devizes, 388. Students of the Pipe Rolls will readily believe the hint given by the Dean of St. Paul's that the king had to give liberal credit for the sums stipulated; Diceto II., 73.

places as well. John was sent down with an army for which a scutage of

Wales. 10*s.* on the knight's fee was levied.[1] No hostilities took place, John halting at Worcester, content with the appearance there of all the Welsh magnates, except Rhys.[2] Further pressure having been been brought to bear on the Southern Prince he allowed himself to be brought under John's escort to Oxford, on the understanding that Richard would come to meet him, as Henry had been in the habit of doing. But Richard, who was at Westminster at the time,[3] could not be troubled with a journey to Oxford, merely to receive the homage of a Welshman, and so Rhys went home in mighty affront.[4]

William the Lion had not attended the coronation, and had neglected other invitations to the English court, demanding the personal escort of

William the Lion. the Archbishop-elect of York ; and, accordingly, Geoffrey was sent up to the Border in November to fetch the King.[5] While he was away, apparently, two grand Councils were held, one in London, the other at Canterbury. The first was held to meet an embassy from Philip who asked for a positive assurance as to Richard's intentions

France. with regard to the Crusade. The Earl of Essex was instructed to assure him that the English King would be at Vézelai by 1st April without fail. The Earl went, never to return, as he died in Normandy on the 14th November.[6]

The Canterbury assembly was convened primarily to settle the terrible

Archbishop Baldwin and the Canterbury Monks. quarrel between the monks and the Archbishop that had harassed the last days of Henry II. The dispute, that originated in Baldwin's attempt to establish a college for secular canons at Hackington near Cambridge, out of revenues that otherwise would have gone to the Canterbury monks, had been aggravated by an injudicious act on his part in appointing one Roger Norrey to be Prior against the wishes of the Convent. Heated discussions held at Westminster in the presence of the King and bishops on the 8th and 9th October had failed to induce the monks to submit their case to arbitration.[7] Baldwin then sent down a body of troops and actually blockaded the monks in their conventual buildings from the 11th to the 14th November in order to starve them into submission.[8] Under this pressure the monks gave way, and then the Grand Council was summoned to consider the whole question.[9] But before it met the situation had been

---

[1] *Red Book Exch.* I. 9, 70, etc. ; apparently some tenants were required to send men and some to send money.

[2] September? Ben. P., II. 87, 88 ; Brut. y. T. 235.

[3] See the charters cited by Bishop Stubbs, Ben. P., II. 97.

[4] October ; Ben. P., *sup.* ; Hoveden III., 23.   [5] Ben. P., *sup.* ; Hoveden, 24.

[6] R. Diceto II., 71, 73 ; Ben. P., 92, 93 ; Hoveden, 19 ; R. Devizes, 389

[7] See *Epp. Cant.*, 308–318 ; Gervase, 459–472. The writer was present.

[8] *Epp.* 318, 319 ; Gervase, 372, 373.   [9] Gervase, 373, 374.

complicated by the unsolicited appearance of a Cardinal, John of Anagni, who landed at Dover on the 20th November. Richard was at a distance, but Eleanor, who was at Canterbury, sent to warn the Legate that he must not proceed beyond Dover without the King's leave, and at Dover he had to remain thirteen days.[1] The Cardinal had been commissioned by Clement III. who favoured the monks, to settle the matter.[2] But Richard, who wisely preferred to determine the question himself, had politely requested the Legate to devote his time to the collection of the Saladin tithe in Poitou; and had given him no invitation to cross the Channel.[3] On the 26th November the King came to Canterbury;[4] on the 28th of the month the monks' affair was taken up, and after two more days of contention a certain settlement was effected, the Archbishop agreeing to cancel the appointment of the Prior, to remove his foundation to another place, and to restore the convent estates of which he had taken possession.[5] In pursuance of this compromise Baldwin gave orders for the demolition of the collegiate buildings at Hackington, and the removal of the **Foundation at Lambeth.** materials to Lambeth, where he had acquired a site of twenty-four acres through an exchange of land effected with the Rochester Chapter. The Hackington chapel remained. But even this could not be tolerated. On the 21st July, 1191, under orders from Celestine III. the services were stopped and the whole fabric pulled down.[6]

The monastic grievance having been got out of the way the Cardinal was allowed to come to Canterbury, and received with all due honour.[7] The attention of the Council moreover could then be given to matters of State.

I. The King of Scots who had been brought to Canterbury by Geoffrey **Treaty of Falaise-Valognes cancelled.** was allowed in consideration of 1000 marks to emancipate himself from the trammels imposed on him by the treaty of Falaise-Valognes, and to recover his castles of Roxburgh and Berwick (Edinburgh had already been restored), with all the estates in Huntingdonshire or elsewhere in England at any time held by his brother Malcolm. Richard also released the homages of the under-tenants of Scotland that had been exacted by Henry, thus making William fully master of his own dominions. For the future it was agreed that

---

[1] Ben. P., II. 97; Diceto, II. 72; *Fpp.*, 321.

[2] *Epp.*, 286, 287.

[3] *Epp.*, 300, 310

[4] *Fœdera*, I. 49.

[5] 30th Nov., Gervase, I. 481; 29th Nov., Diceto, I. 72; the formal award published by the King, apparently to soothe the feelings of the Archbishop, is dated 1st Dec. *Epp. Cant.*, 322. See also Ben. P., II. 97, 98; Hoveden, III. 23, 24; and for the discussion Gervase, 478–481.

[6] See Gervase, 483, 484, 499, 500; *Epp. Cant.*, 335–341; and esp. Bishop Stubbs' rehearsal of the whole affair, lxxiv., lxxix., and xci.

[7] Dec. 3rd? Gervase, 481, 482; Ben. P. and Diceto, *sup.*

William should render to the King of England whatever Malcolm IV. had rightfully rendered, and was bound to render to Richard's predecessors; he again rendering to William whatever his predecessors had rightfully rendered and were bound to render to Malcolm in the matter of safe-conducts to come and go to and from the English court, with suitable entertainment.   Further details were left to be settled by the arbitration of eight barons, four from each side.   The treaty, so far, simply remitted the parties to their former positions, with respect to which, as we know, it had been disputed whether the homage of the Scottish Kings was rendered for the crown of Scotland, or only for the English estates.   But a further clause dealing specifically with the question of future homage declares that William shall be Richard's liege man ' for all lands for which his predecessors had been the liege men of Richard's predecessors,' thus tacitly excluding all homage for the Scottish crown; and so " Benedict " and Hoveden regarded the treaty, taking it as a simple renunciation of all homage for Scotland.[1]

No Homage for the Scottish Crown.

II. How John would behave during his brother's absence must have been one of the gravest uncertainties of the moment.   No place had been assigned to him in the government.   Richard apparently thought that his best chance was to earn John's gratitude by unbounded liberality, and so he now conferred upon him a perfect principality in the West, making over to him all Crown rights over Dorset, Somerset, Devon, and Cornwall.[2]

Grants to John.

III. In Eleanor Richard had a devoted mother, and one whom he could fully trust to defend his interests to the utmost of her power.   He now assigned to her by way of dower all that his father had assigned to her, with all that either Henry I. had assigned to Matilda, or Stephen to his Queen.[3]

Eleanor's Dower.

IV. Geoffrey, through gross imprudence in attacking the King's appointments to the Deanery and Treasurership of York,[4] perfectly regular appointments, had brought down fresh trouble on his own head.   The Bishop of Durham and Hubert Walter, at the instigation of the King,[5] renewed their objections to Geoffrey's election, appealing to the Legate; but the Cardinal, glad of an opportunity of exercising his authority, quashed the appeal, and confirmed the election.[6]

Geoffrey confirmed as Archbishop.

---

[1] See the treaty from the original, *Fœdera*, I. 50, drawn up on the 5th December, the day when Richard left Canterbury; Ben. P., II. 98, 102; Hoveden, III. 25.   The Melrose chronicle, of course, takes the same view of the homage as Benedict and Hoveden.

[2] Ben. P., 99; Hoveden, 27; less correctly, W. Newb., I. 301.

[3] Ben. P. and Hoveden, *sup.*   [4] See above, 271: Ben. P., II. 91, and Hoved., III. 17.

[5] So Giraldus in his *Life of Geoffrey*, IV. 376.

[6] *Id.* ; Ben. P. and Hoveden, *sup.*   John's act was confirmed by the Pope 7th March, 1190; Diceto, II. 79.

V. Another appeal there was that the Legate was able to entertain,
doubtless with equal satisfaction to himself. Archbishop
Baldwin, not content with a mere protest against John's
marriage to the Gloucester heiress, had actually laid her lands
under Interdict. At John's petition the Cardinal dissolved
the Interdict and confirmed the marriage.[1]

Objection to John's Marriage quashed.

On the 5th December the long Canterbury Council at last broke up;
Richard, followed by the Legate and Geoffrey, proceeding to Dover. He
was extremely indignant at the action of the Legate, but Geoffrey, at last
realising that the only access to his brother's goodwill lay through his
pocket, offered 2000 marks for a settlement of all questions. The offer
was accepted, and Geoffrey received the kiss of peace. But on leaving
Dover he was followed by the Vice-Chancellor, John of Alençon, to inform
him that 2000 marks would not suffice, he must make the sum £2000.[2]

On Monday 11th December the King crossed from Dover to Calais,
the Cardinal and others going with him.[3] Short as his stay in England
had been it must have been long enough to dispel all illusions for the
future. Divided rule is seldom satisfactory to the governed,
and Richard's scheme was based on division of authority.
The death of the Earl of Essex, no doubt, left the Bishop of
Durham sole Justiciar, no fresh coadjutor having been appointed. Longchamp, in the minor position of Chancellor, seemed his only rival. But
Hugh's misgivings must have been excited when Richard on leaving
England committed the Tower to the Chancellor, giving Puiset only the
less important charge of Windsor Castle.[4] No two men less
fitted to act together could well have been found. Hugh was
somewhat of a Prince-Bishop of the German type, a man of
the highest connexions, described as nephew to King Stephen, and great-
grandson of the Conqueror.[5] "He had headed the garrisons and trained
the soldiers of his uncle of Winchester when Henry II. was yet a child."
For six-and-thirty years he had ruled the patrimony of St. Cuthbert with
a splendour not yet forgotten. A left-handed connexion with a lady of
the House of Percy added to his local influence. He is described as a
man of commanding presence and grand looks, eloquent and energetic,
of artistic tastes, an experienced intriguer, and a thorough politician.[6]

Outlook in England.

Bishop Puiset.

---

[1] Diceto, II. 72.

[2] For the details see Ben. P., II. 100; Hoveden, III. 27, 28; Giraldus, IV., 378–380.

[3] Ben. P., 101; Hoveden, 28; Diceto makes Richard cross from Dover to Gravelines
on the 14th December; II. 73.

[4] Ben. P., II. 101; Hoveden, III. 28.

[5] Bishop Stubbs, tracing the difficult question of Puiset's relationship to the House of
Blois, comes to the conclusion that his mother Agnes must have been an unknown
daughter of Count Stephen and Adela; Hoved., III. xxxiii.

[6] Bishop Stubbs, *sup.* xxxv., with the authorities there cited.

William of Longchamp was a man of comparatively modest family.[1]
He had gained Richard's confidence as a clerk in his Chancery, rising
to be his Chancellor. He was short and lame; ignorant of
English, and hating all things English; ambitious, resolute,
and unscrupulous; faithful to his master, domineering to all
others; a thorough French fighting official; a true *ministre de combat.*[2]

Chancellor Longchamp.

Such colleagues as Puiset and Longchamp could not fail to quarrel;
and the Chancellor, strong in the confidence of Richard's support, opened
the offensive as soon as he had been fairly enthroned as Bishop.[3] His
first step was to forbid the Justiciar to appear at the council-
table, at which he ought to preside; his next to deprive him
of the sheriffdom of Northumberland. Other recent grants

The Two at War.

were revoked with equal audacity. Godfrey Lucy, the Bishop of
Winchester, was deprived of his county and castles.[4] A whole crop of
complaints speedily followed the King to Normandy. After spending
Christmas at Bures he had held interviews with Philip at the ford of
St. Rémy, near Nonancourt, on the 30th December and the 13th January
(1190), with a third conference on the 15th March. Their treaties of
amity were fully confirmed, but the trysting-day was adjourned from the
1st April to the 24th of June.[5] To meet the complaints from England, the
Queen, Alais, John, Geoffrey, Archbishop Baldwin, and all the leading
Prelates were summoned to Normandy for a Grand Council to be held in
February or March. But the wily Chancellor had taken care to come
beforehand to secure the Royal ear. The result of the Councils was the
confirmation of William's acts, and the further enhancement of his
authority. He was appointed Chief Justiciar for England
South of the Humber, the Bishop of Durham's sphere being
restricted to the districts North of that line; while applications

Longchamp exalted.

were made to the Pope for a Legatine Commission for Longchamp, to be
held during Baldwin's absence on the Crusade, so as to make
him supreme both in Church and State.[6] John and Geoffrey
were bound down on oath not to return to England for three

A Legatine Commission.

years. From Geoffrey there really was nothing to be feared; not so with

[1] His family however were gentle-folk; his grandfather held lands in England, *Id.*,
xxxviii.

[2] See *Id.*, xl.-xliii., 142; R. Devizes, 339; Giraldus, IV. 420–426.

[3] 6th January, 1190, Diceto, II. 75.

[4] R. Devizes, 389. It has been suggested that the purchase money had not been paid,
but such sums could only be paid by instalments.

[5] D.ceto, 73, 77; Ben. P., 104, 105, and notes; Hoveden, III. 30. The death of the
Queen of France, Isabel of Hainault, who died on the day of the last meeting, was one
cause of the delay.

[6] Ben. P., II. 105, 106; Hoveden, III. 32, 33; R. Devizes, 389. Baldwin sailed for
Palestine on the 6th March; Gervase, I. 485. Clement granted Longchamp the
Legatine Commission, 5th June, 1190; Diceto, II. 83.

regard to John.   But Richard, with his usual easy-going trustfulness, at
Eleanor's request, shortly released John from his pledge.[1]

One lamentable outcome of the Crusading movement was the growth of
fanatical intolerance, and the spirit of religious persecution.   It would
seem that after the coronation outrages, Richard had issued a proclamation
taking the Jews under his protection.[2]   But his laxity in dealing

Attacks on Jews. with the original offences must be held responsible for the
disorders that followed.   A series of disgraceful outbreaks took
place early in 1190, beginning at Lynn about the month of January.   The

Lynn. disturbance is described as having originated in a struggle by
the Jews for the recovery of one of their number, a convert to
Christianity, who had eventually taken refuge in a church.   But the end of
it was that the houses of the Jews were plundered, and several of them
killed.   The blame for the pillage, however, was laid on foreign traders,
who, when all was over, sailed off in triumph with their booty.[3]   But their
success encouraged others to follow suit.   From Lynn two waves of disturbance seemed to have spread, one Southward, the other Northward.   On

Norwich. the 6th February a cruel slaughter was perpetrated at Norwich
of all ' unbelievers ' who could be found in their houses, a
remnant escaping to the castle ; so again on a larger scale at Bury St.

Bury. Edmunds on the 18th of March (Palm Sunday).   The malefactors there were mainly young Crusaders about to start for
the East.[4]   In the other direction Stamford was invaded on the 7th March,

Stamford. during a fair, by bands of Crusaders from different quarters.
Most of the Jews escaped to the castle, but their houses were
sacked, and the spoils carried off.[5]   At Lincoln the people were preparing
for an attack, but the Jews warned in time got away to the castle with their
goods.[6]   But the crowning tragedy was enacted at York, that city of wild

York. memories.   There the disturbances had been planned beforehand, partly by Crusaders, partly by local gentry in debt to
Jewish money-lenders.   Chief of these were Philip of Falconberge, Richard
Malebysse, William Percy, and Marmaduke Darrell,[7] all men of undoubted
position.   As elsewhere, the affair began by a nocturnal assault on the
house of a leading Jew, the others escaping to one of the two castles
within the walls.   The reader will notice that everywhere the authorities
were willing to extend to the Jews the passive protection of their strongholds, without taking any active measures on their behalf.   The fugitives,

---

[1] Ben. P. ; Hoved. *sup.*; R. Devizes, 392.

[2] W. Newb., I. 313.   For a charter granting special privileges to one Jew and his
family, see *Fœdera*, I. 51.

[3] W. Newb., I. 308–311.   [4] Diceto, II. 75.

[5] W. Newb., 310, 311 ; Diceto, *sup.*   Gerard of Camville, Constable of Lincoln
Castle, was afterwards accused of complicity in this outrage ; Hoved., III. 242.

[6] W Newb., 312.   [7] Chron. Melsa, I. 251 ; and W. Newb., below.

then, at York having been received by the Constable within his castle, a terrible misunderstanding took place. The Constable having gone out on some business, on his return found the gates closed against him. Losing his temper he applied to John Marshal, the Sheriff, who happened to be at York at the time with his retinue, and he unfortunately, yielding to pressure, gave the word for an assault. We must suppose the Jews to have got the control of the castle. For several days they were besieged in regular form, helping hands from far and near being rallied against them by the wild declamations of a fanatical white-robed hermit. On the night of the 16th March, having been reduced to extremity, the sterner Hebrew spirits, at the suggestion of a leading rabbi, **Semitic Desperation** electing to die by their own hands rather than by the hands of their "Gentile enemies," cut the throats of their wives and children, fired the principal hall over their own heads, and so destroyed themselves and their goods. In the morning a remnant surrendered, offering to submit to baptism; but the mob, again hounded on by the relentless Richard Malebysse, butchered them in cold blood. A rush was then made to the Minster to destroy all the bonds and mortgages deposited there; that done, the Crusaders vanished, leaving the local gentry and the local authorities to bear the brunt of the wrath to come. It is right to add that the chroniclers emphatically condemn the conduct of the rioters.[1]

Shortly after Easter Puiset and Longchamp were sent back to England, the Chancellor being charged to hold strict enquiries as to **Judicial Inquests.** the recent outbreaks.[2] Richard hated insubordination; but we are also told that he was especially vexed at the thought of the valuable Jewish property appropriated by the rioters; the goods of licensed money lenders[3] at their deaths being held to appertain to the Royal fisc. About the 3rd May Longchamp reached York with a considerable force at his back. His first act was to place the Minster under Interdict because the clergy had not received him in procession as a Legate, no Legatine commission having yet been granted to him. His next proceeding was to dismiss the Sheriff John Marshal, and the Constable, Marshal's post being given to the Chancellor's brother Osbert. The estates of the delinquent knights were taken into hand, the culprits themselves having retired to Scotland; a certain number of fines were imposed, and hostages for keeping the peace taken from the citizens; but not a single man was brought to 'justice.'[4]

---

[1] See the full account in W. Newb., I. 312-322; also Ben. P., II. 107; Hoveden, III. 33; Diceto, *sup.*

[2] Ben. P., 108. Puiset and Longchamp were with the King at Lyons-la-Forêt on the 27th March; *Id.,* and 109, notes Stubbs. Probably they would not leave before the close of Easter, 2nd April.   [3] "Fœneratores regios"; W. Newb. 322-323.

[4] Ben. P. and W. Newb., *sup.*; Hoveden, III. 34. The knights eventually recovered their lands for moderate fines; Pipe Rolls, cited Bp. Stubbs, Hoved., *sup.* xlv.

The Bishop of Durham on landing had gone to London to claim his seat in the Council Chamber; but the Barons acting in concert with Longchamp would not admit him. Going homewards he met the Chancellor at Blythe, as Longchamp was going from York to Lincoln to hold

Puiset and Longchamp. another inquest there. Puiset apparently took Longchamp to task for having invaded his jurisdiction by proceeding North of the Humber; and produced his own commission as Chief Justiciar for that district. Longchamp in answer invited him to come to Tickhill Castle at the end of the week to talk the matter over. On the appointed day the Bishop came and was admitted alone to the castle, his men being kept outside; and then the Chancellor politely informed

The Bishop arrested, him that he must consider himself under arrest. It was said that Longchamp produced a commission later in date than that of the Bishop, and over-riding it. Probably the alleged commission was simply the King's orders directing Longchamp to hold the inquest at York.[1] That of course would *pro tanto* interfere with Puiset's jurisdiction. Hugh protested, but in vain. He was taken back to

despoiled, London, and forced to surrender all that he had purchased of the King, castles, Justiciarship, earldom, sheriffdom, Sadberge, and all. Moreover he had to give up his son Henry, and one Gilbert de la Leia, a connexion of the Percies, as hostages.[2] On these terms the unfortunate Bishop was allowed to return homewards. But Longchamp had not done with him yet. Puiset having halted at his manor of Howden in the East Riding was again arrested there by Osbert

and detained. Longchamp, the new Sheriff, and forced to give security not to leave without permission. At Howden Hugh was detained till Richard pitying his case ordered Newcastle and Sadberge to be restored to him.[3]

Having thus got rid of his chief competitor, with Eleanor, John, and Geoffrey all abroad, Longchamp for some ten months lorded it over

Longchamp supreme. England in grand style; holding councils, dispensing Crown patronage, traversing the country with a devouring retinue, surrounded by foreigners and sycophants, levying contributions from the laity as Justiciar, and from the clergy as Legate. But his chief occupation was raising money to meet "the ever-increasing demands" of his master.[4]

One transaction deserves special notice. The succession to the title and

---

[1] I question if the commission of Lieutenancy issued in favour of Longchamp at Bayonne on the 6th June could yet have reached him; much less the Legatine commission granted at Rome the day before. But he was not a man to stick at trifles.

[2] R. Devizes, 390, 391; Ben. P., II. 109; Hoved. III. xlvi. 35.

[3] Ben. P. and Hoved., *sup.*

[4] See Ben. P., II. 143; Hoveden, III. xlvii.-li., and 142 (a letter from Hugh of Nonant); R. Devizes, 390, 391; W. Newb., I. 331-336.

estates of the late William Mandeville Earl of Essex was disputed between
Geoffrey Fitz Peter in right of his wife Beatrice of Say, and her uncle Geoffrey
of Say.[1]   Richard, in November, during the Canterbury Council, accepted
Geoffrey of Say for the enormous fine of 7000 marks ($£4666$ 13s. 4d.) ;
but the instalments not being paid with sufficient regularity Longchamp
resold the estates to Fitz Peter for 3000 marks ($£2000$), and Richard
confirmed the act.[2]

[1] Fitz Peter's wife was granddaughter and heir general of an elder Beatrice of Say, *née*
Mandeville, who was daughter of Geoffrey the 1st Earl.   Geoffrey of Say was the
younger son and heir male of the elder Beatrice.

[2] See Richard's charter dated Messina, 23rd January, 1191 ; Round, *Ancient Charters*,
p. 97 (Pipe Roll Society), with the editor's notes, referring to *Monasticon*. IV. 139, 145.
The real heir to the late Earl was his aunt Beatrice, widow of William of Say.   Geoffrey
of Say, the claimant, was her younger son ; Fitz Peter's wife was the eldest daughter of an ·
elder son William, who was dead ; a younger daughter and co-heiress was altogether
passed over, as the law then stood with regard to the succession to offices.

CHAPTER XVI

RICHARD I. (*continued*)

A.D. 1190, 1191

The Crusade—Richard's Journey to Messina—Affairs there—Alliance with Tancred King of Sicily—Voyage to Cyprus—Conquest of the Island—Marriage of Richard and Berengaria—Landing at Acre

ALL things being ready, on the 24th June Richard formally entered on his pilgrimage at Tours, receiving the scrip and staff at the hands of Archbishop William.[1] For the command of his fleet, raised by petty squadrons from the various harbours of England, Normandy, Brittany, and Aquitaine, constables and justiciars had already been appointed. These included two prelates and three barons, namely Gerard Archbishop of Auch, Bernard Bishop of Bayonne, Robert of Sablon, Richard of Camville, and William of Forz de Oleron. For the maintenance of order and discipline stringent Ordinances were issued.[2] Where the fleet mustered we are not told; most likely it would assemble at Bordeaux, but its orders were to circumnavigate the Spanish Peninsula, and meet the King at Marseilles.[3]

Start for Holy Land.

The Fleet.

The number of the vessels is given by one writer as 106;[4] and by another as 100, with 14 large 'busses' of double the burden.[5] The latter writer describes the average ship as able to carry forty men-at-arms with their horses, and an equal number of foot soldiers. His 100 ships therefore would be transport for 8000 soldiers, half cavalry and half infantry, a very unlikely proportion. The infantry must surely have outnumbered the heavily equipped men-at-arms. A further point to be considered would be the number of horses that each man-at-arms would

---

[1] Hoveden, III. 36. Richard was at Tours 24th and 25th June. I take it that the ceremony would be performed on the 24th, being a Sunday.

[2] Hoved., *sup.*; Ben. P., II. 110, 111.

[3] *Itinerary*, 147; R. Dev., 393.

[4] Ben. P., 120.

[5] R. Dev., 394. This however seems given as the number that reached Messina.

take with him ; surely more than one, as late in the reign we find the mere horse-archers enlisted for war in Normandy required to bring two horses each. But on questions of this sort nothing short of Record evidence is really trustworthy. From the Pipe Roll of the year we learn that the Cinque Ports' squadron, practically the whole English contingent, numbered thirty-three vessels with crews of twenty to twenty-five men each, including one skipper or steersman. The vessels were chartered for a year at the rate of two-thirds of their stated value, the seamen receiving pay in advance, at the rate of 2d. a day, or about £3 a year, and the steerers double.[1]

Leaving Tours apparently about the 26th June, Richard moved to the appointed trysting place at Vézelai, which he reached on the 3rd July.

Allied Muster. Next day Philip arrived with his host; gaudy pennons waved on every height, while the tents shone like a goodly city amid the corn-fields of Burgundy. The Kings struck a fresh treaty pledging themselves to stand by each other in all things, and to divide equally any conquests that they might make, or spoils that **Spoils to be divided.** might fall into their hands,[2] a compact likely to endanger any alliance. Besides they seemed to forget that their mission was to restore the fallen Kingdom of Jerusalem, an enterprise sufficiently arduous in itself. It involved the entire reconquest of Palestine under the most unfavourable circumstances. The men of the First Crusade had only to contend with the Emirs among whom the dominions of Shah Malek had been parcelled out, men divided both by temporal and spiritual jealousies. Now, the whole of Egypt, Syria, and Mesopotamia **Situation in Palestine.** were united in the hands of an able and successful prince, in undisputed command of all the forces of Islam.[3] The fortresses which it had taken the Frank Kings ninety years to build were

---

[1] See the extract given by Mr. T. A. Archer, *Crusade of Richard I.*, p. 11. Some vessels were much larger. The Royal Smack (esnecca), of which we hear constantly under Henry II., carried 61 men ; a ship presented by William of Braose carried 42 men ; *Ib.*

[2] " De omnibus jure belli perquirendis, æqua sorte dividendis ;" *Itiner.*, 149, 150 ; Ben. P., III. 111, and notes. The text of the treaty however is not given.

[3] Saladin whose proper name was Yusuf surnamed Salah-ed-din (Honour to the Faith) was by race a Kurd, born in Armenia in 1138. His father Ayub rose in the service of Zengy, appointed Atabec of Mosul by one of the sons of Malek Shah. Ayub (Job) and his brother Shirkuh became Zengy's right-hand men, and mainly helped to make his son Nur-ed-Din Mahmud Sultan of Damascus. Young Saladin first came into notice in connexion with expeditions to Egypt led by his uncle in 1164, 1167, and 1168. On the last occasion Shirkuh succeeded in establishing himself as Vizir of the Fatimite Caliph, but he died in two months' time when Saladin succeeded him. At the death of Nur-ed-din in 1174, Saladin ousted his son, a mere boy, and by a series of successful campaigns added Mesopotamia and Syria to his original dominion in Egypt. See his Life by Mr. Stanley Lane Poole.

with few exceptions in the hands of the enemy.[1] Ascalon had been surrendered in September 1187 to purchase the liberation of King Guy of Lusignan ; the Holy City had fallen in October ; other reverses had followed, Tyre however having been saved in July (1187) by Conrad of Montferrat, King Guy's enemy.[2] When Guy on the 28th August 1189 undertook the siege of Acre only Tyre and Belfort remained of the old territory of Jerusalem. Three days later Saladin appeared with a greatly superior force, surrounding the Christians and besieging them on the hill on which they were encamped in front of the city gate.[3] Ever since the siege had been maintained at the most frightful cost of life, the losses of one day being made good by the arrivals of the next. The Church with one voice called for succour as if the fate of Christianity as a religion depended on the recovery of Holy Land. Europe responded as it had never responded before. Barons and Knights, priests and pilgrims pressed forward to lay their bones in the vast charnel-house.[4] Finally the three crowned heads of Germany, France, and England had taken the field in person. But before Philip and Richard had met at Vézelai the great

Failure of Barbarossa's Crusade. German host had already come to nothing, used up by the hardships and opposition encountered in the long over-land march through Hungary, Bulgaria, Macedonia, and Asia Minor. On the 10th June the Emperor himself had perished, drowned

His Death. while trying to ford the Saleh or Calycadnus. On the 21st of the month the "scattered remnant" of his forces reached Antioch under his son Frederic Duke of Suabia.[5]

From Vézelai the two Kings marched together to Lyons (July 6th–14th) ; after three days' stay there they parted ; Philip crossing the Alps to Genoa, where he had chartered shipping ; while Richard moved quietly down the

Richard advances to Marseilles. valley of the Rhone to Marseilles (July 17th–31st). To his disappointment the fleet had not arrived ; after waiting some days he lost patience, chartered twenty galleys and ten "busses" for himself and his personal following, and so started on his voyage down

[1] Bishop Stubbs, *Itin.*, cxx. For the strength and size of these fortresses see drawings of remains of them, Archer and Kingsford, *Crusades* 70, 94, 114, 179, 263, 362. Antioch Merkab, Hesm-el-Akrab, Tripoli, and Tyre were the only places retained by the Christians in the summer of 1190.

[2] *Itin.*, 59, 60. Guy was set free in May 1188.

[3] See the news-letter, Diceto, II. 70; *Itin.*, 60–64. Ben. P., II. 93 ; also Lane Poole *Saladin*, 254, 264.

[4] For the leading reinforcements see Bishop Stubbs, *Itinerary*, cxvii.

[5] Frederick Barbarossa started from Ratisbon in April 1189, marching through Hungary and thence crossing the Danube into Bulgaria. In passing through Bulgaria into Macedonia his army was harassed by skirmishing attacks instigated by the Emperor Isaac Angelus. Having wintered at Adrianople, Frederick crossed the Dardanelles in March 1190. In April he entered the territory of the Sultan of Iconium, Kilidj Arslan, where his progress was vigorously opposed. A series of engagements, however, ended

the coasts of the Mediterranean on the 7th August.[1] Sailing in comfort-

Coasting voyage down the Mediterranean. able yachting fashion, by daily trips, putting in to harbour at nights,[2] and again, at times, landing to travel on shore, he reached Genoa on the 13th, and had an interview with Philip. On the 25th August he put in at the mouth of the Tiber, but he was not tempted to turn aside to visit the Eternal City, though invited by the Pope to do so. The light in which Richard regarded Rome was seemingly that of a rival taxing power, which fleeced ecclesiastics of moneys that otherwise might have gone into the King's own pocket. At any rate we are told that when the bishop of Ostia came to pay his respects Richard abused him roundly for the extortions of the *Curia*. At Naples however he found attractions that kept him there eleven days, namely, from the 28th August to the 8th of September. There Archbishop Baldwin, Hubert Walter. Bishop of Salisbury, and Ranulf Glanville, anxious to push on and do something for Holy Land, took leave and sailed direct to Palestine.[3] They reached Tyre on the 16th September, and Acre on the 12th October.[4] The Bishop of Norwich, John of Oxford, satisfied with what he had seen of the Crusade so far, went off to Rome, and obtained absolution from his vow. But Richard thought himself entitled to exact from him a fine of 2000 marks for his consent.[5]

On the 8th September Richard made another stage, riding to Salerno; there at last, at the end of five more days, he heard that his main fleet had sailed past him, and was nearing Messina.[6] Continuing his journey apparently sometimes by sea and sometimes by land, by stages of twenty to twenty-five miles a day, he finally reached La Bagnara, on the Straits of Messina, on the 22nd September. That same day as he was riding from Meleto to Bagnara with only one man in attendance, his freebooting habits involved him in a disagreeable adventure. Having taken a fancy to a fine hawk that he saw in a house by the way-side, he carried it off, without leave or license; where-upon the peasants came after him with sticks and stones; one man drew

A Freebooting King.

in the capture of Iconium, 18th May. The army then descended to the sea coast and at the crossing of the Saleh or Calycadnus the Emperor was drowned. See the *Itinerary* 34–57, with Bishop Stubbs' notes.

[1] *Itin.*, 151–153; Ben. P., 112, and notes.

[2] R. Devizes, 394, 395. [3] Ben. P., II. 112–115.

[4] *Epp. Cant.*, 328, 329; Diceto, II. 87; Ben. P., II. 141. They found the camp in a terrible state of demoralisation between want, sickness, and vice. Among the recent deaths were those of Queen Sybille, her two daughters, Stephen of Blois Count of Sancerre, the Count of Bar, Ferrers Earl of Derby, a brother of the Earl of Herts, etc. Archbishop Baldwin struggled on for a month, and then succumbed 19th November; *Reg. Sacrum.* [5] Ben. P., *sup.*

[6] For the voyage of the fleet, and particularly of its stay in the Tagus and adventures there, see Ben. P., 115–124; and more fully Hoveden, 42–54.

his knife, and Richard in striking him with the flat of his sword broke the weapon. Shipping being in readiness for him at La Bagnara Richard embarked at once, and crossed the Straits, styled by our Norman writers "Le Far (Phare) de Meschines." For the night he slept in a tent on the shore, to enable him to make a state entrance to Messina on the morrow.[1] Amidst a great flourish of trumpets, Richard's galleys, decked out with flags, and glittering with arms and armour, swept proudly into the harbour on the 23rd September. Richard himself, in Royal attire as one prepared to see and be seen, stood aloft on the prow of the tallest vessel. On landing he found his Royal comrade waiting to greet him. Philip having arrived some days before had taken possession of the Royal palace in the city ; Richard therefore had to find quarters in a suburban villa, among vineyards, his men likewise encamping outside the walls.[2]

Entry to Messina Harbour.

At Messina in spite of a friendly reception by the natives Richard found himself in troubled waters. In the first place Sicily was emerging from the throes of a disputed succession. Richard's brother-in-law William II. had died in November 1189 without issue, whereupon the crown of right devolved on his aunt Constance, daughter of King Roger I., and wife of Barbarossa's son Henry, now Henry VI. King of Germany. William had taken steps to ensure his aunt's succession.[3] But the Sicilians, preferring a native ruler, had elected Tancred, Count of Lecce, an illegitimate scion of the Royal family. War ensued, Henry endeavouring to assert his pretensions both in Apulia and Sicily by force of arms.[4]

Affairs in Sicily.

Richard's first step was to send to Palermo to demand the liberation of his widowed sister Jeanne or Johanna, who had been imprisoned by Tancred as a supporter of Constance and Henry. He also required the assignment of her dower and other property ; demanding at the same time a large supply of provisions and shipping for his own use. Tancred sent off the Queen, but took no notice of Richard's other demands.[5] On September 28th Jeanne was received at Messina. To find a suitable residence for her Richard two days later crossed the Straits, seized a strong castle at La Bagnara, the property of the King of Sicily, and established her there ; while again, on 3rd October, to get a depôt for his stores he occupied a Greek monastery in an island in the Straits, expelling all the monks.[6] Southern blood could not fail to rise at such provocation. Even before the King's landing

High-handed Action.

[1] Ben. P., II. 124, 125; Hoveden, III. 54, 55 ; Diceto, II. 84 ; *Itinerary*, 153-156.
[2] *Itin.*, 156, 157 ; Ben. P., 125, 126.
[3] Ben. P., II., 101, 102 ; W. Newb. I., 285, and note.
[4] See Sismondi, *Ital. Rep.*, II. 259-261 (ed. 1826); Ben. P., 140, 141.
[5] R. Devizes, 395, 396.
[6] Hoveden, III. 56 ; R. Devizes, *sup.* ; *cnf.* Ben., 127.

:he unruly conduct of the 'pilgrims' had caused great irritation in Messina.[1]

The Messinese Restive. Richard did something to put down disorders, but in doing so he claimed to hang malefactors of any nationality, no matter whose subjects they might be. On the 3rd October a wrangle over the price of a loaf of bread between a shop-woman and a Crusader led to a serious outbreak, the citizens expelling the foreigners, and closing their gates against them. Richard's men having turned out to retaliate, he had much ado to keep them within bounds.[2] The state of affairs however was felt to be so critical that next day all the Sicilian magnates, the Archbishop, the Admiral of Sicily, the civic authorities, with King Philip, the Duke of Burgundy, and others waited on Richard at his quarters to consider the situation, and arrange for peaceable intercourse in the future.[3] The parties seemed to have come to a satisfactory understanding when a report came in that the townspeople were again

Attack on Richard's Quarters. up in arms, and had attacked the quarters of the Count of La Marche, Hugh Le Brun. Richard, rushing out to quell the disturbance, found himself confronted by an excited mob, who jeered at him as an Englishman, and asked him about his tail.[4] Personal insult is an offence that kings never forgive. Richard in a fury hastened back to his quarters, donned his armour, and blew the trumpets for a general assault. The gates had been closed, and the walls manned; but while Richard's men were busy with a direct frontal attack, he himself with a small following climbed one of the heights at the back of the city, and broke in at a postern that he had previously reconnoitred; from thence, working his way round, he let in the others. Then all was over. ' In less time than a priest could say Matins Messina

Storm and Sack of Messina. was taken!'[5] A regular sack ensued, all valuables being seized, and the better class of women distributed among the victors. Even the Sicilian galleys in the harbour were burned, lest the natives should escape in them with their goods. Philip's quarters in the palace of course were respected, but everywhere else the English flag was hoisted on the walls.[6]

---

[1] *Itin.*, 154, 158. For their gross misconduct at Lisbon, on the voyage out, see Ben. P., 119.

[2] *Itin.*, 158; Ben. P., 127.

[3] Ben. P., II., 128; R. Dev., 399; *Itin.*, 159.

[4] *Itin.*, 160. See R. Devizes, 397, "Græculi enim et Siculi omnes hunc regem (sc. Ricardum) sequentes Anglos et caudatos nominabant." For the popular belief on the Continent that Englishmen had tails, Mr. Howlett cites a thirteenth-century poem, Pertz, xxvii., 77. The taunt was still kept up in the time of the wars of Henry VI.

[5] So the writer of the *Itinerary*, who was present; p. 163. But his account implies a much longer struggle than that phrase would imply; while Richard of Devizes tells us that the whole assault lasted five hours; p. 401 (hora v–x).

[6] 4th October. See *Itinerary*, Richard of Devizes, and Benedict, *sup.*; shorter notices are given by Diceto, II., 85; and W. Newb., I., 324.

Against this assumption of sovereignty, Philip, who, during the fight, had stood on one side, naturally protested. We are also told that he claimed half of the spoils of the Messinese under the Vézelai agreement. After two days' discussion Richard was induced to allow the French flag to be flown alongside of his, and to place the city under the nominal charge of the Templars and Hospitallers. But he insisted on taking hostages from the citizens for a satisfactory settlement with Tancred.[1] Two days later again, Philip and Richard, the Lamb and the Lion, as they were called,[2] sealed a fresh treaty of alliance, issuing ordinances to regulate the intercourse of their followers with the citizens.[3] But as a matter of fact "they were never again friends."

The negotiations with Tancred resulted in a treaty, by which Richard not only entered into a defensive alliance with the King of Sicily, fully recognising him as such, but also agreed to a closer bond by engaging his nephew and heir presumptive, young Arthur of Brittany, to Tancred's daughter. For this honour Tancred 'advanced' by way of his daughter's portion the handsome sum of 20,000 ounces of gold, equivalent at the current rate of exchange to £15,000 sterling.[4] According to the chroniclers Tancred gave Richard a further 20,000 ounces of gold as a free gift. Of this sum, according to the French, Philip was allowed to receive a third.[5] At the same time we are glad to hear that Richard at the suggestion of Walter of Coutances, the Archbishop of Rouen, issued orders requiring the valuables carried off on 4th October to be restored. After that a better feeling began to prevail between the 'pilgrims' and the natives.

Alliance with Tancred of Sicily.

The season for sailing, according to the ideas of the period, being now past, the two kings settled down for the winter at Messina. Richard moved his quarters from the villa among the vineyards to a defensible wooden fortress built by himself on a height overlooking the city. His men who held the "Griffons" or Greek population in supreme contempt, gave it the pleasant name of "Mate-Griffon" or 'Kill-Greek.'[6] There he held his Christmas Feast in great splendour, entertaining his over-lord King Philip, with all his knights.[7]

Winter Quarters.

Richard seldom looked beyond the gratification of the momentary whim, or the needs of the passing hour. Otherwise he would have seen that

---

[1] Hoveden, III., 58.   [2] R. Devizes, 395.

[3] Hoveden, III., 58–61 ; Ben. P., 129-133 ; *Itin.*, 164-166.

[4] November. See the Treaty, Ben. P., 133-136 ; Hoveden, 61-64. On 11th November Richard reported the treaty to the Pope ; Ben., 136. On the Pipe Roll, 1 Rich. I., 106, the ounce of gold is given as equal to 15*s.* in silver.

[5] Ben. P. and Hoveden, *sup.* ; Rigord.

[6] *Itin.*, 168 ; Ben. P., 138. The writers distinguish between the Greek and the Italic populations of the island. The writer of the *Itinerary* calls the latter "Longobardi." For the Apulian Lombardy, see Freeman, *Hist. Geography*, II., map xxxvi.

[7] *Itin.*, 172 ; Ben. P., 150.

by allying himself with King Tancred he challenged the hostility of
Henry VI. and the German party in Palestine.   Philip likewise had had
much to complain of in the conduct of his overbearing vassal.   But there
was worse to come.   In the course of the month of February (1191) the
indefatigable Queen Eleanor was reported as on her way to Messina.[1]
Her mission was twofold.   She was charged to press upon the King's
attention the complaints of the English against Longchamp and his mis-
government; and she brought with her Berengaria, daughter

Richard to marry Berengaria of Navarre. of Sancho VI. of Navarre, a young Princess whom Richard was prepared to marry.[2]   It was natural that Eleanor should wish to see her favourite son settled, and an heir born who would obviate all questions as between Arthur and John.   But the final rejection of the unfortunate Alais involved a gross breach of

Alais rejected. faith on Richard's part, as his undertaking to go on with the marriage was the price that he paid for Philip's support in his last struggle with his father.   Philip complained bitterly of Richard's duplicity;[3] but Richard told him plainly that he would never marry a woman, who, as he could prove had been on terms of improper intimacy with his father.[4]   Once more, however Count Philip of Flanders was able to come forward as a mediator.   Bound for Palestine he had touched at Messina.   Through his efforts another treaty was sealed by which King Philip in consideration of 10,000 marks to be paid by certain

Fresh Treaty with Philip. instalments released Richard from his engagement to Alais Richard promising to restore her to her friends on his return to Normandy.   With regard to Gisors, Neufchâtel, and the Norman Vexin a curious compromise was arranged, the territory being settled on Richard and the heirs male of his body by Berengaria, with remainder to the heirs male of the body of Philip; failing such issue the lands to revert to the

---

[1] Eleanor had left Richard's court in Touraine in the summer to go to Rome; so that perhaps she only came from thence; Diceto II. 81.   As she was married to Louis in 1137, if she was only sixteen then she would be seventy now.

[2] According to the *Itinerary*, 175, Richard had known Berengaria when he was Count of Poitiers, and was attracted by her character and manners ("Morum illecitus elegantia"; so again p. 196, "Puella prudentissima").   Richard of Devizes thought her character her chief attraction ("prudentior quam pulchrior"), 402; and that probably was the case, as she never took her husband's fancy, or got any hold upon him.   William of Newburgh, however, gives her equal credit for qualities and good looks; "famosæ pulchritudinis et prudentiæ"; I. 346.   Of all the writers the original author of the *Itinerary* was presumably the only man who ever saw Berengaria, as she never set foot in England in all her life.

[3] See the interviews with Tancred held at Catania in March; Ben. P., II. 159; Hoveden, II. 98; where, however, Tancred is represented as setting Richard on his guard against Philip's designs.

Ben. P., 160; Hoveden, 98, 99; R. Devizes, 403.   See also Giraldus, VIII. 232, where he asserts that Alais succeeded Rosamond.   But his statements on such points must be received with caution.

U

Duke of Normandy for the time being.   Mutual restitutions in Auvergne and Querci were also agreed upon.[1]

On the 30th March Philip sailed for Acre.   Richard escorted him for a few miles out of the harbour ; then, having seen him safely off, he turned aside to Reggio, took on board his mother and Berengaria, and brought them to Messina.[2]

Till then Richard had turned a deaf ear to all complaints against his Chancellor.   But after hearing what his mother had to say, he

Affairs in England. entrusted Walter of Coutances, the Archbishop of Rouen, with an order to William Marshal Earl of Pembroke and the other members of the Regency Committee directing them, if dissatisfied with Longchamp's conduct, to take the advice of the Archbishop, and act as he

Mission of Walter of Coutances. should suggest.[3]   Another part of Eleanor's errand was to forward the consecration of Geoffrey, whose position had been again attacked at Rome by Bouchard the Treasurer of York, and apparently by Bouchard's uncle Bishop Puiset also.[4]   On the 2nd April, just four days after her arrival, Eleanor was sent back on her return journey. Berengaria remained at Messina under the charge of the widowed Queen Johanna to be married to Richard when Lent was past.   Walter of Coutances took his departure along with Eleanor.[5]   He landed at Shoreham on the 27th April, as we shall see, to find John at war with Longchamp,[6] and that actually on the question of the succession.   Under these circumcumstances, as the dangerous man seemed the brother rather than the Chancellor, he withheld his instructions.   Queen Eleanor was more suc-

Geoffrey Confirmed as Archbishop. cessful; she went to Rome and obtained from the new Pope Celestine III.[7] confirmation for Geoffrey, with orders, under which he was finally consecrated at Tours on the 13th August by Archbishop Bartholomew.[8]   As Eleanor must have been in Rome

---

[1] See the treaty dated in March, before the 25th March ; *Fœdera*, I. 54.

[2] *Itin.*, 175 ; Ben. P., 161 ; Hoved., 100.   Richard had sent for his mother to Naples in February ; but his men found that Eleanor, unable to obtain a safe-conduct from Tancred, had gone to Brindisi ; from thence she went on to Reggio ; Ben. P., 157.

[3] See the fragmentary letter, Diceto, II. 91 ; and the full letter Giraldus, IV. 400. The latter is clearly not a transcript, but a copy from memory, giving the substance of the original.   The bit in Diceto, so far as it goes, is clearly a transcript.   The two may be put together, but I reject the date of Giraldus, 20th February, as too early.   Another letter to the Committee announcing the return of the Archbishop, which is clearly a transcript, and evinces no distrust of the Chancellor, is dated 23rd February ; Diceto, 90.

[4] Ben. P., II. 146 ; Hoved., III. 74 ; *cnf.* W. Newb., I. 339, 240 ; Girald., IV. 382, 383.

[5] *Itin.*, 176 ; Ben. P., 161 ; Diceto, 86.   Though going home on the King's business, Walter was heavily mulcted by him for dropping the Crusade ; R. Dev., 404.

[6] Diceto, II. 90, reading V. Kal " Maii " for " Julii " ; Hoved., III. 135, note.

[7] Clement III. died on 28th March, 1191 ; on the 30th March Jacinto Bobo was elected under the style of Celestine III. ; Diceto II. 89, and *.Epp Cant.*, 332, notes Stubbs.

[8] Hoveden, III. 100 ; W. Newb. I. 340 ; Giraldus, IV. 384 ; *Reg. Sacrum.*

early in April it is only reasonable to suppose that she was there on Easter
Day (14th April), and witnessed the consecration of Celestine, as well as
the imposing ceremony of the morrow, when as the first act of his Pontificate he crowned Henry VI. and Constance of Sicily as Emperor and
Empress of Germany.[1]

On April 10th, Thursday in Holy Week, Richard finally loosed from
Messina. For weeks the pilgrims had been murmuring at the
intolerable delay, and the consequent exhaustion of their means,
at a time when their brethren at Acre were calling so loudly
for help. Richard pacified them by liberal distributions of money.[2]

Departure from Messina.

Johanna and the future bride were sent on somewhat in advance, in one of
the larger vessels or " busses," now otherwise spoken of as " dromonds," in
contradistinction to the lighter rowing galleys.[3] On the 12th the fleet was
scattered by a gale; but Richard, holding on his course, reached Crete on
the 17th of the month, to find some five-and-twenty vessels missing,
including the ship that carried his bride. Re-embarking on the next day
he was driven on to the island of Rhodes, where he remained some days,
detained by illness. Continuing on May 1st he was again driven Northward into the gulf of Sattalia, and did not succeed in working his way to
Limasol or Limisso in the island of Cyprus till the 6th May.
There the Royal ladies were found, safely anchored in the
harbour, but afraid to land. Richard was also informed that
three busses had been wrecked (24th April), and that his Vice-Chancellor and Keeper of the Seal Roger " *Malus Catulus* " (Machell) had been
drowned. His body however had been recovered with the Seal hanging
round the neck. But the natives had shown a hostile disposition. The
wrecked men had been deprived of their arms, and imprisoned pending
orders from the Emperor; and had only been rescued with difficulty after
a smart engagement by a party landed from the ships. Two stalwarts,
Roger of Harcourt and William du Bois are specially mentioned as having
helped the captives to cut their way out.[4]

Landing in Cyprus.

As for the ' Emperor ' in question he was Isaac Comnenus, a scion of
the Imperial House, who had been sent to Cyprus by the
Emperor Andronicus in 1184 or 1185. When Andronicus fell,
dethroned and put to death by Isaac Angelus, the Cyprian
Isaac had declared himself independent, and had maintained
his independence ever since. He was not by any means a man outside

The "Emperor" Isaac Comnenus.

---

[1] Hoveden, *sup.* The writer is the authority for the story that Celestine kicked the
crown from off the Emperor's head. See Bishop Stubbs' note *ad. loc.*

[2] *Itin.*, 171; Ben. P., II. 157; Hoveden, 195.

[3] *It.*, 176. Richard of Devizes gives the fleet as now consisting of 166 ships—*naves*—
say ordinary English craft—24 busses, and 39 galleys, p. 405. Benedict, 162, has simply
153 large ships and 53 galleys.

[4] *Itin.*, 177-181, 184-188; Ben. P., 162; Hoved., 105.

the European circle; he claimed cousinship with Leopold of Austria; [1] and had married a daughter of William I. of Sicily.[2] Like all the Greeks he had a wholesome dread of Frankish visitations, and was generally supposed to be in league with Saladin.[3] Coming to Limasol he promised restitution of the effects of the shipwrecked men; gave the pilgrims hostages to allow them to land, and pressed the ladies to do the same. But his conduct in filling Limasol with armed men excited suspicion, and Johanna and Berengaria preferred to keep afloat. Richard was quite entitled to demand satisfaction for the maltreatment of his followers, but his requirements were not only pretty sweeping in themselves,[4] but also it would seem, couched in terms offensive to Byzantine pride. Isaac, not duly weighing the forces by which he was confronted—or the man— ventured to send a contemptuous answer. Richard without further parley blew his trumpets and manned his boats for a landing, and an attack on the shipping drawn up along the beach. Amidst a storm of arrows and cross-bow bolts showered from either side the pilgrims fought their

Storm of Limasol way inch by inch to the shore, then, charging home, they drove the Cypriots clean out of Limasol, and took possession. The ladies were at once brought ashore, and established in comfortable quarters in the town. But Richard was not satisfied with this measure of redress. The horses were landed during the night, somewhat out of condition from their sea voyage; Richard nevertheless

Further War on Isaac. mounted next day, and rode out to reconnoitre the 'enemy,' who had taken up a position at a little distance from Limasol. The reconnaisance ended in a general engagement, in which the Cypriots were routed, and their camp taken and plundered. Still pressing the unfortunate Isaac, Richard in the course of the next few days forced him to retire to Nicosia or Lefcosia, his capital in the heart of the island.[5]

The Court being comfortably established on shore, and Lent passed, it was thought that the King's marriage ought not to be deferred

Marriage of Richard and Berengaria. any longer, if only out of regard for the bride's reputation;[6] and accordingly on Sunday, 12th May, the Royal pair were united at Limasol, Berengaria being afterwards duly crowned. The

---

[1] R. Coggeshall, 59; Ansbert, extracted Hoved. III. cxl. Leopold's mother Theodora was daughter of the Emperor Manuel; he was son of John Comnenus from whom Isaac of Cyprus was descended. See Tables III. and IV. in Mr. Archer's *Crusade of Richard I.*

[2] So Ernsch and Grüber in their Encyclopædia.

[3] See Ben. P., I. 254–262, and notes; Archer, *Crusade of R. I.*, p. 60; also the Greek chronicle of Cyprus given *Itinerary*, clxxxvi.

[4] "Ad voluntatem suam."

[5] See the clear, impartial narrative of an eye-witness, *Itin.*, 188-194. *Cnf.* the accounts of Ben. P., II. 163, 164; Hoved., III., 105-108; and R. Dev., 423, evidently composed to make a case for Richard, and inculpate Isaac.

[6] "Forte adhuc virgo"; R. Dev. 422.

Archbishop of Bordeaux, with the Bishops of Evreux and Bayonne, and other Prelates officiated.[1]

A few days would naturally be given to wedding festivities. But already Richard had received a distinguished batch of visitors whose presence may have exercised some influence on the subsequent course of events in **Visit from** Cyprus. The new comers were none other than the widowed **Guy of** King Guy of Jerusalem, with his brother Geoffrey, Henfrid **Lusignan.** III. of Toron, Bohemond III. Prince of Antioch, Raymond III. Count of Tripoli, and Leo afterwards King of Armenia, in fact all the chief men of Guy's party. They came to implore Richard's help against their common enemy Conrad Marquis of Montferrat.[2] Sybille, eldest daughter of King Amaury, in whose right Guy had been proclaimed King of Jerusalem, had died at Acre with her two daughters in October 1190.[3]

It then became a question whether Guy should retain the **His Position** crown during his life, or whether the right had not devolved **in Palestine.** on Sybille's sister, Isabel, married to Henfrid III. of Toron. But neither Guy nor Henfrid was, either in social position, or in other respects, suited to the tastes of the great lords of Palestine. The Marquis of Montferrat with his greater wealth, higher connexions, and supreme capacity for intrigue was quite the man to succeed in such an atmosphere. His ambition had naturally been excited by the fact that his elder brother William had been the first husband of Queen Sybille ; and he had always opposed the recognition of Guy.[4] At Sybille's death he saw a way to the **A competitor** throne, and promptly availed himself of it by persuading Isabel **for the** to divorce Henfrid and marry him. Good Archbishop **Crown.** Baldwin forbade the iniquitous marriage. But he died (19th November 1190); and then the amazing transaction was carried out (24th November).[5] King Philip on landing at Acre in April had been induced to declare for the Marquis.[6] An appeal to Richard therefore was Guy's only chance. The King at once promised him his support, and, to do him justice, faithfully kept his word.[7]

But the accession of strength brought by King Guy and his friends, together with the arrival of a further squadron that brought up the number of Richard's armed galleys to one hundred, apparently encouraged

[1] See *Itin.*, 195, 196 ; Ben. P., II. 167. According to the latter the marriage service was performed by the King's chaplain, Nicholas, afterwards Bishop of Le Mans. For Berengaria's dower, dated 12th May, see Martene and Durand, *Ampl. Coll.*, I. 995.

[2] 11th May., *Itin.*, 195 ; Ben. P., 165 and notes.

[3] *Fpp. Cant.*, 329 ; Hoveden, III. 87.

[4] For Guy and Conrad see Bishop Stubbs' sketches, *Itin.*, cxxiv., cxxv. For Conrad's relationship to Frederic Barbarossa and Leopold of Austria see Norgate, *Angevin Kings*, II. 3 0, note.

[5] Ben. P., II. 141 ; Hoved., III. 70, and for the date Bishop Stubbs' notes.

[6] W. Newb., I. 349.

[7] *Itin.*, 195.

him to undertake the out-and-out conquest of Cyprus.[1]   As he pointed out Cyprus would provide a most convenient stepping stone to Palestine[2]; in fact "a strong place of arms"; while Guy of Lusignan and his supporters would be ready enough to attack a Prince closely connected with the hostile Montferrats.   But the Grand Master of the Hospital, who probably did not quite approve of the enterprise, induced poor Isaac to endeavour to disarm Richard by humble submission.   A conference was arranged outside Limasol to settle the terms.   We are told that Richard gladdened the eyes of all beholders by his appearance on a mettled Spanish palfrey, with a gorgeous saddle, carved, gilt, and inlaid : he himself wore a tunic of rose coloured samite, with a mantle thickly spangled with silver crescents, and a scarlet cap embroidered with gold.   After much discussion the Emperor agreed to do homage to Richard for his dominions; to pay an indemnity of 3,500 marks; and to **Submission of Isaac.** follow him to Holy Land with 500 horse; meanwhile however his castles would be placed in the King's hands, to be returned when the provisions of the treaty had been satisfied.

The homage was duly performed, the oath of fealty taken, and the kiss of peace received.[3]   But Isaac was not allowed to depart.   Instead of being dismissed in peace he was conducted to a sumptuous tent, his own tent captured on the 7th May, surrounded with luxuries, but **His Detention.** palpably a mere state prisoner.   This detention of a vassal after having accepted his homage was a gross breach of the feudal tie on the part of Richard.   The hapless man, naturally dissatisfied with his position, made his escape in the night; whereupon **Breach of Feudal Bond.** Richard treating this as a breach of the treaty declared fresh war.[4]   Guy was. sent with an army by land to Famagusta, Richard going round by water.   No Isaac was found at Famagusta ; but envoys appeared from Philip begging Richard to come on, and taking him to task for waging war on a friendly Christian state.   We are told that Richard answered in language that the writer did not care to put on paper.   During an advance to Nicosia a skirmishing action took place in which the Emperor was accused of shooting poisoned arrows at the King.   Hunted from one refuge to another, with all his castles successively **Final reduction and incarceration of Isaac.** reduced, his dearly beloved little daughter in Richard's hands, Isaac at last threw himself on the King's mercy, his only request, doubtless preferred in French, being that he might not be put into irons, "*des fers.*"   The word enabled Richard to grant the

---

[1] "Rex factus erectior arridentem arbitratus est sequi fortunam," *Id.*, 196.

[2] *Id.*, 200.

[3] See *Itin.*, 198, "Omnia prædicta se juravit fideliter observaturum"; also Ben. P., 166, "Juravit fidelitatem regi Angliæ et hœredibus suis sicut ligiis dominis"; also Hoveden, 109, "Homo regis Angliæ devenit"; so too R. Devizes, 424.

[4] *Itin.*, 198, 199.

request, and then escape from his Royal promise through a shameful subterfuge, by placing his prisoner in silver chains.[1]

Cyprus Ransacked Cyprus having been thoroughly ransacked and plundered the pilgrim fleet moved on. The two Queens, with the Emperor's daughter in their charge, must have sailed already, as they reached Acre on the 1st June.[2] The King loosed from Famagusta on the 5th June, having wasted, not to say misused a whole month in Cyprus when within one day's sail of Syria. Isaac was taken with him, to end his days a prisoner in a Syrian fortress. Richard of Camville and Stephen of Turnham were left in command in Cyprus, with orders to arrange for forwarding supplies to Palestine.[3] The Syrian coast was first sighted off Merkab; passing by Tortosa and Jebel, Richard's galleys were nearing Beritus (Beirût) when a large three-masted ship was descried. She proved to be a Turkish vessel from Beirût, bound with reinforcements and munitions of war for the garrison at Acre. After repeated attempts to take her by boarding, Richard, who had wished to save the prize, reluctantly gave the order to ram. The galleys charged and the great 'buss' sank. Of all on board only thirty-five of the 'best' men were saved. Saladin was greatly disconcerted by the news of the loss, which seriously affected the prospect at Acre.[4] On the 7th June Richard anchored off Tyre, Conrad's men refusing to allow him to land. On Saturday 8th June he finally disembarked at Acre.[5]

---

[1] 31st May, *Itin.* 201–203; Ben. P., II. 167; Hoveden, III. 110.

[2] Ben. P., 167, 168; Hoveden, 111.

[3] Ben. P. and Hovenden, *sup.*; *Itin.*, 204.

[4] See the long account, *Itin.*, 205–209. Benedict, 168, and Hoveden, 112, placé the action a day later, between Tyre and Acre. *Cnf.* Saladin's biographer Bohadin (Beha-ed-din) (Palestine Text Society, 1879), p. 249.

[5] *Itin.*, 311; Ben. P., II. 169.

CHAPTER XVII

RICHARD I. (*continued*)

A.D. 1191, 1192

The Crusade Continued—Siege and Reduction of Acre—Massacres of Prisoners—Advance from Acre—Battle of Arsûf—Advance to Joppa and eventually to Beit Nuba—Retirement on Ascalon

GREAT was the joy in the Christian camp at Acre when, after a long deadly winter the King of England, the chivalrous Lord of the Angevin Empire, at last made his appearance. We are told that the very earth was shaken by the jubilant acclamations with which he was greeted; while at night all the lines were illuminated.[1]

The siege as already mentioned had been courageously undertaken by Guy of Lusignan on the 28th August 1189; with the support of the Templars, the Hospitallers, and the Pisans.[2] Acre had to be recovered before anything else could be attempted.

Siege of Acre.

It was the only safe harbour on the coast of Palestine except Tyre; and it commanded the access from Tyre, the Christian stronghold, to Jerusalem. Saladin therefore had promptly come to the rescue, besieging the besiegers. Conrad of Montferrat, though always opposing everything done by Guy, had found it necessary to join the siege; and apparently had remained at it till his marriage with Isabel; when he went off to his comfortable quarters at Tyre (November 1190); leaving the men who were fighting to win him a kingdom to perish from want. From November to the end of February famine was added to the pestilence that was already raging.[3] For both Conrad was held responsible.

Conrad of Montferrat.

'Curse the Marquis and die' was the refrain of the current camp-song.

> Tunc Marchisum detestantur,
> Subtracto solamine,
> Per quem escis defraudantur
> In famis discrimine.

---

[1] "Commota est terra a fremitu"; *Itinerary*, 211, 212.
[2] See the letter, Diceto, II. 70.
[3] *Itinerary*, 123; Ben. P., II. 142; Hoveden III. 69.

296

O tunc plebis vox maledicentis
    Marchisi perfidiam,
Quod non curat tabescentis
    Populi miseriam.[1]

The arrival of a big corn-ship saved the army from starvation.[2] But the Christians could only just hold their own between the sallies of the garrison from within, and the assaults of Saladin from without.

The mortality down to the time of Richard's landing may be gauged by the losses suffered in the highest ranks of society. Among **Losses by Death.** those who had perished were Queen Sybille and her two daughters by Guy; the Patriarch Heraclius; Baldwin of Canterbury and four other Archbishops; some twelve Bishops and Abbots; Frederic Duke of Suabia; Counts Philip of Flanders, Theobald of Blois, Stephen of Sancerre, Rotrou III. of Perche, John of Ponthieu, Roger of Apulia (son of King Tancred), Erard III. of Brienne, William of Férrers Earl of Derby; besides some forty or fifty Knights and Barons of high degree, including the ex-Justiciar Ranulf of Glanville.[3]

With the arrival of King Philip[4] more active operations had been **Dissensions.** resumed. But the dissensions among the leaders also became more virulent. The Marquis came back with Philip to keep him on his side; and Guy was driven over to Cyprus to beg for Richard's support. With the King of England at his back Geoffrey of Lusignan, a great fire-eater, impeached the Marquis of treason and desertion, challenging him to mortal combat. But Conrad prudently declined the encounter.[5] Then Philip started a fresh question by demanding from Richard one half of Cyprus under the Vézelai compact. Richard retorted by claiming half of Artois, a fief that had fallen in through the death of Count Philip of Flanders (1st June).[6] Then, hearing that Philip had gained great popularity by allowing three gold pieces or besants a month to each of his men-at-arms (*milites*), determined not to be outdone, Richard proclaimed an offer of four pieces to every man who would take service with him; whereupon most of Philip's artillerists went over to him.[7]

The Kings however very wisely agreed to join forces, so as to unite all the Christian contingents in one host. Philip had been getting engines ready (*petrariæ, mangonelli*), and an active bombardment began. But before matters were ready for an assault Richard fell ill, of a local

[1] *Itin.*, 125–127.
[2] *Id.*, 136.
[3] See the lists: Ben. P., II. 147–149; Hoveden, III. 87–89; *Epp. Cant.*, 328, 329; *Itin.*, 245; and notes to all.
[4] 20th April, Ben. P., 169; 21st April, *Itin.*, 213.
[5] *Itin.*, 211, 212; Ben. P., II. 169, 170.
[6] Ben. P., 171; and for Philip's death, 168.
[7] *Itinerary*, 213, 214; Ben. P., 170. On the Pipe Roll, 8 John, m. 9, I find the besant given as worth two shillings. If so, Richard's offer would be only 3½d. a day.

complaint, known as *arnoldia*.[1]　Then Philip tired of waiting delivered an assault without him, and was repulsed.　As soon as his men

> **Unsuccessful Assaults.** moved out to attack the city, Saladin, apprised by signals from the garrison, fell on his camp in the rear and forced him to recall the storming party.[2]　Then Philip in turn fell ill of the sickness. Meanwhile however a mine was being driven under the walls.[3]　Again on the 3rd July[4] the French delivered a determined assault, a considerable piece of wall having been brought down ; but again they failed to effect an entrance.[5]

　　Next day the besieged, satisfied that their position was hopeless, opened

> **Negotiations for Surrender.** negotiations.　Karakush and el Meshtub, one the governor of the town, and the other the commander of the garrison, came over, offering to surrender Acre with all contents on receiving assurance of life and limb.　But the Kings made large territorial demands, that could not be granted without Saladin's consent ; while he was protesting against any surrender, and urging the garrison to continued resistance.　For nine days the negotiations went on without any armistice ; the Christians pressing their bombardment without intermission, and Saladin endeavouring to assist his men to break out.[6]　On the 7th July a swimmer had brought him a last despairing appeal ; but no relief was effected.　"On the 12th the same swimmer brought the message that the garrison had capitulated."[7]　The terms extorted from the helplessness of

> **Capitulation of Acre.** the besieged were, the surrender of Acre : the giving up of the True Cross ; the liberation of 1500 prisoners of rank and file, with 100 of higher sort ; and a ransom of 200,000 gold besants, say £20,000,[8] to be paid by three monthly instalments, with 4,000 besants more to the Marquis.　We may hope that the non-combatants were set free, because it is clear that the combatants, one and all, were detained as hostages for the ransom.[9]

---

[1] '*Ægritudo quæ vulgo arnoldia vocatur*' ; *Itin.*, 214 ; Ben. P., 179.　According to Le Breton persons attacked might lose their hair and even their nails ; T. A. Archer.

[2] *Itinerary*, 214-217.　The writer gives the date as the 1st July.　But this does not leave time for the events that occurred before the 3rd July.　Bohadin the Saracen writer speaks of two assaults one on the 14th and the other on the 17th June ; 222-224 (251-253 *ut sup.*) cited Lane Poole, *Saladin*, 291.　Probably this was the affair of the 17th June.　　[3] *Itin.*, 217 ; Le Breton ; Ben. P., II. 170.

[4] See *Itin.*, 214-221 ; Lane Poole, *Saladin*, 291, citing Bohadin, 222-224 (251-253 *ut sup.*) ; Ben. P., 173.　　[5] *Itin.*, 221-224 ; Ben. P. and Lane Poole, *sup.*

[6] Ben. P., II. 174, 175 ; Hoveden, III. 117, 118 ; Lane-Poole, *sup.*, 297.

[7] Lane Poole, *sup.*

[8] Seventy-two besants made a pound of gold, and the pound of gold was worth twelve of silver.

[9] See Bohadin's account, evidently the most correct one, 227, 228, 234-237, cited L. Poole. 302 ; Ben. P., 178.　The English writers seem clearly wrong in stating that Saladin sanctioned the treaty beforehand.　In the Palestine Society's text of Bohadin the reference should be pp. 253-271.

After nearly two years of unremitting efforts the Crusaders had made themselves masters of Acre, that initial step towards the reconquest of Palestine. The difficulties attending further progress soon became apparent. In fact their first entry into the town was marked by an untoward incident. Leopold Duke of Austria, a cousin to the Emperor, and "an enthusiastic Crusader," on taking up quarters within the walls hoisted his flag as an independent Prince. Richard immediately ordered the ensign to be pulled down. His relations with the Duke must have been seriously affected by his treatment of Leopold's kinsman, the Cyprian Isaac. Leopold could hardly fail to be indignant; and he may have ventured to remonstrate. Anyhow Richard took the opportunity of showing his contempt for him. The Duke—like Achilles—retired to his hut, and we may add, lived to be revenged.[1] Philip likewise shortly declared an intention of leaving the field. His health had suffered, and he found it impossible to act with Richard. Then Guy and Conrad demanded a settlement of their rival claims. This matter was smoothed over for a time by a compromise, under which the crown was continued to Guy during his life; the reversion being settled on Conrad and Isabel; Conrad would retain Tyre with Sidon and Beirût; while Guy's brother Geoffrey would receive Joppa and Cæsarea.[2]

Richard and the Duke of Austria.

Guy and Conrad.

Philip was as good as his word. At the end of the month he sailed from Acre for Tyre,[3] taking with him the Marquis, and one-half of the prisoners. A considerable part of his following, however, preferred to remain under the lead of Hugh, Duke of Burgundy, and the martial Bishop of Beauvais. But Philip before leaving was required by Richard to take a public oath that he would keep the peace with him and his during his absence.[4] On the 3rd August Philip left Tyre on his homeward voyage[5]; and then Richard, who wanted to secure the whole of the ransom, sent Hubert Walter to Tyre to demand Philip's half of the hostages. The Marquis Conrad, who had them in his charge, refused to surrender them to the Bishop (5th–7th August): but an embassy led by the Duke of Burgundy proved more successful, and the captives were brought back to Acre on the 12th August. But meanwhile a month from the 12th July had expired, and the time had come when the True Cross, and the

Philip sails home.

His Captives brought back to Acre.

---

[1] See Gervase, I. 514; R. Dev., 428; M. Paris, *Chron. Maj.*, II. 384; Ansbert, extracted Hoveden, III. cxl. Ralph of Coggeshal places the incident at Joppa, p. 59. According to German authorities cited by Dr. Pauli, *Geschichte v. England*, I. 234, the final rupture between Richard and the Duke only took place in the following winter, during the rebuilding of Ascalon.

[2] Ben P., II. 182–184; *Itin.*, 235–237; R. Cogg., 33, 34.

[3] 31st July, Ben. P. 185; Hoveden, III. 126; 1st August, *Itin.*, 239.

[4] Ben. P., 184, 185; *Itin.*, 238, 239.   [5] Hoveden, III. 126.

first instalment of ransom had to be delivered. According to the Saracen

Break-down of the Capitulation. account, the one that seems best entitled to credit, Saladin had accepted the capitulation ; and the Cross, or a " convincing imitation of it," had been shown to English envcys in his camp.[1] The money being ready, and the list of men to be delivered by Saladin having been verified, Richard's envoys

Saracen Account. came on the 11th August, to arrange for fulfilment. Saladin then explained that he would require the Christians either to deliver all their captives at once, on receiving hostages for the ultimate release of the rest of their friends, or to retain their captives, on giving hostages for their ultimate dismissal when all the instalments of ransom had been paid.[2] But Richard would not accept either alternative. After

Massacres of Captives. ten days' further parley, neither side giving way, the Acre captives, 2600 in number,[3] were taken out, in sight of Saladin's camp, and there beheaded, half by Richard's men and half by those of the Duke of Burgundy. As usual a few men good for ransom were saved.[4] Of course Saladin retaliated.

The English story is much less satisfactory. We are told that Richard,

Frank Account. on the 13th August, began pressing for performance, Saladin begging for an extension of time ; that on the 14th and 15th Richard resumed hostilities ; that on the 16th Saladin failed to attend a conference, but sent envoys to say that he could not carry out the convention ; that on the 18th Richard again assaulted Saladin's camp ; that Saladin then butchered his captives ; that Richard heard of this on the 19th, and on the 20th retaliated.[5] Of this version we may remark that with all its chronological exactness it contains nothing incompatible with the Saracen account of the negotiations ; and that it only runs directly counter to it on the point of the prior massacre by Saladin.

On the 22nd August the Crusading host began moving out of Acre, to

---

[1] It appears that the Cross when taken at Hittin was mounted in gold and set with pearls and precious stones. It was sent to Baghdad, where the Kaliph buried it under the threshold of a gate, to be trodden under foot. Yet Bohadin asserts that the True Cross was shown in Saladin's camp at Acre, and afterwards sent to Damascus. From thence it is said to have been sent to Constantinople as a gift to the Emperor Isaac. See Lane Poole, *sup.* 304.

[2] Bohadin, 270-274 : Poole, *sup.* 305.

[3] So Richard's own letter to the Abbot of Clairvaux, Hoveden, III. 131.

[4] 20th August, Ben. P., II. 189 ; Bohadin, *sup.*

[5] See Ben. P., II. 188-190, abridged by Hoveden, III. 126-128. This account of course must have been taken from the diary of some one who was present. But it is right to notice that neither the author of the *Itinerary* who was also present, nor Richard himself in his letter (*sup.*), nor any other of our writers, makes any reference to any previous massacre by Saladin, or offers any excuse for Richard's action. One and all treat the case as one of pure military law ; the appointed day having passed without the stipulated payment, the lives of the hostages were forfeited. But they pass over the matter rather quickly.

undertake its march on Jerusalem. The two Queens with the little
Cyprian Princess were left at Acre, which had been refortified
as a base of operations. Bertram of Verdun and Stephen
Longchamp were left in command.[1] Richard's plan was to
advance along the shore as far as Joppa, so as to have the fleet in
attendance. On the 23rd the Belus was crossed; but there the army
rested a whole day, waiting for the many laggards to come up. The
temptations of Acre, we are told, were great and manifold. On the
25th August, however, the army accomplished its first real stage of some
eight miles to the river Kishon, the effort rendering two nights'
rest necessary. Saladin, hovering on their flanks, had already
begun his attacks, and had cut off part of the baggage train in
a defile. Richard led the way, with his banner displayed from a flagstaff
mounted on wheels and another standard. The Duke of Burgundy
brought up the rear.[2] Resuming on the 27th, they took five days to
make the twenty miles to Cæsarea; but there fleet and army joined hands
again (31st August). Four more marches brought them on the 5th of
September to the *Roche Taillée*, otherwise the Nahr Falik ('River of the
Cleft'), about six miles North of Arsûf (Apollonia),[3] where the
enemy were reported as about to make a more definite stand.
But Saladin's desultory attacks had never ceased; his
horsemen, in small bodies, would, like the Parthians of earlier times,[4]
attack boldly whenever they saw an opportunity; would take to hasty
flight when encountered; and return to the charge the moment that the
pursuit was dropped. The sufferings of the Crusaders
throughout from heat, fatigue, want of transport, and want
of supplies had been intense. The country had been devastated beforehand by the Sultan; the greater part of the pilgrims were
on foot, and had to carry everything for themselves. But the pressure of
this burden was lessened by a system of reliefs, one half of the infantry
being always engaged in the fighting line on the left, and the other half
in carrying *impedimenta* on the protected right by the sea-shore, with
alternate turns of duty.[5] But numbers kept dropping down on the way
to die. The Templars and Hospitallers again were in despair at the
number of horses that they lost, but the flesh of the animals provided a
welcome supply for starving pilgrims.[6]

It would seem that Richard, disconcerted by the difficulties that surrounded him, now offered to treat. Saladin's brother Saphadin came to

(Margin notes: *Advance from Acre.* ; *March to Cæsarea* ; *and Nahr Falik.* ; *Sufferings of the Pilgrims.*)

---

[1] Ben. P., II. 190; *Itin.*, 247, 248.
[2] *Itin.*, 248-252.
[3] See Archer, *Crusade of Rich.*, 146.
[4] " Versis animosum equis Parthum," Horace, Od. I. 19.
[5] Bohadin, 282.
[6] *Itin.*, 252-259.

meet him ; but the King's demands were so exorbitant that nothing could be done.[1] Early on the morning of the 7th September Richard led out his men to fight their way to Arsûf, a distance of six miles, along the sea-shore, **Formation on the March.** with rolling ground and a range of wooded hills at a distance of some three miles on their left. The forces were marshalled in twelve squadrons (*turmæ*), arranged in five lines (*acies*). The Templars formed the van ; next came the Bretons and Angevins ; then the Poitevins under King Guy ; after them the Normans and English in charge of the Standard ; while the Hospitallers brought up the rear. The French, under Count Henry of Champagne and the Bishop of Beauvais, were apparently placed as a wing on the left flank, the flank exposed to attack, with a covering body of infantry outside them again.[2] The rear likewise was closed in by lines of archers and crossbowmen.[3] The baggage train marched on the right, along the shore. We are told that the cavalry were so closely packed that an apple could not have fallen among them without touching horse or man. The whole force must have marched as a solid phalanx of cavalry, shrouded front, flanks, and rear in clouds of infantry.[4] In fact this apparently had been their formation all along, as the Saracen Bohadin gives a precisely similar account of their appearance on an earlier day.[5]

Advancing cautiously, in strict order, with Richard and the Duke of **Approach to Arsûf.** Burgundy riding up and down to direct their movements, the army about 9 a.m. (*hora tertia*) reached the place where the enemy were drawn up abreast of the line of their march, not far from Arsûf, at the foot of the hills. The Saracens, evidently not caring to face the direct impact of the head of the column, had left it room enough to pass,[6] reserving themselves for a flank attack. At a signal from the Sultan the onslaught began. Down came the wild hordes in **Saracen Attack.** torrents (*more aquarum inundantium*) ; first Arabs and Turks ; then Black troops from the Soudan ; then Bedawin from the Desert, only a shade less dusky in complexion than the Soudanese. Behind these pressed on the more regular squadrons of cavalry, with countless flags and banners ; their ardour roused to the highest pitch by wild strains of barbaric music from horns, trumpets, pipes, drums, and cymbals played by regular military bands, an institution, by the way,

---

[1] Lane Poole, *sup.* 313 ; Bohadin, 287-289.

[2] " Comes Henricus Campaniæ custodias agebat a parte montana, semper observans a latere, satellites quoque pedites ; " *Itin.*, 261. See plan.

[3] " Omnium extremi sagittarii et balistarii ordinabantur extremitatem exercitus concludentes ; " *Itin.*, 260, 261.

[4] See again Bohadin, *sup.*

[5] Bohadin, 282.

[6] " Ab exercitu Saracenorum protendebatur exercitus noster usque ad littora maris ; " *Itin.*, 261.

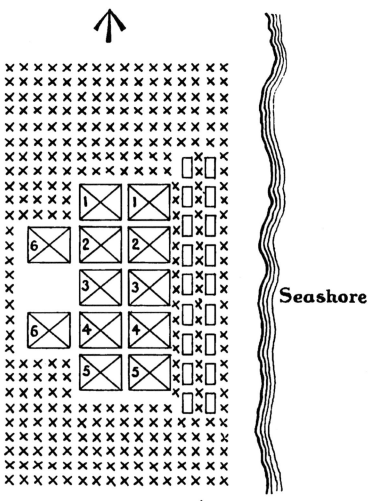

Seashore

THE BATTLE OF ARSÛF
(7TH SEPT., 1191)

[To face page 302.

apparently new to the Europeans.[1]   From front to rear, with an encircling line two miles long, the enemy hemmed in the Christians;[2] the archers and cross bowmen of the latter replying vigorously to the hail of the **Pressure on** enemy's darts and arrows.   But the attack gradually concen-**Christian** trated itself on the Christian rear, where the infantry were **Rear.** obliged to march backwards with their faces to the enemy.[3] It should be noted that even the foot soldiers were not without protection against arrows, most of them being provided with hauberks and *gambesons* or wambais, long padded coats coming down to the knees,[4] while the Moslem wore little or no defensive armour.[5] · The armour of the mounted men-at-arms, of course, was quite impenetrable, but many of them as usual had their horses disabled, and were reduced to marching on foot.   The running fight, however, was kept up under very great difficulties, the heat being excessive, and the advance at last was reduced to a mere crawl.[6] Many of the Emirs discarded their horses to grapple with the Hospitallers on foot.   At last the latter, finding the pressure on their rear intolerable, · applied to Richard for leave to charge.   But he refused, ordering them still to keep their ranks.   The march was continued, the irresistible column still forging slowly ahead, till the infantry of the van began to enter the woods and gardens of Arsûf.[7]   Again the Grand Master begged to be allowed to repel his assailants.   'Good Master,' quoth the King, 'endure yet awhile; I cannot be everywhere at once.'   According to the Chaplain, Richard had a plan which if carried out would have led to the utter destruction of the enemy.[8] To us it seems as if Richard as heretofore wished to accomplish his day's march without risking any general engagement.   With the comparative smallness of his force, and the unlikelihood of any reinforcements coming out from Europe, he could not afford to lose **The** men.   But the Hospitallers could no longer be kept in hand. **Hospitallers** Two of their number broke away, shouting 'Saint George, **charge.** Saint George!' and then, wheeling about, plunged headlong among the enemy in their rear.   Of course their brethren dashed after them; and then the bulk of the army, rank after rank, followed suit, all

[1] See the expression "ad hoc deputati (sc. viri) prœibant." 'Men especially told off for the duty.' *Id.* 262.

[2] " Et a parte maris et terræ solidioris, . . . a duobus circumquaque milliariis," etc. ; *Id.*, 263.

[3] *Id.*, 263, 264, 267.

[4] See Lane Poole, *supra*, 310. Bohadin says that he saw Christians marching with many arrows sticking in them, but that his people could not withstand the cross-bow bolts.

[5] *Itin.*, 247.

[6] " Potius viam carpendo quam eundo ; " *Id.*, 264, 265.

[7] See Bohadin, 290, also Richard's letter to the Abbot of Clairvaux, Hoveden, III. 131, from both of which it appears that the Christians did not charge till their van had reached Arsûf.

[8] See *Itin.*, 265-268.

but the Anglo-Norman force who had to retain their position round the Standard.[1]   But Richard himself was not to be kept out of the scrimmage,

General Engagement. and he and his personal staff were quickly in the forefront, cutting down the enemy right and left.[2]   Half a mile of ground, we are told, was soon covered with corpses.   As seen by Richard's chaplain, the man to whom we owe the narrative of the *Itinerary*, who was doubtless posted by the Standard, the principal feature of the action was the cutting off of the Saracen wing that enveloped the Christian rear, who were driven down to the sea and annihilated.[3]   But Bohadin, the Saracen

The Saracens repulsed, writer, with a fuller view of the battle-field obtained from the heights, saw the whole of their line from right to left flying before the Christian onset.   Weary of slaughter, the Crusaders drew rein, and began to retire, whereupon the whole Saracen force resumed the offensive.[4]   Saladin's nephew, Taki-ed-din, with a body of

But charge again, picked men, fell on the Anglo-Norman contingent in charge of the Standard, and surrounded them.   They were reduced to the utmost straits until rescued by William des Barres, Richard's old antagonist.   Richard himself, in the intoxication of battle, was in wild pursuit of the enemy along the slopes of the hills.   His action, however, may have effected a diversion by taking Taki-ed-din in the rear.[5]   Twice

And again and again are repulsed. again, it would seem, the Crusaders had to charge along the line, before the enemy were sufficiently repelled to allow of their resuming their march.[6]   Finally, however, the column was reformed, and Arsûf was entered in safety.   But the tents could not

Arsûf reached. be pitched without yet another final attack that Richard himself had to assist in repelling.[7]   The chief loss on the Christian side was that of the Fleming James of Avesnes, a very distinguished warrior, who at one time had been in command of the army at the siege of Acre.   The Saracens however likewise only admitted the death of one Emir of the first rank.[8]

On the 9th September, after a well-earned Sunday of rest at Arsûf,

Advance to Joppa. the Crusaders resumed their march; and next day found themselves revelling in the gardens and orchards of Joppa, amidst pomegranates, figs, and grapes.[9]   The coast march had been accomplished; but at a rate of progress that augured badly

---

[1] See *Itin.*, 272, and Richard's own letter *supra*, where he says that on the Christian side, only 4 *turmæ* were engaged; his *turma*, I take it, corresponding to the *acies* of the *Itinerary*.

[2] *Itin.*, 268–272.

[3] See page 269, where he describes the French as driving the enemy "versus maritima a parte sinistra." He also states that the marching order was inverted in the battle, the rear ranks engaging first.   [4] Lane Poole, *supra*, 319; Bohadin.

[5] *Itin.*, 271–274.   [6] Bohadin, 291.   [7] *Itin.*, 274.

[8] *Id.*, Lane Poole, *sup.*, 322.   [9] *Itin.*, 281, 282.

r the future; nineteen days having been required for an advance of
:tle more than sixty miles. Moreover, when the next step to be taken
ime under discussion, great differences of opinion declared themselves.
ichard wished to seize Ascalon which was being demolished by Saladin;[1]
Stay there. but the French insisted on repairing Joppa. Some three weeks
were devoted to that work; and then, towards the end of
eptember, an advance on Jerusalem was ordered; and the forces were
.ken out to a place called the Casal of St. Habakkuk, apparently in
ie neighbourhood of Lydda.[2] During its short stay there, the army
early suffered an irretrievable loss through the capture of its commander-
i-chief. Richard having gone out hawking with a slender escort, and
Narrow Escape of the King. getting tired, dismounted in a cool spot to take a *siesta*,
when he was surrounded and set upon by the enemy; and
in fact only owed his escape to the devotion of one William
es Préaux, who surrendered himself as the King of England, and enabled
ie real Richard to escape.[3]

But now Richard found that the numbers prepared to advance were
uite insufficient, and that he must fall back on Joppa to reorganise his
)rces. Moreover, two trips to Acre were found necessary for the purpose,
ne undertaken by King Guy; the other by Richard in person.[4] In fact,
Negotiations Richard, who had begun to entertain misgivings as to the ultimate success of the campaign, was pressing Saladin with nego-
iations for the surrender of Palestine; while the Marquis had opened
counter negotiations with the Sultan, offering to recover Acre
and Intrigues. for him, on condition of receiving Sidon and Beirût.[5]
Richard's voyage to Acre was clearly undertaken to guard
gainst this intrigue, as he removed Berengaria and Johanna from Acre,
)ringing them with him to Joppa.[6]

On the 31st October a fresh start was made, the army encamping at
?azûr, four miles from Joppa, while advanced posts were being fortified
at places designated as 'the Casal of the Plains,' and 'the
Struggling Advance Casal of Maen,' perhaps Beit Dejan and Saferiyeh on the road
to Lydda.[7] But the army did not get beyond those places
ill the 15th November, when a further advance of a few miles was
made to Ramleh. Saladin, who never ceased to watch and
to Ramleh. confront them, at their advance to Ramleh fell back on
Latrûn; and from thence again to Jerusalem.[8] On the 8th December

[1] See Bohadin, 296-298.
[2] *Itin.*, 285. For the locality see Bishop Stubbs' note.
[3] *Itin.*, 286-289; Bohadin, 301, 302; Hoveden, III. 133.
[4] *Itin.*, 286.   [5] Bohadin, 297, 303.   [6] *Itin., sup.*
[7] *Itin.*, 289, 290, and notes; Bohadin, 307, 308.
[8] *Itin,* 290, 297, 298, and notes; Latrûn, otherwise Netroun, otherwise Toron of the
Knights, lies a little to the S.E. of Beit Nuba.

the army went into winter quarters round Ramleh; while Richard with
the advance guard established himself for Christmas at Latrûn.

Winter Quarters. The army is described as suffering from insufficient supplies,
incessant skirmishing attacks, and heavy rains.[1]

Meanwhile the diplomatic struggle went on. While at Yazûr, Richard
had again demanded the cession of all Palestine.[2] After a while he
came forward with the amazing offer to marry his sister Jeanne to
Saladin's brother Saphadin, if the Sultan would settle

An offer of Marriage. Jerusalem on them. Saladin, treating the proposal as
seriously meant, agreed to consider it, and laid it, together
with the rival offers of the Marquis, before his Council. The Emirs
declared in favour of a treaty with the King of England as against one
with the Marquis; and then Richard had to explain that there were
difficulties in the way of the proposed marriage; that the lady being a
widow, the Pope would have to be consulted (in fact she had refused
to marry a Moslem), and so he now suggested the hand of his niece,
Eleanor of Brittany, who was unmarried and his ward. Saladin answered
curtly that if there was to be a change of woman nothing more need
be said about the matter, and there it ended.[3] The only result of
the negotiations was to create suspicion against Richard in the minds
of the Crusaders, Saladin having been careful to cultivate him with
presents and delicate attentions.[4]

Once more, in the last days of the year (28th–31st December), the army
was set in order, and a march of a few miles to Beit Nuba[5] was accomplished in terrible weather. Everything was soaked with rain,

Advance to Beit Nuba. the biscuit (*panis biscoctus*) and other provisions were spoiled;
the tent-poles blown away. But the pilgrims could console
themselves with the thought that they were within ten miles of the Holy
Sepulchre, almost in sight of the Holy City. Saladin's army was so
utterly worn out[6] that a prompt attack on Jerusalem would certainly have
been successful. But the Syrian Franks were not so much anxious to
capture Jerusalem as to detain the Crusaders in Palestine till their own
possessions had been recovered. They urged that they had not men
enough to hold both Jerusalem and the line of communications to the
coast. To the utter mortification of Richard and most of the pilgrims,
a council of war held on the 13th January,[7] 1192, decided that the

---

[1] *Itin.*, 298, 299; Hoveden, III. 174, 175, and notes; Bohadin, 327.

[2] Bohadin, 308.   [3] Bohadin, 310-312, 317, 320-326.

[4] *Itin.*, 296, 297. Saphadin and Richard had a most friendly meeting on the
8th November, *Id.*, and Bohadin, 320.

[5] For the advance guard at Latrûn the distance would be three to four miles; for the
main body at Ramleh seven to eight miles.   [6] Bohadin, 297, 328; *Itin.*, 309.

[7] Hoveden, III. 179. Richard however had a few days before paid a visit to Joppa,
as he sealed a charter there on the 10th January 1192; *Calendar of Documents* (Round),
103, 104.

reoccupation of Ascalon was the first thing to be taken in hand.[1] With

Retirement to Ascalon. heavy hearts, the army retraced their steps to Ramleh. After a pause of a week or so there, Richard with the Duke of Burgundy and Henry of Champagne, led a reduced host to Ibelin (now Yebneh or Jamnia); and from thence, next day, to Ascalon (22nd January?).[2] There they established themselves within the walls of the dismantled and depopulated city.[3]

[1] *Itin.*, 303-309.

[2] So the *History of Jerusalem* cited by Bishop Stubbs *Itin.*, 312. The *Itinerary* itself places the march from Ramleh to Ascalon on the 19th and 20th January.

[3] *Itin.*, 309-312, and Hoveden, *supra.*

CHAPTER XVIII

RICHARD I. (*continued*)

A.D. 1190–1192

Affairs in England—Longchamp's Administration—Contention with John—Contention with Archbishop Geoffrey—Coalition against Longchamp—Grant of Municipal Incorporation to City of London—Deposition and Banishment of Longchamp

RICHARD on taking his departure from England for the Crusade, had, as we have seen, left as his chief representative his Chancellor William of Longchamp Bishop of Ely, whose position was further enhanced by the receipt of a Legatine Commission from Clement III. Longchamp, making the most of his opportunities, ruled England without opposition, but with ever-increasing unpopularity, for many months. A rival potentate appeared on the scene when Earl John came back, presumably at some time in 1190, to enjoy the magnificent appanage so unwisely conferred upon him by Richard.[1] His rank, wealth, and the splendour of his housekeeping soon gained him popularity. Between John and the Legate there was no ill-feeling to begin with; in fact Longchamp as Legate had absolved John from his oath of absence.[2] But men with grudges against the Chancellor soon began to look to John as a rallying point. A coolness ensued when it became known that Richard had declared Arthur of Brittany his heir, and that Longchamp, in accordance with his master's wishes, was in correspondence with the King of Scots to secure the recognition of his grand-nephew the young Count.[3] John considered himself the heir, and indeed something more, Richard's return being generally considered very doubtful.[4] We hear of a conference between John and Longchamp held at Winchester on the 24th March 1191, as if the two were already more or less at variance. The matters under discussion included the delicate question

Longchamp's Government of England.

Return of Earl John.

The two at Variance.

---

[1] See above, 263, 265, 275.
[2] So Giraldus, I. 86.
[3] W. Newburgh, I. 335, 336; Chron. Melrose, A.D. 1191. Arthur's mother was daughter of Conan by Margaret of Scotland, William's sister.
[4] W. Newb., I. 337 338; R. Devizes, 406.

of the custody of certain castles ; also a question as to pecuniary allow--
ances to John from the royal Treasury.[1]   On the 27th April Walter of
Coutances landed at Shoreham,[2] with the letters authorising him and the
Regency Council to overrule Longchamp's proceedings if his conduct
should seem unsatisfactory.[3]   But the Archbishop soon found that the
man to be feared was not the Chancellor but the brother ; and so he
refrained from publishing his instructions, giving instead a cautious
support to Longchamp as against the questionable proceedings of Earl
John.[4]   No collision occurred till towards Midsummer, when John and
the Chancellor fell out about the case of Gerard of Camville.   This man,
the son of Richard's naval commander, being in right of his wife Nicholaa
de la Haye Constable of Lincoln Castle, had purchased from the King the
Sheriffdom of the county in addition.   But it was a recognised principle of
administration that the control of the county and the castle should never
be left in the same hands.   Camville also laboured under the imputation
of having harboured men concerned in the pillage of the Jews at the fair
of Stamford.[5]   Longchamp, in pursuance of his system of revoking the
King's improvident grants, having first deprived the man of the sheriffdom,[6]
now called on him to surrender the castle also.   In this extremity Camville appealed to John, who ordered the Chancellor to reinstate Camville.

Both parties at once prepared to draw the sword.   Longchamp
War between them. called out levies, and sent abroad for mercenaries ; while Roger
Mortimer of Wigmore enlisted Welshmen on behalf of John.[7]
The Chancellor marched against Mortimer, and by the promptness and
vigour of his action reduced him to submission, and banished him from
England for three years.   From Wigmore Longchamp advanced to
Lincoln, where the Lady Nicholaa had made ready to stand a siege.[8]   But
meanwhile John, through the connivance of underlings in charge, had
been allowed to take possession of Nottingham and Tickhill, castles that
had been intentionally withheld from him.[9]   A conflict between John and
the Chancellor was averted by the Archbishop of Rouen, who persuaded
Longchamp to drop the siege of Lincoln, and meet the Earl in conference.

Both came to Winchester, the appointed place, at the head of regular
armies.   On the 28th July their mutual complaints were considered in an

---

[1] R. Devizes, 402. In confirmation of this writer's authority Mr. Round points out
that Longchamp was at Winchester on the 28th March, *Epp. Cant.*, 327.

[2] R. Diceto, II. 90, reading the corrected date " V. Kal. Maii " for " V. Kal. Julii."
Gervase, however, places his return about Midsummer, I. 497.

[3] See Diceto, II. 91 ; Giraldus, IV. 400 ; and above, 290.

[4] R. Dev., 406.   [5] See Hoveden, III. 242.

[6] See W. Newb., I. 388, and especially the later treaty ; Hoveden, III. 135.

[7] R. Devizes, 407, 409.

[8] After Midsummer, Ben. P., II. 207 ; Gervase, I. 497. Longchamp was at Lincoln
on the 8th July ; Round, *Commune of London*, 214.

[9] Ben. P., II. 207, 232 ; R. Devizes, 406, 407 ; W. Newb., I. 338.

assembly that might be described as a Grand Council.[1] Through the efforts of the Archbishop and others a pacification was arranged on terms conciliatory to John, while the King's interests were carefully safe-guarded.

Public Pacification. John was required to make a formal surrender of Nottingham and Tickhill to the Archbishop on behalf of the King; Nottingham to be placed in the hands of William Marshal the Earl of Pembroke; Tickhill to be virtually restored to John, by being left under the charge of William of Wenneval or Wendiwall one of his followers; all other castles connected with John's possessions in England to remain in the hands of the King's sworn men; Camville to be reinstated in his sheriffdom; and his whole case submitted to legal trial, John pledging himself to abide by the decision of the court. No reference was made to the question of the succession; but we have an interesting testimony to the appreciation of Henry II.'s legislation in a declaration that no freeholder should be disseised by the King's Justices or Ministers except by process of law, in accordance with the legitimate assizes of the realm.[2]

That the Magnates, though anxious to consult John's feelings, were not disposed to abet him in his ulterior designs appears not only from the terms of the pacification, but also from the fact that the sureties for Longchamp included the Earls of Arundel, Salisbury, Norfolk, and Herts while no Baron of first rate position signs for John.[3]

It would seem that John was not quite satisfied with these terms, and refused to disarm, and that Longchamp considering his own unpopularity thought it prudent to conciliate the Earl by further concessions.

Private Compact. A treaty of arbitration, to which the Archbishop of Rouen was not a party, was entered into, with the result that Longchamp agreed to make friends with Camville; to allow John to retain Nottingham as well as Tickhill, and support him against Arthur as heir to the throne.[4]

The excitement of these events had hardly subsided, when a fresh storm burst. The King's brother Geoffrey, as already mentioned, had been consecrated as Archbishop of York at Tours on the 18th August (1191),

---

[1] R. Devizes, 408, 409.

[2] See the treaty Hoved., III. 135, given without date, which I take from R. Devizes, 408.   [3] Hoved., *sup.*

[4] August–September. See R. Devizes, 409, 410, where this treaty is given as the outcome of the meeting of 28th July, but with the insensate date of 25th April (V. Kal. Maii). See also W. Newb., I. 339, and Gervase, I. 497, 498, who agree as to two treaties between John and Longchamp, both executed after the siege of Lincoln. It will be seen that I agree with Mr. Round in holding the treaty in Devizes as later than the one in Hoveden (*Commune*, etc., 217). Bishop Stubbs accepting the treaty in Devizes as really executed on 25th April was obliged to place the seizure of Nottingham and Tickhill in the spring, and to suggest two sieges of Lincoln, one in the spring, the other after Midsummer (Hoveden, III., lvii., lviii.; and 134, note). But there is no allegation of more than one siege of Lincoln in any writer, and the recorded siege clearly fell after

and had received his Pall at the same time.[1]   As the Pope's order for his

Archbishop Geoffrey coming. consecration had to all appearance been issued with Richard's approval[2] he might well consider himself at liberty to return to England, and had lost no time in announcing his intention of so doing.   Longchamp, who was confident that he had the King's mind, was equally prompt in taking measures to prevent his landing, and even

Opposition to his Landing. before Geoffrey's consecration had sent warnings to the Sheriffs not to allow him to set foot in England.[3]   When Geoffrey was reported to be on his way Longchamp wrote to the Countesses of Flanders and Boulogne to forbid his travelling through their territories ; and in consequence of the opposition of the Countess of Flanders Geoffrey had to relinquish the favourite passage from Witsand, and sail from Boulogne. He entered Dover harbour on the 14th September.[4]   As his household had landed on the previous day, the authorities were in waiting for him. Dover Castle was in the hands of Matthew of Clères, who was married to Longchamp's sister Richaut.   She being in charge at the time ordered the Archbishop to be arrested ; but he, disguising himself before landing, and

He takes Sanctuary then mounting a horse made his way to the Priory of St. Martin's and took sanctuary.   A message then came down from the castle requiring him to take an oath of allegiance to Richard and Longchamp.   With his usual hot-headedness he answered that ' he would give the Chancellor the traitor's doom that he deserved.'[5] An alternative offer of permission to leave the kingdom was rejected with

But is dragged from it. equal scorn.   For days he was besieged ; at last on the 18th of September a party of soldiers dragged him from the altar where he was sitting, cross in hand, and marched him off to the castle with the greatest indignity.[6]

Midsummer, in immediate sequence on Longchamp's attack on Mortimer, and the seizures of Nottingham and Tickhill, the whole forming one series of connected events. Lastly Mr. Round has disposed of the supposed meeting at Winchester on 25th April by showing that on the day before Longchamp was at Cambridge (*Commune*, 214).   In further support of the view that there were two treaties between John and Longchamp, I may point to the fact that Benedict, II. 208, and W. Newburgh, I. 389, in their accounts of these affairs both represent Longchamp as promising to support John's claim to the throne, of which there is no word in the treaty in Hoveden.

[1] Diceto, II. 96 ; Ben. P., II. 209.   [2] See above, 290.

[3] See his orders to the Sheriff of Sussex, dated 30th July ; Girald. IV, 389 ; Diceto, II. 96.   It is characteristic of the audacity of the man, that Longchamp, still being or styling himself Papal Legate, orders the seizure of any letters from the Pope.   His original commission expired with the death of Clement III. ; Celestine renewed it, at a date not yet ascertained.   But on the 5th May, before it could well have been renewed, Longchamp, as Legate, consecrated Robert Fitz Ralph to be Bishop of Worcester ; Diceto, II. 89.   [4] Giraldus, IV. 387, 388 ; Diceto, II. 96.

[5] " Nihil aliud facturum nisi quod proditori regis . . . faciendum erat " ; Giraldus.

[6] Giraldus, IV. 388–392 (*Vita Galfredi*) ; Diceto, II. 95 ; Ben. P., II. 210, 211 ; R. Devizes, 411, 412 ; Gervase, I. 504, 505.

Reports of this outrage created an immense sensation, bringing together all who bore any ill-will to the Chancellor. The bishops and clergy naturally took the lead in action. Hugh of Lincoln excommunicated all concerned; while Richard fitz Nigel of London and John of Norwich pressed Longchamp for the immediate liberation of the Archbishop.[1]

Being set free In vain he protested that his orders had been exceeded.[2] After eight days' detention, Geoffrey on the 26th of September was allowed to leave the castle and to return to St. Martin's; but he was required to pledge himself to come to London to submit his case to the bishops and barons in council. From St. Martin's **He goes to London.** he went to Canterbury, and so on to London, where Bishop Richard received him in procession at St. Paul's on the 2nd of October.[3]

Hugh of Nonant, Bishop of Coventry, at one time a friend to Longchamp, but now a bitter enemy,[4] seeing the "greatness of the opportunity," hastened to Lancaster where John was, and brought him to Marlborough to concert measures against Longchamp. The support of the Earl of Pembroke, William Brewer, and Geoffrey fitz Peter, **A Grand Council.** members of the Regency Council, having been secured, as well as that of their coadjutor the Archbishop of Rouen, John issued invitations to a Grand Council, to be held on the 5th of October on the bridge of the Lodden between Reading and Windsor.[5]

When the day came, Longchamp started for the conference, but getting alarmed at the reports of the forces gathered to meet him, turned back to Windsor, requesting a meeting nearer that place. The sitting therefore had to be held without him. It would seem that Geoffrey produced letters from the King authorising his return; and that Walter of Coutances produced his Messina instructions, apparently till then suppressed, empowering **Longchamp to be deposed.** him and the Regency Council to control Longchamp's action. Walter ended by moving the deposition of Longchamp.[6] Next day being a Sunday, the Prelates quartered at Reading for the conference turned the opportunity to account by publicly excommunicating all concerned in the arrest of Geoffrey, including two of Longchamp's agents by name. The Chancellor, on the other hand, in the hopes of breaking up the confederacy, sent men to make private offers to John, but without success.[7] On the Monday, the assembled dignitaries moved from

---

[1] Giraldus, IV. 393, 394; Gervase, I., 505-507.

[2] *Epp. Cant.*, 344, 345.

[3] Diceto, II., 97, 98; Giraldus, IV., 395, 396.

[4] R. Devizes, 415. For Nonant, the clever, ambitious, unprincipled hater of monks, I must refer the reader to Bishop Stubbs; Hoveden, III. liii.

[5] Giraldus, 394-396; Diceto, 98; R. Devizes, 413.

[6] Giraldus, IV. 379-401; Diceto, *supra*.   [7] Giraldus, 401, 402; Diceto, *supra*.

Reading for Windsor, forwarding their baggage to Staines. Again the diminutive Chancellor went some way to meet them, looking, we are assured, not unlike a mail-clad monkey perched on a horse;[1] and again, at the end of a couple of miles, on hearing of the train moving towards Staines, supposing that John was intending to cut him off from London,

A Race to London. returned to Windsor. He gave a few hurried orders for the defence of the castle, and then, crossing the Thames, posted on to London.[2] On reaching the city, he went to the Guildhall,[3] where a meeting had been convened in advance by his friends. He entreated the citizens to resist John as evidently aiming at the Crown ; but he got so little support that he judged it expedient to retire to the Tower.[4] Shortly afterwards John and the Barons arrived, having followed Longchamp so closely that their retinues had come into collision on the way, and blood had been shed.[5] John was given to understand that

The Citizens' Demands. the city would support him if he would grant them municipal independence, or a *commune*, an institution already well known on the Continent. In England the thing was new ; and we are quite prepared to believe that neither Henry II. nor Richard would have listened to such a proposal.[6] But John stuck at nothing, and was prepared to promise whatever was asked.

On the morrow, Tuesday 8th October, John, Prelates, Barons and

Meeting at St. Paul's. Burghers met at St. Paul's ; the citizens having been summoned as to a city meeting by the tolling of the great bell.[7] The suggested compact with the citizens was duly carried out ; and a series of extraordinary measures passed by acclamation.

Longchamp deposed. Walter of Coutances again produced his Messina powers— if indeed he had produced them before[8]—Longchamp was again denounced and deposed from the Chief Justiciarship ;

John Heir to the Throne. John was recognised as heir to the throne, failing issue of Richard, and made virtual if not actual Regent with the control of the royal castles ;[9] Walter of Coutances would be Chief Justiciar under him ; the consultative committee appointed by Richard to go on as before. As a corollary to the deposition of Longchamp some

---

[1] " Quamsi simia equitaret armata," etc., Giraldus.

[2] Giraldus, 402, 403 ; Diceto, 99 : R. Devizes, 414.

[3] " Aula publica quæ a potorum conventu nomen accepit"; Giraldus evidently thought that a Gild meeting involved a drinking bout.

[4] Giraldus, 404 ; Diceto and Devizes, *sup.*

[5] *Id.*, and Hugh of Nonant's letter to Richard, Hoved., III. 218.

[6] So R. Devizes, 416.   [7] Diceto, II. 99.

[8] Benedict, II. 213, and Hoveden, III. 140, assert that the letters were now produced for the first time.

[9] " Constituerunt Johannem comitem . . . summum rectorem totius regni" ; R. Dev., 415. No other writer is so explicit on this point ; but Benedict, 214, states that the Barons swore fealty to John saving their fealty to Richard. That would imply almost as much.

of his more high-handed acts were at once reversed. The Bishop of Winchester would recover his sheriffdom, and the Bishop of Durham his **Municipality** earldom. On the other hand the Magnates one and all, from **of London** John downwards, accepted the *Commune*, and apparently took **granted.** the oaths as freemen.[1] Lastly, as if to clear their consciences towards the Prince whose prerogatives had been so signally invaded, the assembly swore a fresh oath of allegiance to King Richard.[2]

Wednesday was spent in diplomatic efforts by a deputation of Bishops to induce Longchamp to submit; and by him in fresh attempts to make private terms with John. After a long agony, towards night he gave hostages to face his accusers on the morrow.[3] On the Thursday, **Further** 10th of October, a great meeting was held in an open field, **Meeting.** at the East end of London, outside the Tower. We hear of a triple ring, with the Magnates in the centre, the civic authorities round them, and the popular concourse outside all. Hugh of Nonant recapitulated all the charges against Longchamp, and required him to resign the Seal and all his castles except Dover, Cambridge, and Hereford. Longchamp made a spirited defence, asserting the loyalty and integrity of his conduct in the administration of affairs, and his readiness to account for every farthing of the King's revenue received by him. He specially protested against surrendering his castles as a breach of his duty to the King. Of his own free will he resigned nothing conferred upon him by the King; he protested against the decisions of the Council; **Longchamp** overcome by numbers, he yielded to force, as yield he must. **forced to** That same night he surrendered the keys of the Tower.[4] On **submit.** the 11th he removed from the Tower with all his effects, and crossed the Thames to Bermondsey, his brothers Henry and Osbert and his brother-in-law and chamberlain Matthew of Clères being left as hostages for the delivery of the castles. It was also understood that he was sworn not to leave the Kingdom till they had been delivered. On the 12th he was conducted to Dover by the Bishop of Rochester and his friend Henry of Cornhill Sheriff of Kent. A few days later he attempted to escape on board ship in the disguise of a woman. Being detected, he was mobbed and rudely thrust into custody till orders came from the

---

[1] "Concessa est ipsa die et instituta communia Londoniensium in quam universi regni magnates et ipsi etiam ipsius provinciæ episcopi jurare coguntur. Nunc primum in indulta sibi conjuratione regno regem deesse cognovit Londonia;" R. Dev. "Johannes . . . et barones . . . concesserunt civibus Londoniarum communam suam et juraverunt quod ipsi eam et dignitates civitatis Londoniarum custodirent," Benedict. "Omnes . . . magnates juraverunt communam Londoniæ," Diceto. For the Commune in itself and the rights granted see Appendix to this chapter.

[2] R. Dev., 415, 416; Ben. P., II. 213, 214; Diceto, *supra*; Giraldus, IV. 405.

[3] Giraldus, 406; Devizes, 416.

[4] R. Devizes, 417, 418; Giraldus, 405, 407; Diceto, 100.

Archbishop of Rouen for his liberation.　On the 29th of October he was
allowed to cross the Channel.[1]　He landed at Witsand to have
He leaves England. his effects arrested by Flemings, who had claims upon him.
From the coast he made his way to Paris, and from thence
again to Normandy.　In Paris he was received at Notre Dame in procession, but at his own expense.　In Normandy he was treated as excommunicate under the sentences uttered at Reading.[2]

Both sides sent reports to Richard and to the Pope.　Hugh of Nonant,
a traitor in secret league with John, wrote a disgraceful letter to the King,
heaping abuse upon the Chancellor, but prudently omitting all reference
to the things done in London, except the expulsion of Longchamp.[3]　To
the Pope Longchamp appealed with effect.　On the 2nd December
Celestine wrote letters ordering John and those who were acting with
him to reinstate the Chancellor under penalty of excommunication.
Fruitless Papal Intervention. Longchamp with charming irony forwarded the missive for
execution to his dear friend (*sinceræ dilectionis*) the Bishop of
Coventry, suspending the sentence however with regard to
John.　The Pope also accredited two Legates to Normandy; but his
measures fell rather flat.　The Legates were not allowed to enter the
Duchy; while in England the only district placed under ban was Longchamp's own diocese of Ely.[4]

A new piece on the board was introduced by the return of King Philip from
King Philip at Home again. Holy Land, anxious to do Richard any harm that he could.
Passing through Rome he had asked the Pope to relieve him
of his oath to Richard, but Celestine of course refused.　He
reached Fontainebleau in time for Christmas.[5]　His first step was to have
an interview with William fitz Ralph the Seneschal of Normandy, between
Trie and Gisors (20th January, 1192).　He demanded the delivery of
the unfortunate Alais, as promised by Richard at Messina, and with her
the surrender of Gisors, Eu, and Aumâle.　But the Norman authorities
had received no instructions on the subject.[6]　Philip's next move was to
Overtures to John. make overtures to John, offering him the hand of Alais with
his brother's Continental dominions.　At the report of this
intrigue Queen Eleanor hastened over to England, where she
landed on the 11th February.　She found her son preparing to sail for
Normandy.　Very obstinate he showed himself.　Four Councils had to

---

[1] Diceto, II. 100, 101 ; R Dev., 418, 419; Giraldus, IV. 410–413 ; and Hugh of
Nonant's letters, Ben. P., II. 219.　[2] Ben. P., 220, 221 ; R. Dev., *sup.*

[3] See Ben. P., II. 215–220, 221 ; Hoved., III. 141–147, 155 ; R. Dev., 418.

[4] Ben. P., 221–225, 246, 247 ; Hoved., 151–155 ; R. Devizes, 419, 431.　For the
report sent by the Archbishop of Rouen's agents at Rome see Ben. P., 241.

[5] Ben. P., 228–230, 235 ; Hoved., 166 ; Le Breton, *ad loc.*; Norgate.

[6] Ben. P., 236.　Hoveden, 103, places this conference at the end of the year, but
wrongly.

be held, and the sternest threats of confiscation uttered by the Archbish... of Rouen and the Regency Council before he would abandon his purpose Meanwhile however he had induced the Constables of Wallingford and Windsor to place those castles in his hands.[1]

This new overt act was under discussion in London when envoys from Longchamp entered the council chamber. Looking for support from Eleanor, as the true exponent of Richard's views, and still trusting to be able to bribe John, the Chancellor had landed on the previous day at Dover,[2] where he took up his quarters with his sister in the castle.

Longchamp back again. Through his agents he now demanded reinstatement, offering to meet any charge that might be brought against him. Eleanor in fact did do her best to persuade the Justiciars to receive Longchamp, but finding their opposition insurmountable she gave way. John too was prepared to favour Longchamp's petition. wishing to play him off against Walter of Rouen, whose position proved stronger than his own. He ignored successive invitations to attend a Council in London, and when he did come he intimated, by way of explaining his position in the matter, that Longchamp had promised him £500. The Justiciars took the hint; dropped the question of the castles, and placed £500 from the Treasury at the Earl's disposal.

And again banished. After that the order to Longchamp to quit the realm passed at once. On the 2nd April he recrossed the channel.[3]

Eleanor apparently remained in England as peace-maker. She had played a worthy part in these last affairs. She had promised the Canterbury monks her protection against the consequences of having elected an Archbishop of Canterbury without the King's concurrence:[4]

Eleanor as Peace-maker. and she had induced the Archbishop of Rouen and Longchamp to withdraw their mutual excommunications.[5] The never-ending clash of antagonistic pretensions as between Archbishop Geoffrey and the Bishop of Durham no mortal could hope to quell.[6]

---

[1] Ben. P., *sup.* ; R. Devizes, 430–433.   [2] Middle of March ; Gervase, I., 512.
[3] R. Devizes, 433, 434 ; Ben. P., II. 239 ; Hoveden, III. 188 ; W. Newb., I. 345, 346 ; Gervase, *sup.*   [4] Gervase, *sup.*
[5] R. Dev., *sup.* The contention between Walter and Longchamp ramified into Normandy. The Pope sent two Cardinals to settle all questions between them, as already mentioned. But the Seneschal of Normandy William fitz Ralph refused to allow the Legates to set foot in the Duchy without leave from Richard ; whereupon fitz Ralph was excommunicated, and Normandy laid under Interdict. Bishop Puiset was sent over to get the sentences recalled ; but failed to induce the Seneschal to admit the Cardinals. Finally Celestine himself took off the Interdict; Ben. P., II. 246, 247, 249, 250. The Interdict might have given Philip an opening for invading Normandy.
[6] For this dreary business see Hoveden, III. 168, 172, and Bishop Stubbs, Hoved., IV. lii.-lv. Geoffrey's first act as Archbishop was to call on the Bishop to take the due oath of canonical obedience, Hugh having strenuously opposed Geoffrey's appointment. Hugh appealed to Rome, and then Geoffrey excommunicated him, and so on. Geoffrey also promptly quarrelled with his Chapter, and excommunicated them.

APPENDIX TO CHAPTER XVIII.

THE *COMMUNE* OF LONDON OF 1191

ɪ DER the grant of a *Commune* London as a whole would first acquire a corporate unity.
1 then the several Gilds might be incorporated, but the city was not. The essential
tures of a *Commune* as found abroad were three, namely a *Major, Maire* or Mayor ;
elective Council, usually of twenty-four men (*khevins, jurats*) ; and an oath binding
citizens to support their constitution and independence. The oath was so prominent
eature that a *Commune* is often spoken of as a *Conjuratio*, as by Richard of Devizes
ove.[1] As evidence of what the grant of the *Commune* in 1191 established in
ndon we have a document belonging to the spring of 1193 (B. M. Addl. MSS.
,252. f. 112 d.) which gives the communal oath, and the oath shows London as ruled
a Mayor and Councillors, styled "Skivins" ; while another document, dated in the
renth year of King John, tells of twenty-four Councillors sworn to attend to the govern-
:nt of the city with all integrity (Addl. MSS. *sup.* f. 110). The communal oath
acramentum commune) in substance pledges all to be true to the King ; keep and help
keep their own peace ; maintain the *commune* and liberties of the city ; obey the
ayor, Skivins, and other good men acting with them ; and see the right done in all
ɪngs without fear or favour. It has been pointed out that the oath is practically that
ʃen by the Freemen at the present day. As for the other good men referred to they have
·en taken to be the pre-existing Aldermen. The position of the Councillors in whom the
rm of the Common Council has been traced, would be distinguished from that of the
ldermen as representing the interests of the City as a whole, whereas the Alderman
ɪs primarily concerned only with the affairs of his own Ward. With respect to the date
the appointment of the first Mayor, we shall find a Mayor acting with the Regency
ɒvernment in the spring of 1193.[2] Presumably he would have been elected in the
ɪtumn 1192, so that we only want evidence for the official year 1191–1192 to carry back
e start of the Mayoralty to the date of the grant of the *Commune*. At whatever date
: was elected the first Mayor of course was Hentry fitz Aylwin who held the office
l the year 1214.[3]

An incidental benefit derived by the city from the grant of the *Commune* was the
duction of its *firma* from the £547, to which it had been raised in 1169 to the £300 at
hich it had been previously held.[4]

---

[1] R. Dev., p. 416. See also *Foundations*, II. 99 for the same phrase with regard to
e early case of Le Mans, A.D. 1072–1073.

[2] Hovenden, III. 212.

[3] *Liber de Antiquis Legg. Lond.*, p. 1 (Camden Society). This chronicle, however,
nores the grant of 1191, and refers to fitz Aylwin's election to the year 1189.

[4] See the Pipe Rolls of those years cited by Mr. Round, and the whole subject fully
ɪscussed in his able monograph, *Commune*, etc., 219–260.

CHAPTER XIX

RICHARD I. (*continued*)

A.D. 1192

Progress and end of the Crusade—Assassination of Conrad of Montferrat—Henry of Champagne King of Jerusalem—Siege and capture of Darum—Second Advance to Beit Nuba—Capture of Great Caravan—Final retirement from Beit Nuba—Joppa attacked by Saladin and relieved by Richard—Battle of Joppa—Treaty with Saladin and Return to Europe—Imprisonment of Richard by Duke of Austria

THE year 1192 found the Crusaders in Palestine as little able to act in concert as ever. The French at Ascalon finding themselves in want applied to the Duke of Burgundy for wages. Unable to meet their demands he turned to Richard and asked for a loan. But Richard had already lent money, and it had not been repaid; he therefore refused to make any further advance, whereupon the discontented Duke retired to Acre with a considerable part of the French force.[1] Their arrival gave fresh life to the party of the Marquis. At their invitation he left Tyre for Acre, but was kept out by the Pisans who were supporters of King Guy. The report of these dissensions brought Richard from Ascalon to Acre, where he stayed from the 20th February till about the end of March. But his visit accomplished nothing beyond some friendly but futile negotiations with Saladin.[2] By the 31st March he had returned to Ascalon, and next day, much against his will, had to allow the rest of the French to take their departure for Acre. He gave them an escort, but rather meanly sent private instructions to forbid their admission to the town. His nephew, however, Henry of Champagne remained with him.[3]

[marginal notes: The Crusaders at Ascalon. Dissensions. Departure of the French.]

---

[1] February, *Itinerary*, 320, 321, and note.
[2] *Itinerary*, 324; Bohadin, 328; on Palm Sunday, 29th March, Richard knighted Saphadin's son.
[3] *Itinerary*, 326. Henry was son of one of Eleanor's daughters by Louis,

Early in April the fortifications of Ascalon had been sufficiently repaired ; but before anything else could be taken in hand the camp was thrown into a great state of trouble by the arrival of Robert, Prior of Hereford, sent by Longchamp with a report of his expulsion and of John's doings.   It seemed as if Richard while endeavouring to conquer kingdoms abroad, might lose his own inheritance at home.   Naturally his first impulse was to go home ; and he asked his Council if they would be satisfied if he left them 300 men-at-arms and 2000 footmen at his cost and charges.   In answer they urged the primary necessity of settling the question of the Kingdom of Jerusalem, in order to secure unity of action ; and they went on to declare themselves all in favour of the Marquis, Guy having dis-

Final accept-ance of the Marquis Conrad. tinctly failed to obtain recognition.[1]   Richard, for once giving way, sent Henry of Champagne to Tyre to announce his acceptance of Conrad.   The Marquis, overjoyed, was preparing for his coronation when he was stabbed to death

His Assassina-tion. by two fanatical assassins, understood to be emissaries of the Sheykh of Alamût, or of some subordinate chief of the same sect, who bore Conrad a particular grudge (20th April).[2] The French however ventured to give out that Conrad had been murdered at Richard's instigation, and the Moslems were not ashamed to support the calumny.[3]

Just as the Marquis was breathing his last Henry of Champagne came to Tyre.   His appearance solved all difficulties.   Being nephew both to Richard and Philip he would command the suffrages of both nations, and

Henry of Champagne King of Jerusalem. the Crusaders at once proclaimed him King.   But it was made a condition that he should marry the widowed Marchioness Isabel, the heiress of the Angevin line.   Richard having been duly consulted gave his assent.   No time was lost.   On the 5th May, just a week from the time of the death of the Marquis,

---

[1] *Itinerary*, 330-335.

[2] See *Itin.*, 335-340; R. Coggeshall, 35 ; and for the date Diceto, II. 104, and Bohadin, 333.   Alamût lies to the south of the Caspian, but the political sect of the 'Assassins' (*Hashshashiyun*, 'Eaters of hashish,' an intoxicating drug made from hemp, R. F. Burton, *Mecca*, I. 275) had spread into Syria, and were established among the ranges of Lebanon (Archer, *Richard I*, 377).   To the Franks their chief was known as 'The Old Man' (Vetus) or 'Elder' (Senior, Skeykh)   of the Mountain.'

[3] *Itin rary*, 341 ; Bohadin, and R Cogg., *sup.*   In 1195 Richard circulated a letter purporting to be addressed by the Sheykh (Vetus de Monte) to the Duke of Austria, exculpating Richard.   The letter is dated "Messiac in dimidio Septembris . . . anno ab Alexandro millesimo quingentesimo quinto."   R. Diceto, II. 128; *Itinerary*, 444 ; W. Newb., II. 458 ; Messiac is understood to be Massiaf to the east of Tortosa, a stronghold of the sect.   T. A. Archer, *sup.*   The date by the era of the Seleucidæ used by the Arabs is equivalent to the 15th September, 1193.   I am not satisfied that the letter is spurious. Rigord records communications between Philip and the Sheykh denying any evil intentions towards Philip.   I do not believe that any of Richard's followers could have manufactured a consistent date according to the Arab era.

Guy of Lusignan King of Cyprus. Henry and Isabel were married at Tyre, the lady entering the bonds of holy matrimony for the third time.[1] To console the fallen Guy Richard bestowed upon him the kingdom of Cyprus, but always as a fief to be held of himself.[2]

Richard was now able to call for further operations. His plan was to secure all the line of the coast, and the fortresses between **Renewed Operations.** Jerusalem and the coast, before attacking the Holy City. Of the strongholds still in Saracen hands one of the chief was Darum, now represented by the village of Deir-el-Belah, some eight or nine miles to the South of Gaza.[3] The fortifications were held **Siege and capture of Darum.** almost impregnable, but the garrison was weak and ill-found. Richard's force was not strong enough to invest the place; but by confining his attentions to one flanking tower of the outer works, after four or five days and nights of continuous bombardment, he brought it bodily down; a gate also having been battered down the outer works were stormed. At nightfall the survivors, who had retreated to the inner Keep, surrendered themselves as slaves. On Saturday 23rd May (Whitsun Eve) they were marched out, 300 in number, besides women and children.[4] After a tour inland to the East, through places identified with the present Wady-el-Hesi, Râs-el-Ain (Mirabel), and Beit Dibrin (Eleutheropolis Ibelin of the Hospitallers), to clear the country of the enemy, Richard returned to Ascalon (4th June).[5]

But the continued reports of John's intrigues with Philip made the King very uneasy, and anxious to go home. On this point however his followers were, to a man, dead against him. So, again yielding to their wishes, after **Fresh advance on Jerusalem.** a severe struggle with himself, to the great joy of all, he announced a fresh march on Jerusalem.[6] On the 7th June a start was made in grand style, but in terrible heat. Marching by way of 'Blancheguard,' now Tel-es-Safieh, they found themselves on the 9th again at Latrûn, or 'Toron of the Knights.' On the 11th having **Beit Nuba again reached.** been joined by a French contingent they advanced to Beit Nuba, the impassable turning point of the Third Crusade; some thirteen miles from the city. Again we are assured that an immediate attack would have carried Jerusalem. Saladin's biographer however represents him as prepared to offer a vigorous resistance.[7] Richard apparently thought as much, as he insisted on remaining at Beit Nuba till

---

[1] *Itin.*, 342-348; Diceto, II. 104.

[2] *Itin.*, 350, 351; R. Coggesh., 36. Cyprus had actually been bought of the King by the Templars. *Itin.* Guy's descendants retained the Kingdom until 1458.

[3] Archer, *sup.*, 218.

[4] May 17th-23rd; *Itin.*, 352-356: Bohadin, 337. In Diceto the 300 prisoners come out as 5000; II. 104.

[5] *Itin.*, 356-361, 365; Bohadin, 337, 338, and notes; Archer, *sup*, 242.

[6] *Itin.*, 358-365.   [7] *Itin.*, 367-369; Bohadin, 340, 341.

Henry of Champagne had come from Acre with further troops. At Beit Nuba accordingly the host remained until the 3rd July, the French, as if for the mere sake of contradiction, now clamouring for an advance.[1] Richard himself, in his usual daring way, on the day after his arrival, pushed a raid or reconnaisance to the springs of Emmaus, and from thence, as the reward of all his exertions, indulged his eyes with one long gaze at the mystic walls of Jerusalem.[2] The difficulties of the situation however were shown by the repeated attacks of the enemy on the lines of communication with Joppa.[3] But the grand incident of the second stay at Beit Nuba was the capture of a great caravan, bound from Egypt to

A Caravan to be intercepted. Jerusalem, of which Richard had received private reports from scouts and Bedawin. The affair must be considered very creditable to Richard's leadership, as to reach the place where he was advised to attack the enemy a secret march of forty-five miles had to be executed. Towards evening on the 20th June he started with a

Night Marches. flying column of some 500 men-at-arms and 1000 infantry,[4] and by the light of a glorious Syrian moon marched twenty miles through Tel-es-Safieh to "Galatia," identified with the modern Kuratiyeh. There apparently he rested during the day of the 21st, advancing during the night to Tel-el-Hesy. During the 22nd he received further reports as to the progress of the caravan, and again moving on fourteen miles by night was ready at daybreak on the 23rd June to fall on the enemy just as they were taking their animals to water. The place is called the Round Fountain (*Rotunda cisterna*) by the writer of the *Itinerary*, and is identified with the present El-Khuweilfah at the foot of the Hebron hills.[5]

The covering force of the caravan was a strong one, and had been reinforced by Saladin with 500 men on rumours of an intended attack. At Richard's approach they took up their position on a rising ground.

Brilliant Action. The King divided his forces in two, apparently leaving one body in support, while he led the attack. Charging the enemy he rode through them, unhorsing men, and cutting them down right and left. But he pushed his frontal pursuit so far that the enemy on his flanks with their ready skirmishing tactics, began to wheel round, so as to take him in the rear. They were met and discomfited by the

The Spoils. Earl of Leicester and the supports.[6] The rout was complete, and the whole caravan was captured with all its animals and precious stores, including gold, silver, silk, purple, tapestry, embroidery,

[1] *Itin.*, 379.   [2] *Id*, 369.
[3] *Id.*, 370. 371 ; Bohadin, 341, 342.
[4] So the *Itin.* In Hoveden, III. 182, the numbers go up to 5,000.
[5] *Itin.*, 383-386 ; Bohadin, 342, 343, and notes to both.
[6] Robert of Beaumont IV., son of Robert III., and invested at Messina 1st February 1191 ; Ben. P., II. 156.

arms, clothing, drugs, spices, fruits. The number of camels secured was given as 4,700, besides horses and asses.[1]

Richard's movements on this expedition, as well as those on his marches from Ascalon to Toron, and again on to Beit Nuba show that the Crusaders' forces were not necessarily immobile; and that the deplorable slowness of the marches from Acre to Joppa, and from Joppa to Beit Nuba was due to external circumstances, among which might be reckoned a multitude of inefficient pilgrims hanging on to and delaying the really efficient.

Richard returned by easy stages to Beit Nuba. The spirits of the host were greatly cheered by the grand supply of animals brought in, and a liberal distribution of the plunder. But the leaders were as hostile to an advance on Jerusalem as ever, Richard being now satisfied of the impossibility of success. The deficiency of water at the season was the great point insisted on. But the relations of the French and the English had not become more cordial. The Duke of Burgundy circulated scurrilous rhymes at Richard's expense; and he found no difficulty in retaliating in kind.[2]

About the 5th July the Crusaders began their final retreat from Beit Nuba.[3] Simultaneously negotiations were reopened with Saladin; and Richard expressed himself as willing to accept terms previously suggested by the Sultan, namely that the Christians should have the coast, with the level country, and the keeping of the Church of the Holy Sepulchre; the Saracens retaining the hill country and the city of Jerusalem. But since those proposals had been made the Crusaders had captured Toron, and rebuilt Ascalon. Saladin insisted that both must be demolished. After the interchange of several messages Richard ordered Toron to be dismantled, but refused to touch one stone of Ascalon.[4]

Final retirement from Beit Nuba.

On the 26th July Richard reached Acre, but the Sultan had already resumed operations. Advancing from Jerusalem to Joppa he invested the place on the 27th July, and pressed the siege with such vigour that on the fifth day (Friday, 31st July) he stormed the town; reducing the garrison to the citadel. But even there their position was so critical that in the course of the afternoon they agreed to a convention with Saladin, under which they obtained a truce till midday (*horam nonam*) on the morrow, on terms of the usual sort; namely that

Joppa attacked.

---

[1] *Itin.*, 386–391; Bohadin, 341–345. He gives the reported loss of camels as 3000, with as many horses.   [2] *Itin.*, 392–396; Bohadin, 351.

[3] Bohadin, 351, 352 gives the day as the 21st of Jomada II., apparently a Sunday: that would be the 5th July. Bishop Stubbs cites another edition of Bohadin, 238, as giving the 4th July; *Itin.*, 396.

[4] July 4th to 20th. See the summary, *Itin.*, 398, 399; and the details in Bohadin, 353–360. For the earlier offers see 327, 328.

unless relieved before that time they should surrender at discretion, the Sultan to spare the lives of those who could redeem themselves at stated rates, namely ten besants for a man, five for a woman, three for a child.[1]

On hearing of the siege Richard had acted with his usual promptness.

Relief from Acre. He sent off the Templars and Hospitallers by land, taking ship himself. The winds were contrary, but he reached Joppa during the anxious night of the 31st July. Daylight disclosed the shore crowded with Mussulmans. As to the state of affairs in the town Richard remained in the dark till a priest swam out to tell

Richard just in Time. him that he was yet in time. 'If God will that we die with our brethren,' cried the King, 'perish the man who would hang back.' The galleys were run on to the beach, Richard himself being the first man to spring into the water, where he stood covering the landing of his followers with his cross-bow, a favourite weapon. 'The Turks' as the writers call them, having been vigorously assailed and driven off right and left, the King's next step was to make his ships safe by throwing up a hasty breastwork of casks and timber, with a little garrison to hold it. Then he led his men by a winding stair (*cochleam*) through the house of the Templars on to the town wall. He came none too soon. Saladin's officers had been pressing the garrison to come out, the time apparently having expired. Forty-nine men, with their wives and their horses, had surrendered;[2] and seven persons had been slaughtered for non-production of the required ransoms.[3] When the

The Garrison saved. conquering 'Lion Banner'[4] rose from the wall the souls of the despairing garrison came again within them. Sallying wildly with Richard's help they soon cleared Joppa of an unruly mob intent only on plunder. In fact Saladin's officers were busy endeavouring to expel the ruffians in order to ensure a safe exit for the duly ransomed persons from the citadel. But Saladin himself now had to beat a hasty retreat; and Richard, wisely eschewing quarters in the fetid town, established himself on the camping ground just vacated by the Sultan.[5]

The fortifications of Joppa had now again to be repaired, and Richard set his men to work at once. Within two or three days' time a slender reinforcement reached him from Cæsarea; but even then we are told that he could only muster 55 men-at-arms, with 15 horses among them, and 2000 footmen.[6] The weakness of his force induced Saladin to attempt

---

[1] *Itin.*, 400–403; Bohadin, 360–366.   [2] Bohadin, 368.   [3] *Itin.*, 406.

[4] So the *Itinerary* on a later occasion describes it. " Regium cum leone vexillum " ; 418.

[5] *Itin.*, 407–411; Bohadin, 366, 371; R. Coggeshall, 42, 43. The Saracens, who loathed pork, had killed all the pigs in Joppa and laid their carcasses in a row with the bodies of the Christians, a man and a pig alternately.

[6] *Itin.*, 413. Of his original force Bohadin says that Richard came with thirty-five galleys; p. 369.

a night-attack on Richard's open camp, which in fact numbered 'only about a dozen tents,'[1] occupied by about as many knights, Henry of Champagne and the Earl of Leicester being among them.[2] The foot soldiers would bivouac in the open. The hostile movement was discovered just in time to enable the King to arise and make his dispositions for defence. These were very skilful. His communications with the town and the harbour were protected by throwing back one or both of his wings. To meet the main attack in front he made his men kneel in line behind their shields, with grounded spears ; alternately with the shields he placed two crossbowmen, one to shoot, and one to load. The enemy all on horseback, charged in five or six successive lines; they included the best of Saladin's troops, his trained Mamelukes, and his Kurdish bodyguard,[3] but not one of them brought his horse's shoulder into contact with a spear-point. When they came within striking distance line after line turned aside and wheeled about. When the last wave was broken Richard let loose his men to fall on the fugitives, he himself leading the way. According to the reports of Moslems who were present, he rode along the whole of their line challenging an encounter, but no man would face him.[4] We are told that Saphadin was so delighted with his prowess that he sent him two horses on the field.[5]

Battle of Joppa.

Richard's Prowess.

But the battle does not exhaust Richard's doings of the day. Early in the morning while he was marshalling the host he had received a report that in spite of his precautions the enemy were making their way into the town in his rear. Hurrying off with six mounted followers he rode into Joppa cleared the streets, roused the garrison in the citadel, placed them in charge of the gates, and then returned to his post on the battle-field.[6]

Richard had certainly done enough to entitle a friendly writer to describe him as an Achilles, an Alexander, or a Roland. But over-exertion and insanitary surroundings threw him into a fever, and at Joppa he was detained for more than a month. His men at first were inclined to give way to panic, but order was maintained through the good management of Hubert Walter, the Bishop of Salisbury.[7] The

He falls ill.

---

[1] So Bohadin was informed ; 375.　　[2] See the list, *Itin.*, 415.

[3] So the "Meneloues" and "Cordini" of the *Itinerary* seem to be understood.

[4] Wednesday, 5th August. *Itin.*, 412-420; Bohadin, 374-376; R. Cogg. 44. 46-50. Bohadin gives even a lower estimate of Richard's numbers than the *Itinerary* does, making his infantry only 1000.

[5] So *Itin.*, 419, and Ernoul, *Chronique*, 281, 282. Mr. Lane Poole, *Saladin*, 353, points out that at the time Saphadin was ill at Jerusalem, and substitutes Saladin as the donor. But Bohadin describes the Sultan as in a fury at his repulse.

[6] See this episode described by Ralph of Coggeshall from the report of Hugh Neville, one of Richard's Six ; pp. 45, 46 ; see also *Itin.*, 415, 420. According to the latter only ten of Richard's chief followers still had a horse to ride.

[7] *Itin.*, 441-445 ; R. Devizes, 444.

negotiations with Saladin went on, without any truce, but in a friendly spirit, the Sultan at Richard's request sending him snow and peaches. The wily Sultan was only too glad to avail himself of opportunities for spying out the land. Richard begged and prayed to be allowed to retain Ascalon, but the Sultan stood firm. On the 2nd September a truce for three years was negotiated by Hubert Walter; Ascalon to be **Truce with Saladin** demolished; but the Christians to retain the coast towns from Joppa to Tyre, both inclusive, with free access to the Holy Places. "Such was the lame and impotent conclusion of this great and costly undertaking." But it must be said that apart from Tyre and Acre the little that had been won was won by Richard.[1] The French to the last had refused to co-operate with him.[2] The stipulation as to liberty of visiting the Holy Places was honourably observed by Saladin. Bands of pilgrims, one of them led by Hubert Walter, hastened to avail themselves of the concession, and were freely allowed to go the round of Jerusalem. The Bishop himself was treated with marked distinction by Saladin.[3]

The King's state of health did not allow him to complete his pilgrimage. From Joppa he was carried to Haifa for change of air (9th September);[4] and so on to Acre. On the 29th of the month the two Queens with the little Cyprian princess sailed from that port under the faithful **Journeys Homewards.** care of Stephen of Turnham. They reached Sicily in safety; were hospitably received by Tancred; and sent on to Rome where they spent the winter, being afraid to travel farther for fear of the Emperor. In the spring they went by sea to Marseilles, and from thence passed into Poitou.[5] Richard was less fortunate. Loosing from Acre on 9th October[6] he was driven to and fro for a full month. At one time he was off the coast of Barbary within three days' sail of Marseilles. But he had been warned not to make for that port as the surrounding territory would not be safe. The Aquitanian barons had been in revolt; the revolt had ultimately been suppressed through the help of Richard's brother-in-law, young Sancho of Navarre. But Richard's officers had wound up the campaign by invading the territory of the Count of Toulouse; so that within his sphere of influence all roads would be closed against the King.[7] Putting about he finally found himself at Corfu, about the 11th November.[8] His path was beset with danger on all sides. Greeks, Austrians, Germans

---

[1] See Bohadin, 378–387; *Itin.*, cxxxviii., 427–429, and notes; Diceto, II. 105, with the wrong date 9th August.

[2] *Itin.*, 404, 406. To fill up the list of the magnates who perished on the Crusade, the Duke Hugh III. of Burgundy died in July at Tyre.

[3] *Itinerory*, 432–438. The author was with one of these bands.

[4] *Id.*, 430; Bohadin, 389.   [5] Hoveden, III. 228; W. Newb I. 382.

[6] *Itinerary*, 441; Diceto, II., 106. Hoveden, III. 185, has the 8th October.

[7] R. Cogg., 53, who had his facts from Anselm, one of Richard's chaplains; but see also Hoveden 194; and R. Devizes, 431.

[8] " Circa Sancti Martini festum." Diceto, *sup.*; *Itin.*, 442.

and French being all hostile, with their several grudges against him, but mainly in connection with his doings in Sicily and Cyprus.   The German barons had been to a man supporters of the late Conrad, who was cousin both to the Emperor and to the Duke of Austria, and their hostility to Richard knew no bounds.[1]   It was supposed that Richard meant to make for Saxony, where he would find friends.   To conceal his movements he left his own ships, and hired two native galleys, described as 'pirates,' to take him to Ragusa.   The writers speak of landings at Zara, or Pola, as if his voyage ended there.[2]   But it is clear that winds or other circumstances

Shipwreck near Aquileia. took him up to the head of the Adriatic, where he was shipwrecked near Aquileia.   The party then disguised themselves and took horse, pressing through the district of Friuli.   But Richard's enemies were already on the look out for him.   Count Mainhard II. of Goritz, nephew of the late Marquis Conrad, pursued him, and captured eight of his followers ; six more were taken at Freisach in Carinthia by the Count's brother Frederic of Betsau, Richard himself with William de L'Etang, a servant who spoke German, and a third whose position is not described, escaping and pushing on towards Vienna.[3]   But there again watch was being kept by Duke Leopold, the man whom Richard had insulted in Palestine.   Finally on the 20th December,[4] the King was detected and arrested in a cottage in the suburbs of Vienna, utterly exhausted with hunger and fatigue.[5]   His servant who had gone out to buy necessaries betrayed himself by tendering gold besants in payment.[6]   The Duke at once sent him for safe keeping to his castle of Durrenstein on the Danube.[7]

To the modern mind the action of the Germans will seem very base. Churchmen of their own time would regard them as excommunicate for having laid hands on a Crusader ; and as a matter of fact the Duke was promptly excommunicated, and his lands laid under Interdict by Celestine III.[8]   But probably Leopold's conduct would not be severely criticised by the world in general.   Richard had done his best to make a case for all his enemies.

[1] On the special bitterness of the German writers see Bishop Stubbs, *Itin.* xiv. Conrad and Leopold were grandsons, and Henry VI. great-grandson (by a different marriage) of Agnes of Franconia, daughter of Henry IV. ; Norgate, II. 320, note.

[2] R. Cogg., 53, 54 ; Hoveden, III. 185, and notes ; Ansbert, extracted Hoveden, III. cxl.

[3] See the Emperor's report to King Philip of the 28th December, Hoveden, 195 ; also *Id.*, 186 ; R. Coggeshall, 54, 55 ; and *Itinerary, sup.*

[4] Diceto, II. 106 ; *Itinerary,* 443.

[5] See the Emperor's letter, *sup.*, and the covering letter of the Archbishop of Rouen, Hoveden, 196 ; also Ansbert, extracted by Bishop Stubbs, Hoveden, cxl.

[6] Hoveden, 186 ; R. Cogg., 55 ; W. Newb., I. 383.   [7] Ansbert, *sup.*

[8] See the Pope's letter of the 6th June, 1194, prescribing the terms of absolution, Diceto II. 119 ; also Ansbert, *sup.*, cxliii.

CHAPTER XX

RICHARD I (*continued*)

A.D. 1192–1195.

Affairs in England—Invasion of Normandy by Philip—Arrangements for Richard's Liberation—His Ransom—Hubert Walter Archbishop of Canterbury and Chief Justiciar—The King set free—War in Normandy—Reduction of Aquitanian Rebels —Truce with France—Domestic Affairs—Suspension of Archbishop Geoffrey

UNDER the judicious administration of Walter of Coutances, with the support of the Queen-Mother, England passed through the summer and autumn of the year 1192 in peace and quiet. Towards Christmas anxiety as to the fate of the King began to be
Uneasiness in England. felt. Pilgrims who had left Acre at the same time as he did were flocking home, but the only report of him that they could give was that the ship in which he sailed from Acre had been seen at Brindisi.[1] Authentic information, however, reached the country in January (1193), through a copy of the Emperor's letter to Philip, announcing the capture of their common enemy.[2] John at once broke out of bounds. He hastened over to Normandy; and after a fruitless demand for homage from the Norman Barons, went on to
John's Treason. Paris, where it was said that he did homage to Philip for all the Continental possessions of his brother, undertaking to marry Alais, and to cede the Norman Vexin; Philip in return promising to support him to the fullest extent.[3] John then returned to England, bringing with him mercenaries to garrison Windsor and Wallingford castles, that he had been allowed to retain; Welshmen also were enlisted for this service. These bases having been secured he went to London, and demanded recognition by the Justiciars, alleging that the King was dead.

[1] Hoveden, III. 194.
[2] Hoveden, 196.
[3] Hoveden, 204. This compact must be distinguished from the formal treaty given by Rigord, Bouquet, xvii. 39; misdated in Fœdera, I. 57, "January 1193," which being a French document must belong to the year 1194.

They responded by exacting general oaths of allegiance to Richard,
Civil War. putting the Royal castles in order, and calling out levies on
the South coast to guard against invasion.[1]   Walter of
Coutances laid siege to Windsor ; Archbishop Geoffrey occupied Doncaster;
and Bishop Puiset attacked Tickhill.   On the 20th April the hands of
the Government were strengthened by the return of Hubert Walter, with
letters from the King, whom he had visited on his way home from
Palestine ; and then John, disappointed in his hope of support from
Scotland, and finding that Windsor was about to fall, consented to a
A Truce. truce till November ; Nottingham and Tickhill to remain in
his hands ; Windsor, Wallingford, and the Peak to be placed
in Eleanor's hands, but to be restored to John if Richard should not
return.[2]

Concurrently with these affairs Philip invaded Normandy.   Gisors and
Philip invades Normandy. Néaufle were betrayed to him by one Gilbert of Vascœuil
(12th April) a man specially sent by Richard from Messina
to defend the frontier.   Then pushing on the French King
captured Aumâle and Neufchâtel-en-Bray, and overran the whole of the
Norman Vexin, finally laying siege to Rouen.   Finding however that the
city was being defended by the worthy Earl of Leicester, who had returned
safe and sound from the Crusade, he dropped the undertaking (29th April),
and marched home.[3]

Duke Leopold was not allowed to keep his prize all to himself.   His
Imperial suzerain insisted on having his share ; and in the meantime the
custody of the prisoner.   On the 14th February a treaty was settled
Terms of Richard's Liberation. between the two at Würtzburg, to which Richard must have
given his assent, as the provisions could not be enforced
without his concurrence.   The ransom was fixed at 100,000
marks (£66,000 13s. 4d.), to be paid by halves at Michaelmas 1193, and
Mid-Lent 1194, and shared equally between the Emperor and Duke ; but
the Duke's portion would be settled on one of his sons, with the hand of
Richard's niece, Eleanor of Brittany.   Richard was also required to
liberate Isaac of Cyprus and his daughter without ransom.[4]   The first
person to intervene on Richard's behalf was Savaric, the newly appointed
Bishop of Bath,[5] a man who claimed relationship with the Emperor, and

---

[1] Hoveden, III. 204, 205 ; Gervase, I. 514, 515.

[2] Hoveden, 205, 206–208 ; Gervase, I. 515, 516 ; W. Newb., I. 388, 390, 391.

[3] Hoveden, 205, 206, 207 ; R. Cogg., 61, 62 ; Gervase, *sup.*, and for the dates Rigord, Bouquet, xvii. 38 ; Labbe, Bibl. MSS., I. 369.

[4] See the treaty in Ansbert, *sup.*, cxli.

[5] Savaric, previously Archdeacon of Northampton, and Treasurer of Sarum, was consecrated at Rome 19th September 1192, so that perhaps he had not yet returned to England ; Diceto, II. 105, 106.   For Savaric's previous career see Bishop Stubbs' note *Epp. Cant.* lxxxvii.

certainly was on good terms with him.[1] At home the Justiciars on hearing
of the King's fate had sent off the abbots of Boxley and Robertsbridge
to find out his place of detention. After wandering in vain through 'all
Germany' (*Alemanniam*), they entered Bavaria about the 19th March,
and found the King at Ochsenfurt on the Main, on his way to be
delivered to Henry VI. at Speyer. They told Richard of John's doings,
of which he complained bitterly, comforting himself however with the
reflexion that 'brother John was not the man to win land by force if
anybody cared to oppose the least force to him.'[2] On the 23rd March
Richard was handed over to the Emperor;[3] and brought as a State

He is arraigned before the Diet. prisoner before the Diet, that "august but incompetent
tribunal." The King was formally charged with having sup-
ported Tancred in his usurpation of Sicily, in derogation of
the Emperor's rights; with having unjustly deprived Isaac
of his Kingdom; and instigated the murder of the Marquis of Montferrat.
The insult to the Duke of Austria, and Richard's general behaviour to
the Germans in Palestine, formed another count in the indictment. We
are assured that he made a most spirited defence, at the close of which
the Emperor made friends with him, and gave him the kiss of peace, saving
the ransom, of course, to which Richard agreed.[4]

Richard was now joined by Hubert Walter. On landing in Sicily on
his way homewards from Palestine he had heard of his master's captivity,
and had succeeded in making his way to him. Richard sent him home at
once, as already mentioned, with letters to Eleanor, the Justiciars, and the

Hubert Walter named for Canterbury. Canterbury monks, intimating the amount of ransom required
—still 100,000 marks—and directing them to take all necessary
steps for raising the bearer to the See of Canterbury. To
this promotion, as the King said, Hubert's great services fully
entitled him.[5]

Born at Dereham in Norfolk, of a family settled for two generations on

His birth and character. English soil, he was probably as English as anything to be
found in a high position in England at that time could be.
His mother was sister to the wife of the late Justiciar
Glanville [6] who, as his uncle, had taken charge of him and brought him up.
His talents, industry, and integrity soon marked him out for employment
in the public service. In 1185 he appears as a Baron of the Exchequer [7];

---

[1] See the letter of Walter of Coutances to Bp. Puiset, Hoved., 197.

[2] Hoved., III. 198.   [3] Diceto, II. 106.

[4] Hoveden, 199; R Cogg., 58, 59; W. Newb., I. 387, 388; also Richard's letter,
Epp. Cant. 362.

[5] See the letters dated at Speyer 26th-30th March; *Epp. Cant.*, 361-364.

[6] *Monasticon*, VI. 380, 1128. In Latin the family name is spelled alternately and
indifferently "Walterus" and "Walteri." Hubert's brother Theobald "Pincerna
Hiberniæ" was the ancestor of the Butlers Earls of Ormonde, Foss, *Judges*, I. 424,
citing Dugdale.   [7] Foss, *Judges*, II. 123.

in the following year he became Dean of York. It will be remembered that he had been twice suggested for the Province of York; in 1189 he was made Bishop of Salisbury; and all through the Crusade he had taken a leading part in diplomacy and the field. During the famine-winter of 1190–1191 he had initiated charitable collections for the starving poor. He was emphatically a man who did with all his might whatever his hand found to do. For once the Canterbury monks could not find a better man to name. But they were still careful to assert themselves. Having been summoned to hold an election in concert with the suffragan bishops

His Election. in London on the 30th May, they held a Chapter at Canterbury on the 29th, elected Hubert, and then, hastening up to Westminster, presented him next day to the Justiciars, as a ready-made Archbishop-Elect, for simple confirmation.[1]

From Speyer the King was removed to Trifels,[2] in Rhenish Bavaria, a hill fortress, of great strength. There he was visited by his Chancellor William Longchamp, through whose mediation the Emperor was induced to remove his prisoner to more accessible quarters at Hagenau, where Henry was holding his court. Longchamp further succeeded in obtaining

Mission of Longchamp to England. for himself from the two monarchs a commission to go to England to receive and bring over the 200 hostages required by the treaty of Würtzburg. This would be a very confidential task, as the hostages were to be of the highest rank, at the selection of the Emperor, the only persons exempted being the children of the Duchess of Saxony, and Arthur of Brittany.[3]

Richard's instructions to Eleanor and the Justiciars were apparently sent in advance, to prepare for Longchamp's reception. The portion to be paid to the Emperor is now stated as 70,000 marks; the King calls on all good subjects to contribute liberally, and he specially suggests an extensive 'borrowing' of Church treasures.[4] By the Emperor Longchamp was entrusted with a letter sealed with the Imperial Golden Bull, and addressed to the English, urging them to show their loyalty to their King.[5]

The Justiciars, acting promptly on the receipt of Richard's letter, issued

Measures for raising the King's Ransom. orders for raising the sum required. An Aid for the lord's ransom would be exigible in the regular course of things. But, strange to say, no such tax was imposed *eo nomine*. At the supposed legal rate of £1 the knight's fee the yield might come to £7000, a sum altogether inadequate. The Justiciars, therefore,

[1] See the rival accounts, Gervase, I. 518, and Diceto II. 107. On the 7th of November Hubert received his Pall from the Papal envoys, and was enthroned; Gervase, 521–523. He was obliged to take an utterly novel and most stringent oath of allegiance to the Papacy, *Epp. Cant.* 367. Diceto clearly refers to this as "novis verborum formulis" which he would not record, p. 112.

[2] Richard was still at Speyer on the 30th March; *Epp. Cant., sup.*

[3] Ausbert, *sup.*, cxlii.   [4] See the letter, dated Hagenau, 19th April; Hoveden, 208.

[5] Hoveden, 211; also dated Hagenau, 19th April.

apparently called for a general contribution from clergy and laity of one-fourth of all rents and movables, without exemption of any kind, even for Church plate. The Cistercian and Sempringham Orders, having no plate, were required to part with their wool, their only available property.[1]

In due course Longchamp appeared with his Golden Bull. But the mere announcement of his coming had roused all the hostility of the nation. Before he was allowed to set foot on shore he was required to take an oath that he would interfere with nothing but the King's redemption. The Londoners were so excited that the Council to meet him had to be held at St. Albans. On entering the chamber he declared with ostentatious humility that he came neither as Justiciar, nor as Legate, nor even as Chancellor; but simply as a Bishop and the King's envoy. But

Longchamp again rejected. for all that the Archbishop of Rouen could not be induced to give him the kiss of peace, declaring however that their private disagreement should not interfere with the transaction of business.[2] To receive the redemption money as it came in the Council appointed a committee consisting of Hubert Walter, now Elect of Canterbury, the Treasurer Bishop Richard fitz Nigel of London, two Earls, and the Mayor of London, the first appearance of that functionary in State affairs. But with Longchamp they would have no dealings whatever; nobody would entrust him with a son or daughter; and Richard, finding that his presence would only create difficulties, recalled him, and kept him employed on diplomatic business abroad.[3]

The French were doing what they could to prevent or delay Richard's liberation, and with that view they proposed a meeting between

Action of France. Vaucouleurs and Toul on the 25th June. But fortunately for Richard he was not the only man to take alarm at the prospect of this intrigue. His dread of a coalition between Germany and France was shared by a party among the German Princes who were at war with their Emperor, on account of a private feud, arising out of the murder of Albert of Louvain Bishop of Liege, a crime in which he was supposed to have had a hand. Through their combined efforts the meeting

The German Princes. with Philip was averted, and, instead a Diet was arranged to be held at Worms for a general pacification, including the question of Richard's liberation.[4] Henry VI. was playing a very mean

---

[1] See the clear consistent statements of R. Cogg. 60; W. Newburgh, I. 399; Diceto, II. 110; Gervase, I. 519, 520; and the Waverley Annals, 248. Parochial clergy, however, were only asked for a tenth. Hoveden, III. 210, 225, adds a scutage of £1 the knight's fee; but that was imposed at Nottingham in 1194. Nothing of it appears on the Pipe Roll, 5 Richard I. (1192–1193).

[2] Hoveden, 211, 212; Giraldus, IV. 415, 416.

[3] Hoveden, and Giraldus, *sup.* The Council at St. Albans must have been held in June, as Hubert Walter is only styled Elect of Canterbury; Longchamp was again with Richard at Worms on the 25th June.

[4] Hoveden, III. 214, and note. *Cnf.* W. Newb., I. 396–398.

part, making the most of his opportunity, squeezing Richard, and at the same time breaking faith with his partner Duke Leopold. On the 29th June after four days of discussion the Emperor gave a formal pledge to set Richard free, by renewing the treaty of Würtzburg, to which the King was now made a formal party. It will be remembered that this compact, as originally drawn up, was on the face of it merely a treaty between Henry and the Duke of Austria. The actual ransom was still stated at 100,000 marks. But an extra 50,000 marks were now required as commutation for the military service against Sicily stipulated by the original draft. The allocation of the money also was materially changed, the Emperor getting the whole of the primary 100,000 marks, instead of the half;

An Imperial Partner. while of the extra 50,000 marks the Duke would only receive 20,000 marks. In April the Emperor's share had been stated at 70,000 marks, leaving at any rate 30,000 marks for the Duke; now Henry is to have 130,000 marks and Leopold only 20,000 marks. Moreover the whole of the primary 100,000 marks must be ready in London before the King can be set free, hostages being only accepted for the extra 50,000 marks. The stipulations as to the marriage of Eleanor of Brittany, and the liberation of Isaac and his daughter remained as before.[1]

The English, however, were only too glad to have a definite understanding as to the liberation of their King. Philip, regarding the matter as virtually accomplished, sent to John in England the celebrated message that 'the Devil was unchained.'[2] John immediately went over to France to see his friend, and concert measures with him. In the vain hope of breaking up their alliance Richard empowered Longchamp to

Overtures to Philip negotiate and conclude with Philip a treaty of the most hollow and transparent character, a purely one-sided treaty, in which Richard promised everything and asked for nothing. He would recognise Philip's recent conquests in Normandy, leaving it to him to say how much he wished to retain;[3] John would be relieved of his oath not to visit England; and would retain all the possessions on either side of the Channel conferred on him by his brother, on the simple condition of contributing to the ransom; Philip would receive a gratuity of 20,000 marks, to be paid by instalments, with the control in the meantime of sundry castles by way of security. Count Ademar of Angoulême, who had rebelled again and been taken prisoner, would be liberated with all his men; while sundry favours were conceded to Philip's allies, such as Louis the new Count of Blois, Geoffrey III. Count of Perche, Robert of Meulan, and Hugh of

---

[1] See the treaty, Hoveden III., 215, where it is given as settled on the 29th June; Diceto gives the date as 5th July, II. 110. He scornfully styles the Emperor, "*egregius fœnerator.*"

[2] Hoveden, 216.

[3] "Quod, ipse. (*sc.* Philip) tantum inde retinebit, quantum ipse voluerit."

Journay.[1]   The treaty does not give a high idea of the diplomacy, or the
honesty, either of the Chancellor or of his master.

Longchamp then went on to treat with John ; and succeeded in inducing
and John. him to return to Normandy and swear allegiance to his brother,
on condition, however, not only of being admitted to all lands
originally conferred upon him, but also to castles connected with them that
had been intentionally withheld from him.   But the officers in charge,
better advised than their master, refused to act on the reckless concession ;
and the Earl went back to Philip's court to carry on with him their plots
against Richard's liberation.[2]

The collection of the money for the ransom went on both in England
and abroad during the year.   But the amount got in by the first sets
of commissioners sent round proving insufficient a second and a third
levy had to be called for.[3]   By the month of December, however, a
sufficient sum on account having been delivered to the Emperor's agents
in London, he wrote on the 20th December to say that he proposed
to set Richard free on the 17th January, 1194; and that a week later
he would crown him King of Burgundy and Arles.[4]   This of course
was an empty grant of territories over which the Emperor had no control,[5] but it would involve the render of homage on Richard's part;   or
Richard's possibly, it may have been intended as an excuse for detaining
Liberation him after he had been declared free.   In fact Philip and
delayed. John were pressing Henry with large offers of money to
induce him to keep Richard in bonds as long as possible.   Lending
an unworthy ear to these suggestions, when the 17th January came, the
Emperor adjourned the Diet to the 2nd February.   On that day a
final conference was held at Mainz, Eleanor, the Archbishop of Rouen,
Longchamp, and Savaric of Bath being present.   But the Emperor still
hung back, and he was not ashamed to produce letters from France
offering him a subsidy for every month that he should detain the King.
Richard began to despair of ever regaining his liberty.   But the
Free at Last. German Princes, to their credit, revolted at their lord's
conduct; and they spoke out so boldly that he was obliged
to let Richard go.   On Friday the 4th February the King was fairly
set free, after more than thirteen months of most unjust detention.   But
even then he was required to leave hostages for the unpaid balance of

---

[1] See the treaty as executed at Mantes 9th July, and attested by Longchamp William
des Roches, John des Preaux and William Brewer ; Hoveden, III. 217.

[2] *Id.* 237.

[3] W. Newb , I. 399, 400.

[4] Hoveden, 225, 227.   According to this writer the grant was attested by charter; he
also alleges that Richard by his mother's advice made a surrender of his Kingdom of
England to Henry, but this seems very doubtful.

[5] For this Kingdom see Freeman, *Pol. Geography*, I. 148.

his ransom. Nor were the German magnates too proud to accept *douceurs* for their kind offices in the matter.[1]

From Mainz Richard moved in a leisurely way down the Rhine. He rested three or four days at Cologne, where he gave the merchants a charter releasing them from a small annual toll payable in London.[2] At Antwerp he found his smack (*esnecca*), with his favourite skipper Alan Trenchemer waiting for him. Sailing from Antwerp on the 4th March, and coasting in his usual style, he only reached Swine on the 7th March; and Sandwich, apparently, on Saturday the 12th of the month; thus returning to England after an absence of four years and three months. Next day, following the example of his father, he went to pay his first devotions at the shrine of St. Thomas. Advancing towards London he was met at Rochester by the faithful Hubert Walter—now Archbishop of Canterbury—with whom he exchanged most hearty greetings. On the 16th March he made a state entry into London, being received by clergy and people, high and low, in procession, and taken for a thanksgiving service to St. Paul's.[3] Great were

Reception in London. the rejoicings; the city looked so prosperous, and made so brave a show that the Germans who had accompanied the King began to think that he had been let off too cheaply.[4]

But with all the festive loyalty in London Richard as a matter of fact found England in a state of civil war. From the time of the expulsion of Longchamp in October 1191 down to the end of the year 1193 the country had been at peace under the rule of Queen Eleanor and Walter of Coutances. But in Hubert Walter the King had a servant whom he trusted above all others. As soon as he was fairly enthroned at Canterbury [5] the Chief Justiciarship of England was placed in his hands: Eleanor and the Archbishop Walter being directed to join the King in Germany, where we found them on 2nd February.[6] Matters flowed on in quiet till about

John again plotting. January (1194) when it began to appear likely that, in spite of all intrigues, the King would be set free. John then, no longer to be kept under control, broke out afresh. His first move was to seal a fresh treaty with Philip outbidding Longchamp's treaty.

---

[1] Hoveden, III. 232, 233, and especially the letter of Walter of Coutances, Diceto, II. 112, addressed to the Dean. Among the hostages left was Walter Savaric of Bath. In 1197 Boniface of Montferrat received £800, Angevin = £200 sterling as his fee, Stapleton, Norm. Rolls, 301.

[2] Hoveden, 235 and note; Diceto, 114.

[3] See Hoveden, 235; Gervase, I. 524; Diceto, II. 114; R. Cogg. 62, 63. Hoveden and Coggeshall make Richard land at Sandwich on the 13th March. But on this point I prefer to follow Gervase, who was actually at Canterbury, and who tells us that the King came there on the 13th, the day after his landing. Diceto places the events a week too late.

[4] W. Newb., I. 406. [5] 7th November, Gervase, I. 522.

[6] Gervase, 523; Diceto, 112; Hoveden, 226; and Richard's letter there of the 22nd December, evidently addressed to Hubert as Justiciar.

The French King would have not only Normandy East of the Seine, except Rouen, but also Verneuil, Évreux, and the line of the Iton to the West of the Seine, with the best part of Touraine, including Tours, Amboise, and Loches. Nor were his friends the new Count of Blois, or the Counts of Perche and Angoulême forgotten. Large grants were promised to each.[1] Philip acting on this grant had invaded Normandy about February, and made himself master of Évreux, Le Neubourg, and Le Vaudreuil. He then went on to make a second attack on Rouen, which again failed.[2] John on his part prepared for a renewal of the struggle in England, and sent over orders to have his castles put into order. But the bearer of these instructions behaved in London with such imprudence, boasting at the Archbishop's table of his master's influence with the King of France, that he was arrested on suspicion, and, his papers being seized, John's intentions were brought to light. Hubert **His Schemes detected** Walter met the situation with proper vigour. On the very next day (10th February) he held a Council and passed a decree of utter forfeiture against the Earl. Then, calling out troops to enforce the judgment, he himself marched against Marlborough, while Bishop Puiset returned to the siege of Tickhill, and the Scots Earl of Huntingdon, with the Earls of Chester and Derby invested Nottingham. Marlborough yielded in a few days; so did Lancaster, a place that had been held in John's name by the Archbishop's brother Theobald Walter; so did St. Michael's Mount in Cornwall, a monastery that had been seized and fortified for John by one Henry de la Pommeraye.[3]

Such was the state of affairs when Richard landed. Nottingham and Tickhill were still holding out; but the latter place on receipt of positive assurances that the King had returned yielded to the Bishop.[4] For the reduction of Nottingham war material was sent from London.[5] But the King in the first instance felt bound to pay another thanksgiving visit, namely to Bury St. Edmunds.[6] That pious act having been performed, on **and crushed.** the 25th March he came to Nottingham; on the 27th he was joined by Bishop Puiset with the prisoners from Tickhill; while next day the surrender of Nottingham brought the whole rising to a close.[7]

The King had now time and opportunity to hold a Grand Council to

---

[1] See the treaty in *Fœdera*, I. 57, dated at Paris in January 1193. Having been drawn up in Paris that would according to the French computation mean January 1194, and so it is given in Bouquet, XVII. 39.

[2] Rigord, Bouquet, *sup.* 40; G. le Breton, *Id.* 71.

[3] Hoveden, III. 236–238.

[4] *Id.*, 238.

[5] Pipe Roll, 6 Rich. I., "London."

[6] R. Cogg., 63.

[7] Hoveden, 238–240; Diceto, II. 114; W. Newb., I. 406, 407.

discuss affairs of state, and he held it where he was, at Nottingham.
Grand Council. Eleanor and Longchamp assisted, the King still holding to his unpopular Chancellor. The sittings lasted four days (March 30th—April 2nd). Money was the great question. There was the balance of the ransom to provide for, and an expedition to Normandy to be faced. The confiscation and re-sale of offices was again the financial expedient that commended itself to Richard's mind. Gerard **Richard's Finance.** of Camville and Hugh Bardolf were deprived of the sheriffdoms of Lincolnshire and Yorkshire, as well as of the keeping of the castles of Lincoln, York, and Scarborough. These lucrative posts were put up to auction. Archbishop Geoffrey and Longchamp bid against each other, but eventually Yorkshire was secured by Geoffrey for 3000 marks (£2000), 'whereby,' as Hoveden remarks, 'he became the King's servant, and put himself in his power.'[1] For the war in Normandy it was apparently arranged that one third of those liable should be called out for personal service, the rest to pay a scutage of £1 on the Knight's fee, the money to be applied to the liquidation of the ransom.[2] A hidage or Danegeld of two shillings on the carucate of land was also voted for the same purpose.[3] We further hear of a fresh[4] call on the Cistercians for wool, to be eventually commuted for a fine. One day was devoted to the **Judicial Investigations.** cases of Earl John, and his accomplice Hugh of Nonant, the Bishop of Coventry. Hugh stood self-condemned. When summoned by Richard to appear before him in Germany he had taken flight. His brother Robert had actually been John's agent at Mainz, and on his return to England had been imprisoned. Both John and Hugh were now cited to appear within forty days.[5] The last day of the Council was taken up with complaints by the Northern clergy against their Archbishop in connexion with exactions for the ransom, and by more serious charges brought by Longchamp against Gerard of Camville in connexion with the Fair of Stamford. Both sets of accusation were allowed to stand over.[6] But Camville eventually found it expedient to pay the King 2000 marks.[7]

[1] III. 241.

[2] So I harmonise Hoveden's "quod unusquisque faceret sibi tertiam partem servitii militaris," with the entries on the Pipe Roll 6 Rich. I., where we have payments for scutage at the full rate, expressly entitled "Ad redemptionem Regis," with exemptions in favour of those accompanying the King abroad.

[3] Partly raised within the financial year; Pipe Roll. Hoveden absurdly calls this tax a "tenmantale," the Northern word for a tithing. This blunder suggests that he was more French than English. [4] So expressly W. Newb., II. 416.

[5] Hoveden, III. 233, 241, 242. Hugh himself had been arrested at Dover in his flight by Matthew of Clères, the constable, but he was liberated under pressure from the bishops; Diceto, II. 111.

[6] Hoveden, 242, 243. For the struggle between Geoffrey and his Chapter as to the appointment to the Deanery of York see *Id.*, 222, 223. The services had been again suspended and the Archbishop locked out. [7] Bishop Stubbs, Hoved., III. c.

Richard, rather against his will,[1] had been persuaded by his subjects to submit to a re-coronation, as if to wipe off the stain of his bondage.[2] The 17th April was fixed for the ceremony, to be performed at Winchester. Meanwhile the King remained in the Midlands to receive William the Lion, who was coming to court, to welcome him home. They met at Southwell on the 4th April, and travelled together to Winchester, keeping their Easter (10th April) on the way, at Northampton. The King of

Scottish Demands. Scots thought the opportunity a favourable one for pressing for a fresh cession of the three Northern counties, as yielded by Stephen. The further demand for the Honour of Lancaster was preposterous, as that had never been ceded. Richard endeavoured to pacify his ally by framing elaborate regulations for the escort and maintenance of Scottish Kings on their journeys to and from the English court.[3]

The proceedings of the 17th April, with all the importance attached to them by the chroniclers, did not amount to a coronation or a re-coronation, being in fact so ordered as to imply "that the dignity had undergone no diminution."[4] It would seem that precedents had been found at Canterbury in the rites observed at the re-coronation of Stephen and Matilda in

A State Crown-Wearing. 1145.[5] The King was robed and crowned in his chamber by the Archbishop of Canterbury, and then led in procession to the Minster to receive a solemn blessing, the service ending with Mass at which Richard communicated. The King of Scots carried the chief sword of State, the other two swords being borne by Hamelin of Surrey, and Ralph of Chester. Archbishop Geoffrey had been warned that he must not carry his cross within the Province of Canterbury, and rather than appear without it, he stayed away—the never-ending difficulty. The banquet was held in the refectory of the monks, with whom the King had taken up his quarters for the day, the castle being at an

---

[1] So R. Cogg., 64; and Gervase, I. 524.

[2] "Detersa captivitatis ignominia;" W. Newb., I. 408.

[3] The Scottish Kings would be escorted from county to county by the bishop and the earl, with an allowance or "corrody" from the Treasury of £5 a-day. While at court they would receive an allowance partly in kind and partly in money. The allowance included 2 lb. of pepper and 4 lb. of cumin daily, with 4 gallons (sextarii) of superior, and 8 gallons of ordinary wine; Fœdera, I. 62; Hoveden, III. 243-245; Diceto, II. 114. The reader will remember that the Scottish Kings had estates in England for which of course homage would be due. I would also point out that Richard's arrangements give no support to the mysterious "mansiones in itinere" alleged by Roger of Wendover (I. 410) to have been given by Eadgar to Kenneth in 975 for the entertainment of Scottish Kings on their journeys to the English court, and accepted by Dr. Lingard and by Mr Freeman, *Rufus*, I. 304 and II. 544.

[4] l.p. Stubbs; Hoveden, 247; note, where the ceremony is compared to "the great crown-wearing days of the earlier Norman Kings." So too Ann. Waverley, "Coronam portavit."

[5] So Gervase.

z

inconvenient distance from the Minster.[1]   Eleanor of course assisted, with her Maids of Honour; but not Berengaria, who had been left abroad.

Unblushing confiscation was still the order of the day.   Instead of coronation honours we have coronation resumptions.   Richard's first act on reaching Winchester had been to deprive Bishop Godfrey **Resumption of Grants.** Lucy of the sheriffdom of Hampshire, and the castles and estates bought not five years before; while a few days later Bishop Puiset was induced to make a 'voluntary'[2] resignation of the earldom and castles of Northumberland, thus returning to the *status* of a 'simple bishop.'[3]   Puiset however did not part with his acquisitions **Bishop Puiset and his Earldom.** at once, making thie King a fresh offer of 2000 marks for the retention of the earldom (*comitatus*) and castles.   We are told that the King accepted the offer; but that the Bishop and Hugh Bardolf the Sheriff of Northumberland being unable to agree as to the business details of the transaction Richard in a fury ordered Bardolf both to take the Bishop's money and to turn him out.[4]   Further details of the King's proceedings are not supplied; but we are told in a word that whatever appointments could be recalled and turned into money were recalled.   Richard took a direct personal part in this disgraceful business. We are assured that he could assume a lofty moral tone while pointing out to some unhappy victim the impropriety of attempting to urge any private rights against the paramount interests of the Crown.[5]   Thus Longchamp's resumptions that seemed so flagitious were but anticipations of the subsequent proceedings of his Royal master.   On the other hand we are glad to hear of the reconciliation of Geoffrey to the Chancellor effected by Richard at Bishop's Waltham, when hastening to Portsmouth to get away from England.   Regard for Longchamp was doubtless the moving consideration, but Geoffrey recovered his estates in Anjou.[6]

Richard was detained on the South coast by bad weather for nearly three weeks.   On the 2nd May he insisted on putting out to sea, but was **Richard leaves England.** driven back again to Portsmouth next day.   On the 12th May he finally sailed, never to return.[7]   England offered no scope for his restless energies.   Abroad, no doubt, there was plenty to do, as the Continental dominions were all more or less in a state of war and confusion.

[1] Hoveden, III. 246–249; Gervase, I. 524–527.   [2] " Sponte sua, nullo cogente."
[3] " In simplicem rediit episcopum ;" W. Newb., II. 416.
[4] So Hoveden, III. 260, 261 ; where he adds that the King even ordered Sadberge to be resumed.   But Richard in December 1198 granted a confirmation of Sadberge under the new Seal acknowledging payment of the price – viz., 600 marks.   On the Pipe Roll, 8 Richard I. (1195–1196), we find Hugh Bardolf as Sheriff of Northumberland accounting for £666 13*s*. 4*d*. received from Puiset for the county " pro comitatu " (query earldom or sheriffdom ? either might be meant) a further 1000 marks being due, with 600 more for Sadberge.   [5] W. Newburgh, *sup*.   [6] 24th April ; Hoveden, 246, 249–251.
[7] Id. 251 ; R. Diceto, II. 114.   The King landed at Barfleur.

Eleanor's retirement to England in February 1192 had given opportunity for risings against her son in Aquitaine.   The first in arms, apparently,

Recent Events Abroad. was Count Ademar of Angoulême, an old foe.   But he fared badly, as the Poitevins defeated him and carried him off a prisoner.[1]   His liberation was one of the concessions offered by Richard in July 1193 to win Philip from his support of John.[2]   Another revolt of the year 1192 was led by Hélie V. Count of Perigord, and the returned Crusader Hugh le Brun IX. of Lusignan, Count of La Marche. Their efforts, however, were quelled by the Seneschal of Aquitaine, with the support of young Sancho of Navarre, the campaign ending with an inroad on the territory of the Count of Toulouse,[3] a man usually in alliance with Richard's enemies.   These troubles, as we have seen, had interfered with Richard's proposed landing at Marseilles.   The reader has already heard of Philip's invasion of the Norman Vexin in April 1193; and of the treaty of partition between him and John drawn up in January 1194.   In

Situation in Normandy. February[4] the French King again drew the sword to assert the rights conceded in the previous month, and succeeded in reducing Evreux, Le Neubourg, and Le Vaudreuil, returning home for Lent as already told.[5]   By the 10th May he was again in the field, and laid formal siege to Verneuil.   The possession of that place with Evreux and Le Vaudreuil would make him master of the ceded line of the Iton.   By the middle of the third week the walls were tottering, when word was brought that the English had reoccupied Evreux.   Hastening off in person (28th May), he drove the English from Evreux, but the siege of Verneuil came to nothing.   Richard was reported to be at Laigle, whereupon the force left to carry on the siege of Verneuil broke up and went home.[6]

We are told that Richard on landing had intended to hasten to the relief of Verneuil.   But within a few miles of Barfleur, at Bruis, now Brex—the cradle of the immortal House of Bruce—he was met by brother John, who now that his every effort had failed was of course all tears and repentance.   He was allowed to make his peace through the mediation

John makes his Peace. of Queen Eleanor, but Richard, very properly, refused for the time to entrust him with either castles or land, giving him instead pecuniary allowances.[7]   The settlement of these affairs must have delayed the King, as he did not approach Verneuil till the 30th

---

[1] A.D. 1192, Chron. Saint-Aubin of Angers ; Marchegay, *Eglises* (Societé de l'Histoire de France), Norgate, II. 316.

[2] Above, 332 ; and Hoveden, III. 218 ; *cnf.* Chron. Saint-Aubin, *sup.*

[3] Hoveden, 194 ; R. Devizes, 421.

[4] "Superveniente Februario" ; Rigord.

[5] 23rd February, Ash Wednesday ; Rigord, Bouquet, XVII. 39.

[6] Rigord, *sup.*, 40 ; Hoveden, 252 ; Diceto, II. 114, 115 ; W. Newb., II. 418.

[7] The Norman Rolls show the payments.

May, between two and three weeks after landing. A few days were spent in giving some hasty repairs to the walls of Verneuil, and then Richard, leaving Normandy to take care of itself, moved on into Touraine, where also, as we now learn, Philip had done something towards giving effect to John's grants. Loches had fallen into his hands, also Mont-mirail in Maine, a place, by the way, not among the ceded towns. Montmirail however had already been recovered by the Manseaux and Angevins.[1] The recovery of Loches had originally been undertaken by Richard's brother-in-law Sancho; but his father's death intervening he had gone home to be crowned as Sancho VII. of Navarre. By the 13th June Richard had reduced Loches; Tours also having opened its gates, and tendered him a handsome peace-offering, to atone for its previous reception of Philip.[2]

Events in Touraine.

Meanwhile, leading men on either side had proposed in the interests of peace that Philip should meet the Norman Barons at Pont de L'Arche. But the French King instead of attending the conference fell on Les Fontaines, a small place near Brionne, and after four days' siege took it, and demolished it. Returning home-wards in triumph he had the good luck to surprise and capture the gallant Earl Robert IV. of Leicester at the head of a small party of foragers (15th June).[3] Two days later, however, the archbishops of Rheims and Rouen succeeded in bringing about a meeting of barons to discuss the terms of a truce. The French wanted one of three years' duration on the basis of the *status quo*. The English were prepared to agree to a truce for one year on those terms. But Philip further wanted all the allies on either side to be included. To this however, Richard, who had his rebellious Aquitanian feudatories to deal with, could not agree, and so the treaty failed.[4] Operations were then resumed. Philip again fell on Evreux, that once more had reverted to the English, and utterly destroyed it.[5] From the ruins of Evreux the French King marched Southwards, as if to encounter Richard, who, having settled affairs in Touraine, was moving Northwards through the territory of Philip's ally count Louis of Blois. Philip having advanced to Fréteval, while Richard was encamped at Vendôme,[6] polite invitations to an encounter were interchanged. Philip rashly sent to say that he hoped to call on Richard. The latter gladly answered that he would

Events in Normandy.

Evreux again taken by Philip.

[1] Chron. Saint-Aubin, A.D. 1192.

[2] Hoveden, III. 252, 253 ; Chron. Saint-Aubin, *sup.*; Rigord, *sup.*, 40 ; Diceto, II. 116, 117. Philip had visited Tours ; Rigord, *sup.*; W. Newb., II. 418. Richard at first confiscated the estates of the Chapter of Tours, but restored them later in the year ; Diceto, II. 122.

[3] Rigord, *sup.*, 41 ; Hoveden, 253, 254 ; Diceto, 116.

[4] Le Vaudreuil, 17th June ; Hoved., 254, 255.

[5] *Id.* ; W. Newb., II. 418.　　[6] Loir et Cher, both places.

certainly be ready to receive his brother, and that if he did not appear on the morrow he himself would come to meet him. Without waiting for any reply Richard set his forces in motion at daybreak, whereupon

Flight of Philip from Préteval

Philip decamped, but not in time to prevent Richard cutting off his rearguard and baggage train, with the furniture of his chapel, his military chest, and interesting lists of those of Richard's subjects who had subscribed to Philip and John. Philip himself only escaped capture through having left the high road to hear Mass in a parish church at some distance, while Richard in the heat of his pursuit galloped past the cross-road leading to the church.[1]

Relieved of all apprehension of further attacks on Normandy Richard

Reduction of Aquitanian Rebels.

now returned boldly Southwards, and in the course of the next three weeks reduced Taillebourg and the other strongholds of Geoffrey of Rancogne, as well as all those of the Count of Angoulême, apparently the only two outstanding enemies.[2] From Verneuil to the Pyrenees,[3] we are told, not a rebel remained in the field.

A truce for a year from the 1st of November was now, at last,

A Truce.

negotiated in Normandy. The terms were very favourable to Philip, as he was allowed to retain all his conquests of the two preceding years—namely, to the West of the Seine, practically the line of the Iton, from Tillières down to its junction with the Eure, and so down to Pont de L'Arche. To the East of the Seine, Eu, Aumâle and all the Norman Vexin would remain in his hands.[4] These conditions were felt to be very derogatory to England, but in the exhausted state of the Duchy a breathing space was well worth the sacrifice.[5] Unfortunately for their subjects both Kings utilised the interval in pressing for money for the inevitable renewal of hostilities. The clergy, as doubtless being those who had most to spare, were taxed the most.[6] Then Richard's officers in Anjou and Maine were called upon to pay for retention in office, or probably, for dismissal, as the case might be. A novel expedient was that of selling licences to hold or attend tournaments, those ticklish encounters so repeatedly condemned by the Church.[7]

---

[1] 4th July; Hoveden, III. 255; Rigord, 41, 42; Diceto, II. 217, 218; W. Newb., II. 419. Philip rested at night at Châteaudun. Diceto, *sup.*, gives an epigram by Geoffrey of Vinsauf on Philip's flight.

[2] See Richard's report to Hubert Walter dated Angoulême, 22nd July; Hoved., *sup.*; Chron. Saint-Aubin, *sup.*   [3] "Ad crucem Caroli"; Diceto, 118, 119.

[4] 23rd July; Hoveden, 257-260. The treaty was sealed between Verneuil and Tillières.

[5] "Induciæ . . . admodum utiles, licet, ut quibusdam videbatur parum honestæ"; W Newb., II. 420.

[6] So W. Newb., *sup.* See also the treaty of the 15th January, 1196, below.

[7] Hoved., III. 267, 268; W. Newb., II. 422, and for the actual ordinance, *Fœd.*, I. 65, dated Villévêque (Maine et Loire), 22nd August. See also the comments of Diceto, II. 120, on the evils of tournaments.

At home Hubert Walter was carrying on the government with

Affairs at Home.

credit and success. To remedy any laxity or irregularity in the collection of the Revenue that might have crept in during recent troubles a fresh set of instructions were

The Revenue.

issued in September for the guidance of the Justices to be sent on circuit, the Iter being evidently a special one.

Instructions to Itinerant Justices.

The primary duty inculcated is that of strict attention to the rights of the Crown in connection with the multifarious feudal incidents with which the reader is familiar, such

Crown Rights.

as Wardship, Marriage, Escheat, Forfeiture, Forest rights and the like; besides the profits accruing from the ordinary administration of justice. But we also have some special heads connected with recent events; and some points of constitutional interest. The Justices are directed to lay their hands on all the property and effects of the Jews murdered in the late disturbances, as well as on the property and effects of those who murdered them (s. 9). So again account is to be taken of all lands and goods forfeited by John or his followers under decrees issued against them, and not subsequently re-granted or restored by the King (ss. 11-14). Then the Justices must ascertain how far those

Crown Lands.

who had promised contributions for the ransom had paid up (s. 10). Again we have elaborate provisions for the restocking of lands for the time being in the King's hands, and for assessing fair rents as between the King and the persons to whom such lands have been farmed out. It is important to note that in all cases the actual rights of the Crown would be submitted to the finding of local juries (s. 23).

Among the points of constitutional interest are the regulations found

Grand Juries, how to be empanelled.

in the Preamble for empanelling the Grand Juries to sit on Pleas of the Crown and Grand Assizes.[1] As the first step four *milites,* say knights or esquires, are to be chosen (*eligendi*) for the whole county; these are to name two *milites* for each Hundred or Wapentake, and they again appoint the acting jury of twelve; these are to be *milites*—if possible—if not respectable law-worthy men (*legales et liberos homines*). Here, if the primary Four are nominated by the sheriff,[2] the voice of the country will make itself heard through the Twos and the Twelves. As a further piece of elective machinery to assist in the work of government we have in the 20th section a direction for the choice of three

Institution of Coroners.

milites and one cleric in each county as Keepers (*custodes*) of the Pleas of the Crown. The office of Coroner, that has always been elective, is understood to date from this Ordiance. It is easy to see how readily the practice of electing delegates

---

[1] For these Assizes see Pollock and Maitland, I. 147.
[2] So the above writers hold with regard to the Grand Assize, II. 621.

to discharge minor functions would lead up to the election of representatives authorised to speak with authority on matters of general
The Elective Principle. interest.   Returning to our Ordinance, the 21st section forbids
a sheriff to sit as 'Justice' within his own county, thus
marking " a distinct middle stage between the Assize of 1166 in which the
sheriffs share the office of Justice with the itinerant Barons, and the
24th clause of Magna Carta which forbids them to hold any Pleas of
the Crown at all." [1]   A general enquiry as ·to all the receipts of the
sheriffs, constables, foresters and other Crown officers since the King's
coronation was directed (s. 25).   But the opposition offered was such that
Hubert Walter had to withdraw the order.   A more successful financial
measure was one intended to give effect to the constitutional maxim now
being enunciated that the King was the residuary legatee of all defunct
Jews.   We have seen how vexed Richard was at the thought of the
mortgage bonds that had been destroyed, and the property of which
Israelites had been robbed in the riots of 1190, money that ought
Registration of Jews' Property. ultimately to have found its way into his own pocket.   To
prevent the recurrence of such miscarriages in future a general
registration of all Jews' property was taken in hand : houses,
lands, rents, mortgage and other debts (*vadia et debita*), all would have to
be returned and enrolled (*imbrevientur*).   Registries would be established
in four of the chief commercial centres of the kingdom, each with a little
staff of officials, half Christian and half Jewish, and a strong box (*arca*)
for the safe keeping of securities and documents: all advances and
repayments of money to be made in the presence of one of the
officials.[2]

Hubert's scheme took shape; and eventually resulted in the establishment of the Exchequer of the Jews, as a branch of the great
Exchequer of Jews. Exchequer; with Wardens and Justices of the Jews, an office
to shelter and tend them till the time for plucking should
come.   The institution grew and flourished till brought to an end by the
expulsion of all Jews by Edward I.[3]

In the following spring (1195) the Archbishop's position was still further
enhanced by the receipt of a Legatine commission over all
Archbishop Hubert Legate over all England. England, granted by Celestine at the request of the King.[4]
The first use that Hubert made of his new powers was to hold
a visitation of the Church at York, Geoffrey being abroad, as
we shall see.   On the 13th June he deposed the abbot of St. Mary's.
On the two next days he held a Synod, and passed fifteen canons of

---

[1] Bishop Stubbs, *Select Charters*, 250.

[2] Hoveden, III. 262–267 ; Bishop Stubbs, *Select Charters*, 251.

[3] *Select Pleas, etc., Exchequer of Jews* ; J. M. Rigg (Selden Society).

[4] See the commission, dated 18th March, 1195, Hoveden, 290–292 ; Diceto, II. 125 ;
Epp. Cant., 368.

a very sound character for securing the orderly performance of the services,
the due maintenance of the fabric and equipment of the
churches, and the correct lives of the clergy. On the delicate
question of *focariæ* Hubert's tone is distinctly moderate ; he
urges admonition and moral suasion in the first instance, suspension
being only held *in terrorem* over the heads of obstinate offenders as a last
resort.[1]

Visitation of York.

Again under this same year (1195) we have another Ordinance issued
by the Justiciar-Archbishop that has left its mark on our institutions.
Finding it expedient to republish the old English regulations of the Hue
and Cry for the pursuit and apprehension of malefactors, he
adds a direction for the appointment of *milites* to exact oaths
of obedience to the Ordinance from all men of fifteen years
and upwards. This requirement "is probably the germ of the office of
Conservator of the Peace."[2]

Conservators of the Peace.

In one respect however Hubert's conduct does not show to advantage,
and that was in the matter of his treatment of his rival, the Northern
Primate, whom he was evidently determined to ruin. Of Hubert's
hostility we had one instance in his prompt visitation of the Northern
Province, a proceeding not in the best taste. Geoffrey, unfortunately for himself, only gave his adversaries too many
opportunities. At his first appearance at York after consecration[3] he had quarrelled with the Bishop of Durham, and also with his
own Chapter. These difficulties were settled in the course
of the year 1192.[4] A fresh struggle with the Chapter ensued
in 1193. One difference arose from Geoffrey's efforts to
induce the Canons to contribute one fourth of their incomes for the
King's ransom, as other persons were said to have done. Another dispute
broke out over the appointment to the Deanery of York, vacant by the
promotion of Henry Marshal to the See of Exeter.[5] Both Chapter
and Archbishop claimed the right of appointment. Geoffrey began by
naming one Simon of Apulia, a follower of his own, and then revoked the
appointment ; whereupon the Chapter adopted Simon as their nominee.
Both parties appealed to the King in Germany, and also to the Pope.
Geoffrey was on his way to see Richard when he heard that the Canons
had suspended all services, closed the Minster, and barred the private
door from the palace to the church. Returning to York in all haste
(1st January 1194) he excommunicated the chief offenders, and installed
men of his own to perform the services.[6] At the Council of Nottingham

Archbishop Geoffrey

and his Chapter.

[1] Hoveden, III. 293–296.   [2] Hoveden, 299 ; *Select Charters*, 255.
[3] He was received there and enthroned on the 1st November, 1191 ; Giraldus IV., 410.
[4] See Bishop Stubbs, Hoveden, IV. lii.–lv.
[5] 1193. Hoveden, III. 221.
[6] Hoveden, III. 221–223, 229, 230 ; *cnf.* Gervase, I. 523.

(April 1194), as already mentioned, Richard allowed the complaints of the Chapter against Geoffrey to stand over. But in August, the King being again abroad, Hubert Walter thought fit to take up the case. He sent to York a commission of barons, who acted in the most high-handed fashion; declared against Geoffrey on every point; replaced the Canons in their stalls; and summoned the Archbishop to appear before them in person. When he refused they took all his estates into hand, except Ripon, where he was residing. They also practically deprived him of the sheriffdom of York, that he had just bought, by appointing overseers to control the action of his deputy.[1] Not many days later letters came in from the Pope absolving the excommunicated Canons, and ordering them to be reinstated.[2] These mandates were published at York by Hugh of Puiset on Michaelmas Day. Geoffrey then hastened abroad, after entering a fresh appeal to Rome, joined Richard in Maine, and, on giving him security for the balance of the purchase-money of the sheriffdom, obtained from him a letter ordering the restitution of all his lands and other rights.[3] Geoffrey however remained abroad, as we hear that after a period of good understanding the Archbishop's imprudent tongue had again alienated the King.[4] On the 15th January 1195 a fresh battery was unmasked by

Papal Orders. Geoffrey's enemies. On that day the saintly Hugh of Lincoln was brought to York to hold an enquiry directed by the Pope as to Geoffrey's personal character. Celestine had been given to understand that the Archbishop was guilty of devotion to field sports, neglect of duties, misuse of spiritual powers, and disregard of appeals to the Holy See; evidence was to be taken, and remitted to Rome, and a day fixed for Geoffrey's appearance there. "A more outrageous sentence on an ex-parte statement was never issued."[5] The delegates did as they were bidden; they sat, took evidence, and cited

Geoffrey Suspended. Geoffrey and his accusers to appear at Rome on the 1st June.[6] Geoffrey failed to appear. The Pope then enlarged the time to the 18th November; and, the Archbishop having again made default, finally suspended him on the 23rd December.[7]

Simon of Apulia had returned in triumph in February (1195) with letters of confirmation as Dean. Geoffrey's agents endeavoured to prevent his

---

[1] August 119 ; Hoved., III. 261, 262.

[2] *Id.*, 272 ; see also the Pope's letter of the 31st May, 285.

[3] Hoved., 27 -274. The King's letter is dated Mamers, 3rd November. For the 2000 marks refe red to in the letter I would read £2000, as the purchase-money of the sheriffdom of Y rk is clearly referred to.

[4] *Id.*, 287.

[5] Bishop ﾟ ﾟs, Hoveden, IV. lxiii. He thinks that such orders could only have been issued ﾟ c: pressure from the royal agents directed by Hubert Walter.

[6] Hoved., ..I. 278-282. The Pope's letter is dated 8th June, 1194.

[7] Hoveden, 2 .2. See the Papal letters on the subject ; *Id.*, 309-316.

entry into York, even using personal violence, for which they were excommunicated on the spot; and so, without further difficulty, Simon was duly received in the Minster on the 12th of the month. On the next day Bishop Puiset, still eager for the fray, as the last act of his long

Death of Bishop Puiset. pontificate came to York to confirm the sentences against Geoffrey's men. A few days later he took ill on his way to London; was carried back to Howden, and there passed away on the 3rd March (1195) in the forty-first year of his episcopate and the seventieth of his age. Of course the Government laid hands on all his goods.[1]

[1] Hoveden, III. 283, 284; W. Newb., II. 436–440. To Bishop Puiset we owe the valuable survey of the Durham estates known as the Boldon Book (1183); also the elegant Transition Galilee at the West end of Durham Cathedral.

CHAPTER XXI

RICHARD I (*continued*)

A.D. 1195–1198

Intermittent War with France—Treaties of Gaillon—Movement of William Longbeard in London—Question of Liability to Service Abroad—A Force refused—Unsuccessful attempt at New Assessment of England for Hidage—The Hackington Foundation—Resignation of Hubert Walter—Geoffrey Fitz Peter Chief Justiciar

ABROAD the first half of the year 1195 passed in tolerable quiet. By the death of the Duke of Austria (30th December, 1194), Richard had been relieved of the unpaid balance of ransom-money due to him, the clergy having united to extort a remission from Leopold on his death-bed.[1] The King himself was in a most tractable, even penitent mood. He reinvested John with with the Earldoms of Mortain

John reinstated. and Gloucester, and the Honour of Eye, but without the castles ; he pardoned Bishop Hugh of Nonant ; took back Berengaria, with whom apparently he had not lived since he left Palestine ;

Berengaria again with the King. attended daily Mass, 'sitting out the whole service' ; and even began replacing holy vessels taken for the ransom.[2] Lastly he gave up the unfortunate Alais, as he had promised to do. We are glad to record that after all her disappointments she very shortly found a home in Ponthieu by marrying Count William III.[3]

In July, however, the truce broke down, apparently in consequence of intrigues carried on by the Emperor, who was instigating Richard to

[1] The Duke died from an unskilful amputation of a foot crushed by a fall from his horse. Hoveden, III. 276–278 ; W. Newb., II. 431–434 ; Gervase, I. 528, 529. See also Diceto, II. 119 for the letter of the Pope of the 6th June, 1194, ordering the release of the hostages, and the refund of any ransom paid. The hostages, among whom at the last were Eleanor of Brittany and the Cyprian Princess, all came home. According to Hoveden 4000 marks at any rate had been paid ; while William of Newburgh, II. 431, says that there were 20,000 marks more ready to be sent.

[2] Hoveden, III. 286–290. I would suggest that the letter from the Sheykh of the 'Assassins' to the Duke of Austria, acquitting Richard of complicity in the murder of Conrad of Montferrat (above, 319, note) was sent to Richard at this time as a tardy act of justice.

[3] 20 August, Rigord, Bouquet, XVII. 42 ; Hoveden, 303.

attack Philip. The latter, taking the initiative, declared the truce at

Renewed War with France. an end.[1] Petty ravages ensued, ending in conferences near Vaudreuil, to discuss terms more likely to lead to a durable peace than those of the existing truce. Philip, anticipating that he would not be able to maintain the line of the Iton, was preparing for a retirement by quietly destroying the strongholds that he would have to surrender ; and the fact became apparent during the conference, through the sudden collapse of part of the wall of Vaudreuil within sight of the place of meeting. Richard in a fury drew the sword and drove Philip in hasty flight across the Seine.[2] But France was suffering from a famine caused by failure of crops through excessive rain in the previous autumn ; and sheer exhaustion soon brought the Kings again together at Vaudreuil. It would seem that the rectification of the frontier eventually agreed upon was then mooted ; but that through the manœuvres of Henry VI. the question was adjourned, the truce being simply continued to the 8th November.[3] On that day the two Kings once more came to Vaudreuil, but mutual jealousy, or a squabble about etiquette, prevented their actually meeting. Richard went off to lay siege to Arques, and there, according to the French writers, for once in his life, he suffered a repulse at the hands of his overlord, who not only relieved Arques but also burned Dieppe.[4] Against this the English might set off the scattering of the rear-guard of Philip's host on its return march, past the forest of Les Ventes, near Evreux.[5] A more substantial success was the capture of Issudun in Berri effected by Mercadier the captain of Richard's mercenaries (*cotterels*). Both Kings hurried to the rescue ; but the efforts of the clergy and others averted any serious collision. On the 5th December [6] Philip and Richard met, in the usual style, on horseback, between Issudun and Charrost. Richard did homage ; and Philip and he

A Conference. pledged themselves to the terms of a treaty already arranged, the final ratification, however, being left for another meeting, to be held on the 15th January, 1196. On the appointed day the Kings met between Gaillon and Vaudreuil [7] ; and Richard sealed an accord that

Treaty of Gaillon. still involved considerable sacrifices on his part. To the East of the Seine he ceded Gisors, Néaufle, and the Norman Vexin ; retaining Eu, Aumâle, Arques, and Driencourt. To the West of the Seine he gave up Gaillon, Vernon, Pacy, Ivry, and

---

[1] Hoveden, III. 300, 301 ; *cnf.* Rigord, *sup.* Each side blamed the other.

[2] Hoveden and Rigord, *sup.*

[3] September? W. Newb., II. 457 ; Hoved., 302.

[4] Hoveden, III. 304 ; Rigord, *sub.*

[5] Rigord. *sup.*, and Grandes Chron., IV. 101, note Paulin Paris.

[6] See the right date given by the copy of the later treaty in Rigord ; also by W. Newb., II. 462 ; Hoveden has the 9th December, wrongly.

[7] On the 15th January Richard signs at Vaudreuil ; Round, *Calendar*, 107.

Nonancourt; the frontier to be defined by the watershed between the affluents of the Seine and the Eure. Richard also surrendered **Territorial cessions.** all claims on Auvergne. Philip on the other hand yielded Issudun, Graçay, and La Chartre. The Counts of Toulouse, Périgord, and Limoges would be included in the treaty, and the Earl of Leicester liberated on ceding the lordship of Pacy. The treaty also included some curious provisions touching the rights of the Church in **The Kings and Church Rights.** their dominions. By one clause the Kings agreed to procure for each other releases from all claims for damages suffered in the war by the clergy of their respective dominions. Another clause sought to fetter the right of an Archbishop to protect Church property by spiritual censures. The possessions of the See of Rouen included the Rock of Andely, a commanding site on the Seine that had acquired a special value in view of the new frontier. Both Kings evidently wanted to get hold of the place; and so, each hoping to outwit the other, they agreed to clauses subjecting the power of the Archbishop of Rouen of uttering any excommunication or Interdict in respect of Les Andelys to the supervision of a committee [1] to be named by themselves; while at the same time they themselves renounced any rights of property, or claim to fortify any site at Les Andelys. [2]

Great efforts were made by Richard to extort from Walter of Coutances **Normandy under Interdict.** his assent to these provisions, but without success. [3] Determined not to sacrifice Church rights the Archbishop retired first to Cambrai, and then to Paris, finally laying all Normandy under Interdict on the question of the damages. This sentence was dissolved about July, on compensation being promised. [4] A fresh Interdict followed shortly on the question of Les Andelys, as we shall see.

Such a treaty as that of Gaillon could not possibly prove lasting. Probably no terms could have been devised that would have kept the kings at peace. We are told that Richard was anxious to drive Philip to some breach of the treaty; and that even Philip was not content. [5] How Richard came to submit to such terms we cannot understand, unless it was the pressure of the general distress. [6] His acceptance of cessions in Berri, at the expense of the vital Norman frontier, also seems strange, unless it was that as a Poitevin he really cared more for the suzerainty of Aquitaine, which was perpetually in revolt, than for the loyal Northern

---

[1] Dictatores.

[2] See the treaty in duplicate, the copy sealed by Philip being given by *Fœdera*, I. 66; that sealed by Richard, by Rigord, *sup.*, 43; see also Hoveden, III. 302; and W. Newb., *sup.*

[3] See the Archbishop's letter to Diceto, given by the Dean, II. 135; also Hoveden, IV. 3, 4.   [4] See Diceto, 135-146.

[5] So W. Newb., II. 463.

[6] *Id.* Fresh floods came on in March, Rigord; see also for England, Newburgh, 464; and Hoveden, IV. 13.

Duchy that gave him no trouble and filled his purse. As might be
expected he was the first to break the truce. From Philip's

Richard breaks the Truce. biographer we hear of his treacherously seizing Vierzon[1] in Berri, a foolish act of wanton aggression ; while it is clear that in express violation of the terms of the recent treaty he was occupying Les Andelys.[2] Philip retaliated by laying siege to Aumâle ; whereupon

War in Normandy. Richard made his way into Nonancourt, but only with the golden key.[3] He then marched to the relief of Aumâle ; but only to be once more repulsed, and driven off. After a lengthy siege of many weeks' duration the garrison capitulated, and Richard had to allow them to pay heavily for the ransom of their lives.[4] Philip then completed his triumph by going over to Nonancourt and recovering the place. On the other hand John, for a wonder, distinguished himself by seizing Gamaches, between Eu and Aumâle, but within the French frontier.[5] We next hear of troubles in Brittany, caused

Affairs of Brittany. by Richard's demand for the wardship of his nephew the young Count. The King at one time, as we have seen, contemplated making Arthur his heir. That scheme had evidently been abandoned, John being now on the best of terms with his brother. But Richard, of course, wished to keep up his hold on Brittany. Henry II. with that view had obliged Constance within a year of her widowhood to marry Ralph III. Earl of Chester.[6] As the Earls of Chester were hereditary viscounts of the *Avranchin* the union would keep up a connexion between Brittany and Normandy. Unfortunately the Countess and her husband could not manage to live together ; and she, dispensing with his assistance, had for some time been ruling her country without much regard for either Richard or Philip. On the receipt however of Richard's summons, to pacify him, she started for his court, leaving her son in safe keeping at home. But on her way she was intercepted by her husband, and imprisoned at Saint-James-de-Beuvron. Both parties flew to arms : the Bretons to obtain the liberation of their Countess ; Richard to enforce the surrender of her son. As the only means of keeping Arthur from Richard's hands the Bretons sent him to Paris, and placed him under Philip's keeping. But we hear that eventually,

---

[1] Dept. Cher, on the river Cher ; July ; Rigord.

[2] He was there on the 14th July ; *Fœdera*, I. 66.

[3] " Dolo . . . data pecunia," Rigord.

[4] According to Le Breton the siege lasted 49 days ; *Philippis*, Bouquet, XVII. 176. The writer then introduces incidents apparently not found elsewhere, namely an attack on Gaillon by Richard in which he was wounded ; and the slaughter of some thousands of Welshmen near Andelys, p. 177. Richard, no doubt, had Welshmen in his service this year ; but their number was only 700–1000 ; Pipe Roll, 8 Rich. I., ' Southampton,' and ' Hereford.'

[5] Rigord, *sup.*, 46 ; W. Newb., II. 487 ; Hoveden, IV. 5, 14, 16. Gamaches was immediately fortified ; Norman Rolls, II. xiii.   [6] A.D. 1187 ; Ben. P., II. 29.

their lands having been wasted by mercenaries, the Bretons came to terms with the English King.[1]

Meanwhile Richard had quietly taken possession of Les Andelys; and **Fortifications at Les Andelys.** was beginning to build two fortresses there; one on an island in the Seine; the other on a rocky promontory overhanging the river.[2] The site was most important; being situate within the ceded Norman Vexin it gave Richard a footing in that district; it covered Rouen: and it commanded the access to Gaillon and other ceded places to the West of the Seine. But, as already mentioned, the Andelys, both Rock and Island, belonged to the See of Rouen. A fierce struggle for possession at once ensued. Archbishop Walter, who had only just released Normandy from the Interdict on the question of **Normandy again under Interdict.** damages, fulminated a new sentence; following this up by a personal journey to Rome in support of his cause (November). Richard sent an embassy after him; one of the number being Bishop Longchamp, who died on the way, at Poitiers.[3] The Pope and Cardinals were induced to take a moderate view of Richard's offence as he offered compensation. Eventually the Interdict was removed (20th April, **A Settlement.** 1197); and, after months of negotiation Walter was persuaded to accept of Dieppe, Louviers, and other cessions in exchange for Les Andelys.[4]

As a set-off to so much warfare and discord it is a relief to hear of a **Alliance with Toulouse.** pacification described as the ending of forty years of hostilities; namely between Aquitaine and Toulouse, effected through the marriage of Richard's widowed sister Jeanne of Sicily to Count Raymond VI.[5] For Richard this was a most important alliance, as it protected the South-Eastern frontier, and would certainly tend to discourage insubordination on the part of the Aquitanian feudatories. Another disturbing force was removed about this time by the disappearance of Bertran de Born, who, at last, dropping the war-trump, retired to end his days in a monastery.[6]

At home the event of the year (1196) was a movement in London of a **Popular Movement in London.** democratic or social character, arising out of discontent at the pressure of taxation, and unjust taxation, as was alleged, aggravated by the long continuance of dearth and want, which had affected England as well as Normandy.[7] A leader arose in the person

---

[1] Hoveden, IV. 7; G. Le Breton, Norgate, II. 369, 370; W. Newb., II., 463, 491; Chron. Saint-Aubin.

[2] See the plan below; and Stapleton, Norman Rolls, II. xiv.

[3] 31st January, 1197; Diceto, II. 150; *Reg. Sacrum.*

[4] See the Archbishop's letter, Diceto, II. 148-150; Hoveden, IV. 16-18; Stapleton, *sup.* The final agreement was only sealed at Rouen 16th October, 1197. See the documents, Diceto, 153-156. [5] Hoveden, 13, A.D. 1196. [6] See Norgate, II. 371.

[7] For the famine and sickness in England see W. Newb., II. 484; Hoveden, IV. 13.

of one William fitz Osbert, surnamed Longbeard or Bearded William.

William Longbeard. He was a man of good civic position, had joined the London contingent for the Crusade of 1191[1]; and was possessed of considerable oratorical powers. It would seem that the establishment of the *Commune* had not made the government of the City less oligarchical than before. Both echevins and aldermen were apparently taken from the higher merchant classes. Longbeard maintained that the taxes were so assessed as to throw an unfair proportion on the poorer classes, a charge that may well have had some foundation.[2] His harangues on the subject gained him a considerable, in fact an alarming following.[3] But his faith in his cause was such that he crossed

Appeal to the King. the Channel to see the King, and urge financial reform, a subject to which Richard lent a ready ear, and in fact gave the man quite a favourable reception. But on Longbeard's return, Hubert Walter, rightly apprehending the proportions that the movement might assume under such encouragement, began to take precautionary measures, exacting hostages from the citizens for the maintenance of the peace. Nevertheless William, strong in the hope of Royal support, persevered with his meetings, and his inflammatory speeches delivered in St. Paul's Churchyard.[4] Summoned to appear before the Council he came at the head of an armed mob. The authorities then, watching their opportunity, sent men to arrest him in private. He resisted, felling one of the officers with an axe, and then taking sanctuary in the tower of St. Mary le Bow.[5] There he was regularly besieged by the orders of the

Arrest and Execution of Longbeard. Justiciar, and finally smoked out with fire. He was taken to the Tower, tried, condemned, and then drawn at a horse's tail to the gallows at Tyburn, and so hung in chains with eight or nine of his followers.[6] Hubert Walter was bound to assert the supremacy of the law and maintain order. But the Canterbury monks, to whom Bow Church belonged, raised loud protests at the violation of their sanctuary[7]; while fresh trouble was threatened by reports that miracles were being wrought on the spot where the people's champion had suffered.[8]

Another annoyance to which Hubert Walter had been subjected about this same time, was the arrival of a financial expert commissioned by the

---

[1] See Ben. P , II. 116.

[2] So Hoveden seemed to think, p. 5 ; also Diceto, II. 143.

[3] W. Newb., II. 468 ; Gervase, I. 532.

[4] Diceto.

[5] " Intra turrim cujusdam ecclesiæ " ; Diceto. " In turrem contiguam ecclesiæ Sanctæ Mariæ quæ dicitur de Arcu " ; Gervase.

[6] 6th April. See W. Newburgh, II. 466-471, the fullest account ; also Hoveden, IV. 5, 6 ; Diceto, II. 143 ; Gervase, I. 532-534. The last gives the date ; so too the *Liber de Antiquis Legg. London*, p. 2 (Camden Society).

[7] Hoveden, *sup.*

[8] Newb , 471-473 ; Gervase, *sup.*

King to examine the accounts of the Sheriffs and others, a step implying some distrust of the existing Administration. Richard, not unnaturally, was dissatisfied with his English revenue, which had fallen **The Revenue** greatly below that of earlier Kings. The fault lay in the want **falling off.** of any just and equable system of taxation for bringing all the resources of the country into proper contribution. The old assessments of land had become inadequate, as we hear that a hide of land (120 acres, more or less) was still commonly assessed at £1 a year, at a time when an ox was worth 4s.,[1] so that the eight-ox team alone would be worth more than a year's value of the land it had to cultivate.[2] For the taxation of personalty—beyond the spoliation of defunct Jews and ecclesiastics—there was no provision; and the more orderly the country became, and the more constitutionally it was governed the more the profits of justice, and the returns from the feudal incidents would sink. There would be fewer fines, penalties, and forfeitures; fewer opportunities for sweeping *misericordiæ*. Richard however allowed himself to be persuaded that the decay in the revenue was due to malversation, a belief, no doubt, current at the time; and Longbeard's attacks on the city magistracy, who had dealings with the Exchequer, may have confirmed the King in his suspicions. Accordingly **Abortive** he sent over Robert Abbot of Caen, a man of experience in **Financial** the Norman Exchequer, who had confidently assured him that **Investigation.** he could double his revenue for him. The Sheriffs were warned to be prepared for an extra strict investigation at the Easter Audit, but before the day came the Abbot died, and there the matter ended.[3] Worried on all sides Hubert begged to be allowed to throw up the Justiciarship, but after some correspondence with the King he was induced to withdraw his resignation.[4]

With the year 1197 we are told that Richard began to act with greater **The War.** vigour and effect, the old allies of the King of France falling from him, and rallying round the King of England. In fact Philip had already lost ground in that respect. The standing allies of Louis VII. as against Henry II. had been the House of Blois, the relatives of King Stephen. But the present Count of **Richard's** Champagne, Henry King of Jerusalem, was equally related **Allies.** to Philip and Richard, and had throughout kept on most friendly terms with the latter. In another quarter the late Count Philip of Flanders, who died at Acre in 1191, had always sought to hold an even hand as between England and France. But his nephew and

---

[1] See the Instructions to the Justices of 1196, Hoved, III. 265.

[2] The eight-ox team is generally accepted as the complement for a hide of land; Round, *Feudal England*, 35, 36.

[3] 11th April. W. Newb, II. 464, 465; Hoveden, IV. 5. In 1196 Easter fell on the 21st April. [4] Hoveden, 12, 13.

successor, Baldwin, Ninth of Hainault and Seventh of Flanders,[1] having had to cede Artois and Peronne to Philip, was altogether on the side of England.[2] Again the Bretons, unwillingly no doubt, had been forced to take their orders from Richard. What with Philip's domineering tendencies, and what with Richard's liberal use of money, many magnates were changing sides.[3] But we fail to trace any effectual use of these

Feeble Action.

favouring circumstances made by Richard towards the recovery of the Norman Vexin; his operations being still desultory and feeble. Thus we hear on the 15th of April of the burning of Saint Valéry on the Somme, and the capture of some ships there.[4] Next month John and Mercadier made a raid round Beauvais, and laid siege to Milly.[5] Bishop Philip coming to the rescue was taken prisoner with many others (19th May), and then Milly fell.[6] Again Dangu, near Gisors, but within the Norman Vexin, was surrendered by William Crespin to Richard. He took possession, garrisoned the place, and then went off to make useless conquests in Auvergne, where he was said to have won ten towns. But meanwhile Philip recovered Dangu.[7]

To help the King in all the diplomatic work that he had on hand Hubert Walter had been brought over to Normandy in June.[8] Through his good management the friendly relations with Flanders were brought to a point by the execution of a treaty of offensive alliance as against France.[9] On the strength of this support Baldwin took the field to recover lost territory. He captured Douai, and laid siege to Arras. Philip promptly led an army into Artois. At his approach Baldwin raised the siege, retiring slowly so as to entice his enemy into pursuit: then, sending parties round to break down the bridges in Philip's rear, he cut off his communications, putting him in straits for supplies.[10] Prompt co-operation on Richard's part would in all likelihood have been rewarded by some decisive success; but perhaps he was not within striking distance.

---

[1] Baldwin IX. was son of Baldwin VIII. of Hainault by Margaret sister of the late Philip of Flanders. At his death Baldwin VIII. succeeded in right of his wife, but had died since. Baldwin IX. was married to Mary sister of Henry of Champagne. He was the hero of the Fourth Crusade, who became Emperor of Constantinople.

[2] Philip of Flanders held the Vermandois in right of his wife Isabella. At her death in 1182 her rights properly devolved on her sister Eleanor, married to Matthew of Beaumont. But in 1185 King Philip took possession of the Amiénois and part of Vermaudois; and in 1191 he occupied Artois and Peronne. See De Serres, cited *Engl. Hist. Rev.*, XIV. 546.

[3] See W. Newb., II. 492, 495; Hoveden, IV. 19; Rigord.

[4] Diceto, II. 152; W. Newb., 492; Hoved., *sup.*   [5] Oise, near Marseille.

[6] W. Newb., 493; Diceto, *sup.* Hoveden, IV. 16, places this incident under the year 1196, wrongly, his date, Monday, 19th May, being good for 1197, not for 1196.

[7] Hoveden, IV. 20.   [8] 17th June, Gerva~~   ~~5th June, Diceto, II. 158.

[9] *Fœdera*, I. 67, 68; Diceto, 152 (undat

[10] Advancing on Lille by way of Arra   · to cross the Scarpe, the Souchez, and the Haute Deule.

At any rate Baldwin, left to act for himself, was induced to meet his over-lord at Lille on the 8th September ;[1] when he agreed to release him from his difficulty on the simple condition of his holding a conference with Richard in the interests of peace. The Kings accordingly met between Gaillon and Les Andelys on the 17th September, when a long truce was signed, a truce to the 13th January, 1199, no real pacification being possible.[2]

In England the year (1197) witnessed a remarkable rebuff suffered by the King. In a Grand Council held at Oxford on the 7th December[3] Hubert Walter laid before the assembly a proposal that the Baronage, spiritual and temporal,[4] or perhaps, as we might fairly conjecture, expanding slightly the scope of the writer's words, that the military tenants as a whole should provide the King with a force of 300 men-at-arms for one year's service abroad, an entirely novel demand. The Archbishop urged compliance, and so did his colleague Richard fitz Nigel, Treasurer and Bishop of London, who was still living.[5] The next man invited to speak was the Carthusian Bishop of Lincoln, Hugh of Avalon, a man of holy life, upright and inflexible ; one moreover endowed with high artistic feeling, as to him we owe perhaps the most beautiful of England's Minsters. His voice gave no uncertain sound. 'For thirteen years since the Church of Our Lady, Holy Mary the Mother of God,[6] had been entrusted to his rule he had made it his study to defend its rights while fulfilling its duties ; he was aware that the Church of Lincoln owed certain military service within the limits of England but not without them.[7] Rather than subject his church to such a burden as that now proposed he would return to his cell among the hills of Burgundy.'[8] Herbert Le Poer of Sarum, a man closely connected with the court circle and the official world,[9] being next called upon, declared that he could only echo the

Margin notes: Grand Council — Demand for a Force to serve abroad for a year. — St. Hugh of Lincoln. — The Force refused.

[1] Gervase, I. 544 ; where this is given as the final conference.

[2] Hoveden, IV. 22, 24 ; W. Newburgh, II. 495, 496 ; *cnf.* Gervase, *sup.* Ralph of Coggeshall, 77–79, makes the French King advance as far as Ypres, but that seems very unlikely.

[3] Gervase, I. 549 ; *Magna Vita St. Hugonis,* 248 (Dymock, Rolls Series, No. 37).

[4] " Ut barones Angliæ inter quos et episcopi censebantur " ; *Magna Vita, sup.*

[5] He died 10th September, 1198 ; Diceto, II. 163.

[6] " Ecclesiæ dominæ meæ Sanctæ Mariæ Dei genetricis." This meant Lincoln Cathedral.

[7] " Extra metas Angliæ nil tale deberi " ; *Magna Vita,* 248–252.

[8] Before coming to England to take charge of Henry II.'s foundation at Witham in Somerset Hugh had belonged to the Grande Chartreuse near Grenoble ; his father's place, Avalon, was also in the Dept. Isère, near Pontcharra.

[9] Herbert was the son of Richard's agent Richard of Ilchester, made Bishop of Winchester in 1174 ; the surname Le Poer suggests a connexion with Bishop Roger of Salisbury and his family ; Hoved., IV. xci.

words of the Bishop of Lincoln, whereupon the Archbishop in great indignation dismissed the assembly.[1]

Much has been made, and always will be made of the incident as a case of successful resistance to an unjust tax. St. Hugh was quite entitled to object to a demand for which there was no precedent. But the exact ground taken by him, if he has been correctly reported, will not bear investigation. The clergy had been paying and still were paying scutage for war in Normandy without demur. On the face of it, it seems illogical to suppose that men could be called upon to pay commutation for a service for which they were not liable.[2] No doubt it is not safe on constitutional questions to found on the procedure of a government so arbitrary as that of Richard I. But the question seems settled by the fact that the clergy were not only paying scutage, but also paying large extra sums for being relieved from personal service oversea (*Ne transfretent*).[3] We may add that no objection to such service had ever been raised before, unless indeed the opposition of Archbishop Theobald to Henry II.'s exactions for the war of Toulouse may have been partly based on that ground. Again we must express our belief that if St. Hugh objected to personal service abroad he was starting a new constitutional principle, but one likely to prove very popular.

Question of Liability of the Clergy to Foreign Service.

The sequel to the incident is worth telling. Richard in a fury summoned the two refractory Bishops to his presence, at the same time ordering all their property to be taken into hand. The Sarum estates were seized, till Bishop Herbert, hastening abroad, compounded for his offence by a fine. But the awe inspired by St. Hugh's personality, or the dread of his anathemas, was such that no man ventured to lay a finger on anything appertaining to the See of Lincoln ; while for eight months he himself held on the even tenor of his way, ignoring all the King's citations. At last, however, out of consideration for the officials responsible for the execution of the King's orders, who might have got into trouble through his contumacy, he submitted, and crossed the Channel. He found the King at Andely, attending Mass in the chapel of the newly built castle on the Rock, and seated in his stall on the right-

St. Hugh and the King.

---

[1] *Magna Vita*, 249, 250. Hoveden, IV. 40, places the incident in the year 1198, and represents Hubert as asking for pay for the men-at-arms at the rate of three shillings a day, when the rate was only one shilling a day. This is but an instance of the writer's inaccuracy in figures and finance.

[2] Mr. Round, however, *Feudal England*, 531, thinks that such was the case, citing a passage from Joscelin of Brakelond p. 63 (Camden Society) evidently based on the proceedings in the Oxford Council, where the military tenants of Bury are represented as saying that they might be liable for scutage, but not for service abroad. But this story cannot stand against the evidence of the Pipe Rolls.

[3] Pipe Rolls 7 and 8 Rich. I. *passim*. The reader will understand that the service would be performed and the fines p   rgy themselves, but by their *milites*.

hand side of the door. Hugh at once saluted his lord; but Richard after one fierce glance at him turned away his eyes. The Bishop, not a whit disconcerted, demanded the kiss of peace. 'Kiss me O lord my King.' Again Richard refused to notice him. Hugh, then, treating the King as he would a schoolboy or a child, seized his mantle with his two hands, and drawing it tightly round the Royal chest gave him a good sound shaking. 'Thou owest me a kiss as I come from far.' 'Thou deservest it not,' mumbled Richard. 'Nay, but I do. Kiss me then,' retorted the dauntless Bishop, giving his lord a more vigorous shake than before. Richard, unable to hold out any longer, laughed outright and gave the desired salute.[1]

Defeated in their application to the Baronage the Government resolved to fall back on the land, and a levy of hidage or Danegeld. But the returns from this impost as previously tried had been so disappointing that

Hidage or Carucage called for. it was resolved to take it at an enhanced rate, and on the footing of a new assessment, to replace that of the great Domesday Survey. Domesday itself, intended to correct an older and inadequate assessment, had failed to return the full number of taxable hides or ploughlands. Orders therefore were now issued for a new

Proposed new Assessment. survey to ascertain that number, seemingly by the simple process of finding out how many full plough-teams were at work, the scope of the plough-team rather than the actual acreage being in fact the standard of measurement.[2] The rate of 'carucage,' a term that now begins to appear,[3] would be five shillings instead of two shillings the hide; the chronicler adding with palpable inconsistency that every hundred acres of land under plough would be reckoned a hide. The inquest would be held by royal commissioners, a cleric and a knight, in the presence of the sheriff and [four] chosen knights of the shire, who would summon the stewards and bailiffs of the manors, with four good men and the reeve from each township (villa), to appear and give evidence; local interests would be represented by the presence of two knights of the Hundred. Tenants by Grand Sergeanty were excused; but they were required to return their estates, and to present themselves in London by the 31st May to hear the King's pleasure; so that the writs must have been issued early in the year (1198).[4]

The appearance of the representative Knights to superintend the process of assessment is the most interesting feature of the inquest. It has been pointed to as indicating an incipient connexion between representation

---

[1] 28th August, 1198; *Magna Vita*, 251, 252.

[2] "Quot carucarum wannagia fuerint in singulis villis." The fact that the Latin for hide was "carucata," and sometimes simply "caruca," speaks for itself. In English we have "plough" and "ploughland" in the same sense.

[3] W. H. Stevenson *Engl. Hist. Review*, IV. 108; where it is pointed out that carucagium or caruagium is formed from the French caruée.

[4] Hoveden, IV. 46, 47.

and taxation. Financially the tax appears to have been a failure. It
was resisted by the clergy so strenuously that we are told
that an edict was issued putting them outside the pale of the
law.[1] Fragmentary returns by some of the tenants in Grand
Sergeanty have been identified, and compared with the valuations in
Domesday, with the result of showing that in some quarters the old
assessments were lowered instead of being raised.[2] Again we have
counties fining 'to be dealt with gently' in the matter of the carucage;
and others paying to be altogether relieved of the enquiry;[3] while later
in the year instructions to the Justices in Eyre direct them to ascertain
how far the inquests had been held.[4] Of actual payment into the
Exchequer just one sum of £20 is found on the Pipe Roll of 1199
entered after Richard's death as paid by Staffordshire for 'a carucage
assessed in the late King's time'; an entry that might just as well refer
to the levy of 1194 as to that of 1198. On the other hand
we have numerous payments on account of a tallage imposed
on the King's demesnes for the support of 500 foot-soldiers
(*servientes*) abroad.[5] The right to tallage the demesnes was one that as
yet had never been called in question. A most disgraceful act of this
year, however (1198) and one that did excite the indignation
of the Chroniclers was the breaking of the Great Seal, and
the production of a new Seal, to enable the King to call in
all charters sealed with the old Seal for fresh attestation, on payment, of
course, of a fresh fine. The excuse given for discrediting documents given
under the earlier Seal was that it had been out of the King's control on
two occasions, first in 1191 when it was lost (*perditum fuit*) during the
short period when it was still attached to the body of the defunct Vice-
Chancellor before it was recovered and brought to the King; and secondly
while the King was a prisoner in Germany.[6] The old Seal was still in use
on the 1st April 1198; the earliest impression of the new Seal found as
yet is dated 22nd May following. The change therefore must have been
made between those two dates.[7]

Side notes: The Tax a failure. Tallage on Royal Demesnes. Re-sealing of Charters.

[1] Hoveden, IV. 66.

[2] See these returns, picked out of the Testa de Nevill by Mr. Round, *Engl. Hist.
Rev.*, III., 502-505, 508.

[3] See Pipe Roll, 1 John, fol. 7, dorso, Herts and Essex; "Ne fiat inquisitio de
Carruagio"; also the £100 paid by the men of Dorset," "Ut bene tractentur."

[4] Hoveden, 62; Round, *E. H. R.*, III. 501.

[5] Pipe Roll, 10 Rich. I. and 1 John, *passim*.

[6] See this recited on all charters sealed with the new Seal, a mere "common form";
Round, *Feudal England*, 542.

[7] See Round, *sup.* 545; Hoveden, IV., 66; R. Cogg., 93; Ann. Waverley; M. Paris,
Hist. Angl., II. 75. Hoveden in an earlier passage III. 267, had placed the incident
in 1194, coupling it with an alleged   champ for which there is no
foundation.

The efforts to raise the carucage would not lighten the difficulties with which Hubert Walter had to contend.   The Canterbury monks had never ceased attacking him for the violation of the sanctuary of Bow Church ; they complained to the Pope of his engrossment by secular affairs ; while the terrible question of the Hackington Chapel was revived.   As already mentioned Archbishop Baldwin had proposed to found there a college for secular canons out of revenues taken from the monastic endowments of Canterbury, and had to a certain extent carried out his plan.   But the scheme had been fiercely assailed from the first, and at last the Hackington chapel had to be pulled down.   The materials of the Collegiate buildings, however, were transported to a new site acquired at Lambeth.   This had been done partly by Baldwin, and partly by Hubert Walter, who adopted the scheme of his predecessor.   The final confirmation of the new arrangements had only been passed by the King in April 1195.[1]   But the monks now found that the mere existence of a chapel built with stones brought from Hackington was an insult to St. Thomas of Canterbury.   Celestine III. had seen no reason for interfering with the Lambeth chapel.[2]   But he had passed away, and the exalted churchmanship of his successor INNOCENT III.[3] thought otherwise, and the destruction of the objectionable chapel was immediately ordered.[4]   Innocent also took the monks' views of the Archbishop's attention to worldly affairs ; and so the end of it was that Hubert, harassed on all sides, resigned the Justiciarship, and the King, very reluctantly, had to allow him to go.   For his successor he took Geoffrey Fitz Peter, who had been on the Regency Council named in 1189, and had assisted in the work of government ever since.[5]

The Hackington-Lambeth Chapel.

Geoffrey FitzPeter Chief Justiciar.

---

[1] *Fœdera*, I. 65.

[2] *Epp. Cant.*, 371, 372.

[3] Celestine died on the 8th January, 1198. Next day Lothair dei Conti, the youngest Cardinal in the Curia, was elected, and took the style of Innocent III. ; Hoveden, IV. 41 ; Diceto, II. 159. See the new Pope's notification of his accession ; Hoveden, 42 ; *Epp. Cant.* 385.

[4] 24th April 1198 ; *Epp. Cant.* 391 ; Gervase, I. 551, 552. Hubert did not give way till January 1199, the King supporting him to the best of his ability ; but finally in the course of that month the demolition was taken in hand. For the whole struggle, Richard's share in it, and his subsequent persecution of the monks, see Gervase 551-592, and the voluminous correspondence, *Epp. Cant.*, 394-475. The King demanded a view of the Canterbury treasures ; of course it was refused.

[5] See Richard's letter announcing the appointment, dated 11th July, 1198 ; *Fœdera*, I. 71. For Geoffrey Fitz Peter and the Essex inheritance see Hoveden, III. xlviii.

CHAPTER XXII

RICHARD I (*continued*)

A.D. 1198, 1199

Vacancy in the Empire—Otto IV. elected King—Fortifications at Les Andelys—The War—Defeats of Philip—Truce—Death of Richard—Survey of the Reign—Revenue—Commerce—Relations with Scotland, Wales, and Ireland.

ON the 28th September, 1197, a vacancy in the Imperial throne had been created by the death of Henry VI.[1] the mean, cruel Emperor.[2]

Death of Henry VI. It would seem, however, that he had somewhat repented of his treatment of King Richard and had remitted 17,000 marks that were still unpaid.[3] For the choice of his successor the Guelfic party announced an Electoral Diet, to be held at Cologne on the 22nd February, 1198. And now the grant of the titular Kingdom of Arles came into useful purpose, as it enabled the friends of the House of Brunswick to secure the valuable support of the King of England as against the Hohenstaufen by summoning Richard as the chief vassal of the Empire.[4] Richard's first efforts were directed towards obtaining the election of his nephew Henry of Saxony. But the Duke was in Holy Land with a German expedition sent out by the late Emperor; and Richard's agents[5] were obliged to fall back on the younger brother Otho or Otto, already created Duke of Aquitaine and Count of Poitiers by Richard in 1196.[6] His election was opposed

---

[1] Hoveden, IV. 30, 31.

[2] For Henry's barbarites in connexion with his subjugation of Sicily after the death of King Tancred in 1194, see Sismondi, *Italian Rep.*, II. 262 (ed. 1826).

[3] R. Cogg.,72–74; Hoveden, III. 304.

[4] "Sicut præcipuum membrum Imperii"; Hoved. IV. 37.

[5] Among these were Philip of Poitiers, Bishop of Durham, appointed in 1195 in succession to Puiset; the King's Chancellor, Eustace Elect of Ely, appointed in succession to Longchamp; and Baldwin of Bethune, third husband of Hedwise daughter of William I., Count of Aumâle and Earl of York, and so in her right Count of Aumâle; see Hoveden, III. 306, IV. 37 and notes; and G. E. C. Peerage.

[6] Richard had always shown himself very anxious for the promotion of Otto. His first proposal was to make him Earl of York, but the Yorkshiremen would not have

by the Hohenstaufen party, who had their candidate in Philip of Suabia,
brother of the late Emperor, Henry's son Frederick, after-
Otto of Brunswick wards Frederick II., being a mere child, not four years old.
The Suabian Duke had all the support of Philip Augustus;
the Count of Flanders on the other hand declaring for Otto.
Philip of Suabia Innocent III. held aloof, watching the course of events.   Both
parties held Diets and declared their candidate duly elected.
But Otto had the best of it, as he succeeded in ousting his opponent
from Aachen, otherwise Aix-la-Chapelle, where the Regalia were kept;
and so was crowned King of Germany or King of the Romans on the
4th July (1198).[1]

Richard's personal occupation during the first half of the year 1198 was
superintending the works on the Rock of Andely, the tremendous fortress
that in his boyish delight at his own edifice he christened the *Château
Gaillard*, or Saucy Castle.[2]   The site was one pointed out
Château Gaillard by nature, consisting of a jutting chalk cliff, the crest of a
promontory, rising 300 feet above the Seine at its confluence
with the Gambon, and so well protected by water and ravines as to
be accessible only by an isthmus at the foot of the promontory.   The
King's first care had been to fortify a little island in the Seine with bridges
connecting it with the shore on either side.   At the East end of the
bridge, and to the North of the Rock he established a walled town, since
known as Le Petit Andely.   The promontory of which the river-cliff
formed the apex was protected at its lower or North-east end by a
triangular outwork, connected by a drawbridge with the principal
fortification.   This comprised an inner and an outer line of walls, flanked
by towers and bastions.   Richard doubtless had profited by what he had
seen in Palestine, where the circumstances of the Frankish settlers,
surrounded with hostile tribes, had greatly developed the art of fortification.[3]

But Richard would have been better employed in clearing the French
The War. out of Normandy.   In fact the circumstances were eminently
favourable to an effort for the recovery of the lost territory.
We hear of a great coalition that had gathered round Richard as against

him (Hoved., III. 86, A.D. 1190).   The next scheme was to marry him to Margaret
daughter of William the Lion and make him heir to Scotland ; but the Scots would not
have him either (Hoved. III. 298, 308) ; finally in 1196 Richard made him Duke of
Aquitaine, and Count of Poiters (*Id.*, IV. 7 ; R. Cogg., 70).

[1] "Apud Hays capellam" ; Hoveden, IV. 37-39 and notes ; Diceto, II. 163.   For
money borrowed by Richard (2,125 marks) to support Otto's cause at Rome, see *Fœdera*
I. 78.

[2] "Munitionem illam vocavit Gaillardam, quod sonat in Gallico petulantiam."
"Muros Rupis Gaillardæ" ; G. Le Breton, *Gesta* and *Philippis*, Bouquet, XVII. 195, 196.

[3] See Clark, *Mediæval Architecture*, I. 378, and Viollet le Duc., *Dictionnaire*
"*Château*" ; and the engravings of Syrian castles in Mr. Poole's *Crusades* and Mr.
Archer's *Richard I*.

Philip.   Among the names given we find those of Baldwin Count of Flanders, Reginald of Dammartin Count of Boulogne, Louis Count of Blois, Geoffrey III. Count of Perche, Raymond VI. Count of Toulouse, with finally Arthur of Brittany.[1]   On the other hand Philip had secured a treaty with Philip of Suabia.[2]   But Richard was not the man to manage allies.   The only man named as coming actually forward was Baldwin, who had definite ends of his own to attain.   The harvest season over he opened the campaign in September by laying siege to St. Omer.[3]   Pending the siege we hear of a battle between Richard and the French, vaguely indicated as fought somewhere between Gamaches and Vernon, places more than 60 miles apart.   But the action must have been fought much nearer to Vernon than to Gamaches, as we hear that Philip after being defeated was chased into Vernon.[4]   It is possible

Defeat of Philip.

that the French King may have been on his way to relieve St. Omer.[5]   Anyhow as he had been thus driven across the Seine into Vernon, Richard on Sunday 28th September, starting doubtless from the Andelys, crossed the Epte at Dangu, and took Courcelles and Bury (Oise), both within French territory, returning at night to Dangu.   Next day Philip was reported to be hastening—a day after the fair—to the relief of Courcelles.   Richard expecting an attack on Dangu from the direction of Vernon, left the bulk of his force there, on the river bank, himself taking a detachment to reconnoitre the country towards Mantes.   But under his determined leadership the detachment proved more than a match for all that it had to encounter.   Philip advancing from Mantes was attacked on the road, routed, and driven helter-skelter through the town of Gisors across the Epte, into the castle of Gisors.

He is again routed.

As he was crossing, the bridge broke down under him, and he narrowly escaped drowning.   Some 130 prisoners of good position fell into Richard's hands, three of these, one of them a Montmorency, having been unhorsed by the Royal lance.   Writing to England the King could boast that he had forced his enemy to drink of the waters of the Epte.[6]   No relief appearing St. Omer fell, Aire and other places in Artois also passing into Baldwin's hands.[7]   Philip however was able to revenge himself by a

[1] Hoveden, IV. 54, 55; R. Cogg., 77; Rigord.

[2] Rigord, Bouquet, XVII. 49, 50.   [3] Hov. *sup.*; Diceto, II. 163.

[4] Hoveden, 55, 59; Diceto, 164.   I take it that the action described by Hoveden, p. 59, is but an alternative version of the same affair.   Both ended in Philip's being driven into Vernon, and both occurred before Richard's capture of Courcelles.   The casualties given however do not tally.

[5] See Diceto, *sup.*, where succour before the 30th September seems promised.

[6] 28th September.   See Hoveden, IV. 56–60, the list of prisoners there, and especially Richard's letter to the Bishop of Durham; also given R. Cogg., 84.   *Cnf.* Rigord Bouquet, XVII. 49.

[7] Hoveden, 55.   According to Diceto, 163, the siege lasted three weeks from the 6th September.   According to Gervase, I. 572, St. Omer fell on the 13th October.

raid into Normandy pushed almost as far as the line of the Rille ; Evreux,
Le Neubourg, and other places being burnt.[1] Then with short-
sighted economy he disbanded his forces, thus leaving Richard
free to send his standing mercenaries under Mercadier to harry
the *Beauvoisis* and Picardy. Their incursion was carried as far as Abbe-
ville, where they had the good fortune to fall in with and sack a fair.[2]
One of the most painful features of these wars is the evident disposition on
either side rather to damage the enemy than to protect their own people
from harm.

Raids and counter-raids.

Both parties, however, having had their autumn's riding and raiding
were now inclined for peace. To help him through his negotiations
Richard again sent for the indispensable Hubert Walter.[3] According to
the English account, the only one that we have, Philip actually offered for
the sake of peace to surrender all his acquisitions except Gisors, the question of the right to Gisors to be left to arbitration. Richard ought to have
closed with such an offer on the spot. But we are told that with his usual
capriciousness he made difficulties ; he wanted Baldwin and
others to be included, and so no treaty was signed. In the
course of November however the bare truce to the 13th January 1199 was
renewed.[4]

A Truce.

Innocent III., like his great predecessor Gregory VII., had been prompt
to warn the princes of the earth of the subjection that he expected of them.
But we note with interest the difference between the grounds
on which the two Pontiffs based their respective claims to
domination. Gregory thought it expedient to buttress his
Divine commission with territorial pretensions : all islands of
the sea were his ; by one title or another every Christian land had come
to be either demesne of St. Peter, or a fief held of his see.[5] Innocent,
realising more fully where the strength of his position lay, puts forward no
feudal claims. He relies entirely on a spiritual supremacy ; he claims
as the earthly vice-gerent of the Almighty the supreme right of controlling
the actions of men. 'Contempt of him will be contempt of God.'[6] In
this spirit he orders Leopold the young Duke of Austria to refund all the
ransom money received by his father ; the Archbishop of Magdeburg is

Innocent III. contrasted with Gregory VII.

---

[1] Hoveden, 60 ; Rigord, *sup.*

[2] Hoved., *sup.*

[3] Hubert crossed on the 28th September ; Gervase, I. 574.

[4] Hoved., 61, 68.

[5] See *Foundations of England*, II. 110.

[6] "Contemptum nostrum, immo Dei, Cujus locum, licet indigni, tenemus in terris."
So Innocent writes to Richard on the matter of the Lambeth Chapel ; Gervase, I. 589.
Again he says, " Nos ergo præter officii nostri debitum ex quo cum, licet indigni, tempus
acceperimus justitiam judicandi," etc. Id. 385. Of his decision in the Lambeth matter
he says, "Sicut nobis fuit divinitus revelatum." Ib. See also the Pope's circular
calling for a new Crusade ; Hoved., 70-73.

directed to press the Duke of Suabia to the same purpose. To Richard he writes that he has done his best for him in the matter of the ransom, but that he cannot decide all questions between him and the King of France without hearing more; he has ordered the King of Navarre to give up Saint-Jean-Pied-de-Port and Roccabruna, Berengaria's dowry; he is sending the Cardinal Peter of Capua to mediate, but he warns the King that he will not shrink from measures to compel both him and Philip to sheath their swords.[1]

Cardinal Peter duly appeared in Normandy about Christmas time. His **Papal Mission.** instructions were to force the two Kings to make peace, or at any rate to agree to a truce for five years, and that with especial view to a new Crusade.[2] He found them little inclined to come to terms, but he managed to bring them together on the 13th January, 1199, when the existing truce would expire. They met on the bank of the Seine between Andely and Vernon. Richard, having come by water, refused to land, and from his boat carried on his colloquy with Philip sitting on horseback on the shore. The Kings apparently pledged themselves verbally to the desired truce for five years on the basis of the *status quo*; but no treaty was sealed, or hostages **Truce for Five years.** exchanged.[3] The truce, however, almost broke down at once, Philip having begun to establish a new fortress on an island of the Seine. Richard promptly denounced the act, but the Legate persuaded Philip to demolish his work, and even, we are told brought him once more to offer a restitution of all his conquests in Normandy except Gisors; Richard to make over his rights on Gisors, to Philip's son **Suggested Settlement.** Louis, by way of dowry for his intended bride, Richard's niece Blanche of Castile. It will be remembered that by a similar arrangement Gisors, ceded by Count Geoffrey in 1151,[4] had been restored to Henry II. as the marriage portion of Margaret the wife of the young King. But again Richard, in an evil hour for himself, instead of clenching so precious an offer, adjourned the conclusion of the compact in order to prosecute a paltry feud against a petty foe.[5]

[1] 30th, 31st May 1198; *Fœdera*, I. 69, 70. See also the circular calling for help to Palestine; Hoveden, IV. 70.

[2] Hoveden, *sup.*, Rigord, Bouquet, XVII. 50.

[3] Hoveden, IV. 79, 80. He speaks of the truce as being confirmed on oath (sacramento) but Rigord, *sup.* asserts that no guarantees were exchanged. The truce was confirmed by Innocent, 26th March; *Fœdera*, 73. For a long discussion between Richard and the Legate see *W. Mareschal*, II. 47-54. According to the writer Peter pressed for the liberation of the Bishop of Beauvais.

[4] See *Foundations*, II. 443.

[5] Hoveden, 80, 81. No other authority ˗˗tice this offer, nor does either Sismondi or Martin notice it. Miss Norg˗˗ ˗e offer of 1198, but not that of 1199. Lavisse, III. 120, ignores the ˗ treats that of 1199 as accepted.

Some treasure had been found in the *Limousin* near Châlus,[1] on land
belonging to a knight who held of Adémar V. Viscount of
Limoges. Popular rumour probably exaggerated the importance of the "find." Treasure-trove, of course, belonged to
the over-lord, and the landowner had hastened to settle with his viscount.[2]
But Richard put in a claim as lord paramount. Adémar, whose rights
probably included treasure-trove, sent him a share, but the King, of course,
would be satisfied with nothing less than the whole; and, when that was
refused, invaded the *Limousin*, wasting the land with fire and sword, in
utter disregard of the holy season of Lent.[3] On the 24th March[4] he laid
siege to the castle of Châlus. In vain the garrison, conscious
of their inability to resist, offered to capitulate if promised life,
limb, and their weapons of war. Richard swore that he
would hang them all.[5] On the afternoon of the third day (26th March),
after dinner, the King was watching the operations, wearing no armour but
his iron head-piece, when, not keeping properly under cover of a square
shield (*sub quadrato scuto*) that was held in front of him, he was struck by
a crossbow bolt[6] on the left shoulder, at the base of the neck;
the wound apparently passing downwards, under the shoulder-
blade. Bearing the injury very manfully he retired quietly to
his quarters. In the attempt to extract the missile the shaft came off; and
then the surgeon in cutting out the iron head inflicted wounds probably too
serious for the therapeutics of the age. But Richard was a bad subject,
and made his case worse by refusing to attend to the orders of his physicians.[7]
In spite of all treatment the wound grew worse and worse, till mortification
set in. Finding himself sinking he sent for his mother,[8] who was at
Fontevrault, and promptly came at his call. Disposing of his property he
declared John heir to all his dominions. Of his treasures he gave three-
fourths with all his jewels (*baubella*) to King Otto; the remaining fourth he
ordered to be divided between his servants and the poor. The castle
meanwhile having been reduced and the garrison captured, he ordered the
man who had wounded him to be pardoned and set free.[9] Finally he

Marginal notes:

Quarrel with the Viscount of Limoges.

Siege of Châlus.

Richard wounded.

---

[1] Haute Vienne, S.-W. from Limoges.   [2] Rigord, Le Breton.

[3] In 1199, Ash Wednesday fell on the 3rd March, and Easter on the 18th April.

[4] Richard was wounded on the 26th March, that being the third day of the siege,
R. Cogg, 95; Diceto II. 166.

[5] Hoveden, *sup.* Gervase, I. 593.

[6] "Quarellum"; R. Cogg., *sup.*, "Quadratum telum"; Gervase, *sup.*

[7] "In corpore nimis obeso . . . Rege incontinenter se habente et præcepta medicorum
non curante"; R. Cogg, 95, 96; *cnf.* R. Hoveden, 82, 83; and Gervase, *sup.* "Malæ
Veneris gaudia"; also G. Le Breton, Bouquet, XVII. 183.

[8] "Arcessivit"; R. Cogg. *sup.* For Eleanor's presence with Richard on his death-bed,
see her own statement; Round, *Calendar*, 472.

[9] For a high-flown dialogue between the man and the dying King, see Hoveden, IV.
83.

confessed and received the Holy Sacrament,[1] of which probably he had not partaken since his penitent fit at Easter, 1195. His almoner and constant attendant the Cistercian Milo, Abbot of Ste. Marie Du Pin, administered extreme unction, and closed his eyes in death ; and so the lion-hearted

His Death. King passed away about sunset,[2] on Tuesday, 6th April, being Tuesday before Palm Sunday.[3] By his directions his heart, reported to be of unusual size,[4] was sent enclosed in a gilt casket to be preserved at Rouen ; his body would go to Fontevrault, to be laid at the feet of his father, among the good nuns there. On Palm Sunday (11th April), the funeral took place ; the service being performed by St. Hugh of Lincoln,

Burial. who had come out to protest against a fresh attack on his episcopal property.[5] On the day before he was on his way to Angers, where he was to officiate on the Sunday, when he heard of the King's death, and of the intended burial on the morrow. Hastening off at once he called at Beaufort-en-Vallée,[6] where Berengaria was, to inform her of her loss. The poor neglected Queen had not been honoured with an invitation either to her husband's death-bed, or to his funeral ; but we are told that she was deeply affected by the news. St. Hugh rode on to Saumur for the night ; and only reached Fontevrault next day just in time.[7]

Neither the identity nor the fate of the man who discharged the fatal bolt are likely ever to be ascertained. Hoveden calls him Bertrand de Gourdon, and says that he was flayed alive by Mercadier (pp. 83, 84). But "the only man who is known to have borne that name was still living in 1231."[8] Diceto gives the name as Peter Basil ; so do the Annals of Winton, adding that Mercadier sent the culprit to Jeanne, the ex-Queen of Sicily, by whom he was tortured to death. Gervase has John Sabraz, and Guillaume le Breton one Guy, the name being given without further surname or designation.

Richard is described as a tall, well-made man, of fair complexion

\

[1] R. Cogg. *sup.* He alleges that Richard had not communicated for seven years ; but this seems clearly wrong, as he had communicated at his second coronation in 1194, as well as in 1195.

[2] R. Cogg. *sup.*

[3] Hoveden, IV. 84: Diceto, II. 166 ; Gervase, I. 593 ; W. Newb. Cont., II. 504. Ralph of Coggeshall, who gives the best account of Richard's end, gives the 8th April (VII. *Id. Ap.*) as the day, but he corrects himself by telling us, rightly, that he died on the 11th day after he was wounded, that having happened on the 26th March. As to the place the only variant is the "Lautron" of *Mareschal*, II. 59, or "Nantrum" of Gervase, *sup.*

[4] "Grossitudine præstans" ; Gervase.

[5] R. Cogg., *sup.* ; *Magna Vita S. Hugon*

[6] Maine-et-Loire.

[7] *Magna Vita*, 284-286. Berengaria w .... tomb, as she was at Fontevrault with Eleanor on the 21st April

[8] Norgate, II. 345, citing M. Géraud's " .

inclining to red; shapely rather than massive in build, with long supple

The King's appearance

limbs.[1] The effigy on his tomb entirely bears out this portrait. The height would approach six feet two inches; the shoulders are broad, the throat full; the head is small, the face broad rather than long, the features beautifully refined, with a delicately chiselled nose, small mouth with pouting under-lip, and pencilled eyebrows of truly feminine grace. The forehead is smooth, and rather weak. The King wears a neat, well-trimmed beard, moustaches, and whiskers. His whole look is unmistakably French.[2]

These features harmonise with the picture that we should have formed

and Tempera- ment,

to ourselves independently of Richard as a man of nervous, excitable temperament rather than an Ironsides. His frequent attacks of illness do not suggest indomitable strength. He loved war, and he shone in arms.[3] Friend and foe, Frank and Moslem

Courage,

speak with equal admiration of his personal courage. He was, as has been said of a modern hero,[4] "a true leader of men, one to whom danger was a luxury, and battle an excitement." But he was

and Military Talent.

not only a *beau sabreur*, but also a very able commander. His march from Acre to Joppa was a great achievement; and the expedition that resulted in the capture of the great caravan was well planned and cleverly executed. The practical failure of the Crusade was due to moral not to strategic deficiencies on his part. His rude and haughty behaviour made enemies of all his allies. He has been described as "the creation and impersonation of his age."[5] Judged by the most moderate standard he must be pronounced a bad King and a vicious man.

The most favourable view of his character that we can present

General Character.

is that to the end of his days he remained a boy, a high-spirited, reckless, overbearing schoolboy, without sense of responsibility or duty, but fully satisfied in his own mind that might made right. He meant no harm himself, and was little given to suspecting harm in others. He was hot-tempered, but not ill-natured or vindictive. Towards John he was most forgiving. Lavish to prodigality, he stuck to his friends, and they in return served him loyally and lovingly. The affection evidently felt for him by men like St. Hugh of Lincoln, and Hubert Walter is a speaking fact. In his love of dress and show, again, Richard showed a boyish disposition, and St. Hugh in the Andely incident evidently treated him as a boy. Towards enemies he did not hold himself

---

[1] "Procerus, . . . elegantis formæ, inter rufum temperata cæsarie et flavum, membris flexilibus et directis . . . brachia productiora"; *Itin.* R. 144.

[2] See the portrait above, and better still the careful reproduction of the original at Fontevrault to be seen in the Crystal Palace at Sydenham.

[3] "Vir operi Martio deputatus," Diceto, II. 166.

[4] Sir Sydney Smith, W. H. Fitchett, *How England Saved Europe.*

[5] Bishop Stubbs. So too Pauli, I. 291.

bound by any laws of honour or otherwise. Treaties with them were simply made to be broken. Of any regard for the rights or wants of his subjects he was equally innocent. His dealings with them in money matters were simply shameless. He had no policy at home or abroad, and in all matters of business was altogether unreasonable and impracticable. A *Poitevin*, and something of a troubadour, he could write verses of a sort:

Musical Tastes. he was fond of music, and he took great interest in the services of his chapel. We are told that he would walk up and down the choir, beating time, and encouraging the choristers to sing out. Unlike his father he kept reverential silence during the *Secretum Missæ*, refusing to answer even if spoken to.[1] But though the age accepted Richard as a hero, and the champion of Christendom,[2]

Views of his own age. it was by no means blind to his defects. The hostile epigrams balance the friendly ones.

> "In hujus morte perimit formica Leonem.
> Proh dolor, in tanto funere mundus obit."

> "Virus, avaritia, scelus, enormisque libido,
> Fæda fames, atrox elatio, cæca cupido
> Annis regnarunt bis quinis, arcubalista
> Arte, manu, telo prostravit viribus ista."[3]

> "Neustria sub clypeo regis defensa Ricardi,
> Indefensa modo, gestu testare dolorem."[4]

With the clergy the seizure of Church treasures was one of the King's worst offences; and so we have the following effusion :—

> "Christe, tui calicis prædo fit præda calucis;
> Ære brevi deicis qui tulit æra crucis."[5]

It was said that Fulk of Neuilly, the celebrated preacher, had ventured to address Richard in pretty plain terms bidding him to get rid of three bad daughters, Pride, Avarice, and Luxury. 'Hear me ye' said the King, turning to his courtiers, 'Pride I give to the Templars, Avarice to the Cistercians, and Luxury to the Benedictines.'[6] But Richard was a friend

---

[1] R. Coggeshall, 97.

[2] "Ricardus . . . totius militiæ speculum." Lavisse, *France*, III. 121, quotes the troubadour Gaucelm Faidit to the effect that Europe for a thousand years had not suffered such a loss as Richard's death.

[3] Hoveden, IV. 84.

[4] Geoffrey Vinsauf, *De Nova Poetria*, extracted N. Trevet, 161. See also *Itin.* R. 447; Giraldus, VIII. 248; Gervase of Tilbury, Leibnitz, *Scriptt. Rer. Brunsvicarum*, I. 927, and *Chron. Turon.* Martene and Durand, *Ampl. Coll.*, V. 1037, cited Bishop Stubbs.

[5] Giraldus, *sup.* 326. For criticism, especially of Richard's later days, see R. Cogg. 89-93.

[6] See the story given with variati⸢⸣   IV. 76; Giraldus, VI. 44, and W
Hemingburgh, I. 229. Acc⸢⸣rding   ⸢⸣n, "Luxury" was to be given to
the bishops; Hemingburgh makes   ⸢⸣e speaker.

and patron of the Cistercians. Two of their abbots, besides Milo Du Pin, were said to have been with him at the last.[1] The grant of a pension of 100 marks a-year to their general Chapter graced his coronation.[2] For them he founded the Abbey of Bonport, rebuilt Du Pin, and re-roofed Pontigny, besides other benefactions. He also founded a House of Premonstratensian canons in Aquitaine.[3]

But whether for good or ill, the point to be borne in mind is that Richard was a simple Frenchman, and that in him England in reality had neither part nor lot.

Our investigation of the Pipe Rolls of the reign has established
Finance of Reign. a fact that had already been suspected, namely that the whole of the moneys taken in the King's name do not always appear on these records. Emoluments there were of which no government would care to preserve testimony against itself, such as the appropriation of the effects of deceased ecclesiastics, or other
Pipe Rolls. invasions of Church property. The fact was made clear in the case of Geoffrey Riddel, Bishop of Ely, who died in 1189, where we had the sum charged by the sheriff of Cambridgeshire for bringing the Bishop's goods to London,[4] but no entry at all of what the goods realised for the Treasury. Again we suggested in connexion with the Saladin tithe that possibly only persons connected with the Revenue in the ordinary course of things would render account at the Exchequer audits ; and at any rate that collections for special purposes made through special commissioner might not find their way into the Pipe Rolls. Still we believe that for all ordinary revenue these give sufficient and trustworthy evidence.

It was not to be anticipated that in the matter of finance, we should find the haphazard Richard, with all his greed for money, succeeding where his careful, business-like father had failed. Continued decay
Falling Revenue. is still the leading feature of the revenue. Apart from the extraordinary contributions raised for the ransom, the income drawn by the King from England was very moderate ; while, so far as the testimony of the Pipe Rolls goes, the sums received for the ransom did not amount to very much after all. But of this anon. Four scutages were
Scutages. imposed during the reign, namely one at the reduced rate of 10s. the knight's fee in the first year (1189) for the expedition to Wales, and three at the usual rate of £1 the knight's fee. Of these one was voted at Nottingham in 1194 ; this was distinguished as the Redemption Scutage, though in fact only two-thirds of the tenants were

---

[1] N. Trevet, 160.
[2] Diceto, II. 69.
[3] R. Cogg, 97. For Richard's friendly relations with "such of the clergy as he had not cheated of their money"; see further *Itinerary, xxiv.*
[4] Pipe Roll, 1 Rich., I. 188 (Hunter).

called upon for money payment, the others being required to give personal attendance abroad. The other two scutages were levied in 1195 and 1196 for the war.[1] Carucage, otherwise hidage or Danegeld, was called for twice. Once in 1194 at the ordinary rate of 2s. the hide, and again in 1198, at the enhanced rate of 5s. the hide, as already mentioned. Tallages also, as

Hidage. under Henry II., were at times imposed, at the King's discretion, but only the Royal demesne lands, and boroughs of the King's demesne were liable to these assessments, which were fixed by the Justices in Eyre. The tallages appear to have been paid pretty strictly. Not so the scutages or the carucates. Under the head of the Redemption Scutage within the year 1194, the year of its assessment, we only find £1660 paid, with something less than £500 in the following year as the collective yield of arrears of the Welsh scutage, arrears of the Redemption Scutage, and payments on account of the new scutage for the war in Normandy. One scutage alone ought to have yielded £5000 to £6000. Petty payments on account of all the scutages were still coming in at Michaelmas 1199, six months after John's accession. As for the carucages, we find in 1194 the four counties of Cumberland, Worcester, Somerset, and Dorset paying between them a total sum of £635 5s. 10d., those being the only entries except a few compositions of trivial amount. Of the 5s. hidage of 1198, not a penny is entered as paid down to Michaelmas 1199. A 2s. hidage ought to have yielded at least £2500, as when last levied. To come to the total of the Revenue, we found that for the year of Richard's accession (1188–1189) it amounted to £15,347. With a reign of only ten years' duration, we thought that the summation of the entries for one other year would give a sufficient basis for estimating the average revenue, and we took the 8th year (1195–1196) as that appearing to offer the largest total, and in round numbers it amounts to £20,000. Of this sum the items specially connected with the ransom, namely fines, gifts,

Total Revenue. tallages, scutages, and tenth of goods (one entry) come to £5,704, leaving just £14,300 for ordinary revenue.[2] The ransom items for the previous financial year (1194–1195) make up as nearly as possible the same sum, namely omitting shillings and pence £5,734.[3] We might, therefore, conjecture a total revenue of £20,000 for that year also. In the later years the receipts sink visibly. Probably the totals would not reach £15,000 each. Roger of Hoveden has given us his estimate of the King's revenue for the two years 1194–1195, and 1195–1196—a most valuable illustration of the worth of chroniclers' figures, and he tells us gravely that within that period Hubert Walter transmitted to Normandy no less than 1,100,000 marks,[4] or £733,333 6s. 8d. If the whole of the ransom had been paid, and paid out of

---

[1] Pipe Rolls *passim*, and esp. 8 Ric. I. m. 10.
[2] Pipe Roll, 8 Rich. I.   [3] Pipe Roll, 7 Rich. I.   [4] IV. 13.

English funds; and if Hubert in addition had sent over a sum equal to the entire amount accounted for at the Exchequer during those two years, say in all £140,000, an impossible amount, that impossibility would still have to be multiplied five-fold to bring it up to the level of the chroniclers' imagination. On the Norman Roll for the year 1195, which is extant, we have a sum of £5722 sterling drawn from the treasury at Caen, being apparently the amount remitted from England during the year.[1] The chroniclers evidently made the most of their grievances. We might say that the taxpayer of the 12th century was as little disposed to suffer in silence as the Nonconformist of a later age.

With respect to the King's ransom, the most interesting point connected with the finance of the reign, we are quite in the dark as to **The King's Ransom.** how far, or how, or by whom it was met. The total demanded was 150,000 marks or £100,000. Of this under the final arrangement the Emperor would receive 130,000 marks or £86,666 13s. 4d., and Duke Leopold 20,000 marks or £13,333 6s. 8d. According to Hoveden, if he can be trusted, Henry VI. remitted 17,000 marks (£11,333 6s. 8d.),[2] reducing the sum received to £75,333 6s. 8d. Then it is also clear that Leopold was not paid in full.[3] Probably £80,000 or £85,000 was as much as was paid. That would be four or five times the largest revenue of the reign. But it must not be supposed that the whole of this would come from England. Richard had also the rich lands of Normandy, Maine, Anjou, and Touraine to draw upon, without counting Poitou, or the more Southerly Aquitanian districts over which his hold would be less effectual. Of the sums that may have been contributed by these latter territories we know nothing whatever. For Normandy we have a fragment of the year 1194, and fuller Rolls for 1195 and 1198, and they show the Duchy contributing, and contributing in much the same way as England did, by 'gifts' from religious houses, heavy tallages from the towns, and mulcts from the Jews, only to much larger amounts than in England, just as the Norman revenue of the time exceeded the English revenue. Thus Caen pays £2,700 9s. 6d. sterling, and the city and *Vicomté* of Rouen about £2,500, when London merely promises a *Donum* of £1,000. But the only actual payment to the Emperor recorded on the extant Norman Rolls is one of £4,000 in 1195, the money having come from England.[4] Reverting to the Pipe Rolls, on that for the financial year ending at Michaelmas, 1193 (5 Rich. I.), we have no reference whatever to the ransom: on that for the following year we seem to have not quite £2,300 paid in, with large promises of payment in the future;

---

[1] Rot. Norm., I. 136 (Stapleton).

[2] III. 304.

[3] Hoveden, III. 277; W. Newb., II. 431. The latter gives the sum due as 20,000 marks, the whole sum stipulated, but that must be wrong.

[4] Rot. Norm., I. 136.

for the seventh and eighth financial years the contributions come to £5,734 and £5,704, as already mentioned. We may therefore claim it as a satisfactory confirmation of our researches that on the Norman Roll for 1195, corresponding to the Pipe Roll of the seventh year, the sum stated as transmitted from England for the ransom, namely £5,722 16s. 10d.,[1] is within a few pounds of the sum we make out from the Pipe Roll. The reader will see how little on the whole can be made of these facts, the only ones we have. Our own beliefs are, first that the bulk of the whole ransom came from abroad; secondly that the primary instalments to secure Richard's liberation, those from England at any rate, were procured by the seizure of Church treasures,[2] Cistercian wool, and the like measures, of which no account appears on the Rolls; and thirdly that money continued to be levied for the ransom after all payments to Henry or Leopold had ceased.

With reference to the comparative yields of the English and the **Norman Revenue.** Norman Exchequers we have been at the pains to add up the Norman Roll for the year 1198 which is extant, and the total comes to £98,193 Angevin,[3] equivalent to £29,048 sterling, as against the English revenue which did not quite reach £20,000.

With respect to Richard's extravagance it must be stated that the Norman Rolls show that his means were not spent on personal indulgence, but on fortifications and military expenditure, with a certain amount of subsidies to political allies.

With respect to trade and commerce we find that the manufacture of **Commerce.** cloth was already a widespread industry, as entries of the time of King John show some twenty towns, including Worcester, Gloucester, Newcastle, Lincoln, Nottingham, and Norwich, fining for leave to deal in cloth as they did under Henry II.[4] We also get a glimpse of the Customs' duties. The general rate is given as £10 per cent. For the Port of London, the Chamberlain of London accounts for £475 8s. 4d. as the produce of two years, tin and woad for dyeing being specially mentioned.[5] Again we have another account of the same official for a year and ten months, 1197–1199, amounting to £466, but including a large amount for contraband goods seized and sold.[6] For the other ports of the kingdom we do not seem to have any definite accounts.

---

[1] Rot. Norm., I. 136. The £4,000 paid to the Emperor's agents, as stated above, was taken from this sum, the rest being applied to other purposes.

[2] So the writer of the Welsh *Brut.* understood; p. 237.

[3] Rot. Norm., II. 189, etc. (Stapleton). The Norman Rolls have pitfalls of their own, not encountered in the Pipe Rolls: we have at times a given sum first entered as paid out of the Treasury to A. B., and later a detailed account of how the money was expended by A. B. But I think that my total is fairly correct.

[4] Pipe Roll, 4 John, cited Madox, *Hist. Excheq.*, I. 468.

[5] Pipe Roll, 8 Rich. I, fol. 1., dors; Madox, I. 775.

[6] 10 Rich. I., fol. 12, dors; Madox, 775, 776.

We also now hear of the Prisage of wines, or the right of taking one tun (*tonnel*) of wine from before, and one from behind the mast of each ship at the low rate of 15*s.* the tun ; the wine so taken being usually resold for the King's benefit.[1]   The profits of the Mints (*Cambium*) for all England, except Winchester, for the third year of King Richard are returned at £400.[2]

With respect to wages and prices ; we find that footsoldiers abroad got 2*d.* a day ; their captains (*magistri*) a shilling a day.   Appar-

Wages and Prices. ently the men were organised by twenties, as we have nine *magistri* for 180 men.   Mounted infantry with two horses each got 6*d.* a day ; *milites* a shilling a day.[3]   Earlier in the century the foot-soldiers at home got a penny a day, and the *milites* 8*d.* a day.   Cattle on the average were worth 4*s.* each, and agricultural horses the same.   In Normandy we have £30 *Angevin*, or £7 10*s.* sterling, given for a horse for the King ; and again £80 *Angevin* given for three more horses.   In England sheep were mostly worth from 1*d.* to 1¼*d.* each ; but a Hampshire pig was worth 6*d.*

In 1197 Hubert Walter made an attempt to establish an uniform system of weights and measures for the whole of England.   But local custom, very tenacious in such matters, refused to give way.   The ordinance fell a dead letter, and had to be withdrawn.[4]

No English coins bearing the names either of Richard or John have been found, Henry II.'s type being retained.[5]

With Scotland, thanks to a non-intervention policy on the part of

Relations with Scotland. England, the mostly friendly relations were kept up from the time of the treaty of Canterbury, by which the obligations of the treaty of Falaise-Valognes were cancelled.[6]   William the Lion had condescended to accept the hand of a Norman lady, Ermengarde, daughter of Richard, Viscount of Beaumont-le-Vicomte, the latter being son of the Viscount Roscelin by Constance natural daughter of Henry I.[7]   William had also found homes for two natural daughters by marrying them to Anglo-Norman Barons ; one, Margaret by name, was wedded to Eustace de Vesci of Alnwick, and Isabel the other to Robert de Ros of Hamlake.[8]   The King's brother David, the Earl of Huntingdon, was married to Matilda or Maud, daughter of Hugh II. Earl of Chester ;[9] he had given the help of his sword to repress John's attempts ; both he

---

[1] Madox, *sup.* 665, 675.   The wine might be worth £1 to £3 the tun.
[2] Pipe Roll, 3 Rich. I., fol. 12, dors ; Madox, II. 132.
[3] Pipe Roll, 8 Rich. I., fol. 9.   [4] Hoveden, IV., 33, 172.
[5] E. Hawkins, *Silver Coins of England.*
[6] 5th Dec., 1189 : *Fœdera*, I. 50, and above, 274.
[7] Chron. Melrose, A.D. 1186 ; Ben. P., I. 347 above, 230.
[8] Hoveden. IV., 140, and note Stubbs.
[9] Chron. Melrose, A.D. 1190 ; Doyle *Official Baronage.*

and his brother had attended Richard's second coronation, and William had contributed 2000 marks towards the ransom.[1] From the Scottish writer Fordun we hear that intercourse between the two countries was absolutely free and unrestricted.[2]

In North Wales David son of Owain Gwynedd had been ruling as King

Welsh Affairs.

since 1174 or thereabouts; he had received as his Queen Emma, natural sister of Henry II., and had been further conciliated by the grant of Ellesmere to the value of £10 a year.[3] We hear of no trouble caused by him. But in spite of that,

North Wales.

possibly on that very account, in 1194 he was deprived of his kingdom by his nephew Llywelyn son of Jorwerth.[4] But he retained a certain footing in Wales till 1197, when he was taken prisoner by a fresh aspirant to Cambrian rule, Gwenwynwyn, son of Owain Cyfeiliog Prince of Powys. David however and Emma were allowed to retire to England, where they were living at the time of Richard's death; and in England David died in 1203.[5]

South Wales, a district that under Henry II. had, on the whole, been so

South Wales.

quiet, was in a state of constant disturbance during Richard's reign, Rhys son of Gruffudd being perpetually at war with the English in Pembroke, or the Flemings in Ros, or the March Lords, or his own sons. His invasion of Ros and Gower, and his attack on Carmarthen in September 1189 were thought sufficiently serious to call for the levy of a Royal army under Earl John. When in the following month Rhys was induced to come to Oxford to render homage, Richard did not trouble himself to meet him. In subsequent hostilities the defence of English interests was mostly left to William of Braose the lord of Brecon,[6] Roger Mortimer, and Hugh of Say. But once if not twice Hubert Walter as Justiciar had to bring an army to their aid.[7] On the 28th April 1197 Rhys was gathered to his fathers.[8] The succession was disputed between his elder son Gruffudd and a younger Maelgwn. Gruffudd went to England, and obtained recognition from the Government. But shortly after his return home (August) he was attacked by his brother with the support of Gwenwynwyn of Powys, taken prisoner, and handed over to the English,

[1] Chron. Melrose, A.D. 1193.

[2] p. 274.

[3] Brut. y T., 225; Pipe Roll, 20 H. II.; Ben. P., I. 162.

[4] Ann. Camb.; Brut., 241. Jorwerth and David were both sons of Owain Gwynedd.

[5] Brut., 251, 253; Pipe Roll, 8 Rich. I.

[6] Through his mother Bertha, daughter of Milo and sister of Roger Earls of Hereford, William had inherited the fiefs of Bernard of Neufmarché, the conqueror of South Wales. In 1176 he had treacherously massacred a number of Welshmen at Abergavenny Castle, nominally in revenge for the death of his uncle Henry of Hereford. See Mr. Round's Article in the National Dictionary.

[7] Ann. Camb. and Brut. y T., Gervase, I. 543; Hoveden, IV., 35.

[8] Brut., p. 245; Hoveden. IV. 21; Ann. Camb., 60.

who to be rid of him shut him up in Corfe Castle.[1] Meanwhile Gwen-

Powys.
wynwyn having got the upper hand both of David son of
Owain, and of his competitor Llywelyn, with a certain control
over South Wales, was mustering all his forces for a grand effort to shake
off the Saxon yoke. To divide the South Welsh the English liberated
Gruffudd; while Geoffrey Fitz Peter led an army to attack the confederates
who were besieging de Braose in a fortress, known as Maud's Castle,
otherwise Colwyn in modern Radnorshire. Gwenwynwyn was defeated
with great slaughter, and Gruffudd reinstated.[2] We shall find him shortly
doing homage to John.

For the Dominion in Ireland, administered in the name of Earl John,[3]

Governors of Ireland.
the historian finds little beyond the succession of governors
to record; the extent of territory occupied, and the general
relations of the English to the natives not undergoing any
material change. At Richard's accession Hugh de Lacy, second son of
the former Viceroy, held rule. In 1190 we have one William Le Petit,
a Baron settled in Meath; while from 1191 to 1194 the chief officer was
William Marshal. Through his marriage with Strongbow's daughter
Isabel he had become lord of a principality described as extending over
one hundred and twenty miles, " comprising Ossory with the three counties
of Wexford, Carlow, and Kildare," being of course the inheritance of King
Dermot, Isabel's grandfather.[4] The mark of Marshal's governorship was
the building of a castle, and the establishment of a chartered settlement
on the banks of the river Nore in the central plain of Ossory. Castle
and town were named after a local saint Cill Cannigh, otherwise Kilkenny.
In 1194 William was succeeded by one Peter Pipard, and he again in
1197 by Hamo of Valognes, an Anglo-Norman from Suffolk. Hamo
quarrelled with the Archbishop John Cumin, the founder of St. Patrick's
Cathedral Dublin. Cumin, refusing to submit to Hamo's encroachments,
excommunicated him, laid the whole See under Interdict, and then
retired to Normandy to appeal for redress to Richard and John, but
without effect.[5]

In Ulster John de Courcy still ruled as an independent potentate, in
alliance with Godred King of Man, whose daughter "Affreca" he had

[1] Ann. Camb., 61 ; Brut., 249, 251 ; Ann. Winton.

[2] 13th August, 1198; Diceto, II. 163 ; Hoveden, IV. 53 ; Brut., 253; Ann. Camb.,
sup. The Welsh writers speak of the siege as being that of Pains Castle in " Elwail."

[3] See *Historic Documents of Ireland*, J. T. Gilbert, 49-56 ; and next note below.

[4] From the Earl's biographer we hear that in 1194 Richard pressed him to do
homage to him for his lands in Ireland, but that William refused, as he held of John.
Mareschal, II. 6. This is another proof that the Conqueror's rule had never established
itself.

[5] Hoveden, IV. 29. Innocent III. addressed a severe rebuke to John for the
treatment of Cumin ; *Epp. Inn., III.*, Vol. I. 215 (Baluse), 18th September, 1198
See J. T. Gilbert, *Viceroys of Ireland*, 55-58.

married, and also on friendly terms with Duncan mac Gilbert of Galloway. Duncan assisted de Courcy in his wars against the natives, and was rewarded by him with lands wrested from the Irish.[1]

The King's Issue. By Berengaria daughter of Sancho VI. of Navarre Richard had no issue. She died after the year 1230, having lived mostly in Maine, dowerless and dependent on her sister Blanche Countess of Champagne.[2] We hear of a natural son Philip, who must have been a grown man at Richard's death, as he had been invested with the castle and Honour of "Cuinac" (Cognac?). To avenge his father he slew the Viscount Adémar of Limoges.[3] Under John we find him in receipt of a pension of a shilling a day.[4]

ENGLISH OF THE TIME OF RICHARD I.

Prophecy published *circa* 1190.

Whan thu seches (seest) in Here herty-reret,
Than sulen Engles in thre be y-deled (divided),
That an (ane, one) sal into Yrlande alto late waie (alto, into, lead way),
That other into Puille (Apulia) mid prude bileve (with pride abide, tarry)
The thridde into her bahen herd (their own heart) alle wreke y-drehegen [5]
                                  (wretchedness drie, endure).

---

[1] Hoved., IV. 25, 162.

[2] *National Dicty. of Biog.* For repeated applications by the Pope to John for payment of Berengaria's jointure see *Fædera*, I. 84, 97 ; Ann. Waverley, 278.

[3] Hoved., IV. 97.

[4] Pipe Roll, 8 John.

[5] Hoved., III. 68. The place Here where the stag was to be seen lifted up has not been identified. For comments see Academy, 1886, II. 189, 380.

CHAPTER XXIII

JOHN, 'LACKLAND'

(JEHAN, JOHAN SANS TERRE; JOHANNES SINE TERRA.¹)

"Johan rois sans tere
Murra en bere."²

Born at Oxford 24th December 1167;³ Invested as Duke of Normandy 25th April 1199; and crowned King of England 27th May following (Ascension Day). Died at Newark 19th October 1216

A.D. 1199–1201

Accession and coronation—Treaty with France—Divorce of Isabel of Gloucester, and re-marriage with Isabel of Angoulême—Hostilities with the De Lusignans—Visit to Paris

WITH the death of Richard I. we may say that we take leave of the 12th century, with its "hard-headed, hard-handed industry," and enter on the brilliant thirteenth century, that era of grand ideas and great men, the age of Innocent III., Dante, and Giotto ; of St. Dominic and St. Francis, a period dear to all lovers of poetry and art.⁴ But for the House of Anjou Richard's end gave the signal for "the break-up" of its dominions.⁵ The question of the succession as between Arthur and John was opened up. Arthur was the heir according

Accession.

---

¹ Rigord, Bouquet, XVII. 39 ; *W. Mareschal,* passim ; *Magna Vita S. Hugonis,* 287 ; Le Breton, *Philippis,* VI. 590, adds that John had the *sobriquet* from his father.

² Paris, *Hist. Angl.,* II. 190. marginal addition. Compare the fellow distich on Richard above, 262.

³ R. Monte, 233 (ed. Howlett). He records an appearance of meteors in the sky on the same evening ; N. Trevet, 60, follows him. Diceto, whose dates often differ from those of other writers, simply gives the year, and gives it as 1166 (I. 325). Wendover and Matthew Paris follow him. The circumstance that he was born at Oxford comes from Robert of Gloucester, 484 (ed. Hearne). He adds that the birth took place at the King's Manor House there, that by the time when he wrote had become the house of the White Friars.

⁴ "A period more productive of ideas in every department of culture the world has never seen. But it was in some respects a precocious age. Many of the ideas which it produced luxuriantly, and for which its heroes risked all, were premature. Hence it is a period of great failures answering to too great designs." Bishop Stubbs, *Select Charters,* 307.

⁵ Norgate, II. 388.

to modern ideas of representation ; but the theory of strict representation
had not yet established itself. John was nearer in blood to
the late King, an important point in the estimation of the period.
Arthur was only just twelve years old,[1] and unknown outside of
Brittany.   John had not done much to make him either popular or
respected, but he had taken an active part in the affairs of England and
Normandy ; he had large estates, and consequently a certain amount of
personal following on either side of the water ; while his brother's final declaration in his favour secured the support of the ruling officials, with
Hubert Walter, Geoffrey fitz Peter, and William Marshal at
their head.   To these men and to the energy and devotion of
his mother John owed his crown.   The Justiciars would secure England :
and England and Normandy were so closely linked in many ways that
acceptance by the one would surely carry acceptance by the other.   Not
so with regard to the other Continental possessions, where feudalism was
still rampant.   In Aquitaine, no doubt, John was safe under the ægis of
his mother's rights, which were indisputable.   But elsewhere the rule of a
boy-Duke [2] of Brittany seemed preferable to that of a grown-up King of
England.   At the first word of Richard's death Maine and Anjou [3] declared
for Arthur and primogeniture ; and Constance and her son at
the head of the Breton forces entered to take possession.   On
Easter Day (18th April) they were received at Angers.[4]   Philip
likewise, taking advantage of the ' happy opportunity,' [5] occupied Evreux.[6]
John had not been with Richard at the last.   In the course of the
winter he had been accused of having again conspired with the King of
France, Philip himself, strange to say, being the informer.
John's estates had once more been confiscated, and he had
been driven out to find shelter with his nephew Arthur in
Brittany.[7]   His first care now was to hasten to Chinon, the seat of the
Angevin treasury, under the charge of Stephen of Turnham, Seneschal of
Anjou.   He reached the place on the 14th April.   John having solemnly
sworn to observe all good laws and customs the hoard was surrendered, and

Arthur's Claims.

John's Supporters.

Arthur's Adherents.

John's Movements.

---

[1] Arthur was born on the 29th March, 1197, after his father's death.   Benedict Pet.,
I. 361 ; Diceto, II., 48.

[2] I gather from Mr. Round's *Calendar* that Arthur and his father before him adopted
the style of *Dux* or Duke of Brittany ; their predecessors having been content to call
themselves *comites*, counts.

[3] The writer of the *Mareschal* includes the Aquitanians.   ' Neither Gascon, Limousin,
Poitevin, Angevin, nor Breton assented to count John ' ; II. 65.

[4] Chron. Saint-Aubin of Angers.

[5] " Statu rerum sibi in melius mutato " ; Rigord, Bouquet. XVII. 50.   Le Breton
speaks still more plainly, " Visitavit Deus regnum Francorum nam Ricardus occiditur ; "
Id., 74.

[6] Hoved. IV. 85 ; Rigord and Le Breton, *sup.*

[7] *Magna Vita, sup.* ; *cnf.* Hoveden. IV. 81.

homage done to him by certain magnates assembled there. Among these, seemingly, was St. Hugh of Lincoln, to whom we are told that John paid great court. The Bishop took him to Fontevrault to keep his Easter (18th April) there with his mother, by the graves of his father and brother. But great as John's need of ecclesiastical support was he could not be brought to communicate; and he tendered his offering at the altar with such levity, making a joke of it, that St. Hugh refused to take the gold piece from him, or to allow him to kiss his hand, as was usual.[1]

John remained with his mother till the 21st April when they parted. Eleanor went off with Mercadier and his men to establish her authority in

Queen Eleanor in Poitou. Poitou, making an inroad into Anjou on the way.[2] John turned his steps to Rouen to be elected,[3] and installed as Duke. But on his way thither he found time to sack the rebellious city of Le Mans.[4] The investiture with Ducal cap and sword was duly performed on Sunday 25th April by Archbishop Walter. John

John Duke of Normandy. took the proper oaths; but again he shocked the clergy by his irreverent behaviour. When the Archbishop handed him the lance with the banner of Normandy he turned round to make some jesting remark to the young men behind him, and in so doing let the lance fall—a bad omen, as was thought.[5]

To secure England Hubert Walter and William Marshal had already been sent over, as coadjutors to the Chief Justiciar, Geoffrey fitz Peter.

The usual disturbances had broken out through the suspension of the reign of law by the abeyance of the King's Peace during the interregnum.[6]

Affairs in England. Magnates had begun to indulge in brigandage, and all who had castles hastened to man and victual them.[7] Order, however, was soon restored by the vigorous action of the Justiciars, who, with the help of the sheriffs, exacted oaths of allegiance to John from all

---

[1] *Magna Vita*, 291, 292; Hoveden. IV. 86, 87. The latter represents John as keeping Easter at Beaufort, but I follow the *Magna Vita*.

[2] Hoveden, 88. Eleanor was at Loudun on the 29th April, and at Poitiers on the 4th May; Round, *Calendar*, 389, 390. 473. It must have been on this trip that Eleanor was taken prisoner by Hugh IX. Le Brun, Count of La Marche, and forced to surrender some land. *Art. de Vérifier les Dates*, X. 228–229.

[3] The elective theory comes out clearly in the *Mar schal*, II. 63. The writer represents his hero as urging Archbishop Walter to "haster d'eslire" John. So too R. Cogg. 99: "Communi procerum electione et civium acclamatione;" where the respective parts of the baronage and people are accurately distinguished.

[4] Hoveden, 87, where the incident seems to be placed before Easter; R. Cogg. 99.

[5] *Magna Vita*, 293; Hoveden, and R. Cogg., *sup.*

[6] The proceedings in the Curia Regis are dated as of the tenth year of Richard down to 2nd May; from 9th May they run in the name of Duke John; Rot. Cur. R. I. 259, 264, etc.; Pauli.

[7] Hoveden, IV. 88, 89; R. Cogg., 98.

and sundry. They also held a Grand Council at Northampton, to which

Acceptance of John. they were careful to summon the men from whom opposition might be feared, such as David Earl of Huntingdon, William II. Earl of Derby, and Roger de Lacy Constable of Chester, men who had all acted with Longchamp against John. De Lacy had hanged two knights for having surrendered Tickhill and Nottingham to John.[1] Another man to be conciliated if possible was Richard of Clare Earl of Hertford, married to Amice one of the Gloucester heiresses passed over in favour of John. Then Ralph III. of Chester was husband to Constance of Brittany, and so stepfather to Arthur ; while Waleran Earl of Warwick,[2] and William Mowbray of Axholm, apart from personal considerations, were members of a class whose influence had been considerably curtailed during late reigns. Some of these men were inclined to make terms. The King of Scots sent to demand the Northern counties. But Hubert Walter pacified them with arguments and promises ; even the demands of the Scots would receive consideration when John came over. Not a voice was raised for Arthur ; all gave in their adhesion to John.[3]

William Marshal then went back to Normandy to report the favourable situation of affairs. On the 21st May he was at Dieppe with John preparing to sail ;[4] on the 25th they landed at Shoreham. Next day they went on to London, and on the day again after that, being Holy Thursday or Ascension Day,[5] John was duly hallowed at Westminster by Archbishop

Coronation. Hubert (27th May). The concourse of magnates, spiritual and lay, was great, seventeen archbishops and bishops, and ten earls being named as present. But Geoffrey of York was still kept at a distance ; nor do we hear anything of Isabel of Gloucester the King's despised wife.[6] No details as to the proceedings are given by the actual writers of the time ; but from those of the next generation we have statements which, whether strictly correct or not, imply adherence to the original ritual. From Roger of Wendover, who, presumably, was a grown man at the time,[7] we hear that after the coronation oath had been

The Oath. administered, Hubert Walter adjured John not to assume ' this honour ' (*hunc honorem*)—evidently the crown—unless he meant conscientiously to act up to his pledges ; and that John had

---

[1] Ben. P. II. 232-234 ; Hoveden, III. 172.

[2] Brother to William, the third Earl who died in Holy Land in 1184.

[3] Hoved. ; R. Cogg., *sup.*

[4] Round, *Calendar*, 36.

[5] During the reign the absurd system was adopted of dating the regnal years from the Ascension Day of the year, a movable feast ; so that sometimes the same date occurs twice in a regnal year. See Foss, *Judges,* II. 1, and the tables of regnal years there, and in Nicolas, *Chron. Histy.* 325.

[6] Hoved. IV., 89, 90.

[7] He died in May 1236. F. Madden.

answered that with God's help he would.[1] The very same appeal had been addressed by Baldwin to Richard. But in fact for a homily addressed to the King in connexion with the coronation oath we have the precedent of St. Dunstan.[2] Matthew Paris, re-writing Wendover's work some years later,[3] introduces a further speech as delivered by the Archbishop to the assembled magnates before the coronation. In this address Hubert is represented as dwelling on the elective character of the royal office, citing the cases of Saul and David, Kings chosen for their qualifications. The Primate concluded with these words. 'We therefore after appeal for the guidance of the Holy Spirit have elected the illustrious Count John, as well on the ground of his merits as of his relationship to the late King.' The writer adds that with one accord the assembly answered (of course in French) ' *Vive le Roy Johan !* ' (*Vivat Rex Johannes !*)[4]

Formal Election.

Whether Hubert Walter spoke these very words or not we have here a clear reference to the form of election in Westminster Hall prior to the procession to the Abbey, an essential part of the original ritual.[5] In confirmation however of the substantial accuracy of Matthew's report it has been pointed out that Louis of France in his declaration against John in 1216 laid stress on the fact that Archbishop Hubert in crowning John had warned him that he was King 'not by succession but by election.'[6]

A King by Election.

But with all his good professions John again shocked public feeling by refusing to partake of the Sacrament at the Coronation Mass, an omission alleged to be without precedent.[7] The coronation honours included the final investiture of William Marshal and Geoffrey fitz Peter as Earls of Pembroke and Essex respectively ; while the Great Seal was taken from Eustace the Bishop of Ely and given to Hubert Walter.[8] A little later Wm. of Ferrers II. was recognised as Earl of Derby with the 'third penny' of his county.[9] On the other hand a

Coronation Honours.

[1] R. Wendover, III. 146. The words, though coming so near, are not a transcript of the account of the incident at Richard's coronation. Wendover, however, again misquotes the coronation oath, making the King only to swear to hold the Church and its ministers in good peace.

[2] See *Foundations of England*, I. 330, note. Bishop Stubbs refers to the case of Lanfranc and Rufus, for which see *Id.* II. 156, 157.

[3] Matthew died in 1259.

[4] " Idcirco dixerimus pro inclito comite Johanne . . . . quem nos invocata Spiritus Sancti gratia ratione tam meritorum quam sanguinis regii unanimiter elegimus universi, etc." M. Paris, *Chron. Maj.*, II. 454. " Vivat rex " clearly represents not an English but a French utterance.

[5] See *Foundations*, I. 319.

[6] " Quod non ratione successionis sed per electionem eum in regem coronabat " ; *Fædera*, I. 140 ; Pauli, *Geschichte v. Eng.*, I. 297 ; Bp. Stubbs, W. Coventry, II. xxviii.

[7] *Magna Vita S. Hugonis*, 293 ; Norgate.

[8] Hoved., 90 ; Foss *Judges*, II. 10.   [9] *Fædera*, I. 75, June 6.

scutage at the extra rate of two marks the knight's fee (£1 6s. 8d.) was called for from the Baronage, ecclesiastical and lay.[1]

Envoys from William the Lion appeared in London demanding Northumberland and Cumberland as the price of his support. John evaded the demand, asking for a personal interview. To facilitate a meeting he went as far as Nottingham (6th June). But the King of Scots came not. On the contrary he sent envoys to inform John that he was raising an army; and that he would assert his rights by force **Scottish** if he did not get a satisfactory answer within 40 days. John **Pretensions.** met the threat sufficiently by placing the two counties and their castles under William de Stuteville *vice* Bardolf. At the same time he restored Pontefract to Roger de Lacy, taking his son however as a hostage. To conciliate the Northern Province he ordered the revenues of York to be paid over to Geoffrey's agents. 'But the King kept the Whitsunday rents all the same, promising to repay them.'[2]

Less than a month sufficed for such business as John cared to transact in England, pilgrimages to Bury St. Edmund's and Canterbury included. On the 20th or 21st June he crossed from Shoreham to Dieppe; on the 24th of the month he was at Rouen, and had a friendly meeting with Archbishop Geoffrey; while a truce to the 16th August was signed with Philip.[3]

Both sides had been active during his absence. Philip had **Truce with** met Constance and Arthur at Le Mans; had taken Arthur's **France.** homage for Anjou and Maine, at the same time kindly undertaking to keep his castles for him.[4] On the other side Queen Eleanor advanced from Poitiers, where she had been on the 4th May, to Bordeaux.

She was at Soulac in the Gironde, apparently on her return **Eleanor in** journey, on the 4th July.[5] On the 28th August she met **Aquitaine.** Philip at Tours, and renewed her title by doing homage to him for Aquitaine. Philip then went back to Paris taking Arthur with him.[6] Coming back to Normandy Eleanor invested John with Aquitaine as a fief to be held of her. Then by an ingenious piece of feudal conveyancing she took from him a regrant to herself of all his interest during her life, so as to make her position safe against any possible forfeiture by her son.[7]

At the expiration of the truce (16th August) envoys met near Andelys,

---

[1] *Red Book Exchequer*, I. 10; R. Cogg., 102; Pipe Roll, 2 John.

[2] Hoveden, IV. 91, 92.

[3] Diceto, II. 166; Hoved. 92, 93; *Itinerary* of John, Hardy, Introduction to Patent Rolls.

[4] Rigord, *sup.*, 50; Le Breton, 74; Hoveden, 87, 94. Arthur and his mother were at Le Mans in June; Round, *Calendar*, 363, 473.

[5] Round, *sup.*, 389, 391, 450.

[6] Rigord, *sup.*

[7] Rot. Cart. 30, 31; *Fœdera*, I. 77.

between Boutavant and Gouleton, otherwise Le Goulet.[1] On the third

Conferences. day the Kings came together. We are told that Philip demanded the Norman Vexin for himself; and for Arthur Anjou
and Maine.[2] Now with regard to the Vexin we have seen that
French it was ceded to Philip by John in January 1194, while Richard
Demands. was still in captivity; that the cession was accepted by Richard
in July of that same year; and again confirmed by him in January 1196;
nor have we heard of any recovery of the district by Richard. We must
therefore suppose that what the chronicler meant was a fresh ratification
of the cession on the part of John.[3] The claims put forward in the name
of Arthur were clearly inadmissible, and Philip was in no position to enforce
his demands. Otto, who had just been finally accepted by
Philip's Innocent, was advising John not to be in a hurry to come to
Difficulties. terms with Philip.[4] Ecclesiastical censures were hanging over
Philip's head for his hasty repudiation of his second wife the Danish
Ingeborg, and his subsequent marriage to Agnes of Meran.[5] The French
magnates, who had more reason than ever to be alarmed at Philip's
schemes, were rallying round John, as they had rallied round Richard.
John's Baldwin of Flanders had already done homage to John; the
Opportunity. break up of the conference was followed by the execution of
treaties of defensive and offensive alliance on the part of
Baldwin, and Reginald of Boulogne with the King of England; minor
lords were following suit.[6] In short John had before him an extraordinary
opportunity for a coalition, with, for once in a way, both Pope and Emperor
in accord, and on his side. But John of course was even less capable of
utilising an alliance than his brother.

---

[1] Boutavant was a fort in an island of the Seine, established by Richard in 1198, as an outpost to Andelys. Le Goulet was a counter-work set up by Philip; R. Hoved., IV. 18; Miss Norgate states that the two places were four miles above Les Andelys, II. 403.

[2] Hoveden, IV. 94, 95.

[3] Martin, the historian of France, has not a word about the question of the Vexin, and Sismondi is equally silent as to the recent history of the affair. Lavisse, *France*, III. 120, has it that at Richard's death Philip in fact had nothing of the Norman Vexin but Gisors, and that was probably the case.

[4] Hoveden, 95, 96.

[5] Philip's first wife Isabel of Hainault died 15th March, 1190 (Diceto, II. 77; Rigord, 29). On the 14th August, 1193, Philip married Ingeborg sister of Cnut VI. of Denmark, but taking a sudden aversion to her dismissed her the very next day. Her brother refused to take her back, and the unfortunate Queen was bandied about from castle to convent between France and Flanders. Celestine III. did his utmost to induce Philip to take her back, but in spite of him he procured from the French clergy a divorce on pretended grounds of consanguinity; and eventually in June 1196 married Agnes. daughter of Berthold Duke of Meran (Rigord, 38, 46, 50, 51; W. Newb., I. 368–370, and notes; Hoved. III. 224, 306, and notes; Pauli, I. 303).

[6] Hoved. *sup*,; *Fœdera*, I. 77.

War of the usual desultory character ensued.   Philip advancing from his outpost at Evreux captured Conches, the old stronghold of the House of Tosny.   But he " opened the eyes " of Arthur's friends by seizing and dismantling Arthur's castle of Ballon in Maine. Thereupon William des Roches, Arthur's Seneschal for Anjou,[1] on receiving satisfactory assurances from John,[2] took the young Duke to him, and surrendered Le Mans.   But John in his turn was so little able to conceal his feelings towards his nephew that Constance and her chief supporters carried him off in terror on the very next night after his arrival.[3]

War.

The year ended with a truce, negotiated by the Cardinal Peter of Capua, who was still in France, prosecuting the Pope's case against Philip.   A suspension of hostilities, to the 13th January 1200, was agreed upon.[4]

Truce.

At the expiration of the truce conferences were held between Andely and Gaillon, when a provisional agreement was arrived at for a pacification on the footing of a matrimonial arrangement, much on the lines of the compact of 1151, a solution that had been suggested a year before, in Richard's time.   By the final treaty, as sealed four months later, Philip's son Louis not yet thirteen years old,[5] would marry John's niece little Blanche of Castile.   As her marriage portion John would cede to Philip on her behalf Evreux and a district extending half way to Danville, Conches, Le Neubourg, and Acquigny ; also Issudun, Graçay and other fiefs in Berri : he would also pay Philip 20,000 marks as *rachat*, otherwise Relief, on being admitted as heir to all Richard's possessions not ceded by the treaty, including the Norman Vexin, now apparently abandoned by Philip.[6]   The French Vexin, of course, in its entirety, would remain his.   John would do homage to Philip, and receive the homage of Arthur for Brittany and the Earldom of Richmond.   Lastly he agreed, shabbily enough, to give up the cause of his nephew Otto, of course out of regard for the French King's alliance with Philip of Suabia.[7]

Matrimonial Settlement.

Blanche of Castile.

In England men sneered at the concessions made by their ' peace-loving ' King.[8]   The treaty no doubt was a compromise, but one distinctly

[1] Round, *Calendar*, 363, 473.   [2] 18th September, Rot. Cart. 30.

[3] Hoveden, IV. 96, 97 ; Diceto, II. 167.   John was at Le Mans 22nd, 23rd September, *Itiny.*, Hardy.   Constance then threw up her husband Ralph of Chester, and married Guy of Thouars, brother of the Viscount Amaury ; Hoved., 97.

[4] October ? Hoveden, 97.

[5] He was born in September 1187 ; Rigord, 24.

[6] So I read the rather obscure clause on the subject in the treaty.   My view seems supported by the fact that the French were not to fortify on the Norman side of Gamaches, the frontier town (Somme).   R. Cogg., however, 100, asserts the contrary.

[7] See the treaty as finally executed, *Fœdera*, I. 79 ; Hoveden, 148 ; Rigord, 51.

[8] " Utpote pacis amator " ; R. Cogg. 101.   The writer, however, I think misunderstood the treaty.

advantageous to John, who would be relieved of all immediate anxiety
on the score of Arthur's claims, and would himself be
recognised as lord of Maine, Anjou, and Aquitaine. For Philip
the treaty was not a bad one either, as Normandy West of the
Seine would not now have even the line of the Iton to defend it, and
Normandy doubtless was what his eyes were fixed upon.   Besides all that,
he was not in a position to demand high terms.   His throne at the time
might be supposed to be shaken to its foundations.   On 11th January
France had been threatened with all the terrors of an Interdict, proclaimed
to take effect from Mid-Lent Sunday (19th March), unless her King in the
meantime would submit to the Pope's decision in the matter of his
marriage.[1]   Queen Eleanor, as the most experienced politician in Europe,
appreciated the value of the treaty in the interests of her son ; and so,
though now eighty years old, she started once more on a matrimonial
embassy, crossing the Pyrenees under the escort of Mercadier,
to fetch her grand-daughter, while John went over to England
to raise the 20,000 marks.   Landing about the 27th February
he was at Westminster from the 6th to the 8th March.[2]   A carucate of
three shillings on the hide was called for ;[3] and then the King
moved on to York, hoping to receive the King of Scots.   But
again he was doomed to be disappointed, as William never came.

As we have seen the homage, technically, was only supposed to be
due for the English estates.   But from the importance attached to the
recognition it is clear that the moral significance of the act went much
farther.   The chief incident of the King's visit to the North was a quarrel
with the Cistercians, who protested that they could not contribute to John's
tax without the authority of a General Chapter of the Order.
The King in a fury ordered them to be put out of the protection
of the law.   With difficulty was he prevailed upon to withdraw
the edict by the promise of 1000 marks conveyed through Hubert Walter.[4]
Another man who fell into disgrace through resistance to the carucate
was the incorrigible Archbishop Geoffrey of York.   Long kept out of
England by the persistent hostility of Hubert Walter,[5] he had apparently
come over with the King, only to have his possessions again seized for
refusing to contribute to a lay impost.[6]

Marginal notes: A Working Compromise. / Queen Eleanor in Spain. / John in England again. / Taxation of Ecclesiastics.

---

[1] This was the outcome of a Synod that met at Dijon on 5th December, 1199, under
the Cardinal Peter of Capua, the sittings being adjourned to Vienne on the Rhone.
But the sentence was not promulgated till the 11th January, 1200. Diceto, II. 167, 168 ;
Hoveden, IV. 112 ; Rigord, *sup.* 51 ; Sismondi, *France*, VI. 191, citing Labbe, *Conc.*
XI. 11, 12 ; Martin, *France*, III. 161.

[2] Hoveden, IV. 107 ; *Itin.*

[3] R. Cogg. 101 ; Hoved., *sup.* No notice of the tax appears on the Pipe Rolls.

[4] R. Cogg. 102, 103.   [5] Hoveden, IV. 99.

[6] R. Wendover, III. 154. A further offence was Geoffrey's refusal to go back to
Normandy with John for the wedding. Doubtless he opposed the treaty as derogatory.

About the 1st May John returned to Normandy.[1] Little **Blanche** arriving shortly afterwards the treaty embodying the terms above given was formally executed at Le Goulet on Thursday, Ascension

Treaty of Le Goulet. Day (18th May). John did homage to Philip; while Arthur was produced to do homage to John for Brittany, being taken back to Paris as soon as the ceremony had been performed. On the

Marriage of Louis and Blanche. following Monday, the 22nd, Louis and Blanche were married by Hélie Archbishop of Bordeaux. But the service had to be performed at Portmort, on Norman soil, France being now under Interdict. Eleanor, too exhausted to finish the journey, had remained at Fontevrault.[2]

Again the King of England could boast of a territory stretching from the Channel to the Pyrenees.[3] The treaty executed, and the

John in Aquitaine. wedding over, John started on a progress to the far South; but only to take the first opportunity of making fresh enemies and creating trouble for himself. We have seen that John's wedded wife Isabel, third daughter of Earl William of Gloucester, had not been allowed to share his coronation. Married in August 1189 she had borne him no child; the earldom that he had received with her was no longer of any importance to him, and he probably wished for an heir to secure the succession. Anyhow being, from whatever motives, resolved to get rid of her, he fell back on the relationship on the ground of which Archbishop

Divorce of Isabel of Gloucester. Baldwin had originally condemned the marriage; and either late in 1199, or early in 1200 obtained from some of the Norman or Aquitanian bishops a divorce, overruling the dispensation of Clement III.[4] John then despatched an embassy to Portugal to apply for the hand of the King's sister, of whom he had heard great reports. The envoys had not returned when John started on his Aquitanian tour, in the course of which he came across another Isabel, the beautiful daughter of Ademar Count of Angoulême, and fell violently in love with her. She had been formally betrothed to Hugh Le Brun the younger of Lusignan, son of the crusading Count of La Marche;[5] but the marriage had not yet been celebrated, the girl being only about

---

[1] He signs at Valognes on the 2nd May; *Itin.*

[2] Hoveden, IV. 114, 115, and for the treaty *Fœdera*, *sup.* The dates come from Rigord, 51–53. Mercadier the soldier of fortune who had escorted Eleanor to Castile lost his life on the way back, falling a victim to assassination at Bordeaux.

[3] So the Angevin Chron. Saint-Aubin points out; "Ad Crucem Caroli."

[4] Diceto, II. 166, 167, under 1199; Hoved., 119, 120, under 1200. R. Cogg., 103. Not content with discarding Isabel, John also deprived her of her patrimony, conferring the Earldom and estates of Gloucester on her sister's husband Amaury of Montfort, Count of Evreux, in exchange for rights that he had to cede to Philip to make the cession of the *Evrecin* complete; Round, *Calendar*, 474; R. Cogg, 101.

[5] The younger Hugh is styled Count of La Marche, but in fact his father Hugh IX. lived till 1206, Norgate II. 401.

twelve years old.[1] Ademar, allured by the offer of a crown, removed
his daughter from the custody of her betrothed, and gave her
An Impolitic Marriage. over to John, who married her forthwith at Angoulême, without even communicating with his ambassadors in Portugal.[2]
By this rash act John had earned all the hostility of the war-
The House of Lusignan. like and ambitious House of Lusignan,[3] whose pretensions
had been raised to the highest pitch by the conspicuous part
played by the family in Eastern affairs.[4]

From Angoulême John hastened to England for the coronation of his
youthful bride. In the first week of October they crossed the Channel
presumably from Barfleur to Portsmouth.[5] On Sunday the
Coronation of the Queen. 8th of the month Isabel was hallowed at Westminster by
Archbishop Hubert, the King wearing his crown at the same
time, doubtless in order to give greater *éclat* to the ceremony.[6] Immediately
afterwards a third invitation to render homage was addressed to William
the Lion, a meeting being appointed to be held at Lincoln on the 21st of
November. Gruffudd ap Rhys of South Wales also received a safe-
conduct to enable him to appear.[7] Both Kings duly came to Lincoln on
the day, with most imposing retinues. The city must have been filled to
overflowing, as John brought with him pretty nearly the whole collective
Baronage of England. Three archbishops, thirteen bishops—English,
Scots, Welsh, and Irish—ten earls, and seventeen barons are named as
present, besides Gruffudd of Wales and Roland mac Uhtred, Prince of
Galloway. By entering the city John, like Stephen, braved the old tradition
that forbad Kings to set foot in Lincoln. But John even ventured to
enter the new Minster,[8] then in course of construction, and to offer a gold
chalice at the altar of St. John the Baptist, part of the new work
(22nd November). John then went outside the walls, and received the

---

[1] So Ralph of Coggeshall judged by her appearance at her coronation in the autumn;
" quæ quasi duodennis videbatur "; 103.

[2] August (26th?) Hoveden, IV. 119, 120; Diceto, II. 170; John was at
Angoulême on the 26th August; *Itin.*; Isabel's settlement is dated 30th August;
Rot. Cart., 75.

[3] " Ci commença l'achaison De la honte et de la guerre," *Mareschal* II. 67. See
also R. Wend., III. 148. It may be worth noticing that the Lusignans were the
descendants of Roger of Poitou (son of Roger of Montgomery) who had married the
heiress of La Marche.

[4] Amauri of Lusignan was now King of Cyprus in succession to his brother Guy.

[5] John was at Valognes on October 1st; and at Fremantle near Southampton on the
6th October, *Itin.*

[6] Hoved. 139; R. Cogg. 103 distinguishes the two functions accurately. "Rex . . .
coronam gestaturus; . . . uxor sua in reginam consecranda."

[7] Hoveden, 140; *Fœdera*, I. 81.

[8] " Rex intrepidus, et contra consilium multorum, intravit ecclesiam "; Hoved. 141;
R. Wendover, III. 161. They seem to limit the superstition to the cathedral; but the
earlier writers extended it to the whole city: see *Foundations of England*, II. 428.

Scots' King's homage.   William in return again pressed for the cession
Homages of Scotland and Wales. of Northumberland, Cumberland, and Westmorland ; and
John again put him off, promising an answer at Whitsun-
tide.[1]   The third day at Lincoln saw the Scots depart, and the
sad procession arrive that brought the remains of the Sainted Bishop
Death of St. Hugh of Lincoln. Hugh.   Returning to England about October, after a journey
to Rome, he was laid up in London with a quartan fever,
doubtless contracted abroad.   John, when in Town for the
coronation, visited him at his lodgings in the Old Temple Holborn, and
promised to respect his Will, and also the Wills of other prelates.   On the
16th or 17th November St. Hugh died.[2]   When the funeral reached
Lincoln the whole assembled concourse went out to meet it, and the King
and the chief barons took up the coffin and bore it on their shoulders to
the Minster door.   There the clergy received it, and carried it to the
choir, to be entombed next day at the altar of the Baptist.[3]

John staid on three more days at Lincoln, the last day (26th November)
being marked by a final reconciliation with the Cistercians.
The Cistercians. On landing in October, being still furious with them, he had
issued orders forbidding any of their animals to be allowed to
pasture within the royal forests, a severe blow at the beginning of winter.
By the advice of Hubert Walter the Cistercian abbots in a body came to
Lincoln to plead their cause face to face with the King.   Hubert managed
matters with such tact that John revoked his hostile orders, apologised for
his past conduct, and promised by way of amends to found a new abbey
for the Order.[4]   The pledge was shortly redeemed by the establishment
of Beaulieu Abbey in the New Forest.[5]

From Lincoln John moved through Northampton and Abingdon into
Wilts and Hants, passing again into Surrey to keep Christmas at Guildford.[6]
Immediately afterwards he started with his young Queen on a
Progress to the North. winter progress to the far North.   On the 12th and 13th
January he was again at Lincoln, and endeavoured to arrange
for the appointment of a new bishop.   But the canons wanted a free

---

[1] Hoveden, IV. 141, 142 ; J. Fordun, 275, where the homage is correctly given as
merely rendered for the English estates.   R. Cogg., 107.

[2] Hoveden, 141 gives the 16th November (XVI. Kal. Dec.), Wendover, III. 161,
gives the 17th November (XV. Kal. Dec.).   So too the *Registrum Sacrum* of Bishop
Stubbs.   Matthew Paris in the *Chron. Maj.* follows Wendover, and in the *Hist. Angl.*
goes back to the 16th November.

[3] Hoveden, 142, 143 ; Diceto, II. 171 ; R. Cogg., 110, 111.   The last admires the
unfinished cathedral as the finest in England.

[4] See the whole story, R. Cogg., 103–110 ; also Hoveden, 144, 145.   With respect to
the special position of the Cistercians it may be noted that they, the Premonstratensians,
Carthusians, and monks of Grammont were exempted even from the Fortieth being now
levied by Innocent for the relief of Palestine ; R. Cogg., 116.

[5] R. Cogg., 147 ; Ann. Waverley, A.D. 1204.   [6] *Itin.* ; Hoveden, 156.

election, to which of course he could not give in.   On the 24th January
the Royal pair crossed the Humber to Cottingham, resting next day at
Beverley.   From thence they passed on to Scarborough, Durham, Newcastle, Bamborough, and Hexham : then following the line of the Roman

Carlisle visited. Wall the King and Queen on the 21st February reached
Carlisle,[1] a city more used to receiving visits from Scottish
than from English Royalty.   In fact Carlisle had not been
honoured by the presence of any member of the English Royal family
since May 1149, when young Henry of Anjou went down to be knighted
by his great-uncle David I. of Scotland.[2]   By the 1st March John and
Isabel had come southwards as far as York.   They found Geoffrey there,
and a friendly agreement for a reference to arbitration on all points in
dispute was entered into.   With his Chapter and his clergy generally the
Archbishop was bound to go on quarrelling as fiercely as ever.[3]   Easter

Easter Crown-wearing. (25th March) was kept at Canterbury.   Both King and Queen
wore their crowns in the cathedral in the olden style, receiving
them, of course, at the hands of the Archbishop.[4]

John's abduction of Isabel was in itself a sufficient challenge to the
Lusignans.   A wiser man than he would have sought to avert any further
breach with the family.   John on the contrary, treating their hostility as
inevitable, thought it wise to anticipate their action, and adding injury to
insult, began wantonly to attack them.   He had already seized some of

War against the Lusignans. their castles in Poitou; and at this very time was declaring
war on Ralph of Exoudun, brother of the elder Le Brun, and
Count of Eu by marriage.[5]   Guérin de Glapion, Seneschal of
Normandy was being sent to attack Driencourt (Somme, W. of Peronne),
a place given to Ralph by King Richard.   The siege resulted in the
capture of the place, the blow being followed up by Ralph's expulsion from
his wife's heritage of Eu.[6]   In view of these affairs John on the 1st May
issued writs summoning the military tenants to be ready at Portsmouth
on the 13th for an expedition to Normandy.[7]   The Barons,

Baronial Opposition. who probably did not sympathise with the war in hand, demurred.   They held a meeting at Leicester, and sent a message
to the King to say that they would not attend unless 'he gave them their

---

[1] *Id.*   [2] See *Foundations*, II. 438.

[3] *Itinerary*; Hoveden, IV. 157-160, and Innocent's letter there warning Geoffrey to
respect the rights of others.   The disputes turned mainly on questions of patronage.

[4] Hoveden, 160; Diceto, II. 172.

[5] He was married to Alais daughter of Henry Count of Eu who died in 1183, his two
sons dying shortly afterwards ; Stapleton, Norm. Rolls, II. ccxxxii.

[6] See G. Le Breton, *Philippis*, 185, 186 (Bouquet); Hoveden, 160; and especially
Stapleton's extracts from the Patent Roll 2 John, given Rot. Norm. II. ccxxi.   See
also *Fœdera*, I. 81 for Eleanor's efforts to keep Amauri of Thouars loyal ; and his letter to
John hinting that if terms were not made with him he might join the Count de La Marche.

[7] Hoveden, *sup.* ; Diceto, II. 172.

rights.'[1] Now we have seen that at John's accession Hubert Walter had to promise the Barons 'their rights' (*jura sua*). But no hint was given to us as to the nature of the rights or privileges that they wished to have respected ; nor are we told anything now, except that the Royal Progress had been found very burdensome to the people.[2] But if we take the charter of Henry I. as our standard of constitutional right we can see at a glance how much the Baronage had to complain of in the practice of the Crown on such points as the sale of heiresses and widows, the wardship of minors, reliefs, amerciaments, and the like. With regard to the liability to personal service abroad on which the Barons took their stand we take it that they had no case at all. But it often happens that burdens, technically legal, and warranted by precedent, become in course of time obsolete and vexatious, through changes of circumstance. The growing

Question of Service over-sea. severance between English and Norman interests would make personal service abroad more and more irksome. We would suggest that the Barons either having special grounds of complaint against John, or wishing to better their general position as against the Crown, took a hint from St. Hugh of Lincoln, and started the theory of non-liability to personal service abroad as a lever for bringing pressure to bear on the King. But they were not organised for resistance ; and John met them by threatening to seize their castles, and demanding hostages, making a beginning with the Earl of Arundel (William III. of Aubigny), who was only allowed to retain Belvoir on giving up his son. The result was that the Barons came to Portsmouth, when John, following

The Opposition Quelled. Richard's extortionate practice, dismissed them on payment of a scutage of two marks (£1 6s. 8d.), *plus* fines for being allowed to pay instead of serving in person, thus completely turning the tables on them.[3] William Marshal and Roger de Lacy were sent in advance with 200 hired men-at-arms to defend the borders of Normandy, while Hubert de Burgh, the King's Chamberlain, was appointed Warden of the Welsh March, with another 100 men-at-arms. King and Queen sailed shortly, Isabel going first, and John a few days later. Normandy was found to be quiet, Philip, whose cue at the moment was to keep on good terms with John, having been exerting himself to maintain peace.

John in Paris. The two had a friendly meeting near Andelys ; and then John went on to Paris, where he had a most hospitable reception, Philip vacating his own palace for him.[4] It was perhaps at this time that a treaty of a very dangerous character of which we hear as

---

[1] " Nisi ille reddiderit eis jura sua."
[2] R. Wend. III. 166.
[3] Hoveden, 163 ; see the entries " De finibus et scutagio militum ne transfretent " ; *Red Book Ex.* I. 11, and Pipe Roll 3 John, *passim.*
[4] Hoveden, 161, 163. John was at Andelys 25th-27th June and in Paris 1st July ; *Itinerary* ; Rigord, 53, 54.

entered into by the two Kings was executed.   By this compact the barons
on either side who had been named as guarantors of the treaty of
18th May 1200 would be released from their allegiance if their King
committed any breach of the convention.[1]   From Paris John went on to
Chinon, where he met Berengaria and settled her jointure, agreeing to
pay her 1000 marks a year, to be provided, in substance, half from the
English treasury, and half from the Norman treasury at Caen.[2]   For
getting rid of the rebel Poitevin barons we are told that John had conceived
a notable plan, a scheme in truth of the most childish character.   He
would impeach them, one by one, for treasonable conduct both as against
his brother and himself; he would challenge them to clear themselves
according to the laws of chivalry, having prepared a set of accomplished
swordsmen to fight the duels on his behalf.   Of course the
Visit to Poitevins declined to enter the lists with such antagonists.[3]
Poitou.
From Poitou the King returned to Normandy, to keep his
Christmas at Argentan.

[1] Hoveden, IV. 175.   R. Cogg., 135, 136, refers to a treaty executed without the
concurrence of the Count of Boulogne that enabled him to break with John.

[2] 2nd August, *Fœdera*, II. 84 ; *cnf.* Hoved., 173.

[3] Hoved. 176.   John was at Mirebeau in Poitou (Vienne) 9th October, being the
farthest point South visited by him in the year ; *Itin.*

CHAPTER XXIV

A.D. 1202–1204

Breach with France— Citation of John to Paris—Capture and murder of Arthur of Brittany—War, and loss of Normandy, Anjou, Maine, and Touraine

WITH the year 1202 the affairs of Normandy entered on a new stage. John persisting in his operations against the De Lusignans they appealed for help and redress to Philip as Lord Paramount,

Philip and the Lusignans. complaining of John's attacks.[1] Philip could now afford to throw off the mask, as he had settled the quarrel with Innocent III. that hitherto had hampered his action. The Interdict which came into operation 19th March 1200 was dissolved on the 7th September following, Philip having condescended so far as to make a show of taking back Ingeborg. In May 1201 matters were further simplified by the death of Agnes of Meran, and then the Pope to conciliate Philip agreed to declare her children legitimate.[2] With his hands thus free Philip apparently took up the grievances of Hugh le Brun and Ralph of Eu. He had an interview with John at Le Goulet on the 25th March, 1202;[3] but not an interview of a very friendly character, as apparently it ended by Philip requiring John as a vassal of France to appear in Paris before his court to answer certain charges brought against him, and to submit to the judgment of his peers.[4] In vain John protested

John cited to Paris that the Dukes of Normandy owed no suit to the Courts of the French Kings, and that they had always met as equals on the frontier. Philip refused to accept the excuse. After further interchanges to no purpose a formal citation for the 28th April was served upon John.[5]

---

[1] G. Le Breton, 75; R. Cogg., 135. John after dividing the month of January between Maine and Touraine passed at the beginning of February into Poitou, going as far as Angoulême, Cognac, and Saint-Jean d' Angely; by the 20th of the month he had returned to Normandy; *Itinerary*. [2] Hoved. IV. 137, 138, 173; Rigord, 53, 54.

[3] Diceto, II. 174, the last entry in the work; R. Wend. III. 167; Rigord.

[4] "De illatis injuriis responsurus, et juri quod pares sui decernebant pariturus"; R. Cogg.

[5] Rigord, 54; R. Cogg., 135, 136. The exact charges brought against John do not appear, but I reject the allegation of Wendover that Philip called on John to surrender

According to the account that seems best entitled to credence John sent Eustace Bishop of Ely and Hubert de Burgh to ask for a safe conduct to enable him to appear. Philip was willing to give the safe-conduct for John to come ; but would only grant the warrant for his safe return subject to the finding of the Court ; and with that of course John's envoys could not be satisfied. With respect to John's claim of exemption from jurisdiction on the ground of his royal dignity Philip is represented as meeting that by answering that John's ancestors were Dukes of Normandy before they became Kings of England, and that the rights of an overlord could not be affected by a subsequent accession of dignity to his vassal. John

and con- failed to appear whereupon the Court declared all his fees
demned. forfeited for breach of feudal duties.[1] Philip confirmed the finding of the Court, and to put it in force, at once entered Normandy, sweeping victoriously through the Vexin and Bray. His

French first operation was to capture and demolish Boutavant, the
conquests in outwork of the position at Les Andelys ; pushing on he quickly
Normandy. made himself master of Les Thilliers-en-Vexin, Longchamps (by Etrépagny), Lyons-la-Forét,[2] La Ferté Sanson (by Forges), Mortemer (by Neufchâtel), and Aumâle ;[3] finally reducing the town and county of Eu, thus gaining the control of all the country up to the walls of Arques. Reginald of Boulogne, rejecting his treaty with John, declared for Philip, and was rewarded with the custody of Aumâle. Hugh of Gournay alone, worthy scion of a loyal House, held out, till Philip by cutting the embankment of a reservoir let loose a flood of water that made his stronghold untenable.[4] In honour of this success Philip knighted Arthur, now sixteen

Normandy, Anjou, and Poitou to Arthur. That would be inconsistent with the treaty of 1200 and a false move.

[1] See the note on this matter appended by Matthew Paris, *Chron. Maj.*, II. 658, to his transcript of Wendover's report of the discussion on Louis' case against John held at Rome in 1216 ; also R. Cogg., 135, 136 ; and especially Innocent's letter of the 7th March, 1205, to the Norman Bishops in answer to an enquiry as to Philip's right to their homage. The Pope states that he was aware that Philip claimed to have taken possession of Normandy under a judicial decree ; but that, as he was not acquainted with the exact circumstances under which the decree was passed, he could not give any opinion as to its validity ; *Epp.* VIII. No. 7. See also his letter to John of the 31st October, 1203 (*Epp.* VI. 167), in which without referring to any actual condemnation he reminds him that he had been cited to appear before Philip's Court as his liege man, but had failed to appear. If there is any substance of truth in Wendover's account of the discussion at Rome in 1216 (III. 373-378 and Paris, *sup.*), the only point in dispute was the validity and effect of a condemnation of John by the Court of King Philip, the fact of the condemnation being undisputed. Miss Norgate rejects the condemnation in 1202, as well as that in 1203. But she does not notice the proceedings in Rome of 1216 or the note in Paris above ; *Transactions Royal Historical Society*, N.S. XIV. 53.

[2] Eure, all three.   [3] Seine Inf., all three.

[4] R. Cogg., 136 ; Rigord, *sup.* G. Le Breton, *Gesta*, 75 and *Philippis*, 186-188 ; R. Wendover, III. 167, 168.

years old, and gave him the hand of his little daughter Jeanne, with the
investiture of Brittany, Anjou, Maine, Touraine, and Poitou.
Arthur, Duke of Brittany. To Brittany Arthur was now fully entitled, his mother being
dead;[1] but the other fiefs were only granted 'when, God
willing, they should be conquered.' Normandy Philip evidently intended
" to conquer and keep for himself."[2]

To follow up his advantages Philip advanced from Gournay to attack
Radeport on the Andelle, some ten miles from Rouen (8th July). After an
eight days' siege, John, who all the time had been sitting idly at or near
Rouen, came to the rescue, and chased him away (15th July).[3]

After a short stay in Paris Philip and Arthur took the field again. The
King led the bulk of his forces to the siege of Arques; while the young
Duke was sent with 200 men-at-arms to win his spurs by co-operating with
the Lusignans in Poitou. On joining forces at Tours they heard that
Queen Eleanor had left her favourite retirement at Fontevrault in order
once more to assert her position beyond the Loire; and that she was
established with a slender garrison in the castle of Mirebeau (Vienne).

Attack on Queen Eleanor. She was their chief antagonist, and John's shield and prop in
Poitou, where her rights could hardly be affected by sentences
against him. Thus Arthur was induced to join in a most
ungracious attack on his grandmother, now fully eighty years old. The
town of Mirebeau, and the outworks (*castrum*) of the castle were quickly
carried, and Eleanor reduced to the Keep (*castellum*). To secure themselves
against attack from without the besiegers established themselves within the
outworks or baileys, walling up all the gates but one.[4] But Eleanor had
contrived to send an urgent appeal for help to her son. It would seem
that John was already on the march to Poitou, with his Flemish mercenaries,[5] as he tells us that he received his mother's message on the
30th July as he was approaching Le Mans,[6] his previous stay having been
in Normandy.[7] Between Le Mans and Mirebeau a good hundred miles

---

[1] Constance died 3rd or 4th September, 1201; Morice, *Bretagne*, Preuves, I. c. 6, 106
cited Norgate, II. 404. Her mother Margaret of Scotland, who had taken Humphrey of
Bohun as her second husband, died about the same time; Hoved. IV. 174.

[2] See the act of homage dated at Gournay, July 1202, Round, *Calendar*, 475; and
Rigord, 54: R. Cogg., 137; Norgate.

[3] R. Wend.. *sup. Itinerary.*

[4] " Castrum intraverant, et omnes portas terrari fecerant, excepta una sola "; R. Cogg.

[5] Chron. Turon, Martene, *Ampl. Coll.*, V. 1039.

[6] See his letter, R. Cogg., 137, 138.

[7] Sir T. D. Hardy's *Itinerary* represents John as having been at Bonport on the
30th July. But if he was nearing Le Mans on that day he could not not have been at
Bonport, say 110 miles distant, on the same day. The fact is that entries on the Patent
Rolls are not always proof of the King's presence at the place named on the day, as
Record students know. Orders given by the King might be afterwards drawn up by the
officials and marked " Per ipsum Regem."

of road extend ; but John in one of his spasmodic fits of energy covered
the distance with such expedition that he reached Mirebeau
John to the rescue. in the early hours of the 1st August, and, catching the enemy
encaged in their walls, like rats in a trap, overpowered
them almost without a struggle.[1]   Among the prisoners mentioned by
John as taken were Arthur, young Hugh le Brun and his
Capture of Arthur. uncle Geoffrey of Lusignan, and the Gascon Baron Savary of
Manléon.   Geoffrey of Lusignan, brother of King Guy, was
the man by whose hand Earl Patrick of Salisbury was understood to have
fallen in 1168.   He was an "inveterate fighter," who after strenuously
opposing Richard in Poitou, had been "one of his best supporters in
Palestine." [2]

The use that John made of this signal success was in the first instance
to raise up a fresh host of enemies, and, eventually, to cover himself with
undying infamy.   William des Roches, Seneschal of Anjou, had
William des Roches. in various ways largely contributed to the victory at Mirebeau.
In 1199, when placing Arthur in John's hands he had exacted
from him a formal pledge as to his dealings with the young Duke.[3]   He
now ventured to approach John on the subject, and was coolly told to
mind his own business.   The man at once went into revolt.[4]

From Mirebeau John went back to Normandy with a long train of carts,
laden with captives, all safely bound in fetters.   Arthur was deposited at
Falaise, under the charge of Hubert de Burgh, the others being distributed
among various castles in England and Normandy.[5]   Philip on hearing of
the disaster at Mirebeau raised the siege of Arques, and, to vent his fury,
pushed a savage raid as far as Tours, which he burned, leaving a garrison
in the citadel.   Then John came up in turn, expelled Philip's garrison,
and in doing so burned down whatever Philip's conflagration had spared.[6]
There the recorded operations of the year end ; Philip retiring to Paris,

[1] See R. Cogg., *sup.* and John's letter there ; Ann. Waverley ; R. Wend. 168, 169 ;
Le Breton, *Gesta*, 76, and *Philippis*, 188-192.   From the latter it appears that John
reached Mirebeau in the night ; and Wendover tells us that his march was accomplished
in a day and a night.

[2] Norgate, II. 405.

[3] See the compact, Rot. Cart. 30.

[4] *Mareschal*, II. 83-86 ; R. Cogg., 139 ; Chr. St. Aubin.   G. Le Breton, *Philippis*,
sup., represent Des Roches as taking pledges from John as to his treatment of Arthur and
the Lusignans while on the way to Mirebeau.

[5] R. Wendover, III. 169 ; R. Cogg., 139, 140 ; *Itin.*   The Lusignans were liberated
after a while on surrendering their castles ; but many of the minor prisoners languished
and died in prison, among others Arthur's sister Eleanor, who had also fallen into John's
hands, and was kept in custody for forty years.   See Hardy, *Introdn. to Patent Rolls*,
36-46, and Ann. Margan, A.D. 1202.

[6] Rigord, 55 ; Le Breton, *Gesta*, 76 ; R. Cogg., 138 ; R. Wend. 169, 170.   John was
at Tours 22nd-23rd August, and again from the 30th of the month to the 1st of
September ; *Itin.*

while John, to keep his enemies in check, moved up and down Maine and Anjou all the autumn, returning in December to Normandy, to hold his Christmas at Caen.[1]   He had scored another petty success in the capture of the Viscount of Limoges, Guy son of Ademar;[2] the latter had fallen a victim to the vengeance of Richard's natural son Philip of Cognac.

But the ground was slipping from under John's feet.   His

John losing ground. allies were falling away, while his enemies were mustering their forces.   Baldwin of Flanders had gone to the East, to win an 'Imperial Crown; Otto for the time had been estranged and renounced.[3]   On the other hand the Bretons had held a provincial assembly of clergy and barons to demand Arthur's release;[4] and William des Roches, joining hands with them, organised a league that was able to establish itself at Angers in October.[5]

What was to be done with Arthur must have become a question in John's inner circle.   The well-informed Abbot of Coggeshall tells us that the King was advised to mutilate his nephew, so as to render him incapable of rule ; that officers charged with that duty were sent to Falaise, but that

Arthur in John's Keeping. Hubert de Burgh refused to execute the barbarous order.[6] It may have been this squeamishness on the part of his servants that induced John early in 1203 to remove Arthur from Falaise to Rouen to have him in his own keeping.[7]

Shortly after Easter, 1203, ghastly rumours began to run both abroad and in England ; Arthur was no more, murdered, and as men even said

His fate. murdered by the very hand of his uncle.[8]   The exact circumstances attending Arthur's death must remain in doubt, as of the accounts transmitted to us there is no one whose authority we are bound to accept as conclusive, and the writers of the time speak with natural reserve.   But the only substantial question is whether the deed was done by John's orders only, or in his actual presence, if not by his very hands.   His guilt in one or other of these degrees is either expressly asserted or tacitly implied in every page of his subsequent history.   No friend ever ventured to assert John's innocence, nor did he ever venture to assert it himself, though repeatedly taxed with the murder.   It is no doubt hard to believe that he could have had any difficulty in finding an agent, or that he would unnecessarily embrue his hands in his nephew's

[1] *Itinerary.*
[2] Rigord ; bef. 7th September ; Hardy, *sup.* 43 ; Hoveden, IV. 97.
[3] Hoveden, IV. 116.   Richard's legacies had been withheld.
[4] Daru, *Hist. Bretagne*, I. 415 ; Pauli.
[5] Chron. Saint-Aubin ; Norgate ; R. Cogg., 139.
[6] R. Cogg., 139, 140.
[7] R. Wend III. 170; R. Cogg., 143 ; G. Le Breton, *Philippis*, 192.
[8] R. Wendover, III. 170, 171 ; M. Paris, *Chron. Maj.*, II 479, 480.   Chron. Lanercost (Bannatyne Club) A.D. 1201.

. blood; yet it seems clear that the prevalent belief of his own time was that

The belief of the age. he had done so. This much is beyond question, viz. that while Arthur was under his uncle's charge at or near Rouen he suddenly vanished, never to reappear.[1] The Annals of Margan assert that John murdered Arthur after a drunken orgy on the Thursday before Easter (April 3rd); that the body was thrown into the Seine, but that eventually it was fished up, and buried privately in Notre-Dame des-Prés.[2] The latter part of the story is clearly wrong; Le Breton, the French King's chaplain gives a much more likely account. He tells us that John after spending three days quietly at Moulineaux came back by water to Rouen at night, reaching the castle steps at high tide; that Arthur was then brought down to the boat from his cell, stabbed, and thrown into the Seine.[3] The stealthy cunning of this mode of proceeding would be quite worthy of John. If we accept the date of the Margan writer we get a distinct confirmation of Le Breton's story in the fact that John was at Moulineaux on the 2nd April, and that he appears at Rouen on the 3rd April.[4] If the murder was committed on the 2nd April after 6 o'clock p.m. that would be the 3rd April according to the computation of the time.

General horror. The whispers of Arthur's fate created general horror. Society was becoming too humane to tolerate such barbarism. Within fifteen days of Easter Philip was in communication with the Bretons, who wanted to know what had become of their Duke. A demand for his deliverance in return for proper hostages was addressed to John. It is also clear that he was again summoned to appear before Philip's court, and that he again made default.[5]

John again cited. But in spite of allegations to the contrary it seems doubtful whether in the absence of definite evidence Philip ventured to charge the King with the actual murder of Arthur.[6]

[1] " 'Arthurus subito evanuit . . . . Rex Johannes suspectus habebatur ab omnibus quasi illum manu propria peremisset"; R. Wend. *sup.* Paris in his *Chron. Maj., sup.,* copying Wendover, substitutes for the last passage "modo fere omnibus ignorato; utinam non ut fama refert invida." In his *Hist. Angl.,* II. 95, he cancels this, and suggests suicide, or death by drowning during an attempt at escape.

[2] P. 27. (Rolls Series No. 36); so too in substance, R. Cogg., 145. "Rex Philippus . . . . sæviebat . . . . pronece Arturi quem in Sequana submersum fuisse audierat."

[3] *Philippis,* 193, 194.

[4] *Itinerary.*

[5] R. Cogg. 143; Rigord, 56; Innocent, *Epp.* VI. 167 (31st October 1203).

[6] For the allegation that John was formally condemned for the murder of Arthur see Ann. Margan, 27; Chron. Lanercost, 2; and especially Louis' proclamation in 1216. "Satis notum est quomodo de murdro Arturi nepotis sui in curia domini Regis Franciæ . . . tandem fuit condemnatus," *Fædera,* I. 140. The "tandem" seems to leave the date of the trial uncertain. Against this we may set the silence of all the French Records, and French writers of the time. In October Philip frankly admitted that he did not really know whether Arthur was alive or not (so a charter to Guy of Thouars,

John having offered no satisfaction hostilities were resumed. Philip directed his first steps towards the Loire, capturing Saumur; while

French Successes. William des Roches and his allies made themselves masters of Beaufort and Châteauneuf (Vienne).[1] But Robert of Turnham was making a vigorous stand on John's behalf; and so the King turned Northwards for an attack on central Normandy, marching apparently through Maine by Beaumont-le-Vicomte, and Alençon, both of which places were already in friendly hands.[2] At Philip's coming Séez, Conches, Montfort-sur-Risle, and many other places opened their gates. Séez was surrendered by its Count, Robert by name; and Montfort by the loyal Hugh of Gournay, who, no longer able to keep loyal, joined the King of France with all his men. Another noteworthy defection was that of Guérin de Glapion, who only the year

Norman defections. before had been Seneschal of Normandy; his defection involved the loss of Exmes, a fief conferred on him by John.[3] From Montfort Philip led his forces against Le Vaudreuil. But before his siege train was well in position, before a single projectile had been hurled, Robert fitz Walter and Saer de Quincy yielded at discretion. The next stage brought Philip face to face with Richard's fortifications at Les Andelys. These consisted first of the rocky promontory of the Château

Château Gaillard. Gaillard, protected by the Seine on one side, and the Gambon on the other side; next of Le Petit Andely, a fortified town across the Gambon, facing the Rock, surrounded with water, and connected by a bridge with the third member of the group, namely the Island fort in the Seine. Le Grand Andely was an open village at a little distance to the West, and outside the system of fortification. The defences also included a triple stockade thrown across the river above the Island to cut off operations by water from the upper Seine. At Philip's approach the garrison in the Island destroyed the bridge between themselves and

Operations. the left bank of the Seine, retaining their communication with Le Petit Andely on the right bank. Philip's first care after establishing his camp opposite the Island was to destroy the stockade. That having been done, and the water-way cleared, barges and ferry boats were collected and a pontoon bridge thrown across the river below the Island, to enable the French to draw supplies from either side, while in fact the

Delisle, *Catalogue*, 783, cited Bémont). Again on the 31st of the same month Innocent, in the letter already cited, writing to remonstrate with John on his defaults towards Philip, refers to his second citation in the previous month of April, but without any reference to Arthur's murder. See the matter discussed by M. Charles Bémont, *Revue Historique*, XXXII. 33 and 290.

[1] Chron. St. Aubin, Norgate; Rigord, *sup.* and Le Breton, *Gesta*, 76, but both under the year 1202.

[2] R. Cogg., 139; Rigord and Le Breton, *sup.*

[3] *Id.*; Wendover, III. 172; and Stapleton, Rot. Norm., II. ccxv.

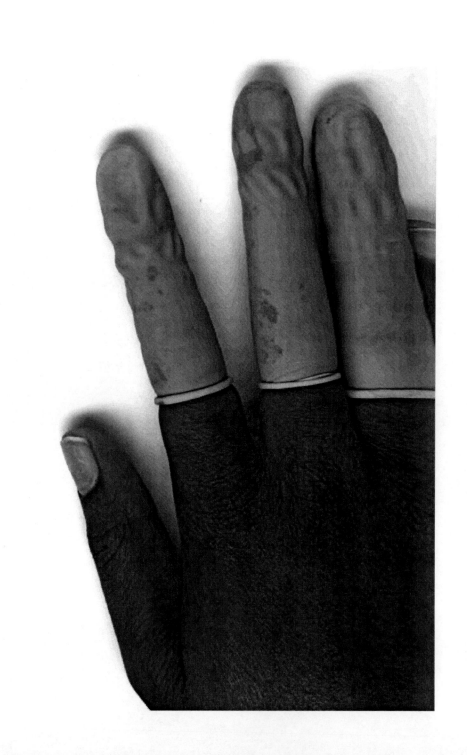

)ulk of the French army was transferred to more comfortable quarters on
he right bank.[1]

John meanwhile had not made an effort to retrieve the situation, living
t his ease, mostly at or near Rouen, with occasional tours through the
Western parts of the Duchy.[2]   ' Let alone ' he would say with

John's inaction. insensate vanity when told of some fresh loss, ' I will regain
all in a few days.'[3]   The only enterprises credited to him
/ere a four days' siege of Alençon, dropped at Philip's approach ; and an
qually feeble attempt to capture the border fort of Brézolles (Eure et
.oir, near Verneuil).[4]   But with Château Gaillard in danger he was at
1st stirred to serious action.   A considerable force was got together for
the relief of the Andelys ; but John thought it best to delegate

Attempted relief of Château Gaillard. the chief command to the trusty Earl of Pembroke, William
Marshal.   A night attack on the French leaguer on the left
bank of the Seine—the weaker part of their forces—was the
)lan resolved upon ; a flotilla of boats would co-operate in order to
estroy Philip's pontoon bridge, cut the communication between the two
·anches of the French army, and refresh their own garrison in the Island.
1e expedition failed utterly.   The Earl of Pembroke coming by land, by
hort cut across the windings of the Seine, was first on the spot, and
dc fell slaughter among followers found outside the French camp.   The
'p itself was thrown into some disorder ; but the English failed to press
· advantages in the darkness : reinforcements to the French soon came
om the other side, under William des Barres and others, and then the
sh dispersed.   The fleet, arriving too late to act in concert with the
failed to break through the French pontoon bridge so as to reach
and, while the latter itself was captured by the French through a
ınce not less daring than ingenious.   An accomplished diver, one
of Mantes, managed to make his way unobserved to the far side
of the Island, towing after him by a string a floating vessel
filled with live coals.   With these he fired the palisades surrounding the fort.   Fairly smoked out the garrison fled over
ʒe to Le Petit Andely, and Philip took possession.[5]   The
Island involved that of Le Petit Andely, itself described
as another island, surrounded with water.   Roger de Lacy,
vho was in command on the Rock, with more humanity than
ru dence, allowed the bulk of the panic-stricken inhabitants to·
him.[6]

1, 77 ; *Philipp.* 196, 197.   [2] See the *Itinerary.*   [3] Wendover, 171.
sta, 76.   John was at Alençon 11th-15th August ; *Itin.*   Philip drove
y invoking the help of a party of knights assembled at Moret-en-
ıent.
very glowing account of Le Breton, *Philippis*, 198-202 ; R. Cogg.,.
ndely cum castello."   [6] Le Breton, 78, 202.

From Le Petit Andely Philip led his forces to renew the siege of
Radepont (31st August).   At the end of fifteen days the place
Investiture
of the Rock yielded.[1]   Then, after an interval of repose, Philip, in
of Andely. September, went back to Andely   But the walls of the
Château Gaillard, and the unshaken fidelity of de Lacy seemed to defy
assault, and so for the winter the King resolved to content himself with
the slow sure process of blockade.   To effect this he proceeded to cut off
all access to the Rock from the landward side by a series of tremendous
entrenchments, in fact an entrenched camp extending from the Seine to
the Gambon.[2]

By December John had begun to realise that without support from
England all in Normandy would soon be lost.   The extent of
The King to the defection so far may be gauged by comparing the receipts
England.   of the Norman Exchequer for the year 1203 with those for the
year 1198, both Rolls being extant.   Of fifteen administrative districts that
appear in the earlier year, only six come forward in the later period, the
only substantial receipts being from the Cotentin and Mortain.[3]   On the
5th or 6th of December the King took final leave of Normandy, crossing
from Barfleur to Portsmouth.[4]   Furious with the barons for whose
defection he blamed his losses, John, we are told, at once demanded
from them a seventh of their movables, the exaction being
Financial extended even to monastic Houses and parochial clergy.   We
measures.   are further assured that in enforcing the King's demands
Hubert Walter and Geoffrey Fitz Peter spared nobody.[5]

But the King's needs were felt to be so urgent that at a Grand Council
held at Oxford on the 2nd January 1204 a scutage at the rate of two marks
the knight's fee was again voted.[6]   But in spite of frantic appeals for men
and money addressed to all and sundry[7] we fail to trace the smallest force
set on foot for the relief of Château Gaillard.

In view of John's subsequent history it is interesting to note his relations
with the Papacy at this time, as if Innocent's keen eye had already
detected a weakness that might be turned to profitable account.
John and the Already he had attempted to mediate between Philip and
Papacy.   John, his intervention being resisted by the French as conceived in John's interest.[8]   Hard on this we find John setting a fatal

---

[1] Rigord, 57 ; Le Breton, *sup*.   [2] Sept.   Rigord, 57 ; Le Breton, 78, 202, 203.
[3] Stapleton, *Rot. Norm.*, II. 289 etc. ; 503, etc.   [4] Wendover, III. 173 ; *Itin.*
[5] R. Wend. III. 173 ; *cnf.* R. Cogg. 144.   Not an entry of this levy appears on the
Pipe Rolls.
[6] R. Wend. 174, 175, where the rate is wrongly given as 2½ marks.   On the Pipe Roll,
4 John, the rate is two marks, with extra fines.
[7] See John's letters to the Gascons, the Irish clergy, the men of Jersey and Guernsey ;
Fœdera, 89, 90.
[8] July–August 1203 ; Rigord, 57, and the letters of the Duke of Burgundy and others,
Fœdera, 89; Sismondi, *France*, VI. 225, and Innocent's letter, Duchesne, *Hist. France*, V. 712.

precedent by acquiescing in the Pope's proposal to find a maintenance for the Archbishop of Ragusa, who could not live at home, by quartering him on the vacant See of Carlisle.[1]—The first of those Papal ' Provisions ' of which we shall hear so much.

All through the autumn and winter (1203–1204) the blockade of Château Gaillard had been strictly kept up. Thrice had de Lacy to save his

Blockade of Château Gaillard. stores found it necessary to expel non-combatants, useless mouths that he had unwisely admitted within his walls. Two bands were allowed by the French to pass through. At the appearance of a third and larger party Philip ordered them to be driven back into the ditches between the two lines of fortification, there to support existence as best they might. At last, however, moved by a personal sight of their misery he allowed the survivors to escape.[2] An appeal to John by the Constable was answered by directions to hold out as best he might.[3] About the 22nd February[4] Philip, weary of the blockade, began an active assault, pushing a covered gallery up the slopes of the hill to the apex of the triangular outwork, the men at the front working under cover of movable mantlets (*musculos ductiles*). Through the covered gallery material was brought up for filling the ditch, and setting up a 'belfry' or movable tower, to command the besieged battlements. A mine was then driven in under the foundations of the great tower at the apex, the undermined building being supported in the mean time by pit-props. When all was ready the props were fired,

The outworks undermined. and a great piece of the wall came tumbling down, " swelling out . . . suddenly at an instant."[5] De Lacy then had nothing for it but to fire his buildings and retire across a drawbridge to the outer ward of the principal work, another fortress for the French to reduce. The labour of a regular siege however was saved them by the discovery of a weak spot in the fortifications, due to some recent works of King John. He had built a chapel abutting on the curtain or outer wall,[6] the vaulted basement of which was used as a store-house. This lower story had a window looking through the outer wall. A reconnoitring party having found that access to this aperture could be gained by a man standing on another man's shoulders on the brink of the ditch, boldly made their way into the underbuilding and established themselves there.

The outer bailey carried. An attempt to expel the intruders by fire turned against the besieged; the escaladers got possession of the drawbridge leading to the outwork, and admitted their friends in force.[7]
The English then had to fall back on the citadel, or inner ward of the

[1] *Fœdera*, I. 90. The letter ascribed to Innocent III. on the next page belongs to Innocent IV.

[2] Le Breton, 78 and 203–205. He appears to have been present during the siege.

[3] *Fœdera*, 90.   [4] Rigord, 57.   [5] Le Breton, 79, 206, 207 ; Isaiah xxx. 13.

[6] See Plan.   [7] " Funibus abruptis pontis versatilis " ; Le Breton, 79, 208, 209.

fortress, over which again towered the Keep. But the fate of a garrison left to its own resources, and too weak to attempt offensive operations can only be a question of time. Philip's engines succeeded in battering down a piece of wall contiguous to the gate of the citadel, Richard apparently having allowed the foss there to be spanned by a solid bridge capable of supporting any weight.[1] A storming party rushing in over-

Storm of the citadel

powered de Lacy and his gallant band, who struggled to the last, refusing to surrender. But their ransom-value protected their lives ; and some forty knights, and one hundred and twenty men-at-arms were carried off as prisoners of war (6th March). Of knightly rank only four had fallen during the siege.[2]

One month after the loss of Château Gaillard John bestirred himself to the extent of commissioning Hubert Walter, the Bishops of Ely, and Norwich,[3] and the Earls of Leicester, and Pembroke to treat for peace. But Philip who now had Normandy lying at his feet scouted all idea of terms, and asked sarcastically what had become of Arthur.[4] Lent and Easter fairly past, in May he led a fresh host into Normandy. Falaise

Further French conquests.

resisted for a week ; Domfront and Caen yielded without a struggle ; Bayeux, Coutances, Cherbourg, and Barfleur followed suit. Guy of Thouars, the latest husband of the Duchess Constance, who had been governing Brittany since Arthur's capture,[5] attacked and burned Mont-Saint-Michel ; sacked Avranches, and harried all the country up to Caen, where he joined forces with Philip. The King sent him back to reduce Pontorson, and Mortain ; while he himself completed the reduction of the East side of Normandy. By the end of the month only Rouen, Arques, and Verneuil still held out.[6] On the 1st June the men of Rouen signed a truce with Philip, agreeing to surrender if not relieved within thirty days. In answer to their appeals John told them, as he had

Surrender of Rouen.

told de Lacy, that they must help themselves. On the 24th of June, Rouen ' the unconquered city,' without waiting for the expiry of the truce, opened its gates, and Rolf's fair Duchy, wrung three centuries before from the weakness of Charles the Simple, again became part of the demesne of France.[7]

Normandy, no doubt, was lost " without one strong blow struck to save

---

[1] " Pons erat ex imo quo scandebatur in arcem Excisus saxo quem sic diviserat olim, Quando profundavit fossas, Richardus utrimque."

[2] Le Breton 79, 209; Rigord, 57; R. Wend. III. 180 ; Deville, *Château Gaillard,* 86–89.

[3] Eustace Bishop of Ely, had been chancellor in the late reign ; he was consecrated in 1198 ; Diceto, II. 159; John Gray, domestic chaplain to King John, was consecrated Bishop of Norwich in succession to John of Oxford in September 1200; *Id.* 169.

[4] R. Cogg., 144, 145.

[5] Guy had an infant daughter by Constance also named Constance, who was recognised as the heir, Eleanor being in captivity in England ; Norgate, II. 424, and note.

[6] Rigord, 57 ; and Le Breton 79, 80, both under the year 1203 ; R. Cogg., 145.

[7] Rigord, 57, 59 ; R. Cogg., *sup.*

t." It has been further suggested that "it was lost needlessly."[1] The ties
between England and Normandy, of course, were still strong ;
Loss of Normandy. but we have seen that even under the fighting Richard
Normandy was slipping away.[2] The separation from France
was too anomalous a state of things, too prejudicial to the interests of
the people to last. The men of double allegiance accepting the inevitable,
made submission to Philip to save their Norman estates.
England's gain. For the English the loss of Normandy was pure gain. Their
Kings " could no longer look on Normandy as their natural
home, but found themselves obliged to live face to face with their
people. . . . England began to be ruled more distinctly on natioual
principles, for English purposes and by Englishmen."[3] The fusion of
the races at last began to make real progress.

The tide of French conquest did not spend itself in Normandy.
Maine, Anjou, and Touraine were already won, all but Chinon and
Maine, Anjou, and Touraine gone. Loches, held, the former by Hubert de Burgh ; and the latter
by Gerard of Athys.[4] In Poitou John's Seneschal, Robert of
Turnham, with the help of the Gascon Savary of Mauléon,
strove to hold his ground against William des Roches and the Lusignans.
Savary on being liberated by John had joined him heart and soul. In
August, however, Philip mustered his forces for a third campaign. On
the 10th of the month Poitiers surrendered ; the Poitevin barons then,
with few exceptions, came forward to tender their allegiance
Some hold on Aquitaine. By the close of the autumn Niort, Thouars, and La Rochelle
were the only places remaining to John in Poitou. Further
South the Count of Angoulême was kept in tow by the family connexion ;
while beyond the Dordogne the wine-trade of Bordeaux, and the instincts
of the Gascon lords declared in favour of English suzerainty.[5] Balance
of power was pre-eminently a feudal doctrine. The younger Bertran de
Born laments the days of King Richard whom his father had persistently
attacked.[6]

Queen Eleanor had not lived to witness the loss of her inheritance.

---

[1] Bishop Stubbs, W. Coventry, II. xxxv.

[2] According to the writer of the *Mareschal*, II. 89, John lost the hearts of the Normans
through the licence of his mercenaries under Lupecaire or ' Lovrekaire,' as he gives
the name. [3] Bishop Stubbs, *sup.*, xxxvii.

[4] R. Cogg., 146. Mr. Round in his *Calendar* identifies Athie or Athys with the
present Authie in Calvados.

[5] Rigord 59 ; Le Breton, *Philipp.* 214-217 ; R. Cogg., 146, 147 ; Wendover, III. 181 ;
Norgate, II. 426 ; Chron. Saint-Aubin.

[6] See the passage given by Pauli, I. 316, from Raynouard, *Choix.* IV. 201.

> " Por que tota Guiana plaing
> Lo rei Richard, q'en deffenden
> En mes mant aur et mant argen ;
> Mas acest (*this one*, i.e. John) no m'par n'aia soing."

She passed away at Poitiers on the 1st April,[1] being about 82 years old.

Death of Queen Eleanor. a most wonderful woman. A beauty in her youth, and throughout life a keen politician,[2] she had outlived both her husbands, most of her children, and several grandchildren. Fifty years had elapsed since her " political meddling " had troubled the

Her career. mighty hosts of the Second Crusade ; while only four years before her death she had journeyed to Castile to establish a granddaughter in marriage. In her long career sixteen years of captivity " appear but an episode." [3]

It would seem that during the autumn Philip, to strengthen his position, had effected an alliance, expressly aimed at England, with Henry Duke of Louvain, and his brother-in-law Reginald of Boulogne.[4] Rumours of

Alarm of invasion. impending invasion became rife in England.[5] John took advantage of the panic to raise an army for the recovery of his lost possessions. On the 3rd April 1205 writs were issued requiring the military tenants to provide forces for the defence of the

Call for troops. realm on the footing of one fully equipped man-at-arms being provided by every ten knights' fees, the men sent out to receive pay at the rate of 2s. a day, double the usual amount. The men were directed to be in London three weeks after Easter, to await orders, again, 'for the defence of the realm.' Further provisions called for mass levies in case of the actual landing of foreigners. The writs refer to the previous consent of the Magnates ; we must therefore suppose that they had been summoned to some Grand Council of which no record seems to have been preserved.[6] We next hear of an actual Grand Council held at Northampton, after Easter,[7] presumably 21st–25th May, when the King was at Northampton.[8] Some modification

---

[1] Ann. Waverley ; R. Cogg., 144. Her death was known in England on the 15th April, when John issued an Act of Grace to all criminals in prison for the good of her soul. *Id.* 90. Her death at Poitiers is recorded by the Angers chronicle of Saint-Aubin, the year being omitted, but the concurrent events showing it to be 1204. The death at Beaulieu Abbey (barely founded yet) given by Matthew Paris in his *Hist. Angl.*, II. 102, seems due to a careless copying of the original entry in the *Chron. Maj.*, II. 488, where a reference to the founding of the abbey follows the notice of Eleanor's death.

[2] " Admirabilis domina pulchritudinis et astuciæ," M. Paris, H. A. II. 102.

[3] See Bishop Stubbs' sketch, W. Cov., II. xxix., where he holds that the imputations on her conjugal fidelity in Palestine really grew out of her divorce, which, as we have seen was in fact a separation by consent. " The divorce was the origin not the result of the accusations."

[4] Reginald was married, as her fourth husband, to Ida eldest daughter of Matthew of Boulogne by Mary daughter of King Stephen ; the Duke was married to her sister Matilda. See Hoveden, II. 131 ; Ben. P., I. 269, and notes.

[5] R. Cogg., 148.

[6] *Fœdera*, I. 92. For remarks on the writ see *Select Charters*, 272.

[7] R. Cogg., 152.

[8] *Itinerary.*

of the plans may have been agreed to, as from Northampton the King
went to Porchester (there 31st May) to muster a considerable army;[1]

Service abroad resisted. with shipping collected for transport abroad. But the proposal to take the forces over-sea met with strenuous opposition from the Barons, Hubert Walter and William Marshal being put forward as spokesmen.[2] Their remonstrances are represented as based on the risky and impracticable character of the enterprise; but one is inclined to surmise that the constitutional objection that the force had been granted for home defence may have come into play also. A less pleasing suggestion is this, that William Marshal may not have been the only English baron who, to save his estates in Normandy, had become Philip's ' man.'[3] After a long struggle, the actual shipment of stores and munitions having begun,[4] John was forced to give way: but as a compromise he was allowed to send detachments, under a natural

Succour to La Rochelle. son Geoffrey, and the Earl of Salisbury, for the relief of La Rochelle. Then a fresh wrangle ensued over the King's proposal that the men allowed to go home should find the pay for the men going out. The discontent at the trouble and expense already incurred for nothing was great and general; but the loudest in their complaints were the unfortunate seamen who, after being summoned from far and near, were dismissed without compensation.[5]

Mortified and depressed John left the coast for Winchester on the 11th June, returning in a whimsical manner next day; when, as if to put his subjects to shame, he embarked, and put out to sea to beat about the coast for three days, and then returned to land at Studland on the Dorsetshire coast.[6] But for want of succour by the end of the month Loches and Chinon had been stormed, and Robert of Turnham and Hubert de Burgh were prisoners in Philip's hands.[7]

[1] "Cum maximo et nobili exercitu"; "nunquam copiosior exercitus"; R. Cogg., 152, 154.

[2] R. Cogg., *sup.* "Prohibente sibi Cantuariensi archiepiscopo et multis aliis"; Wend. III. 182. "Consilio Huberti et magnatum Angliæ complurimorum"; Ann. Waverley; so too Ann. Margan.

[3] See the *Mareschal*, II. 103-114, where Marshal's objection to serve in Poitou is based purely and simply on the fact that he had done homage to Philip. John in return took the Earl's eldest son as hostage.

[4] R. Cogg. John paid visits to Portsmouth, doubtless superintending the shipment, June 5th–9th; *Itin.*

[5] R. Cogg., 152-154.

[6] *Id.*; R. Wend. *sup.* 13th–15th June; *Itin.*

[7] Cogg., 152, 154; Wendover, *sup.* Rigord, 59; Chron. Saint-Aubin, 53, 54, the number of the year being again omitted; Le Breton, *sup.* During Turnham's captivity Savary of Mauléon was appointed Seneschal of Poitou. Rot. Pat., I. 49.

CHAPTER XXV

A.D. 1205–1209

Death of Archbishop Hubert Walter—Struggle over the appointment of a successor—
England laid under Interdict and the King excommunicated

ON the 13th July (1205) Archbishop Hubert Walter, the able administrator and diplomatist, the faithful Prime Minister, passed away
at his manor of Teynham, in Kent.[1] He is described as a

Death of Archbishop Hubert Walter. man of fine presence, pure life, and general capacity, but not
an orator.[2] His career exhibits him as a shrewd, tactful man
of business; one who sought the interests of his country, not
those of his mere order: whatever his hand found to do it did

His character thoroughly. Even the great Glanville by whom he was
brought up bowed to his judgment. In Palestine his military per-
formances excited Richard's admiration. His ability as a

and career. ruler was shown most conspicuously in the prompt reduction
of England to order after Richard's capture. When the Archbishop
landed the whole country was in a turmoil; at his appearance everything
fell into place again. With Richard his relations had been most cordial,
and his influence unbounded.

John at his accession appointed him Chancellor; but the King's wilful-
ness chafed at any controlling influence; and a man of Hubert's

Measures to standing and character could not fail to exercise influence.
be attributed When informed of the death of the Archbishop John did not
to him. attempt to conceal his sense of relief.[3] If we are not mistaken
Hubert's administration has left more enduring marks on our institutions
than is commonly understood. To him we would ascribe the legal
measures of Richard's time, such as the regulations for empanelling of
grand juries, and the institution of Coroners and Conservators of the Peace:
to him also credit must surely be given for the great series of Chancery

[1] Gervase, II. 413 (*Act. Pontt.*) ; R. Cogg, 165; Wendover, III. 183.

[2] Gervase, *sup.*, 406; "Non eloquio pollens."

[3] Wendover, 183. Paris in his *Hist. Angl.*, II. 104, makes John exclaim : " Nunc
primum sum rex Angliæ." For a passing jar between John and Hubert, see Gervase,
sup. 410.

Records that sprang into existence while he held the Great Seal. The Charter Rolls, Patent Rolls, Close Rolls, and others were all started during that period. Like Becket Hubert kept an almost regal household; and like him was taxed with being jealous of power and emolument.[1] More successful in litigation than his predecessor he recovered for Canterbury Rochester Castle, the de Ros and de Clare fiefs, and other possessions,[2] for which Becket had struggled, and struggled in vain. We have noticed the Synod held by Hubert at York in 1195 (above 343). Another set of very instructive canons were passed by him at Westminster in September, 1200.[3] But essentially a statesman he was deficient in scholarship and theological learning.[4] On the day after his death he was laid in his tomb at Canterbury.[4]

At successive vacancies in the Primacy we have seen the Canterbury monks striving to give substantial effect to the form of canonical election introduced by William the Conqueror.[6] The utmost concession that they had ever obtained was that of taking their choice among names laid before them by the King. In no case had they carried a man of their own against the Royal will. In 1173, no doubt, they had induced Henry II. to accept Prior Richard, a man not originally suggested by him: in 1191 at a meeting held before the day of election named in the King's writ they had chosen Reginald Bishop of Bath, again a man not proposed by the King. But the election came to nothing, as Reginald died within a few days, and before consecration. On the present occasion the monks went greater lengths than ever in their efforts to defeat the royal prerogative. A section of them, without waiting for any writ at all, held a secret meeting, and agreed upon a list with the names of three men, namely the Prior, the Sub-prior, and the Precentor, pledging themselves to accept the man who should eventually obtain most votes in full assembly. Two days after Hubert's death John hastened to Canterbury to look after the late Primate's effects.[7] The proceedings of the monks transpiring the suffragan bishops of the Province, who had usually concurred in the 'election' of archbishops, came forward to assert their position. They appealed to Rome against the action of the monks; the latter, of course entering a

The Canterbury Monks and the Primacy.

---

[1] R. Cogg. 160.   [2] Gervase, *sup.* 411.   [3] Diceto, II. 169.

[4] For a survey of his career see Gervase, II. 406–414 ; and Bishop Stubbs, *Memorials of Richard*, II. cxiv.–cxvii.

[5] Gervase, 413.

[6] Dr. Lingard, II. 155, misrepresents the legal state of the case by asserting that the kings at their coronation promised "to maintain the immunities of the Church, among which was numbered the right claimed by the chapters of choosing their prelates." The coronation oath contained no such promise : the king only swore to hold Church and people in good peace. The supposed promise to maintain the immunities of the Church was an invention of the monastic writers.

[7] 15th July ; *Itinerary.*

counter-appeal against the bishops, and claiming the sole right of election for themselves.   Subsequently, however, it was said that they were induced to agree to withdraw their appeal, and to hold an election in concert with the bishops.[1]   Nevertheless in violation of this pledge, if it really was given, they went on to hold a private election of their own, when the majority of votes fell to the Sub-prior Reginald.   He was immediately sent off to Rome in quest of confirmation, with

A secret election. strict injunctions as to secrecy.   But the man's vanity proved too much for his prudence, and as soon as he had crossed the Channel he gave himself out as the Elect of Canterbury, exhibiting his credentials.[2]   With respect to the participation of the bishops it would seem that in strictness they had no right to any.   Nothing of the sort is heard of in connexion with ' elections ' at York.   The intervention of the suffragans at Canterbury is first heard of in connexion with the appointment of William of Corbeil in 1122, having been, as we believe, introduced by Henry I. as a useful counterpoise to the action of the monks, as indeed it proved to be.[3]   But without doubt an assent on their part had become usual.   Meanwhile the monks, or some of them, becoming alarmed at the possible consequences of their action, offered to drop Reginald, and hold a fresh election.   John gave a willing assent, recommending

Counter-election. to their notice John Gray, Bishop of Norwich, one of his confidential agents.   On the 10th December the King came to Canterbury, and on the next day, being a Sunday, the monks in his presence elected Gray.   John put him in possession of the temporalities, also writing at once to Innocent to notify the ' election.'[4]   This step was followed up by the despatch on the 20th December of an embassy, that included six monks from Canterbury, charged to support the

Appeals to Rome. cause of the Bishop of Norwich.[5]   Confirmation by the Pope was of course usual and necessary, as he alone could confer the Pallium, the seal of an archbishop's investiture.   But it is clear that both the bishops in disputing the validity of a canonical election on the mere ground that it had been held without their concurrence ; and the King in contending for an election held in derogation of a prior election, and in his actual presence, would have considerable difficulties to contend with at Rome.

---

[1] So Peter of Englesham, the Bishops' agent, informed the Pope.

[2] See Innocent's account of the statements laid before him, *Epp*. VIII. 161, and again IX. 34.   For the current popular account see Wendover, III. 183, 184.

[3] Dr. Lingard inverts the relation of the bishops to the king. "the king always confederated with the bishops." In fact, the bishops always supported the king's nominee.

[4] Wendover, III. 184, 185 ; *Itinerary* ; and especially John's letter dated 11th December 1205 ; Rot. Pat., I. 56.   The King alleged that before the election both parties had renounced their appeals in his presence.   This statement was repeated to the Pope by the Archdeacon of Richmond, one of John's envoys.   [5] Rot. Pat., I. 57.

John was not so engrossed with the Canterbury question as to forget his lost dominions. Thouars, Niort, and La Rochelle were still his.

The Viscount Amaury was calling for help. At Thouars, **The lost dominions.** in the North of Poitou, he found himself in a very isolated position. He had been working with his brother Guy, Regent of Brittany on behalf of his, Guy's infant daughter Constance, to bring him round to John's side.[1] Philip met his manœuvres by capturing and demolishing Guy's castle of Brissac on the Loire, from thence paying visits to Angers and Nantes, and making all safe in those quarters.[2] Meanwhile John, having, as we may suppose, come to terms with his English barons, was mustering in considerable force at Portsmouth **Expedition to Aquitaine.** (21st–23rd May, 1206). On the 1st June he was at Yarmouth in the Isle of Wight, preparing to sail; on the 8th he signs at La Rochelle.[3]

In Aquitaine we hear that John received a hearty welcome; that the natives flocked to his standard; and that with their help he subdued 'no inconsiderable tract of territory.'[4] He remained no doubt on Gaulish soil for full six months, moving about without encountering direct opposition. But his itinerary shows that for the first three months at any rate his peregrinations were confined within the limits of a line drawn from La Rochelle to Niort, and from thence Southwards to La Réole on the Garonne.

The great achievement of this period was the reduction of **Capture of Bourg.** Bourg on the Gironde, which had become the head-quarters of Philip's partisans. The place was carried by storm on the 1st August after fifteen days of bombardment.[5]

Philip on hearing of John's landing had hastened to Poitou, where he set Chinon, Poitiers, and Mirebeau in order. Having made his Marches safe in that quarter he went back to 'France.'[6] The coast being thus clear John advanced to the Loire, marching on Nantes by way **Advance to the Loire.** of Montmorillon and Clisson. But Nantes was not prepared to receive the King; so he turned up the river to Chalonne, then, crossing by a ford he fell on Angers on the 6th September, sacking the town, and plundering even the churches. At Angers he remained, pushing raids into Anjou and Brittany, till the 21st September, when he fell back on Thouars, Philip being then reported as coming to the rescue.[7]

---

[1] Rigord 60; Le Breton; Sismondi *France*, VI. 240.

[2] May; Chron. Saint-Aubin.

[3] R. Wendover, III. 186, 187; *Itinerary.*

[4] "Partem sibi non modicam terræ illius subjugavit," Wend. *sup.* So too the Angevin Chron. of Saint-Aubin.

[5] So the Chron. Saint-Aubin, correcting Wendover, *sup.*, who gives the place taken as Montauban. John was never near Montauban; while the *Itin.* shows him at Bourg 17th July–5th August.   [6] Rigord, 60.

[7] Chron. Saint-Aubin; *Itin.* John was at Thouars by the 3rd October.

Philip followed him to Thouars, offering battle. But no battle came of.
On the contrary, negotiations were opened, through which, on the 5?

Truce for two years. October, a truce for two years from the 13th was sworn.
Each King would retain the allegiance of the men who had
actually sided with him in the war, but no right to any lands
or allegiance North of the Loire would be recognised in John.[1]

John returned to La Rochelle to spend the autumn at the sea-side. In
December he sailed to England, landing apparently at Wareham, as on the
13th of the month[2] he signs at Beer-Regis, a few miles inland.

In dealing with the double election at Canterbury the Pope gave a
decision that might well have been anticipated. The agents of both

The Pope's orders. parties having laid their cases before him he writes to the
monks on the 30th March 1206 reproving them indignantly
for their vacillation in submitting to hold a second election,
and venturing to meddle with a matter under the consideration of the
Holy See. With respect to Gray's election he quashes that summarily,
as having been made after appeal, and under undue influence. With
respect to the election of the Sub-prior he expresses himself as being left
in doubt by the conflicting statements that he had received. But it is
pretty clear that he had made up his mind as to how he would act,
because, while ordering the Bishop of Rochester and the Abbot of St.
Augustine's to take evidence as to the past proceedings at Canterbury, he
directs the Monks, the Bishops, and the King to send delegates to Rome
by the 1st October, with all necessary powers for holding a valid
canonical election.[3] In requiring all parties to send representatives the

His intentions. Pope was preparing for a bold stroke, for which probably
nobody was prepared. The Papacy has seldom missed an
opportunity of pushing an advantage, and Innocent was not
the man to be false to that tradition. On the 26th May John in answer

John's action. to the Pope's letter of the 30th March accredited Thomas of
Erdington and Anfrid of Dene, as his representatives, but
without any special powers: at the same time he begs His Holiness to
respect the prerogatives enjoyed by himself and his ancestors in the matter
of appointments to Canterbury and other cathedral churches.[4] But along

---

[1] "Ita tamen quod . . . ultra Ligerim . . . non remanebit nobis (sc. Johanni)
terra, homo, vel imprisius per hanc treugam"; *Fœdera* I. 95; Rigord, *sup.*

[2] *Itin.* Wendover gives the landing as on the 12th December at Portsmouth, the
place being clearly wrong

[3] See the Pope's letters to the various parties; *Epp.* IX. 34, 35, 36, 37; Bishop
Stubbs, W. Cov. II. li.

[4] "Destinamus ad pedes sanctitatis vestræ latores presentium, rogantes quatenus
dignitates nostras quas nos et patres nostri habuimus super provisionibus tam ecclesiæ
Cantuariensis quam aliarum cathedralium sedium integras et illæsas conservare velitis, et
ecclesiæ Anglicanæ et Regno in arcto positis paterna provisione providere"; Rot. Pat.
I. 65; Lingard.

with their credentials John gave his agents letters of credit for large sums of money to be used in bribing the Papal officials.[1] But that would not be an out of the way proceeding. As a bit of "secret history" Matthew Paris tells us that John assured the Canterbury delegation that he would accept any man elected by them, at the same time binding them by an oath to elect no man but Gray.[2] With respect to this allegation, on the truth or falsehood of which our judgment on the conduct of the parties must largely depend, it must be said that it does not appear to be borne out by any documentary evidence, certainly not by John's letter of the 26th May; and that Paris himself in his later work modifies his statement, simply representing the King as charging the monks to consent to no election but that of Gray.[3]

Innocent's decisions were not published till the 20th December. The appointment of Gray had already been disposed of. There remained however two questions, one between the convent and the suffragans as to the right of election; the other between the Prior and the Sub-prior, both of whom claimed to have been elected. Dealing first with the broad question of the right of election he declared, no doubt rightly on strict canonical grounds, that it appertained to the monks, and to the monks alone; and he forbade the bishops ever again to interfere.[4] With respect to the election of the Sub-prior he found himself obliged to condemn it for irregularity, secrecy, and haste. The ground having been so far cleared, on the 21st December Innocent was able to announce that the monks at Rome had held an election, and had chosen a man suggested by himself, a personal friend, a man of the highest character and attainments, Stephen of Langton Cardinal Priest of St. Chrysogonus, "an Englishman and a scholar, not a monk, but also no courtier."[5]

The Pope's final decisions.

Cardinal Langton to be Archbishop.

We may take it that all these matters had not been settled in a day. The Pope admitted in his letters that considerable efforts had been made at Rome by the supporters of the rival claims of Reginald and Gray; and that the election of Langton was not obtained without difficulty.[6] Then it appears that the monks when first sounded on the subject had protested that the Royal assent, and the concurrence of the whole convent, were necessary; but that they had been silenced by the ready assertion that their powers were quite sufficient; and that no assent was needed for an election held at the Holy See.[7]

Papal trickery.

---

[1] Erdington and Dene had letters of credit for 3000 marks, of which they spent 2000 marks before they returned; Rot Pat. I. 65; Bishop Stubbs, W. Cov., II. li., liii.

[2] *Chron. Maj.*, II. 514.

[3] See *Hist. Angl.*, II. 111, where he omits the words of the earlier work, "ut quemcunque eligerent ipse acceptaret." I cannot see why John should give such a pledge.

[4] *Epp.*, IX. 205; Wendover, III. 188.

[5] Bishop Stubbs, W. Cov., II. lii.; Innocent, *Epp.*, IX. 106, 107, 21st December.

[6] "Post multas deliberationes," *Epp.*, 206.   [7] Wendover, III. 212-214.

Then the King's agents utterly refused to give the Royal assent, having doubtless no authority to agree to any election except that of Gray. Innocent therefore, who wished to keep up an appearance of strict legality, had to write to John for his assent, explaining however that it was not necessary.[1]

John, of course, had every justification for refusing. He had been palpably tricked out of his rights. It is impossible to suppose that either the powers given by him, or those given by the Canterbury convent had been conferred in contemplation of an absolutely fresh election at Rome, a proceeding of which nobody could have dreamed. The Pope had applied the letter of their instructions to a purpose never intended. In fact we shall find him complaining that the King had not given his agents 'sufficient' powers; i.e., powers to commit him to anything that the Pope might please to do. The right thing would have been to direct the holding of a fresh election in England. That of course would have meant the promotion of John Gray, and to that Innocent was utterly opposed. John however again showed his knack of putting himself in the wrong. He used rough language. Instead of confining himself to protests against the plain invasion of his prerogatives he ventured to take exception to Stephen Langton, as an obscure individual of whom he had **Royal assent refused.** never heard. He insisted on the promotion of the Bishop of Norwich, and failing that threatened to cut off all intercourse between England and Rome.[2] It would seem that the King's agents insisted that no proper request for his consent had ever reached their master, and that they begged Innocent to suspend further action till suitable application had been made. Innocent in his answer, after rebuking John for the tone of his language, vindicates Langton's position; he had attained to the Doctorate in the University of Paris both in Arts and Theology: he was a Prebendary of Notre Dame in Paris, and St. Peter's York; John had written thrice to him since his promotion to the Cardinalate, regretting that he could not have his services in England. As for applications to the King for his assent he had evaded receiving them. Monks sent with letters to him had been arrested at Dover : but no assent of his was really needed, and no further steps to gain his concurrence would be taken. He, Innocent, would not swerve from his purpose; and he urges the King to render him due honour, 'and so earn more fully God's goodwill and the Pope's,'[3] lest worse should befall him.[4]

---

[1] *Epp.*, IX. 206 ; Wend. *sup.* Innocent suggests that John should say that he had assented from the first (!) *Ib.* c. 1045 (Migne).

[2] See the summary of the letter given by Wendover, III. 215, 216, with the further points reflected in the Pope's answer, *Id.*, 216–219. Erdington and Dene who took John's letter out received their credentials on the 20th February, 1207, with letters of credit for 2000 marks, and a charge not to spend them unless sure of the result ; *Rot. Pat.*, l. 69. Stubbs.   [3] " Ut gratiam divinam et nostram uberius merearis."

[4] Wendover, 216–218. The letter is not known from any other source ; Luard.

Innocent was as good as his word. On the 17th June, being then at Viterbo, he consecrated Langton.[1] John was furious. Cursing the monks

Consecration of Langton. as the authors of all the annoyance, on the 11th July he ordered Fulk Cantilupe and Reginald of Cornhill to seize all their property.[2] Three days later the monks left Canterbury in a body, to find a refuge at St. Omer, in the

Expulsion of the monks. great monastery of St. Bertin.[3] The archiepiscopal estates were also taken into hand, and all appeals to Rome (*placita domini Papæ*) forbidden.[4]

A tax voted at Oxford in February (1207) marks a distinct stage in the history of our national finance, and a step towards the system of subsidies,

A tax on rents and movables. a mode of taxation destined shortly to become the mainstay of the Revenue. The first precedent had been set by the Saladin Tithe of 1188;[5] followed by Innocent's Fortieth for Holy Land in 1200.[6] A beginning in the way of raising money in this manner for secular purposes was made in 1203, on John's return from Normandy, when we heard of the exaction of one seventh of their movables from the Barons. The impost then, however, was described as a mere arbitrary fine for desertion. On the present occasion the procedure took a more constitutional shape. A demand for a contribution from clergy and laity was laid before a Grand Council held at Westminster on the 8th January. In consequence of the opposition of the clergy the assembly was adjourned to the 9th February, to meet at Oxford. The sitting apparently was held on the 11th, the King having only reached Oxford on the 10th.[7] The clergy still withholding their consent, the grant officially announced was that of a thirteenth, or twelve pence on the mark, of all rents and movables from the laity.[8] Nevertheless, it clearly appears that the clergy, after all, were forced to contribute. Archbishop Geoffrey of York again protested energetically, and eventually left the Kingdom for Rome; but not till he had denounced an excommunication on all who should venture to meddle with the clergy of his Province.[9] Of course his temporalities were again taken into hand, a fresh challenge to Innocent.

The Pope did not shrink from the struggle. Already, on the 27th August, on hearing of the expulsion of the monks from Canterbury, he had written

---

[1] Wendover, 213; see the announcement to the Convent, Wilkins, *Conc.*, I., 518; dated 24th June (reading VIII. Kal. Julii).   [2] Rot. Pat., I. 74; Stubbs.

[3] Wendover, 215.   [4] Ann. Waverley, 259.   [5] Above, 236 and Ben. P., II. 30.

[6] Diceto, II. 168; R. Cogg., 116.   [7] Ann. Waverly, *Itin.*

[8] *Fœdera*, I. 96; Ann. Waverley.

[9] Rot. Pat., I. 72; Wendover, III. 209, 210; Ann. Winton, Dunstable, and Bermondsey; Ann. Margan, A.D. 1206; and *esp.* the letter of Innocent giving the whole history of the matter, *Epp.*, XI. 87; Bishop Stubbs, W. Cov., II. lxix. Dunstable paid 100 marks besides the Sheriff's commission (præter munera vice-comitis). But the Pipe Rolls again ignore the impost.

to the Bishops of London, Ely, and Worcester[1] to use their influence with the King to induce him to receive Langton; ordering them, in case of his refusal, to impose an Interdict.   But he tells them to remind

An Interdict threatened. John that he had stood by him in former times of trouble, and had incurred odium through so doing.[2]   On the 18th November he writes to the bishops of England and Wales in general, reminding them of the paramount duty of obedience; and warning them not to show themselves lukewarm (*tepidos*), or afraid of persecution in the cause of the 'liberty of the Church:'[3] the English Barons are urged to show their true loyalty to the King's best interests by turning him from the courses of a Rehoboam, offensive to God (*contra Deum*).   Wales must be included in the Interdict if it should be laid on.[4]   A month later he directs the Bishops of Worcester, Ely, and Hereford to insist on amends being made to Geoffrey, again under pain of Interdict.[5]

John did not entirely ignore the Papal demands.   On the 21st January, 1208, he sent a brief note to the Bishops of London, Ely, and Worcester

A shuffling offer. saying that he was prepared to obey the Pope's mandate relative to the Church of Canterbury,[6] transmitted by them, 'saving his prerogatives and those of his heirs.'   What John meant by this last reservation it is not easy to say, unless it was to stipulate that the case should not be made a precedent.   Most likely it was a mere shuffle; but he clung to it at an audience given on the 12th March to Simon Langton, who, according to the King, refused all concession, declaring that his brother's reception must be unconditional.[7]   We also hear of an interview with the three Bishops, and a last appeal to the King's piety to induce him to submit; accompanied, however, by formal notice of the day on which, failing submission, the Interdict would come into operation.   John lost all self-control, swearing by God's teeth[8] that if they, the Bishops, or any other men, dared to lay his lands under

Frantic threats. Interdict the whole ecclesiastical community of England would be sent packing off to Rome; messengers from Italy venturing to land would have their eyes torn out.   With that he ordered them out of

---

[1] The Bishop of London was William of Sainte-Mère Eglise (Manche), an official much employed by Richard in Revenue work, and appointed Bishop in 1199.   The Bishop of Worcester was Mauger, appointed in 1200; the Bishop of Ely was Eustace, the ex-Chancellor.   The first and the last, and probably all three, were Frenchmen.

[2] *Epp.*, X. 113; Wilkins, *Conc.*, I. 519.   [3] *Epp.*, X. 159.   [4] *Id.*, 160, 161.

[5] *Id.*, 172.   The Bishop of Hereford was Giles of Braose, son of William, appointed in 1200.

[6] "Quod parati sumus obedire domino Papæ . . . et mandatum ejus super negotio Cantuariensis ecclesiæ . . . implere"; *Fœd.*, I. 99.

[7] "Dixit nobis quod nichil inde faceret."   So John in a proclamation to the men of Kent, *Fœd.*, I. 100.

[8] The *Mareschal*, II. 109, gives us this John's favourite oath, as he would utter it, "Par les denz Dieu."

his presence.[1] That John had been warned of the exact date at which the Interdict would begin appears from the fact that on the 18th March he issued prospective orders for the confiscation of the property of all clergy who should refuse to perform Divine Service from and after the 24th of the month, the appointed day.[2]

On Passion Sunday, 23rd March, the dread sentence was at last fulminated, to take effect from the morrow.[3] From that time throughout England and Wales the altars would be stripped, the church

Interdict proclaimed. doors closed, and all public ministrations of the sacraments would cease, except baptism of infants, and the viaticum to the dying. Most trying of all to the feelings of the age would be the burial of their dead, like lost malefactors, in silence and on unconsecrated ground.[4] Marriages, however, and the churching of women would be performed in the porch of the church ; and sermons might be preached on Sundays in the churchyards.[5] In the following year Innocent intimated some further concessions. With regard to chrism, or the special holy oil used in baptism and confirmation, if by reason of the Interdict new chrism could not be made as usual on Maundy Thursday, the old chrism might be eked out by the admixture of unconsecrated oil ; while he further gave out that he might not object to the performance of Low Mass within closed doors in privileged Houses once a week.[6] On the other hand the Cistercians who had ventured openly to disregard the Interdict were sharply taken to task, and ordered to conform.[7] The object of an Interdict of course was to impress the people with a sense of being in the land under a curse, abhorred of God and forsaken. But the reckless use of their spiritual weapons made of late by the clergy, either in their squabbles among themselves, or their struggles to assert the 'liberty' of the Church must have greatly impaired the terrors of excommunication and Interdict.

The three Bishops of London, Ely, and Worcester having executed their dangerous mandate fled from the wrath to come. Their example was followed by Joscelin of Bath, Giles of Hereford, Herbert

Flight of the bishops. le Poer of Salisbury, and Gilbert Glanville of Rochester, the two last retiring to Scotland, with John's leave.[8] Geoffrey of York was already in exile ; Chichester, Exeter, and Lincoln were

---

[1] Wendover, III. 221 ; *cnf.* Ann. Waverley. [2] *Fœdera*, I. 100.

[3] W. Cov., II. 199 ; R. Cogg, 163 ; Ann. Wav., Winton and Dunstable. Wendover mixes up the two days, giving the Monday as the 23rd March (X. Kal. April) and Paris in both works copies him faithfully.

[4] Innocent, *Epp.*, X. 113 ; R. Wend., 222. For the formula of Interdict see Martene, *Thesaurus* IV. 147.[5] So Ann. Dunstable. Holy bread and water might also be distributed.

[6] *Epp.*, XI. 102 *bis*, 214 ; W. Cov., II. 201.

[7] W. Cov., 199 ; Innocent, *Epp.*, XI. 141, 259, 260.

[8] Wendover, III. 223 ; Ann. Waverley and Dunstable ; *Fœdera*, I. 100. The Bishops of Worcester and Hereford did not retire at once ; the Bishop of Bath is found again at court by the end of the year. Rot. Cart. ; *Fœdera.*

vacant ; Philip of Durham died in April ; and Geoffrey of Coventry was probably in failing health, as he died in October.   Of the whole episcopate apparently only two remained to support the King, namely John Gray of Norwich and the recently appointed Bishop of Winchester, Peter des Roches.[1]

It was to be expected that the possessions of the absconding prelates would be seized, and their relations persecuted.   But John with his usual **Persecution of the clergy.** recklessness at once proceeded to declare war against the whole ecclesiastical community, monks, parish priests, and all, taking their temporalities into hand, and putting them on pittances[2] The parochial clergy who were married, or had housekeepers (*focariæ*) living with them were forced to redeem them.[3]   The confusion and alarm created were such that at the end of a few days John found it necessary to issue a proclamation forbidding the clergy to be molested or annoyed in word or deed.[4]   Yet we hear that a highwayman on the Welsh March having robbed and murdered a priest, the King said, ' Let him go ; he has only killed one of my enemies ! '[5]

Towards barons suspected of sympathising with the clergy John acted with equal violence, exacting hostages from them, a monstrous practice **The Laity and the Interdict.** peculiar to himself of which we have already heard.   One case perhaps not specially connected with the quarrel with Innocent excited wide-spread interest.   William de Braose the lord of Brecknock, ranked for territiory and connexions among the greatest of the land.   His eldest son was married to a daughter of William Marshal the Earl of Pembroke; one daughter was married to Walter de Lacy: **Case of De Braose.** two others to magnates of equal rank.   The Earl of Derby was his sister's son.[6]   Braose had been a great supporter of King John, and much favoured by him.   In 1200 he had been appointed Sheriff of Herefordshire, with a grant of all lands that he could conquer from the Welsh.   He had also received a grant of lands in Munster, for which he was to pay 5000 marks by ten yearly instalments.   In 1201 he had received the Honour of Limerick, but without the city.[7]   He had been with John at the relief of Mirebeau, and Arthur had fallen into his hands, to be surrendered by him to the King.[8]   It is therefore only natural

---

[1] Peter, a Poitevin of high connections and military reputation (vir equestris ordinis et in rebus bellicis eruditus, Wend.. III. 181), who had been chaplain to John (Rot. Cart., I. 34), had been appointed Bishop in 1205 and consecrated at Rome by Innocent, Wend., *Reg. Sacrum.*

[2] Lingard, II. 159 ; and Close Rolls (Hardy), 107. cited Coxe.

[3] Wendover, 223 : Ann. Waverley.   See also R. Cogg., 163 ; W. Coventry, II. 199.

[4] 11th April, *Fœdera*, I. 101.   [5] Wendover. *sup.*

[6] See Gilbert, *Viceroys of Ireland.* 67, 68.

[7] See *Fœdera*, I. 83, and John's statement, *Id.* 107 ; also Mr. Round's article in the *Natl. Dicty.* and Hoveden, IV. 152.

[8] John's letter given, R. Cogg., 138.

to suppose that the young Duke's fate weighed on his mind;[1] but he remained at Court during the year, while in 1205 Grosmount, Skenfreth, and White Castle were conferred upon him.[2] Not long afterwards however, he fell into disgrace. According to an explanatory

The King's story. statement subsequently published by the King their differences simply arose from proceedings to enforce the payment of the 5000 marks, of which it is clear that only 700 marks had been paid by 1207.[3] Through the mediation of friends de Braose was allowed to come to Hereford, and make his peace on surrendering his castles of Hay, Brecknock, and Radnor (November, 1207). Still he paid nothing. When the Interdict was laid on his younger son Giles the Bishop of Hereford was one of the Pope's agents; but John admits that de Braose gave hostages when required.

From Roger of Wendover we hear that he was one of the suspect Barons of whom hostages were demanded, and that when the

Wendover's account. Royal officers appeared for that purpose his wife Matilda of Hay imprudently declared that no child of theirs should be entrusted to the hands of the murderer of Arthur. De Braose must soon have been driven to extremities, because after an ineffectual attempt at a rising, in which Leominster was sacked, he and his wife and all his family were forced to retire to Ireland—the old refuge—there

Flight of De Braose. to be received by their friends the Marshals and de Lacies.[4] Thus John was doing his best to bring the Barons into line with the clergy.

Still, as the Pope had other and sharper arrows in his quiver, the King could not afford to neglect a show of negotiation. Ten days

Hollow negotiations. after the promulgation of the Interdict, on the very day when the King modified his attitude towards the clergy, the Abbot of Beaulieu was instructed to go to Rome to say that the King was prepared to reinstate the Canterbury monks; to place the temporalities of the See in the hands of the Pope; and to receive Langton, but not as a friend.[5] This was the old difficulty of the kiss of peace; and John shirked conferring the temporalities with his own hands for the same reason, namely that it would involve receiving the Archbishop's homage. Innocent in answer urged John to confer the temporalities himself; but, as if to meet

[1] See Le Breton, *Philipp.*, 192. [2] Rot. Pat., I. 57.

[3] Pipe Roll, 8 John, m. 6; cited Round.

[4] Michaelmas. R. Wend., III. 224, 225; *Fœdera*, and Round, *sup.*; Brut. y T.; Ann. Wav. and Dunstable, and *Mareschal*, II. 125, 145–148, where it clearly appears that the fall of de Braose involved delicate questions of State, dangerous to speak of. The Earl of Pembroke had in 1206 with difficulty obtained leave to visit his estates in Ireland (*Id.* 115), and when he did go the King took another son, Richard, as hostage (119).

[5] "Nondum . . . ut familiarem eidem archiepiscopo gratiam exhiberes." So John's words quoted in the Pope's letter in answer; XI. 89.

E E

him half way, he authorised the three Bishops of London, Ely, and Worcester to receive the temporalities and confer them in his, Innocent's name; and also to relax the Interdict if John's offers were fulfilled.[1] Later in the year John issued safe-conducts to Simon Langton and the three Bishops to come to England; also one to Stephen himself, but only under the title of Cardinal.[2] The Archbishop therefore, naturally did not care to avail himself of the invitation. The Bishops did come over, and waited two months without being admitted to an audience.[3] As it was becoming clear that the King had no intention of keeping his word,[4] Innocent on the 12th January 1209 addressed him in terms amounting to an ultimatum. If the promises made by the Abbot of Beaulieu were not fulfilled within three months' time from the receipt of that letter, the King would stand and be excommunicate; and the three Bishops were ordered to promulgate and enforce the sentence.[5] But, as if still clinging to the hope of a peaceful solution, Innocent followed up his minatory letter with one written in gentler strains.[6] He also gave Langton authority to absolve the officers who had dispossessed the Canterbury monks.[7] But the three months came and went without any submission on John's part. The three Bishops, therefore, forced to act, entrusted the task of publishing the excommunication to their brethren in England— the King's men—who, of course, neglected the duty; and so for a while matters again remained in suspense. Towards August John, being on his way to the Scottish Border, sent invitations for the three Bishops to come to England to treat.[8] They came over, and had conferences at Canterbury with the King's agents, when terms were agreed upon, and a formal treaty signed. The compact being reported to John partial restitution was ordered to be made to Langton, and the Bishops of London, Ely, Worcester, and Hereford; £100 being allotted to each, by way of earnest. But the King intimated that he could not go the length of full restitution. To this the Bishops demurred, insisting on complete reinstatement, as under the treaty; failing that they threatened excommunication by the 6th October.[9] The term approaching the futile attempt to forestall the sentence was repeated. On the 2nd October Langton, with the Bishops of London, and Ely, landed at Dover under safe-conducts to meet the King at Canterbury. On the 8th the King, anticipating the movements

Marginal notes: Papal ultimatum. / Terms agreed upon / and then evaded.

---

[1] *Id.* also 90, and 91; 27th May; also 141, 22nd August. Full restitution is required.
[2] Rot. Pat., I. 82, 85, 86; Bishop Stubbs, *sup.*, lvi.
[3] Ann. Waverley.
[4] " Rex . . . se satisfacturum . . . spopondit ; sed minime tenuit ;" R. Cogg., 163.
[5] *Epp.*, XI. 211, 218 (12th and 13th January anno. XI.).
[6] *Epp.*, XI. 221, 23rd January, 1209.   [7] *Epp.*, XI., 216.
[8] Wendover, 229; Bishop Stubbs.
[9] Ann. Waverley, without date; August, Ann. Dunstable.

of the Prelates, advanced from Rochester to Chilham,[1] sending on the
Justiciar Geoffrey Fitz Peter and the Bishop of Winchester to impart certain
requirements. These doubtless involved the modifications of the treaty
already demanded by John, as we hear that Langton and the Bishops
refused, again insisting on entire fulfilment ; whereupon they were politely
escorted back to their ships, without having seen the King.[2]

**John excom-
municated.** In the course of November the excommunication was finally
published, but only in France, not in England.[3] The news no
doubt would soon cross the Channel. But John had guarded against the
possible consequences of the blow by calling for a general performance of
homage from his subjects ; even the Welsh gentry, to their great annoyance,
being brought to Woodstock for the purpose.[4] By Christmas

**The country
still loyal.** time it was generally known that the anathema had fallen on
the King's head ; but nevertheless we are told that at the
festivities at Windsor there was no falling off in the attendance of the
nobility.[5] The revenues of the vacant Sees and impounded Abbeys
enabled the King to dispense with direct taxation. The scutages, of
which so much has been made, though accompanied by arbitrary fines
" *ne transfretent*," really came to nothing ; all the big landowners being
systematically excused payment.[6] As during the Becket struggle the
chroniclers, afraid to speak, tell us nothing. The literary life of England,
at any rate, during the period was in a state of suspended animation.

[1] *Itinerary*.
[2] Ann. Waverley and Dunstable.
[3] Ann. Dunstable ; Florence, Cont. II. 168.
[4] Wendover, III. 227 ; W. Cov., II. 200 ; Ann. Winton. John was at Woodstock,
16th–19th October. *Itinerary*.
[5] Wend., 231.
[6] See Pipe Rolls, 8 and 9 John, *passim* and below.

CHAPTER XXVI

A.D. 1208–1210

The Interdict—Foreign affairs—Wales—Treaties with Scotland—Expedition to Ireland —The de Braose family

CUT off from Continental schemes John had been consoling himself by lording it over his vassels and neighbours at home. Llywelyn son of Jorwerth had been Prince of North Wales since 1194, when he ousted his uncle David, as already mentioned. In July 1201 he obtained recognition from John, who took his homage (through Fitz Peter), and confirmed him in all his holdings;[1] in 1205 he received a regrant of the £10 in Ellesmere previously enjoyed by his uncle David, with the castle;[2] while about the same time or a little later he received the hand of Johanna, a natural daughter of King John.[3] With Gwenwynwyn of Powys Llywelyn had continued pretty continuously at war. John had given some support to the former, doubtless as a counterpoise to the Prince of Gwynedd, as we find him in receipt of a pension of £13.[4] But in September 1208 he is charged with deforcing lands ; and thereupon we find John and Llywelyn joining hands against him, and seizing him at Shrewsbury, to be detained till he had given hostages for his good behaviour.[5] Llywelyn at once took advantage of this opportunity by occupying Powys. He then proceeded to attack the Princes of South Wales, Maelgwn and Rhys, sons of Rhys. It would seem that these men and their nephews Rhys and Owain, sons of Gruffudd son of Rhys, between them controlled perhaps all modern Cardiganshire, with the western parts of Caermarthenshire up to the line of the Towy ; Dynevor, Llangadog, and Llandovery being theirs. The nephews apparently had their portion in Caermarthenshire, the uncles in Cardiganshire. Llywelyn seized Aberystwith, taking Cardiganshire North of the Ystwith for himself—if indeed he was not

(marginal notes) Foreign affairs. Wales. Llywelyn and South Wales.

---

[1] *Fœdera*, I. 84. Llywelyn is not recognised as 'King,' only as 'Princeps.'

[2] Pipe Roll 9 John, m. Order for payment with arrears ; Rot., Pat, I. 51.

[3] *Fœdera*, 1. 102. See also Prof. Tout's article in the *National Dicty.* ; Rot. Cart., I, 147 ; Ann. Worcester.

[4] Pipe Roll, 5 John ; "Notts." [5] Rot. Pat., I. 86 ; *Brut y T.* 263 ; *Fœdera*, 101.

already in possession of it—giving the district between the Ystwith and the Aeron to the nephews ; and restricting the two uncles to Cardiganshire South of the Aeron.[1]   The ensuing struggles between the uncles and the nephews apparently brought John to the Welsh March early in 1209,[2] when it would seem that his support was given to the uncles, who in 1210 are found in friendly alliance with him ; while in the same year Gwenwynwyn was set free and reinstated in Powys.[3]

But to go on with the year 1209 ; from Shrewsbury John moved to the Northern Border, where William had given distinct provocation. A fort

Scotland. had been set up at Tweedmouth—apparently by Philip the late Bishop of Durham—as a counter-work to Berwick. The Scots, determined to have the control of the river in their own hands, had destroyed the fort once if not twice.[4]   A safe conduct for a conference on the matter was sent to the King of Scots.[5]   They met at Norham on the 23rd April ; but no agreement was effected.[6]   John then called out an army, and again appeared on the banks of the Tweed on the 3rd August. William took up his position at Roxburgh. The two armies being thus face to face terms were adjusted.   John agreed to acquiesce tacitly in the

A treaty. demolition of the Tweedmouth fort ; while William entered into a treaty by which he agreed to pay 15,000 marks (£10,000) by four half-yearly instalments, and to place his daughters Margaret and Isabel in John's hands[7]   But the King of Scots

Reciprocal concessions. did not make these concessions for nothing. His daughters were to be provided for in marriage ; the Scots maintaining that the understanding was that the Lady Margaret was to be married to John's eldest son.[8]   As matters turned out, however, we shall find her given to Hubert de Burgh, and her sister Isabel to Roger Bigod II., Earl of Norfolk.[9]   A further point agreed upon was this that William should

[1] *Brut y T.* under 1207.

[2] Ann. Wav. John was at Shrewsbury 26th-29th January, 1209 ; *Itinerary.*

[3] *Brut.* (under 1209).

[4] J. Fordun, 276, 277 ; Chron. Lanercost, 4. The ground of difference alleged by Trevet, namely that William was proposing to marry a daughter to Count Reginald of Boulogne, will not bear investigation. Reginald held the county in right of his wife Ida, and she lived till 1216 ; E. W. Robertson, *Scotland under Early Kings*, I. 418.

[5] 10th April, Rot. Pat., I. 91 ; Pauli ; Chron. Melrose ; *Itiny.*

[6] Chron. Melrose ; J. Fordun, *sup.* The *Itinerary* shows John at Alnwick on the 24th April, there being no entry for the 23rd.

[7] *Fœdera*, I. 103, where the notification of the treaty is dated 7th August at Northampton, clearly a misreading for Norham, as the *Itinerary* shows John at Fenwick in Northumberland on the 7th August, on his way Southwards ; see also J. Fordun ; and Chr. Melrose, *sup.* Mr. E. W. Robertson gives the names of the youths surrendered as hostages from the close Roll of the year f. 137 b   More than half of them are Anglo-Norman ; *Scotland under Early Kings*, I. 422.

[8] Fordun, *sup.*, and the allegation of King Alexander II. ; *Fœdera*, I. 233.

[9] Chron. Melrose, p. 138 ; Wyntoun, II. 229 ; *Complete Peerage*, etc.

surrender his English estates to be granted to his son.   This arrangement
was duly carried out, Alexander being invested and doing homage to John
in the course of the ensuing year.[1]   Years and infirmity, and the natural
wish to secure the succession of his youthful son induced William to
assume towards England an attitude not altogether pleasing to his subjects.
He had also in Moray and Ross the representative of a rival dynasty to
contend with, namely Guthred son of Donald Bane MacWilliam, who
claimed descent from Duncan the son of Malcolm Canmore by his first
wife Ingeborg, which Duncan himself had been King of Scotland for some
months in 1094.[2]   English support being thus of great importance
William again met John at Durham on the 2nd February 1212, the Queen
of Scots also being present.   The conference was adjourned to Norham ;

Further treaty. and there apparently about the 7th February a treaty was
sealed by which William granted to John the privilege of
marrying young Alexander, then in his fourteenth year, to
whomsoever he would at any time within the next six years, but always
'without disparagement.'   William also pledged himself on behalf of
himself and his son that whatever might happen to John 'they would

Allegiance to John's heir. bear faithful allegiance to John's son Henry as their liege
lord.[3]   Alexander then accompanied John to London, and
there, on Mid-Lent Sunday, 4th of March, received the honour
of knighthood at Clerkenwell where John was keeping the Festival.[4]
Sixty-three years before had old King David conferred the like honour on
John's father young Henry of Anjou.   But it must be admitted that these
transactions placed Scotland very much in the position of a vassal state ;
and so we shall find it treated by Pope Innocent III.

During the course of the year 1209 John had made praiseworthy

Ecclesiastical affairs. attempt to fill up his vacant sees.   Hugh Archdeacon of
Wells was appointed Bishop of Lincoln ; Henry Archdeacon
of Stafford being named for Exeter, Walter Grey the Chancellor for Coventry, and Nicholas of Laigle for Chichester.[5]   Hugh was
sent over to France with orders to seek consecration from the hands of
Walter of Coutances, the Archbishop of Rouen.   But it would seem that
Walter was already dead.[6]   Anyhow Hugh went to Stephen Langton and

[1] Fordun, *sup.*   Mr. E. W. Robertson, *Scotland under Early Kings*, I. 424, quotes
the Melrose Charter No. 168 as showing that the homage was rendered 10th May, 1210.
If so it cannot have been rendered to John in person, as he was at Odiham on that day.

[2] See *Foundations of England*, II. 178; Skene, *Celtic S.*, I. 476, 482; W. Coventry,
II. 206.

[3] "Tanquam ligio domino nostro . . . . fidem et fidelitatem tenebimus ;" *Fœdera*,
I. 104; Fordun, 278.   Alexander's seal was to be affixed after he was knighted, as till
then he would not be considered of age.

[4] Wendover, III. 238 ; Chron. Melrose ; Fordun, *sup.*

[5] Ann. Dunstable and Waverley.

[6] So Ann. Dunst.

was consecrated by him at Melun on the 20th December (1209). But John, incensed at the recognition of the Archbishop, refused to allow him to come home.[1] After that miscarriage the nominations to the other bishoprics were allowed to stand over.

Towards May 1210 we hear of fresh invitations to Langton to come over to meet the King, John's safe-conducts being backed up by the private guarantees of the chief men in the kingdom. On the 4th May John went down to Dover, hoping to meet the Archbishop, who had come to Witsand. But at the last Langton refused to cross the Channel. We are told that he was dissatisfied with the form of the safe-conducts. Probably he was again simply addressed as 'Cardinal.'[2]

But the great event of the year was a Royal expedition to Ireland,

Expedition to Ireland. giving occasion to extortionate demands for money from the clergy and the Jews. A scutage, no doubt, the eighth of the reign, was called for, but we have already seen that a scutage at this time did not count for much. John did not want to tax the

Taxation. Magnates unduly,[3] while the clergy having no bishops to protect them were very much at his mercy.[4] The object of this, John's first visit to the Dominion since 1185, was to punish the de Lacies, Walter and Hugh, sons of Hugh assassinated in 1186. After repeated struggles, the brothers in 1204 had finally got the better of John

De Courcy and the de Lacies. de Courcy, ousting him from his petty kingdom in Ulster.[5] For this service Hugh de Lacy was rewarded with the grant of de Courcy's Ulster (Antrim and Down), to be held as an earldom, the first creation of an English title in Ireland.[6] But in 1207 Walter de Lacy had the presumption to set up a 'new assize' (*Nova assisa*), *i.e.*, a private court of High Justiciary, with powers co-ordinate with, if not superior to those of the King's Court. John contented himself with protesting.[7] But this misdemeanour was followed by one that touched the King more nearly, namely, the harbour given to de Braose

De Braose. and his wife, who had stigmatised John as the murderer of Arthur. The Earl of Pembroke had shared this guilt. But by extraordinary prudence and tact; by prompt attendance at court when summoned; by ready delivery of sons as hostages; he had earned forgiveness.[8] In 1208 John Gray the Bishop of Norwich had been sent out in

[1] Wendover, III. 231 ; Florence, Cont. II. 168.
[2] Ann. Winton, Waverley, and Dunstable ; R. Cogg., 164.
[3] The scutage however was paid, partly to the King direct, partly into the Exchequer.
[4] R. Cogg., 163; W. Cov., II. 201, 202; Ann. Winton, Waverley, Margan, and Dunstable.
[5] Ann. Ulster (Macarthy) and Loch Cé.
[6] 29th May, 1205; Rot. Cart., I. 151. The supposed earlier creation of John de Courcy has no foundation.   [7] Rot. Pat. 72 ; and again 9 November 1207.
[8] For the intrigues of Meiler fitz Henry the Justiciar appointed by John in 1200, and Marshal's prudent conduct since his visit to Ireland in 1207, see *Mareschal*, II. 119–145.

pursuit of de Braose.[1] But he did not possess sufficient local influence t.
effect a capture ; and John had now to take the task in hand himself. I:

John again in Ireland. the course of June a flotilla was mustered in Milford Haver
on the 20th of the month the King landed at Crook ne:
Waterford.[2] In his train came the Earl of Pembroke, and
John de Courcy. The latter, after keeping aloof for some time had
finally submitted in 1205, and obtained restitution of a small estate i.
England.[3] He now came to enjoy the sight of the fall of his enemies.

From Crook John advanced by Kilkenny and Naas to Dublin. There he

Homages of natives. rested 28th–30th June, receiving homage from a train of native
chiefs, headed by Cathal O'Conor (O'Conchdebhair) King of
Connaught, and Donough (Donnchadh) O'Brien Prince of
North Munster. But the promptness of these men in coming to meet the
King of England must not blind us to their hostility to the 'Foreign'
settlement. The copious native annals can hardly bring themselves to
notice the presence of the Saxon King. John pressed on in pursuit of his
enemies through Trim and Kells to Carlingford, the de Lacies retiring
before him and firing their castles. From Carlingford he advanced by
Downpatrick—de Courcy's old seat—to Carrickfergus—where, at last,
de Lacy's men, making a stand, withstood his efforts for some days
(19th–28th June).[4] The reduction of Carrickfergus was followed by the

Siege of Carrick-fergus. welcome news that Matilda de Braose, as we may call her,
with a married daughter, wife of the son of Roger Mortimer,
her son the younger William and his wife, and his two sons,
had all been arrested in Scotland, and were in the hands of the King's
friend and ally Duncan of Galloway, recently created Earl of Carrick.
The de Lacies and the elder William were at large ; the latter having gone
back to Wales when John's coming to Ireland was announced ; while the
de Lacies made good their escape to France, there to remain for various
periods of time.[5] The de Braose captives were immediately sent for and
taken in charge by the King. To finish the gruesome incident. According
to John's account Matilda offered 40,000 marks, to be paid by certain
instalments, for amnesty and reinstatement for herself and her

The de Braose family. family ; and a formal agreement on that basis was drawn up
and sealed. Matilda having been sent to Bristol for safe
keeping, her husband was allowed to visit her there, to arrange for raising

---

[1] Ann. Dunstable ; *Mareschal*, II. 144.   [2] *Itiny.*
[3] See Mr. Round's article in the *National Dicty.* On the 7th Sept. 1205 a safe-
conduct to come to England was granted to de Courcy, Rot. Pat. 50. He lived on in
favour with John and Henry III. in receipt of a pension, and died before September
1219 ; Round, *sup.*   [4] *Itiny.* John was at Carrickfergus 19th–28th June.
[5] Walter was pardoned in 1213 ; but Hugh joined the Albigensian crusade, and was
not allowed to return to England till 1221. See Mr. Kingsford's article in the
National Dicty.

the ransom. But the sum was utterly beyond their means, as all their property was confiscate ; and the alleged ' offer ' of the marks was doubtless in fact a crushing amerciament imposed by John to legalise ulterior proceedings. In short the term fixed for the tender of the first instalment passed without payment, whereupon, as the King calmly tells us, the law was allowed to run its course.[1] De Braose was proclaimed an outlaw from county to county : he retired to France, and died next year at Corbeil, near Paris, on the 9th August.[2] As for Matilda and her eldest son, according to all the chroniclers, they were removed from Bristol to Windsor, and there deliberately starved to death.[3] The sensation caused by these events led John in 1212 to publish the explanatory statement from which we have quoted.

John retraced his steps to Dublin, where he was from the 18th to the 23rd or 24th August.[4] His time there must have been well **English Law in Ireland** employed, as he is credited with having taken important steps for introducing into Ireland the rules of English law, and the English system of administration by sheriffs and other officers deriving authority from the Crown. The Anglo-Norman Barons were made to swear observance of the laws of England, transcripts of which were deposited in the Irish Exchequer ; while the territory supposed to recognise the King's authority was mapped out in twelve counties. Seven of these, **Counties** namely Uriel or Louth, Meath, Dublin, Kildare, Catherlagh or Carlow, Wexford, and Kilkenny lay within the borders of Leinster. The other five, being Waterford, Tipperary, Cork, Limerick, and Kerry, took in Munster South of the Shannon. Munster North of the Shannon, Connaught, and Ulster were not meddled with.[5] In connexion with the military organisation of the Dominion we hear of tenure by ' foot-service ' as well as by knight-service. Tenants under the former category were required to provide men armed with spears, shields, and long knives.[6] All these were sound measures ; but we should be inclined to attribute their real authorship to Bishop Gray, who about this time, to **Halfpence and farthings.** meet the wants of the country, had the good sense to initiate the practice of coining halfpence and farthings, instead of leaving people to break up pennies for small change. John ordered the new currency to be received in England as well as in

---

[1] "Quod consideratio regni nostri de eo fieret," *Fœdera*, I. 107, 108 ; Ann. Margan.

[2] M. Paris, *Chron. Maj.*, II. 532 ; Ann. Margan.

[3] Wendover, III. 253 ; W. Cov., II. 202 ; Ann. Waverley ; etc. A few days before his death John granted a site for a monastery to be founded for the good of the souls of William de Braose, his wife and their son.

[4] *Itinerary.*

[5] So Gilbert, *Viceroys*, 74, where he seems to be quoting records, though all reference to the authority is suppressed. County Wicklow seems to be omitted, unless it was included in some other county.

[6] *Ib.*

Ireland.[1] Finally Gray was left in Ireland to continue as Chief Justiciar,
with the Earl of Pembroke as military adviser.[2] By the 26th August John
had landed at Fishguard on the coast of Pembrokeshire.[3]

Dissatisfied with the contributions for the war obtained from the
monastic Houses in general, and the Cistercians in particular,
Taxation of the Clergy. John towards the end of October summoned a sort of Synod
or Convocation to meet in St. Bride's Church, Fleet Street.[4]
We are told that abbots, abbesses, priors, Templars, Hospitallers,
even wardens (*custodes*) of Priories Alien, were brought together to give
reluctant consent to money grants. The Cistercians were forbidden to
attend the annual general chapter of the Order, or even to receive brethren
from abroad, till they had complied with the King's demands. The monks
at Waverley broke up their establishment and dispersed.[5] John's bitterness against the Cistercians was of course connected with the fact that
their Order was actively pressing the crusade against his brother-in-law and
ally Raymond VI. of Toulouse. It was their 'abbot of abbots,' Arnaud
Amaury of Citeaux, who in the previous autumn at the storm of Beziers
had been credited with the inhuman war-cry, 'Kill all ! God will know
His own.'[6] But the allegations of the chroniclers as to
Chronicler's figures. the sums raised by John must be received with the greatest
reserve. Wendover tells us that £100,000 were extorted, of
which amount the Cistercians alone paid £40,000. The Waverley Annals
reduce the contributions of the Order to 33,000 marks, and the Annals of
Margan to 27,000 marks, or £18,000. Against these figures we may set
the fact that the Dunstable writer honestly tells us that what his House
paid was just 20 marks (£13 6s. 8d.). The Jews too, no doubt, were
heavily mulcted. On the 1st of November a general tallage
Tallage on the Jews. on them was assessed at Bristol. The Waverley writer again
asserts that the King pillaged them to the tune of 66,000
marks ; and other chroniclers tell us that many Jews left the country in
despair.[7] Wendover has preserved the well-known story of the Bristol Jew
who was condemned to lose a tooth a day until he had paid 10,000 marks.
For seven days he held out ; when it came to the eighth tooth he gave in.[8]
This man must clearly be identified with Isaac the Bristol Jew who under
the tallage in question was called on to pay 5,100 marks for himself and

---

[1] Wendover, III. 234. Of course a prophecy of Merlin's was found to fit the innovation : " Findetur forma commercii, dimidium rotundum erit." For engravings of these
Dublin pennies and halfpennies see Ruding, *Annals of Mint*, II. 305 ; and III. Pl. II.

[2] Ann. Waverley.

[3] *Itinerary.*

[4] Paris, *Chr. Maj.*, II. 531. John was at the Tower on the 27th October ; *Itiny.*

[5] Wendover, III. 234, 235 ; Ann. Wav. and Margan.

[6] 22nd July 1209. See Martin, *France*, IV. 34 ; Milman's *Latin Chr.*, IV. 210.

[7] W. Cov., II. 203 ; Paris, *sup.*

[8] Wend., III. 231, 232 ; Paris.

his family, but only by instalments. On the Pipe Roll for the ensuing year (13 John) we find him paying in £1,336 9s. 6d. ; the total accounted for from the Jews being £1,785 2s. 5d. ; while two years later the total got in comes to £2,159 11s., including a further instalment from Isaac.[1] In comparison however with the estimates usually given to us by chroniclers, Wendover's figures here, representing the sum as only double the real amount, and that to be paid all at once and not by instalments, may be considered quite a creditable approximation to the truth.

[1] See Madox, *Hist. Excheq.*, I. 223, citing Pipe Rolls 13 John, m. 22 ; and 15 John, m. 9.

CHAPTER XXVII

A.D. 1211–1213

The Interdict—Efforts at settlement—Preparations for war with France—Disaffection in England—The Pope's ultimatum—Submission of the King—His absolution—Reforming movement—England and the Papacy

WITH the year 1211 John in spite of excommunication and Interdict seemed to have reached the zenith of power.[1] Innocent, engrossed with his struggle with Otto in Italy on the one hand, and with his horrible Albigensian crusade in Languedoc on the other hand,[2] seemed for the moment content to leave England to itself. Strict watch of course was kept at the English seaports against the introduction of Papal letters;[3] while rather inconsistently John ordered all self-exiled ecclesiastics to return to England by Midsummer under pain of forfeiture.[4] This, however, might be regarded as simply a cloak for spoliation. Still the King's position, at bottom, must have been a very anxious one. A list of the men acting as his advisers and confidants at this time includes only three names of first-rate position, namely, those of his natural brother William Longsword Earl of Salisbury, Aubrey de Vere II. Earl of Oxford, and the Chief Justiciar Geoffrey Fitz Peter, besides the two faithful Bishops Gray and des Roches.[5]

The King's position.

Negotiations re-opened.

Under these circumstances John reopened negotiations with Innocent, asking that envoys might be sent to treat.[6]

As yet however the only man in Great Britain who ventured to defy John openly was the irrepressible Llywelyn son of Jorwerth, a man destined for thirty years to come to be a thorn in the side of the English government. "Even in Bardic verse Llywelyn rises high out of the mere mob of

---

[1] So W. Cov., II. 203.

[2] See Innocent's Letters, XI., Nos. 156–159 calling for a crusade "ad exterminandum pravitatis hæreticæ sectatores." October 1208; also Le Breton, 219, etc.

[3] Ann. Waverley, 266, 267.

[4] R. Cogg., 164; Ann. Wav. 267.

[5] Wendover, III. 237; Paris.

[6] Ann. Winton, and Waverley; and Burton, 209.

chieftains who live by rapine, and boast as the Hirlas-horn passes from
hand to hand that they take and give no quarter."[1]   The
Troubles in Wales. Prince had gone to war with the hereditary foe of his people,
Ranulf or Randolf III. Earl of Chester; and that on the old
grievance, English castle-building in Wales.   Llywelyn had demolished
the English frontier fort at Dyganwy on the Conway; the Earl rebuilt
it, and refortified Holywell in modern Flintshire.   The Prince retaliated
by furious raids on the Earl's territory.[2]   Two expeditions led
John in the field. by the King in person were required to reduce Llywelyn to
seeming subjection.   The first, undertaken about the month
of May 1211, failed utterly, in spite of the co-operation of Llywelyn's
enemies Gwenwynwyn of Powys, and the Southern chieftains Maelgwin
and Rhys, sons of Rhys.   In the face of such a coalition Llywelyn withdrew with all his substance to 'the mountain of Ereri' otherwise the ranges
of Snowdon.   The English advancing along the North coast to Dyganwy
found themselves starving and helpless in the face of an enemy whom
they could not reach.[3]   The second expedition, undertaken in July and
August,[4] in greater force and with fuller supplies, was pushed as far as
Bangor, where the Bishop, Robert of Shrewsbury, was taken prisoner in
his cathedral.   A new fort was also founded at Aberconway, otherwise
Conway, on the farther side of the river of that name, opposite Dyganwy.
Thus hemmed in, with his communications with Anglesea cut off, Llywelyn
condescended to treat, using his wife John's natural daughter as a go-
between.   Under safe-conduct he himself subsequently came to the
Llywelyn makes peace. English camp, and was admitted to peace on condition of
giving hostages, paying a heavy fine in cattle, and submitting
to a certain curtailment of territory.[5]   "The ink of the treaty
was hardly dry before Wales was again on fire."[6]

From the Welsh March John in the latter part of August went to
Northampton to meet the subdeacon Pandulph and Brother Durand of
the Temple, the Papal envoys sent at his request.   They met
Papal envoys. apparently on Tuesday, 30th August.[7]   It would seem that
the King was prepared to receive Langton, and to reinstate
the monks and bishops who had left England; but that the treaty broke

---

[1] J. R. Green, *History English People*, I. 289 (ed. 1878).

[2] *Brut y T.* 265 (A.D. 1210, given as 1209).

[3] Ann. Camb ; *Brut y T.* (under 1210); Ann. Margan ; W. Cov., II. 203.   John was
at Chester 16th and 17th May; *Itiny.*

[4] John mustered his forces at " Album Monasterium," *i.e.* Whitchurch in Shropshire
on the 8th July, and was back there on the 15th August; Wendover, III. 235.

[5] Ann. Camb. ; *Brut.* 269–271 ; Wendover, *sup.*; Ann. Margan.   [6] Green, *sup.* 287.

[7] Tuesday after St. Bartholomew's Day; Ann. Wav., where by an obvious error the
meeting is placed under the year 1212, the report of the interview being borrowed from
the Burton Annals, which give it rightly under the year 1211, as do all the other writers,
including the Waverley chronicler himself in an earlier entry.   John can be proved to

down on the question of the arrears, the point on which the negotiations
between Henry II. and Becket always failed. As during that
Failure of the mission. struggle, so again now the Church refused to be satisfied with
anything short of an absolute victory.[1] John, like his father,
would not, in fact could not refund all the money, and so the pacification
failed.[2] But it would seem that Pandulf in public audience ventured to
notify, or remind John to his face of the fact that he was excommunicate ;
and to warn him that unless he gave way further sentences would follow.[3]
The Annals of Burton profess to give a verbatim report of this colloquy.
Pandulf, they tell us, finding the King contumacious, proceeded then and
there to release all his subjects and vassals from their allegiance, and to
declare him incapable of ever thereafter wearing the crown.[4] This
precious story may be dismissed on the simple ground that Pandulf and
Durand had no authority to utter any sentence against John. They were
directed if he proved obdurate to leave the prosecution of the struggle in
the hands of Langton, and to return to Rome.[5] We are however quite
prepared to believe that John affected to treat the Legate's warnings with
contempt. We are also told that he endeavoured to impress them with
a sense of his judicial power by sitting in person on criminals ; but that
even there Pandulf had the best of it ; for, when it came to condemning
a cleric to be hung for coining, he took the man out of the King's hands,
and set him free.[6] The reader will notice that the ' liberty of the Church '
was still quite a reality. The efforts to come to terms cannot have been
abandoned at once, as the Papal envoys did not leave England till
Michaelmas, and when they did go John thought it prudent to send
agents of his own with them.[7]

According to Roger of Wendover, Innocent on the return of his envoys
issued the further sentence against John placed by the Burton annalist in
the mouth of Pandulf, releasing all his vassals from their alle-
Question of further sentences against John. giance.[8] But we have just seen that failing John's submission
the Pope ordered the matter for the time being to be left with
Langton ; and no real evidence of the issue of any further
sentences has ever been adduced, wide-spread as the popular belief in

---

have been at Northampton at any rate on the 29th August 1211; but he was not there
at all in the latter part of August 1212; *Itiny.*

[1] See the Pope's instructions to Pandulf and Durand, *Fœdera*, I. 109, as again presented to John in 1213.

[2] Wendover, III. 235, 236; Paris. [3] So the Annals of Margan. [4] Ann. Burton, 209–219.

[5] *Fœdera, sup.* One point that disposes of any claim of the Burton report to be considered contemporary is this, that John is made to admit that he knew that Otto had been
deposed in favour of another. Nothing of the sort had happened in August 1211.
Frederic was only accepted by the Pope in October 1211; and could not have been
styled Emperor in any sense till the autumn of 1212.

[6] Ann. Burton, 217. [7] Ann. Margan, 31; Burton, *sup.*; Winton, 81.

[8] Wend., III. 237; followed by Paris, *Chr. Maj.,* II. 532; and *Hist. A.,* II. 125.

them has been, and still is.   But Innocent's action has been left in some uncertainty owing to the subsequent destruction by his orders of certain of his Bulls against John, and especially of one beginning with the ominous words "*Expectantes hactenus quæ expectavimus*," addressed to the prelates of France, England, Scotland, and Ireland.[1]   We may take it however that the fact that John was excommunicate could not be suppressed or ignored after the mission of Pandulf and Durand ; and that circumstance alone will account for the disposition to keep aloof from him that now begins to appear.   We shall find the Welsh shortly proclaiming that they understood that they had been absolved from all their oaths and obligations to John.[2]

The King's movements in the early part of the year 1212 have already been noticed.   In May we find him at Lambeth receiving the homage of Reginald of Dammartin, Count of Boulogne, who had been expelled by Philip.[3]   Reginald, a warrior of some distinction, and an old ally of England, had been acting as envoy between John and his nephew Otto.[4]   He was

Continental alliances. now commissioned by the King to effect alliances on joint account of himself and the Emperor with the Princes bordering on the North East frontier of France, including Ferrand the new Count of Flanders,[5] the old Countess Margaret of Flanders, and the Dukes of Brabant and Limburg ; even Theobald Count of Bar, being a kinsman to Reginald, was induced to join the league through which John hoped to recover his lost possessions.[6]   By one writer John is also given credit for a diplomatic move of a very venturesome, one might almost say of a desperate character, namely an offer of alliance to Mohammed el

Embassy to Morocco. Nassir, Emperor of Morocco.   The proposal of course must have been made in strictest secrecy, as the mere rumour of such a step would have covered the King with infamy in the eyes of a Crusading age.   But far-fetched as the proceeding might seem to

[1] *Fædera*, I. 166.   "Litteras . . . destinandas."   This expression suggests that the letter may never have been issued ; if it had been so widely disseminated some copy must have survived.

[2] *Brut.* 273 ; W. Cov., II. 206.

[3] Reginald held the county in right of his wife Ida who was still living.   But Philip proposed to confer the fief on their daughter Matilda, whom he had married to his son by Agnes of Meran, Philip surnamed Hurepel.

[4] *Fædera*, I. 104 ; Le Breton, *Philipp.* Bouquet, XVII. 227 ; Pauli.

[5] Dom Ferdinand, commonly called Ferrand, was son of Alphonso II. of Portugal, and nephew of Matilda of Portugal, the widow of Count Philip of Flanders who died at Acre in 1191.   Ferrand became Count in January 1212 by marrying Jeanne the daughter of Baldwin IX., the Emperor-Count, who died in Bulgaria in 1206.   The marriage of Ferrand and Jeanne was celebrated in Paris, under Philip's auspices, in his chapel, and the Count did homage to him.   But during the festivities Philip sent his son Louis to seize Aire and St. Omer ; Le Breton, *Philipp*, 232 ; Lavisse, *France*, III. 170.   Artois and Peronne had been appropriated by King Philip in 1191.   Hence the hostility of Flanders.   [6] *Fædera*, 104–107.

be it would not be unintelligible. About the time when John's embassy must be supposed to have gone out Mohammed was taking hordes of Arabs over to Spain to assist his countrymen there in a final struggle for supremacy. His action did in fact act as a temporary diversion in favour of Raymond of Toulouse, as part of the Crusading hosts were called off to Spain; and it was not till after the utter defeat of the Moslems at Las Navas de Tolosa (16th July 1212) that Simon of Montfort was able to dispose of Raymond under the walls of Muret (Haute Garonne; 12th September 1212).[1]

Another step taken by John at this time, obviously in contemplation of war, was the issuing of orders for an Inquest of Service to ascertain the services due by the tenants in chief, so as to correct or super-**An Inquest of Service.** sede the returns from the Inquest of 1166. The new Inquest had points of resemblance to the Inquests of 1086 and 1198, being based on the sworn verdicts of juries empanelled for the purpose, and in that respect differing entirely from the Inquest of 1166, where each tenant-in-chief was left to make his own return of his fees. Now the enquiry was to be conducted by the Sheriff, Hundred by Hundred, for the County, the final lists to be compiled by the officials from those returns.[2] The present Inquest also differed from that of 1166 by including the towns,[3] that before were not dealt with.

The writs were apparently issued on the 1st June, the returns to be sent in by the 25th of the month. Concurrently with this Inquest an enquiry was directed as to ecclesiastical benefices held under the gift of prelates in exile.[4] Unfortunately the returns of the military service due that have come down to us are incomplete;[5] so that the number of the knights' fees in England in 1212 cannot be positively stated, but the most careful computation estimates them at 7000 or thereabouts, a number already quoted by us.[6]

---

[1] See Martin, *France*, IV. 48–53. I accept the bare fact of the embassy to Mohammed on the authority of Paris, *Chron. Maj.*, II. 559–564; the account being also given in the *Gesta Abbatum S. Albani*, I. 236–243 (Riley). The writer places the mission in the year 1213, but in correct sequence, before the battles of Las Navas and Muret. He names as envoys Thomas of Erdington, a well-known man, and Thomas of London, a cleric placed by the King in charge of the estates of St. Albans, from whom Paris got the facts; "audiente Mathæo qui et hæc scripsit"; p. 564. But Paris uses his authority as a mouthpiece for pouring calumnious abuse on John and Queen Isabella.

[2] Round *Commune*, 274.

[3] "Omnimodis tenementis infra burgum sive extra"; see the writ, *Testa de Nevill* 54; *Red Book Exchequer*, cclxxxv.

[4] Round, *sup.*, 267; Ann. Waverley, 267.

[5] The *Red Book of the Exchequer*, 469–574 gives abstracts for 31 counties: the *Testa de Nevill* "returns or fragments for 25 counties." See these collated, Round, *sup.*, 275. The *Testa*, a bundle of miscellaneous returns from landowners strung together about the time of Edward I. will be found among the publications of the Record Commission, 1807.

[6] See *Feudal Statistics*; A. H. Inman, p. 50 (1900).

From London John early in June started on one of his rambling
progresses through Lincolnshire and Yorkshire to Westmorland
Progress to   and Cumberland.   Whether undertaken from policy or rest-
the Border.   lessness these journeys would certainly add to the King's
influence, by impressing the people with a sense of his omnipresence.
From the 23rd to the 26th of the month he rested at Carlisle, returning by ·
Welsh rising.   Hexham, Durham, and York to the South and West.[1]   In
August the Welsh rose, alleging a Papal call to arms, as
already mentioned.   Llywelyn, Gwenwynwyn, and Maelgwn,[2] acting in
concert, made simultaneous assaults on the English strongholds throughout
the country.   In Gwynedd all their forts except Dyganwy and Rhuddlan
fell ; and the territory cut off in the previous year was recovered.   Gwenwynwyn won back his ancestral seat Mathrafal ;[3] while Maelgwn burnt
Swansea, and devastated all Gower.[4]   John, again incensed to fury, called
out his forces, vowing to exterminate the Welsh ; he then went to Nottingham, where the boy-hostages delivered to him in the previous year were
kept, to glut his eyes with the sight of their execution.[5]   We are next told
that as he was sitting down to his midday dinner, a messenger came
in from the King of Scots to warn him that he was surrounded with
treachery ; and then it would seem that immediately afterwards he
received another letter, from his daughter in Wales, to assure him
that his followers could not be depended on ; and that if
Disaffection   he ventured on a campaign he would be left in the lurch.[6]
in England.
Whether these graphic details are to be considered strictly
authentic or not, it certainly appears that John got warnings that gave him
such a scare that he disbanded his feudal levies (16th August)[7] and shut
himself up for some days in the Castle at Nottingham, surrounding himself
with mercenaries.[8]   He then went back to London, to give orders for
seizing castles, and exacting hostages from suspect barons.   The Scots Earl
Flight of   David of Huntingdon was required to give up Fotheringay,
Eustace de   with a son as hostage : the Earl of Pembroke had again to
Vescy and   deliver his eldest son William, his second son Richard being
Robert
FitzWalter.   already in the King's hands.[9]   Eustace de Vescy of Alnwick,
and Robert fitz Walter of Baynard's Castle Blackfriars, and
Dunmow in Essex, men it was said with grievances of their own, deemed it

---

[1] *Itinerary.*

[2] Maelgwn was in rebellion by the 26th May, when the Honour of Cardigan was taken
from him, and given to his nephew, Rhys son of Gruffudd ; Rot. Pat., I. 93.

[3] Montgomeryshire, between Llanfair and Welshpool.

[4] *Brut.*, 271, 272, where the events are given partly under 1211 and 1212 ; Ann. Camb.
and Margan ; Lewis, *Topog. Dict.*   [5] Wendover, III. 239 ; *Brut.*; 273.

[6] Wend., *sup.*   See also Paris, *Hist. Angl.*, II. 128.   [7] Rot. Pat., 94.

[8] R. Cogg., 165 ; Ann. Margan and Dunstable ; W. Cov., II. 207 ; Wend., *sup.*, John
was at Nottingham 10th–17th September.   On the 20th he signs at the Tower.

[9] Rot. Pat., 94, 95 ; *Mareschal*, II. 158–161.

F F

prudent to retire : the former to Scotland, and the latter to France. They were promptly outlawed, and all their possessions confiscated.[1] We even hear of men in the official circle venturing to leave the King's service, and suffering in consequence. One of these persons, Geoffrey Archdeacon of Norwich, was imprisoned at Bristol in a leaden cope, and done to death by starvation and pressure.[2]

John's nerves were ready to take fright at every shadow. A poor hermit, Peter of Pontefract, who lived on bread and water, and **Peter of Pontefract.** was held a prophet by his neighbours, declared that it had been revealed to him in a dream that John would reign fourteen years and no more, and that his reign would have come to an end by Ascension Day 1213, his regnal years beginning with that festival. The prophecy having been reported to the King he had the man arrested. Peter on being examined could not explain how his vaticination would be fulfilled, but persisted in asserting that the reign would end by Ascension Day ; and offered to stake his life on the issue. John took him at his word, and shut him up in Corfe Castle to abide the event. But by foolishly noticing the prophecy the King had given it publicity and importance.[3]

While still persecuting the Cistercians for their share in the Albigensian Crusade, John now sought to clear himself of the charge of having oppressed **Popular measures.** the clergy by the shallow contrivance of extorting from the Abbots and others letters declaring that whatever he had had from them had been freely given.[4] Nevertheless we do also hear of creditable efforts to conciliate the people by remissions of Forest penalties, by a mitigation of the restraints of late imposed on intercourse with the Continent ; and by more careful attention to the administration of justice.[5]

But, apart from domestic warnings, John was far from being ignorant of the course of events in the outer world, or of the fate that had

---

[1] Wendover, 239, 240 ; Paris, *Hist. Angl.*, II. 128 ; R. Cogg., 165 ; W. Cov., II. 207 ; Rot. Pat., *sup.*, Robert fitz Walter was a scion of the illustrious House of Brionne and Clare, descended from the Conqueror's Guardian Count Gilbert. Robert's father Walter was son of the *Dapifer* Robert, who died in 1136, a younger son of Richard of Bienfaite, the son of Count Gilbert. The *Dapifer* Robert received Baynard's Castle and Dunmow from Henry I. in 1111, on the forfeiture of William Baynard. Eustace de Vescy was son of William de Vescy, son of Eustace fitz John of Bamborough and Alnwick, who fell in Wales in 1157 (above, p. 14) by Beatrice, heiress of Yvo de Vescy, who came over with the Conqueror ; William had adopted his mother's surname ; Foss, *Judges*, I. 115.

[2] Wendover, 229 ; R. Cogg., *sup.* ; Paris, *Hist Angl.*, II. 126.

[3] So W. Cov., II. 209. See Wendover, 240 ; and Annals of Dunstable, Tewkesbury, and Lanercost.

[4] See the letter, Ann. Waverley, 268 ; also R. Cogg., 165 ; W. Cov., 207. The Pope was indignant ; *Fœdera*, I. 110, and cancelled all the bonds.

[5] W. Cov., *sup.*

befallen other Princes who had come under the ban of the Third

Innocent III. and his opponents. Innocent. The career of his Saxon nephew interested him deeply. Otto IV. had been crowned Emperor at Rome on the 4th October 1209,[1] money for the expenses having been apparently provided by John.[2] "But the Guelfic Emperor trod in the

The Guelfic Emperor Otto IV. steps of the Hohenstaufen." Otto began to assert Imperial rights, invading territory claimed as the Patrimony of St. Peter, or under the protection of the Church. After eighteen months of transient success he was excommunicated on Holy Thursday (31st March) 1211.[3] A declaration in Germany in favour of the young King of Sicily, Frederic of Hohenstaufen, followed. In October he was accepted by the Pope: in the course of 1212 he made an adventurous journey from Palermo through Italy to the banks of the Rhine: the partisans of his House received him with enthusiasm: King Philip held out his hand to him, and sent his son Louis to have an interview with him near Vaucouleurs (November). The rejected Otto had to retire to his estates in Brunswick, to concert with John the formation of their Northern League.[4]

John's brother-in-law Raymond VI. of Toulouse had fared even worse.

Raymond VI. of Toulouse. He was no heretic; but as a humane and tolerant ruler he refused to sacrifice peaceable subjects merely because their religious tenets were not those of Rome. In consequence he had been excommunicated, and his subjects released from their allegiance: the North and East of France had been launched in crusade against him: his territories had been wasted with fire and sword; and at the point that we have reached Toulouse and Montauban was all that was left to him. The most infatuated of men could hardly fail to take warning by such examples as these; and John had the obvious contingency to take into consideration that Philip might be commissioned—perhaps already had been commissioned—to draw the sword of the flesh in the cause of the Lord. Under these circumstances he once more reopened negotiations,

Envoys to Rome. and on the 11th November instructed the Abbot of Beaulieu and others to proceed to Rome.[5] It was doubtless on hearing of this embassy that Langton, the Bishops of London and Ely, and some laymen of rank hastened to Rome to represent the state

[1] Wend., III. 227; Ann. Winton, and Waverley.

[2] In the previous month of March Otto's brother Duke Henry of Saxony received in London 1000 marks; *Fœdera*, I. 103. Otto had himself visited England in 1206.

[3] Pauli, from Hürter's *Innocent*; Milman.

[4] Milman, *Latin Chrt.*, IV. 54-61. On the 2nd December Frederic was elected King of Germany at Frankfort. For confidential intercourse between John and Otto at this time see *Fœdera*, I. 104, 105. His brother Henry the Count Palatine came to London in March (Ann. Dunst.) and received 500 marks in August as a year's pension Rot. Claus., I. 121; Pauli.

[5] Rot. Claus, I. 126; Bishop Stubbs.

of things in England, and press for strict dealing with John.[1]   By Wendover again we are told that at their instance a Conclave was held, and

Alleged
Papal
sentences. 'definitive sentence' for John's deposition passed ; further that letters were drawn up directing Philip to undertake the expulsion of King John, with a grant of the kingdom of England to him and his heirs ; also letters to divers magnates urging them to support Philip in his crusade : further we are informed that these documents were entrusted to Pandulf, ostensibly for immediate delivery, but with private instructions to withhold them if John could be brought to terms.[2]   This story has received an amount of credence to which it seems little entitled. From Innocent himself writing to John we learn that the King had put himself in the hands of a collective delegation of six, assuring the Pope that he would abide by anything they should agree to ; but that only three of the number had appeared at Rome, and that they could not act without the others, a circumstance, by the way, we may note, of which the Pope had had to complain before.   Innocent goes on to say that the three who had reached his court, realising, as we may suppose, the urgency of the situation, had taken it upon them to say that their master would give in to the terms propounded by Pandulf and Durand in 1211. 'Those gracious offers'[3], says Innocent, 'had been rejected by John, who by his subsequent conduct had shown himself unworthy of grace : nevertheless to overcome

Innocent's
ultimatum. evil with good, and deprive him of any excuse, the Pope would still stand to those terms, if the King should pledge himself to them as more fully expounded by Innocent in a supplemental paper appended to prevent misunderstanding.'[4]   Failing compliance John is threatened in the plainest language with 'ruin,' *i.e.* deposition.   The terms of 1211 forming the basis of the negotiation, a copy of the instructions then given to Pandulf and Durand was inclosed in the letter, with the supplemental 'expositions.'[5]   These do not essentially vary

---

[1] Wendover, III. 241, copied by Paris. They agree in making the prelates return from Rome in January 1213 ; but Walter of Coventry and Ralph of Coggeshall make them start for Rome in 1213 ; and that date suits Wendover's narrative much better than his own date.   No one of the writers seems to know anything of John's embassy.

[2] Wend., 241, 242 : Paris, *Chr. Maj.*, II. 535, 536. In his *Hist. Angl.* the latter omits all reference to Pandulf and his instructions, and represents the deposition of John as formally proclaimed in France ; II. 132. Walter of Coventry, II. 209, does not go so far, but has letters from the Pope authorising the invasion if John should not repent. Coggeshall, 166, knows of no deposition at all, and regards Philip as acting simply on the advice of his barons ; and so too do the French authorities, Le Breton, 89, and Rigord. Sismondi, VI. 328, takes the same view ; but Martin, IV. 68, treats Philip as expressly authorised by the Pope.

[3] "Formam . . . quæ pro majori parte gratiam continebat."

[4] "Secundum expositiones et explanationes quas ad omnis dubitationis scrupulum removendum duximus exhibendas."

[5] For the letter, dated 27th February, 1213, see Innocent, *Epp.*, XV. 234 ; Ann. Burton,

the conditions of pardon, which still remain the full and friendly acceptance of Langton as archbishop; and the reinstatement of the exiled
bishops, monks, and 'all others concerned'[1], with plenary restitution, and
compensation for damages. But the names of Robert fitz Walter and
Eustace de Vescy are now introduced; and the Pope's requirements become
more stringent and explicit, indicating an increased distrust of John. All
contracts interfering with restitution are declared void: £8000 sterling to
be provided at once for the immediate wants of the exiled clergy[2]; all
outlawries against clergy or laity to be withdrawn; with a disclaimer of
any right on the King's part to issue decrees of outlawry against ecclesiastics in future. The form of pledge to be given by the King was also
carefully prescribed. Four barons would swear to the King's observance of
the terms on his soul, in his presence, and at his command; he would give
his own letters patent to the same effect; while prelates and barons might
be called in as guarantors at Langton's discretion.[3] Neither the Pope's
letter to the King, nor the explanatory appendix give any countenance to
the view that further decrees against John had been issued since 1211.
The Interdict and the King's excommunication are the only sentences
referred to.[4]

But while negotiating or pretending to negotiate with the Pope, John,
in spite of domestic disaffection was still cherishing hopes of getting the
John's
schemes. better of Philip through the help of his Continental allies.
The Pope too would be attacked through Philip. On the
28th January, John being at Bamborough laying hands on
de Vescy's effects, ordered 9000 marks (£6000) to be paid to his nephew
out of money in deposit at the Temple.[5] Such a sum could only be
Preparations
for War. intended for Otto's military chest. On the 3rd March stringent orders were issued for all ships capable of carrying six
horses or more to be at Portsmouth by the 24th of month; as
if some expedition oversea was in contemplation;[6] while on the 27th of
the month the ranks of the Northern League were filled up by the

---

217; *Fœdera*, I. 168. For the original instructions to Pandulf and Durand, and the
present 'expositions,' *Fœd.* 109.

[1] " Cæteris clericis et laicis ad hoc negotium contingentibus."

[2] Of this money Langton would receive £2500; the Bishops £750 each; and the
Canterbury monks £1000.

[3] *Fœdera*, I. 109; Ann. Burton, 218–221; Innocent *Epp.*, *sup.*

[4] Bishop Stubbs in his note to W. Cov., II. lix., seems mistaken in stating with
reference to Innocent's letter to John that "the Pope thus declares that the mission of
Pandulf and Durand had failed, and that severer measures had been taken against the
King in consequence." Innocent refers to further misdoings by John, not to any further
action of his own.

[5] *Fœdera*, I. 108.

[6] See the Writ, Wendover, III. 244, dated at the New Temple; John was there on
that day.

accession of William of Holland. The Count came to London, did homage to the King, and undertook to send 25 men-at-arms (*milites*) and 500 or more footsoldiers (*servientes*) to England in case of invasion, receiving in return a pension of 400 marks for himself and his heirs.[1]

Philip had not waited for a formal Papal commission to attack King John. Innocent had not gone that length; but friendly messages sent to Paris by Cardinal Robert of "Corzon," said to be an Englishman, would give Philip sufficient encouragement without committing the Pope too deeply.[2]

Innocent and the King of France. He could hardly call for war against John while offering him terms; but the presence of a French army on the coasts of the Channel would materially strengthen the hands of the Papal negotiators. On the 6th April the French King held a Grand Council or Parliament of Magnates at Soissons. Most of the chief feudatories were there, and all except Ferrand of Flanders were prepared to invade England. Even Savary of Mauléon had now turned against John. The objects given out were the redress of the wrongs of the Church of England, and the punishment of John for his murder of Arthur and other crimes.[3]

Philip's aims. But the real aim was the establishment of young Louis as King of England in vassalage to France, a grand conception.[4] A general muster was ordered for the 21st April. John met this move by calling for mass levies for the same day. All men capable of bearing arms were required to turn out under penalty of being proclaimed 'culverts,'[5] the equivalent of the Old English "nidering," involving forfeiture of all property. As usual John's orders

England under arms. were obeyed: more men came than the King could maintain, and numbers had to be sent home. Even Bishop Gray was recalled from his government in Ireland. The main body was established in a central position on Barham Down, near Canterbury; detachments being posted at Dover, Feversham, Ipswich, and other places where landings might be feared.[6] The King moved from one seaport to another superintending.[7] But all immediate danger of invasion had been dispelled by the activity of the English fleet, which had not waited to be attacked. The shipping at the mouth of the Seine, and at Fécamp had been captured or destroyed, and Dieppe burnt.[8]

[1] *Fœdera*, I. 110.

[2] April. The Cardinal had a general mission to France to call for aid to Holy Land; but his instructions to the King were private. Innocent, *Epp.* XVI. 31-33.

[3] G. Le Breton *Gesta*, Bouquet XVII. 89; *Philipp. Ib.* 230, 231. In neither place is there any reference to any Papal commission; the King's holy zeal prompted him.

[4] See the pledges taken from Louis with respect to his government of England in the event of his winning the crown; *Fœd.* 104, dated at Soissons.

[5] The word is said to be a corruption of *colibert*, and must not be taken as meaning "Turntail"; see Godefroy, and Ducange.

[6] Wendover, III. 244-246; Paris; W. Cov., II. 209; Ann. Dunstable.

[7] See the *Itinerary.*   [8] Ann. Dunstable, a year behind the time, as usual.

While the two armies were thus facing each other across the Channel Pandulf reached Calais with the Pope's ultimatum. The King's envoys accompanied him, to testify to the pledges that they had given.[1] John now found himself in a great strait. There were the Papal terms so bitter and humiliating;[2] but there also was the plain threat of deposition, with Philip ready to give effect to it. Against that John might set the English army, strong enough in point of numbers—if it could be depended on—but that was just the question. Rumour whispered that many of the Barons were in communication with the King of France.[3] Probably the wish to get safely over Ascension Day, and falsify Peter's prophecy had also something to do with the King's final resolution.[4] Anyhow Pandulf was invited to come over. Preliminaries having been adjusted, on the 13th May John, who for some time had been staying at the Templars' house at Ewell, between Barham Down and Dover, came to Dover, and sealed letters patent binding himself to Innocent's requirements word for word—*mutatis mutandis*. The Earls of Salisbury, Surrey (Warenne), Derby (Ferrers), and Reginald of Boulogne took the required oath on the King's behalf.[5]

John in a fix.

Peter's prophecy.

The King gives in.

The world, or the shrewder part of it may have been prepared for this result, Innocent's ascendency being felt to be irresistible.[6] But great must have been the astonishment of all to hear that two days later John surrendered his kingdoms of England and Ireland to the Pope, to be held as fiefs of the Holy See, at a yearly rent of 1000 marks, namely 700 marks for England, and 300 marks for Ireland. This gratuitous act of humiliation, as he himself described it, the King submitted to, he said, in order to show his sense of his offending against God and the Church, and to earn remission of sins for himself and all his kin, living and dead. Henry the new Archbishop of Dublin,[7] John Gray of Norwich, and eleven Earls and Barons subscribed the charter. A formal record of the homage was sealed at the same time.[8]

Surrender of England to the Papacy.

At whose instigation John took this extraordinary step does not appear.

---

[1] W. Cov., II. 209; Ann Waverley; Wendover, 246.

[2] Paris, *H. E.*, II. 135.

[3] W. Cov., 211.

[4] So at least Wendover, 248. Paris, *Cr. Maj.*, II. 541, copies him, as usual. In the *Hist. Angl.* he omits this reference to Peter.

[5] Wendover, 248–252; Paris, *Hist. Angl. sup. Fœdera*, I. 111.

[6] "Eo quod ab universis metuebatur papa Innocentius supra omnes qui eum a multis annis præcesserunt"; W. Cov. 210.

[7] Archbishop John Cumin, whose architectural work still adorns the city of Dublin, died in 1211; W. Cov., II. 208. In March 1213 Henry of London, Archdeacon of Stafford, an official of the Exchequer, was appointed to succeed him; Foss, *Judges*, II. 90.

[8] 15th May, *Fœdera*, 111, 112. Wendover, 252–255, etc. The charters however do not appear on the Charter Rolls.

Whether Pandulf suggested it or not Innocent accepted it freely.[1]   Already
on a previous occasion he had received the surrender of a Kingdom from
Pedro II. of Arragon (1204).   Not content with the purely spiritual
supremacy for which we were inclined to give him credit at the first, the
Vicegerent of Christ upon earth was lowering himself to aspirations after
territorial sovereignty, the infatuation of the Papacy.   The English,
mortified and humiliated in their national pride,[2] regarded
English opinion. the proceeding with very natural suspicion.[3]   But Pandulf
harangued them energetically, dwelling on the duty of alle-
giance to their King now that he had been reconciled to the
Church, and making large promises of reform on his behalf.[4]   Public
confidence was to a certain extent restored, and the 23rd May (Ascension
Day) passed without incident.   John was in high spirits: he
Ascension Day. set up a marquee in a field near Ewell and gave a grand
banquet in honour of the day.   But still there were persistent
believers in the Seer of Pontefract—the wish doubtless being father to the
thought—who ventured to suggest that the fatal day might be the anniversary of the original Ascension Day of the coronation, namely the 27th
Execution of the prophet. May, and that something might yet happen before that day.
The second anniversary however having also passed in peace
Peter and a son were sent to the gallows (28th May).   But
people on thinking over recent events began to protest that the poor
hermit had been a true prophet after all: John had ceased to be a King
by the 23rd May.[5]

Pandulf was now sent back with the £8000 to fetch the exiles, letters of
protection couched in the amplest terms being also forwarded to them.[6]
The Legate also proceeded to inhibit Philip from waging war on a vassal
of the Holy See.[7]   This was rather hard on the King, as John, strong in
the sense of Papal support, was beating up recruits for an
Plans against France. expedition to Poitou, to attack France from the South; while
Otto and his allies would invade it from the East.   Moreover
John had just found an opportunity for dealing an annoying blow at his

[1] See his Golden Bull of the 4th November 1213 accepting the surrender and regranting the kingdom to be held of the Holy See; *Epp.*, XVI. 131 ; also 135.   The order for
the destruction of the letters against John had been given on the 31st October ; No. 133.

[2] "Licet id multis ignominiosum videretur, et enorme servitutis jugum"; W. Cov.,
210.   Matthew Paris, who was strongly antipapal, is loud in his condemnation.   "Carta
detestabilis . . . sic humiliatus est rex Johannes"; *Hist. Angl.*, II. 135, 136.

[3] "Quia non credebant rem fide agi," W. Cov. 211.

[4] "Regem . . . per omnia in proximo satisfacturum"; W. Cov. *sup*.   See also the
proclamation ; *Fœdera*, 112.

[5] W. Cov. 212 ; Wendover, 255 ; and for the date Ann. Wav. 278.

[6] Wendover, 256 ; *Fœdera*, *sup*.   But of the actual payment of the £8000 (12000
marks) I find no entry till the 1st of January following ; Rot. Pat., I. 107.

[7] Wendover, *sup*.   R. Cogg, 166, and the proclamation above cited from *Fœdera*.

adversary. Philip was overrunning the territories of John's ally, Ferrand of Flanders, and had an auxiliary flotilla with supplies in attendance at Damme. The place at that time was the seaport of the city of Bruges; but the retreat of sea has now left it some miles inland. At Ferrand's call for help John despatched an armament under the Earl of Salisbury, the Count of Holland, and Reginald of Boulogne, who achieved a great

Destruction of French fleet. success, capturing or destroying most of the French vessels (30th May).[1] But John's proposed expedition to Poitou made no progress, the Barons declining to follow him under various excuses, one being that he was still excommunicate.[2]

Langton had been in no hurry to come to England. For one thing, he waited to see the stewards and bailiffs of the exiled clergy put into actual possession of their lands. Then it was clear that he was well acquainted with the wants of the nation, and that he did not regard John's absolution as a matter simply concerning the King and the clergy, but as one in which the demands of the laity also ought to have a voice.[3] Satisfactory

Langton in England. progress, however, in the matter of restitution having been made,[4] he left his retreat at Pontigny, and crossed the Channel, landing at Dover in July.[5] His party included the Bishops of London, Ely, Hereford, Bath, and Lincoln. Mauger or Malger of Worcester had died abroad; likewise the ill-starred Geoffrey of York, whose troubled career had come to an end on the 12th December, 1212.[6] We must suppose that the Prelates on disembarking made their way first to London; and that there they were directed to join the King at Portsmouth, as we are told that a Royal escort was waiting them at Guildford, a place that could hardly be reached from Dover except by way of the metropolis. The King himself met them on the 18th July on a height outside Porchester.[7] We are told that he fell at Langton's feet, saying 'Welcome Father.'[8] But of course Stephen could not accept the due kiss of peace

[1] W. Cov., II. 211; Wendover, III. 257; Le Breton, *Philipp.*, 233–236. The date of the action is given by M. Paul Meyer, *Mareschal*, II. 162. John's commission to the leaders is dated May 25th; *Fædera*, 113.

[2] Wendover 259; W. Cov. 212.

[3] See the Pope's letter to Langton of the 15th July acknowledging the receipt of one from him in which the Archbishop must have suggested grounds for delaying John's absolution, as Innocent presses on him the importance of absolving the King as soon as possible, " propter instantem necessitatem "; Epp., XVI. 89. As the Pope's letter could not have reached Langton before the absolution we may suppose that in that matter Stephen's proceedings followed the course that he had indicated to the Pope.

[4] *June*; Ann. Dunstable, 37. The orders for restitution of temporalities were issued on the 1st of the month; Rot. Pat., I. 99.

[5] 9th July, Ann. Worcester; 16th July, Wendover, 260.

[6] *Reg. Sacrum.* A good likeness of him may be seen in his monumental effigy now at Pont l'Evêque; A. Hartshorne.

[7] Ann. Dunstable, 37; *Itinerary.*

[8] So at least Wendover, 260, and the Waverley Annals.

from lips that were still excommunicate.   John however, to show his
friendly feeling made a semblance of kissing the Archbishop or in children's
phrase "blew him a kiss."[1]   Next day they all moved on to Winchester.
But Langton was firm in his purpose not only of binding the King once
**The King's
absolution.**   more to the fulfilment of the Pope's requirements, but also of
exacting from him pledges for better government in the future.
Accordingly, when on Sunday 20th July John was taken to the
door of the cathedral to be absolved, he was required to repeat in public
his coronation oath,[2] as well as the oath to the Papal compact.[3]
**Langton's
conditions.**   Then the 51st Penitential Psalm was sung,[4] and so, 'under the
usual discipline' the King received absolution from the Archbishop.   The kiss of peace could then be given and the King be allowed
to enter the church.   The *Te Deum* was sung, followed by High Mass
celebrated by Langton, and so John coming forward to offer was finally
reconciled 'at the horns of the altar.'   A banquet at which the Prelates
assisted ended the day.[5]   But the Interdict had not yet been dissolved,
and Langton in presuming to celebrate was held at Rome to have been
guilty of a grave offence, and in fact "was never forgiven." [6]

The King had been relieved of his personal sentence.   But that did not
clear the whole situation.   He was still bent on his expedition to Poitou,
**State of
England.**   so persistently resisted by the Barons ; there was the terrible
question of the compensation due to the clergy ; there were
endless vacancies in the Church to be filled up ; while the
whole realm was still under the cloud of an Interdict.   But John as usual
would attend to nothing but the gratification of his own purposes.   After
**The King's
purposes.**   issuing a few orders placing the Regency in the hands of
Geoffrey Fitz Peter and Peter des Roches, and leaving them
to discuss the state of the realm in a Grand Council to be held
at St. Albans [7] he hastened down to the Dorsetshire coast, to find that the

---

[1] So I interpret the words of the Waverley writer : "Rex . . . osculatus est eum
(sc. Langton) ore tantum," p. 276.

[2] See Wendover, *sup.*, where the coronation oath seems intended, though loosely and
inaccurately given.   That the King before absolution had in some shape or other been
made to swear to respect the old liberties of his subjects also appears from Coggeshall, 267.

[3] " In conspectu cleri et populi juravit rex quod servaret concordiam ibi publice lectam
in causis pro quibus fuerat excommunicatus" ; Ann. Dunstable, *sup.* ; also Bermondsey, 438.

[4] As an instance of Wendover's inaccuracy, he, a monk, actually gives the 50th as the
Penitential Psalm, and the scribe who copied out his work as a basis for the history of
Matthew Paris repeats the error.

[5] Ann. Dunstable, Bermondsey, and Waverley, *sup.* ; W. Cov., II. 213 ; Wendover,
260, 261.

[6] Hook, *Archbishops*, II. 701.

[7] Wendover, III. 261.   I accept his statements to that extent ; but I utterly reject the
actual writ that he professes to give, by which the King is represented as summoning four
good men and the reeve from all the royal demesnes to meet in one place on one day, to
give evidence as to the damages suffered by the Church lands, of which of course they

barons whom he had summoned to follow him again refused to go, insisting
that their tenure did not involve liability to foreign service.
Baronial resistance. In point of strict constitutional law this position was untenable,
as we have shewn.   But with the loss of Normandy it was
clearly fair that some new understanding on the subject should be come
to.   The Northern barons are specially mentioned in this connexion.
Perhaps they had not been called out in April, and therefore were required
to turn out now.   John as if to show his determination of purpose put out
to sea with his personal household, as he had done in 1205, sailing as far
as Jersey, and returning within three days to Studland Bay.[1]   Vowing to
be revenged on the men who had failed him John moved
Civil War imminent. Northwards with a crushing force.   The barons might have
been made to pay dearly for their contumacy had not Langton
come to the rescue.   He hastened after the King, overtaking him at
Northampton, and remonstrated with him, insisting that to
Langton intervenes. wage war on subjects without judicial investigation would be
a breach of the oath that he had just taken at Winchester.
John, who probably could not understand an ecclesiastic troubling himself
about lay rights, told him angrily to keep to his own sphere, the Church;
and then, as if to pacify him, and detach him from the Barons' cause,
issued writs ordering the officers who had been in charge of the impounded
Church lands to arrange with the bishops for meetings to settle as to
damages.[2]   Next morning the King, still boiling with rage, moved on to
Nottingham.   But Langton followed him; and by threats of ecclesiastical
censures forced him to agree to submit all questions between him and his
barons to legal decision.[3]   To keep up appearances, however, John continued his march North as far as Durham, returning to London by the end
of September.[4]

The Grand Council at St. Albans for which John had arranged was
held on the 4th of August, and was duly attended by Langton and the
chief peers, Spiritual and Lay.   Of the question of damages
Grand Council. for which the meeting was said to have been convened we
now hear nothing.   Reform is the only question; and it
would seem that large promises of amendment were made in the King's
name; and that orders were issued to the sheriffs, foresters, and other

could know nothing.   The genuine writs on the subject issued later require the King's
officers who had been in possession to render account; *Fœdera*, I. 114.   Thus all
question of "early representation" falls to the ground.

[1] 5th–9th August; W. Cov., II. 212; R. Cogg., 167; Wendover, III. 261, 262;
Itinerary.   See also John's letter of the 17th August to Raymond of Toulouse, lamenting
that he had been unable to make out his expedition; *Fœdera*, 114.

[2] 31st August, *Fœdera*, *sup.*   The reader will contrast this with the alleged writ in
Wendover which has been accepted so long.

[3] Wendover, 262, 263; W. Cov., *sup.*; R. Cogg., 167.

[4] *Itiny.*

officials to keep strictly within their legal duties. We are even told that

Promises of Reform. the 'Laws' of Henry I., *i.e.* his coronation charter, were referred to as the standard of constitutional right.[1] A reverter to the principles of that compact would involve very considerable modifications in the practice of the administration.

The meeting at St. Albans was followed by one in London on the 25th August, of which two wholly different reports have been handed down. According to one narrative, whose details suggest infor-

Synod at Westminster. mation at first hand, Langton preached at St. Paul's, the day being a Sunday. He then adjourned to Westminster, to hold a Provincial Synod—the first of his episcopate. The question of the arrears is the only one reported as touched upon, the clergy being urged to make out full claims of all that was due to them[2] From Wendover, the constitutional writer, we hear of a private meeting at St. Paul's of clergy

Charter of Henry I. and laity, when Langton, referring to recent promises of reform, produced an actual copy of Henry's charter. The barons, deeply impressed by its contents, pledged themselves to risk their lives if necessary to gain such rights, and the Archbishop promised them his best support. That the day included proceedings of a strictly ecclesiastical character appears even from this writer's account, as he tells us that Langton granted to the clergy, parochial as well as conventual, certain relaxations of the Interdict.[3] Of course it is quite possible that two meetings may have been held, one a mixed assemblage at St. Paul's, and the other a clerical Synod at Westminster. But it does not seem quite likely that Langton would choose a day of concourse and a place of

Patriotism of the Archbishop. publicity for holding a secret meeting ; to hatch a scheme that would be regarded by the King as a simple conspiracy.[4] Langton's conduct in lending the support of the Church to the assertion of lay rights is deserving of special notice. Since the Conquest the clergy in any struggles with the Crown had seldom cared for anything but the 'liberty' of the Church ; the 'liberty' of the Church involving inroads on private lay rights quite as much as on Crown rights.

John had returned to London to receive a fresh Papal Legate, a man of higher position than Pandulf, being a member of the Sacred College, Nicholas, Cardinal Bishop of Tusculum (Frascati). The scope of his

---

[1] So Wendover, 262, again the sole authority ; the transcript by Paris is so mechanical that it adds no weight to the original.

[2] Ann. Waverley, 277. The writer gives the text of the sermon, "In Deo speravit cor meum, et adjutus sum, et refloruit caro mea ; " ' My heart trusted in God, and I was holpen and my flesh revived ' (*Psalm* XVI. 1, 9?) ; whereat one of the congregation shouted out, ' You're a liar ; you never trusted in Him ! '

[3] Wendover, III. 263-266. The writer gives a copy of the charter. Paris, as usual, transcribes him in the one work, and abridges him in the other.

[4] "Confœderatione facta ; " Wend., *sup.*

mission included not only the settlement of the outstanding questions
A fresh between the King and his clergy, but also a general control
Papal of the affairs, foreign as well as domestic, of the whole king-
Mission. dom. Philip of France and John's subjects alike are invited
to pay ' humble attention ' (*humiliter intendentes*) to the monitions of the
Cardinal.[1] Later instructions direct him in the filling up of vacant
benefices to act decisively on his own responsibility, rejecting all appeals
to Rome.[2] But his subsequent conduct showed that he was intended to
give a general support to the interests of the King.[3] Pandulf who was
still in England would act with him.

Nicholas had landed on the 27th September. John came to London
Fresh on the 28th, and on the 3rd October he renewed his surrender
homage to of the Kingdom, and did fresh homage to the Legate; the
the Papacy. charters, this time, being sealed with golden ' bulls ' to mark
their importance.[4]

In the matter of ecclesiastical affairs alone, there was plenty of work to
be done. The Archbishopric of York, and the Sees of Durham, Worcester,
Exeter, Lichfield, and Chichester, with some ten abbeys were vacant,
without counting minor preferments.[5] The clergy were pressing for
strictly canonical elections, while John was insisting on the rights of the
Crown. But the question that comes most to the front, certainly in the
reports of the chroniclers, is that of the arrears. These had risen to
gigantic proportions[6] through John's improvident rapacity. Instead of
farming out the benefices at reasonable rents, he had been
Ecclesiastical stripping them of everything that could be turned into money,
damages. selling off stock, felling timber, and the like. In the case of
the Canterbury estates he had squeezed out £5169 19s. 5d. in the course
of one year, while his father had been content with a rent
Three Grand of £1,300.[7] We hear of the damages as being discussed at
Councils. three successive Grand Councils held during the autumn,
namely one in London, one at Wallingford, and one at Reading. The
King and the Legate were present at each ;[8] and on each occasion we have

[1] *Epp.*, XVI. 79–83 ; *Fœdera*, 111.

[2] See the Pope's letter of the 1st November, Wendover, 277; *Epp.*, XVI. 138; *cnf.* Nos. 130, 132.

[3] See the Pope's letter to the King of the 4th November telling him that as long as he stands on the rock of St. Peter he will have nothing to fear; *Epp.*, XVI. 130; also No. 134 in which the Legate is directed to dissolve all "conjurationes et factiones" formed in England through the King's quarrel with the Church.

[4] Ann Waverley, 277; *Fœdera*, 115; *Itinerary.*

[5] See the list given by W. Cov., II. 113; and *Reg. Sacrum.*

[6] " Damna in summam excreverunt incredibilem ;" W. Cov. ; *sup.* See the schedule *Red Book Exchq.*, II. 772, where a total of £100,000 is brought out.

[7] Pipe Roll, 8 John ; so too with Hyde Abbey, m. 4 dors. See also Ann. Waverley, 265 ; and Wendover, 276.   [8] Ann. Dunstable, 38.

the King pressing the clergy to accept of a sum down ; the clergy resisting, and the Legate siding with the King.   The London Council, we are told, lasted three days, rising on the 2nd October, the day before the surrender to Nicholas.[1]   The Wallingford Council met apparently on the 1st of November;[2] and included other business besides that of the damages, as we are told that it was marked by a reconciliation between the King and the Northern Barons, who received the kiss of peace.   But we are also informed that the pacification proved short-lived, the pledges mutually interchanged not having been kept.[3] This breakdown may perhaps be explained by a gleam of light derived from writs issued on the 7th November, referring to earlier writs, which may fairly be supposed to have been issued at Wallingford, or in consequence of some agreement entered into there.   The earlier writs, which have not been preserved, had summoned a Grand Council of an entirely novel character, in fact a national Parliament to meet at Oxford on the 15th November.   The King had called for the attendance not only of the magnates usually summoned, but also of *milites*, and four discreet men from each shire—a clear beginning of county representation.   By the writs of the 7th November the King directs the sheriffs to send up the *milites* with their arms, but the Baron's men without arms.[4]   He was evidently hoping to play off the lesser county gentry against their natural leaders, the local magnates, a hopeless attempt.   Of course nothing more is heard of the parliament.   But we are told that the Barons had now generally resolved to make a stand for national rights.[5]

The King and the Northern Barons.

An abortive Parliament.

The Barons combine.

The Reading Council met apparently on the 8th December.[6]   Inquests as to losses sustained had been held, and accounts taken during the autumn, and the clergy were full of hope.[7]   Again we are told that the wrangle lasted three days.   The end of it was that at the close of the

---

[1] So Wendover, III. 275.   In his account of the meeting the writer represents John as offering the Bishops 100,000 marks, when on the very next page we find them fain to accept 15,000 marks, another good instance of Wendover's utter inaccuracy.   I take it that he got his 100,000 marks from the Pope's letter to Nicholas of the 23rd January, 1214, instructing him to insist on that sum ; *Epp.*, XVI. 164.

[2] So Ann. Dunstable, 40.   Wendover places the meeting on the 5th November, when the King was at Woodstock.   He was at Wallingford on the 1st November; *Itin.*

[3] Ann. Dunst., *sup.*; R. Cogg., 167.

[4] See the writ rightly dated, *Select Charters*, 279; in *Fœdera*, I. 117, the date is wrongly given as 15th November.

[5] "Omnes fere barones Angliæ confœderantur sibi ad tuendam libertatem ecclesiæ et totius regni ; " R. Cogg., 167.

[6] Both Wendover, 276, and the Waverley Annals, 278, make the Council meet on the 6th December; but the King did not go to Reading till the 8th December ; remaining there till the 14th of the month.

[7] Ann. Wav., *sup.*; Dunstable, 39.

sittings, when most persons had left, the King persuaded the Bishops to
accept of 15,000 marks, and there, for the time, the matter
A sop to the Bishops. rested.[1] Towards the filling up of the bishoprics no progress
whatever had been made by the end of the year. The King
and the Chapters could not agree; and Innocent, as represented by his
Appointments to benefices. Legate, had become suddenly forgetful of capitular rights;
and, we might add, of the spiritual wants of the flocks left
without pastors. The Worcester Chapter having made an
unanimous election in favour of their Prior Ralph, the proceedings were
quashed by Nicholas in order to make way for John's man, Walter Gray
the Chancellor, to whom they had to resign themselves a few weeks later.[2]
It was even hinted that the Pope was prepared to indulge the King with
the custody of the vacant benefices a little longer.[3] In connexion with
this it is well to point out that in his ultimatum to John the Pope had
intimated a willingness to sanction that uncanonical prerogative, holding
the loss of it over the King's head *in terrorem* if he should break his
word.[4] Even under Innocent the Papacy could subordinate Church
principles to political considerations.

During the autumn John had lost his right-hand man the Chief Justiciar,
Death of Geoffrey Fitz Peter. Geoffrey Fitz Peter, Earl of Essex, who passed away on the
14th October.[5] Paris, enlarging Wendover's bare record of the
death, gives Geoffrey a high character, as a 'pillar of the State,'
and a man on good terms with all the chief men of the realm. He tells us,
as he told us at the death of Hubert Walter, that John with a sense of
undisguised relief exclaimed ' By God's Feet now am I at last King and
Lord of England '; adding ' Let him go to Hell and greet Hubert Walter
there.' [6] The writer goes on, ' At his death England became as a ship in a
storm without a rudder. The storm broke at Hubert's death; after the death
of Geoffrey, England could not even breathe.' As far as we can judge
of his career Fitz Peter had been but the faithful executant of his master's
orders. No word of any opposition or remonstrance is ever recorded.
But he probably kept the King in some measure in touch with the
Baronage. The one measure of conciliation towards the Magnates that we
know of, the practice of exempting them from the payment of the scutages
exacted from the lesser gentry and the clergy, may have been his doing.[7]
At any rate, John after his death broke away from his Barons more
decidedly than ever.

---

[1] Wendover, and Ann. Wav., *sup.* The writ for payment of the 15,000 marks is dated
12th December; Rot. Pat., I. 106.   [2] Ann. Worcester, 402, 403.   [3] W. Cov., 214.

[4] See the words dictated to John. "Si forte . . . contraverimus . . . nos perpetuo
vacantium ecclesiarum custodiam amittamus;" Ann. Burton, 219, etc.

[5] Wendover, 271.   [6] *Chron. Maj.*, II. 558; *Hist. Angl.*, II. 144.

[7] The practice, however, began under Richard in connexion with the so-called
Redemption 'Scutage.'

CHAPTER XXVIII

A.D. 1214

Futile Campaign in Poitou—Campaign and Battle of Bouvines

THE year 1214 found England still under the Interdict. Not one of the six vacant Sees had yet been filled up; the attitude of the Barons towards the King was sulky and defiant. But a partial settlement, a settlement on account, so to speak, had been effected with the Bishops who had been in exile; and so John, content to leave his interests in the hands of the Papal Legate, could turn his whole thoughts once more towards setting in motion the long-prepared coalition against **Preparations for War.** France. The unfortunate Count Raymond VI. of Toulouse, utterly defeated by Simon of Montfort at the battle of Muret (12th September, 1213),[1] had come to London in December, to the great scandal of the Legate, who insisted on his prompt dismissal.[2] Ferdinand or Ferrand of Flanders came over in January, and, renouncing his recent allegiance to France,[3] did homage to John. William of Holland also appeared about the same time to concert plans of operation. They were shortly sent back in company with the Earl of Salisbury, and Reginald of Boulogne, the former having the command of the small English contingent detached for service in Flanders.[4] Towards the end of January the King himself went down to Southampton Water. On the 1st February, being at Portsmouth, as his last act before sailing, he appointed the Bishop of Winchester, Peter des Roches, to the vacant post of Chief **Regency.** Justiciar, thus making him Regent of England during his absence.[5] The choice was not a popular one, the Barons being indignant at having a Frenchman and a priest, not to say a noted in-**The King's crossing.** triguer, set over their heads.[6] On the 2nd February apparently the King put out to sea. The Queen, his second son Richard, just five years old,[7] and Eleanor of Brittany went with him. He took

---

[1] See Martin, *France*, IV. 49-53.
[2] Ann. Dunstable. 39; Waverley, 280. On the 16th January, 1214, an order for his journey money to leave England was issued; Rot. Pat., I. 108. [3] See above, 431, note.
[4] W. Cov., II., 215 R. Cogg.. 168; Ann. Waverley. [5] *Fœdera*, I. 118.
[6] R. Cogg.; Ann. Wav., *sup.* [7] Born 6th January, 1209; Ann. Winton and Wav.

out 40,000 marks ($£26,000 13$_. 4_d.) in cash, and a certain force of hired soldiers. But the only Englishmen of rank were the Earls of Chester and Derby, and Walter de Lacy. He had received a pardon in the previous year, but still had to earn full restitution.[1] Bad weather, however, must have come on, as on the 3rd February the King is found at Yarmouth in the Isle of Wight ; tbere to remain till the 9th February. On the 15th of the month he signs at La Rochelle.[2]

The campaign proved even more humiliating than that of 1206. At first all went smoothly enough, the Poitevins willingly accepting John's nominal suzerainty. On the 8th March he writes to England that the lords of six-and-twenty castles had tendered their allegiance : even Savary of Mauléon had come in and been pardoned, at the request of the Archbishop of Bordeaux. Only one fort, Melle (Deux Sèvres), had to be reduced by force.[3] We next learn from his *Itinerary* that during the ensuing month he made a tour to Angoulême, Aixe (near Limoges), and La Souterraine (Creuze), returning by Limoges, Angoulême, and Cognac to La Réole, the most Southerly place visited by him in 1206. The reader will notice that his round did not include Poitiers a place that rejected him.[4] B> the 22nd April he had returned to La Rochelle, and between that place, Niort, and Fontenay he kept rotating till the 14th May, when at last he began a definite march toward the Loire, resting at Partenay. From another letter of his to England we gather that the only men who had rejected his overtures were his old foes the Lusignans ; that he had called for their submission by a given day, and that as the term had expired he intended to attack their outlying strongholds. Accordingly on the 16th May he appeared before Mervent (Vendée), a few miles to the North of Fontenay, a castle belonging to Geoffrey of Lusignan. The place must have been unprepared, because John, exerting all his strength, carried it by storm on the morrow, Whitsun Eve. Next day again, regardless of the Feast (Whitsunday) he moved on some three miles to Vouvant, where Geoffrey himself and two sons were established. After three days' bombardment the Count de La Marche appeared to negotiate a surrender on behalf of his relatives. John drew off to Partenay, and there on Trinity Sunday (25th May) he received the homages of the Lusignans, namely Hugh le Brun X., Count of La Marche,[5]

Marginal notes: Campaign in Poitou. Promising beginning. Advance towards the Loire. The Lusignans attacked, And brought to terms.

---

[1] R. Cogg., *sup.* ; *Fœdera*, I. 122, 125; and Mr. Kingsford's Article on de Lacy in the *Nationl Dicty.*   [2] *Itinerary.*

[3] *Fœdera*, 118. For the submission of the Viscount of Limoges see Rot. Pat., I. 115, Pauli.

[4] R. Cogg., 169.

[5] Son of Crusader Hugh IX., who died in 1207-1208 ; *Art de vérifier les Dates*, X. 229.

his son Hugh, Ralph Count of Eu, and Geoffrey.   He also entered into a curious matrimonial agreement contracting his daughter Jeanne or Johanna, not four years old,[1] to the younger Hugh, son of the man who was to have married her mother.   The infant bride would have a handsome dowry in lands in Poitou, Anjou, and Touraine—when conquered—meanwhile her affianced lord would be appointed Seneschal of Saintonge and Oleron ; and the Count of Eu would he admitted to Tickhill Castle, and the Rape of Hastings, to which he had claims through his wife.[2]

With respect to his move to Partenay John tells us that he was on his way to relieve Moncontour, a Lusignan stronghold that was being attacked by young Louis of France.   Louis had been sent by his

Young Louis at Chinon. father with a considerable army to defend the line of the Loire; and had taken up his position at Chinon.[3]   We are told that he had 1200 men-at-arms (*milites*), 2000 light horse (*equis vecti*), and 7000 foot-soldiers.[4]   He must have marched on Moncontour on hearing of the Lusignans' alliance with John.   The latter made a further advance towards Moncontour, as on the 28th May he was at Chiché (Deux-Sèvres, near Bressuire).   Of Louis' attack on Moncontour however we hear no more : probably he dropped it, as four days later John is found at L'Epine,[5] apparently the place of that name in La Vendée, near Les Essarts.   From

Operations on the Loire. that base he began pushing forays up and down the valley of the Loire, with one across the river to the gates of Nantes.

Robert of Dreux the younger, whose brother Peter Mauclerc had just married the Breton heiress Constance, venturing to cross the bridge at Nantes to rescue the booty was surrounded and taken prisoner.[6] On the 11th June John crossed the Loire and occupied Ancenis.   Next day, recrossing, he pushed a raid through St. Florent to Rochefort ; and so again on to Blaison (near Brissac), returning by the 15th to Ancenis. Angers and Beaufort then opened their gates to him.[7]   Ordering Angers

Siege of La Roche-au- Moine. to be strongly fortified, he set to work to reduce la Roche-au-Moine, a fort on the North bank of the Loire,[8] recently erected by William des Roches, the Seneschal of Anjou, as a counterwork to Rochefort on the South side of the river.   The new castle, being on the North bank, cut the line of communication between Angers and

---

[1] Born 22nd July, 1210; Ann. Worcester.

[2] See John's letter written 27th or 28th May, Wendover, III. 280.   The King's dates are entirely borne out by the *Itinerary*.   For the treaty see Bouquet XVII., 90, and Rot. Pat., I. 116.   In *Fœdera*, I. 125 the marriage is given as contracted with Geoffrey of Lusignan.   [3] Le Breton, Bouquet, *sup.* 90, 93.

[4] Le Breton, *Philippis*, 245 ; Delpech.   [5] " Spina" ; *Itinerary*.

[6] Le Breton, 91 : " Al pont de Nantes," *Mareschal*, II. 170 ; 4th-7th June.   I cannot identify " Pilem " and " Chezelles," places here named in John's *Itinerary*.

[7] 17th June ; *Itiny.* ; Le Breton, 92, 93.

[8] 19th June.   The place does not appear on the maps ; it is stated to have been five leagues, say 15 miles, below Angers ; Paulin Paris.

Ancenis.   For fourteen days John pressed the siege with vigour.   Young
Louis as yet had shown no disposition to come to close quarters with the
King, contenting himself with watching his operations at a safe distance.
Suddenly, about the 2nd July, Louis was reported as advancing in force on
la Roche.   From what ensued one is inclined to surmise that he had
          ·intelligences in John's camp, and knew what the state of
Defection of feeling there was; because when John proposed to move out
the Poitevins.
          boldly to meet the foe the Poitevin barons refused to follow,
telling him plainly that they had not come to fight pitched battles.[1]   John,
          panic-stricken at the thought of treachery and desertion, raised
Flight of the the siege, and recrossed the Loire in such haste that he left
King.
          behind him his tents, baggage, and artillery.   Two days later
he rested at Saint Maixent, near Niort, seventy miles off.[2]   On the
9th July, being at Rochelle, he addressed a last piteous appeal for help
to his English barons : everything would be forgiven to those who came at
once.[3]   Of course John was disgraced in the eyes of the world.   But the
real reproach lay with the Poitevins who had failed their lord and paymaster
so basely.   Louis soon recovered the places that John had won.   Then
moving across the Loire he occupied himself ravaging the lands of Thouars,
and capturing and demolishing Moncontour.[4]   His energies as we shall
see might have been more usefully employed elsewhere.

    The troops sent by John to Flanders in the winter, or to speak more
          correctly, those retained for him there, had for a time found
The coalition occupation in ravaging Artois, and Ponthieu.[5]   That done
campaign.
          they had to possess their souls in patience awaiting the ap-
pearance of their Imperial leader.   On the 12th July, at last, Otto met his
          confederates at Nivelles, and a general concentration was
Muster at ordered to be held at Valenciennes, with a view to a march
Valenciennes.
          on Paris.[6]   All John's allies had come forward.   Ferrand of
John's allies. Flanders, William of Holland, Henry of Brabant (son-in-law
to Philip, but father-in-law to Otto, who had just married
his daughter Mary), Henry of Limburg were there ; also Duke Theobald
of Lorraine, and the young Count Philip of Namur.[7]   In the English

---

[1] " Dixerunt se ad campestre prælium non esse paratos."
[2] 2nd-4th July : Wendover, III. 286, *Itinerary* ; Le Breton, 92, 93.
[3] Rot. Pat., I. 118 Pauli ; *Fœd.*, I. 123 (15th July).   [4] Grandes Chroniques.
[5] Wendover, III. 279, 280, 287.   Artois had been taken from Flanders by Philip after
the death of Count Philip in 1191 as the portion of his late wife Isabel, and made the
appanage of his son Louis : see above p. 354, note.   The Count of Ponthieu was William
III., who married the rejected Alais in 1200.
[6] Vita Odiliæ, Pertz, XXV. 187.   A biography of an unknown woman, with some
general history interwoven, and written before 1247.
[7] Vita Odiliæ, *sup.*   Kohler *Kriegswesen i.d. Ritterzeit*, I. 122 ; Le Breton, 94.   The
Count of Namur was son of the Countess Yolande by Peter of Courtenay II., Count of
Auxerre, who was on the French side.

contingent we now find Hugh of Boves (Somme), nephew of Hugh of Gournay,[1] associated in command with the Earl of Salisbury, and Reginald of Boulogne.[2] Otto's personal following included the Saxons and Westphalians. In drawing the sword against Philip he doubtless

Their motives. considered that he was attacking the chief supporter of his enemies Frederic of Hohenstaufen, and Innocent III. Other men, such as the Count of Flanders, and Reginald of Boulogne, no doubt, had direct accounts to settle with the King of France. But as a whole the allies might fairly be said to have turned out because John had hired them to fight Philip.[3]

On the French side an army had still to be left with Louis to watch John's movements in the South. But Philip, we are told

Philip's supporters. took 400 men-at-arms from his son,[4] still leaving him 800 men-at-arms, if the chroniclers' figures can be trusted. The Duke of Burgundy was the only great feudatory who joined the King. Theobald the Count of Champagne being under age (13 years old) was kept at home; but a contingent of 180 men-at-arms came on his account. The Archbishop of Reims, with the Bishop of Laon, and Philip of Dreux, the fighting Bishop of Beauvais, represented the Church Militant. Besides these men Philip had the lesser nobility and gentry of the Isle of France, Normandy, and Picardy, with the levies of the *communes*. Among these the men of Corbie, Amiens, Arras, Beauvais, and Compiègne are specially mentioned. The consideration of the question of the numbers on either side may be deferred till we come to the actual field of battle.

The French muster had been held at Péronne. On the 23rd July Philip

Muster at Péronne. began a forward movement from that place. Entering the *Cambresis*, then appertaining to Hainault, he laid all waste before him. Apparently he had been advised not to attack the enemy's position at Valenciennes by the direct road from Cambray, through Bouchain, but to endeavour to turn their flank, or even get at their rear from the North and East, because from the neighbourhood of Cambray he turned towards Douai, and on the 25th July rested at the Bridge of Bouvines, on the little river Marcq, a tributary flowing Northwards to join the Lys. Next day crossing the Marcq he made some ten

French advance to Tournai. or eleven miles along an old Roman road to Tournai. The place had been occupied by Ferrand in the previous year, but had recently been recovered by Philip. He now doubtless thought himself on the flank of the allies. But in fact Otto, keeping an

---

[1] Pauli, I. 398, citing Rot. Misæ, 160 (Hardy).

[2] Wend., III. 287 ; Le Breton, 94, 249.

[3] " Retenus en soudées " ; Grandes Chroniques, IV. 167.

[4] Vita Odiliæ, *sup.*, copied by Gilles d'Orval, Bouquet, XVIII. 253. This certainly tallies with Le Breton's statement that Louis who before had 1200 men-at-arms still retained 800 ; p. 244.

eye on his movements, had advanced along the Scheldt from Valenciennes
to Mortagne, about halfway to Tournai, and was facing him there.[1]
Philip, we are told, was keen for action, but again it was pointed out that
with his dependence on cavalry it would be madness to attack the enemy
established with a narrow front between the river on one hand, and a
forest on the other hand. The French accordingly at day-
Retreat to break on the 27th July began to fall back on Bouvines,
Bouvines. with the intention of drawing the enemy into the more open
country between Lille and Cambray.[2]

Between Tournai and Bouvines the road at first follows the crest of a
rolling plateau culminating at a point a little to the West of Bois, from
whence a good view can be obtained of the surrounding country, and
especially of the low-lying ground to the South and East. After Bois the
plateau sinks, and the road finally reaches Bouvines through a little hollow,
between sloping ridges, one rising towards Cysoing, the other towards the
bank of the river Marcq. About midday Philip with the main body of his
army had reached the banks of the Marcq; the leading division having
already crossed over. The day was very hot, and the King had disarmed,
and was resting under the shade of an ash tree to refresh himself and
drink of the waters of a neighbouring spring, when a scouting party from
the rear reported that the enemy were following in fighting
The allies trim, with banners displayed, light infantry in front, and horses
pursue. with all their housings on; 'certain signs of battle.' A general
halt was ordered, and a council of war held. It was a Sunday. A good
many were in favour of pushing on, so as to adjourn fighting till the
morrow; but Philip very prudently ordered the men who had crossed
the river to be recalled.[3] These included the communal levies with the
Oriflamme. This force, apparently the main infantry force of the army,
was intended to form part of the centre in line of battle. But they were
some three miles off, preparing to encamp at l'Hotellerie;[4] and with the
narrow bridge to cross they did not get back till after the battle
The outposts had begun. Meanwhile a covering party in the extreme rear
engaged. were reported as hard pressed, and the Duke of Burgundy,
who was in command of the rear, was ordered to support them.[5]

The allies on hearing of the French retirement from Tournai, naturally
regarding it as more or less of a flight, were eager to pursue in the hope of
cutting off their force at the crossing of the Marcq. But again some had

---

[1] Le Breton, *sup.*; *Genealogia Com. Fland.,* Bouquet, XVIII. 566; *Vita Odiliæ, sup.*

[2] Le Breton, 94, 254.

[3] Le Breton, 94, 95, 254-256. *Geneal. Com. Fl.,* Bouquet, XVIII., 566.

[4] "Jusques près des hostieux"; Grandes Chron., 181; "Hospitia," Le Breton, 97;
Delpech.

[5] J. Iper, Bouquet, XVIII. 605; Le Breton, 95. The Duke of Burgundy was Eude
or Odo III., son of Hugh, who died at Tyre in 1192.

scruples about the Sunday; while Reginald of Boulogne deprecated any attempt to force on a general engagement, urging that the French should be allowed to continue their retreat, a movement sure to lead to discouragement and desertion, while expected reinforcements of their own would be given time to come up. But the fire-eating counsels of Hugh of Boves prevailed against him.[1] We need not suppose that the allies followed the French round by Tournai, in which case they would never have caught them up as they did. They must have taken a short cut by some of the

Line of the Allied advance. many roads with which that open country abounds, probably through Hovardries and Mouchin, but at the last certainly approaching Bouvines by the commanding ridge that comes down from Cysoing. Had they followed the Tournai road they would have had to approach through a hollow commanded on either side; whereas we are expressly told that the allies occupied ground slightly higher than that occupied by the French. The only ground higher than the line clearly pointed out as that held by the French lies towards Cysoing.[2]

On came the allies. But it appears that their pursuit was pressed with a degree of haste not altogether compatible with strict formation.[3] In fact the battle to a certain extent developed itself out of a running fight between the allied van and the French rear.

Philip after offering up a hasty prayer in the chapel at Bouvines (now **French order of battle.** replaced by a memorial church) proceeded to set his men in order, deploying to the left towards Gruson, with his right extending across the road from Cysoing. A wooden cross on the upper Gruson road marks the extreme French left; a memorial stone by the side of the Cysoing road gives the position that we would assign to the King's right centre.[4] The right wing would extend along the lower slopes of the Cysoing heights past the private grounds marked on the map. The left would occupy an eminence or ridge already mentioned as overlooking the Tournai road; the centre would stand on lower ground between the slopes held by the wings. From end to end the French stood with their backs to the river, and along its bank. The King himself, we are told, took up his position, in the front rank, with no one between him and the enemy.'[5] His post of course would be with the centre, and

---

[1] *Geneal. Com. Fland.*, *sup.*, 567; Wendover, III. 288, 289. Le Breton, 254; Vita Odiliæ, 188.

[2] See the letter of Guerin the Bishop-Elect of Senlis who took such a leading part in the battle; he describes it as being fought "inter Bovinas et Tornacum juxta abbatiam quæ diciter Cyson"; Bouquet, XVII. 428.

[3] Vita Odiliæ, 188; Le Breton, 254.

[4] These landmarks refute the views of those who like Köhler, Delpech, and Lavisse align the two armies East and West along the road from Bouvines to Tournai. Mr. Oman places them athwart the road; *Art of War*, 450.

[5] "Rex ponit se in prima fronte belli ubi nullus inter ipsum et hostes imminebat"; Le Breton, 95.

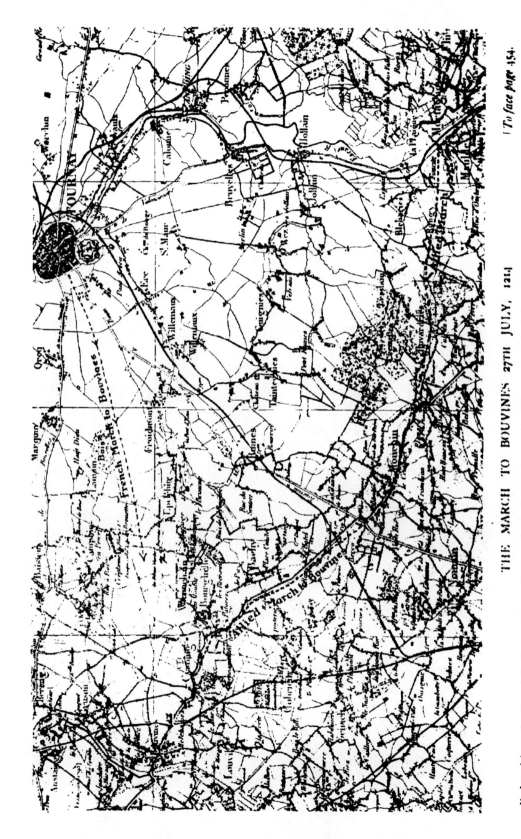

THE MARCH TO BOUVINES 27TH JULY, 1214

Reduced from the French Ordnance Map. The positions of the two armies at the beginning of the action are also shown by dotted crosses; the Allies to the right on right hand side, and the French to the left on left hand side, after the march from Cysoing and Tournay to their new

[To face page 494.

in the middle of it. That at the outset there was nothing in front of him, nothing between him and the enemy, was true ; but it was the result of an accidental circumstance. He was intended, as will clearly appear further on, to take post behind the main body of his infantry ; but they had not yet recrossed the river, and so Philip, for the time, had to confront the enemy face to face. A party of foot-soldiers was detached to hold the bridge of the Marcq in the rear.

The French line would face about due East. We are told that when the action began they had the sun at their backs ; from which **Aspect of the French line.** circumstance we may gather that the forces did not come together till the afternoon, as might be expected from the distances that they had marched that day.

The position taken up by the allies was determined by that of the French. We hear that they deployed to the right of the road **Allied position and order of battle.** by which they had come, moving obliquely towards the West and North, taking up ground slightly higher than that of the French, and having a broiling sun full in their faces.[1]

On each side there were as usual three divisions, a centre, and two wings. Philip's left wing was commanded by the Count of **Marshalling of the lines.** Dreux, supported by his brother Philip, Bishop of Beauvais, and the Counts of Ponthieu, Auxerre, and Soissons. The infantry of this division was mainly furnished by a contingent, estimated as 2000 strong, brought by Thomas of Saint Valéry, lord of Gamaches.[2] The King himself, as already mentioned, stood in the centre, not in a line with the front of his army, but at a point in the rear, with a vacant space left in front of him for his infantry, when it should arrive. But he had

---

[1] " Hostes diverterunt ad dexteram partem itineris quo gradiebantur, et protenderunt se quasi ad occidentem, et occupaverunt eminentiorem partem campi, et steterunt a parte septentrionali, solem qui die illa solito ferventius incaluerat ante oculos habentes. Rex etiam alas suas nihilo minus extendit e regione contra illos, et stetit a parte australi cum exercitu suo, per spatia campi non parva linealiter protenso, solem habens in humeris : et ita steterunt hinc inde utræque acies, æquali dimensione protensæ, modico campi spatio a se invicem distantes." Le Breton, *sup.*, 95. In his *Philippis* the writer says of Otto's movement, " A læva paulum retrahit vestigia parte, componensque acies gressus obliquat ad Arcton " ; p. 257. Le Breton was evidently hazy as to the points of the compass, as he speaks of the farther side of the Marcq as being to the South ("ad austrum," p. 256) ; of course it was to the West. The Chronicle of Tours again represents Otto as moving towards the North ; " versus septentrionem " ; Bouquet, XVIII. 298. M. Delpech, *Tactique au XIII. Siècle*, I. 70, taking his stand on the literal words of Le Breton, and ignoring local tradition arranges the French in an extraordinary position along the South side of the Tournai road, and the allies on the North side of it ; General Köhler, *Kriegs-wesen*, I. 144, and Mr. Oman, *Art of War*, 467, arrange the forces more as I do, but they make the fatal error, as it appears to me, of assuming that the allies reached the field of battle by the Tournai road.

[2] Le Breton, 99, 250, 257, with the identifications supplied by Köhler, 140, and Delpech, 116.

the support of 70 men-at-arms from Normandy, and of his household body-guard, with the flower of French chivalry, Richard's old antagonist,
William des Barres at their head. They would have a certain
Philip's Bodyguard. complement of lighter horse, of course. But we may point out
that as a whole they were men more distinguished for personal prowess than for large followings. Of all the men connected by the chroniclers with this corps the only ones likely to bring substantial contingents were Henry Count of Bar, and Ingelram of Coucy, so that until the levies from the *communes* came up the King's division must have been represented by a thin line of glittering mail. Over Philip's head fluttered his banner, golden *fleur de lys* on an azure ground.[1] The right wing, the post usually appertaining to the van of the marching column, had to be left open for the rear-guard under the Duke of Burgundy, who apparently only came up just in time to fall in. With him came the men of Champagne, the Counts of Beaumont and St. Pol, Matthew of Montmorency, the Viscount of Melun, and the Hospitaller, Brother Guérin, Bishop-Elect of Senlis. This man, who had been in command of a covering party in the rear, is represented as being virtually in command of the whole right wing.[2] Philip addressed his men in a few simple words. Otto and all his had been excommunicated by their Holy Father the Pope; they, the French were Christians, sinners may be, as other men were, but still conforming to the laws of God and the Church; they were fighting the cause of the Church, and Heaven would surely bless their arms.[3]

On the other side the allies leaving their van, which was still entangled with the French rear, on the left, deployed to their right, as
The Allied forces. already stated, with the Emperor in the centre, and the English,
who had been in the rear, pushed forward to the right hand position, opposite the French left. The allied right included, besides the small actual contingent from England under the Earl of Salisbury, foreign mercenaries, apparently mainly footmen, enlisted by Reginald of Boulogne and Hugh of Boves; with a body of Flemish horse under Arnold of
Oudenarde.[4] A special feature of this division was the forma-
Formation of Infantry. tion adopted by Reginald for his infantry, who were drawn up
in a hollow circle, two ranks deep, with one opening, doubtless in the rear, to enable his cavalry to take shelter inside when hard pressed.[5] We may suppose the cavalry to have been aligned to the right and left of

---

[1] Le Breton, 95, 97, 250; Köhler, 139; Delpech, 114. *Contra*, Lavisse, III. 190, who makes Philip's banner "rouge semée de fleur de lys."

[2] Köhler and Delpech, *sup.*   [3] Le Breton, 95; *Geneal. Com. Fland.*, *sup.*

[4] Le Breton, 263, and P. Mousket, cited Delpech, I. 117.

[5] Le Breton, 98, 263; G. Guiart, cited Delpech, 153; *Geneal. Com. Fland.*, 567; Köhler, 143. The Flemish writer gives the number in the ring as 400; Le Breton, 98, makes them 700.

this circle.　The Emperor in the central division was surrounded by troops massed in very deep formation,[1] and mainly composed of infantry, these being placed in the forefront.　Besides his own German following he had the contingents of the Dukes of Lorraine, Brabant, and Limburg, with that of the Count of Namur, and perhaps also that of the Count of

The Emperor's Bodyguard. Holland.　His Standard, bearing the old Saxon emblem of a golden eagle perched on the back of a dragon, was mounted on a lofty pole, set up on wheels, a regular Italian *carroccio*, like the celebrated Standard of 1138.　For its defence and that of his own person he had, like Philip, a bodyguard of picked knights under Counts Conrad of Dortmund and Otto of Tecklenburg, assisted by Gerard of Randerode and Bernard of Hortzmar, all men of renown.[2]　The allied left, as already stated, was led by Count Ferdinand or Ferrand of Flanders with divers Flemish gentlemen of minor note under him.　The Count of Holland however may have been attached to this division.　No footsoldiers are spoken of in connexion either with this corps, or with the opposing French right; nor do we get much information as to the tactical arrangements of the various bodies of troops engaged, except as to the ring of infantry on the allied right; and the dense formation of the allied centre, these points being clearly stated.　Philip's chaplain who was present tells

Length of the lines. us that the French front as originally drawn out covered a space of 1040 paces (*passus*); but that the allied front when it was deployed was found to extend to 2000 paces, so that Philip to save being completely outflanked had to extend his line to a corresponding length.[3]　Of the operation as carried out on the French right, where the movement would begin, we hear that Guérin met the situation partly by leaving an extra interval between himself and the centre,[4] partly by extending his line; and that it had to be opened out to such an extent that he now had only first-class men-at-arms enough to man his front rank.[5]　Corresponding movements must have taken place on

---

[1] "Stabat Otho in medio agminis consertissimi"; Le Breton, 95.

[2] Le Breton, 94, 98, 248, 249; Köhler, 142; Delpech, 115.

[3] Le Breton, 96.　"Sic etiam Rex ipse suæ protendere frontis Cornua curavit, ne forte præoccupari, Aut intercludi tam multo possit ab hoste"; Id. 257.

[4] "Spatiis a Rege remotis"; *Id.* 258.

[5] "Omnes isti (sc. milites) erant in una acie; Electo sic disponente, qui quosdam . . . de quorum probitate et fervore certus erat in una et prima acie posuit, et dixit illis, 'Campus amplus est; Extendite vos per campum directe, ne hostes vos intercludant. Non decet ut unus miles scutum sibi de alio milite faciat; sed sic stetis ut omnes quasi una fronte possitis pugnare"; Le Breton, 96; and again in the *Philippis.*

  "Summopere caveant ne ipsos numerosior hostis
   Cornua protendens forte intercludere possit;
   Ne seria series sit longior hostis eorum;
   Ne scutum miles faciat de milite, sed se
   Quisque sua sponte opposita fronte offerat hosti"; p. 258.

the French left and centre also; because it is clear that when the action began the two centres confronted each other.

But the general question how the men, horse and foot, light-armed and heavy-armed, were marshalled within their respective divisions, remains open to doubt. One modern writer would arrange the cavalry **Question of formations.** in three distinct lines, each line being three ranks deep; and he brings the entire lines into action one after the other; he also subdivides each line in each division into four squadrons, all numerically equal.[1] These may have been usual arrangements, but we have no evidence of them in connexion with the battle of Bouvines.

Another authority regards the contingent of each of the **Modern theories.** greater feudatories as constituting a squadron or unit, the respective vassals fighting under their own lords; and the accounts of the fighting on the French right clearly point to this arrangement.[2] But again the same writer would divide these contingents into two lines, one the fighting line in front, the other a deeper line in support behind. On the French wings the fighting line would be one man deep.[3] This writer further lays it down that the infantry were posted in front of the cavalry. But at Bouvines this was only the case with the two centres, to which the main infantry corps were assigned. On the whole the impression left on our mind by the course of the engagement is that the French right charged in little columns of squadrons, or feudal contingents, possibly in wedge formation,[4] the men-at-arms supplying the steel tip and the casing of the mass, and their followers the backing[5]; that the allied left facing them, also composed entirely of cavalry, was probably arranged in successive lines and squadrons; that at the other end of the battle the French left and the allied right both had the support of bodies of infantry, in defensive positions, the offensive falling wholly on the cavalry. With respect to the two centres we believe that the Imperial and Royal leaders, when the lines were fully made up, were posted with their household bodyguards behind masses of infantry, with possibly some flanking cavalry.

One word as to numbers. Of the foot-soldiers on either side we would

---

[1] Köhler, 136–139, 141, 144. The "tres acies" of Wendover on which the General relies clearly refer to the three divisions of the whole army; and the "tres ordines" of *Vita Odiliæ,* p. 188, doubtless mean the same.

[2] Speaking of the light cavalry (*servientes*) Le Breton says : "Scalasque suorum quisque magistrorum, densant," p. 256. "Scalas," rendered échelles in the Grandes Chroniques, whence the modern échelon, is used by Le Breton as a squadron or contingent.

[3] Delpech, 119, 120.

[4] On this formation, retained by the Germans till the end of the fifteenth century, but beginning to fall into disuse in France in the thirteenth century, see Köhler, 136.

[5] See again Le Breton's description of this formation, "Scalas suorum magistrorum densant," p. 256." 'They fill up the squadrons of their leaders.'

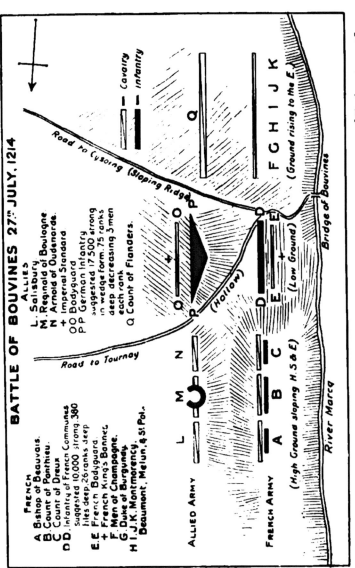

BATTLE OF BOUVINES 27ᵗʰ JULY, 1214

FRENCH
A Bishop of Beauvais.
B. Count of Ponthieu.
C. Count of Dreux.
DD. Infantry of French Communes
  suggested 10,000 strong. 380
  files deep. 26 ranks deep
E.E French Bodyguard.
+ French King's Banner.
F. Men of Champagne.
G. Duke of Burgundy.
H. I. J. K. Montmorency.
  Beaumont, Melun, & St Pol.

ALLIES
L. Salisbury.
M. Reginald of Boulogne.
N. Arnold of Oudenarde.
+ Imperial Standard.
OO. Bodyguard.
P.P German Infantry
  suggested 17,500 strong
  in wedge form. 75 ranks
  deep decreasing 3 men
  each rank.
Q. Count of Flanders.

Road to Cysoing (Sloping Ridge)

Road to Tournay

(Hollow)

(High Ground sloping H. S. & E.)

ALLIED ARMY

FRENCH ARMY

River Marcq

(Low Ground)

Bridge of Bouvines

(Ground rising to the E.)

Cavalry
Infantry

[To face page 458.]

rather not pledge ourselves to any estimate, as we have really nothing to
go by. But as a plan of the battle seemed indispensable,
and infantry had to appear, we have set on foot 17,000 men
on the allied centre, and 10,000 men on the French centre,
besides the foot specially noticed as attached to the French left and the
allied right. With regard to the cavalry a contemporary writer tells us
that prisoners taken by the French declared that the allies had only
1500 men-at-arms (*milites*); while another writer reduces the number
to 1300, and these figures have been accepted by modern scholars.[1] The
light horse (*servientes equites*) would be much more numerous, probably
4000 or 5000, as it seems that the Flemings were strong in that arm.[2]
For the heavy cavalry of the French we seem to have a basis for an
estimate in the facts given as to the extension of their front. At first
it measured 1040 paces or yards. From that we must deduct something
for the intervals between the centre and the wings, say 40 yards for each
interval, or 80 yards in all. That would leave 960 yards of frontage to be
shared by the three divisions. If equally divided the space would give
320 yards to each division. But when the allied front was deployed the
French found that they had 2000 yards to face. To meet that we have
seen that the intervals between the divisions had to be increased, say
from 40 yards to 80 yards each, or 160 yards in all. There would
remain 1840 yards to be divided between the three divisions, making
613 yards or thereabouts for each—just double the original allowance.
But Guérin with this increased front to cover had only men-at-arms
enough for one rank. Does it not seem to follow that with his original
front he would have had two ranks of such men? The question then
follows how many mounted men would fill a given space; how much
are we to allow for each horse? Mr. Oman in his *Art of War* thinks
three feet enough for the heavy mediæval charger with all his housings.[3]
General Köhler allows him four feet,[4] and M. Delpech two metres or
six feet six inches.[5] Taking five feet as a medium estimate two ranks of
320 yards would require 380 men. If we could assign an equal strength
of such cavalry to each division we should have a total of 1150 men in
round numbers. But we question if the details of cavalry mentioned by
Le Breton in connexion with the centre could be regarded as suggesting
numbers equal to those connected with either of the wings, while the right
wing having no infantry at all ought surely to have had a larger allowance
of cavalry than the left. Thus 1000 full men-at-arms would seem to be as

Question of
numbers.

---

[1] Chron. Turon., Bouquet, XVIII. 229; Chron. S. Columb. Sens, *Id.* 722; Köhler,
124; Delpech, 4; Oman, *Art of War*, 463.
[2] So Kohler, *sup.*
[3] P. 468.
[4] P. 141.
[5] P. 123.

much as we could estimate for the French army.[1]　As for light horse the proportion assigned by Le Breton to Louis' army in Poitou was only 2000 to 1200 men-at-arms.　There may have been a larger proportion of them at Bouvines, but on the whole we can see no reason for supposing more than one rank of the very finest heavy cavalry, with a backing of two or three ranks of light horse.　But of course the order in which they fought on this occasion was exceptionally open.

As for the tactical arrangements of the allies they seem to have followed very closely those of the French.　In the matter of numbers we are bound at any rate to recognise on their side an excess corresponding to the extent by which their front exceeded the original French front, say by the ratio of five to three.

Fighting began on the French right—where the two armies had already been in contact—and it began apparently without orders from headquarters,

The action. and possibly even before the forces had been fully arrayed, certainly before the infantry of the French centre had arrived. Guérin by way of breaking ground, and as if to feel for an opening, sent out a body of 150 light horse to provoke the enemy.　But the

The French Right. Flemish gentry declined to break their ranks for such foes, and apparently disposed of the attack by simply spearing or unhorsing any who ventured to come within reach.[2]　Some hand to hand encounters followed, all in favour of the French.　Then there ensued on the part of the latter a series of brilliant charges to which the result of the day was mainly due.　Walter Count of St. Pol led off by dash-

Comet-charges. ing furiously uphill with his contingent against the ranks in front of him, cutting his way through them, then wheeling shortly round he recharged them from the rear, the sweeping tail of his force enveloping the intervening files as in a net; galloping home without attempting to take prisoners St. Pol returned to his original ground to take breath, and prepare for another swoop.[3]　The use of the word

[1] M. Delpech also takes the French heavy cavalry as 1000 in number, but he arrives at that figure by a very different route from mine.　He assumes that the 400 men taken from Louis' army were practically the only 'knights' (chevaliers) in Philip's army; however he raises the number to 500, and then assigning to each knight the 'traditional' esquire man-at-arms he gets the 1000 total.　Of light horse he allows 4000, and 20,000 foot.　On the numbers of the allies he becomes utterly wild, giving them 12,500 horse and 74,500 infantry (!), I. 1–13 and the Table p. 37.　General Köhler with his three lines, each three ranks deep, and four feet for each horse, gives the French 2500 heavy and 4000 light horse, with 50,000 foot, I. 126, 141.　Mr. Oman gives the French 1500–2000 "knights," 4000 light horse, and 20,000–25,000 foot; for the allies he has 1500 "knights," 5000 mounted "serjeants," and 40,000 foot, pp. 467, 468.

[2] Le Breton, 96, 258.

[3] "Perforavit eos per medium eorum mira velocitate transiens . . . et ita reversus est per aliam partem, multitudinem eorum quam maximam intercludens quasi in sinu quodam"; Le Breton, 98.　And again "Sinu facto . . . implicat innumeros quasi pisces rete retentos," p. 260.

perforavit, and the whole description of the Count's action not as riding down the enemy, but as piercing their ranks, and cutting off a certain number of files, implies a formation if not in the shape of a wedge at any rate in column with a very narrow front.   Similar comet-charges by the Count of Beaumont, Matthew of Montmorency, the Viscount of Melun, and the Duke of Burgundy followed, Ferrand's extreme left being the point especially assailed.[1]   In one attack the Duke, a big heavy man, had his horse killed under him, and was mightily incensed thereat.

Neither the Count of Flanders nor Reginald of Boulogne had failed to notice the hollow state of the French centre, with its main force wanting.
Weakness of the French Centre. Both endeavoured by oblique movements inwards to make for the French King's position.   Had Otto co-operated the French line must have been cut in two.   But for infantry deliberately to attack heavy cavalry would no doubt be something very novel, in fact unheard of in the warfare of the times, and so the Emperor remained where he was, blocking the way in fact.   But it must be pointed out that to attack the French centre he would have to descend from the slope of his hill to lower ground.   On the other side the men of Champagne on the French right, and the Count of Dreux on the left throwing themselves into the breach, arrested the attempted concentration against their centre, and kept the two Counts fully employed in defending their positions each on his own original ground.[2]

By this time the levies of the *Communes* had at last come up.   Pressing through the wide interval left by Guérin between himself and the French
French infantry arrive. centre, they took up their appointed position, in front of their King and his household bodyguard.   Otto now saw before him foes with whom he could rightly grapple, and so setting his sturdy pikemen in motion he slid down on the communal infantry like
Their defeat. an earthslip, and overwhelmed them.   It has been suggested with great probability that the Germans charged in wedge formation,[3] because we hear that the French foot breaking off to the right and left in utter rout left their King exposed to the brunt of the German
Philip unhorsed. onslaught.   He was hooked by a man with the crook of his halbert,[4] and dragged to the ground.   But for his armour he might have been killed.   He was rescued by desperate exertions on the part of his standard bearer Gales or Galon de Montigny,

[1] Le Breton, *sup.*; Delpech, 134, 138.

[2] Le Breton, 96, 98.   [3] So Delpech, 142.

[4] The German foot are described as armed with long spears fitted with a battle-axe on one side and a hook on the other—halberts.   We also hear of another weapon new to the French writer, a three-edged sword-dagger, obviously the old Anglo-Saxon *seax* ; "cultellos longos graciles, triacumines, quolibet acumine secantes a cuspide usque ad manubrium, quibus utebantur pro gladiis"; Le Breton, 97, 261.   For engravings of these see *Foundations of England*, I. 174.

and a few others of the bodyguard who drove back his assailants, and remounted him. Philip's exposed position was due to the impetuosity of William des Barres and the Household Knights, who, panting to be at the Emperor, pressed forward on the right hand and the left in advance of their master, to throw themselves on the flanks of the German infantry. A lengthy and desperate struggle ensued, ending in the break-up and dispersal of the phalanx.[1]

On the allied left the battle had already come to an end. The demolition of their outer wing by Guérin's repeated charges enabled him to throw his whole force against Count Ferrand and the inner section **Defeat of the Allied left.** of his wing, who had been fighting the men of Champagne. Dismounted, wounded, and utterly exhausted the gallant Count had to yield himself a prisoner. His followers and allies then made off as best they could.[2]

Meanwhile Philip's bodyguard, having disposed of the German infantry, had fairly fought their way to the Emperor. One man seized his bridle-rein and tried to lead him off. Another, aiming a blow at his head, **Otto's horse killed.** stabbed his horse through the eye. The animal rearing up, and wheeling round in his agony, set his rider free, and then galloped off wildly to drop down dead at a little distance. Bernard of Horstmar, sacrificing his own chance of safety for that of his master, quickly remounted him, giving him his own horse. Otto abandoning the struggle continued his flight; the Duke of Brabant accompanied him; the two never rested till they reached Valenciennes.[3] In the medley, we are told, des Barres had twice got his arm round the Emperor's neck, wrestling with him on horseback, but had been unable to keep his hold in the crush.[4] The Imperial Household, cover-**Dispersal of Allied Centre.** ing their lord's retreat, like true vassals, held their ground, fighting to the last. Des Barres was unhorsed, and reduced to fighting on foot. The scale was finally turned by the assistance of horse and foot, brought from the French left under Thomas of St. Valéry. Des Barres was rescued, the Imperial Standard beaten down, the Eagle captured; while, surrounded by overpowering numbers, Conrad of Dartmund, Otto of Tecklenburg, Gerard of Randerode, and Bernard of Horstmar, all had to give up their swords.[5]

On the allied right and the French left the struggle was kept up longer and on more equal terms than anywhere else. In fact we are **The Allied Right.** told that the result remained long in doubt.[6] This was clearly due to the good generalship and staunchness of Reginald of Boulogne, who fully justified his military reputation. His central ring

---

[1] Le Breton, 97, 98, 261, 262.   [2] Le Breton, 97, 261.
[3] Chron. S. Columb. Sens, Bouquet, XVIII. 722; Chron. Fland. Köhler, 153.
[4] Le Breton, 97, 98. In the *Philippis*, 265, 266, he gives a rather different account of des Barres' attempt.   [5] Le Breton, 98, 99, 266.   [6] Le Breton, 266.

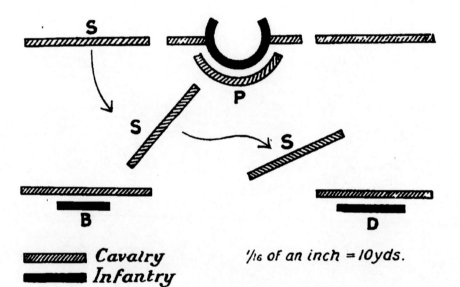

Cavalry

Infantry

¹/₁₆ of an inch = 10yds.

BATTLE OF BOUVINES, 27TH JULY, 1214

ATTACK OF THE EARL OF SALISBURY ON THE COUNT OF DREUX

S Earl of Salisbury.
P Count of Ponthieu engaged with infantry in the ring.
B Bishop of Beauvais.
D Count of Dreux.

[To face page 403.

of trained Flemish foot maintained an unbroken position till the very last

Reginald of Boulogne and his Infantry. stage of the action : while the ready shelter to be found within their ranks enabled his cavalry to take breath from time to time, and watch an opportunity of sallying out again with effect.[1] On his right hand he had the Earl of Salisbury ; Hugh of Boves and Arnold of Oudenarde were also attached to his division ; but their exact position is not indicated. Hugh being in the English service would probably stand with the Earl ; and Arnold might assist Reginald in directing the movements of the centre and left of their division. On the side of the French the Bishop of Beauvais confronted Longsword ;[2] the Count of Ponthieu led the centre, while Dreux and Auxerre stood on the right of the division, next to King Philip.[3]

As already mentioned, Reginald at the outset endeavoured by a flank movement to get at King Philip, but was held in check by the Count of Dreux. This would be an engagement of cavalry. The next movement that we hear of at that end of the battle is the attack of the Count of Ponthieu with cavalry on the infantry ring (*globum*). This lasted the whole of the day. Again and again the horsemen charged, but to no purpose: in vain they hacked and hewed at the steadfast lines of pikes ; when their horses were disabled they fought on foot, but still without success, Reginald with his horse giving every support to his infantry.[4] Ponthieu having been practically defeated Salisbury, at last, came forward. The operation that might be expected of him would be an attempt to turn the French flank. Instead of that we hear of an attack on the Count of

Longsword's charge. Dreux, who was on the right hand or innerside of the French left, and next to the King. That would involve a cross-attack on Longsword's part against an enemy not in front of him, but to his left. To get at the Count he would have to wheel, first to the left, round the infantry ring, and the struggle connected with it, past the front of the Bishop of Beauvais, and then to the right, leaving both the Bishop and Ponthieu in his rear.[5] Perhaps the Earl despised the Bishop as being a mere churchman. A more material circumstance that may have induced him to risk so bold a movement was this, that, as we have seen, the contingent of Thomas of Saint Valéry had been taken from the French left to complete the discomfiture of the German centre. If Longsword despised the Bishop he paid dearly for his contempt. The gallant Prelate, like Odo at Senlac, carried a club as his only weapon. This was done to avoid any canonical question as to shedding of blood. He had

---

[1] *Id.*, 98, 267.

[2] " Longus Gladius ; " Vita Odil. ; *sup.*, 186 ; " Cui . . . Angligenæ longo dederant agnomen ab ense ; " Le Breton, 266.

[3] Le Breton, 98.

[4] *Geneal. Com. Fland.*, Bouquet, XVIII. 567. This part of the battle is not noticed by Le Breton.   [5] See plan.

taken no part in the battle as yet.   But to come forward to save his brother's men from destruction would be defensive action, and strictly legitimate.[1]   Hastening to the rescue he came down on the *Its discomfiture.* Earl, who must have been taken in the rear while engaged with another enemy in front.   In Le Breton's verse the contest resolves itself into a short hand to hand encounter between the Bishop and the Earl.   The Bishop smites his antagonist on the head with his club, and fells him to the ground ; the Earl and a few others are secured ; 'the rest they run away.'[2]   Be this as it may have been the Bishop's charge finally settled the issue of the day of Bouvines.   Salisbury's force having *Reginald of Boulogne overcome.* been dispersed the dauntless Reginald and the doomed pike-men in the ring remained alone on the field.   The ex-Count of Boulogne, the one man who on the eve of the battle advised Fabian tactics, was the last to succumb.   He had fulfilled his vaunt that he would live to see Hugh of Boves take to his heels while he, Reginald, fought it out to the bitter end.[3]   Only six mounted followers remained with him, striving to drag him from the field.   A foot-soldier stabbed his horse ; the animal fell, with his master under him.   The Count was then secured and led away on a sumpter horse.   Arnold of Oudenarde endeavouring to come to the rescue shared his fate.[4]

But the doomed ring of foot-soldiers still remained.   Thomas of St. *End of the Battle.* Valéry, to complete his signal services of the day, brought his men to surround them and cut them off.   According to Philip's chaplain they were butchered to a man.

Little pursuit was attempted.   The sun was setting ;[5] the battle must have lasted three or four hours[6]—a long time for a mediæval action, and Philip was chiefly concerned with keeping his numerous prisoners in safety. *Victory of the French.* Besides, pursuit would not be free from risk ; the allied army had been broken up and defeated, but not destroyed ; and they were returning by fifties and hundreds.   The King called off his men and sent them to their bivouacs.[7]   He might well be satisfied with the success that he had achieved.   The mere lists of important

---

[1] Le Breton is very explicit on the point that Dreux's contingent was the one attacked by Salisbury.

> "Nam Belvacensis ut vidit Episcopus Angli
> Regis germanum, cui cum sit viribus ingens
> Angligenæ longo dederant agnomen ab ense,
> Sternere Drocenses et damnificare frequenti
> Cæde sui fratris acies, dolet."   p. 266.

[2] *Id.*, 267.
[3] Wendover, III. 289 ; *Mareschal*, II. 168.
[4] Le Breton, 99, 268.
[5] Le Breton, 290.   At Bouvines on the 27th July the sun sets at 7.44 p.m. Delpech, 265.
[6] See Le Breton, 97.   [7] *Id.*, 99.

captives sent to different quarters for safe keeping shewed 131 names of men of position, with five Counts and twenty Bannerets.[1]   But the political

Future of France assured. consequences were infinitely greater.   The future of France was settled; the ultimate reduction of the soil of Gaul under the rule of the Kings of Paris could only be a question of time.   The question of the Imperial Crown was also settled.   Otto after a few months' stay at Cologne had again to retire to Brunswick, there to end his days on the 19th May, 1218.[2]   The battle has been claimed as an illustration of the advantages of fighting in open order.[3]   Clearly the French lost nothing by being obliged to extend their ranks.   Then the absolute supremacy of the mail-clad cavalry on the field of battle is still manifest.   The age had no missiles that could harm them.   Neither the bow nor the cross-bow of the period were of any avail; the men-at-arms were really only vulnerable through their horses, who as yet were not protected by defensive armour.[4]   But Reginald of Boulogne might claim to have shown the world, how, under more favourable circumstances,

Prowess of the French chivalry. infantry might be led to victory.   Lastly we cannot withhold our tribute of admiration for the gallantry of the martial gentry of the Northern and Eastern districts of France—the endemic home, by the way, of the tournament.   These were the men, who, the year before at Muret, under the leadership of Simon of Montfort, had, against immense odds, defeated all the forces of Arragon and Languedoc.

Utterly worsted in both his campaigns John had to resign himself to peace.   On the 11th September a truce on the basis of the

Truce with France. *status quo* was signed with Philip; hostilities to be suspended till Easter 1220.[5]   The King himself remained for some weeks touring in the neighbourhood of La Rochelle, paying visits to Angoulême and Limoges with a trip as far North as Le Blanc.[6]   On the 2nd October he was still at La Rochelle; on the 15th of the month he signs at Dartmouth.[7]

[1] Bouquet, XVII. 101–107.
[2] Pauli, I. 409, 410.
[3] Delpech, I. 173.
[4] Delpech, 422.   In 1298 they were only receiving short housings of mail ; *Ib.*
[5] *Fœdera*, I. 124, 125.
[6] Indre—midway between Poitiers and Châteauroux.
[7] *Itinerary.*

H H

CHAPTER XXIX

A.D. 1214, 1215

The Interdict dissolved—Reforming Movement—Demand for the Charter of Henry I.—
Grant of Magna Carta

AT the time of John's departure for Poitou we left Langton chafing at the presence of the Legate Nicholas, and protesting against his interference with canonical elections, and private rights of Ecclesiastical patronage. A Provincial Synod held at Dunstable by the affairs. Archbishop about the middle of January (1214) resolved on an appeal to Rome. Their case was entrusted to Simon Langton, while the Legate sent his coadjutor Pandulf to defend his proceedings.[1] Innocent quietly ignored Langton's complaints, calling the attention of the parties before him to the primary importance of settling the arrears, and relieving England of the Interdict. He had already fixed on 100,000 marks as the sum to be paid by John, before the Interdict could be dissolved.[2] Now to facilitate matters he suggested that John should only be required to pay 40,000 marks down, credit being given him for all sums already paid, and that for the balance of the 100,000 marks he should give security for its settlement by instalments spread over five years.[3] John being then at Angers accepted the compromise, and gave the required undertaking.[4]

On these terms the Interdict was finally dissolved. A grand The Interdict ecclesiastical function was held at St. Paul's on Wednesday, dissolved. 2nd July, the Legate presiding, when the Bishop of Ely, with all due formality, declared the terrible sentence at an end.[5] Six years and

---

[1] Wendover, III. 278; W. Coventry, II. 216. On the 1st January 12,000 marks were ordered to be given to Pandulf, a payment that I cannot explain, unless it refers to the money understood to have been sent abroad in May. Rot. Pat., I. 107. This was independently of his journey money for which £1000 was ordered on the 3rd of the month; *Ib.*

[2] See the Pope's letter of the 23rd January, 1214, *Epp.*, XVI. 164. This was doubtless the letter presented to John in Poitou on the 4th March, which he forwarded to England with a request for contributions from the chief towns; *Fœdera*, I. 118.

[3] See the letter, Wendover, III. 281. It is not known from any other source.

[4] 17th June; *Fœdera*, 122; *Itinerary*.

[5] W. Cov., II. 217; R. Cogg., 169; Ann. Winton, Waverley, Bermondsey, and Wykes. Wendover, III. 284, gives the date as the 29th June.

a quarter, and more, it had lasted, namely since the 24th March 1208. Church services were resumed, and church bells might again ring out their merry peals.   But of the stipulated 40,000 marks 23,000 marks had already been received by the clergy who had been in exile, namely 12,000 marks through Pandulf, and 15,000 marks at Reading, leaving only 23,000 marks available for more general distribution.   In consequence the Legate was assailed by a hungry crowd of abbots, priors, abbesses, Templars, Hospitallers and others who had not been in exile clamouring for a settlement of their claims.   Nicholas could only tell them that he had nothing more to give.[1]

Of the bishoprics left vacant when the King went abroad only two had been filled by the time of his return.   Walter Gray the Chancellor had been duly installed at Worcester, and Simon of Apulia at Exeter.[2]   This last man's relations with the late Archbishop Geoffrey will be remembered.[3]

Vacant Sees. On the other hand Gilbert Glanville Bishop of Rochester had died, while another vacancy followed shortly through the demise of the faithful John Gray of Norwich, who fell ill in Poitou on his way back from Rome.[4]   His death was a distinct loss to the King.

John had returned to England beaten and discredited, with all his plans frustrated, and his treasure squandered for nothing.   The men whom he had left in England to represent his interests, the Legate and Peter des Roches, had done nothing to make themselves popular; and **Discontent in England.** their injudicious action had added to the general discontent.[5]

But the absence of the King during eight continuous months would give the malcontent barons great opportunities for meeting and concerting measures.   That the administration of the country was carried on under difficulties appears from a letter of the 5th November from the Pope to Eustace de Vescy, reminding him that now that the Church questions had been settled there could be no justification for any 'confederacies' or opposition to the King; and forbidding any interference with the King's officers in the discharge of their duties.[6]   Altogether the situation was one calling for tact and prudence on the part of a ruler.   John met it by demanding a scutage from the barons who had refused to follow him to Poitou, thus raising the most burning question of the hour.[7]   He had his answer in the shape of a meeting held at Bury St. Edmunds under

---

[1] Wendover, *sup.*; Ann. Waverley.

[2] Ann. Worcester; *Reg. Sacrum.*   Both were consecrated at Canterbury on the 5th October.

[3] See above, 344.

[4] Glanville died on the 24th June and Gray on the 18th October.   *Reg. Sacr.*

[5] See Ann. Waverley, 281.

[6] "Cum . . . sit omnino sopita discordia quæ olim inter regem et sacerdotium in Anglia vertebatur . . . concordia reformata cum causa cessare debet et effectus"; *Fœd.,* I. 126.

[7] W. Cov., II. 217; Rot. Pat, I. 141.   See also the Pope's letter of the 1st April, 1215, ordering it to be paid; *Fœdera,* I. 128.

pretence of a pilgrimage ; men from all parts of the Kingdom attended.
Charter of Henry I. demanded. The Barons again pledged themselves to demand the charter of Henry I. ; but they made a distinct step in advance by resolving that the time for action had come, and that preparation should be made for a possible recourse to arms after Christmas.[1] It is pretty clear however that some conferences were held with the King, and that the Legate endeavoured to mediate.[2] But John shortly lost the benefit of such support as Nicholas could give, as the Pope yielding to the representations of the English clergy recalled him.[3] John endeavoured to divide his enemies by detaching the clergy from the laity. A real solidarity of the two would seem to him impossible. On the 21st November he offered the right of free canonical election to the cathedral and monastic chapters ;[4] and next day he placed the advowson (*jus patronatus*)
John's intrigues. of the vacant See of Rochester, with all rights, at the disposition of Archbishop Langton ; while Thorney Abbey was given to the Bishop of Ely.[5]

John kept his Christmas at Worcester, for a change, and was allowed to keep it in peace. After a short tour through the Midlands he came to London, establishing himself in safe quarters at the Temple, still distinguished in the records of the time as the New Temple (7th–15th January 1215).[6] True to time at the Epiphany the confederate barons appeared, and in glittering array,[7] with their demand for the
The Barons in London. Charter of Henry I. They insisted that the King had already promised as much at the time of his absolution at Winchester.[8]
John shuffled and evaded, and begged to be allowed to defer his answer on such weighty matters till the Octave of Easter (26th April). The request for so much time was not well received, but eventually the barons
Their demands evaded. gave in to it, the King having induced Langton, the Earl of Pembroke, and the Bishop of Ely to pledge themselves on his behalf that he would give all legitimate satisfaction at that time.[9] John employed the respite in fresh efforts to sow dissensions

---

[1] Wendover, 293, copied by Paris. No other writer notices this meeting in terms ; but see R. Cogg., 170, for the broad facts ; also W. Cov., 218. Bishop Stubbs dates the meeting before John's return ; *Const. Hist.*, I. 567. Pauli suggests that it may have been held on St. Edmund's Day, 22nd November. I feel inclined to connect it with a hasty run to Bury made by John on the 4th November. The agreement to defer action till after Christmas suggests the approach of Advent.

[2] W. Cov., *sup.*   [3] Id., 217.

[4] *Statutes of Realm, Charters of Liberties*, 5 ; *Select Charters*, 280.

[5] *Fœdera*, I. 126.   [6] *Itinerary*.

[7] " In lascivo satis militari apparatu."

[8] This point was again pressed on the Pope at Rome, see the report to the King, *Fœdera*, I. 129, wrongly given under 1214 instead of 1215.

[9] Rot. Pat., I. 126 ; Wendover, III. 295, 296 ; W. Cov., II. 218. Bishop Eustace died shortly, namely on the 3rd February ; *Reg. Sacrum.*

among his enemies, and in preparations for war.[1] He ordered fresh oaths
of allegiance to himself to be taken, with a special clause disclaiming the
Charter.   The demand was resisted ; and in fact it turned against him, as
the publicity given to the terms of the Charter greatly strengthened the
Barons' cause.   'From the time when this Charter was shown to the people
The Charter it carried all men with it.   There was but one voice and one
and the   mind; all would stand as a wall in defence of the liberties of
People.   Church and Realm.'[2]   John had thus for the first time since
the Conquest arrayed the Commons on the side of the Barons as against the
Crown.[3]   Continuing his efforts, on the 15th January he republished the
grant of canonical elections to the clergy;[4] while a little later he went
through the transparent farce of taking the Cross,[5] to clothe
John takes himself with the immunities attaching to the person of a
the Cross.   Crusader; and also, no doubt, to curry a little extra favour
with the Pope.

Of course John had appealed to his Lord Paramount.   His agent was
followed by Eustace de Vescy who went to support the Barons' cause.
Eustace insisted that they were only keeping John to his oath; he
reminded Innocent of the support given by the Barons to the Church
in her struggle with the King, and hinted that the result was largely due
to their action.[6]   The Papal view of the situation however was still the
same ; the Church having got all that she wanted resistance to
The Pope on the King's authority could no longer be tolerated.   He writes
the situation.   to Langton expressing astonishment that he could have con-
nived at, if not abetted, 'questions' raised against the King after the happy
pacification with the Church ; and he orders the Archbishop to quash all
'conjurations and conspiracies' against John.   In a letter to the Barons
he annuls all the 'conjurations and conspiracies' off-hand; and warns
them that they must not presume to put armed pressure on their King:
he has urged the King to grant whatever is right.   A separate mandate
orders the Barons to pay the scutage of Poitou.[7]

[1] See the Patent Rolls for February, March, and April, *passim*.

[2] " Ex quo autem primo vulgata est carta hæc assertoribus ejus omnium conciliati sunt
animi," etc., W. Cov.; and Wendover, *sup.* For John's demand for a rejection of the
Charter see also his agent's report of the account of the proceedings in London given to
the Pope by the Barons; *Fœdera*, I. 120 (misplaced).   The Bishop of Winchester, the
Earl of Chester, and William Brewer were said to be the only men who approved of the
King's action.

[3] So Bishop Stubbs remarks, W. Cov., II. lxxii.

[4] *Fœdera*, I. 126 ; the Pope confirmed the grant in March, *Id.* 127.

[5] Ash Wednesday, 4th March ; W. Cov., II. 219 ; Ann. Winton, Worcester, and
Wykes.   Wendover, wrong as usual, has the 2nd February.

[6] See the report sent to John by his agent W. Mauclerc, *Fœdera* 120, but wrongly
placed under the year 1214.   Mauclerc reached Rome on the 17th February 1215, and
de Vescy on the 28th.   [7] *Fœdera*, 127, 128, 19th March, and 1st April.

As John was importing mercenaries[1] and evidently preparing for a trial of strength, the Barons saw that they could not affort to wait till Easter.

Both sides preparing. The steps taken by them cannot be traced with any certainty, owing to the confused and contradictory statements of the chroniclers. But it would seem that a preliminary meeting was held at some place not named, doubtless in the North, where the strength of the party lay. So much so was this the case that they were commonly spoken of collectively as the North-country Men.[2] A warning message was sent to the King; but an uncompromising answer was returned.[3] An armed muster was then held at Stamford.[4]

The Barons in arms. From Stamford they marched to Northampton, which place they were allowed to enter, no hostilities having yet taken place. The King kept sending messages challenging their proceedings; but they held on their way to Brackley in Northamptonshire, the King then being at or near Oxford.[5] This fact which seems fairly established enables us to fix approximately the time of the Barons' appearance at Brackley; as John's Itinerary shows that he was at Woodstock from the 4th April to the 6th April; at Oxford from the 7th to the 13th of the month; and that he did not again visit that neighbourhood till July.[6]

The Barons' ranks presented a formidable array. At Stamford the Northern contingent had been joined by Giles of Braose, Bishop of Hereford, who could not forget the cruel wrongs of his family; also by Robert fitz Walter, and by Geoffrey of Mandeville, the new Earl of Essex. This man in the previous year had been forced, much against his will, to take to wife the King's discarded Isabel of Gloucester.[7] John had made

---

[1] W. Cov., II. 219. For men from Flanders see *Fœdera*, I. 128; Rot. Pat., I. 128, 130. John was also evidently looking for help from Wales. In December he sent back Llywelyn's hostages; on the 2nd March, 1215, William of Cornhill the newly appointed Bishop of Coventry was sent with proposals to the Welsh Prince; *Fœdera*, 126, 127. William of Cornhill had been consecrated on the 25th January 1215; *Reg. Sacrum.*

[2] "Aquilonares," W. Cov.; "Boreales"; "Norenses," Ann. Dunst.; "Barones Northumbriæ," R. Cogg.

[3] "Cum duriuscule eis rex respondisset."

[4] W. Cov., II. 219. I reject his date of Easter week for this gathering.

[5] *Id.* and Wendover, III. 296. See also the rhythmical summary given Chron. Melrose, 117, where it appears that the King was at Oxford when he finally rejected the Barons' 'Articles.'

[6] Matthew Paris in his *Hist. Angl.*, II. 155, for once in a way correcting Wendover and his own *Chronica Majora*, tells us that the Barons came to Brackley some time before Easter week (19th–26th April); "Ebdomada Paschali adveniente." Wendover and the *Chronica Majora* had spoken of a meeting on the Monday after the Octave of Easter, 27th April, the day originally appointed. If worth anything this might be read as Monday after Passion Sunday or April 6th. On the 27th April John instead of being at Oxford was going from Clarendon to Corfe.

[7] Rot. Pat., I. 109; W. Cov., *sup.* Geoffrey was son of the late Justiciar FitzPeter, but had assumed the name of his maternal grandmother through whom the Essex Earldom came.

many enemies. A list of the principal insurgents gives forty-four barons of rank, among whom we have Richard of Clare II. Earl of Hertford; Robert de Vere Earl of Oxford; Roger Bigod Earl of Norfolk; ✓ **Strength of** Henry Bohun Earl of Hereford ; Saer de Quincy Earl of **their party.** Winchester, the last a title created by John. Among the names of North-country association we have Mowbray, de Vescy, Percy, de Ros, Bruce, de Stuteville, de Lacy, Malet, Multon, Vaux, Fitz John, Fitz Alan, Gresley, and Fitz Warine, the bearer of the last of these a hero of romance.[1] Connected with the South were the Barons Fitz Walter, Beauchamp, Montacute, Montfitchet, and William Marshal the younger. His father the Earl of Pembroke, whose prudence was not to be lured into any rash step, still sided with the King.[2] It would seem that the example of this pair was followed in a good many cases, the sons going "out," while the fathers staid at home ;[3] a course by the way adopted in times of revolution as late as the year 1745. But every class and interest, and families of the most varied traditions, were represented in the insurgent camp. The Barons were also strong in the known sympathy of the Archbishop, the Bishops, and the parochial clergy. The monastic clergy would probably be inclined to bow to the ruling of the Pope.[4]

The King, then, being at Oxford, and the Barons at a convenient distance at Brackley, conferences were opened, John communicating with his adversaries through Langton and the Earl of Pembroke. John having finally asked what the exact concessions required of him were the **The** insurgents tendered a schedule containing doubtless the **"articles"** Articles subsequently produced at Runnymede. When they **rejected.** were read out by the Archbishop, John lost all self-control. He swore with furious oaths that he would never submit to such slavery. ' They might as well ask the Kingdom at once.'[5]

The King's rejection of their terms having been reported to the Barons they proceeded at once to ' defy ' him ; that is to say to renounce their homages and allegiance as a necessary preliminary to hostilities.[6] **War** John had already left Oxford, and the hostile messages had **declared.** to follow him, either to Wallingford or Reading, at which places he rested on the 13th April and 14th April.[7] The Barons' next

[1] See the Legend of Fulk Fitz Warine, printed by Mr. Stevenson with his edition of Ralph of Coggeshall, 277.

[2] See the list ; Wendover, III. 297.

[3] W Cov., II. 220.

[4] The tone of the monastic chroniclers is by no means entirely in favour of the Barons ; *e.g.*, W. Cov., 220, 221.

[5] Wendover, III. 268; W. Cov., II. 219.

[6] " Regem diffiduciantes . . . et hominia sua reddentes ;" W. Cov., *sup.* "Homagia quæ barones . . . reddiderant ;" Ann. Dunst , 43 ; R. Cogg., 171.

[7] The Dunstable Annals, *sup.*, name Wallingford as the place. The *Liber de Antiquis Legibus Lond.*, p. 201, gives Reading as the place where, and the 5th May as the day

step was to choose a Commander-in-chief, and they took fitz Walter, giving him the remarkable style of ' Marshal of the army of God and the Church.[1] But strong as they were the insurgents did not feel prepared for a march on London ; and so they fell back in a rather aimless way on Northampton. As they now came in hostile array, with banners displayed, the gates were closed against them, the town being held by a foreign garrison. This must have happened just after Easter (19th April), as John subsequently dated the beginning of hostilities from that day.[2]   Some fifteen days were

Occupation of Bedford. spent in assaults which came to nothing for want of siege artillery. From Northampton the Barons were induced to advance to Bedford, a place in the hands of William of Beauchamp, one of their number (3rd May ?).[3]   By this time the Pope's letters must have come to hand : and John on the strength of

Negotiations. them again reopened negotiations.   After whining appeals for consideration on the double ground of his being a vassal of the Church, and under crusading vows, John went on, by way of complying with Innocent's requirements, to make an offer of putting down any abuses (*malas consuetudines*) that might have crept in either during his brother's reign or his own.   This very insufficient offer not having been accepted John called on the Archbishop to excommunicate the Barons.   But Langton, with the general assent of his suffragans,[4] declined to do so, alleging that he knew the Pope's real mind better than the King did ; at the same time he urged John to dismiss his mercenaries.   The King then fell back on a proposal for a reference to eight arbitrators, four to be chosen on either side, with the Pope as umpire.[5]   But such an offer could deceive no one.

Matters thus remaining somewhat at a standstill, the King negotiating

---

when, the King received the Barons' defiances ; adding that hostilities began on the 3rd May.   John, no doubt, was at Reading on the 5th May, as well as on the 14th April. But the date of the 3rd May as that of the beginning of hostilities leaves no room for the siege of Northampton and the occupation of Bedford ; and the renunciation of homage must have preceded those operations, and so Ralph of Coggeshall tells us, *sup.* The Continuation of Florence, 171, says that hostilities began about the 19th April (Easter Day) say on the 20th April, a likely date that would bring the move to Bedford about the 3rd May.

[1] Wend., *sup. Fœdera*, I. 133.

[2] See Magna Carta, s. 62.   Select Charters, 296, and below.

[3] Wendover, and W. Cov., *sup.*   The 3rd May given by the *Liber de Ant., sup.,* as the day when hostilities began might be the day of the occupation of Bedford.   For the struggle for the possession of Bedford between Milo of Beauchamp on behalf of Matilda and Stephen's, Earl of Bedford, see *Foundations*, II. 364, 402, 426.

[4] John could only claim Pandulf and Simon of Apulia, the new Bishop of Exeter, as agreeing with him, so his own letter to the Pope, below.

[5] See John's letter to the Pope of the 29th May, *Fœdera*, I. 129.   The proposal for arbitration was made on the 10th May ; Rot. Pat., 141 ; Blackstone, *Charters*, xiii. ; Stubbs.

and intriguing,[1] a determining impulse was given to the Reforming cause by the action of the leading citizens of London, who sent a message to the Barons at Bedford, offering to admit them to the Metropolis. No time was lost in seizing the opportunity. The main body moved on the same day to Ware; while a detachment, pressing on through the night, entered by Aldgate next morning without opposition, the citizens being mostly in attendance at Mass (Sunday, 17th May).[2] The Mayor at the time was Serlo le Mercer,[3] who must have taken a leading part in the business. But the old connexion of the Mandeville family with the city, and the influence of Robert fitz Walter as an Essex landowner, and the lord of Baynard's castle Blackfriars, should also be taken into consideration. Earl Geoffrey claimed the Constableship of the Tower as of hereditary right; but the fortress had been placed in other hands, and was held for the King.

The Barons received in London.

The occupation of the capital brought a large accession of strength to the Barons' cause. The sittings of the Courts at Westminster and throughout the country were suspended, and the whole administration of the country was brought to a standstill.[4] Popular risings took place at Exeter and Northampton; a party of Northerners established themselves at Lincoln in Whitsun week (7th–14th June),[5] while Philip of France was promising all the support that he could give.[6] On the other hand it must be pointed out that John had in his hands a formidable array of castles; among these we find Wallingford, Berkhampstead, Oxford, Winchester, Marlborough, Exeter, Bristol, Gloucester, Bridgnorth, Newcastle-under-Lyne, Chester, Norwich and Orford. The Tower of London was his, and he was making great efforts to get Rochester castle out of Langton's hands.[7] With the instincts of a despot he never grudged money for the repair of castles: the chartered boroughs also were attached to him by their trading privileges. Altogether he saw that time would be on his side, and to gain time he resolved to concede all that was asked.

The King feigns compliance.

On the 8th June, John, being at Merton in Surrey, issued a safe-conduct for the Barons to meet him at Staines, between the 9th and the 11th of the month, the 'truce' being afterwards extended to the 15th June. The Barons, who were established in London, came down to Staines, and pitched their tents there on the historic sward of Runnymede, between Staines and Windsor, at which latter place John was staying. Langton

---

[1] See Rot. Pat., I. 134, 136.

[2] See the notice sent out by the King next day, Rot. Pat., I. 137.

[3] *Liber de Ant.*, 4.

[4] Wendover, III. 300; R. Cogg., 171.

[5] W. Cov., II. 220, 221.

[6] R. Cogg., *sup.*

[7] Rot. Pat., I. 137-141. The custody of Rochester Castle was claimed by the Archbishops under a grant from Henry I.. See above, p. 35.

and the bishops acted as mediators between the malcontents and the King's
adherents.　But John made the task easy; as he intended to
The Articles accepted. be bound by nothing, so he made no difficulties.[1]　Forty-nine
articles were produced, being doubtless the demands so fiercely
rejected at Brackley.　After a due show of discussion they were accepted;[2]
Magna Carta. and from them the GREAT CHARTER was drawn up and
sealed on the 15th June.

Magna Carta deserves all the praise that it has received as a great
constitutional compact between the different orders of the body politic,
A great national compact. stipulating for the essential bases of fair dealing and just
government, not only as between Crown and subject, but also
as between subject and subject.　The rights granted by the
King to his tenants in chief are to be granted by them to their under-
tenants.[3]　The following provisions alone seem to establish all the leading
principles of constitutional government.　' Justice not to be sold, or delayed,
or refused to any man' (s. 40).　'No freeman to be taken, or imprisoned, or disseized, or outlawed, or in any way destroyed except by the
lawful judgment of his peers (*parium suorum*)[4] or by the laws of the
land' (s. 39).　'No scutage, or Aid (except the regular three) to be imposed
except by the Common Council of the Realm' (s. 12).　In modern
language this clause would run " No new direct tax to be imposed except
by consent of Parliament."　' Merchants from friendly states to be free to
come, and go, and trade, subject only to the payment of established
Customs' duties' (s. 41).　Native subjects, not under sentence of law, to be
free to leave the realm, and free to return, except in time of war (s. 42).
The reader need hardly be told that these rules implied an absolute reversal
of the practice of the administration on every point.　Justice was freely
bought and sold; the restrictions on trade reflected in the official records
of the time almost pass belief.　Apparently nobody could safely enter or
leave the Kingdom without special Royal licence.[5]

But Magna Carta as a tentative measure is open to criticism in various
respects.　On some points it goes before, on others it lags behind the

---

[1] *Fœdera*, I. 129; Wendover, 301, 302; R. Cogg., 172.

[2] *Fœdera, sup. Select Charters*, 282.

[3] Sect. 60.

[4] However these "famous words" may have come to be understood in later times the
view of modern scholars is that they were not intended to imply trial by jury.　What the
Barons aimed at was that no man should be judged by his inferior, the trial of an inferior
by his superior being left open.　See Pollock and Maitland, *Hist. Eng. Law*, I. 173.
See also the view expressed by Innocent III. with reference to the alleged condemnation
of John by the French Barons, that the inferior could not judge the superior; Wendover,
III. 373; and again, s. 21 of Magna Carta.

[5] See the constant entries on the Patent Rolls of leave to this or that individual to
import or export certain articles, and nothing else.　The state of affairs however was all
the time more or less one of war.

charter of Henry I. on which it was understood to be based.   On some
questions it is timid ; on others sweeping and extravagant.
Points open to criticism. Archbishop Langton had not given his support to the Barons
for nothing.   The first words of the Charter proclaim the
absolute 'liberty' of the Church in the fullest sense.[1]   This 'liberty,' as
then understood, involved the surrender of all that Henry II.
"Liberty" of the Church. had contended for in his Constitutions of Clarendon ; it would
relieve the clergy of all lay control, and of all liability to contribute to the needs of the State beyond the occasional scutages due from
the higher clergy for their knights' fees.   The clergy would be in the happy
position of having their property and rights protected for them *gratis*, by
Courts whose decisions if adverse to themselves they would be free to
reject.   The grant of the absolute 'liberty' of the Church, with the free
canonical election already granted and now expressly confirmed, would
establish a self-elected corporation as the ruling power in the Kingdom.
We are told, no doubt, that the Charter of Henry I. also 'secured the
rights of the Church.'[2]   But how did that King understand the measure
of liberty that he was prepared to concede?   Why that he would neither
sell nor farm out preferment, and that he would not impound the revenues
of vacant Sees.   That was all that he promised.[3]   The difference between
Henry's view of the due rights of the Church and the views entertained in
John's time marks the expansion of ecclesiastical pretensions made during
the 12th century.

Of the incidents of military tenure developed by Norman lawyers on
English soil 'Wardship' and 'Marriage' were the most cruel.[4]
"Wardship" in chivalry. The former of these prerogatives gave the King the entire
disposition of the person and property of an infant heir, without
any liability to render account, or do more for his ward than provide him
with a decent maintenance.   'Marriage' in the technical legal
"Marriage" in chivalry. sense entitled the King to sell and dispose of the hand of a
female heiress for the best price that he could get, the only
requirement being that she should be married 'without disparagement'
that is to say to a man not beneath her in social rank.   Even widows and
elderly women were brought into the market.   Magna Carta deals timidly
with both of these monstrous prerogatives.   Henry I. promised that the
custody of the person and estate of the heir should rest with his mother or
other nearest relatives—the Old English rule.   The Runnymede Barons
only stipulate that the guardian (*custos*) appointed by the King shall be
content with taking the ordinary rents and profits, without 'wasting' the
property (ss. 4 and 5).   The sale of heiresses also had been fallaciously

---

[1] " Quod libera sit et habeat jura sua integra et libertates suas illæsas."
[2] Bishop Stubbs, *Const. H.*, I. 572.
[3] See *Select Charters*, 97 ; *Foundations of England*, II. 230.
[4] See *Foundations*, I. 141, 142.

disclaimed by Henry; but Magna Carta only intervenes on behalf of widows who wish to remain single. They must not be 'distrained' to marry again, or fined for leave to escape an unpalatable connexion (ss. 7 and 8). Again we notice that no attempt was made to settle the great moot question of liability to service abroad; the Barons apparently being content to leave the matter to be dealt with from time to time as the circumstances of each particular case might suggest. One provision bears a somewhat invidious appearance. The county farm-rents must not be raised—an impossible requirement; but the King's right to lay tallages on the Crown demesnes is expressly reserved (s. 25). Again the great question of Purveyance, that standing grievance of centuries to come, seems dealt with imperfectly. 'No constable of a castle or other royal officer (*ballivus noster*) shall take a man's corn or goods without payment' (s. 28); 'nor shall any sheriff, royal officer, or other man impress any freeman's horses or carts for transport without his leave' (s. 30). This seems to leave the King's personal right open. In the next clause he disclaims for himself expressly, as well as for his officers, the right of taking timber for fortifications or other works (s. 31).

Purveyance. [marginal note]

Among the provisions to be specially noticed are the following :—

For the constitution and meetings of the national assembly (*Commune Concilium Regni*), the Grand Councils whose consent was declared necessary to the imposition of a scutage or a novel 'aid,' it is arranged that the archbishops, bishops, earls, and greater barons shall be summoned by special writs addressed to them individually; the lesser tenants in chief by a general writ addressed to the sheriff of the county; forty days' notice to be given, and the time and place of meeting, and business to be transacted to be stated in the writ (ss. 12, 14).

Special provisions. [marginal note]

The Court of Common Pleas not to follow the King's Court, but to be settled in some fixed place (s. 17).

The three great inquests of *Novel Disseisin, Mort d' Ancestor,* and *Darrein Presentment* to be taken in the County Court, before two Justices in Eyre to be sent into each county four times a year; the Justices to have four chosen Knights of the Shire to sit with them as assessors (s. 18).

No sheriff, constable, coroner, or other royal officer to hold Pleas of the Crown (s. 24).

No royal officer (*ballivus*) to bring any man to justice on his mere word (*simplici loquela sua*) without witnesses (s. 38).

No man to be called upon to render more than his due services for any knight's fee or other holding of free tenure (*de libero tenemento,* s. 16, also 29).

Freemen to be amerced only in proportion to the measure of their offence, and upon the finding of a jury of the neighbourhood. Earls and barons to be amerced by their peers; amerciaments in no case to be so heavy as to deprive the party amerced of his means of livelihood, such ιs the tenement of a freeman, the stock-in-trade of a merchant, the ⁊ainage of a villein. Clerks to be amerced only to the extent of their ιon-ecclesiastical property (ss. 20, 21, 22).

The chattels of a deceased layman to be made over to his executors o answer the purposes of his will—if he have left one—after deducting ll debts due to the Crown. The chattels of an intestate to be distributed ⁊y his next-of-kin under the direction of the Church (ss. 26, 27).

Uniform weights and measures to be established throughout the kingdom ⌐ s. 35).

London and all other cities, boroughs, and ports to retain all their old ⌐ ights and liberties (s. 13).

Weirs and stake nets (*Kidelli*) for catching salmon to be allowed only in he estuaries of the rivers (s. 33).

Forests created by John to be disafforested ; and recent extensions of ⁊orest Law (*malæ consuetudines*) to be enquired into by juries, and ⌐ ᴄondemned (ss. 47, 48.).[1]

Justice to be done to Llywelyn and Welshmen who had been dispos-ᵢessed of their lands in England or Wales ; also to Alexander II., the young King of Scots (ss. 56–59)[2]. On the other hand John agreed to remove from office (*de balliva*) a set of objectionable foreigners, and to dismiss all his foreign mercenaries (ss. 40, 41).[3] Taken all in all it must be admitted ⌐ that these enactments, for such they were, breathe a healthy spirit of moderation and equity. They are still "the keystone of English liberty." Yet five hundred years of struggle, the execution of a King, and the final banishment of a dynasty were needed to bring the Crown to acquiescence.

But the sealing of the Charter would have been of little use without provisions for enforcing its execution. John accordingly was required to

Executive Commission. give in to the Barons' demand for a standing commission of five-and-twenty, to be chosen by them, whose duty it should be to receive complaints of any violation of the Charter by ⌐ him or his officers ; failing redress within forty days the whole community (*communa totius terræ*) to be at liberty to wage war on the King and his

---

[1] Wendover, III. 311, followed by M. Paris, *Chr. Maj.* II. 598, appends here a Forest Charter, being apparently that issued by Henry III. in 1225, a signal instance of their inaccuracy.

[2] William the Lion died at Stirling 4th December, 1214 ; Alexander was installed at Scone on the fifth or sixth of the month ; *Chr. Melrose* ; J. Fordun, 279, 280.

[3] *Select Charters*, 288. For a suggested unknown "Charter of Liberties" printed by Mr. Round from Rymer's Transcripts in the Record Office, see *Engl. Hist. Rev.*, VIII. 288. The original is in the Paris archives in "a French hand of the early years of the thirteenth century" ; and appears to be a rough summary of a few of the provisions of the Great Charter sent to France for the information of Philip and Louis. The writer however has inserted a clause of his own relative to scutage and service abroad ; a clause not found elsewhere. On the subject see Mr. Round, *sup.*, and Mr. G. P. Prothero and Mr. H. Hall, *Engl. Hist. Rev.*, IX. 117, 326.

possessions, saving his own person and those of the Queen and Royal children.   The barons further claimed the right of exacting oaths of obedience to themselves from all classes, as if they contemplated taking the administration of the country into their own hands.   But they were fully justified in requiring John to pledge himself not to procure directly or indirectly any revocation of any of the conceded liberties, declaring any such revocation null and void (s. 61).[1]

On the 15th June the Great Charter was executed.   But it was not till three days later, when another meeting was held at Runnymede, that
Ostensible pacification.   John could proclaim that the Barons had renewed their homage, that peace had been restored, and that his officers must levy no more contributions of war or "tenserie."[2]   From this we learn that he had been levying protection money, just as was done in the anarchic days of Stephen.[3]   But the questions as to performance, and mutual guarantees must have been endless : and three more sittings from the 21st to the 23rd June led to little result.   John pledged himself to do his best to meet all requirements by the 15th August; and in the meantime he agreed to place the Tower in Langton's keeping, and to allow the Barons to remain in London till then, or longer if necessary.[4] Notice of the Charter was sent to the sheriffs, with orders to exact the oaths to the Twenty-Five, and to impanel juries to enquire into Forest grievances.[5]   Castles and hostages were restored in a few cases, and Hugh of Boves ordered to dismiss his mercenaries.[6]   But the vital question would be that of the composition of the Executive Commission upon which everything would depend.   Matthew Paris gives a list, not found in the earlier writers, wholly taken from the side of the malcontents.[7] In the preamble to Magna Carta John in mentioning the men by whose advice he was guided only gave the names on his own side, ignoring all others.   It is impossible to suppose that he gave his assent to the Commission given by Paris ; but without that assent their authority would always be disputable.   Apparently while issuing the formal orders for obedience to the Twenty-Five John left it uncertain who they might be, leaving them to assert themselves as best they might.   But questions
Hollow situation.   of personal redress were probably those with which he would most be pressed, and for their discussion a further Council was agreed upon to meet at Oxford about the 16th July.[8]   On the 15th

---

[1] *Select Charters*, 288-296 ; *Fœdera*, I. 131, 132.
[2] A French word, literally " Protection."   [3] *Fœdera*, 133.   [4] *Id.*
[5] *Id.*, 124 ; W. Cov., II., 221, 222 ; R. Cogg., 172.   [6] Rot. Pat., I., 143, 144.
[7] *Chron. Maj.*, II. 604.
[8] Wendover, 318, 319, where the place of meeting is wrongly given as Westminster. The Melrose Chronicle gives the place of meeting rightly, with the date of the 20th July, p. 119.   Walter of Coventry again, II. 223, names Oxford, but gives the date as the 16th August.   There was another meeting of the Barons there on the 30th August ; Rot. Pat., I. 153.

July however John wrote that he could not attend, sending the Archbishop of Dublin, Pandulf and others to represent him.[1] The Barons were so dissatisfied with the King's attitude that but for the harvest they would have recommenced regular operations. In the North the royal demesnes were being freely plundered.[2] To keep their party together the malcontents had recourse to tournaments. We hear of one in particular that was to have been held at Stamford, but for prudential reasons was adjourned to Hounslow, nearer London.[3]

APPENDIX TO CHAPTER XXIX

TEXT OF MAGNA CARTA

JOHANNES Dei gratia rex Angliæ, dominus Hyberniæ, dux Normanniæ et Aquitanniæ, comes Andegaviæ, archiepiscopis, episcopis, abbatibus, comitibus, baronibus, justiciariis, forestariis, vicecomitibus, præpositis, ministris et omnibus ballivis et fidelibus suis salutem. Sciatis nos intuitu Dei et pro salute animæ nostræ et omnium antecessorum et hæredum nostrorum, ad honorem Dei et exaltationem sanctæ ecclesiæ, et emendationem regni nostri, per consilium venerabilium patrum nostrorum, Stephani Cantuariensis archiepiscopi totius Angliæ primatis et sanctæ Romanæ ecclesiæ cardinalis, Henrici Dublinensis archiepiscopi, Willelmi Londoniensis, Petri Wintoniensis, Joscelini Bathoniensis et Glastoniensis, Hugonis Lincolniensis, Walteri Wygornensis, Willelmi Coventrensis, et Benedicti Roffensis episcoporum ; magistri Pandulfi domini papæ subdiaconi et familiaris, fratris Eymerici magistri militiæ templi in Anglia ; et nobilium virorum Willelmi Mariscalli comitis Penbrok, Willelmi comitis Saresberiæ, Willelmi comitis Warenniæ, Willelmi comitis Arundelliæ, Alani de Galweya constabularii Scottiæ, Warini filii Geroldi, Petri filii Hereberti, Huberti de Burgo senescalli Pictaviæ, Hugonis de Nevilla, Mathei filii Hereberti, Thomæ Basset, Alani Basset, Philippi de Albiniaco, Roberti de Roppelay, Johannis Mariscalli, Johannis filii Hugonis et aliorum fidelium nostrorum.

1. In primis concessisse Deo et hac præsenti carta nostra confirmasse, pro nobis et hæredibus nostris in perpetuum, quod Anglicana ecclesia libera sit, et habeat, jura sua integra, et libertates suas illæsas ; et ita volumus observari ; quod apparet ex eo quod libertatem electionum, quæ maxima et magis necessaria reputatur ecclesiæ Anglicanæ, mera et spontanea voluntate, ante discordiam inter nos et barones nostros motam, concessimus, et carta nostra confirmavimus, et eam optinuimus a domino papa Innocentio tertio confirmari ; quam et nos observabimus et ab hæredibus nostris in perpetuum bona fide volumus observari. Concessimus etiam omnibus liberis hominibus regni nostri, pro nobis et hæredibus nostris in perpetuum, omnes libertates subscriptas, habendas et tenendas, eis et hæredibus suis, de nobis et hæredibus nostris.

2. Si quis comitum vel baronum nostrorum, sive aliorum tenentium de nobis in capite per servitium militare. mortuus fuerit, et cum decesserit hæres suus plenæ ætatis fuerit et relevium debeat, habeat hæreditatem suam per antiquum relevium ; scilicet hæres vel hæredes comitis, de baronia comitis integra per centum libras ; hæres vel hæredes baronis, de baronia integra per centum libras ; hæres vel hæredes militis, de feodo militis integro

---

[1] Rot. Pat., I. 149 ; W. Cov., II. 223.

[2] W. Cov., II. 223.

[3] See Fitzwalter's letter, Wendover, III. 321. A lady of high rank had offered a bear as a prize. See also R. Cogg, 172, 173.

per centum solidos ad plus ; et qui minus debuerit minus det secundum antiquam consuetudinem feodorum.

3. Si autem hæres alicujus talium fuerit infra ætatem et fuerit in custodia, cum ad ætatum pervenerit, habeat hæreditatem suam sine relevio et sine fine.

4. Custos terræ hujusmodi hæredis qui infra ætatem fuerit, non capiat de terra hæredis nisi rationabiles exitus, et rationabiles consuetudines, et rationabilia servitia, et hoc sine destructione et vasto hominum vel rerum ; et si nos commiserimus custodiam alicujus talis terræ vicecomiti vel alicui alii qui de exitibus illius nobis respondere debeat, et ille destructionem de custodia fecerit vel vastum, nos ab illo capiemus emendam, et terra committatur duobus legalibus et discretis hominibus de feodo illo, qui de exitibus respondeant nobis vel ei cui eos assignaverimus ; et si dederimus vel vendiderimus alicui custodiam alicujus talis terræ, et ille destructionem inde fecerit vel vastum, amittat ipsam custodiam, et tradatur duobus legalibus et discretis hominibus de feodo illo qui similiter nobis respondeant sicut prædictum est.

5. Custos autem, quamdiu custodiam terræ habuerit, sustentet domos, parcos, vivaria, stagna, molendina, et cetera ad terram illam pertinentia, de exitibus terræ ejusdem ; et reddat hæredi, cum ad plenam ætatem pervenerit, terram suam totam instauratam de carrucis et wainnagiis secundum quod tempus wainnagii exiget et exitus terræ rationabiliter poterunt sustinere.

6. Hæredes maritentur absque disparagatione, ita tamen quod, antequam contrahatur matrimonium, ostendatur propinquis de consanguinitate ipsius hæredis.

7. Vidua post mortem mariti sui statim et sine difficultate habeat maritagium et hæreditatem suam, nec aliquid det pro dote sua, vel pro maritagio suo, vel hæreditate sua quam hæreditatem maritus suus et ipsa tenuerint die obitus ipsius mariti, et maneat in domo mariti sui per quadraginta dies post mortem ipsius infra quos assignetur ei dos sua.

8. Nulla vidua distringatur ad se maritandum dum voluerit vivere sine marito, ita tamen quod securitatem faciat quod se non maritabit sine assensu nostro, si de nobis tenuerit, vel sine assensu domini sui de quo tenuerit, si de alio tenuerit.

9. Nec nos nec ballivi nostri seisiemus terram aliquam nec redditum pro debito aliquo, quamdiu catalla debitoris sufficiunt ad debitum reddendum ; nec pleggii ipsius debitoris distringantur quamdiu ipse capitalis debitor sufficit ad solutionem debiti ; et si capitalis debitor defecerit in solutione debiti, non habens unde solvat, pleggii respondeant de debito ; et, si voluerint, habeant terras et redditus debitoris donec sit eis satisfactum de debito quod ante pro eo solverint, nisi capitalis debitor monstraverit se esse quietum inde versus eosdem pleggios.

10. Si quis mutuo ceperit aliquid a Judæis, plus vel minus, et moriatur antequam debitum illud solvatur, debitum non usuret quamdiu hæres fuerit infra ætatem, de quocumque teneat ; et si debitum illud inciderit in manus nostras, nos non capiemus nisi catallum contentum in carta.

11. Et si quis moriatur, et debitum debeat Judæis, uxor ejus habeat dotem suam, et nihil reddat de debito illo ; et si liberi ipsius defuncti qui fuerint infra ætatem remanserint, provideantur eis necessaria secundum tenementum quod fuerit defuncti, et de residuo solvatur debitum, salvo servitio dominorum ; simili modo fiat de debitis quæ debentur aliis quam Judæis.

12. Nullum scutagium vel auxilium ponatur in regno nostro, nisi per commune consilium regni nostri, nisi ad corpus nostrum redimendum, et primogenitum filium nostrum militem faciendum, et ad filiam nostram primogenitam semel maritandam, et ad hæc non fiat nisi rationabile auxilium : simili modo fiat de auxiliis de civitate Londoniarum.

13. Et civitas Londoniarum habeat omnes antiquas libertates et liberas consuetudines suas, tam per terras, quam per aquas. Præterea volumus et concedimus quod omnes

aliæ civitates, et burgi, et villæ, et portus, habeant omnes libertates et liberas consuetudines suas.

14. Et ad habendum commune consilium regni, de auxilio assidendo aliter quam in tribus casibus prædictis, vel de scutagio assidendo, summoneri faciemus archiepiscopos, episcopos, abbates, comites, et majores barones, sigillatim per litteras nostras; et præterea faciemus summoneri in generali, per vicecomites et ballivos nostros. omnes illos qui de nobis tenent in capite; ad certum diem, scilicet ad terminum quadraginta dierum ad minus, et ad certum locum; et in omnibus litteris illius summonitionis causam summonitionis exprimemus; et sic facta summonitione negotium ad diem assignatum procedat secundum consilium illorum qui præsentes fuerint, quamvis non omnes summoniti venerint.

15. Nos non concedemus de cetero alicui quod capiat auxilium de liberis hominibus suis, nisi ad corpus suum redimendum, et ad faciendum primogenitum filium suum militem, et ad primogenitam filiam suam semel maritandam, et ad hæc non fiat nisi rationabile auxilium.

16. Nullus distringatur ad faciendum majus servitium de feodo militis, nec de alio libero tenemento, quam inde debetur.

17. Communia placita non sequantur curiam nostram sed teneantur in aliquo loco certo.

18. Recognitiones de nova dissaisina, de morte antecessoris, et de ultima præsentatione, non capiantur nisi in suis comitatibus et hoc modo; nos, vel si extra regnum fuerimus, capitalis justiciarius noster, mittemus duos justiciarios per unumquemque comitatum per quatuor vices in anno, qui, cum quatuor militibus cujuslibet comitatus electis per comitatum, capiant in comitatu et in die et loco comitatus assisas prædictas.

19. Et si in die comitatus assisæ prædictæ capi non possint, tot milites et libere tenentes emaneant de illis qui interfuerint comitatui die illo, per quos possint judicia sufficienter fieri, secundum quod negotium fuerit majus vel minus.

20. Liber homo non amercietur pro parvo delicto, nisi secundum modum delicti; et pro magno delicto amercietur secundum magnitudinem delicti, salvo contenemento suo; et mercator eodem modo salva mercandisa sua; et villanus eodem modo amercietur salvo wainnagio suo, si inciderint in misericordiam nostram; et nulla prædictarum misericordiarum ponatur, nisi per sacramentum proborum hominum de visneto.

21. Comites et barones non amercientur nisi per pares suos, et non nisi secundum modum delicti.

22. Nullus clericus amercietur de laico tenemento suo, nisi secundum modum aliorum prædictorum, et non secundum quantitatem beneficii sui ecclesiastici.

23. Nec villa nec homo distringatur facere pontes ad riparias, nisi qui ab antiquo et de jure facere debent.

24. Nullus vicecomes, constabularius, coronatores, vel alii ballivi nostri, teneant placita coronæ nostræ.

25. Omnes comitatus, hundredi, wapentakii, et trethingii, sint ad antiquas firmas absque ullo incremento, exceptis dominicis maneriis nostris.

26. Si aliquis tenens de nobis laicum feodum moriatur, et vicecomes vel ballivus noster ostendat litteras nostras patentes de summonitione nostra de debito quod defunctus nobis debuit, liceat vicecomiti vel ballivo nostro attachiare et inbreviare catalla defuncti inventa in laico feodo, ad valentiam illius debiti, per visum legalium hominum, ita tamen quod nihil inde amoveatur, donec persolvatur nobis debitum quod clarum fuerit; et residuum relinquatur executoribus ad faciendum testamentum defuncti; et, si nihil nobis debeatur ab ipso, omnia catalla cedant defuncto, salvis uxori ipsius et pueris rationabilibus partibus suis.

27. Si aliquis liber homo intestatus decesserit, catalla sua per manus propinquorum parentum et amicorum suorum, per visum ecclesiæ distribuantur, salvis unicuique debitis quæ defunctus ei debebat.

I I

28. Nullus constabularius, vel alius ballivus noster, capiat blada vel alia catalla alicujus, nisi statim inde reddat denarios, aut respectum inde habere possit de voluntate venditoris.

29. Nullus constabularius distringat aliquem militem ad dandum denarios pro custodia castri, si facere voluerit custodiam illam in propria persona sua, vel per alium probum hominem, si ipse eam facere non possit propter rationabilem causam ; et si nos duxerimus vel miserimus eum in exercitum, erit quietus de custodia, secundum quantitatem temporis quo per nos fuerit in exercitu.

30. Nullus vicecomes, vel ballivus noster, vel aliquis alius, capiat equos vel caretas alicujus liberi hominis pro cariagio faciendo, nisi de voluntate ipsius liberi hominis.

31. Nec nos nec ballivi nostri capiemus alienum boscum ad castra, vel alia agenda nostra, nisi per voluntatem ipsius cujus boscus ille fuerit.

32. Nos non tenebimus terras illorum qui convicti fuerint de felonia, nisi per unum annum et unum diem, et tunc reddantur terræ dominis feodorum.

33. Omnes kydelli de cetero deponantur penitus de Thamisia et de Medewaye, et per totam Angliam, nisi per costeram maris.

34. Breve quod vocatur *Præcipe* de cetero non fiat alicui de aliquo tenemento unde liber homo amittere possit curiam suam.

35. Una mensura vini sit per totum regnum nostrum, et una mensura cervisiæ, et una mensura bladi scilicet quarterium Londoniense, et una latitudo pannorum tinctorum, et russettorum, et halbergettorum, scilicet duæ ulnæ infra listas ; de ponderibus autem sit ut de mensuris.

36. Nihil detur vel capiatur de cetero pro brevi inquisitionis de vita vel membris, sed gratis concedatur et non negetur.

37. Si aliquis teneat de nobis per feodifirman, vel per sokagium, vel per burgagium, et de alio terram teneat per servitium militare, nos non habebimus custodiam hæredis nec terræ suæ quæ est de feodo alterius, occasione illius feodifirmæ, vel sokagii, vel burgagii ; nec habebimus custodiam illius feodifirmæ, vel sokagii, vel burgagii, nisi ipsa feodifirma debeat servitium militare. Nos non habebimus custodiam hæredis vel terræ alicujus, quam tenet de alio per servitium militare, occasione alicujus parvæ sergenteriæ quam tenet de nobis per servitium reddendi nobis cultellos, vel sagittas, vel hujusmodi.

38. Nullus ballivus ponat de cetero aliquem ad legem simplici loquela sua, sine testibus fidelibus ad hoc inductis.

39. Nullus liber homo capiatur, vel imprisonetur, aut dissaisiatur, aut utlagetur, aut exuletur, aut aliquo modo destruatur, nec super eum ibimus, nec super eum mittemus, nisi per legale judicium parium suorum, vel per legem terræ.

40. Nulli vendemus, nulli negabimus, aut differemus, rectum aut justiciam.

41. Omnes mercatores habeant salvum et securum exire de Anglia, et venire in Angliam, et morari et ire per Angliam, tam per terram quam per aquam, ad emendum et vendendum, sine omnibus malis toltis, per antiquas et rectas consuetudines, præterquam in tempore gwerræ, et si sint de terra contra nos gwerrina ; et si tales inveniantur in terra nostra in principio gwerræ, attachientur sine dampno corporum et rerum, donec sciatur a nobis vel capitali justiciario nostro quomodo mercatores terræ nostræ tractentur, qui tunc invenientur in terra contra nos gwerrina ; et si nostri salvi sint ibi, alii salvi sint in terra nostra.

42. Liceat unicuique de cetero exire de regno nostro, et redire, salvo et secure, per terram et per aquam, salva fide nostra, nisi tempore gwerræ per aliquod breve tempus, propter communem utilitatem regni, exceptis imprisonatis et utlagatis secundem legem regni, et gente de terra contra nos gwerrina, et mercatoribus de quibus fiat sicut prædictum est.

43. Si quis tenuerit de aliqua escæta, sicut de honore Walingeford, Notingeham, Bononiæ, Lainkastriæ, vel de aliis eskætis, quæ sunt in manu nostra, et sunt baroniæ, et

obierit, hæres ejus non det aliud relevium, nec faciat nobis aliud servitium quam faceret baroni si baronia illa esset in manu baronis ; et nos eodem modo eam tenebimus quo baro eam tenuit.

44. Homines qui manent extra forestam non veniant de cetero coram justiciariis nostris de foresta per communes summonitiones, nisi sint in placito, vel pleggii alicujus vel aliquorum, qui attachiati sint pro foresta.

45. Nos non faciemus justiciarios, constabularios, vicecomites, vel ballivos, nisi de talibus qui sciant legem regni et eam bene velint observare.

46. Omnes barones qui fundaverunt abbatias, unde habent cartas regum Angliæ, vel antiquam tenuram, habeant earum custodiam cum vacaverint, sicut habere debent.

47. Omnes forestæ quæ afforestatæ sunt tempore nostro, statim deafforestentur ; et ita fiat de ripariis quæ per nos tempore nostro positæ sunt in defenso.

48. Omnes malæ consuetudines de forestis et warennis, et de forestariis et warennariis, vicecomitibus et eorum ministris, ripariis et earum custodibus, statim inquirantur in quolibet comitatu per duodecim milites juratos de eodem comitatu, qui debent eligi per probos homines ejusdem comitatus, et infra quadraginta dies post inquisitionem factam, penitus, ita quod numquam revocentur, deleantur per eosdem, ita quod nos hoc sciamus prius, vel justiciarius noster, si in Anglia non fuerimus.

49. Omnes obsides et cartas statim reddemus quæ liberatæ fuerunt nobis ab Anglicis in securitatem pacis vel fidelis servitii.

50. Nos amovebimus penitus de balliis parentes Gerardi de Athyes, quod de cetero nullam habeant balliam in Anglia ; Engelardum de Cygoniis, Andream, Petrum et Gyonem de Cancellis, Gyonem de Cygoniis, Galfridum de Martyni et fratres ejus, Philippum Mark et fratres ejus, et Galfridum nepotem ejus, et totam sequelam eorumdem.

51. Et statim post pacis reformationem amovebimus de regno omnes alienigenas milites, balistarios, servientes, stipendiarios, qui venerint cum equis et armis ad nocumentum regni.

52. Si quis fuerit disseisitus vel elongatus per nos sine legali judicio parium suorum, de terris, castellis, libertatibus, vel jure suo, statim ea ei restituemus ; et si contentio super hoc orta fuerit ; tunc inde fiat per judicium viginti quinque baronum, de quibus fit mentio inferius in securitate pacis : de omnibus autem illis de quibus aliquis disseisitus fuerit vel elongatus sine legali judicio parium suorum, per Henricum regem patrem nostrum vel per Ricardum regem fratrem nostrum, quæ in manu nostra habemus, vel quæ alii tenent, quæ nos oporteat warantizare, respectum habebimus usque ad communem terminum crucesignatorum ; exceptis illis de quibus placitum motum fuit vel inquisitio facta per præceptum nostrum, ante susceptionem crucis nostræ : cum autem redierimus de peregrinatione nostra, vel si forte remanserimus a peregrinatione nostra, statim inde plenam justiciam exhibebimus.

53. Eundem autem respectum habebimus, et eodem modo, de justicia exhibenda de forestis deafforestandis vel remansuris forestis, quas Henricus pater noster vel Ricardus frater noster afforestaverunt, et de custodiis terrarum quæ sunt de alieno feodo, cujusmodi custodias hucusque habuimus occasione feodi quod aliquis de nobis tenuit per servitium militare, et de abbatiis quæ fundatæ fuerint in feodo alterius quam nostro, in quibus dominus feodi dixerit se jus habere ; et cum redierimus, vel si remanserimus a peregrinatione nostra, super hiis conquerentibus plenam justiciam statim exhibebimus.

54. Nullus capiatur nec imprisonetur propter appellum fœminæ de morte alterius quam viri sui.

55. Omnes fines qui injuste et contra legem terræ facti sunt nobiscum, et omnia amerciamenta facta injuste et contra legem terræ, omnino condonentur, vel fiat inde per judicium viginti quinque baronum de quibus fit mentio inferius in securitate pacis, vel per judicium majoris partis eorumdem, una cum prædicto Stephano Cantuariensi archi-

episcopo, si interesse poterit, et aliis quos secum ad hoc vocare voluerit : et si interesse non poterit, nihilominus procedat negotium sine eo, ita quod, si aliquis vel aliqui de prædictis viginti quinque baronibus fuerint in simili querela, amoveantur quantum ad hoc judicium, et alii loco illorum per residuos de eisdem viginti quinque, tantum ad hoc faciendum electi et jurati substituantur.

56. Si nos dissaisivimus vel elongavimus Walenses de terris vel libertatibus vel rebus aliis, sine legali judicio parium suorum, in Anglia vel in Wallia, eis statim reddantur ; et si contentio super hoc orta fuerit, tunc inde fiat in marchia per judicium parium suorum, de tenementis Angliæ secundum legem Angliæ, de tenementis Walliæ secundum legem Walliæ, de tenementis marchiæ secundum legem marchiæ. Idem facient Walenses nobis et nostris.

57. De omnibus autem illis de quibus aliquis Walensium dissaisitus fuerit vel elongatus sine legali judicio parium suorum, per Henricum regem patrem nostrum vel Ricardum regem fratrem nostrum, quæ nos in manu nostra habemus, vel quæ alii tenent quæ nos oporteat warantizare, respectum habebimus usque ad communem terminum crucesigna-torum, illis exceptis de quibus placitum motum fuit vel inquisitio facta per præceptum nostrum ante susceptionem crucis nostræ ; cum autem redierimus, vel si forte remanserimus a peregrinatione nostra, statim eis inde plenam justiciam exhibebimus, secundum leges Walensium et partes prædictas.

58. Nos reddemus filium Lewelini statim, et omnes obsides de Wallia, et cartas quæ nobis liberatæ fuerunt in securitatem pacis.

59. Nos faciemus Allexandro regi Scottorum de sororibus suis, et obsidibus reddendis, et libertatibus suis, et jure suo, secundum formam in qua faciemus aliis baronibus nostris Angliæ, nisi aliter esse debeat per cartas quas habemus de Willelmo patre ipsius, quondam rege Scottorum ; et hoc erit per judicium parium suorum in curio nostra.

60. Omnes autem istas consuetudines prædictas et libertates quas nos concessimus in regno nostro tenendas quantum ad nos pertinet erga nostros, omnes de regno nostro, tam clerici quam laici, observent quantum ad se pertinet erga suos.

61. Cum autem pro Deo, et ad emendationem regni nostri, et ad melius sopiendum discordiam inter nos et barones nostros ortam, hæc omnia prædicta concesserimus, volentes ea integra et firma stabilitate gaudere in perpetuum, facimus et concedimus eis securitatem subscriptam ; videlicet quod barones eligant viginti quinque barones de regno quos voluerint, qui debeant pro totis viribus suis observare, tenere, et facere observari, pacem et libertates quas eis concessimus, et hac præsenti carta nostra confirmavimus, ita scilicet quod, si nos, vel justiciarius noster, vel ballivi nostri, vel aliquis de ministris nostris, in aliquo erga aliquem deliquerimus, vel aliquem articulorum pacis aut securitatis transgressi fuerimus, et delictum ostensum fuerit quatuor baronibus de prædictis viginti quinque baronibus illi quatuor barones accedant ad nos vel ad justiciarium nostrum, si fuerimus extra regnum, proponentes nobis excessum : petent ut excessum illum sine dilatione faciamus emendari. Et si nos excessum non emendaverimus vel, si fuerimus extra regnum, justiciarius noster non emendaverit infra tempus quadraginta dierum computandum a tempore quo monstratum fuerit nobis vel justiciario nostro si extra regnum fuerimus, prædicti quatuor barones referant causam illam ad residuos de viginti quinque baronibus et illi viginti quinque barones cum communa totius terræ distringent et gravabunt nos modis omnibus quibus poterunt, scilicet per captionem castrorum, terrarum, possessionum, et aliis modis quibus poterunt, donec fuerit emendatum secundum arbitrium eorum, salva persona nostra et reginæ nostræ et liberorum nostrorum ; et cum fuerit emendatum intendent nobis sicut prius fecerunt. Et quicumque voluerit de terra juret quod ad prædicta omnia exsequenda parebit mandatis prædictorum viginti quinque baronum, et quod gravabit nos pro posse suo cum ipsis, et nos publice et libere damus licentiam jurandi cuilibet qui jurare voluerit, et nulli umquam jurare prohibebimus. Omnes autem illos de terra qui per se et sponte sua noluerint jurare viginti quinque

baronibus, de distringendo et gravando nos cum eis, faciemus jurare eosdem de mandato nostro, sicut prædictum est. Et si aliquis de viginti quinque baronibus decesserit, vel a terra recesserit, vel aliquo alio modo impeditus fuerit, quo minus ista prædicta posset exsequi, qui residui fuerint de prædictis viginti quinque baronibus eligant alium loco ipsius, pro arbitrio suo, qui simili modo erit juratus quo et ceteri. In omnibus autem quæ istis viginti quinque baronibus committuntur exsequenda, si forte ipsi viginti quinque præsentes fuerint, et inter se super re aliqua discordaverint, vel aliqui ex eis summoniti nolint vel nequeant interesse, ratum habeatur et firmum quod major pars eorum qui præsentes fuerint providerit, vel præceperit, ac si omnes viginti quinque in hoc consensissent; et prædicti viginti quinque jurent quod omnia antedicta fideliter observabunt; et pro toto posse suo facient observari. Et nos nihil impetrabimus ab aliquo, per nos nec per alium, per quod aliqua istarum concessionum et libertatum revocetur vel minuatur; et, si aliquid tale impetratum fuerit, irritum sit et inane et numquam eo utemur per nos nec per alium.

62. Et omnes malas voluntates, indignationes, et rancores, ortos inter nos et homines nostros, clericos et laicos, a tempore discordiæ plene omnibus remisimus et condonavimus. Præterea omnes transgressiones factas occasione ejusdem discordiæ, a Pascha anno regni nostri sextodecimo usque ad pacem reformatam, plene remisimus omnibus, clericis et laicis, et quantum ad nos pertinet plene condonavimus. Et insuper fecimus eis fieri litteras testimoniales patentes domini Stephani Cantuariensis archiepiscopi, domini Henrici Dublinensis archiepiscopi, et episcoporum prædictorum, et magistri Pandulfi, super securitate ista et concessionibus præfatis.

63. Quare volumus et firmiter præcipimus quod Anglicana ecclesia libera sit et quod homines in regno nostro habeant et teneant omnes præfatas libertates, jura, et concessiones, bene et in pace, libere et quiete, plene et integre, sibi et hæredibus suis, de nobis et hæredibus nostris, in omnibus rebus et locis, in perpetuum, sicut prædictum est. Juratum est autem tam ex parte nostra quam ex parte baronum, quod hæc omnia supradicta bona fide et sine malo ingenio observabuntur Testibus supradictis et multis aliis. Data per manum nostram in prato quod vocatur Runingmede, inter Windelesorum et Stanes, quinto decimo die Junii, anno regni nostri septimo decimo.[1]

---

[1] *Select Charters*, 288-297.

CHAPTER XXX

1215, 1216

War between the King and the Barons—Crown offered to Louis of France—He comes over to England—His Campaign there—Illness and Death of King John

JOHN'S chief hope was in the Pope, and Innocent, to do him justice, did not neglect the cause of his vassal and Crusader. Finding that Langton had disregarded his injunction of the 19th March he issued a fresh Bull excommunicating in the most solemn words 'all the men who were disturbing the King and country' (*perturbatores regis et regni*), the execution of the sentence being committed not to the Archbishop, but to the Bishop of Winchester, Pandulph, and the Abbot of Reading.[1] This mandate was laid before the Council of the 16th July at Oxford that John failed to attend.[2] The clergy now found themselves in a difficulty. The summonses for the Fourth Lateran Council had gone forth ; and the prelates would shortly have to present themselves at Rome. It was not a time to disregard the orders of the Pope. Still they resolved to suspend the sentence till they had made one more effort to bring the King to a real understanding with the Barons; and in that hope they appointed another Council to be held at Staines on the 26th August. But again John refused to come, insisting that he was not the obstacle to peace. The bishops then, following the Pope's own words, proclaimed the excommunication of all 'disturbers of the King and country'; an anathema that either side might interpret as they liked.[3]

Innocent in the Field.

Disturbers of the Peace excommunicated.

The confederate Barons, satisfied that further negotiation with the King would be useless, resolved to take the actual administration of the country, or so much of it as was under their control, into their own hands, dividing it into seven districts. The Earl of Essex would take his own county ; Fitz Walter Northamptonshire ; Roger of Cresci Norfolk and Suffolk ; the Earl of Winchester Cambridge and Huntingdon ; William of

---

[1] Wendover, III. 336. Prynne, *Hist. King John*, 17, has a letter of the 18th June addressed to the Barons, but it does not read quite like one of Innocent's utterances.

[2] W. Cov., II. 223.

[3] W. Cov., II. 223, 224 ; *Liber de Ant.*, 202 ; R. Cogg, 173. On the 30th August John sent messages to Langton and the Barons then being at Oxford ; Rot. Pat., I. 153.

Aubigny Lincolnshire; Roger de Lacy, the Constable of Chester, would govern Yorkshire and Nottinghamshire; and Robert de Ros Northumberland.[1] They must have known that John all along had been preparing for

John still arming. a struggle, gathering shipping, enlisting mercenaries, calling in money and jewels deposited with monasteries.[2] He now took up his quarters on the coast to prepare for the reception of his allies and mercenaries.[3] Peter of Dreux, the Duke of Brittany, had been offered the earldom of Richmond held by his predecessors.[4] Hugh of Boves had been commissioned to enlist all and sundry.[5] It was understood that Michaelmas had been fixed for a general muster at Dover. The Barons, as if finding themselves driven to extreme measures, resolved to depose John, and offer the Crown to Louis of France, the only quarter from whence effectual aid could be expected. Overtures

The Crown offered to Louis of France. to him to that effect had already been made in 1213. A Council was summoned to authorise the measure. The thoroughgoing partisans agreed to renounce John, and Saer de Quincy was sent across the Channel to settle matters.[6]

But the confederates had overshot the mark. John's supporters, the men by whose advice (according to him) he had granted Magna Carta,[7] the Earls of Salisbury, Chester, Pembroke, Surrey, Derby, and Warwick,[8] declared that they were now released from their oaths to the Twenty-Five; while Albemarle[9] one of the Twenty-Five went over to the King. The clergy also fell away, pointing out that the men who renounced their allegiance would fall under the Papal ban. We are even told that some of the leading confederates were excommunicated, and London

Langton suspended. laid under a futile Interdict. The prelates on their way to Rome mostly stopped to pay their respects to John, at Dover.[10] Finally the Bishop of Winchester and Pandulph suspended Langton, just

---

[1] W. Cov., II. 224.

[2] Rot. Claus., I. 217–223; Rot. Pat., I. 144–149, 160. The number of deposits of plate and jewels that John had is quite remarkable.

[3] John was at Sandwich 28th–31st August, and at Dover 1st–19th September; *Itinerary.*

[4] Rot. Pat., I. 152; Stubbs.

[5] Wendover, III. 320; R. Cogg., 174.

[6] W. Cov., 225; R. Cogg., 176; Ann. Waverley, 283; Wendover, III. 349 (misplaced). The author of the *Mareschal* also places the offer to Louis before the siege of Rochester, II. 179.   [7] See the preamble to Magna Carta.

[8] Henry of Beaumont, II., who succeeded his father, Waleran, in 1204.

[9] William of Forz de Oleron II., son of William of Forz, I., second husband of Hawise or Hedwise of Blois. This Lady, the daughter and heiress of Count William of Aumâle, created Earl of York by Stephen, was married first to William of Mandeville, Earl of Essex (he died *s. p.* 1189; above 273); secondly to William of Forz I.; and at his death in 1195 to Baldwin of Bethune, who became Count in her right (above 360, note) till his death in 1213, when her son succeeded. See Doyle, Official Baronage.

[10] W. Cov., II. 224, 225.

as he was embarking for the Council.[1]   Pandulph followed him to tell his own story.[2]

The Pope's view of Magna Carta probably reached England not long afterwards, say towards the end of September.   He gave no uncertain

Magna Carta quashed. sound.   By a Bull dated the 25th August he utterly condemned the whole, not only as having been extorted by force, but also as being in itself 'vile, base, and illicit' (" *vilem, turpem, et illicitam* ").   All stipulations for its observance were quashed. By a letter of even date to the Barons he orders them to renounce the 'composition' made with their king.[3]   All this could only widen the breach between the parties, and accordingly, we hear that the Confederates

War again. again drew the sword, laying fresh siege to Northampton, and also to Oxford.[4]   But John's mercenaries were now coming over in formidable numbers.   One squadron, no doubt, under Hugh of Boves, while making for Dover from Calais, was caught by a sudden storm, and finally wrecked on the East Anglian coast, Hugh's own body being washed ashore near Yarmouth.[5]   But in spite of this mishap large bands recruited in Gascony, Poitou, Flanders, and Brabant joined the Royal Standard at Dover;[6] and John found himself strong enough to detach forces sufficient to dispel the sieges of Northampton and Oxford.[7]

This success, however, for the moment seemed counterbalanced by the loss of Rochester Castle, that suddenly passed into the hands of the confederates.   The fortress had been made over by John to Langton, as an appendage to the See of Rochester, then vacant, in November (1214),[8] as mentioned above.   Two months later Benedict of Sansetun had been consecrated as bishop of Rochester.[9]   But the castle was still regarded as appertaining to Langton; and with his consent it was entrusted to Reginald of Cornhill the younger, who had succeeded his father as Sheriff of Kent, on the express condition that he should redeliver it to the Archbishop within a stated time.   On the 25th May, however, John had pressed that the castle should be given over to Hubert de Burgh and Philip of Aubigny;[10]

---

[1] *Id.* ; R. Cogg, 174 ; Wendover, III. 340.   The suspension was confirmed by the Pope 4th November ; *Fæd.*, I. 139.

[2] *Fædera* I. 135.   Langton was apparently still at Dover on the 10th September, when the King took his possessions under his protection ; Rot. Pat., 154.   Pandulf was still at Dover on the 13th September ; Rot. Cart., I. 218.

[3] *Fædera, sup.*

[4] W. Cov., II. 226.

[5] Wendover, III. 332 ; R. Cogg, 174, 175 ; 26th September, Chron. Melrose, 119.

[6] Wendover, 331.   [7] W. Cov., *sup.*   [8] *Fædera*, I. 126, above 468.   [9] *Reg. Sacrum.*

[10] *Fædera*, 121, but under the year 1214, wrongly.   Mr. Foss, *Judges*, II. 52, represents the elder Reginald as living until 5 Henry III. ; but he was clearly dead by the year 1210, when his son accounted for all moneys due from himself or his father to the King ; Pipe Roll, 12 John, f. 11.   On the next year's Roll Reginald of Cornhill— obviously the son—appears as Sheriff of Kent.

while a few days later Hubert was appointed Sheriff of Kent vice Reginald, who was no longer trusted.[1]   On the 9th August the King returned to the charge, begging that the fortress should be committed to the Bishop of Winchester; but Reginald remained in charge;[2] and by him Robert fitz Walter and William of Aubigny were quietly allowed to enter and garrison the place (30th September?).[3]   As Reginald had been put in **Rochester** possession by John, and not by Langton, no blame seems to **Castle seized** attach to the Archbishop, who was in fact out of the country **by the** at the time.   Within three days, we are told, John appeared **Barons.** in the Medway, with a force brought by water.   He attempted to burn down Rochester Bridge, to cut off the garrison's communications with London.   But fitz Walter repelled the whole attack, and saved the Bridge.   But not till two of his knights in their eagerness to secure prisoners had been taken captive themselves.   One of these men, Oliver of Argentan, an active partisan, would have been starved to death by John but for the devotion of an elder brother, who to save Oliver's life agreed to change sides, and so joined the King 'in body if not in heart.'[4]

On the 13th October John, returning to the attack, took up his quarters in Rochester, stabling his horses in his Cathedral, and investing the castle.[5]   For seven weeks a garrison of some five or six score **Besieged by** men under Reginald of Cornhill and William of Aubigny **John,** held all the King's forces at bay, in spite of a bombardment kept up by night and day.   At first the outworks (*castrum*), enclosing some $4\frac{1}{2}$ acres of ground, now laid out as a public garden, had to be held. These were first stormed by the Royalists; then recovered by the garrison; then finally lost.   On the 27th October a feeble attempt at relief was undertaken by fitz Walter, who marched out of London with some 700 men.   But his forces never crossed the Darent.   A bitter gale assailed them, while John, apprised of their coming, was found to be holding the line of the river in strength.   Fitz Walter returned to London, leaving the garrison of Rochester to their own resources.[6]   The walls of the lofty inner Keep (*turris*) defied all bombardment; but mining operations were undertaken with success at the South East angle, where the underlying chalk comes near the surface.   A piece of wall, the extent of which may yet be discerned, was brought down; and a practicable breach effected. But the whole of the Keep was not yet won.   It was divided laterally from East to West by a massive party wall, and the garrison were able to hold

[1] June, Rot. Pat., 144, 145.
[2] Rot. Pat., I. 181 ; R. Cogg, 173.
[3] R. Cogg, 174, 176. On the 2nd October Reginald's estates were confiscated.
[4] R. Cogg, 175 ; Wendover, 331.
[5] R. Cogg, 176 ; *Itinerary*.
[6] W. Cov., II. 226 ; Wendover, III. 333 ; Paris, *Hist. Angl.*, II. 664.

out for a while longer in the Northern half, the half that fortunately contained the well.[1]   But their provisions were running out.   On the 30th November, their last horse having been eaten, they surrendered at discretion.   Again we are told that John would have hung all the leaders; but that Savary of Mauléon interfered, pointing out that no mercenaries would serve in a war in which no quarter was to be given.[2]   As a matter of fact it would seem that only one man was put to death, a cross-bowman who had been personally connected with the King.[3]

And captured.

During the last days of the siege detached parties had captured Tonbridge Castle, the old de Clare stronghold; and wrested Bedford from the servants of William Beauchamp.[4]

Having settled matters in Kent, Surrey, and Hants, John, on the 16th December moved to Windsor.   Two days later he appeared at St. Albans, when he was able to inform the monks that the Pope had confirmed Pandulf's suspension of Langton; and ordered the York Chapter to take for their Primate the King's nominee Walter Gray, Bishop of Worcester, quashing their previous election of Simon Langton, Stephen's brother.[5]   Encouraged by these fresh marks of Papal approval, and also no doubt by the obvious helplessness of the confederate Barons, John proceeded to inflict on his offending subjects such a winter harrying as England had not seen since the early days of the Conquest.   To do the work more thoroughly he divided his forces.   One army, under the Earl of Salisbury, Savary, Fawkes of Bréauté, and the Brabanter Walter Buck was detailed to keep a watch on London, and operate in the Eastern counties; while the King himself, with the Earl of Albemarle, Philip of Aubigny, and John Marshal[6] would lead another army through the Midlands Northwards.[7]   Salisbury again subdivided his force, leaving part to blockade the roads to London, while he himself led the rest to overrun Herts, Middlesex, Essex, and Cambridgeshire.   All hostile estates were devastated, protection money being exacted from the towns, as if no longer under the King's Peace.[8]

England harried.

Longsword and Savary

---

[1] See the plan in Clark's *Mily. Antiqs.*, II., 410.   It bears interesting testim~~ony~~ accuracy of the narrative preserved by Walter of Coventry.

[2] So Wendover, III. 335.

[3] W. Cov., II. 227.   See also R. Cogg, *sup.*   Reginald's wife Isabel ~~paid~~ marks for his ransom.   Rot. Pat., I. 189.   The wife of the elder Reginald had die~~d~~ year before (Foss, *sup.*); so that the son was clearly the man of the siege.

[4] Wendover, 349.   John gave the place to Fawkes of Bréauté with the hand of Margaret Rivers; Paris, *Chron. Maj.*, II. 638.

[5] Wendover, 344, 346; W. Cov., II. 227, 228; *Itinerary.*

[6] Presumably the son of the late John, elder brother of the Earl of Pembroke, who may have been jealous of the position to which his uncle had attained.

[7] Wendover, III. 347, 348.

[8] Wendover, 349.

On Christmas Eve Savary captured Pleshey, Mandeville's castle;[1] and
on Christmas Day itself he plundered Tilty Abbey, during
In East Anglia. the celebration of Mass; following up that act of sacrilege by
a similar act at Coggeshall on the Feast of the Circumcision
(1st January, 1216). From Coggeshall he moved on to Bury, and
from thence again he went to join hands with his chief, for an attack
on the Isle of Ely, that had become a centre of refuge.[2] The men
gathered there were prepared to resist. But a severe frost had deprived
Ely of its watery defences. This circumstance however worked two ways,
as, when the soldiers burst in by the Stentney bridge, the refugees were
Ely ravaged. enabled to escape in all directions over the ice. The cathedral
and other churches were plundered, prisoners put to the
ransom, and the whole Island gutted.[3] Savary was then sent to attack the
old Roman walls of Colchester, but at the end of five days, hearing that
relief was coming from London, he retired.[4]

The King's personal campaign extended over a much greater area.
Pushing like a firebrand through Beds, Bucks, Northamptonshire, and
The King in the Midlands. Leicestershire, he stayed one whole day in Nottingham, to
hold there a soldier's Christmas in camping fashion.[5] No
resistance had been attempted anywhere, all the leading
castles being in the King's hands. But nothing belonging to the hostile
party was spared. Everything that could not be carried off was destroyed.
Men caught outside the sanctuaries were put to the ransom.[6] These
severities of course would only be indulged in towards ostensible rebels;
but we may fairly surmise that the King's foreign troops would not be too
particular in verifying the politics of the places they visited. Resuming
his march on the 26th December John halted a day at Langar to receive
the submission of Belvoir Castle, extorted from the men of William of
Aubigny under threats of death to their lord. He of course had been
Northumbria overrun. taken prisoner at Rochester.[7] Continuing by Newark, Doncaster, Pontefract, York, Thirsk, Darlington, and Durham the
army entered Northumberland, where Mitford, Morpeth,
Alnwick, and Wark were successively given to the flames.[8] About the

---

[1] Earl Geoffrey himself died on the 22nd February (1216), of a wound received in a
tournament, and was buried at the Priory of the Holy Trinity Minories; R. Cogg., 179;
Ann. Dunst., 459, *q.v.* for the forced marriage to Isabel of Gloucester; above, 470.

[2] R. Cogg., 177. [3] R. Cogg., 177, 178; Wendover, III. 358; W. Cov., II. 229.

[4] 31st January–3rd February, 1216; R. Cogg, *sup.*

[5] "Ibi Natale Domini, non tamen ex more, sed sicut in expeditione positus, egit;"
W. Cov., II. 228; *Itinerary.*

[6] So Wendover, III. 348; Paris, *Chron. Maj.*, II. 636; *Hist. Angl.*, II. 170;
W. Cov., 229; R. Cogg, 178.

[7] Wendover, 350. Aubigny had been called from Belvoir to take the command at
Rochester; *Id.*, 329.

[8] *Itinerary*; Chron. Melrose, 122.

13th January, 1216, John occupied and sacked Berwick with the greatest cruelty, even torturing prisoners for ransom.[1]

The attack on Berwick was not unprovoked. Alexander II. from the time of his accession had been in communication with the English malcontents. Scottish bands had swelled the army of fitz Walter:[2] Magna Carta, as we have seen, contained stipulations on behalf of the Scots, and John had issued some orders for giving effect to them.[3] But when hostilities fairly broke out in the autumn Alexander crossed the Border, and laid unsuccessful siege to Norham ; but he received homage from divers Northern barons at Felton on the Coquet (October 1215).[4]   In fact the South of Scotland was now full of English gentry who had fled at John's coming ; and fresh homage to Alexander had been rendered in the Chapter House at Melrose on the 11th January.   John did not adventure his own person any farther beyond the Border ; but he sent *Lothian wasted.* his men 'to chase the red Scottish fox from his lair.'[5]   For nine days they repeated on Scottish soil the deeds so often wrought in England by the Scots.   They wasted the country to the Firth of Forth, burning Roxburgh, Dunbar, and Haddington.   Beyond the latter place it was not thought prudent to advance, as Alexander had an army on the Esk, at the foot of the Pentlands.   On their way back the English plundered Coldingham Abbey, though a dependency of Durham.[6] About the 23rd January John evacuated Berwick, burning down the town and its bridge behind him.   We are told that he set the example by setting fire with his own Royal hand to the hospitable roof that had sheltered him.[7]   Northumberland having already been sufficiently dealt with he moved through the Palatinate of Durham into Cleveland, a specially offensive district.   A whole fortnight was devoted to overrunning the land ; but a successful resistance was at last encountered at Helmsley, where de Ros' men defied all John's assaults.   On the 15th February the *Yorkshire* King slept at York.[8]   Knaresborough and Pontefract were then honoured with visits ; and after that the King passed *via* Tickhill into Lincolnshire, another county that had been fertile in *and Lincoln-shire visited.* rebels.   But the city of Lincoln was allowed to buy peace by giving hostages for a fine of 1000 marks.   Leaving Lincolnshire on the 23rd February, and resting at Fotheringay—the Scotch Earl David's seat—John spent eight days at or near Bedford ; turning

---

[1] *Id.*, Wendover, III. 352.

[2] Ann. Dunstable. Allan of Galloway, described as constable of Scotland, was at Runnymede, but his name appears as on John's side. *Fœdera*, I. 131.

[3] Rot. Pat., 144, 150.   [4] Chron. Melrose, 121.

[5] "Sic fugabimus rubeam vulpeculam de latibulis suis ;" Paris, *Chron. Maj.*, II. 642.

[6] Chron. Melrose, *sup.* Fordun, 284.   [7] *Id.*

[8] Wendover, 351, 353 ; *Itinerary.* York city was fined £1000 for supposed sympathy with the rebels. Rot. Fin. et Obl., p. 574 ; Pauli.

ıence into East Anglia, where, after a circuit through Cambridge, Bury,
Framlingham (Bigod's castle), and Ipswich, he settled down
:eduction of to the reduction of Colchester that Savary had failed to effect.[1]
Colchester.

At the end of six days the mixed garrison came to terms ;
ıreigners to be allowed to retire to London ; natives to be kept as
risoners for ransom.[2] The reduction of the Earl of Oxford's castle at
Iedingham (Essex) brought the winter's campaign to a close.[3] London,
ıe one outstanding rebel hold of importance, was much too strong to
e attacked ; and so John contented himself with taking up a position
f observation at a prudent distance—now at Windsor, and now at
ʟeading—to await the course of events.[4]

England had been devastated, every place attacked except Helmsley
ı Yorkshire and Mountsorrel in Leicestershire had been reduced.[5] But
England in spite of ceaseless offers of amnesty on John's part not
unsubdued. a malcontent had been won over.[6] On the contrary the
Northerners were up again and attacking York.[7] It is note-
ʒorthy that of all the Earls professedly on John's side only his natural
ırother Salisbury, and Albemarle, a Poitevin, could be entrusted with
:ommands in the field. The only two English barons in whom John had ·
ıntire confidence were Hubert de Burgh and John Marshall the nephew of
he Earl of Pembroke. John had the keeping of Sherborne and Dorchester
ʟastles.[8] Hubert had been appointed Chief Justiciar, Sheriff of Hereford,
ʃorfolk, Suffolk, and Kent, and Constable of Dover Castle.[9]

Concurrently with the action of the fleshly sword the spiritual arm had
ıeen playing its part. On the 16th December (1215) Innocent had
excommunicated thirty-one of the leading malcontents by
The Pope name, the Bull being addressed to the Abbot of Abingdon
again. and others. It reached England and was published towards
the end of February ;[10] but it produced so little effect that
Excommuni- the commissioners shortly found it necessary to anathematise
cations. a further batch of some thirty minor offenders, besides all
he Londoners.[11]

The Barons, thus, being unable to cope with John, and John being

[1] *Itinerary.*　　[2] 14th–19th March ? R. Cogg., 179 ; *Itinerary.*
[3] 25th–28th March ; R. Cogg., 180 ; *Itinerary.*
[4] *Id.* ; W. Cov., 229.　　[5] Wend., 353.
[6] For offers of safe-conducts see Rot. Pat., *passim* : the close Rolls claim numerous
ʃubmissions, *valeat quantum.*
[7] R. Cogg, *sup.*
[8] Rot. Pat., I. 150.
[9] *Id.*, 143, 144, 149, 150.
[10] *Fædera*, I. 139 ; R. Cogg, 179. The confirmation of Langton's suspension issued
₄th November apparently only reached John towards the 20th December, above 487, 488.
[11] Wendover, III. 353-357. For a further excommunication of Louis' agents in London
ʃee *Id.*, 360, 361.

unable to reduce them to submission, the future seemed to depend on
the action of the King of France. Some six months had elapsed since
a formal offer of the Crown of England had been made to his son Louis.
The chief leaders of the Baronial party had gone over in turns to Paris ;
terms had been agreed upon ; and hostages placed in Louis' hands. For
constitutional government he doubtless cared no more than John did ;
but the offer of a kingdom was not to be refused ; and small successive
forces had been sent to London in anticipation of his coming.[1] Finally
he had written to say that he would be at Calais ready to sail by Easter
(10th April).[2]

There again the Pope exerted himself on behalf of John. As soon as
he heard of the offer of the Crown to Louis he wrote to him and his

Louis forbidden to cross. father forbidding him to meddle with a feudatory of the
Church.[3] When the invasion of England seemed imminent
he sent Cardinal Gualo to exert himself on the spot to
frustrate the scheme. Philip received the Legate in audience at Melun
on the 24th April. He demurred to the allegation that John

Mission of Gualo. was, or could be, a vassal of the Pope ; no King could
alienate his realm without the consent of his Barons, a doctrine
loudly applauded by the French Magnates. But for himself personally
the King washed his hands of the whole affair, protesting that it lay simply
between his son and King John. " Mediæval morality did not recognise
political expediency as a justifiable cause of war ; it required some claim
of right, or some plea of provocation." [4] For the consideration of Louis'
case against John, therefore, a formal sitting was held next day.

Louis' case against John. Louis' spokesman—a well-born knight of course (*miles*)—
contended that it was matter of public notoriety that John
had been condemned by his Peers in the court of the King of France for
the murder of Arthur, committed with his own hands ; that subsequently
he had been rejected for his crimes by the Barons of England, who would
no longer have him to rule over them : by surrendering his crown to the
Pope without the assent of his Barons he had simply created a vacancy ;
and the Barons had filled it, by electing Louis in right of his wife, whose
mother the Queen of Castile was at the time the only survivor of John's
brothers and sisters.[5] The Legate, without entering on these delicate
questions of fact and constitutional law, called the speaker's attention to
the circumstance that John had taken the Cross, and that under the

---

[1] R. Cogg, 176, 178 ; W. Cov., II. 228 ; Chron. Auxerre, Bouquet, XVIII. 283 ; Le
Breton, *Id.*, XVII. 109 ; Wendover, 359–362.

[2] Wendover, 363.   [3] W. Cov. II. 228.

[4] Bishop Stubbs, *Const. Hist.*, II. 12.

[5] Eleanor was still living at the time of the surrender to the Pope ; but she died not
long afterwards, namely 21st October, 1214. Her sisters Matilda and Johanna died
before her.

decrees of the recent Lateran Council he was entitled to peace and the protection of the Holy See for four years.   The answer to that was that John, long before the assumption of the Cross, and ever since, had been at war with Louis, burning Aire, overrunning the county of Guisnes, etc., so that Louis could lawfully wage war against him.[1]   The end of it was that Gualo once more forbade Louis to go under pain of excommunication; but that Louis declined to accept the sentence, on the plea that he had sent envoys to Rome, and that therefore the matter was actually in the Pope's own hands.[2]

On Friday, 20th May, Louis embarked at Calais, with a considerable fleet, led by the noted Channel 'pirate' Eustace 'the Monk.' But the only

Landing of Louis.

men of rank mentioned as going with him were the Count of Nevers, and the Viscount of Melun, the latter one of the heroes of Bouvines.   They encountered head winds, and only landed at Stonar in Thanet the next day.[3] John, fully prepared for Louis' coming, had also gathered shipping to resist his landing; and had himself been on the look-out, moving backwards and forwards between Sandwich, Dover, Folkestone, and Romney since the 26th April.   But a gale had scattered his fleet and left the coast clear.   No sooner were the French reported to be fairly at sea than he lost heart, and retired to Canterbury (20th May). Most of his mercenaries were vassals of France, and could not be trusted to act against Louis, a consideration that had doubtless weighed with the Barons in their choice of him.[4] John did not rest at Canterbury, retiring to Seaford, and Bramber on the Sussex coast; thus leaving the way open to Louis, who immediately advanced to Canterbury.   There he halted a few days, to collect his forces, and explain his position to the people of

Proclamation to the English.

England.   For this purpose he issued a proclamation re-stating the case laid before Gualo at Melun, with some amplification. John had not only been condemned in Philip's court for the murder of Arthur, but had already, before his accession, been sentenced by his Peers in England for treason against Richard.[5] The

John's defaults.

Queen of Castile then became Richard's heir; and she and her heirs had made over their rights to Blanche and Louis. The election of John announced by Archbishop Hubert Walter at the coronation was invalid, being made in derogation of Eleanor's prior rights:

[1] "Unde justum bellum potest movere contra ipsum."

[2] See Wendover, III. 363–367. For Louis' agents at Rome, and the long discussion held there before the Pope, see *Id.*, 371–378. On the question of the murder of Arthur it is well to notice that Innocent made no attempt to deny the fact, but some attempt to justify it; p. 374.

[3] Wendover, 368; "per biduum in mari"; R. Cogg, 181; Ann. Winton and Waverley. According to the Chron. Auxerre, Bouquet, XVIII. 284, Louis only moved from Thanet to Canterbury on the 23rd May.

[4] *Itinerary*; Wendover and R. Cogg, *sup.*; W. Cov., II. 229.

[5] For the actual proceedings at Nottingham in March 1294, see above, 336.

he, Louis, had done nothing to disentitle him to take advantage of those
rights, as he had been at war with John ever since, and had been no party
to any compacts entered into by his father with John (*i.e.* the various
truces): again John had violated his coronation oath by surrendering the kingdom to the Pope, without the consent of his Barons, in
derogation of the old liberties of the realm. Finally he had specially
authorised his subjects to take up arms against him in case of misconduct
on his part, and after that had misbehaved more grossly than ever.
       Wherefore the Barons by common consent had voted John
Louis' rights. unworthy of rule, and had elected him, Louis, as their lord and
King, thus giving him a double and unimpeachable title.[1] The allegations
of fact here are audacious; but the mixture of good and bad reasoning is
very curious. The stress laid on Blanche's shadowy pretensions calls for
explanation. Louis himself was a timid man, of a pious sort, much in awe
of the Pope. But much as he feared the Pope, we are told that he feared
his wife more; and it is believed that he only embarked on the English
adventure to gratify her ambition.[2]
  But the proclamation doubtless served its purpose, and natives and
foreigners flocked to Louis' standard. On the 30th May Rochester
       Castle, that had defied John so long, opened its gates to him.
Louis in On the day before, being Whitsunday, Gualo, who had followed
London. hard in his wake,[3] and had joined John at Winchester, had
re-excommunicated Louis and all his with every possible formality.
Undeterred by this thunderbolt the Londoners received the French
Prince in triumph on the 2nd June.[4] Homage was done to him, while he
swore in a general way to observe the 'good laws' of his new subjects,
and to restore to all men their forfeited estates. Simon Langton was
appointed Chancellor, and letters were sent to the King of Scots, and
absent magnates, claiming their allegiance. The Tower however was
still held by John.[5]
  But Louis and his supporters were fully aware that England had to be
won with the sword. As soon as the first necessary pieces of business had
       been transacted they sallied forth, North and South. William
Confederates of Mandeville,[6] the new Earl of Essex, with Robert fitz Walter
in the field. moved into East Anglia, to recover their lost hold on those
districts; that is to say to ravage all places that had submitted to John;
and especially the larger towns, attached to the King by their chartered
privileges. In fact two armies are spoken of as operating; one Baronial,

---

[1] *Fœdera*, I. 140. The document bears no date, but would probably be issued very
shortly after Louis' landing. [2] Martin, *France*, IV. 92.
[3] According to the Continuation of Florence Gualo landed on the 20th May; p. 172.
[4] *Liber de Antiq.*, 202; W. Cov., II. 230.
[5] W. Cov. and *Liber de Antiq.*, *sup.*; Wendover, III. 368–370.
[6] Brother to Geoffrey who died in February.

the other mainly French. Essex, Suffolk, and Norfolk appear to have
been visited by both. The foreigners captured Norwich and Lynn ; while
East Anglian the Barons were credited with having sacked Cambridge,
towns Yarmouth, Dunwich, Ipswich, and Colchester,[1] all rich, com-
sacked. mercial towns. Farther North too the Barons were raising
their heads. Gilbert of Gant, the Lincolnshire magnate, captured the city,
but not the castle of Lincoln. That fortress held out under the intrepid
Lady Constable, Nicholaa de la Haye. Gilbert was then directed by
Louis to keep a watch on the King's garrisons at Nottingham and Newark.
Beyond the Humber De Ros, Bruce, and Percy had recovered the
control of most of Yorkshire.[2]

Louis himself marched against his principal enemy, who was reported to
have raised the old Dragon Standard at Winchester.[3] On the 7th June
Louis in the he captured Reigate; Guildford on the 8th June, and Farnham
South. on the 10th June. Four days later he entered the city of Win-
chester, John having retired to Ludgershall some days before.
On the 25th June Savary of Mauléon evacuated the Castle of Winchester;
Wolvesey Castle, the bishop's palace being yielded on the same day.[4]

Royalists Some of John's best friends now came forward to give in an
wavering. ostensible allegiance to Louis. Hugh Neville tendered the
keys of Marlborough; and Longsword those of Salisbury.[5]
The Earls of Surrey and Sussex (Warenne and Arundel) also appeared;
even Albemarle professed to change sides for a time.[6] Independent
risings were taking place in the West. On the 21st June the Earl of
Devon (William of Redvers) had been authorised to compound for protection for his estates, presumably those in the Isle of Wight.[7] On the 7th
July Exeter was reported to be in danger;[8] while about the same time
Worcester passed into the hands of William Marshal the younger.[9] John
was in such alarm that on the 17th July he left Corfe, as if no longer safe
there, and made for Bristol and the Severn Valley. For Louis every thing
seemed to point to the expediency of a prompt advance. Had he pushed
on at once he might have hemmed in John at Corfe.[10] But instead of
Impolicy of pressing his advantage the French Prince fell back to lay
Louis. siege to Odiham, as if to complete the conquest of Hampshire, which, with Sussex, had been placed under his chief
Lieutenant the Count of Nevers. The appointment of a foreigner of

[1] Wendover, III. 371, 378, 380. He names Louis as acting in these raids, which must be wrong; R. Cogg., 182.   [2] Wendover, 379; W. Cov., 230.   [3] R. Cogg., *sup.*
[4] Ann. Winton, 82 ; Waverley, 285 ; *Itinerary.*
[5] Wendover, 371 ; R. Cogg., *sup.*; *cnf.* W. Cov., II. 231.
[6] W. Cov., *sup.* But see the permission given to the Earl of Devon, next note.
[7] "Quod terram vestram contra Ludovicum tensetis"; Rot. Pat., I. 188. For the estates in Wight see *Complete Peerage.*   [8] Rot. Pat., 190.
[9] The city however was recovered on the 17th July by Fawkes; Ann., Worcester.
[10] John remained at Wareham and Corfe 18th June–17th July; *Itin.*

course was unwise, and gave great offence.[1]   Odiham having fallen **Louis**

Sieges of Windsor divided his forces, sending Nevers to lay siege to **Windsor**, while he himself marched off to blockade Hubert de Burgh at Dover.   For some fifteen weeks he lay there in an entrenched camp, bombarding the Castle with engines brought over from France.

and Dover. One huge catapult was dignified with the name of *La Malvesine.*[2] The chief incident of the siege was a visit from the **King of** Scots, who, at Louis' invitation, made his way through England to render homage, rendering it for the English holdings.   The journey

Scottish homage. however cost the party the life of Eustace de Vescy, who fell, struck by a cross-bow bolt, during an unsuccessful attack on Barnard Castle, held for King John by Hugh of Balliol.   After a fortnight's stay at Dover Alexander regained his Kingdom, eluding John's efforts to have him intercepted at the fords of the Trent.[3]   On the 14th October, de Burgh, finding his position untenable, signed a convention to surrender by a given day, if not previously relieved.[4]

The state of England by this time must have been deplorable.   Between the King and the Barons the 'people were ground down as between

State of England. whirling millstones.'[5]   The anarchy must have been as complete as in any days of Stephen's time.   The worst of it was that both sides seemed equally to go downhill.   Both John's

Balance of Parties. cause and that of the Barons seemed daily to grow more and more hopeless.   Louis' incapacity was obvious.   His followers gave themselves offensive airs, treating the English as a conquered people.

> " Qui si érent plen de vantance
> Qu' il disoient que Engleterre
> Ert lor, e voidassent la terre
> Engleis; quer nul dreit n'i aveint."[6]

One William Vaux of Collingham gathered a band of guerilla archers in the Weald of Sussex for the express purpose of killing Frenchmen;[7] while the men of the Cinque Ports, always strongly national, harassed Louis' shipping.[8] John still retained the control of all the chief fortresses, besides the allegiance of a string of influential Barons, including the Earls of

---

[1] R. Wend., III., 371 ; Ann. Dunst., 46; *Mareschal*, II. 180.

[2] Wendover, 371, 380 ; R. Cogg., 182 ; *Liber de Ant.*, 202.

[3] Chron. Melrose, 123 ; J. Fordun, 284 ; Wendover, 382.   Alexander had crossed the Border into England on the 5th August.

[4] R. Cogg. and *Liber de Ant., sup.*

[5] Paris, *Hist. Angl.*, II. 184.

[6] *Mareschal*, II. 180.   See also the so-called 'confession' attributed to the Viscount of Melun ; Wendover, II. 383, 384.

[7] Paris, *Chr. Maj.*, II. 655 ; Ann. Dunstable, 46 ; *Mareschal, sup.*   The author of the last says that he had seen the bodies of 100 Frenchmen lying between Winchester and Romney.

[8] Aun. Dunst., *sup.*

Pembroke, Chester, Derby, Warwick, Surrey, Sussex, and Devon.   It may however be questioned whether they were as much in earnest as their opponents; while John with all his efforts, all his offers of amnesty and what not, failed to bring over one single malcontent.[1]   No man who had once given him serious offence could trust him.

For a whole month (19th July–19th August) John had remained out of sight on the Welsh March.   The district was a loyal one, but he could find land to harry at any rate in the Braose estates recently restored to Reginald son of the late William.[2]   At the very time when the Scottish bands were traversing England with impunity John must have been shocked by the news of the death of his prop and mainstay, **Death of Innocent III.** Innocent III.[3]   His cause seemed indeed lost.   A new Pope doubtless would inaugurate a new policy.[4]   But Honorius trod in the tracks of Innocent; and the messenger who brought word of the death of the late Pope, must also have brought John the assurance of the unshaken support of his successor.[5]

It may have been the comfort of this intelligence that induced the King to make a sudden effort for the relief of Windsor.   Leaving Chippenham **The King again in action.** on the 1st September, and marching through Cirencester and Burford, he reached Oxford on the 3rd September; advancing to Reading and Sonning, he halted there from the 6th to the 13th of the month, at a distance of some 18 miles from Windsor.   Finding however that the Count of Nevers was prepared to give him battle, and coming forward to meet him, he lost heart, and fell back on Wallingford, from whence he started on a final tour of furious devastation through the Eastern counties.   It seemed as if despairing of success for himself he wished to involve the whole rebel Kingdom in destruction.   Passing **A last raid.** through Aylesbury and Bedford he went to Cambridge, and from thence along the borders of Essex and Suffolk as far as Hedingham, devastating everything.   The Barons on hearing of his movements dropped the siege of Windsor, and hastened after him, as far as Cambridge, a party from London joining in the pursuit.   But he eluded them by rapid marches through Rockingham to Stamford; not however without finding time to burn the barns at Oundle, a cell of Peterborough, though the monks had given him all the ready money they had to offer.[6]

[1] For John's offers to his opponents see the entries on the Patent Rolls for his last year *passim.*

[2] Ann. Dunst., 47. For terms made with the de Braose family see Rot. Pat., I. 157, 184.

[3] The Pope passed away at Perugia on the 16th July; R. Cogg, 183; Ann. Waverley, 286; Hurter; Pauli.   On the 18th July Cardinal Cencio Savelli was elected, and took the style of Honorius III.; H. Nicolas.

[4] So W. Cov., II. 230.

[5] See the notification of his accession sent by Honorius to Gualo; *Epp.*, I. 6; Raynaldi, *Ann.* XX. 393; Pauli.   [6] Paris, *Hist. Angl.*, II. 189.

From Stamford John pushed on to Lincoln (22nd September) where he had the satisfaction of raising the siege of the Castle, pressed by Gilbert of Gant.[1]   From Lincoln as a centre, without giving himself one day's rest, he began a series of vindictive raids, first Northwards to Axholm and Grimsby ; then round by Louth and Boston to Spalding. ' Was never so much burning in so short a time remembered in our age.'[2]   At Spalding he staid two days, apparently to enable him to visit Croyland, to whose Abbot he bore a grudge. Savary was ordered to lay the whole place in ashes, the King waiting outside to see the work done. But the Gascon Lord allowed himself to be moved by a humble procession of barefooted monks, with relics, and an image of the Virgin ; he accepted 50 marks as a peace offering. But to pacify his indignant master he had to destroy all the autumn's crops laid up in store.[3]

After spending seventeen days in Lincolnshire John on the 9th October moved from Spalding to King's Lynn in Norfolk, either in pursuit of refugees, or to establish a garrison there. His exact object does not appear. At Lynn he was attacked by dysentery, brought on The King's by over-eating and over-drinking.[4]   Returning to Lincolnshire illness. on the 12th October he marched through Wisbeach to Swineshead, crossing the dangerous sands at the mouth of the Welland without a proper guide,[5] and at a wrong time of the tide. The King passed over in safety, but his followers were caught by the rising tide, or engulfed in quicksands. A good many perished, but, sadder still, the precious baggage train, with all the furniture of the King's chapel, the relics, the money, plate and jewels that he had been so carefully taking under his own charge were lost.[6] Vexation and rash indulgence in a supper of peaches and new cider brought on fever.[7] At Swineshead Abbey he rested a whole day. On the 14th October, restless as ever, he started for Sleaford ; but after riding a few miles, finding the effort too great, he called for a litter. But there was neither litter, nor horse trained to litter work in his following ; an extemporised couch made of osiers and horse-cloths shook him so painfully that he had to be placed on a pack-horse, and so was gently carried on to Sleaford.[8]   There he was duly bled, according to the medical practice of the times ;[9] and on the 16th October was conveyed one more stage to

[1] R. Cogg, 182, 183; Wendover, III. 381, 382; W. Cov., 231 ; *Itinerary*. The Scots had been at Lincoln not long before.

[2] W. Cov., *sup. Itinerary.*

[3] Paris, *Chron. Maj.*, II. 667 ; *Hist. Angl.*, II. 189. In the former work the incident is clearly placed on the way to Lynn.

[4] W. Cov. ; R. Cogg., *sup.*

[5] " Sine duce " ; Paris.

[6] Wendover, 384 ; Paris, *Hist. Angl.*, II. 190 ; R. Cogg., 183, 184.

[7] Wendover, 385 ; Paris, *sup.*

[8] Paris, *sup.*, 191, 192.

[9] R. Cogg., 183.

Newark. From Sleaford he had already written to Honorius, commending his son to his charge.[1] He now declared young Henry heir to the Throne, and took such measures as he could to ensure his succession, in the way of orders to the sheriffs and constables of castles. He also made a short Will appointing thirteen executors, to whose care he committed all his affairs, with special injunctions as to the satisfaction due to the Church, the sending of help to Palestine, and the succession of his son. He also directed his body to be buried at Worcester.[2] Among the executors were the Legate, the Bishops of Winchester, Chichester,[3] and Worcester;[4] the Master of the Temple; and the Earls of Pembroke, Chester, and Derby. Finally he made his confession to the Abbot of Croxton, who was acting

His death as his physician, and so passed away in the early hours of Wednesday, 19th October, in the eighteenth year of his reign,[5] and apparently the forty-ninth of his age. The Bishop of Winchester and John Marshal were among the few with him at the last.[6] Again we hear of a disgraceful looting of the death-chamber, and the prompt disappearance of all the attendants.[7] The body was embalmed, and duly carried to

and Burial Worcester by the soldiery, and there laid between the tombs of St. Oswald and St. Wulfstan—the latter only just canonised in the Lateran Council. "*Inter sanctos collocabitur*" was a prophecy adduced from the current Merlin.[8] By his own desire John was laid to his rest in the habit of a monk, "a posthumous tribute" to the beliefs that he had lived to outrage.[9]

The political see-saw had gone on to the last. John's dying hours had been disturbed on the one hand by the report of the convention at Dover; on the other hand by offers of submission that came all too late.[10]

---

[1] Raynaldi, XX. 397, Pauli.

[2] *Fædera*, I. 144; from the original still shown at Worcester.

[3] Richard le Poer, consecrated 25th January, 1215. *Reg. Sacr.*

[4] Silvester of Evesham, consecrated by Innocent at Perugia, 3rd July, 1216. *Id.*

[5] " In nocte quæ diem Sancti Lucæ Evangelistæ (18th October) proxime secuta est "; Wendover, III. 385; W. Cov., II. 231; Ann. Winton, 82; Wav., 286.

[6] See *Mareschal*, II. 182, where John of Monmouth, Walter Clifford, and " Sire Rogier," are also named.

[7] R. Cogg., 184.

[8] Ann. Worcester, 405, 407. " Entre les souvereins " is another version of the prophecy; *Mareschal*, 184. The date of the King's burial does not appear.

[9] See the effigy on his tomb. The coffin was opened in 1797, and the habit found to be as there represented, but with a monkish cowl round the head. Nash, *Worcestershire*, II., *Additions*, 88.

[10] R. Cogg., 183; Wend., III. 386; Paris, *Hist. Angl.*, II. 192, 194.

CHAPTER XXXI

1199-1216

Survey of the Reign—John's Appearance—Character, and Government—Finance— Revenue—The Boroughs—Gild Merchant—University of Oxford—The King's Issue

IN bodily make John, like his father and his brother Geoffrey, was a stout man, strongly built, but rather under middle size. The effigy on his tomb gives an apparent height of five feet six inches. In his latter days he was corpulent and bald. Giraldus Cambrensis gives him credit for a certain amount of good looks; and the monument, seemingly taking him as at his best, exhibits a thick head of curly hair, trim beard and whiskers, and a small delicate mouth, with corresponding moustaches turned neatly downwards at the points. The eyebrows are finely arched, like those of Richard, and the forehead smooth. But the face is short and broad, with high cheek bones, and is altogether smug and destitute of expression.[1]

John's personal appearance.

Sprung from a very bad family, John was a selfish cruel tyrant of the worst type, extortionate and unjust, treacherous and vindictive, without regard either for the spirit or the form of law, and wholly destitute of religious feeling. Giraldus Cambrensis, who had accompanied him to Ireland as his Mentor, ventured to express some hopes of him in his youth. At the close of his career he felt bound to pronounce him the most atrocious tyrant on record.[2] In the matters of taxation, fines, amerciaments, and the general abuse of feudal rights it is

His character.

---

[1] Giraldus, writing of Geoffrey and John as young men, described them as "ambo staturæ grandis, paulloque plus quam mediocris, et formæ dignæ imperio"; *Top. Hib.*, p. 198. Re-writing the passage years later for insertion in his *De Principis Instr.* he says of John "staturæ modicæ, paulloque mediocri plus pusillæ, et formæ pro quantitatis captu satis idoneæ"; p. 177. In his later years John was described as "Omnino canus; corpore fortis, nec procerus, sed potius compactus et formæ ad robur convenientis"; so John's envoy to the Emperor of Morocco; Paris *Chr. Maj.*, II. 561. "Eo quod corpulentior esset." So of John at his death, W. Cov., II. 232. When the tomb was opened in 1797 the skeleton was found to measure about 5 feet 6 inches. Nash, *Worcestershire, sup-*

[2] "Atrocius cæteris tyrannis omnibus tam in sacerdotium quam in regnum . . . debacchari . . . vitiosos vincere cunctos," *De Prin. Instr.*, 310; comparing *Top. Hib.*, 198-200.

not clear that John went beyond the practice of his predecessors. The extra scutage-fines "*Ne transfretent*" were Richard's invention. The abominable practice of exacting hostages as an ordinary method **His government.** of government was of course John's own. But what distinguishes his rule from that of others is its pettiness, meanness, and spitefulness; its generally irritating character, and the utter absence of any redeeming features. He was not wanting in cleverness, or spasmodic energy. But there is no splendour in any of his doings to gild his sins; nothing but failure. He has no policy, foreign or domestic; he never looks beyond the immediate future. Through thirty years of public life we search in vain for one good deed, one kindly act to set against his countless offendings. He loved petty successes, and to take his revenge "on the innocent and in the dark." He had faithful servants; but they served him without loving him;[1] and for choice he employed "creatures" whom he could sacrifice at will.[2] Hubert de Burgh was probably his most attached servant. His private life from boyhood upwards was **Licentious habits.** profligate. The dishonour to which noble families had been subjected by his *amours* is given as one leading grievance.[3] Even his brother Salisbury's wife was not safe from him.[4] Yet in John's case, if ever, the faultiness of the sovereign proved the salvation of the people. Had John been less intolerable, Clergy, Baronage, and Commons might never have banded together to win Magna Carta.

One tardy act of recognition must not be overlooked. A few days before his death John granted a piece of forest land for a site for a House of Religion to be founded for the souls of William de Braose, his wife, and their son.[5] The Cistercian abbey of Beaulieu in the New Forest was the only actual foundation of John's own.[6] But the buildings were really the work of his son.

With all his strictness in Forest exactions John was not a great sportsman; but he liked hawking, and paid large sums for falcons from Norway. The Wiltshire Downs seem to have been the favourite hawking ground, as the King's hawks were kept in that county[7]

---

[1] This point comes out clearly in the case of the Earl of Pembroke, who evidently remained loyal, not from love of the King, but from inborn prudence, and a determination not to imperil his great position. See the *Mareschal, passim*, and esp. II. 180–183.

[2] Bishop Stubbs, W. Cov., II. xvi., *q. v.* for a grand full-length portrait of the King.

[3] So Wendover, III. 240; Ann. Waverley, 282; and Wykes, 53. Of John in his youth Giraldus wrote: "Magis addictus . . . veneri quam virtuti"; *Top. Hib.*, 200.

[4] So Le Breton, Bouquet, XVII. 110.

[5] 10th October, 1216; Rot. Pat. I. 199, Pauli. There was at any rate one son, Reginald, still living, and two grandsons, Giles and Philip; Rot. Pat., I. 158, 184.

[6] Ann. Wav., 256; A.D. 1204. See above, 388. The foundation charter is dated 25th January, 1205; *Monasticon*, V. 682; Pauli.

[7] See the Wilts accounts in the Pipe Rolls, *passim*, where the charges for the keeping of the hawks appear regularly.

Under John it becomes even more clear than in the time of his brother that the Pipe Rolls do not represent the whole of the King's revenue.

Finance of the Reign. Of the hidage in course of collection at Richard's death, of that of the year 1200, of the Seventh of movables said to have been taken from the Barons in 1203, of the Thirteenth taken from clergy and laity in 1207, we find nothing on these Records. Of

The Revenue not fully recorded. scutages and amerciaments we seem to get fair accounts; while of some sources of revenue, that ought to have been constant, we get occasional and only occasional accounts. The numerous hoards of money kept by the King at the Temple, with the

Imperfect accounts. Hospitallers, and in Houses of Religion up and down the country may have had something to do with the silence of the Exchequer accounts. The large payments made through the King's Chamber or Privy Purse will not account for it, because these, or some of them, are noticed on the Pipe Rolls. Probably we may ascribe the irregularities in the Accounts to the haphazard, we might almost say childish character of John's government, and his readiness to swallow any bait offered in the shape of ready-money. For a satisfactory view of the Royal Revenue we must bear to wait for the next reign, when the fine series of Pell Issue and Receipt Rolls will give us full information on both sides of the account. We have therefore contented ourselves with adding up one Pipe Roll of John's reign; and we have taken the eighth year as a sort of average year, not marked by any special circum-

Total on one Pipe Roll. stances. The total paid or accounted for comes to the handsome sum of £34,516 12s. 3d., the largest total on any Pipe Roll that we have had to record. As to the items of which this total is made up, the county farm-rents might yield £12,000, as

Heads of Revenue. at the close of Richard's reign: the scutages and fines *ne transfretent* only amount in round numbers to £436. But the stripping of the Canterbury estates seized in July brought in £5169 19s. 5d.; while the abbey lands of Hyde and Ramsey

County Farm Rents. yielded £500 more. The only other noteworthy item appears to be a fine of £1000 extorted from Philip of Poitou, the Bishop of Durham.[1] Deducting these sums there will still remain £15,000, mainly derived from similar sources, namely Church lands in hand, fines, amerciaments, tallages on the Royal demesnes lay estates in hand and the like. With respect to the scutages of the reign, of which so much has been made, we have already pointed out that owing to the system of granting remissions they came to very little.[2] Of the miscel-

---

[1] The Bishop died 22nd April, 1208. On the Pipe Roll, 10 John, his executors are entered as owing 4000 marks; 2000 marks for the late Bishop's jewels, and 2000 for offences committed by him or his relations; fol. 9 dorso "Nova Oblata."

[2] For the scutages, eight in number, see *Red Book of Exchequer*. The last scutage raised was that for the expedition to Ireland; Pipe Roll, 12 John. The scutage for the

laneous receipts of various years the following may be taken as samples.

Pines. Walter Gray had to pay 5000 marks (£3333 6s. 8d.) for being appointed Chancellor ;[1] and William de Stuteville £1000 for being appointed Sheriff of Yorkshire.[2] Saer de Quincy had to promise £4000 for getting his moiety of the estates of the late Robert fitz Parnell, Earl of Leicester ;[3] and the Countess of Perche had to offer 1600 marks (£1066 13s. 4d.) to be admitted to lands in Essex belonging to her late husband.[4] Then the wardship of the lands of Gilbert of Laigle was sold to Earl Warenne (Surrey) for £2000 ;[5] while William Mowbray, apparently a minor, or in custody, had to promise 2000 marks 'to be treated fairly and according to custom.'[6] Reginald of Cornhill the younger, son of the old Sheriff of Kent whom he had succeeded, paid 10,000 marks (£6,666 13s. 4d.) to clear himself of all claims against his father or himself.[7] For his treason at Rochester, as we have seen, he lived to pay £2000 more. But the Church presents the biggest single item of all. On the Pipe Roll of the thirteenth year we find the prodigious sum of

Vacant Sees. £16,787 brought into account as representing the revenues of the See of Durham for three years and four months. The reader will bear in mind that to give their equivalents in modern money these sums should be multiplied twenty-fold and more. Most characteristic of the times and the man were John's dealings with the property of his first wife Isabel of Gloucester. She was only the third daughter

A rich heiress. of her father William fitz Robert ; but was made his heiress for the benefit of her Royal husband. After her divorce from John her title and estates were made over to Amaury of Montfort, the husband of her eldest sister, in compensation for his county of Evreux, ceded to King Philip under the treaty of Le Goulet (A.D. 1200; above 386, note). By the ninth year of King John (1207–1208) the 'Honour' of Gloucester is again found in hand (Pipe Roll). But in 1214, John being presumably in want of money, he re-endowed his discarded wife with her inheritance ; and compelled Geoffrey of Mandeville, the Earl of Essex to marry her, in order to obtain from him an impossible fine, one that he could never pay.[8] The marriage was simply a device for turning the Gloucester estates into money.

Of two sources of revenue that ought to have appeared regularly on the

expedition to Poitou for which John called in 1214 would have been a ninth levy, but it was never paid, in spite of the Pope's injunction.

[1] Foss, II. 78.   [2] Pipe Roll, 3 John.

[3] Pipe Roll, 9 John, f. 19, dors.   Half the amount was eventually remitted.

[4] Pipe Roll, 10 John, f. 15, dors.   The Count was Geoffrey III., who died in 1202; his son Thomas succeeded.

[5] Pipe Roll, 8 John.

[6] " Ut Rex faciat eum deduci juste et secundum consuetudinem Angliæ ;" Pipe Roll. 3 John, f. 12, dors, Madox, I. 428.   So again 5 John.

[7] Pipe Roll, 12 John, f. 11.

[8] See *Complete Peerage* ; Doyle, *Official Baronage*, and Ann. Dunst., 45.

Pipe Rolls, namely the Customs, and the profits of the Royal Mints, we
get some isolated accounts.   From one of these we learn that
Profits of the Mint.   the Mints were farmed out to Hugh Oisel for £566 13s. 4d. a
year.[1]   Under Richard the yield without Winchester was only
£400.[2]   For the Customs in like manner we have one full account, and
Customs.   that tells us that the general rate of duty was a fifteenth, or
7½ per cent., instead of 10 per cent. as the rate seemed to be
under Richard.   The yield for some twenty-nine months from thirty-two
ports, mostly on the East coast and without Bristol, is £4958 7s. 3d.
That would represent something over £2000 a year.   The four chief
contributors were London, sending in £836 ; Boston, £730 ; Southampton,
£712 ; and Lynn, £651.[3]   After that we have only casual accounts of
duties on sundry articles, such as corn, tallow, and woad, the last evidently
an important article in the Eastern counties, being used for dyeing cloths.[4]
We also hear of the Prisage of Wines, being the profits from the King's
right of taking two tuns ("*tonnels*") from each ship at 15s. the tun, the
market rate running from £1 to £2 6s. 8d. the tun.[5]   We also find a very
small duty of four pence on the tun of wine,[6] doubtless of old standing.

A few notes of prices may be given.   We find an ox valued at 3s. ; a
pig and a hive of honey at 1s.   Sheep ran from 1¼d. to 2¼d.
Agricultural prices.   each.   A palfrey or good riding horse might be worth £3 to
£4 ; while animals good enough for the King's general purposes
could be had for less than 30s.   We find an entry of agricultural land let,
namely a virgate, or about 50 acres, for 13s. 4d., or not quite 3d. an acre.
We have already noticed the failure of crops and dearth through excessive
rains between the autumn of 1202 and the summer of 1205.   In 1201–1202
Norfolk wheat could be had for 2s. 3d. the *summa* or quarter (Pipe Roll
3 John).   In the Accounts for the next two years we have wheat quoted
in different places at 4s. 9d., 6s. 8d., 7s. 3d., and 8s. the quarter.   According
to the chroniclers wheat by the spring of 1205 had risen to 13s. 4d. and
14s. the quarter.[7]   In 1204 when an attempt was made to regulate the
price of bread, or rather the size of the loaf—as that and not the price
was to vary—it was assumed that wheat might run from 1s. 6d. to 6s. [the
summa].[8]   As for wages, the services of an able-bodied man
Wages.   to act in a position of some trust, such as the keeping of a
gaol, could still be had for a penny a day.   Miners received 3d. a day.   A

---

[1] He accounted for £1133 6s. 8d. as the 'farm' for two years ; Pipe Roll, 3 John,
fol. 35, dors.   [2] Pipe Roll, 3 Rich. I., fol. 12 ; Madox, I. 133.

[3] Pipe Roll, 6 John, f. 16, cited Madox, I. 772.

[4] See the details, Madox, 772, 773.   The tax on woad is distinguished as an "assisa,"
as if there was a special duty on it.

[5] Pipe Rolls, *passim*.   [6] Madox, I. 773.   [7] R. Cogg., 151 ; Wendover, III. 182.

[8] Paris, *Chron. Maj.*, II. 481.   The measure is not stated, being evidently taken for
granted.

ounted master-arblaster or crossbowman, with three horses, received 6*d.*
day ; an ordinary arblaster, with two horses, had 4½*d.* a day.

Of John's expenditure one point should be noticed, the constant outlays
ι the keeping-up of castles, a piece of forethought that stood him in good

The Public Records. stead. With this reign we have a great expansion in our public
Records, the most perfect collection in Europe. The Charter
Rolls begin with the first year of King John ; the Patent Rolls
th the third year, and the Close Rolls with the sixth year. The Charter
olls preserve the Charters granted by the King ; the Patent Rolls the
etters Patent issued by him ; and the Close Rolls the closed or private
tters sent out.[1] A charter testifies to a solemn act, such as the grant of
nds, or a pardon ; it requires witnesses, and is addressed to the several
ders of society. 'To the Archbishops, Bishops, Earls, etc.' Letters
atent, or open letters, are addressed generally 'To all to whose sight or
nowledge these shall come ;' and they contain a public order ; the Close
tters are addressed to an individual person, and contain private instruc-
ons. But the entries on the Rolls are multifarious, and not confined to
ieir proper class of document. Other Rolls were also started in the
eign, such as the Rolls of Fines and Offerings (*Oblata*) ; the Liberate
tolls, for orders for payment of money ; the Prestita Rolls, recording
dvances made to public servants on account ; and the Misæ Rolls
letailing the King's daily household expenditure.

John, like Richard, dispensed borough charters with a liberal hand, both

The Boroughs. Kings being always ready to sacrifice prospective rights for
ready money or other immediate object. Their grants show the
Borough in every stage of development from the lowest to the
iighest, the last, or full municipal incorporation, being probably only to be
ound in London.

The Borough, as distinguished from a simple town or village, may be
lescribed as having been in its inception a fortified town—as in fact the

Essential features. very name (*burh*) implied. Commonly, but not necessarily, it
was a county town, a place, at any rate, that through its im-
portance had obtained either by charter or prescription the
distinction of ranking as a Hundred,[2] and so of sending twelve representatives to the county court, instead of the four men sent by a township.[3]
A further primary feature would be the market, held with the right of
levying tolls, under the protection of a special borough peace, an extension
of the old limited King's Peace.[4] The borough also would have its own

---

[1] See Foss., *Judges*, II. 2.

[2] See this in John's charter to Dublin as an essential feature of a borough ; Gilbert,
Municipal Documents Ireland 52.

[3] See John's charter to Dunwich, Rot. Cart., 51 ; *Select Charters*, 303.

[4] See F. W. Maitland, *Domesday and Beyond*, 172, and *Township and Borough*
(Cambridge, 1858); also Pollock and Maitland, *Hist. Engl. Law*, I. 636, etc.

court, its burhmote or portmote, with its franchise of soke, sake and
infangthief, held by the sheriff, or some portreeve appointed by him.   In
consequence, probably, of their having been early social centres, in which
various persons would acquire property, the boroughs in their entirety were
never absorbed in the manors of individual lords, the burgages being held
of various landlords, the King usually being the chief, but seldom if ever
the sole immediate landlord of a whole borough.[1]   But the privileges
granted by the royal charters tended to exclude the manorial rights of the
lesser landlords, making the boroughs more and more the King's own.[2]
But, under whatever landlord, the burgages would be held at money-rents,
free from all agricultural services, whence the chartered town gained the
name of 'Free Borough' (*liber burgus*).   From the first, then, these communities would enjoy certain powers of self-government.   One of the
first concessions that they would seek would be that of being
allowed to 'farm' themselves, that is to say the right of compounding with the sheriff for the burgage rents (*gafol*), share of
judicial fines, market dues, and other profits falling to the King.   Many
boroughs had reached this stage by the time of Domesday.[3]   If granted in
fee-farm, that is to say in perpetuity, the amount of the *firma burgi* would
be fixed ; but in general the composition was only allowed to stand for a
term of years, or at will.[4]   A further distinct gain would be the right of
electing their own reeve or bailiff, subject always to the King's approval.[5]
The exclusive jurisdiction of the borough courts within their own sphere
is a point carefully asserted by the charters ; the burgesses are not to be
called upon to plead outside the walls except in respect of 'foreign'
holdings, pleas of the Crown, or the like.[6]   This exemption would clearly
infringe on the rights of lords who might have burgages within the borough
precincts, but attached to distant manors.   Again, among the 'liberties'
conceded, we have modifications of the common law ; such as the right of
testamentary disposition of land ; a freer right of selling land ;[7] free right
of disposing of daughters in marriage ;[8] immunity from the judicial combat ;
rights of compounding for amerciaments at fixed rates ;[9] and the like.

*Chartered
Privileges.*

[1] Pollock and Maitland, *sup.*, 367, 368.   [2] *Id.*, 645.

[3] Maitland, *Domesday, sup.*

[4] See John's grant to Helston (*Select Charters*, 306 ; Rot. Cart., 93), where a confirmation of the existing composition, with an increment of £4, is only granted at the
King's pleasure.

[5] So John's charter to Lincoln, *Select Charters*, 303 ; Rot. Cart., 56 ; an advance on
Richard's charter which gave no such right ; see also John's charter to Nottingham, Rot.
Cart., 39.

[6] See John's charters to Dunwich and Helston, *sup.*   Also Richard's charters to
Winchester, *Select Charters*, 257, and to Lincoln, *Fœdera*, I. 52.

[7] Pollock and Maitland, *sup.*, 645.

[8] Dunwich, *sup.*

[9] Richard's charters to Winchester and Lincoln, *sup.*

The man who lived a year and a day in a borough in time of peace unchallenged became free of any lord except the King. This rule would greatly tend towards the emancipation of serfs; yet it would seem that the townsfolk were not at all anxious to have serfs admitted to rights of citizenship.[1]

A singular but constant privilege, and one that would be highly valued by the trading community was that of exemption from tolls, pontages, harbour dues (*lestuage*), market dues, and the like throughout the Kingdom, and, sometimes even throughout the foreign dominions. The King, while empowering the favoured burgesses to levy toll on all who might set foot within their precincts, authorises them to invade the jurisdictions of all other communities, except those of London. Metropolitan rights were always to be respected.

The grant of the privilege of having an elective Mayor has always been considered the crowning concession, constituting a perfect
Full in-
corporation. municipality.[2] This right was first extorted by the Londoners in an irregular manner from Earl John and the Barons in 1191, as the price of their support against Longchamp. The man first chosen was Henry fitz Aylwin, and he held office for twenty-two years,
A Mayor of
London. in fact till his death.[3] The requirement that the Mayor should be elected annually, and presented for Royal approval, and re-presented if re-elected was introduced by John in his confirmation charter of the 9th May, 1215;[4] and from that time the municipality of London must be considered to have been fully established. John's charter of course was granted in the hope of securing the allegiance of the citizens; but it failed signally, as eight days later the Barons entered London in triumph. What the headship of a Mayor would import above that of an elective Reeve or Bailiff does not appear, the approval of the Crown being equally necessary in either case. But the distinction of a novel title is always appreciated.

Apart from this dignity we seem to find something very like full incorporation in other places than London. At Oxford, in connexion with a
Commune
at Oxford. quarrel with the University referred to below, we hear of a commune (*communia*) capable of binding the citizens by a charter under their common seal.[5] Then at Ipswich, under a charter granted by John in May 1200, we have open air meetings of the
Ipswich. whole population, resulting in the election of two Bailiffs, four Coroners and twelve chief Portmen, all sworn well and faithfully to govern the borough, and defend its liberties and customs; we have also a common seal; and lastly we have the general oath, held the essential

[1] John's charter to Nottingham, Rot. Cart., 39; *Select Charters*, 300; Pollock and Maitland, 649.   [2] *Select Charters*, 299.   [3] *Liber de Ant.*, 1, 3.
[4] *Select Charters*, 306; Rot. Cart., 207.
[5] *Munimenta Academica*, I. 3 (Rolls Series, No. 50; Anstey).

feature of a *commune*,[1] the oath by the whole population to obey their Bailiffs, Coroners, and Portmen, and to stand by them in defence of their borough and its liberties as against all persons, except the King and Queen.[2]

But the most curious feature of the mediæval borough was the Gild Merchant so constantly associated with it. Gilds were an essential part of the old English constitution. But of the Gild Merchant nothing is heard till after the Norman Conquest.[3] But it appears that at that time the Gild Merchant was already to be found in Flanders and the North-East of France,[4] so that in England it may have been a reconstruction, or adaptation of old institutions on a plan borrowed from abroad, and prompted by the development of trade consequent on the Conquest. Trade is gregarious; men of one calling gather together: the fullers or weavers of a town would live in the same quarter, and arrange to be arrayed in the same tithing. For leave to do this they were willing to pay substantial sums to the King; without his leave it could not be done.[5] The advantages derived from the incorporation of individual trades must have suggested the bold idea of incorporating all the trades of a place in one big or general Gild. The charters sanctioning Merchant Gilds are not troubled to explain in detail the force of the grant, its meaning being known to all. From legal proceedings taken to test the validity of some of these charters, and other sources, we learn that the brethren of a Gild Merchant claimed nothing less than the monopoly of all the trade of the town, nobody being allowed to trade or deal in any article who was not a member of the Gild.[6] Further the Gild was apparently free to admit to its circle only such men as it pleased, and to exact from its members such contributions (hanse) either by way of entrance money, or annual subscriptions, as it might think fit to impose.[7] We also hear of leave to establish a hans-hus or Gild-hall as an incidental concession.

A corporate body. The Merchant Gild therefore was clearly a corporate body, able to own property. It is worthy of notice that in some of the charters, the grants, and specially the exemptions from tolls and

---

[1] So Mr. Round maintains. [2] *Domesday of Ipswich*, Gross, II. 115–121.

[3] The earliest references to the Gild Merchant are said to be found in documents connected with Burford and Canterbury, dating 1087–1109; Gross, *Gild Merchant*, I. 5.

[4] *Id.*, 4, and the authorities there cited.

[5] Under Henry II. we have 18 Gilds in London amerced because 'adulterine,' *i.e.* set up without license; Madox, I. 562; from Pipe Roll, 26 H. II., f. 11, dors.

[6] "Ita quod nullus qui [non] sit de gilda illa mercandisam aliquam faciat in eadem villa nisi ad voluntatem burgensium prædictorum;" *Record of Caernarvon*, 158–161. Gross, II. 16. "Ita quod aliquis qui non sit de gilda illa aliquam mercaturam non faciat cum eis in civitate, vel burgo, vel villa vel in socagiis;" Bedford, Gross, 17; so also at Berwick, 19. So we hear of a man being 'presented' for keeping an open shop, not being a burgess; *Nottingham Records*, Stevenson, I. 317.

[7] The origin of the word hanse or hansa, which is clearly not English, is obscure; but we have it explained as "proficuum" or "custuma;" Gross, I. 194.

dues, are only made in favour of the members of the Merchant Gild, not of all the burgesses of the borough.[1] But the whole system was devised to oust competition, and to benefit petty "rings" at the expense of the community. In London there never was any Gild Merchant: the commercial interests were much too big to be incorporated.

We have seen that in John's struggle with the Barons the boroughs were apparently reckoned on his side. The royal charters would account for the fact, as by them the leading men were attached to the Crown by links of personal interest.

The boroughs were improving their position. We wish that we could say as much for the agricultural population, the great bulk of the community.

The agricultural population. No distinct improvement in their position is yet distinguishable; they had not as yet been able to commute or shake off the bonds of attachment to the soil: servile service was still the daily lot of most Englishmen.

Of the University of Oxford,[2] about the year 1187 or 1188, Giraldus Cambrensais gives us a glimpse, as a leading educational centre, with duly

University of Oxford. organised Faculties, and an academic concourse worthy of being entertained with a recitation of the writer's newly published *Topographia Hiberniæ*. Three days the reading out lasted, and on each occasion the learned author gave a general entertainment at his lodgings. On the first day he received all the poor of the town; on the second day the Doctors of the chief Faculties and their most promising pupils; and on the third day all the rest of the students, besides the chief gentry (*milites*) and burgesses of the place.[3]

Some twenty to twenty-two years later a shocking outrage brings the University again into light as flourishing in numbers, and enjoying the largest measure of ecclesiastical 'liberty,' under the fostering care of its

Liberty of the Church. diocesan, the Bishop of Lincoln (Hugh II. 'of Wells'). A girl having been outraged to death by students at a hostel known as Mayden-Hall, John condemned two culprits to be hung; whereupon, according to the chroniclers, the schools were closed in indignation, Masters and Scholars retiring, some to Reading, some to Cambridge, some to Paris (January, 1210).[4] From a decision on the whole case given four years later by the Legate Nicholas of Tusculum we learn that the schools had been closed by superior order, presumably that

---

[1] So apparently Richard's charter to Winchester; *Select Charters*, 257.

[2] "Universitas Oxoniensis"; *Munimenta Academ. Oxon.*, Vol. I. 8. The word is used in its original mediæval sense as merely a collective noun, applicable to any body of men with some distinctive attribute.

[3] Giraldus, *De Gestis*, I. 72, 410. "Apud Oxoniam, ubi clerus in Anglia magis vigebat."

[4] W. Cov., II. 201, and note; Chron. Lanercost, 4; Wendover, III. 227; Ann. Osney, 54; Dunstable, 32.

of the Bishop, or his representative the Chancellor of the University, and that the schools had been closed to punish the town for the acts of their fellow citizens, who had been concerned in the arrest and execution of the guilty clerks. Lastly we hear that the townspeople, alarmed, as we may suppose, at the prospect of losing the custom of the University, agreed to submit absolutely to the decision of the Church. The Legate's sentence was that for ten years lodgings should be let to the students at half the rates previously established, and that the *Commune*[1] of Oxford should bind themselves by a charter under their common seal to pay fifty-two shillings a year for the benefit of poor scholars, and also to provide a dinner of bread, beer, pottage, and one plate of fish or meat for a hundred poor scholars on every 6th December (St. Nicholas' Day). It was specially provided that in future any clerk arrested by the townspeople should at once be delivered to the Chancellor or other person appointed by the Bishop.[2]

If we might ascribe to the time of King John the state of things at Oxford that we find obtaining there a few years later, as doubtless we safely might, we should find the germs of the collegiate system already appearing; the students mostly live in Halls, under a Principal; and each student has his name entered on the list of a Regent Master,[3] who would stand to him very much in the relation of a modern tutor to an undergraduate. From his tutor the student would receive at any rate one lecture a day, independently of any other courses that the pupil might like to attend.[4]

Germs of the collegiate system.

As to the probable numerical strength of the University, Wendover in connection with the recession ventures to talk of 3000 Masters or Scholars. The numbers were clearly on the increase, as we hear of new houses being built to let. But we may ask how many men could Gerald have received at his lodgings in the course of two entertainments, some townspeople also being included? Reading is within easy reach of Oxford. Paris was the great centre of learning. But the retirement to Cambridge, a place not particularly accessible from Oxford, suggests that letters had already found a home there.

Numbers of Students.

With John's reign and the thirteenth century, the English tongue, after a suspended animation of some fifty years since the close of the Peterborough Chronicle, reappears as a literary language. Shortly after the year 1205, one Lazamon son of Lovenath, priest of a place identified with Areley Regis in North Worcestershire, published his *Brut*, a translation of Wace's *Brut* or History of the Kings of Britain, itself taken from the romance of Geoffrey of Monmouth.

The English Language.

[1] "Communia."
[2] *Munimenta Acad.*, I. I.
[3] "Quod quilibet Scholaris habeat Magistrum proprium actu regentem"; *Id.* 17.
[4] *Id.*, 13-19. These Statutes are conjecturally dated as not later than 1250.

Worthless as history Lazamon's poem is invaluable as a specimen of pure Saxon English.

> " An preost wes on leoden,
>   Lazamon wes iholen.
>   He wes Leovenathes sone :
>   Lithe him beo Drihte :
>   He wonede at Ernleze
>   Uppan Severne stathe."[1]

> ' A priest was on the land
>   Lazamon was he hight ;
>   He was Lovenath's son ;
>   Gracious to him be the Lord :
>   He dwelled at Ernley,
>   On Severn's bank.'

John's reign of course was not an era of church-building. But in the chancel of St. Mary Overeye, now St. Saviour's Southwark, we have a **Architecture.** good specimen of the pure Lancet Style of the period. The rebuilding of the church, destroyed in 1212, was undertaken shortly afterwards.[2] In connexion with the city of London we hear of the **London Bridge.** rebuilding of London Bridge in stone, a work said to have been begun by Peter chaplain of St. Mary Colechurch in the Old Jewry, as far back as the year 1176.[3] The progress made being slow, John in 1201 brought over Isambard, Master of the Schools at Saintes, to finish the undertaking. Isambard had already distinguished himself by building bridges at Saintes and La Rochelle ; and his plan included the construction of houses or shops on the bridge, the rents of which would go to the maintenance of the fabric.[4] The chaplain Peter died in 1205 ; and was buried in a chapel on the central pier of the bridge.[5] But one may express a doubt whether the work had been wholly carried out in stone ; because we hear in 1212 that the great fire in Southwark, that destroyed St. Mary Overeye, burned part of the bridge, and spread over to the city ;[6] while two years later, concurrently with the rebuilding of St. Mary's, we have the laying of an arch of the bridge.[7] About the same time we hear of a great ditch or moat being dug at the East end of London, to the detriment and annoyance of the Canons of Holy Trinity.[8] This work may fairly be identified with the modern Houndsditch.

[1] Ed. Madden, (1847) I. 2.   [2] Paris ; Ann. Tewkesbury ; *Liber de Ant.*
[3] " Pons lapideus " ; Ann. Waverley, p. 240 ; Ann. Cambriæ.
[4] *Fœdera*, I. 83.
[5] Ann. Waverley, 257 ; Wheatley and Cunningham, *London*, II. 418.
[6] *Liber de Antiq.*, p. 3 ; Paris.
[7] " Fundatio archæ pontis Londoniæ " ; Ann. Bermondsey, 451 ; but under the year 1209, the fire being placed in 1207.
[8] Ann. Dunst., A.D. 1211 ; Ann. Bermondsey, A.D. 1213.

By Isabel of Gloucester John had no issue. Divorced from him in
1200 she was remarried in 1214 to Geoffrey of Mandeville.
John's Issue. Earl of Essex, and died s.p. in 1217.[1] By Isabel of Angoulême
John had—

(1) HENRY III., born at Winchester 1st October, 1207.[2]

(2) Richard, afterwards Earl of Cornwall, and King of the Romans:
born at Winchester 6th January, 1209;[3] married first, Isabel Marshal,
widow of Gilbert of Clare I., Earl of Gloucester; secondly, Senche or
Sanchia, daughter of Raymond Berenger of Provence; and thirdly, Beatrice
of Falkenstein; died 2nd April, 1272, leaving by his second wife a son.
Edmund, who succeeded him.[4]

(3) Johanna or Jeanne, born 22nd July, 1210;[5] married to Alexander II.
of Scotland, 1221, died s.p. March, 1238.[6]

(4) Isabel, married 15th July, 1235, to the Emperor Frederic II.; and
died December, 1241.

(5) Eleanor, born 1214 (?);[7] married first to William Marshal II., Earl
of Pembroke (1224)) and secondly to Simon of Montfort II., Earl of
Leicester (1239); died 13th April, 1275.[8]

Queen Isabel herself in 1220 remarried her first love, Hugh le Brun X.,
Count of La Marche; died in 1246;[9] and was buried at Fontevrault.
The effigy on her tomb shows an elongated face, with large eyes, a long
straight nose, and a very small well-shaped mouth.[10] The continuous
series of her children by John, down to the year 1214 at any rate, contra-
dicts the allegations against her character introduced by Matthew Paris
in his account of the embassy to Morocco in 1211-1212.[11]

John's illegitimate offspring were numerous.[12] Among these we have
Johanna or Jeanne, married to Llywelyn ap Jorwerth in 1205
Natural children. or 1206.[13] By him she left David who succeeded him; and a
daughter Eleanor married first to John the Scot, Earl of Chester;
and secondly to Robert de Quincy.[14] She herself died in 1236 or 1237.[15]

---

[1] Above, 505, and Doyle, *Official Baronage*, and G.E.C., *Complete Peerage.*

[2] Ann Winton, and Waverley; Wendover, III. 219.

[3] Ann. Winton., and Waverley; 5th January, Ann. Bermondsey.

[4] Doyle and G.E.C., *sup.*

[5] Ann. Worcester, and Tewkesbury.

[6] Chron. Melrose, 138, 148.

[7] Sandford, *Genealogical History*, 87, gives this date as that of the birth of Isabel, whom
he makes the third daughter of John; but as the marginal entry to Paris, *Chron. Maj.*
II. 87, makes Eleanor the third daughter, this may have been the date of her birth.

[8] G.E.C., and Doyle, *sup.*

[9] *Fœdera*, I. 160; Paris, *Chron. Maj.*

[10] See the copy in the Crystal Palace at Sydenham.

[11] *Chron. Maj.*, II. 563.

[12] So Giraldus, Camb. V., 409; a late addition to the *Expurg. Hibernia.*

[13] Rot. Cart., l. 147; Ann. Worcester.

[14] *Complete Peerage*, "Chester."   [15] Ann. Tewkesbury; Ann. Camb. and *Brut.*

Geoffrey, who received the manor of Selling in Kent in 1204, and was sent with troops to La Rochelle in 1205.[1]

Richard of Warenne, who killed Eustace the monk in 1217 ; was sheriff of Berkshire and Staffordshire, 1221–1222 ; and still living in 1242.[2]

John, mentioned in Rot. Claus., I. 121.

Richard, married to the daughter and heiress of Geoffrey of Lucy.[3]

Oliver, who received lands in Kent in 1213, and the manor of Frome in 1215.[4]

[1] Rot. Claus., I. 8, b ; 27 ; 52 ; R. Cogg., 154.
[2] Madox, *Hist. Excheq.*, I. 286, 329, 233.
[3] Rot. Claus., 230.
[4] *Id.*, 234, 312 b.

LIST OF AUTHORITIES

Anglia Sacra, H. Wharton, 1691.

Annales Cambriæ, A.D. 444–1288.¹ This important Welsh Chronicle is believed to have been started originally at St. David's about A.D. 954, probably from Irish materials, and subsequently continued at various intervals. (J. W. ab Ithel ; Rolls Series, No. 20.)

Anonymous Life of Becket, I. (The Roger of Pontigny of Dr. Giles' edition). The writer became acquainted with Becket during his exile, possibly at Pontigny, but he does not seem to have had much personal knowledge of the Archbishop ; wrote 1175–1176, see p. 2. (*Materials for History of Archbishop Becket* ; J. C. Robertson, Rolls Series, No. 67, vol. IV. 1–79.)

Anonymous Life of Becket, II. (The Lambeth MS. of Dr. Giles' edition). Henry Wharton says that the writer was a Canterbury monk, and at Canterbury at the time of the murder, as might be gathered from his narrative. He mentions Henry's reconciliation with the Church in 1172, but not his pilgrimage to Canterbury in 1174, so that he may have written between those dates. (*Materials for History of Archbishop Becket* ; J. C. Robertson, Rolls Series, No. 67, vol. IV., 80–144.)

Archer, T. A., *Crusade of Richard I.*

Aubin, Saint (Angers), *Chronicle of*, A.D. 768–1220, a boiled-down text from various sources. (Marchegay, *Eglises d'Anjou*, Société de l'Histoire de France, 1869.)

Becket, Materials for History of (J. C. Robertson, Rolls Series, No. 67. 8 vols.).

Bermondsey, Annals of, A.D. 1042–1432 ; probably written up in the year 1433 ; a compilation from various sources, chiefly valuable for the history of the House itself, and also for the later entries. (H. R. Luard, Rolls Series, No. 36, vol. III.)

Blois, Peter of. A man of letters with a ready pen, employed on secretarial work by a series of persons in the highest position, including Archbishop Rotrou of Rouen, Archbishops Richard, Baldwin, and Hubert Walter of Canterbury, Queen Eleanor, and Henry II. Born of Breton parents about 1135 ; died before 1212. See the *Natl. Dicty. of Biog.* His Letters are printed by Dr. J. A. Giles.

Bohadin (Baha-ed-din), a learned Arab, native of Mesopotamia, born 1143, entered the service of Saladin (Salah-ed-din), in June 1188, and remained with him during his subsequent campaigns down to his death. (Palestine Text Society, 1879.)

Bosham, Herbert of, *Vita S. Thomæ.* This man, apparently a native of

Sussex, became secretary to Becket when he was appointed Archbishop, and remained with him throughout his career, leaving England when his master left it, and returning when he returned, but he was not present at his death, having been sent on a mission to France a few days before; was writing his Life of Becket 1183–1185, and again in August 1186 (pp. 192, 461, 497). The reference to the King's death July 6th, 1189 seems a later addition. His close connexion with Becket gives importance to his work, but "for bad literary taste, irrelevancy, and vanity" he stands perhaps unrivalled in English literature. (*Materials for History of Archbishop Becket*; J. C. Robertson, Rolls Series, No. 67, vol. III.)

Bouquet, *Recueil des Historiens de la France.*

Breton, Guillaume le, *Gesta Philippi*, and *Philippis*. This man, sometimes cited as Guillelmus Armoricus, was chaplain to Philip II. of France, and in particular was with him at the Battle of Bouvines; he wrote a Continuation of the *Gesta* of Rigord, from the year 1208, where it ended, down to the death of Philip in 1223. He subsequently composed a metrical Life, the *Philippis*, which he presented to Louis VIII. Both are printed by Bouquet, *Recueil*, vol. XVII.

Bromton, John, Abbot of Gervaulx, *Chronicon*, A.D. 597 (given as 588) –1200. A mere compilation from earlier works put together in the latter half of the Fourteenth Century. (Twysden, *Scriptores Decem.*)

Brut-y-Tywysogion, or *Chronicle of the Princes of Wales*, in Welsh, A.D. 681–1282 (Rolls Series, No. 17, Rev. J. W. ab Ithel). This Chronicle is believed to have been originally compiled by one Caradoc of Llancarvan before 1150; but subsequently revised and continued by later hands.

Burton, Annals of, A.D. 1004–1263, imperfect at end: very brief till A.D. 1189, when it begins to copy Hoveden, to whom it refers; becomes important after A.D. 1211. (H. R. Luard, Rolls Series, No. 36, vol. I.)

Canterbury, William of, *Vita S. Thomæ*. This man was a monk, and ordained a deacon by Becket a few days before his murder, of which the writer was an eye-witness; probably wrote 1175–1184, having previously published a book of Becket's miracles. (*Materials for History of Archbishop Becket*, J. C. Robertson, Rolls Series, No. 67, vol. I.)

Chron. Melsa; Chronicle of the Abbey of Meaux; A.D. 1150–1406. (Rolls Series, No. 43.)

Clark, G. T. *Mediæval Military Architecture in England*, 1884.

Coggeshall, Ralph of, *Chronicon Anglicanum*, A.D. 1066–1227. This man was elected Abbot of the Cistercian House of Coggeshall in 1207 (p. 162). He died in 1228. His work is only valuable from about the year 1187; he was a good observer of events at home; his account of the Crusade was taken from the narratives of persons who had been engaged in it. (J. Stevenson, Rolls Series, No. 66.)

Coventry, Walter of, *Memoriale*. This, from the earliest ages to A.D. 1225, is a compilation or condensation from earlier materials made between A.D. 1293–1307. The valuable part of the Work is that from 1201, where it incorporates a Barnwell Chronicle (MS. College of Arms, No. 10) written early in the reign of Henry III. (Bishop Stubbs, Rolls Series, No. 58.)

Devizes, Richard of, *De Rebus Gestis Ricardi Primi*. From the Prologue, and facts noticed in the work, it appears that the author, a Winchester monk, wrote after 1191 and before 1199. His work is therefore the earliest record of the reign of Richard I. (English Historical Society, J. Stevenson.)

Diceto, Ralph of—the only name used by himself or his contemporaries—*Imagines Historiarum*, 1148-1202. The writer was a Frenchman, probably deriving his name from Dissay or Dissé (both in Sarthe); he may have been born 1120-1130; man of extensive reading; may have studied at Paris; Archdeacon of Middlesex in 1152; personal friend of Gilbert Foliot, but not hostile to Becket; employed on several missions during the struggle; in 1180 became Dean of St. Paul's; did not begin to write till after that time; his relations with leading Churchmen gave him every opportunity of learning facts, but his critical power was not great; to him we owe the survey of the Capitular Estates known as the *Domesday of St. Paul's*; (Archdeacon Hale, Camden Society) died in 1202 or 1203. (Rolls Series, No. 68; Bishop Stubbs.)

Doyle, James E. *Official Baronage of England* (1886).

Draco Normanicus (*i.e.*, Standard of Normandy). A metrical chronicle in Latin of events connected with Gaul, Normandy, and England, chiefly valuable for the detailed contemporary notices of events, 1167-1169; written before December, 1170; supposed to be the work of one Etienne of Rouen, a monk of Bec, hostile to Becket. (R. Howlett, Rolls Series, No. 82, vol. II.)

Dunstable, Annals of, A.D. 1-1297; this chronicle down to the end of the year 1241 was compiled by Richard of Morins, who became Prior of the Monastery in 1202, and died in 1242; apparently he began his work in 1210 (see p. 3, where the authorship is distinctly claimed); after 1221 the entries appear to have been posted up year by year. After 1241 various hands are employed, none of them later than the Thirteenth Century. (H. R. Luard, Rolls Series, No. 36, vol. III.)

Epistolæ Cantuarienses, Canterbury correspondence, 1187-1199. (Memorials of Richard I., vol. II., Rolls Series, No. 38, Bishop Stubbs.)

Ernoul, *Chroniques* (Paris, 1872). The writer was Esquire to Balian of Ibelin, a Frank lord in Palestine.

Eyton, Rev. R. W., *Court, Household, and Itinerary of Henry II.* (1878).

Fantosme, Jourdain, *Chroniques de la Guerre*, etc. The writer, a foreigner, clerk in the household of Henry of Blois, Bishop of Winchester, has left us a metrical chronicle in Norman-French of the war between England and Scotland in 1173 and 1174, he having been an eye-witness of some of the events, and notably of the capture of William the Lion at Alnwick. (R. Howlett, Rolls Series, No. 82, vol. III.; also printed by F. Michel for the Surtees Society.)

Fitz-Stephen, William, *Vita S. Thomæ*. A native of London, employed by Becket when Chancellor in the work of the office, and afterwards as domestic chaplain; his work shows an acquaintance with legal questions; was with Becket down to the time of the Council of Northampton, but did not leave England with him; on the contrary, made his peace with the King by composing a metrical prayer for him (pp. 78-81), and so remained in England; rejoined Becket on his

return to Canterbury in Dec. 1170, and was with him at the end;
died perhaps in 1191 (Foss, *Judges*). (*Materials for History of Arch-bishop Becket*; J. C. Robertson, Rolls Series, No. 67, vol. III.)

Fœdera Conventiones, etc. T. Rhymer. (Clarke and Holbrooke, 1815.)

Foliot, Gilbert of, Bishop of Hereford and London, *Epistolæ*. (T. A. Giles.)

Fordun, John of, *Chronica Gentis Scottorum* (W. F. Skene, Edinburgh, 1871), written apparently 1363–1387.

Foss, Edward, *Judges of England* (1848).

Garnier (of Pont-Sainte-Maxence), *Vie Saint Tomas*. This "trouveur" wrote a metrical Life (*Sermun*) of Becket in French. He tells us that he went over to Canterbury to collect information from monks and others, and particularly from Becket's sister Mary, Abbess of Barking, and that he finished it in the fourth year. He clearly had no personal knowledge of the events (pp. 6, 205, 206); he complains that others borrowed from him, but his work in the main looks like a compilation from other known writers (C. Hippeau, Paris 1859).

G. E. C., *Complete Peerage*, etc. (Cockayne).

Gervase of Canterbury : *Chronica* (1), A.D. 1100–1199. *Chronica* (2), *seu Gesta Regum*; Mythical Ages, Brutus, etc., to 1210 with Continuations by different hands to 1328. *Actus Pontificum Cantuariensis Ecclesiæ*, from the mission of Saint Augustine to the death of Hubert Walter, 1205. The writer, a Canterbury monk, may have been born about 1141, as he received the tonsure in 1163. His Chronicle was probably begun in 1188, and from that time onward may be considered strictly contemporary. The second Chronicle or *Gesta Regum* and *Actus Pontificum* were not taken in hand till after 1199. The above were first printed, in part, by Sir R. Twysden in his *Scriptores Decem*; now fully, and in thoroughly scholarly style, by Bishop Stubbs. Rolls Series, No. 73.

Gilbert, J. T., *Historic Documents of Ireland*.

—— *Viceroys of Ireland*.

" Giraldus Cambrensis." Gerald of Barry, Glamorgan, commonly known by the above name, was the son of William of Barry, a Norman settled in Wales, by Angareth, daughter of the Lady Nest, daughter of Rhys ap Tewdwr, the last King of South Wales. Gerald was born about 1147, studied in Paris, was appointed Archdeacon of Brecknock, and chaplain to Henry II., and sent with the King's son John to Ireland in 1185. He was still writing in his seventieth year, say A.D. 1217. See Mr. J. S. Brewer's Introduction to Gerald's works. Rolls Series No. 21, 8 vols.

Godefroy, F., *Dictionnaire de l'Ancienne Langue Francaise* (Paris, 1880).

Green, M. A. E., *Princesses of England* (1849).

Grim, Edward, *Vita S. Thomæ*, an Englishman, native of Cambridge; a clerk in Holy Orders; had gone to Canterbury on a visit to Becket a few days before his murder; was with him at the last, and received a severe wound in the arm in attempting to shield him; wrote after Henry's penance in 1174, but seemingly before 1177. (*Materials History Archbishop Becket*; J. C. Robertson, Rolls Series No. 67, Vol. II.)

Holyrood, Chronicle of, B.C. 55–A.D. 1163; compiled apparently in the time of Henry II. (*Anglia Sacra*, Wharton, vol. I., 152.)

Hoveden, Roger of, *i.e.*, of Howden in the East Riding of Yorks
Chronica, A.D. 547-1201. Educated at Durham under Bishop H
of Puiset; in 1174 he is found a clerk in the King's household
apparently continued in his service till 1189; apparently did not
to write till after that. For our period his work is meagre dow
the year 1169; from that year till 1192 it is a rewritten copy
Benedict of Peterborough (q.v.); after 1192 it becomes origin
probably died 1201. (Bishop Stubbs, Rolls Series, No. 51.) Tho
taking his name from Howden, perhaps as incumbent of the liv
the incorrect use made by our author of the few words of English t
he introduces suggests that he was not an Englishman.

Ibn-el-Athir, a native of Mesopotamia, born 1160: he was attached to d
service of various princes upset by Saladin, and consequently writ
in a spirit hostile to him.

Itinerarium Regis Ricardi. A valuable record of the events of the Thi
Crusade, by one who was with Richard in Palestine. The *Libellus a
Expugnatione Terræ Sanctæ* (printed by Mr. Stevenson with his *Ral*
of Coggeshall, Rolls Series, No. 66), itself the work of a man who wa
wounded at the siege of Jerusalem in 1187, tells us that the *Itinerariu*
was a translation from the French, made by the direction of the Prio
of Holy Trinity (pp. 243, 257). Nicholas Trevet, writing at the
beginning of the fourteenth century, repeats the statement, giving the
name of the translator as Richard, Canon of Holy Trinity, Aldgate
(pp. 116, 117 Ed. Hog). Richard, in fact, became Prior of Holy
Trinity in 1222. It now appears that the original was a poem in
French by one Ambrose, a clerk of the King's chapel, Richard's work
being not so much a translation as a paraphrase. See W. Malmesbury
Gesta Regum II., xvii. (Rolls Series, No. 90), where Bishop Stu.bs
recalls the views adopted by him in the introduction to the *Itinerarium.*
Portions of the work of Ambrose are given by Pertz, *Mon. Hist. Gern*.,
vol. XXVII., 533. The *Itinerarium* must have been published before
the year 1220, as Giraldus was familiar with it. The mistaken
ascription to Geoffrey Vinsauf was probably due to the fact that one
MS. of the *Itinerarium* appends some verses by him. (*Memorials of
Richard I.*, vol. I., Rolls Series, No. 38, Bishop Stubbs).

Itinerary of Henry II. (*See* Eyton.)
Itinerary of King John. (T. D. Hardy, *Introduction to Patent Rolls.*)
Itinerary of Richard I. (*See Itinerarium.*)
Labbe, *Concilia* (1671).
Lanercost, Chronicle of (Bannatyne Club, J. Stevenson).
Lavisse, E., *Histoire de France*, 1901.
Loch Cé, Annals of, A.D. 1014-1590. (W. M. Hennessy, Rolls Series,
No. 54.) The solitary MS. of this chronicle (Trin. Coll., Dublin, H.
I. 19) is expressed to have been transcribed 1580-1590 from an older
work, one that seemingly had been used by the Four Masters in
their compilation. Gaps in the MS. have been filled up from other
sources.
Madox, T. *History of the Exchequer* (4°, 1749).
Magna Vita S. Hugonis, a life of St. Hugh, the Bishop of Lincoln, written
by one Adam, a monk, probably of Eynsham, of which he ultimately
became Abbot; he was chaplain to St. Hugh during his later years,

and wrote during the Interdict, apparently A.D. 1212–1213 (pp. 282, 290, Dymock, Rolls Series No. 37).

ap, Walter, *De Nugis Curialium*. The writer, a native of Herefordshire, of good parentage, was born *circa* 1140, studied at Paris under Girard la Pucelle (1160), became clerk in Henry's household; Justice in Eyre 1173, 1185; sent to Lateran Council 1179; held much preferment; Archdeacon of Oxford 1197; died *circa* 1210; a witty courtier, with a profound hatred for monks. His *De Nugis* are the personal reminiscences of a man of the world with a satirical turn. (S. T. Wright, Camden Society, 1850.)

Mareschal, Willeme le; Metrical Life of William Marshal, Earl of Pembroke and Regent under Henry III.; written at request of his son William Marshal II., about the year 1226, perhaps by "Jean d'Erlee," but more likely by an unknown rhymer from materials supplied by Jean. The latter was probably an Englishman, who should be described as John of Earley, in Berkshire, near Reading; this John apparently joined the Earl about 1188, and remained in personal attendance on him till his death. *See* the Introduction by M. Paul Meyer, vol. III., ii–xi. (*Société de l'Histoire de France*.)

Margan, Annals of (now Margam in Glamorganshire), A.D. 1066–1232; the earlier part is apparently copied from William of Malmesbury, with notes of its own from the time of the foundation of the Abbey in 1147; becomes fuller after 1184; Thirteenth Century hand throughout. (H. R. Luard, Rolls Series, No. 36, vol. I.)

Martene, E. and Durand, M., *Thesaurus Novus* (1717).

—— *Amplissima Collectio* (1724).

Martin, H., *Histoire de France*, 1855.

Maskell, W., *Monumenta Ritualia* (1846).

Melrose, Chronicle of, A.D. 731–1270. Down to 1120 it is taken from Symeon of Durham; after that it becomes original; and from 1136, when Melrose Abbey was founded, it becomes in fact contemporary. (J. Stevenson, Bannatyne Club, 1835.)

Monte, R. de, *Chronica*, 1100–1185. Robert of Torigny-sur-Vire (Manche), was born *circa* 1110, took vows at Bec, and was finally elected Abbot of Mont-Saint-Michel in 1154; hence he is commonly known as Robert *de Monte*. He died in 1186. He began writing soon after the death of Henry I., so that from that time his work may be considered contemporary. (R. Howlett, Rolls Series, No. 82, vol. IV.)

Muratori, *Annali*, etc. (1744).

Newburgh, William of, *Historia Rerum Anglicarum*, A.D. 1066–1198, with a continuation to the year 1298. The writer, who styles himself Willelmus Parvus, was born at Bridlington in 1136; became Canon of the Augustinian Priory of St. Mary Newburgh in the North Riding; died prob. in 1198. A writer of great good sense and judgment. (R. Howlett, Rolls Series, No. 82, vols. I. and II.)

Niger, Radulfus; studied in Paris after 1160; supporter of Becket; banished from England by Henry II., perhaps on that account; still living 1184; has left two chronicles extending down to his own time; bitter enemy to Henry II. (Metcalfe, Caxton Society, 1851.)

Norgate, Miss K., *England under the Angevin Kings*. (London, 1887.)

Osney, Annals of, A.D. 1016–1347. Down to the year 1233, that is to say for all that concerns the present work, this chronicle is a compilation from known sources, put together in 1233, with a few original facts added relating chiefly to the affairs of Osney itself, or of Oxford. (H. R. Luard, Rolls Series, No. 36, vol. IV.)

Paris, Matthew of, Chronica Majora (H. R. Luard, Rolls Series, No. 57) *Historia Anglorum* (Sir F. Madden, Rolls Series, No. 44). *Vitæ Abbatum* (Wats, 1640). Monk of St. Albans, took vows there January 21st, 1217, being then 17 years old. At death of Roger of Wendover, in 1236, succeeded him as historiographer at St. Albans, starting his own *Chronica Majora*, which, for the period now in question, is a practical transcript of the *Flores* of his predecessor with all errors faithfully reproduced. The *Historia Anglorum* is an abridgment of the *Chronica Majora* with modifications, and some new matter introduced.

Pauli, R., Geschichte von England (Hamburg, 1853).

Pertz, Monumenta Germaniæ Historica.

" Peterborough, Benedict of," *Gesta Henrici Secundi*, and *Gesta Regis Ricardi*, 1169–1192. A primary, contemporary authority for the period he covers. The authorship is unknown ; the ascription to Abbot Benedict is due to the fact that the leading extant MS. (Julius A. XI.) was transcribed by Abbot Benedict, of Peterborough, previously Prior of Canterbury. It is probable that the author had the benefit of the lost work of Bishop Richard Fitz Nigel, the Treasurer, entitled *Tricolumnis*. (Rolls Series, No. 49, Bishop Stubbs.)

Pipe Rolls. The Roll for the thirty-first year of Henry I., the earliest yet discovered, those for the second, third, and fourth years of Henry II., and those for the first year of Richard I., and the third year of John, have been printed by Mr. Hunter for the old Record Commission ; those for the sixth to the twenty-first years of Henry II. have been printed by the Pipe Roll Society ; all the others are in MS. at the Record Office, Chancery Lane.

Red Book of Exchequer, H. Hall (Rolls Series, No. 99).

Registrum Sacrum, Bishop Stubbs (1858 ; an enlarged ed. 1897).

Reuter, H. Geschichte Alexander des Dritten (1860).

Rigord, Gesta Philippi Augusti. The writer, originally a physician, and afterwards in Holy Orders at St. Denis, wrote a Life of Philip, first published about 1200, and afterwards continued down to 1208. His work was again continued down to the death of Philip in 1223, by Guillaume le Breton. (Bouquet, *Recueil*, etc., vol. XVII.).

Rot. Cart. Rotuli Cartarum, Charter Rolls.

Rot. Claus. Rotuli Litterarum Clausarum ; Close Rolls.

Rot. Pat. Rotuli Litterarum Patentium ; Patent Rolls.

Round, J. Horace, Calendar of Documents preserved in France, 1899.

—— Commune of London (1899).

—— Feudal England (1895).

Ruding, R. Annals of the Coinage of Great Britain (1817).

Salisbury, John of.

—— *Metalogus* (J. A. Giles).

—— *Epistolæ* (*Id.*).

—— *Polycraticus* (*Id.*).

alisbury, John of, *Vita S. Thomæ*; John the most distinguished English scholar of his time; went to Paris, 1136–1137, and studied there under Peter Abelard and others for some ten years; introduced to Archbishop. Theobald at Council of Reims in 1148; came back to England with him and became his secretary; on friendly terms with Hadrian IV.; strong supporter of Becket as Primate; banished by Henry before the Council of Clarendon; joined Becket in exile; returned with him in 1170; was in the Cathedral at the time of the murder; appointed Bishop of Chartres by Louis VII. in 1176; died 1180. His Life of Becket was written before he became Bishop. (*Materials for History of Archbishop Becket*; J. C. Robertson, Rolls Series, No. 67, vol. II.).

Sismondi, J. C. de, *Histoire des Francais*, 1823.

—— *Républiques Italienes.*

Song, *The, of Dermot and the Earl*, a Norman-French poem detailing the events connected with the invasion of Ireland, 1166–1176; the work, as we have it, appears to have been written not later than 1225, perhaps earlier, but avowedly from a pre-existing *Geste* by, or based on materials supplied by Morice Regan, at one time "Latimer" (read Latinier) or secretary to King Dermot Macmurrough ; it therefore gives an original version of the occurrences by an Irishman, but. one no doubt on the side of the English. The reader will notice the early misreading by which Latinier, a man versed in Latin writing, became the unmeaning Latimer. (G. H. Orpen, Oxford, Clarendon Press, 1891. A previous edition by M. Michel, 1837, has generally been cited as Regan.) The occurrence of a mass of matter common to this writer and Giraldus suggests that the latter had access either to the Song or to the pre-existing work on which it was based ; and therefore that the two narratives are not altogether independent.

Stubbs, W., Bishop of Oxford.

—— *Constitutional History of England*, 1887.

—— *Registrum Sacrum*, 1858 (New Ed., 1897).

—— *Select Charters*, 1870.

Symeon, *Historia Regum* (*continuation*); *Historia Dunelmensis Ecclesiæ* (*continuation*); (T. Arnold, Rolls Series, No. 57).

Tewkesbury, Allan of, *Vita S. Thomæ*; an Englishman by birth who having been in Italy for some years, on returning to England in 1174, entered the monastery of Christ Church, Canterbury, of which he became Prior in 1179; Abbot of Tewkesbury, 1189; wrote A.D. 1176–1180; died 1202. His work was intended to supplement the imperfect Life of Becket by John of Salisbury (q.v.) ; (*Materials for History of Archbishop Becket*; J. C. Robertson, Rolls Series, No. 67, vol. II.).

Tewkesbury, Annals of, A.D. 1066–1263, imperfect at end; very meagre till A.D. 1200; after that in various hands of Thirteenth Century. (H. R. Luard, Rolls Series, No. 36, vol. I.)

Vic and Vaissète, *Histoire de Languedoc* (ed. 1872).

Vigeois, Geoffrey of; a monk of Saint Martial's, Limoges, and Prior of Limoges (Corrèze, near Uzerche) has left a chronicle of Aquitanian History from the time of Robert I. down to 1183, when he ceased writing. He was at Limoges during the siege in that year, and saw the funeral procession of the young King Henry enter Uzerche on June 12th. (Labbe, *Nova Bibliotheca MSS.*, vol. II.)

Waverley, Annals of, Incarnation to A.D. 1291 ; imperfect at end ; down to 1119 written in three Twelfth or early Thirteenth century hands; from that time in various contemporary hands, with blanks for further matter to be added. (H. R. Luard, Rolls Series, No. 36, vol. II.)

Wendover, Roger of, *Flores Historiarum,* A.D. 447–1235. Monk of St. Albans ; first of the existing series of chroniclers connected with that Abbey ; probably began to write 1220–1230 ; died May 6th, 1236 ; his work, so far as it goes, is the basis of the chronicles of Matthew Paris ; down to the year 1202 Roger's work is a compilation from pre-existing materials, possibly based on a compilation already made at St. Albans ; from the year 1202, being the end of Hoveden's work, it becomes original ; Wendover is a careless, inaccurate writer, on whom, however, we are dependent for a great mass of matter.

Wickham Legg, L. G. *Coronation Records* (1902).

Winton or Winchester, Annals of, A.D. 519–1277. Down to the year 1202 this Chronicle appears to be a compilation by Richard of Devizes, being in the same hand as his Gesta Ricardi, contained in the same volume. The remainder is by other hands not contemporary. (H. R. Luard, Rolls Series, No. 36, vol. II.)

Worcester, Annals of, A.D. 1–1308, with a few entries going down to 1377 ; original after 1285 ; possibly the work of Nicholas of Norton, the Sacrist, mentioned in 1300 (p. 546). (H. R. Luard, Rolls Series, No. 36, vol. IV.)

Worcester, Florence of, *Continuation of* (Eng. Historical Society, 1849 ; B. Thorpe).

Wykes, Thomas, *Chronicon,* A.D. 1066–1289. For what concerns the period covered by the present work this chronicle is but a repetition of the annals of Osney, themselves started in the year 1233. (H. R. Luard, Rolls Series, No. 36, vol. IV.)

INDEX

Acre, Siege of, 234, 296-299; losses there, *ib.*; surrender of garrison on terms, 298.

Agnes of Meran, third wife of Philip II. of France, 383 and note; dies, 392.

Alais of Blois, third wife of Louis VII. 23, 205.

—— of France, engaged to be married to Richard, son of Henry II., 96, 175; the solemnisation evaded, 198 and note, again, 229: suggestion for marrying her to John, 234; marriage to Richard again evaded, 235, 240; Richard promises to marry her, 264; present at his coronation, 266, 277: finally rejected by Richard, 289; sent back to France, and married to the Count of Ponthieu, 347.

—— of Maurienne, betrothed to John, son of Henry II., 163, 164, 175; dies, 195.

Albert, Cardinal, commissioned to absolve Henry on terms, 150, 151, 156; absolves him, 159.

Alexander, son of William the Lion, invested with his father's English estates, and knighted by John, 422. *See* Scotland, Kings of.

Alphonso II.. king of Arragon, meets Henry at Montferrand and Limoges, 164; supports Richard against the young king, 217.

—— III., king of Castile, married to Eleanor, second daughter of Henry II., 193; submits disputes with Navarre to Henry's arbitration, 197.

Angevin Currency, ratio to Sterling, 229 note.

Angoulême, Counts of—
> William Taillefer IV. in revolt, 168, 191; surrenders to Richard, 192.
> Wulgrin Taillefer III., son of the preceding, attacks Poitou, 191; surrenders, 192.
> Ademar or Aimar, brother to preceding, in arms against Richard, 237; again, 332, 339, 341; his daughter Isabel married to King John, 386, 387.

Anti-popes—
> Victor III., 23.
> Pascal III., 98.
> Calixtus III., 98.

Apulia, Simon of, Dean of York, 344-346. *See* Exeter, Bishops of.

Architecture of Henry II.'s reign, 255-257; of John's reign, 513.

Arundel or Sussex, Earls of—
> William of Aubigny I., 465, 467.
> William of Aubigny II., son of preceding, 195; supports Longchamp against John, 310.
> William of Aubigny III., 390: supports John, 497, 499.

Assize of Arms, 208, 209.
—— of Clarendon, 76.
—— of Northampton, 189.
—— of Novel Disseisin, 81.
—— of Mort d'Ancestor, 190.
—— Grand, 202.
—— of Forests, 223.
Aubigny, Philip of, 488, 490.
—— William of, beseiged at Rochester, 488, 491.
Aumâle or Albemarle, Counts of—
    William, taken prisoner by rebels, 168.
    William de Mandeville (Earl of Essex), Count of Aumâle in right of wife Hawise, daughter of preceding, 233 and note.
    Baldwin of Bethune, third husband of Hawise, 360 note.
    William of Forz, son of Hawise above, by second husband, supporting John, 487, 490, 493.
Austria, Leopold, Duke of, insulted by Richard in Palestine, 299 ; arrests him on way home at Vienna, 326 ; surrenders him to Henry VI., terms for Richard's liberation, 328 ; remits unpaid balance of ransom and hostages, dies, 347 and note.
Baldwin IV. King of Jerusalem, a leper, 224 ; offers crown to Henry, *ib.*
—— V., his nephew, dies shortly, 234.
Balliol, Bernard of, opposes inroad of William the Lion, 178.
—— Hugh of, holds Barnard Castle for John, 498.
Bar, Henry, Count of, at battle of Bouvines, 456.
Bardolf, Hugh, on Regency Council, 271 ; deprived of Sheriffdon of Yorkshire, 336 ; again Sheriff, 338 and note ; again deprived, 382.
Barres, William des, French knight, unhorsed by Richard, 239 ; at battle of Arsûf, 304 ; at siege of Château Gaillard, 399 ; at battle of Bouvines, 456, 462 ; wrestles with Emperor Otto on horseback, 462.
Bath, Bishops of—
    Reginald of Bohun appointed, 167, 168, 182, 200 ; at Richard's coronation, 267 ; elected to Canterbury by the monks, but dies before consecration, 316, 407.
    Savaric, consecration, visits Richard in captivity, 328 and note, 333.
    Joscelin, 415, 441.
Beauchamp, William of, 471, 472.
Beaumont, Count of, at battle of Bouvines, 456, 461.
Beauvais, Philip of Dreux, Bishop of, on the Crusade, 299, 302 ; taken prisoner by John, 354 ; at the battle of Bouvines in command of French left, 455 ; defeats and captures Earl of Salisbury, 463, 464.
Becket, Agnes, sister of Thomas, married to Thomas Fitz Theobald, 30.
—— Mary, sister of Thomas, appointed Abbess of Barking, 30, 167.
—— Thomas, Archdeacon of Canterbury, appointed Chancellor, 4, 9 ; sent on embassy to Paris, 16 ; instrumental in taxing clergy, 20 ; active in campaign of Toulouse, 21, 34 ; objects to marriage of an abbess, 22 ; given the charge of the King's son, 25 ; named for Canterbury, 26 ; form of election, ordained priest and consecrated, 27 ; birth, parentage, and earlier life, 30, 31 ; relations with King as Chancellor, duties and emoluments, 32, 33. *See* Canterbury, Archbishops of.

Berengaria of Navarre, brought to Messina to marry Richard, 289; her character and looks, *ib.* note, 290; voyage from Messina to Cyprus, there married to Richard and crowned, 291, 292; sails to Acre, 295, 301; brought to Joppa, 305; voyage home to Ppitou, 325; not brought to England, 338; again with Richard, 347; not invited to his death-bed or his funeral, 366; her latter years and death, 376; meeting with John, 391.

Bernard of La Coudre, Papal envoy, his unsuccessful mission, 101-104.

—— Bishop of Nevers, on Papal mission, 115, 120-122.

Bertran de Born, great troubadour; incites Henry's sons to rebel against him, 192 and note; hostile to all the family, 212, 213, 215, 217; dies in a monastery, 351.

Besant, gold coin worth 2 shillings sterling, 297 note; 72 besants = one pound of gold, 298, note.

Blanche of Castile, daughter of Alphonso III. and Eleanor of England suggested marriage to Louis, son of Philip, 364, 384; married to him, 386.

Blois, Counts of Blois and Chartres—

Theobald II., surrenders Amboise and Fréteval to Henry, 18; 23; 24, 90, 91; 114; 124; supports Henry's sons in revolt, 165; 182; breach with Philip Augustus, 205; refuses to support him against Henry, 239; dies at Acre, 297.

Louis, 332; in alliance with Richard, 362.

—— William of, Archbishop of Sens, friend of Becket, 102, 110, 120; lays Henry's continental dominions under Interdict, 136, 182; translated to Reims, crowns Philip II., 203; slighted by him, 205, 206.

—— Stephen of. *See* Sancerre.

Bohun, Humphrey of, Constable of England, repels Scottish inroad, 173.

Boroughs, Borough Charters, their privileges, 507-510.

Boulogne, Counts of—

William, younger son of King Stephen, 12, 22.

Matthew, in right of wife Abbess Mary, daughter of King Stephen, 22, 90, 91, 98; supports Henry's sons in revolt, 165; invades Normandy, mortally wounded, dies 170.

Peter, Bishop-Elect of Cambrai, brother to preceding, 170 note.

Reginald of Dammartin, in right of wife Ida, daughter of Matthew, 362, 431 note; allied with John, 383; breaks with him, 393, 404 and note; again in alliance with him, 431, 439; destroys French fleet, 441; sent to Flanders to raise troops, 448; on Bouvines campaign, 452; advises retreat, 453; his good generalship, 456, 462, 463, 465; last man to succumb, taken prisoner, 464.

Boves, Hugh of, on English side at battle of Bouvines, 452; urges action, 454, 456, 463; takes to flight, 464; in command of John's mercenaries, 478, 487; dies, drowned at sea, 488.

Brabant, Henry, Count of, on Allied side at Battle of Bouvines, 451, 457; flies, 462.

Braose, Giles de, younger son of next-named. *See* Hereford, Bishop of.

—— William de, lord of Brecon, his parentage, 374 note; his family connexions and relations with John, 416; quarrels with him, retires to Ireland, 417; driven from Ireland, dies in France, 424, 425.

—— William de, eldest son of preceding, starved to death by John, 424, 425.

Braose, Matilda de, wife of first-named William, refuses to give hostages to 'murderer of Arthur,' 417 ; taken prisoner and starved to death by John, 424, 425.

—— Reginald de, son of William II., reinstated, 499.

Bréauté, Fawkes of, foreigner in John's service, 490.

Brewer, William, on Regency Council, 271, 312 ; faithful throughout to John, 469 note.

Brittany, affairs of 9, 10, 16, 17, 89, 90, 92, 97, 100, 114, 171, 203, 350, 378, 384, 394–398.

Brittany, Counts of (afterwards Dukes)—

Allan Fergant, 9.

Conan III., 9.

Allan, Earl of Richmond, in right of wife Countess Bertha, 10.

Eude of Porhoet, in right of Bertha, 10, 89, 92, 97, 114 ; at war with Henry, 171, 185 note.

Conan IV., son of Allan of Richmond, 10 ; relegated by Henry to Rennes and Upper Brittany, 16, 17 ; married to Margaret of Scotland, 89 ; marries his daughter Constance to Henry's son Geoffrey, surrenders government, 90, 92 and note ; dies, 151.

Geoffrey, fourth born son of Henry II. (*see* "Geoffrey"), becomes Count in right of betrothed wife Constance, daughter of Conan IV., 151, 172 ; at war with his father, 165 ; comes to terms at Montlouis, 182, 183 ; reduces Eude of Porhoet, 185 note ; in England, 191, 198 ; Knighted by his father, 200 ; subdues Breton rebels, 204 ; supports Philip II., 210 ; supports Richard against rebels, 212 ; does homage to young King, 213 ; at war with his father and brother, his treachery and sacrilege, 214, 215 ; makes peace, 217 ; again at war with Richard, goes over to England with him, 219, 222 ; dies, 231 ; his issue, 232 ; style of Duke assumed by him, 378 note.

Constance, daughter of Conan IV. and widow of Geoffrey, remarried by Henry II. to Ralph Earl of Chester, rules Brittany, separates from her husband, 350 ; at Richard's death occupies Angers, 378 ; meets Philip, 382, 384 ; divorces Earl of Chester and marries Guy of Thouars, 384, note ; dies, 394.

Arthur, son of preceding, by Geoffrey ; his wardship claimed by Philip of France, 231 ; recognised by Richard for a time as his heir, 308 ; that purpose having been abandoned he is taken to Paris by the Bretons to keep him in Richard's hands, 350 ; acting with Richard, 362 ; assumes title of Duke ; at Richard's death accepted by Maine and Anjou, 378 and note ; does homage to Philip for them, 382 ; goes to Paris with him, *ib.* ; taken to John's court, and then again removed, 384 ; does homage to John, 386 ; Knighted by Philip and invested with Brittany, Anjou, and Poitou, 393, 394 ; besieges Queen Eleanor at Mirabel, 394 ; taken prisoner by John, 395 ; his ultimate fate, 396, 397 and note.

Constance, daughter of Constance above, by Guy of Thouars, 402 note ; married to Peter Mauclerc of Dreux, Duke in her right, 450.

Peter Mauclerc, younger brother of Robert of Dreux II., taken prisoner by John, 450 ; exchanged for Earl of Salisbury, 487.

Brock, Ralph of, farmer of Canterbury Estates, 68, 84, 105, 127, 129.

Burgh, Hubert de, Chamberlain to John, appointed Warden of Welsh

March, 390 ; on mission to Philip, 393 ; in charge of Arthur, 395, 396 ; refuses to mutilate him, 396 ; at Chinon, 403 ; taken prisoner, 405 ; appointed Sheriff of Kent, 488, 489 ; fully trusted by John, Sheriffdoms held by him, 493 ; besieged at Dover, signs convention with Louis, 498.

Burgundy, Dukes of—

Hugh III., 210, 211, 215, 287 ; on the Crusade, 299, 302, 307, 318, 322 ; dies at Tyre, 325 note.

Eude, or Odo, III., son of preceding, on French side in campaign of Bouvines, 452 ; commanding the rear, his horse killed under him, 461.

Cambridge University, possibly started by migration from Oxford, 512.

Camville, Gerard of, buys Sheriffdom of Lincoln, 272 ; accused of complicity in attacks on Jews, 278, note ; deprived of Sheriffdom by Longchamp, 309 ; reinstated by Walter of Coutances, 310 ; again turned out by Richard, 336 ; fined for attack on Jews, 336.

—— Richard of, in command of Richard's fleet, 284 ; left in command at Cyprus, 295.

Canon Law, 39, 42, 63.

Canterbury, Archbishops of—

Theobald, crowns Henry and Eleanor, 3 ; protests against taxation of clergy, 11 ; dies, 25.

Becket, Thomas, election and consecration of, institutes Feast of Trinity Sunday, 27, 28 ; change of life, 34 ; asserts Church claims, 35 ; at Council of Tours, 36 ; resists the King, 'the Sheriff's Aid,' 37 ; protects clerks charged of crimes, 40 ; claims all Canterbury livings, 41 ; 'must obey God rather than man,' 44 ; agrees to observe Henry's 'customs,' 45 ; under pressure accepts *Constitutions* of Clarendon, 45-50 ; repents, and suspends himself, 51 ; attempts to leave England, 52 ; cited to answer complaint of John Marshal, 53 ; fresh citation to Northampton, 54 ; proceedings there, 54-62 ; flight, 63 : assumes disguise and crosses Channel, 65, 66 ; journey to St. Omer and Soissons, 66 ; audiences with Pope and Cardinals at Sens, 68-70 ; removes to Pontigny, 70 ; quarrels with Owain Gwynedd, 75 ; calls on Henry to surrender, 82 ; excommunicates his Ministers, 83, 84 ; leaves Pontigny for Sens, 88 ; rejects mediations of Cardinals Otto and William, 91-93 ; also that of Simon and Bernard, 101-104 ; issues fresh excommunications against Henry's agents, 105, 106 ; yet again more, 107 ; threatens an interdict, 110 ; excessive demands at Montmartre, 111-114 ; admitted to peace by King at Fréteval, 121, 122 ; last interview with him, 124, 125 ; fresh suspension of Prelates, and return to England, 126, 127 ; last sermon, 129 ; assassination, 130-134 ; estimate of his conduct, 135 ; canonisation, 136, 168.

Richard, previously Prior of St. Martin's, Dover, 129 ; proceedings preliminary to his election, 166, 167 ; consecration arrested by young King, finally consecrated, 168, 182 ; holds Synod at Westminster, 186 ; yields St. Peter's, Gloucester, to the Archbishop of York, 188 ; struggle for precedence, 190, 191 ; escorts Royal bride, 193 ; truce with York, 194 ; dies, 221.

M M

Canterbury, Archbishops of (*continued*)—

Baldwin, proceedings prior to his election, 221; election, 222; marries William the Lion to Ermengarde of Beaumont, 231; preaches Crusade in Wales, 237; quarrel with Canterbury monks, *ib.*; on mission to Philip II., 238; absolves Richard for warring against his father, 263; protests against marriage of John to Isabel of Gloucester, 265, 276; crowns Richard, 269; quarrels with Canterbury monks over the Hackington foundation, 273; leaves England, 277; joins the Crusade, dies at Acre, 285 note, 293, 297.

Hubert Walter, translated from Salisbury, his parentage, appointment, and election, 329, 330, 331; appointed Chief Justiciar, 334; outlaws John in rebellion, 335: re-crowns Richard, 337; domestic adminstration, institutes office of Coroner, 342; and Registry of Jews' Property, 343; appointed Papal Legate, holds visitation of York, deposes Abbot of St. Mary's, 343; holds Synod and passes Canons, 344; institutes Conservators of Peace, 344; appoints commission to try Geoffrey of York, 345; arrests William Fitz Osbert, 352; attacked for violation of sanctuary, offers to resign Justiciarship, 352, 353; called to Normandy, 354; asks for force to serve abroad, 355; transports materials of Hackington Chapel to Lambeth, obliged to pull it down, resigns Chief Justiciarship, 359 and note; attempts to introduce uniform system of weights and measures, 373; leads armies against the Welsh, 374; at Richard's death declares for John as against Arthur, 378, 379; secures allegiance of Magnates, crowns John, 380, 381; appointed Chancellor, 381; mediates between John and the Cistercians, 385, 388; crowns Queen Isabel (of Angoulême), 387; levies taxes, 400; sent to treat with Philip, 402; opposes John, 405; dies, his character and life's work, 406, 407.

Stephen Langton, Cardinal of St. Chrysogonus, named for Archbishopric of Canterbury by Innocent III., 411; consecrated by him, 413; declines to come to England, 418; comes and returns without meeting John, 419, 423; comes to England, 441; absolves John on terms, 442; restrains him from making war on his Barons, 443; holds meetings and produces copy of Henry I.'s charter, 444; appeals to Rome against Legate Nicolas, 465; pledges himself for John, 468; mediating between him and Barons, 471, 473; suspended, 487.

Carucate. *See* Danegeld.
Cashel, Synod of, 154.
Champagne, Counts of—

Henry I., married to Mary, daughter of Louis VII. and Eleanor, 23; at war with Henry II., 24, 95, 96; breach with Philip Augustus, 205.

Henry II., son of preceding, quarrels with Philip II., 210; on the Crusade, 302, 307, 318; elected King of Jerusalem, 319; marries Isabel, widow of Conrad of Montferrat, 320; reinforces Richard, 321; at Battle of Joppa, 324; friendly to Richard, 353.

Chester, Earls of—

Hugh II., joins the young King in revolt, 166, 169; taken prisoner, 171, 174, 175, 181; pardoned, 195, 197.

Ralph III., son of preceding, resists John when in revolt, 335,; at court, 337; married to Constance of Brittany, 350, 380; taken to Poitou, 449; on John's side throughout, 469 note, 487, 499, 501.

Chichester, Bishops of—
Hilary, 44, 57, 61, 65, 94.
John, appointed, 167.
Richard le Poer, executor of John's will, 501.
Cinque Ports, Barons of, their functions at coronations, 267.
Cistercians (*Albi Monachi*), receive Becket at Pontigny, 70; forced by
Henry to dismiss him, 88; convent for them founded by Henry
at Witham in Somerset, 256; legacy to them, 259; their wool
demanded for Richard's ransom, 331; so again, 336; patronised
by Richard, 366, 369; quarrel with John, 385; their connection
with Albigensian Crusade, taxed by John, 426.
Clarendon, *Constitutions of*, 46-48; not officially condemned by Alexander
III., 69; quashed by Becket, 84, 93.
Comyn, Cumin, John. *See* Dublin, Archbishops of.
Constance of Brittany, daughter and heiress of Count Conan IV., engaged
to Geoffrey, son of Henry II., 89; becomes Countess at father's
death, 151; in Henry's keeping, 175. *See* Brittany, Counts of.
—— of Castile, second wife of Louis VII., dies, 23.
—— of Sicily, wife of Henry VI. of Germany, 286.
Cornhill, Henry of, Sheriff of Kent, 314.
—— Reginald, the younger, Sheriff of Kent, delivers Rochester Castle to
Confederate Barons, 488, 489.
Cornwall, Earl of, Reginald, 49, 57, 124, 167, 169; lays siege to Leicester,
172, 173; dies, 196 note.
Coucy, Ingelram of, at Battle of Bouvines, 456.
Courcy, John de, his conquests in Ulster, 197, 227; employed by Henry,
228; in alliance with King of Man and men of Galloway, 375, 376;
driven from Ulster by the de Lacys, 423; makes friends with John,
424.
Courts, Christian, 38, 39.
Coventry, Chester, and Lichfield, Bishops of—
Richard Peche, 111, 119.
Hugh of Nonant, 232 note; buys Priory of Coventry, 272; organizes
resistance to Longchamp, 312; impeaches him, 314; in secret
league with John, 315; summoned by Richard, absconds, 336;
pardoned by him, 347.
Geoffrey, 416.
William of Cornhill, 470 note.

Danegeld, hidage, or carucate, 252, 336, 357, 370, 385.
David of Scotland, brother to William the Lion, styled Earl of Huntingdon,
in revolt against Henry, 169, 175, 176. *See* Huntingdon, Earls of.
—— son of Owain, Welsh Prince, 72; married to Emma, natural sister of
Henry II., receives a grant in Ellesmere, 196; dethroned, retires to
England, dies there, 374.
Derby, Earls of—
Robert of Ferrers III. in revolt, 169, 177; submits, 181.
William of Ferrers I., dies at Acre, 297.
Williams of Ferrers II., 335, 380; finally recognised as Earl, 381,
416, 439; taken to Poitou, 449; supporting John, 487, 499,
501.

Dermot MacMurrough, King of Leinster, expelled, 141, 142; allowed to raise troops in England and Wales, returns home, 142; recovers his position, 143; invades Ossory, 144; recognises Roderic O'Connor as over-lord, attacks Dublin, 145; again, 147; invades Meath, dies, 148.

Devon. Earls of—

    Baldwin of Redvers, his marriage, 265, note.

    William of Redvers, supporting John, 497, 499.

Dortmund, Conrad, Count of, on Otto IV.'s bodyguard at Battle of Bouvines, 457; taken prisoner, 462.

Dreux, Robert II., Count of, at Battle of Bouvines, in command on French left, 455, 463.

Dublin, Archbishops of—

    Laurence O'Toole, 147, 257.

    John Cumin (before appointment), employed by Henry, 87; archbishop, 257; at Richard's coronation, 266; his death, 439; architectural work at Dublin, *ib.*, 257; quarrel with Hamo of Valognes, 375.

    Henry of London, 439, 479.

—— Sieges of, 145, 147, 148, 149; charter from Henry II., trading rights to men of Bristol, 156 and note.

Duncan MacGilbert, a Galloway chieftain, 231.

Durand, a Templar, on Papal mission to England, 429, 430.

Durham, Bishops of—

    Hugh of Puiset, 119; acting with rebels, 167, 176; submits, 181; fined, 196; commission to Scotland, 237; at Richard's coronation, 267; joint Justiciar, 271; buys Earldom and Sheriffdom of Northumberland and Wapentake of Sadberge, 272; opposes Geoffrey, 275; given charge of Windsor Castle, his character, 276; driven from the Council by Longchamp, 277; arrested and deprived of his offices, 280; recovers his Earldom, 314; quarrels with Geoffrey, 316 and note; resists John, 328; so again, 335; deprived of Earldom of Northumberland, but retains Sadberge, 338 and note; publishes Papal mandates revoking acts of Archbishop Geoffrey, 345, 346; dies, his architectural work, and the Boldon Book, *ib.*, note.

    Philip of Poitiers, 360 note; dies, 416.

Edward the Confessor, first translation of his remains at Westminster, 44.

Elder (Sheykh) of the Mountain, clears Richard of complicity in murder of Conrad of Montferrat, 319 and note.

Eleanor of Brittany, daughter of Geoffrey and Constance, 232; proposal for her marriage to Saphadin, brother of Saladin, 306, for her marriage to a son of Duke of Austria, 328; hostage in Austria, sent home, 346; taken prisoner by John and sent to England, 395 and note; taken with him to Poitou, 448.

—— Countess of Poitiers and Duchess of Aquitaine, divorced wife of Louis VII. of France, re-married to Henry II., her possessions, 1 and note; mentioned, 9, 12, 15, 18, 71; supports her sons against their father, 163; arrested and kept in custody, 165, 175, 213; brought to Winchester on more liberal footing, 220;

at Christmas feast at Windsor, 223; nominally re-invested with Aquitaine, 227; comes back to England with Henry, 229; not guilty of poisoning Rosamund, 261; finally liberated at accession of Richard, acts as Regent on his behalf, 265; at his coronation, 266; her dower assigned, 275; goes over to Normandy, 277; brings Berengaria of Navarre to Messina, 288, 290; sent home, *ib.*; at Rome, 291; hastens to England to check John's intrigues with Philip, 315, 316; supports Longchamp, *ib.*; at Mainz, 333, 334; at Council at Nottingham, 336; at Winchester, 338; brings Richard and John together, 339; sent for by Richard on his deathbed, 366; supports John, 379; invests him with Aquitaine, 382; travels to Spain to fetch granddaughter Blanche, 385, 386; dies, 403.

—— second daughter of Henry II., born, 260; proposal for her hand, 71; married to Alphonso III. of Castile, 193, 260; dies, 494 note.

—— daughter of John, 514.

Ely, Bishops of—

Nigel, Chancellor for a time, then Treasurer, 4.

Geoffrey Riddel, appointed, 167, 194; dies, his treasures seized by Richard, 266.

William of Longchamp, 270, 271, 272; given charge of the Tower, 276; his character, 277; ousts Bishop Puiset from his offices, 277; his action confirmed by Richard, appointed Papal Legate, *ib.*; holds inquests as to outrages on Jews, 279; arrests and despoils Bishop Puiset, becomes supreme in England, 280, 308; opposed to John, the two at war, 309; public pacification between them, followed by private compact, 310; arrests Geoffrey, Archbishop of York, 311; shuns meeting on bridge of Lodden, 312; retires to London, and the Tower, deposed from Justiciarship, 313; surrenders Tower, and leaves England, 314; attempts to return, without success, 316; again sent to England on a mission by Richard and the Emperor, 330; recalled, 331; authorised to conclude treaty with Philip, 232; also with John, 333; at Nottingham with Richard, 336; dies at Poitiers, 351.

Eustace, Chancellor, 360 note; resigns Seal, 381; on mission to Philip, 393, 402; proclaims the Interdict, 414, 415, 418; returns to England, 441; dissolves the Inderdict, 466, 468 (bis).

Emma, natural sister of Henry II., married to Owain Gwynedd, 374.

Essex, Earls of—

William of Mandeville, 79, 109, 233, 242, 267; Joint Justiciar, 271; dies, 273.

Geoffrey Fitz Peter, buys Essex estates, 281; his claim to the office, *ib.* note; on Regency Council, 312; appointed Chief Justiciar, 359; defeats the Welsh, 375; at Richard's death declares for John, 378, 379; finally invested as Earl, 381, 400, 409, 428, 442; dies, 447.

Geoffrey of Mandeville, son of preceding, forced to marry John's discarded wife, Isabel of Gloucester, 470, 473; with Barons against John, 487; dies, 496 note.

William of Mandeville, brother to preceding, acting against John, 496.

—— Henry of, Constable of England, drops the Royal Standard at Consilt, 14; impeached, 36.

Eu, Counts of—
> Henry, 170 ; his death, 389 note.
> Ralph of Lusignan, in right of wife Alais, daughter of preceding, 389, and note ; attacked by John, *ib.*, 449, 450.

Eustace, the Monk, Channel pirate, brings Louis to England, 495.

Exeter, Bishops of—
> Bartholomew, 57, 65, 85, 111, 119.
> Henry Marshal, 344.
> Simon of Apulia, 467.

Faye, Ralph of, uncle to Queen Eleanor, setting the young King Henry against his father, 156 note, 162, 168.

Fines, Legal mode of conveyance of land, first appearance of, 201.

Fitz Peter. *See* Essex, Earls of.

Fitz Walter. *See* Robert.

Flanders, Counts of—
> Dietrich of Alsace, at Henry's coronation, 3 ; treaty of retainer, 35, 65 ; dies, 95 note.
> Philip, son of preceding, refuses safe-conduct to Becket, 66 ; acting against Henry, 90, 91, 95, 98, 109 ; supports Henry's sons in revolt, 165 ; threatening to invade England, 175, 176 ; sends over troops, 177 ; attacks Rouen, 181 ; makes peace, 186 ; at coronation of Philip II., 203 ; becomes his Mentor, 205 ; cedes Artois, and promises Vermandois, etc., 206 ; receives pension from Henry, 206 ; at war with France, 210 ; surrenders Pierrefonds, etc., 211 ; marries Matilda of Portugal, 220 ; refuses to support Philip against Henry, 239 ; at Messina on Crusade, mediates between Philip and Richard, 289 ; dies at Acre, 297.
> Baldwin VII. of Flanders (Ninth of Hainault), sister's son to preceding, married to Richard's niece Mary of Champagne, makes treaty with Richard and invades Artois, 354 and note ; draws Philip into difficulties, but lets him off, 355 ; supports candidature of Otto for Imperial Crown, 361 ; in alliance with Richard, 362, 383 ; goes on Crusade, 396 ; dies in Bulgaria, 431 note.
> Ferdinand or Ferrand of Portugal, Count in right of wife Jeanne, daughter of preceding, in alliance with John, 431 and note, 438 ; attacked by Philip, 441 ; does homage to John in London, 448; joins Bouvines campaign, 451 ; the battle, 452-461, taken prisoner, 462.

Flemings settled in Pembrokeshire, 4.

Foliot, Gilbert, an Angevin, and old Cluniac monk. *See* Hereford, and London, Bishops of.

Forests, Forest Assize, 223.

France, Kings of. *See* Louis, Philip.

Gant, Gilbert of, Lincolnshire magnate, acting against John, 497, 500.

Geoffrey of Anjou, younger brother of Henry II., 2 ; lays claim to Anjou and Maine, 8 ; reduced to submission, 9 ; established as Count of Nantes, 10 ; dies, 16.

—— fourth born son of Henry II., 259 ; married to Constance heiress of Brittany, 89 ; does homage to brother Henry, and receives homage of Bretons, 114 ; becomes Count. *See* Brittany, Counts of.

Geoffrey, natural son of Henry II., appointed to See of Lincoln (*see* Lincoln, Bishops of), resigns and is appointed Chancellor, 230, 233, notes; with his father in his last campaign, 242, 243 ; nurses him on his deathbed, 244 ; delivers the Seal to Richard, 262 ; named for Archbishopric of York, 263. *See* York, Archbishops of.

—— natural son of King John, 405, 515.

—— Fitz Peter, on Regency Council, 271 ; admitted to Essex estates, 281. *See* Essex, Earls of.

Gerald of Windsor, Constable of Pembroke, his sons by the Lady Nest, daughter of Rhys ap Teudwr, 13.

Germany, Emperors of—

Frederic I. "Barbarossa," supports Anti-pope Victor III., 23 ; suggests a show of the two Popes, 29 ; overtures to Henry, holds Diet at Würtzburg, 71 ; proclaims Anti-Pope Calixtus III., 98 ; condemns Henry the Lion to forfeiture, 207 ; banishes him, 211 ; goes on Crusade and dies, drowned in fording a river, 284.

Henry VI., son of preceding, King of Germany, by rights King of Sicily in right of wife Constance, at war with Tancred, actual King of Sicily, 286 ; takes Richard from custody of Leopold of Austria, terms for Richard's liberation, 328 ; arraigns him before Diet, 329 ; mean conduct towards Richard and Leopold, 331, 332 ; finally induced to release him, 343 ; dies, 360.

Otto IV., younger son of Duke Henry the Lion and Matilda of England ; created Duke of Aquitaine by Richard, 360 and note ; candidate for Imperial Crown with support of Richard ; elected and crowned King of Germany, 361 ; Richard bequeaths jewels to him, 365 ; relations with John, 383, 384, 396 ; crowned Emperor by Innocent with John's support, 435 ; falls out with Innocent, 428, 435 ; in alliance with John, 431 ; excommunicated by Innocent, subsidised by John, 437 ; joins the Bouvines campaign, 451, 452 ; at the battle, his horse killed under him, escapes, 456-462 ; retires to Cologne, and again to Brunswick ; dies, 455.

Frederick II., son of Henry VI., a child at his father's death, 361 ; taken up in Germany and accepted by Innocent III., supported by Philip II., 435.

Gilbert fitz Renfrid, married to heiress of Lancaster, 263.

Gild Merchant, a close trading corporation, 510.

" Giraldus Cambrensis," otherwise Gerald of Barry, the historian, with John in Ireland, 227 ; accompanies Archbishop Baldwin on Welsh tour, 237 ; entertains Masters and Scholars of Oxford at his lodgings, 511.

Glanville, Ranulf of, Sheriff of Yorkshire, captures William the Lion at Alnwick, 178, 179 ; appointed Chief Justiciar, 202, 218, 221, 222, 227, 232 ; his book, " De Legibus Angliæ," 258 ; resigns Justiciarship, 271 ; joins the Crusade, and dies at Acre, 285 and note, 297.

Gloucester, Earls of—

William, son of Robert, 56, 169, 181, 186 ; settles estates on youngest daughter Isabel and King's son John, 195.

John, King's son in right of wife Isabel, daughter of preceding. *See* John.

Amauri of Montfort, created by John, 386 note, and errata.

Grand Councils, 4, 5, 6, 13, 23, 25, 37, 45, 54, 82, 152, 175, 186, 193, 194, 195, 198, 202, 225, 236, 270, 273, 277, 310, 312, 315, 316, 335, 355, 380, 400, 404, 413, 444, 446.

Gratian, Papal envoy, his unsuccessful mission, 107-110.

Gray, Walter, Chancellor 422 ; afterwards Bishop of Worcester, *q.v.*

Grim, Edward, Cambridge monk. Biographer of Becket. With him and wounded at time of his murder, 134.

Gruffudd, son of Rhys, Prince of South Wales, 374, expelled, reinstated, 375 ; does homage at Lincoln to John, 387.

Gualo, Cardinal, his mission to arrest Louis' invasion of England, 494, 495 ; follows him to England, and excommunicates him and all his followers, 496 ; named executor of John's Will, 501.

Guérin, Hospitaller, Bishop-Elect of Senlis, in command of French right at Battle of Bouvines, 456, 457, 459, 460.

Guthfrith, or Godfrey, King of the Western Isles, 90 and note.

Guthred, King of Man, assists Irish in siege of Dublin, 148, 149 ; his daughter Affreca married to John de Courcy, 227.

Gwenwynwyn, Prince of Powys, 374 ; defeated by Geoffrey Fitz Peter, 375 ; 420, 421, 429, 433.

Hackington, attempted foundation at, by Archbishop Baldwin, from Canterbury revenues, 237, 242, 273 ; removed to Lambeth, 274 ; demolition of Lambeth chapel, 359 and note.

Hastings, Richard of, Grand Master of the Temple in England, 24, 50.

Henry II., "Curt Mantel"; birth, etc., 1 ; Continental dominions at accession, *id.* ; recalls alienations of Ducal demesnes in Normandy, recognised by Louis VII. of France, 2 ; comes over to England, is crowned with Eleanor, issues a charter, 3 ; passes decrees for expulsion of mercenaries and demolition of adulterine castles, 4 ; reduces refractory Magnates, 5, 6 ; indicates a family policy, exacts homage to his sons, schemes a conquest of Ireland, obtains the Papal Bull, *Laudabiliter*, 6-8 ; crosses the Channel, does homage to Louis, 9 ; reduces brother Geoffrey, and then establishes him as Count of Nantes, 9, 10 ; returns to England, 12 ; recovers Northern Counties from Scots, 12 ; invades Wales and forces Owain of Gwynedd to submit, 13, 14 ; wears crown in State for last time at Worcester, 15 ; goes over to Normandy, arranges marriage of his son Henry to Margaret of France, 17 ; occupies Nantes, 18 ; lays claim to Toulouse, 18, 19 ; unsuccessful campaign, 19-22 ; resumes county of Mortain, *ib.* ; settles Boulogne on Matthew of Flanders, *ib.* ; recognises Pope Alexander III., 23 ; recovers Norman Vexin, 23, 24 ; signs truce with France, reduces castles in Aquitaine, 25 ; receives Alexander III., crosses to England, 29 ; treaty with Flanders, 35 ; campaign in Wales, 36, 37 ; breach with Becket, " the Sheriffs' Aid," 37 ; criminal clerks to be punished, 39 ; scheme for that end, 42 ; resisted by Becket, 43 ; upbraids him at Northampton, 44 ; propounds *Constitutions of Clarendon*, 45-50 ; makes application to the Pope, 51, 52 ; at Council of Northampton, 54-62 ; sends ambassadors to Louis and Alexander, 65 ; confiscates Becket's property and banishes his friends, 68 ; crosses to Normandy, interview with Louis, 70 ; sends envoys to Diet at Würzburg, 71 ;

disavows them, 72 ; invades Wales, 72, 73, punishes heretics, 75, 76 ; publishes *Assize of Clarendon*, 76-79 ; *Assize of Novel Disseisin*, 81 ; crosses to Normandy, 81 ; levies Palestine tax, 82 ; reduces rebel barons, 88, 89, occupies Brittany, 89, 90 ; meets Count of Toulouse, 91 ; at war with France, 92 ; reduces Brittany again, 92 ; annoyed at failure of Papal mission, 95 ; propounds dynastic scheme, 95, 96 ; reduces Poitevins, 96 ; and Bretons, 97 ; abortive conferences with Louis at La Ferté Bernard, 97, 98 ; war, and truce, 98 ; does homage for the third time, 100 ; fruitless conferences with Becket at Montmirail, 101-104 ; so with Gratian and Vivian, 107-110 ; guards against threatened Interdict, 110, 111 ; fruitless interview with Becket at Montmartre, the kiss of peace refused, 111-114 ; crosses to England, 116 ; orders Inquest of Sheriffs, 117 ; crowns his son, 119 ; crosses to Normandy, meets Louis and Becket at Fréteval, agrees to reinstate Becket, 121, 122 ; proclaims peace to him and his, 124 ; loses self-control, 130 ; horrified at report of Becket's murder, 136 ; jealous of Strongbow's success in Ireland, 151 ; leaves Normandy, calls out levies, and goes over to Ireland, 152 ; receives submission of natives, kings, and clergy, 153 ; keeps Christmas at Dublin, convenes Synod of Cashel, 154 ; returns to England, 156 ; goes over to Normandy and is reconciled to the Church at Avranches, 159 ; ceremony repeated, 162 ; treaty with Count Humbert III. of Maurienne, 163 ; meetings with Alphonso II. of Arragon and Raymond V. of Toulouse, homage done by latter, revolt of young king, 164 ; Henry (elder King) prepares for war, 165 : fills up vacant see, 167 ; relieves Verneuil, besieged by Louis, 171 ; captures Dol after forced march from Rouen, 171 ; makes fruitless offers to his sons and King Louis, 172 ; hasty visit to England, 174 ; reduces rebel castles in Poitou, *ib.* ; reduces Saintes and Ancenis, holds Grand Council, and crosses to England, 175, 176 ; does penance at tomb of Becket, 179 ; advances to London, Huntingdon, and Northampton, and receives William the Lion as prisoner, 180, 181 ; crosses to Normandy and raises siege of Rouen, 181, 182 ; brings his sons to terms, arrangement of Montlouis, 182, 183 ; crosses to England with the young King, progress to the North, Forest Prosecutions, receives homage of William the Lion and his subjects, 186, 187 ; publishes *Assize of Northampton*, 189 ; appoints son John Lord of Ireland, 196 ; arbitrates between Castile and Navarre, 197 ; crosses to Normandy, 198 ; seals treaty at Ivry with Louis VII., 198, 199 ; enters Berri and Auvergne, contracts to purchase county of La Marche, *ib.* ; goes over to England, knights Geoffrey, 201 ; rearranges Circuits of Judges—Court of King's Bench started, 201, 202 ; mediates between Philip II. of France and his relatives, confirms treaty of Ivry, 206 ; grants pension to Count of Flanders, *ib.* ; holds interview with Philip, 207 ; mediates between him and Flanders, crosses to England, 208 ; publishes Assizes of Arms, 208, 209 ; crosses to Normandy, and mediates between France and Flanders, 211 ; supports Richard in Poitou, 212 ; requires his younger sons to do homage to the young King, 213 ; supports Richard in Poitou, endeavours to bring young King to his duty, 214 ; grief at his death, 216 ; suggests cession of Aquitaine

Henry II. (*continued*)—

to John, 218, 219; refuses to part with Norman Vexin, but does fresh homage to Philip, and settles Margaret's dower, 218, 219; finds a new wife for Count of Flanders, 219, 220; crosses to England, allows Queen Eleanor to join Duchess of Saxony at Winchester, 220; accepts Baldwin as Archbishop of Canterbury, 222: issues new Forest Assize, 223; declines offer of Crown of Jerusalem, 225, 226; knights son John, grants Earldom of Huntingdon to William the Lion, crosses to Normandy, *ib.*; reinvests Eleanor with Aquitaine, 227; sends John to Ireland, *ib.*; holds conferences with the French and agrees to marry Richard to Alais, 228, 229; returns to England, *ib.*; fills up vacant sees, 230; crosses to Normandy, 232; takes the Cross, 235; imposes Saladin Tithe, 236: crosses Channel for last time, declares war, and raids French territory, 239; holds abortive conferences at Châtillon and Bonmoulins, 240; his last Christmas, thinly attended, 241; out of health, last efforts for reconciliation with Richard, *ib.*; driven from Le Mans, 242; forced to accept Philip's terms, 243; signs treaty of Colombières, his end, 244, 245; his appearance and character, 246; estimate of his foreign and domestic policy, 247, 248; legal reforms, 249, 250; revenue, 251-254; works and buildings, 255; architecture of the reign, 256: his foundations, 225, 256; his Will, 258; issue, 259.

—— second born, but eldest surviving son of Henry II. (the Young King), homage done to him, 6; does homage to Louis VII. for Normandy, 23; married to Margaret of France, *ib.*; does homage for Anjou, Maine, and Brittany, confers Brittany on brother Geoffrey, 100; receives his homage, 114; is crowned King, 118, 119; receives homages, 120; attached to Becket, 122, 128; ruling in Normandy, 152; concurs in father's oaths to the Papacy at Avranches, 159, 160; shabbily treated by his father, 161; re-crowned with his wife, 162; insidious advice given to him, 163; demands an independent establishment, *ib.*; leaves his father's court in revolt, 164; lavish grants to supporters, 165; attempts to veto appointment to Canterbury, 168; invades Normandy, 170; rejects liberal offers of his father, 172; attacks Seez, 175; preparing to invade England, 176; attacks Rouen, 181; comes to terms with his father at Montlouis, 182; crosses to England with him, 185, 186; again discontented, goes to France, 191; co-operates with Richard, 192; meets his father, 198; carries the crown at Coronation of Philip II., 203, 206; supports him against coalition, 210; supports Richard against rebels, 212; intrigues against him, 213; demands oath of fealty from him, 214; supports rebels against him, treacherous conduct towards his father, takes the Cross, last campaign and death, 215, 216.

—— eldest son of John, born, 514.

—— Cardinal, Bishop of Albano, on mission to England and France, dies, 241.

—— the Lion, Duke of Saxony and Bavaria, married to Henry's daughter Matilda, 71, 99; his estates forfeited, 207; sentenced to banishment, retires to Normandy, 211, 213; in England, 223; at coronation of Richard I., 266.

Henry II. of Saxony, son of preceding, Count Palatine, on Crusade, not candidate for Imperial Crown, 360.

Heraclius, Patriarch of Jerusalem, his mission to England, 225; and France, 226; dies at the siege of Acre, 297.

Hereford, Bishops of—

Gilbert Foliot, opposes promotion of Becket to Primacy, 26, 77; translated to London, 36. *See* London, Bishops of.

Robert of Melun, 44, 59, 62, 85

Robert Foliot, appointed, 167.

William de Vere, appointed, 230.

Giles de Braose, 414, 415, 418, 441, 470.

—— Earls of—

Roger, son of Milo, in rebellion, dies, 5.

Henry Bohun, opposing John, 471.

Heresy, Heretics. *See* Nonconformists.

Hertford, Earls of—

Roger of Clare, at war with Welsh, 72; loyalty to Henry, 169.

Richard of Clare II., 181; married to Amice of Gloucester, 195; supports Longchamp against John, 310, 380; opposes John, 471.

Hidage. *See* Danegeld.

Holland, William, Count of, does homage to John in London, 438; comes over again, 448; on allied side at battle of Bouvines, 451, 457.

Hortzmar, Bernard of, on Bodyguard of Otto IV. at battle of Bouvines, 457; taken prisoner, 462.

Humez, now Le Hommet, Richard of, Constable of Normandy, 89, 90, 96.

Huntingdon, Earl of, David, 226; at coronation of Richard, 267; resists John in rebellion, 335; married to Maud, daughter of Hugh II., Earl of Chester, 373, 380, 433.

—— Earldom of, granted to Malcolm IV., the Maiden, King of Scots, 12; granted, after interval, to William the Lion, and by him passed on to his brother David, 226, and note.

Ilchester, Richard of, Archdeacon of Poitiers, employed by Henry II., 51, 65, 71, 72; excommunicated, 84, 105; again employed, 159; appoii ˄d Bishop of Winchester, 167. *See* Winchester, Bishops of.

Ingeborg of Denmark, second wife of Philip II., hastily repudiated by him, 383, and note; 385, 392.

Inquest of Service, 79; of Sheriffs, 117.

Ireland, early intercourse with England, ecclesiastical relations, 138; primitive state of society, 139, 140; music and poetry, 141; Provinces of, *ib.*; course of partial conquest of by Welsh adventurers, Earl Strongbow, and Henry II., 141-150, 152-157; submission of Roderic of Connaught, 187; King's son John to be Lord of Ireland, 196; conquests of John de Courcy, 197; governors under Richard, 275.

Isaac Comnenus, "Emperor" of Cyprus, 291; rejects Richard's demands, driven from Limasol, and again defeated, 292; carried off to die a prisoner in Syria, 294, 295.

Isabel of Gloucester, contracted to John, son of Henry II., 195, 263; married to him in spite of objections of Archbishop Baldwin, 265;

Isabel of Gloucester, (*continued*)—

    not crowned with him, 380; divorced, 386; deprived of her inheritance, *ib.* note; re-endowed and married to Geoffrey, Earl of Essex, 470; dies, 514.

—— of Angoulême, second wife of King John, 386; crowned, 387; sails with him to La Rochelle, 448; her children and death, 514.

—— daughter of John, 514.

—— of Hainault, married to Philip II. of France, 206; dies, 383 note.

—— heiress of Vermandois, married to Philip, Count of Flanders, 206; dies, 211, 219.

Jeanne or Johanna, third daughter of Henry II., married to William II. of Sicily, 104, 193; left a widow, taken in charge by Richard, 286; voyage from Messina to Cyprus, 291; on to Acre, 295, 301; brought to Joppa, 305; voyage home to Poitou, 325; suggestions for her marriage, 306; married to Raymond VI. of Toulouse, 351.

—— or Johanna, natural daughter of King John, married to Llewelyn son of Jorwerth, 420, 514.

Jerusalem, Kingdom of, its weakness, 207, 224; kings of, *ib.*; again, 234; captured by Saladin, 235.

Jews, false charges against, 205, 254; protected by Henry II., 269; outrages on them at Richard's coronation, 268; further attacks on them at Lynn, Norwich, Bury, Stamford, York, 278, 342; registry of their property established, Exchequer of the Jews, 343; tallages on them in Normandy, 371; in England, 426.

John ("Lackland," "Sansterre"), youngest son of Henry II., born, 377; contracted in marriage to Alais of Maurienne, 163, 175; then to Isabel of Gloucester, 195, 213; cession of Aquitaine to him suggested, 218, 219; in England, 222, 223; unsuccessful expedition to Ireland, 227, 228; proposal for his coronation as King of Ireland, 228, 232; with Henry abroad in command of an army, 233; so again, sent into Normandy, 242; castles there to be given to him, *ib.*; in secret complicity with Richard, 244; confirmed by him as Count of Mortain, and Earl of Gloucester, etc., 263; married to Isabel of Gloucester, 265; further grants to him, 266; at Richard's coronation, 267; sent into Wales with troops, 272; four Western counties granted to him, 275; being in Normandy sworn not to return to England for three years, 277; returns, absolved by Longchamp, 308; coolness between them, then war, 309; pacification and private treaty, 310; summons meeting on bridge of Lodden, 312; grants *Commune* (Municipal Corporation) to City of London, 313; intriguing with Philip, but kept quiet by Eleanor, 315, 316; on report of Richard's capture does homage to Philip, and fortifies castles in England, forced to sign truce, 327, 328; makes fresh treaty with Philip, 334; renews struggle in England, but outlawed, 335; makes friends with Richard, 339; re-invested with Mortain and Gloucester, 347; seizes Gamaches, 350; takes Bishop of Beauvais prisoner, 354; at Richard's death seizes treasure at Chinon, 378; installed as Duke of Normandy, 379; crosses to England and is crowned, 380, 381; restores Geoffrey's revenues, 382; crosses to France, signs a truce, 382; at war again, betrays hostility to Arthur, 384 ; agrees to pacification with France, Philip's son Louis to marry Blanche of Castile, 384; crosses to England, quarrels with the Cistercians and Archbishop Geoffrey, 385 ; returns to Normandy, signs treaty of Le Goulet, divorces Isabel of Gloucester and marries Isabel of Angoulême, 386 ; returns to England, crowns Isabel of Angoulême, receives homage of Gruffudd of South Wales, 387 ; and of William the Lion, attends funeral of St. Hugh of Lincoln, is reconciled to the Cistercians, 388 ; progress to the North, 389 ; wages war on the Lusignans, calls for army for service abroad, exacts a scutage instead, 389, 390 ; crosses to Normandy, visits Philip in Paris, *ib.* ; settles Berengaria's jointure, 391 ; summoned by Philip to answer complaints of Lusignans, condemned to forfeiture in default of appearance, 392, 393 and note ; relieves Queen Eleanor besieged at Mirebeau, and captures Arthur and others, 394, 395 ; makes away with Arthur, 396, 397 and note ; feeble resistance to Philip in Normandy, attempts relief of Château Gaillard, 399 ; crosses to England, levies a Seventh of movables, 400 ; allows Château Gaillard to fall, 401 ; attempts to treat, loses Normandy, 402 ; fails to raise an army for service abroad, 404, 405 ; nominates John Gray, Bishop of Norwich, for Canterbury, 408 ; sails with troops to La Rochelle, 409 ; campaign in Poitou, signs truce, returns to England, 410 ; refuses to accept Stephen Langton as Archbishop, 412 ; expels Canterbury monks and seizes Archiepiscopal estates, levies a Thirteeenth, 413 ; threatens clergy if Interdict should be proclaimed, 414 ; Interdict having been proclaimed wages war on clergy, 415, 416 ; attempts to negotiate with the Pope, 417 ; excommunicated, 418 ; invites Langton to England, but fails to meet him, 419 ; recognises Llywelyn, son of Jorwerth, and gives him Ellesmere, with hand of natural daughter, Johanna, 420 ; called to Welsh March, makes treaties with Scots, 421 ; knights Alexander, son of William the Lion, 422 ; appoints to vacant Sees of Lincoln, Exeter, Coventry, and Chichester, 422 ; again invites Langton to come over, crosses to Ireland to punish the de Lacys, 423 ; reduces Carrickfergus, starves Matilda de Braose and her son to death, 424 ; measures for administration of Ireland, 425 ; returns to England, taxes clergy and Jews, 426; enters Wales (twice) to reduce Llywelyn to submission, 429; fruitless conferences with Papal envoys, Pandulf and Durand, 430; contracts alliances with Flanders and Netherlands, 431 ; alleged embassy to Morocco, *ib.* ; calls for Inquest of Service, 432 ; proposes to reduce Welsh rising, disbands his forces on reports of disaffection, 433 ; reopens negotiations with Innocent, 435 ; forms a Northern League against Philip and Innocent, 437 ; calls out troops, 438 ; submits to Innocent's terms, and surrenders England, 439 ; receives Archbishop Langton, and is absolved by him, 441, 442 ; unable to force Barons to serve abroad, threatens them, 442, 443 ; does homage again for England to Legate Nicholas of Tusculum, 445 ; pays 15,000 marks for damages to the Bishops, 447 ; appoints Peter des Roches Chief Justiciar, crosses to La Rochelle, 448 ; his campaign in Poitou, 449 ; operations on the Loire, flight from La Roche-au-Moine, 451 ; contracts infant

John (*continued*)—

daughter Jeanne to young Hugh le Brun, 450 ; signs truce, returns to England, 465 ; calls for a scutage, 467 ; endeavours to detach clergy from laity, 468 ; calls for fresh oaths of allegiance, 469 ; imports mercenaries, 470 ; rejects Barons' Articles, 471 ; proposes arbitration, 472 ; grants Magna Carta, 473, 474 ; refuses to meet Barons, 486 ; imports mercenaries, 488 ; besieges and captures Rochester Castle, 489-490 ; appoints Walter Gray Archbishop of York, 490 ; harries England, 490, 491 ; halts at Berwick, 492 ; ravages Yorkshire and Lincolnshire, 492 ; captures Colchester, 493 ; on the watch to resist Louis' landing, retires to Sussex and Hampshire at his landing, 495, 496 ; thence to Corfe Castle and Severn valley, 497 ; returns to the valley of the Thames, thence into East Anglia and Lincolnshire, his last raid, 499, 500 ; dies, 501 ; his personal appearance, character and government, 502, 503 ; finance, 504, 505, 506 ; Public Records started, 507.

—— natural son of King John, 515.

—— de' Conti, Cardinal of St. Mark, on mission to France and England, 241, 242.

—— of Anagni, Cardinal on mission to England, 274 ; confirms Geoffrey as Archbishop, 275 ; also John's marriage to Isabel of Gloucester, 276.

King's Bench, Court of, Institution of, 101.

Knights' Service, knights' fees, 11 ; number of, 21, 73, 79, 80, 81, 432.

Lacy, Hugh de, employed by Henry in Ireland, 153 ; appointed Justiciar with grant of Meath in fee, 156 ; brought to Normandy, 170 ; superseded, 194 ; again Justiciar, 196, 227 ; deprived of military command, 228.

—— Hugh de, second son of preceding, Justiciar of Ireland in 1189, 375 ; created Earl of Ulster, 421 ; driven from Ireland by John, 422.

—— Walter de, brother of preceding, 416 ; sets up private Court of Justiciary, 423 ; driven from Ireland by John, 424 ; pardoned, taken to Poitou, 449.

—— Roger de, Constable of Chester, 380, 382 ; sent to Normandy, 390 ; in command of Château Gaillard, 399, 401 ; obliged to surrender, 402.

Langton, Simon of, 414, 418, 466 ; election to York quashed, 490 ; Chancellor to Louis, 496.

—— Stephen of. *See* Canterbury, Archbishops of.

L'Aumône, Philip, Abbot of, 44, 45.

Leicester, Earls of—

Robert of Beaumont II. appointed Chief Justiciar conjointly with Richard of Lucy, 3, 9, 49, 57, 62, 71 ; dies, 99.

Robert of Beaumont III., son of preceding, in rebellion, 169, 170 ; lands with force in Suffolk, 172 ; defeated and taken prisoner at Farnham, 173, 174, 175, 181 ; pardoned, 195 ; reinstated by Richard, 264 ; at his coronation, 267.

Robert of Beaumont IV., son of preceding, on the Crusade, 321 and note ; at battle of Joppa, 324 ; returning home defends Rouen against Philip, 328 ; taken prisoner by him, 340 ; liberated on ceding Pacy, 349 ; on mission to France, 402.

Limburg, Henry, Count of, on Allied side at battle of Bouvines, 451, 457.

Limoges, Viscounts of—

Ademar, in rebellion against Count Richard, 191 ; submits, 192 ; quarrels with him about treasure trove, 365 ; killed by Richard of Cognac, 396.

Guy, son of preceding, taken prisoner by John, 396.

Lincoln, Bishops of—

Robert, 57.

Geoffrey, Elect of, appointed, 167 ; acting vigorously against rebel barons, 177 ; appointment confirmed, 187 ; finally cancelled, 232 note.

Walter of Coutances, 230, 232, notes. See Rouen, Archbishops of.

Hugh of Avalon (St. Hugh), appointed, 232 ; removes Rosamund's tomb, 261 ; excommunicates Longchamp's agents, 312 ; holds enquiry on Geoffrey of York, 345 ; denies liability to service abroad, 355 ; ignores Richard's citations, 356 ; forces him to give the kiss of peace, 356 ; buries him, 366 ; with John, 379 ; dies, 388.

Hugh of Wells, 422, 441.

Lisieux, Arnulf, Bishop of, 44, 51, 83, 122, 159, playing double game, 167 ; forced to surrender his see, *ib.* note.

Llywelyn ap Jorwerth ousts his uncle David from North Wales, 374, 375 ; receives grant of Ellesmere, with hand of Johanna natural daughter of King John, 420 ; at war with the English, reduced to submission, 428, 429 ; in arms again, 433 ; his hostages returned, 470 note, 477.

London, Bishops of—

Gilbert Foliot, translated from Hereford, 36 ; urges Becket to submit to King, 44 ; again, 57, 58, 59, 65, 67, 74, 85, 94, 105, 106, 116, 119, 127, 128, 222.

Richard fitz Nigel, 270, 312, 331, 355 ; dies, *ib.* note.

William of Sainte-Mère-Église, 414 and note ; proclaims the Interdict, 415, 418 ; returns to England, 441.

—— Grant of *Commune*, i.e., Municipal Corporation to, 313, 317 ; first mention of Mayor, 331.

—— Mayors of—

Henry fitz Alywin, 317 ; 331.

Serlo le Mercer, 473.

—— Bridge built in stone, 513 ; Houndsditch excavated, 513.

Longchamp, William of, Chancellor, 270 ; see Ely, Bishops of.

Lorraine, Theobald, Duke of, on Allied side at Battle of Bouvines, 451, 457.

Louis VII., King of France, recognises Henry II. as Duke of Aquitaine, and restores Neuf Marché and Vernon, 2 ; sanctions Henry's occupation of Nantes, and agrees to marry daughter Margaret to Henry's son, 17 ; opposes Henry's attack on Toulouse, 21 ; receives Pope, 29 ; refuses to expel Becket, 67 ; visits him, 68 ; at war with Henry, 91, 92, 94 ; supports Poitevins, 96 ; abortive conference at La Ferté Bernard, 97 ; accepts Henry's dynastic scheme, 100 ; annoyed at Becket's obstinacy, 103, 104 ; meets Henry at Montmartre, 112, 114 ; again at Fréteval, 121 ; setting the young King Henry against his father, 162, 163, 165 ; lays siege to Verneuil, sacks part of town and retreats, 170, 171 ; attacks

Louis VII. (*continued*)—
>Rouen and is repulsed, 181, 182; presses for marriage of Alais to Richard, 198; seals treaty of Ivry, 199; visits Canterbury on pilgrimage, 202; struck with paralysis, 203; end of his reign, 205; dies, 206.
—— son of Philip II. of France, afterwards Louis VIII., suggested marriage to Blanche of Castile, 364, 384; married to her, 386; confronting John on the Loire, 450; drives him from La Roche-au-Moine, 451; preparing to invade England, defends his case against John, 494; lands in Thanet, issues a proclamation, 495; enters Rochester and London, 496; drives John from Winchester, 497; lays siege to Dover Castle, 498.
Lucy, Geoffrey of, at Richard's coronation, 267.
—— Richard of, appointed Chief Justiciar in conjunction with Robert, Earl of Leicester, 3, 9, 27, 41, 66, 79; excommunicated, 84, 97, 105, 167, 169; lays siege to Leicester, 172, 173; repels Scottish inroad, 173, 177; condemns King's action, 186, 194, dies, 202.
Lusignan, Geoffrey of, 96, 97, 168, 237, 293, 297, 395, 449.
—— Guy of, married to Sybille, sister of Baldwin IV., King of Jerusalem; becomes King in her right, 234; signs truce with Saladin, *ib.*; taken prisoner by him, 235; ransomed, lays siege to Acre, attacked by Saladin, 284; visits Richard in Cyprus, his position in Palestine, 293; assists Richard to conquer Cyprus, 294; at Acre again, 297; compromise with Conrad of Montferrat, 299; at battle of Arsûf, 302; 305; finally rejected from being King of Jerusalem, 319; made King of Cyprus, 320.
—— Hugh le Brun IX. of, acquires County of La Marche, 199, note; at Messina, on Crusade, 287; in revolt, 339.
—— Hugh le Brun X. of, 386 and note; appeals to Philip against John, 392; taken prisoner by him, 395; makes terms with him, 449.

Madog, son of Maredudd, Lord of Powys, 13.
Maelgwn, younger son of Rhys, son of Gruffudd, disputes succession his elder brother, 374, 420, 429, 433.
Magna Carta, comments on, 474-478; text of, 479-485.
Marche, La, Counts of. *See* Lusignan.
Margaret, daughter of Louis VII., married to the young King Henry, son of Henry II., 23; not allowed to be crowned with him, 119; subsequently crowned with him, 161; in custody, 175; at liberty, 191, 213; her dower settled, 219; but not paid, 229, 233; re-marries Bela III. of Hungary, *ib.*
—— natural daughter of William the Lion, married to Robert de Ros of Hamlake, 373.
Marshal, John, the elder, 53, 55.
—— John, the younger, 490, 493; with John at his death, 501.
—— William, afterwards Earl of Pembroke, supporter of the young King Henry, knights him, 119; in revolt against the elder King, 168; goes on pilgrimage to Holy Land on behalf of the young King, 216, 217; with the King as against Richard, unhorses the latter, 242; engaged to Isabel of Clare, 263. *See* Pembroke.

Marshal, William, the younger, opposing John, 471 ; 497.

Mary, daughter of King Stephen, Abbess of Romsey, removed from her convent, made Countess of Boulogne, and married to Matthew, younger son of Count Dietrich of Flanders, 22.

Matilda, The Empress, mother of Henry II., 2 ; objects to invasion of Ireland, 8 ; opposed to promotion of Becket to Primacy, 26 ; smiles at his anathemas, 84 ; dies, 93.

—— eldest daughter of Henry II., born, 12 ; proposal for her hand from Henry the Lion, 71 ; married to him, *id.* note, 193 ; comes to Normandy with him, 211 ; 213 ; goes over to England, and gives birth to son William at Winchester, 220 ; at Windsor, 223 ; her death, 259.

Mauléon, Savary of, taken prisoner by John, 395 ; joins his service, 403 ; allied with Philip, 438 ; joins John, 449 ; in his service, 490 ; captures Pleshey, attacks Colchester, 491 ; surrenders Winchester Castle to Louis, 497 ; spares Croyland Abbey, 500.

Maurice fitz Gerald, Welsh adventurer, concludes treaty with Dermot, King of Leinster, 143 ; storms Wexford, 144 ; brings further troops, 145 ; placed under Hugh de Lacy, 156.

Mauriénne, Humbert III., Count of, contracts daughter Alais to Henry's son John, 163.

Meiler, fitz Henry, Welsh adventurer in Ireland, 143.

Melun, Viscount of, at battle of Bouvines, 456, 461 ; with Louis in England, 495.

Mercadier, Captain of Richard's mercenaries, 348, 354, 363, 366, 379, 385 ; assassinated, 386.

Milo of Cogan, adventurer in Ireland, 147, 148, 149, 196.

Montferrat, William of, first husband of Queen Sybille, 293.

—— Conrad of, younger brother of preceding, saves Tyre from Saladin, enemy to Guy of Lusignan, 284 ; supported by King Philip, marries Mabel, sister of late Queen Sybille, 293 ; keeps Richard out of Tyre, 295 ; at siege of Acre, his unpopularity, 296, 297 ; compromise with Guy of Lusignan, 299 ; intriguing with Saladin, 305, 306 ; finally accepted as King of Jerusalem by Richard, assassinated, 319.

Montfort l'Amauri, Simon of, Count of Evreux, in revolt, 168.

—— Amauri of, created Earl of Gloucester by John, 386 note, and errata.

Montfort-sur-Risle, Robert of, in revolt, 168.

Montmorency, Matthew of, at battle of Bouvines, 456, 461.

—— Hervé of, 143, 144, 151.

Mortimer, Hugh of, forced to surrender Bridgenorth, Cleobury and Wigmore, 5, 6 ; contends with the Welsh, 13.

—— Roger of, supporting John against Longchamp, banished, 309.

Morville, Hugh of, assassinates Becket, 130-134 ; his subsequent history, 137.

Mowbray, Roger, of Axholm, in revolt, 169, 176, 177, 179.

—— William, of Axholm, 380.

Namur, Philip, Count of, on Allied side at battle of Bouvines, 451, 457.

Nest, the Lady, daughter of Rhys ap Teudwr, last King of South Wales, her children, 13, 14, 142, 158, 227.

Nevers, Count of, with Louis in England, 495; appointed Governor of Hants, 497; besieges Windsor Castle, 498; offers battle to John, 499.

Neville, Hugh, with Richard at Joppa, 324 note; in command at Marlborough, 498.

Nicholaa de la Haye, hereditary Constable of Lincoln Castle, wife of Gerard of Camville, 309; resists John, *ib.*; holds the Castle for him against the Barons, 497.

Nicholas, Cardinal, on mission to England, receives homage for England from John, 444, 445, 467; recalled, 468.

Nonant, Hugh of, Archdeacon of Lisieux, 59. *See* Chester, Coventry, and Lichfield, Bishops of.

Nonconformists in England persecuted, 75, 76; in Languedoc, their tenets, proceedings against them, 199, 200.

Norfolk, Earls of—
    Hugh Bigod, deprived of castles, and of 'third penny' of Norfolk, 12, 74, 105; in revolt, 169, 174, 177; surrenders, 180.
    Roger Bigod, son of preceding, 310; opposing John, 471.

Northampton, Earls of—
    Simon of St. Liz III., 169, 170, 177.

Norwich, Bishops of—
    Roger, 44; 111.
    John of Oxford, 187, 285, 312.
    John Gray, 402 and note; named by John for Archbishopric of Canterbury, and elected by monks, 408; election quashed by Innocent, 410; remains with John after the Interdict, 416; sent to Ireland, 423; coins halfpence and farthings, 425; brought back to England, 438, 439; dies, 467.

Novel Disseisin, Assize of, 81.

Octavian, Cardinal, commissioned by Urban III. to crown John King of Ireland, 232; mediates between England and France, 233.

Oliver, natural son of King John, 515.

Otho, Cardinal, his unsuccessful mission, 93, 95, 97, 98.

Oudenarde, Arnold of, on English side at battle of Bouvines, 456, 463; taken prisoner, 464.

Owain, son of Gruffudd, Prince of Gwynedd, inflicts reverse on Henry II., 14; forced to submit, 15; serves on campaign of Toulouse, 20; does homage, 37, 73; dies, 152.

—— son of Gruffudd, son of Rhys, Prince in South Wales, 420, 421.

Oxford, Earls of—
    Aubrey de Vere, 428.
    Robert de Vere, opposing John, 471.
—— John of, employed by Henry II., 51, 71, 72; excommunicated, 84, 87, 125, 127. *See* Norwich, Bishops of.
—— University of, *circa* 1187, probable numbers and system of tuition, 511, 512.

Pandulf, Sub-Deacon, Papal envoy to England, warns John to remember that he is excommunicate, 429, 430, 436; brings Papal ultimatum, receives John's homage for England, 439, 440, inhibits Philip from waging war on John, 440; sent to Rome, 466, 479; suspends Archbishop Langton, 487.

Pembroke, Earls of—

Gilbert of Clare, "Strongbow" I., 13.

Richard of Clare, "Strongbow" II., contends with the Welsh, 13; makes alliance with Dermot, King of Leinster, 142; his character and appearance, 146; lands in Ireland, 147; marries Eva of Leinster, and captures Dublin, 147; submits absolutely to Henry, 148; defeats Roderic O'Connor, 149; his Irish policy, 150; goes to meet Henry, 152; surrenders regalian rights to him, 156; loyal in time of trouble, 169, 170; appointed Justiciar of Ireland, dies, 194.

William Marshal (*q.v.*), married to Isabel, daughter and heiress of preceding, 263; at coronation of Richard, 267; on Regency Council, 271, 310, 312; Justiciar or Viceroy of Ireland, founds Kilkenny, 375; at Richard's death declares for John, 378, 379, 380; finally invested as Earl, 381; sent to Normandy, 390; fails to relieve Château Gaillard, 399; on mission to France, 402; opposes John, does homage to Philip for estates in Normandy, 405, and note, 416; his prudence and tact, 423, 424; in command in Ireland, 426; required to give son as hostage, 433; pledges himself for John, 468, 471, 487, 499; executor of his will, 501.

Perche, Counts of—

Rotrou (third of the name in the history of the county) surrenders Moulins-la-Marche and Bonmoulins to Henry, receiving Bellême in return, 18; supporting the young King against his father in 1173 (name omitted, p. 168), joins him in an attack at Séez, 175; dies at Acre, 297.

Geoffrey (third of the name), son of preceding, prepared to support Richard against Philip, 362.

Peter of Capua, Cardinal, on Papal mission, 364; brings Philip and Richard to meet *ib.*; threatening Philip for having neglected Ingeborg, 384.

—— of Pavia, Cardinal, on Papal mission, 198.

Philip II., "Augustus," King of France, born, 111, note; crowned King during father's life, 203; accession, marries Isabel of Hainault, confirms treaty of Ivry, 205, 206; attacked by a coalition, 210; presses for retrocession of Norman Vexin, and for marriage of sister Alais to Richard, 218, 219; unable as yet to join Crusade, 226; claims guardianship of young Arthur of Brittany, complains of Richard's conduct, makes truce, 232; again at war, captures Graçay and Issoudun, 233; signs truce at Châteauroux, 234; takes the Cross, 235; imposes Saladin Tithe, 236; attacks Richard in Berri, 238; cuts down historic elm-tree, 239; demands recognition of Richard as Henry's heir, 240; so again, with celebration of marriage with Alais, 241; presses campaign against Henry in concert with Richard, 242, 243; captures Tours and obliges Henry to submit to his terms (treaty of Colombières), 243, 244; interview with Richard, latter to marry Alais, 264; agreement as to Crusade, 264; so again, 277; joins muster at Vézelai, agreement as to partition of conquests, 283; reaches Messina 286, 287; coolness between him and Richard, 288; releases Richard from promise to marry Alais on terms, 289; sails for Acre, 290; supports Conrad of Montferrat, 293; remonstrates with Richard for war in Cyprus, 294; contends

Philip II. (*continued*)—

with him at Acre, 297 ; sails home, 299 ; intrigues with John, 315 ; on report of Richard's imprisonment invades Normandy, 328 ; intriguing against Richard's liberation, 331 ; makes fresh treaty with John, and again invades Normandy, 334, 335, 339 ; captures Earl of Leicester, abortive conference with English, destroys Evreux, 340 ; shuns battle with Richard, 341 ; at war again, obtains cessions of territory for peace (treaty of Gaillon), 348, 349 ; truce being broken by Richard, wins towns in Normandy, 350 ; supports Philip of Suabia against Otto for the Imperial Crown, 361 ; twice defeated by Richard, 362 ; signs a truce, 363 ; meets him on the Seine, suggested settlement of Norman Vexin and Gisors, 364 ; at Richard's death occupies Evreux, 378 ; takes Arthur of Brittany under his charge, 382 ; fruitless meeting with John, 383 ; at war again, alarms Arthur's friends, 384 ; repudiates Ingeborg of Denmark, and marries Agnes of Meran, 383 note ; agrees to pacification with John, his son Louis to marry Blanche of Castile, 384 ; incurs Papal censures, 385 ; submits to Innocent's terms, summons John to answer charges, 392 ; invades Normandy and reduces Eu and Aumâle, 393 ; knights Arthur and invests him with Brittany, Anjou, etc., 393, 394 ; burns Tours, 395 ; again summons John, 397 ; invades Normandy and lays siege to Château Gaillard, 398-400 ; reduces it, 402 ; likewise all Normandy, 402 ; Anjou, Maine, Touraine, and Poitou, 403 ; opposes John in Poitou, 409 ; signs truce, 410 ; prepares to invade England, 438 ; overruns Flanders, 441 ; on the Bouvines campaign, 452 ; resolves on action, 454 ; unhorsed, 461 ; restrains pursuit, 464 ; declines responsibility for his son's invasion of England, 494.

—— of Suabia, brother to Henry II., candidate for Imperial Crown, 361, 364.

—— of Cognac, natural son of Richard I., kills Ademar, Viscount of Limoges, 376.

—— of Broi, 30.

Poitiers, Counts of—

William VIII., 19.

William IX., father of Queen Eleanor, his dominions, 1 note ; claim on Toulouse, 19.

Pontefract, Peter of, his prophecy, 434 ; put to death, 440.

Ponthieu, Counts of—

William Talevas I., son of Robert of Bellême, by Agnes of Ponthieu, 88 ; surrenders Ponthieu to eldest son—namely :

Guy, 89.

John, son of preceding, offends Henry, who ravages Vimeu, 98 ; supports the young King, 168 ; dies at Acre, 297.

William, son of preceding, at Battle of Bouvines on French side, 455, 463.

Popes—

Adrian IV., approves of invasion of Ireland, the Bull *Laudabiliter*, 6, 7, 155 ; his earlier life, 7 note ; dies, 23.

Alexander III., recognised by Henry, 23, 24 ; leaves Italy and comes to Gaul, reception by Louis and Henry, 28, 29 ; holds Council at Tours, 36 ; moderate support to Becket, 44, 51 ; delusive grants,

52; audience to Henry's envoys, 67; to Becket, 68; annuls judicial sentences, 74; restrains Becket's action, 75; grants him Legatine Commission, 82; friendly tone to Henry, 87, 88; accredits mission of Cardinals William and Otho, 87, 93; then that of Simon and Bernard, 101; then that of Gratian and Vivian, 104, 107; remonstrates with Becket, 107; instructs fourth mission, Rotrou of Rouen, and Bernard of Nevers, 115; pardons Foliot, 116; inhibits coronation of young King Henry by Roger of York, 119; authorises Becket to suspend English prelates, 123, 126, 127; canonises him, 136; excommunicates his murderers, and accredits mission of Cardinals Albert and Theodine, 150, 151, 156; sanctions Henry's conquests in Ireland, 155; calls for help to Jerusalem, 207; dispute with William the Lion, 208; dies, 209; success of his career, *ib.*

Lucius III. election, sends Golden Rose to William the Lion, 210; attempts to tax English clergy, 221; refuses to make John King of Ireland, 228; his death, *ib.* note.

Urban III., his election, approves of John as King of Ireland, 228 and note; his death, 235.

Gregory VIII., his short Pontificate, 235 and note.

Clement III., his election, 235 note; accredits missions to make peace between England and France, 241; authorises Richard to excuse men from Crusading vows, 271; accredits John of Anagni to England, 274.

Celestine III. elected, confirms Geoffrey as Archbishop, 290 and note; crowns Henry VI. and Constance, 291; orders Longchamp to be reinstated, but without effect, 315; grants Legatine Commission to Hubert Walter, 343; suspends Geoffrey of York for non-appearance to citation, 345; sanctions Lambeth Chapel, dies, 359 and note.

Innocent III., orders demolition of Lambeth Chapel, *ib.*; his attitude to temporal princes, 363; accredits Peter of Capua to mediate, threatens both Richard and Philip, 364; friendly to John, 400; quashes rival elections to Canterbury of Bishop Gray and Sub-prior Reginald, 410; nominates Stephen Langton, 411; consecrates him, 413; threatens John with an Interdict, 414; and again with excommunication, 417, 418; sends him an ultimatum, 436, 438; accepts surrender of England, 440; gives John time for payment of damages, orders Interdict to be dissolved, 466; condemns opposition to the King 467; so again, 469; again excommunicates all disturbers of England, 486; confirms suspension of Langton, 488 note; quashes Magna Carta, *ib.*; excommunicates leading Barons by name, 493; forbids Louis to invade England, accredits Cardinal Gualo to stop him, 494; dies, 499 and note.

Honorius III. supports John fully, 499.

Prendergast, Maurice of, Adventurer in Ireland, 143, 145.

Quincy, Saher de, in revolt, 168. *See* Winchester, Earl of.

Randerode, Gerard of, on Bodyguard of Otto IV. at Battle of Bouvines, 457; taken prisoner, 462.

Raymond, IV., V., and VI. *See* Toulouse, Counts of.

Raymond Beranger IV., Count of Barcelona, in alliance with Henry II., 19.
—— Fitzwilliam, "The Stout," Welsh adventurer in Ireland, 146, 147, 148.
Reginald, fitz Urse, assassinates Becket, 130, 134; subsequent history, 137.
—— Sub-prior of Canterbury, elected by the monks Archbishop of Canterbury, 407, 408; election quashed by Innocent, 411.
Rhys, son of Gruffudd, Prince of South Wales, 13; gives trouble, reduced, and does homage, 36, 37, 72, 73, 142; meets Henry, 152; acting against rebels, 177; leads force to Normandy, 181; at court, 186; receives a grant in Radnorshire, 196; seizes Llanstephan, 272; comes to Oxford to do homage, 273, 374; dies, *ib*.
—— son of Rhys, Prince in South Wales, 420, 429.
Richard, *Cœur de Lion*, third born but eldest surviving son of Henry II. born, 15; invested with Poitiers and Aquitaine, 96, 100, 161; in revolt, 165, 175; engaged to marry Alais of France, 96, 175; hunted down by Henry, comes to terms at Montlouis, 182, 183, 185; comes to England for succour, 191; returns and reduces rebels, 192; meets his father, 198; contends successfully with Aquitanian rebels, 203, 204; goes over to England, 204; supports Philip II. against coalition, 210; his government in Poitou unpopular, fresh risings, 211, 212; intrigues against the young king, 212, 213; in revolt, and himself at war with Poitevin rebels, 214; reduces them, 217; refuses to cede territory to John, 218, 219; at war with Geoffrey, goes over to England with him, 219, 222, 223; back to Poitou, 224; suspended by his father, 227; again sent into Aquitaine with troops, 229; siding with Philip against his father, returns to his duty on being re-invested with Aquitaine, 233, 234; takes the Cross, 235; subdues rebels in Aquitaine, 237; at war with Tolouse, 238; again with his father, unhorses William des Barres, goes off to Berri, 239; deserting his father does public homage to Philip, 240; rejects his father's overtures, 241; wages active war against him in concert with Philip, 242; kneels by his father's corpse, 245; absolved from war against him, makes friends with John and others, installed as Duke of Normandy, 263; makes treaty with Philip II. and promises to marry his sister Alais, 264; crosses to England, and liberates Earl of Leicester and Queen Eleanor, 264, 265; crowned, 266, 269; banquet, outrage on Jews, 269; Richard's laxity, 270; wholesale traffic in offices to raise money, 271, 272; releases the Scots from treaty of Falaise-Valognes, 274; grants four Western Counties to John, assigns his mother's dower, 275; crosses the Channel, has interview with Philip of France, confirms Longchamp's action in England, 277; takes pilgrim's scrip and staff; numbers of his fleet, 282; meets Philip at Vezelai, compact for division of spoils, 283; advance to Marseilles, 284; journey down Mediterranean coast to Messina, 285; entry to Messina, affairs there, obtains release of sister Jeanne, 286; difficulties with the natives, sacks Messina, 287; coolness between him and Philip, 288; establishes himself in a fortress outside Messina, alliance with Tancred, King of Sicily, 288; finally refuses to marry Alais, 289; sends Archbishop of Rouen home on special

mission, 290; voyage to Cyprus, 291; storm of Limasol, and war against Isaac Comnenus, marries Berengaria, 292; conquers Cyprus, and carries off Isaac and his daughter, 294; voyage to Acre, and landing there, 295; falls ill, 297; massacres Acre prisoners in default of ransom, 300; advances from Acre to Nahr Falik, 301; defeats Saladin at Arsûf, 301-304; advances to Joppa, 304; further advance towards Lydda, Richard nearly captured, advance to Ramleh and Beit Nuba, offer of matrimonial alliance to Saladin, 306; retirement to Ascalon, 307; repairs the fortifications, *ib.*; visits Acre, 318; finally accepts Conrad of Montferrat as King of Jerusalem, and at his death supports Henry of Champagne, 319; grants Cyprus to Guy of Lusignan, 320; captures Darum, and advances again to Beit Nuba, *ib.*; captures a great caravan, 321; retires finally from Beit Nuba, 322; relieves Joppa, 323; defeats Saladin in battle there, 324; falls ill, makes truce for three years with Saladin, 325; carried back to Acre, adventures on voyage home, taken prisoner by Leopold of Austria at Vienna, 325, 326; given over to Henry VI., terms for his liberation, 328; arraigned before Diet, 329; appoints Hubert Waller Archbishop of Canterbury, 329; sends Longchamp on mission to England, 330; authorises him to conclude treaty with Philip, 332; free at last, 333; returns to England, 334; visits Bury, 335; holds Grand Council at Nottingham, confiscates and re-sells offices, 336; calls for scutage, 336; goes through form of re-coronation, 337; resumes further grants, 338; reconciles Geoffrey and Longchamp, *ib.*; leaves England for ever, *ib.*; reconciled to John, 339; moves from Normandy into Touraine, 340; puts Philip to flight, 341; reduces Aquitanian rebels, signs truce with France, 341; reinvests John with Mortain and Gloucester, pardons Hugh of Nonant, and cohabits with Berengaria, 347; again at war with Philip, makes territorial cessions for sake of peace (Treaty of Gaillon), 348, 349; breaks truce, fresh war in Normandy, demands custody of young Arthur of Brittany, 350; fortifies Les Andelys, 351; makes peace with Tolouse, *ib.*; listens to William Fitz Osbert, 352; sends financial expert to England, 353; at war again, burns Saint Valéry, and wins towns in Auvergne, 354; signs a truce, 355; forced by St. Hugh of Lincoln to give him the kiss of peace, 357; produces a new Great Seal to compel re-sealing of charters, 358; appoints Geoffrey Fitz Peter Chief Justiciar, 359; builds *Château Gaillard* on the Rock of Andely, 361; fails to make use of friendly coalition round him, makes Philip drink of the waters of the Epte, 362; signs a truce, 363; meets Philip on the Seine, suggested settlement of the Norman Vexin and Gisors, 374; quarrels with Adémar, Viscount of Limoges, wastes *Limousin*, and lays siege to Castle of Châlus, wounded, last dispositions, 365; sends for his mother, dies, buried at Fontevrault, 376; his issue, 376; his appearance, character, and military talents, 367; estimates of his own age, 368; his revenues, 369, 370, 372; his ransom, 371; Customs duties, etc., 372, 373; relations with Scotland, 373; with Wales, 374; with Ireland, 375.

- second son of King John, his birth, taken to Poitou, 448 and note, 514.

Richard of Warenne, natural son of John, 515.

—— a Breton, assassinates Becket, 130-134.

Riddel, Geoffrey, Archdeacon of Canterbury, employed by Henry, 51, 105, 109; appointed Bishop of Ely, 167. *See* Ely.

Robert of Barry, brother to "Giraldus Cambrensis," enlisted by King Dermot, 143.

—— Fitz Stephen, Anglo-Norman adventurer, enlisted by King Dermot, 142, 143; storms Wexford, 144; sent to Limerick, 145; taken prisoner, 149, 150; set free, 153; ruling under Hugh de Lacy, 156; receives grant of Cork, 196, 227.

—— Fitz Walter, in Normandy, 398; absconds in revolt, 433, 437, 470, 471; elected Marshal of Confederate army, 472, 473, 487; occupies Rochester Castle, 489; fails to relieve it, *ib.*; ravages East Anglian towns, 496, 497.

Roches, William des, Seneschal of Anjou for John, brings Arthur to him, 384; pleads for Arthur, and failing to obtain satisfaction revolts, 395, 396, 398, 403, 450.

Rochester, Bishops of—
    Walter, 62, 85, 119.
    Gilbert of Glanville, 415; dies, 467.
    Benedict of Sansetun, 488.

Roderic O'Connor, King of Connaught, High King of all Ireland, 141; expels Dermot MacMurrough, King of Leinster, 142; makes terms with him, 143, 145; repulsed from blockade of Dublin, 149; keeps aloof from Henry, 153; submits to rule under him and pay tribute, 187, 188.

Ronald mac Uhtred, Prince of Galloway, 230, 231.

Ros, Robert de, married to Margaret, daughter of William the Lion, 373; Confederate Baron, 487; his castle at Helmsley resists John, 492, 497.

Rosamund Clifford, 260.

Rouen, Archbishops of—
    Rotrou of Beaumont, 71 note, 83, 94, 96, 111, 116; on Papal mission, 115, 120-122, 125, 136, 150, 161, 193.
    Walter of Coutances, 230 note, 232; absolves Richard for warring against his father, a Crusader, instals him as Duke of Normandy, 263; at his coronation, 266; in Sicily on Crusade, 288; sent to England on special mission, 290; supports Longchamp as against John, 309; mediates between them, 309; moves deposition of Longchamp, 312; appointed Chief Justiciar, 313, 327; resists John, 328; refuses kiss of peace to Longchamp, 331; at Mainz, 333; refuses to remit damages due or to surrender property at Les Andelys, lays Normandy under Interdict (twice), 349, 351; accepts of a compromise, *ib.*; instals John as Duke of Normandy, 379; dies, 422.

Saint-Pol, Walter, Count of, at Battle of Bouvines, 456, 460, 461.

Saint Valéry, Thomas of, on French side at Battle of Bouvines, 455, 462, 463, 464.

Saladin, Sultan of Egypt and Damascus, threatening Jerusalem, 207, 224; makes truce with Guy of Lusignan, 234; truce having been treacherously broken by Reginald of Chatillon defeats Christians, and captures Guy of Lusignan, Jerusalem, and other cities of Palestine, 235, 283, 284; attacks the Christians besieging Acre, 296, 298; negotiates concerning ransom of Acre prisoners, butchers his captives, 300; his skirmishing attacks on Crusaders on the march, 301; defeated at Arsûf, 302-304; negotiations, 305, 306, 322; attacks Joppa, *ib.*; driven off by Richard, 323; again defeated in battle, 324; signs truce for three years, 325.

—— Tithe, how assessed in England and France respectively, 236.

Salisbury, Bishops of—

Joscelin of Bohun, 49, 58, 85, 87, 94, 104 note, 105, 119, 127, 128.

Hubert Walter, 270, 271 and note, 275; on Crusade, 299; maintains order when Richard ill, 324; negotiates truce with Saladin, 325; returns home, visiting Richard on the way, 328; named for Canterbury, 329. *See* Canterbury, Archbishops of.

Herbert le Poer, 355 and note, 356, 415.

—— Earls of—

Patrick, 4 note, 96 : killed, 97.

William, son of preceding, 169, 260.

William, *Longespée*, natural son of Henry II., married to Ela or Isabel, daughter of preceding, 260; at Richard's coronation, 267; supports Longchamp against John, 310; sent to La Rochelle, 405; true to John, 428, 439; destroys French fleet, 441; sent to Flanders, 448; commands wing at Battle of Bouvines, 452; his charge, 463; defeated and taken prisoner by Bishop of Beauvais, 464; true to John, 487, 490, 493, 497.

—— John of, distinguished scholar, friend of Becket, 123, 129; with him at his death, 132.

Sancerre, Stephen of Blois, Count of, 205, 210; dies at Acre, 297.

Sancho VI., King of Navarre, submits disputes with Castile to Henry's arbitration, 197.

Saxony, Dukes of. *See* Henry.

Scotland, Kings of—

Malcolm IV., 'The Maiden,' surrenders Northern Counties, does homage to Henry II., and receives Earldom of Huntingdon, 12; serves on campaign of Toulouse, 20; Knighted by Henry, 21; does homage, 37; dies, 81.

William the Lion, hallowed, follows Henry to Normandy, 81; there again, 90; does homage to young Henry, 120; acting with barons in revolt, 169; invades England, 173; again twice, 176; taken prisoner at Alnwick, 177-179, 182; released under treaty of Falaise-Valognes, 183, 184; at court, 198; summoned to Normandy in connexion with ecclesiastical dispute, 207, 208; marries Ermengarde of Beaumont, 230, 373; offers to contribute to Saladin Tithe, 237; relieved by Richard from obligations of the treaty of Falaise-Valognes, 274; definition of Scottish homage for the future, 275; welcomes Richard home, 337; demands Northern Counties from John, 382; evades a meeting, 385; comes to Lincoln, and does homage, 387, 388; demolishes English fort at Tweedmouth, makes treaty with John, and surrenders his daughters Margaret and Isabel, 421; hands over his English estates to his son Alexander, 422; further treaty with John, 422; dies, 477 note.

Scotland, Kings of (*continued*)—

 Alexander II., installed at Scone, 477 note ; in correspondence with Barons opposed to John, receives homage from English Barons, 492 ; retires before John's forces to the Pentlands, 492 ; does homage to Louis at Dover, 498.

Scottish homage question, 12, 81, 120, 183, 184, 198, 274, 275, 337.

—— Kings, regulations for their entertainment on visits to English court, 337.

Scutage, history of the tax, 10 ; levied, *ib.*, 13, 20 (Great Scutage of Toulouse), 73, 153 note, 252, 273, 336, 369, 382, 390, 400, 423.

Sens, William, Archbishop of. *See* Blois.

Simon fitz Peter, Justice in Eyre, 40.

—— of Mont Dieu, Papal Envoy, his unsuccessful mission, 101-104.

Surrey or Warenne, Earls of—

 William, younger son of King Stephen, Earl in right of his wife Isabel of Warenne, 12 ; dies, 41.

 Isabel of Warenne, Countess in own right, widow of preceding, not allowed to marry King's legitimate brother William, but allowed to marry his illegitimate brother Hamelin, 41.

 Hamelin, Earl in right of wife Isabel, 41, 169, 337.

 William, son of preceding, faithful to John, 487, 497, 499.

Sussex, Earls of. *See* Arundel.

Sybille, sister of Baldwin IV., King of Jerusalem, married first to William of Montferrat, secondly to Guy of Lusignan, 224 ; at death of her son Baldwin V. becomes Queen, and confers the Crown on Guy, 234 ; dies at Acre with her daughters, 293, 297.

Synods, Cashel, 164 ; Westminster, 176 ; London, 186 ; Westminster, 190 ; Eynsham, 230 ; Marlborough, 231 ; York, 343 ; Westminster, 407.

Talevas, family of, 88, 89, 98, 168. *See* Ponthieu.

Tancarville, William of, Chamberlain of Normandy, in revolt, 168, 170.

Tancred, elected King of Sicily, his dealings with Richard at Messina, 236 ; in alliance with him, 288.

Tecklenburg, Otto, Count of, on Otto IV.'s Bodyguard at Battle of Bouvines, 457 ; taken prisoner, 462.

Theodine, Cardinal, commissioned by Alexander III. to absolve Henry for murder of Becket, on terms, 150, 151, 156 ; absolves him, 159.

Thouars, Amaury, Viscount of, 389 note, 409.

—— Guy of, third husband of Constance, Countess of Brittany, 384 note ; governing Brittany, 402, 409.

Tiernan O'Rourke, Under-King of Breifny, enemy to Dermot MacMurrough, 142, 143, 145, 147.

Toulouse, Counts of—

 William IV., 19.

 Raymond IV., 19 ; attacked by Henry, 21, 22 ; meeting with Henry, assassinated, 91.

 Raymond V., does homage to Henry, 164 ; opposes, Nonconformists, 200 ; supports young King against Richard, 215 ; attacked by Richard, 238.

 Raymond VI., pacification with Richard, marries his sister Jeanne, widowed Queen of Sicily, 351, 362 ; defeated by Simon de

Montfort at Muret, 432 ; excommunicated by Innocent, 435 ; comes to London for help, obliged to depart, 448 and note.

Turnham, Stephen of, Seneschal of Anjou, 242, 263 ; left in command in Cyprus, 295 ; brings Berengaria home, 325 ; at Chinon, 378.

—— Robert of, 398, 403, 405.

Ugo, Ugoccione (Hugh), Cardinal, on Papal Mission to England, questions between Canterbury and York, 188, 190.

Vaux, William, of Collingham, Guerilla chief, 498.

Vermandois, Question of, 206, 211, 219, 226, 354 note.

Vescy, William de, repels Scots from Bamborough, 176, 178.

—— Eustace de, married to Margaret, natural daughter of William the Lion, 373 ; absconds in revolt, 433, 437 ; sent to Rome by the Barons, 469 ; killed, 498.

Vivian, Papal envoy, his unsuccessful mission, 107, 110, 114.

Walter, Hubert. *See* Salisbury and Canterbury ; for early life, 329.

Warwick, Earls of—

William of Beaumont, 169 ; dies in Holy Land, 380 note.

Waleran, brother of preceding, 380 ; dies, 487 note.

Henry of Beaumont II., son of preceding, supporting John, 487, 499.

Welsh affairs, 13-15, 36, 37, 72, 152, 237, 273, 374, 375, 420, 429, 433.

William II., King of Sicily, on friendly relations with Henry, marries his daughter Johanna, 193 ; his death, 286.

—— eldest born son of Henry II., 2 ; homage done to him as Heir Apparent ; dies young, 6.

—— of Anjou, younger brother of Henry II., 2 ; prevented marrying Isabel of Warenne, dies, 41.

—— younger son of King Stephen, Count of Boulogne, forced to surrender castles of Mortain, Pevensey, and Norwich, 12 ; dies, 22.

—— of Pavia, Cardinal, 88 ; his unsuccessful mission, 91-93, 97, 88.

—— Fitz Aldelin, employed by Henry in Ireland, 153, 155, 156 ; Justiciar there, 194 ; superseded, 196.

—— Fitz Ralph, in command in Normandy, 242 ; Seneschal of Normandy, meets King Philip, 315 ; keeps out Papal Legates, 316 note.

—— Fitz Osbert, "Long Beard," movement in London excited by him, his arrest and execution, 351, 352.

Winchester, Bishops of—

Henry of Blois, brother of King Stephen, at coronation of Henry II., 3 ; retires for a times to Cluny, 8 ; announces "election" of Becket, 27 ; consecrates him, 28 ; declares sentence on him, 55 ; urges him to resist, 57, 58, 85, 111 ; his Church policy and death, 152.

Richard of Ilchester, appointed, 167, 175, 194.

Godfrey of Lucy, appointed, 270 ; buys Sheriffdom, etc., of Hants, 272 ; deprived of it, 277 ; recovers it, 314 ; again deprived, 338.

Peter des Roches, appointment, remains with John after the Interdict, 416 and note, 419, 442, 469 note ; suspends Langton, 487 ; named executor of John's Will, 501 ; with him at the last, *ib*.

Winchester, Earl of, Saer de Quincy, 398, 471; with Barons against John, 487.

Worcester, Bishops of—

Roger of Gloucester (King's cousin), 57, 62, 94, 136, 161.

Baldwin, appointed in 1180; translated to Canterbury, his antecedents, 221. *See* Canterbury.

William of Northall, appointed, 230.

Mauger, appointed, 414, note; proclaims the Interdict, 415, 418; dies abroad, 441.

Walter Gray, the Chancellor, 447, 467. *See* York, Archbishops of.

Silvester of Evesham, executor of John's Will, 501.

York, Archbishops of—

Roger of Pont l' Eveque, jealous of Becket, 31; at Council of Tours, 36; urges Becket to submit, 44, 50, 51, 54, 59, 65, 94, 115, 116, 119; suspended by Becket, 127, 128; absolved and reinstated, 161: resists Scottish inroad, 178; struggles with Canterbury for precedency, 188, 190; a truce, 194; in charge of Scarborough Castle, 195; lays Scotland under Interdict, dies, 209, 210, 221.

Geoffrey, natural son of Henry II., appointed, 263; appointment confirmed, 270, 271 note; sent to Scotland, 272, 273; again confirmed, 275; buys Richard's goodwill, 276; being abroad sworn not to return to England for three years, 277; finally consecrated, 290, 310; returning to England, arrested at Dover by order of Longchamp, 311; released, comes to London, 312; quarrels with Bishop Puiset, 316 and note; resists John, 328; buys Sheriffdom of Yorkshire, 336; quarrels with Chapter, *ib.* note, 344; not allowed to carry his cross within Province of Canterbury, 337; reconciled to Longchamp, 338; his estates seized, 345; goes abroad, summoned to Rome by Celestine, suspended for non-appearance, 345, 380; his revenues restored, 382; again taken from him for resistance to carucate, 385; protests against a tax of a Thirteenth, and leaves England, 413; dies abroad, 441.

Walter Gray, 490.

—— Earl of—

William of Aumâle, surrenders Scarborough Castle, 4, 5.

Printed by Hazell, Watson & Viney, Ld., London and Aylesbury.